DEMOGRAPHIC
AND ECONOMIC CHANGE
IN
DEVELOPED COUNTRIES

National Bureau of Economic Research

Special Conference Series

1. Problems in the Study of Economic Growth
   (in mimeograph)
2. Conference on Business Cycles
3. Conference on Research in Business Finance
4. Regularization of Business Investment
5. Business Concentration and Price Policy
6. Capital Formation and Economic Growth
7. Policies to Combat Depression
8. The Measurement and Behavior of Unemployment
9. Problems in International Economics
   (February 1958 Supplement to the *Review of Economics and Statistics*)
10. The Quality and Economic Significance of Anticipations Data
11. Demographic and Economic Change in Developed Countries
12. Public Finances: Needs, Sources, and Utilization
13. The Rate and Direction of Inventive Activity: Economic
    and Social Factors
14. Aspects of Labor Economics

Demographic
and Economic Change
in
Developed Countries

A CONFERENCE OF THE
UNIVERSITIES–NATIONAL BUREAU COMMITTEE
FOR ECONOMIC RESEARCH

A REPORT OF THE
NATIONAL BUREAU OF ECONOMIC RESEARCH, NEW YORK

PUBLISHED BY
PRINCETON UNIVERSITY PRESS, PRINCETON
1960

Relation of National Bureau Directors to
Publications Reporting Conference Proceedings

SINCE the present volume is a record of conference proceedings, it has been exempted from the rules governing submission of manuscripts to, and critical review by, the Board of Directors of the National Bureau. It has, however, been reviewed and accepted for publication by the Director of Research.

(Resolution adopted July 6, 1958, and revised November 21, 1949.)

Universities-National Bureau Committee for Economic Research

Contents

INTRODUCTION   3
Ansley J. Coale

PART I
THE ANALYSIS OF POPULATION CHANGE

AN INTERNATIONAL SURVEY OF RECENT FERTILITY TRENDS   17
Halvor Gille

    C O M M E N T   34
Frank Lorimer

DIFFERENTIAL FERTILITY IN EUROPEAN COUNTRIES   36
Gwendolyn Z. Johnson

    C O M M E N T   72
Ronald Freedman

DIFFERENTIAL FERTILITY IN THE UNITED STATES   77
Clyde V. Kiser

    C O M M E N T   113
Robert Gutman

THE STRUCTURE AND TEMPO OF CURRENT FERTILITY   117
Norman B. Ryder

    C O M M E N T   131
Edward P. Hutchinson   ·   Ansley J. Coale

SOME RECENT DEVELOPMENTS IN AMERICAN FERTILITY RESEARCH   137
David Goldberg

    C O M M E N T   151
Charles F. Westoff

DIFFERENTIAL FERTILITY IN UNITED STATES CENSUS DATA   155
Richard and Nancy Ruggles

    C O M M E N T   190
Pascal K. Whelpton

ix

CONTENTS

AN ECONOMIC ANALYSIS OF FERTILITY   209
  Gary S. Becker

    COMMENT   231
    James S. Duesenberry   Bernard Okun

THE INFLUENCE OF BUSINESS CYCLES ON MARRIAGE AND BIRTH
RATES   241
  Dudley Kirk

    COMMENT   257
    Dorothy Swaine Thomas

MORTALITY, FERTILITY, THE SIZE–AGE DISTRIBUTION, AND THE
GROWTH RATE   261
  Frank W. Notestein

    COMMENT   275
    John V. Grauman · Conrad Taeuber

PART II
THE ECONOMIC EFFECTS OF POPULATION CHANGE

AN ECONOMIC AND DEMOGRAPHIC MODEL OF THE HOUSEHOLD
SECTOR: A PROGRESS REPORT   287
  Guy H. Orcutt and Alice M. Rivlin

    COMMENT   318
    Robert Solow · Reply by Orcutt and Rivlin

POPULATION CHANGE AND AGGREGATE OUTPUT   324
  Simon Kuznets

    COMMENT   340
    Richard E. Quandt · Milton Friedman · Reply by
    Kuznets

POPULATION CHANGE AND DEMAND, PRICES, AND THE LEVEL OF
EMPLOYMENT   352
  Ansley J. Coale

    COMMENT   371
    Margaret G. Reid · William J. Baumol

x

CONTENTS

POPULATION CHANGE AND THE SUPPLY OF LABOR 377
Stanley Lebergott

COMMENT 414
James N. Morgan · John Durand

POPULATION CHANGE AND RESOURCES: MALTHUSIANISM AND
CONSERVATION 423
Harold J. Barnett

COMMENT 451
Edgar M. Hoover · Theodore W. Schultz

POPULATION CHANGE AND THE DEMAND FOR FOOD 457
Jean A. Crockett

COMMENT 484
Karl Fox

POPULATION CHANGE AND THE DEMAND FOR SERVICES 496
Robert Ferber

COMMENT 517
Richard A. Easterlin · Reply by Ferber

COMMENT on Crockett and Ferber 522
Elizabeth W. Gilboy

INDEX 527

DEMOGRAPHIC
AND ECONOMIC CHANGE
IN
DEVELOPED COUNTRIES

Introduction

ANSLEY J. COALE

OFFICE OF POPULATION RESEARCH, PRINCETON UNIVERSITY

THIS conference was planned to discuss the mutual influences in industrially advanced countries between changes in national population and changes in national economies. The conference was limited primarily to the causes and effects of variations in fertility and mortality, which are the principal determinants of changes in national populations. Questions of *local* population changes, often dominantly influenced by migration, were deliberately omitted. So were the causes and consequences of population change in underdeveloped economies. It was not the view of the planning committee that these topics were any less important than those we chose to emphasize; rather it was our view that demographic-economic relations on a national level in industrially advanced countries constitute more than adequate scope for one conference. The ensuing proceedings indicate that whatever weaknesses it had, the conference did not suffer from too narrow a focus.

The proceedings make accessible in a single volume a description of what demographers and economists think about economic influences on fertility and mortality, and about the influences of demographic factors on important economic variables. The papers are of first-rate quality and the discussion was lively and acute. The exchange of views between experts from two disciplines on something of mutual interest was, I believe, stimulating to both groups and it is to be hoped that the proceedings will have an interest as well for those who were not present.

When nearly twenty scholars are asked to write papers (each on a subject in which he has a special interest), the natural result is a somewhat diverse collection, each paper more easily understood and usually more immediately interesting to those who share the author's specialty. So it is with these papers. There are few readers indeed who would be equally at home with the technical demography in Norman B. Ryder's paper, the social-psychological survey material covered by David Goldberg, the theory of consumers' behavior in Gary Becker's paper, the statistics used by Richard and Nancy Ruggles, and the econometrics employed by Guy Orcutt and Alice M. Rivlin.

In other words, the proceedings do not and could not provide an

3

integrated account of demographic-economic relations. In this situation I felt that the most useful introduction would be one devoted to a short statement of the theme of the conference to provide a background against which more highly specialized papers could be read. The informal essay that forms the rest of this introduction attempts to describe what the conference was about, without, however, trying to summarize the views of the participants.

Just as in the conference, there is more emphasis in this introduction on variations in fertility than in mortality. Fertility is emphasized because only industrially advanced countries are considered. Among such countries mortality differences are relatively slight. Moreover, mortality changes in the next decades are not likely to be strongly influenced by economic forces, nor is it probable that these changes will have major economic consequences. Expectation of life at birth varies only from sixty-four to seventy-three years among the industrialized countries, including under this term the European countries (except Iberia and the Balkans), Oceania, America north of the Rio Grande, Japan, and the Soviet Union. Also mortality is declining most sharply in the countries with the lowest life expectancy, so that differences are rapidly diminishing. In the countries with the lowest mortality there is little room for further declines in death rates except at the older ages. Unless on the one hand we are victims of a nuclear war or, on the other, the beneficiaries of a major break-through in the treatment of degenerative diseases, we can look forward to rather gradual further increases in life expectancy. These increases will not affect population growth nearly so profoundly as the variations we can expect in fertility. Nor will mortality improvements produce nearly such pronounced changes in age distribution as those already "built in" by past variations in fertility, or those to be expected in response to future fertility changes.

Fertility, on the other hand, has recently followed diverse courses in industrialized countries, and has a much wider current range than mortality. Gross reproduction rates vary from 1.03 in West Germany to 1.88 in Canada. The substitution of a gross reproduction rate of 1.88 for one of 1.03 would contribute an additional annual natural increase of 2.0 per cent to the rate of growth if mortality risks were unchanged. On the other hand, the range of mortality in industrially advanced countries —from a life expectancy of about sixty-four in the Soviet Union to one of about seventy-three in Norway—would yield rates of annual increase differing by only about 0.3 per cent, if fertility rates were the same in both instances.

4

Economic Influences on Fertility

Until the 1940's many demographers believed it possible to describe a characteristic course of fertility that one could expect in any area undergoing industrialization. This course was downward from the high fertility levels typical of pre-industrial agrarian economies to levels that they believed would be (without state intervention) even below the low rates found in western Europe in the 1930's.

Indeed until the 1930's every area that had reached an advanced stage of industrialization had experienced a prolonged and essentially unbroken decline in fertility. In the countries of northern and western Europe (and the overseas areas peopled by their emigrants) the decline had lasted at least forty years, and in some instances more than a century. Moreover, nearly universal patterns of differential fertility could be interpreted as evidence that the small-family custom had not yet completed its diffusion. Hence the slight revival of fertility in the late 1930's and early 1940's was viewed as merely a transitory interruption of the unfinished decline in response to economic recovery.

The classic pattern of differentials was a negative association between socio-economic status and fertility. Fertility tended to be lower among urban than rural families, among the educated than among the uneducated, among high income families than among low, and so forth. These differentials were attributed to a "cultural lag" in the acceptance of small families as desirable and in the mastery of the means to attain them. It was expected that the ultimate association of fertility to income would be positive, but that this correlation would arise when low-income families had accepted the restriction of births and had decided that they could afford only very small numbers of children. In fact a widely cited positive association between income and fertility existed in Stockholm in the 1930's, but Stockholm fertility was about the lowest in the world—at only some 40 per cent of replacement.

After more than twenty years of rising fertility in the United States it is clear enough that the revival in the late 1930's was anything but a temporary quirk. However, the interpretation of the baby boom as the natural consequence of prolonged prosperity is hardly more tenable than the earlier interpretation of the reversal in the 1930's as momentary. The next earlier period of notable prosperity in the United States—the 1920's—was a period of sharply falling fertility. In fact, as Dudley Kirk points out, the depressed 1930's produced *more* births by far than one would expect on the basis of an extrapolation of the trend of the prosperous 1920's. The observed high correlation between economic fluctuations and fluctuations in births is an association between deviations from trends. A prophet fully aware of this correlation and gifted with perfect foresight of the economic future would not have predicted in 1940 eighteen years of bumper birth crops.

Another basis for doubting any simple explanation of the postwar baby boom as the result of postwar prosperity is the variety of courses followed by fertility since World War II in industrialized countries. In countries where fertility had fallen to low levels by the mid 1930's there was a fairly general rise during the early years of World War II, and a nearly universal peak in 1946 or 1947 at a level much above the 1930's.[1] After the postwar spurt, however, trends in these countries have been quite varied. Following a brief decline during 1948–1950, fertility in the United States, Canada, Australia, and New Zealand rose rather steeply to levels that in 1956–1958 were well above the immediate postwar peak. Fertility in Norway in the mid 1950's was slightly above the level just after the war, while in the remaining countries of northwestern Europe the trend since 1947–1948 has been generally level or moderately declining. In no instance has there been a decline to the prewar levels. These countries have shared in the general prosperity since the war. But while immediately after the war the increase in fertility experienced, for example, by Sweden and New Zealand was similar—48 per cent above 1935–1939 in New Zealand, and 40 per cent in Sweden—continued postwar prosperity has been accompanied by fertility in New Zealand 7 per cent higher in 1956 than in 1945–1949, and in Sweden 10 per cent lower.[2]

At the same time countries with relatively high fertility in the 1930's (Russia, Italy, Spain, Portugal, and countries of eastern Europe) generally experienced continuing declines during and after World War II. Indeed, almost all of these countries now have lower fertility than the United States. Japan, after a brief postwar revival, has had an extraordinary decline, so that in 1957 Japanese fertility (as measured by the gross reproduction rate) was among the two or three lowest in the world. Yet many of these countries—for example, Italy and Japan—have enjoyed relative prosperity in many of the postwar years.

If depression and recovery do not explain the fertility reversal in the 1930's and the sustained rise since, how can we account for them? The

---

[1] West Germany was an exception.

[2] See Frank Lorimer's discussion for hypotheses about possible special factors affecting fertility in the English-speaking non-European countries.

explanation is necessarily noneconomic in part. A reduction in average age at marriage, an increase in the proportion ever married, and a new record low in childlessness were developments not previously strongly associated either with national prosperity or with individual affluence; yet they account for much of the baby boom.

A hypothesis that would further diminish the importance of prosperity in accounting for the recent course of fertility was suggested during the conference discussion. This hypothesis is that when the custom of family limitation is in the later stages of its spread through a population, the fertility of that population is temporarily depressed below any tenable long-term level. There are two bases for the hypothesis. One is that *period* fertility will tend to fall below an equilibrium level because birth restriction by different cohorts will be bunched in the same period. The other basis is that a few cohorts at the peak of the fashion of birth control will carry the practice further than later cohorts who view family limitation more as a matter of course.

Period fertility would fall temporarily below an equilibrium level (defined as equal to the average fertility of cohorts long after family limitation has completed its spread) because many couples just taking up contraception might already have had all the children they wanted. A couple of this sort might have had, for example, three children when the wife is twenty-seven and, having discovered birth control, decided to have no more. Had they practiced contraception from marriage the third birth would have occurred, say, when the wife was thirty. Thus the diffusion of contraception through the population could mean that members of a series of marriage cohorts would simultaneously reduce fertility to an unusual degree.[3]

But the fertility of the marriage *cohorts* whose childbearing occurs at the culmination of the spread of contraceptive practice also tends to fall below the fertility of later cohorts. When birth control is still a new idea, keeping up with the Joneses means having fewer children. But when voluntary control of family size has become nearly universal, infertility no longer conveys any invidious distinction. In fact a large family may even take on a Veblenian value as a form of conspicuous expenditure.

The hypothesis that period fertility tends to swing below its equilibrium level suggests that there would have been a fertility minimum followed

[3] In fact, as Norman Ryder shows, if the spread of contraception results in a rising average age of childbearing and an increasing dispersion about the average age, period fertility is necessarily depressed relative to the fertility of cohorts then at the central ages of childbearing.

by a revival in the 1930's even if there had been no depression and no subsequent boom. These economic events may have caused merely an accentuation of a sequence that would have occurred anyway. If this notion has validity, fertility in Japan should soon reach bottom, even under favorable economic circumstances, and then recover somewhat, an eventuality that seems the more likely in view of the drastic role played by abortion in achieving the low current levels. This hypothesis is not put forward with any real confidence, but merely as a possible alternative to a view that overemphasizes economic factors.

Data on differential fertility, while too complex to be summarized here, can be described in brief as showing for recent years only a slight relation between income and family size. In recent interview surveys specifically designed to explore the factors affecting fertility, income is found to be very weakly related to desired or expected family size, while a similarly slight relationship is found in Current Population Survey data between achieved fertility and income.[4]

While it can be confidently asserted that short-run economic fluctuations have a fairly predictable impact on short-run fertility variations, we can only guess what fertility would accompany an extended continuation of prosperity on the one hand, or a prolonged depression on the other.[5]

Economic Influences on Human Mortality

The effect of economic variables on risks of dying in the industrially advanced countries is probably weaker and less direct than effects on fertility. From a very long-run point of view, of course, there has been a fairly intimate causal association between increases of life expectancy and industrialization. Mortality reduction has been the result of law and order and regularity of food supply, but overwhelmingly the consequence of purer water supplies, environmental sanitation, the gradual development of vaccines and serums, and in recent years remarkable progress in perfecting insecticides, chemotherapeutics, and antibiotics. It is hard to imagine that these developments in medicine and public health would have occurred *without* changes in industrial organization and techniques. An examination of the periods of most rapid mortality improvements in Europe or the United States makes it clear that the proximate force at work was some innovation in medicine or public health, not a period of unusual prosperity or industrial progress. Thus

[4] See David Goldberg's and Clyde V. Kiser's papers.
[5] See papers by Dudley Kirk and by Orcutt and Rivlin.

mortality reduction was accelerated when large cities acquired better water supplies in the nineteenth century, and when such recent scientific advances as antibiotics and insecticides were introduced.

Perhaps the most remarkable instances of mortality reduction largely independent of economic change are to be observed in the low-income areas of the world today. In these areas medical innovations are being introduced from the industrialized parts of the world with startling effects on death rates, both in areas that are developing economically and in areas that are not. There may be some question about the permanence of the gains in longevity achieved in low-income areas unless profound economic and social changes occur soon. But it seems probable that the course of mortality in *industrialized* areas can be safely discussed without reference to prospective variation in strictly economic forces.

Mortality, Fertility, and Population Change

Population growth equals net immigration plus the excess of births over deaths. Many national populations no longer experience large changes from net migration, and growth depends very largely on the balance of mortality and fertility.

The age structure of a population is an important determinant of births and deaths. Reproduction is limited to a particular segment of the life span, in industrialized countries births occur mostly to women twenty to forty, and mortality is increasingly concentrated in relatively advanced ages. The death rate is about eleven per thousand in England and Wales, where the life expectancy is seventy years, and only eight in Japan, where the life expectancy is sixty-six. The cause of this apparent anomaly is differences in the age distributions. Japan's population has a much smaller fraction over age fifty.

The age distribution of a population is also of major direct economic significance because age is a determinant of economic behavior. For example, consumption patterns are very different at different ages, and labor force participation is highly correlated with age.

The age structure of a population that has been affected neither by heavy recent gains or losses through migration nor by very large military losses is almost wholly the result of the past history of its fertility. Continued high fertility produces a population with many children and with numbers that rapidly diminish with age; continued low fertility produces a population with relatively few children and with a high proportion of the aged. A *decline* in fertility will yield a population that has few children and a temporary "bulge" in early adult ages, while a rise in fertility produces many children and a temporary deficit in early adult ages. These effects are illustrated by the United States age distributions of 1940 and 1957. The 1940 age distribution shows the effect of the preceding prolonged fertility decline, with a scarcity of children and relatively many persons in early adult ages. The 1957 age distribution has a high proportion of young children because of recent high fertility, a conspicuous trough resulting from the minimum fertility of the 1930's, and a high proportion over fifty, reflecting the high fertility before 1910.

Changes in mortality that have occurred to date have had very slight effects on the age distribution. In brief, the United States age distribution is very similar to the one that would exist had current mortality risks always prevailed while fertility followed its actual historic course.[6] However, our population is much *larger* and is growing faster than would be the case if mortality had failed to decline.

The interrelations in a closed population of growth, size, age distribution, fertility, and mortality can be described in a few summary statements.

1. Population size depends on the size at some previous date and the interim rate of growth.

2. The rate of population growth depends on fertility, mortality, and the age distribution. Growth increases with fertility, and decreases with mortality. It also is increased by an age distribution with high proportions in the ages of childbearing, and with low proportions in the ages of high mortality.

3. The age distribution is almost wholly determined by the past course of fertility.[7]

Population Change and Per Capita Output

In this very brief statement the sort of population changes brought by high fertility will be contrasted with those brought by low fertility.[8] Mortality will be neglected as a contributing variable for reasons already given. I shall first discuss the effect of demographic variables on aggregate

[6] For an explanation of this fact see Frank W. Notestein's paper, and the references there cited.

[7] However, future variations in mortality may have a substantial impact on the age distribution if there is an unprecedented improvement in survivorship at advanced ages with trivial improvement at young ages.

[8] High fertility here means simply above low fertility, which in turn is taken as a gross reproduction rate at least high enough to insure replacement or, to be more concrete, high fertility means a level comparable to that now current in the United States or Canada, and low fertility means a level like that in France, England or Scandinavia.

demand. Subsequently it will be assumed that deficiencies in demand can be ignored, and questions of the influence of population on the aggregate production function will be discussed.

POPULATION AND EFFECTIVE DEMAND

The sort of population change produced by high fertility serves as a stimulus to aggregate demand. High fertility, of course, promotes more rapid growth than low fertility. Fast growth implies higher and more secure returns from producers' investment and a stronger tendency for consumers to buy durable equipment such as homes and furniture. High fertility also produces an age distribution with only a small proportion in the ages of labor-force participation. If the population of labor-force age is used as the invariant element in comparing age structures, it is clear that the labor force has more dependents to support if current and recent fertility are high. More dependents per earner tend to raise the consumption function at the expense of savings and exert an upward pressure on government expenditures, especially for education. In short, higher fertility raises the demand, *ceteris paribus*, for goods currently consumed, for durable consumers' goods, for producers' goods, and puts upward pressure on government expenditures.

A high fertility population in an industrialized country, where low mortality can be assumed, thus has many children relative to its adult population, and many persistent pressures toward higher expenditures— pressures toward inflation and high levels of employment.

POPULATION AND PRODUCTIVITY

This section is a very short outline of how variations in fertility and mortality affect output per capita in industrialized countries. Full employment is assumed. The underlying concept employed is an aggregate production function where total output depends on inputs of labor, capital, and resources.

The principal analysis compares output per capita with low fertility and with high. Consider first labor input in relation to the size of the population. Low fertility tends, *ceteris paribus*, to yield a larger labor force relative to total population, for two reasons: because low fertility brings about an age distribution with a higher proportion in the ages of usual labor-force participation, and because low fertility increases the possibility of women's entering the labor force.

Next there is the question of the relation of labor inputs relative to resources. If we assume for the moment that the supply of capital is equally favorable with high or low fertility, the relationship to resources becomes essentially a question of economies of scale. High fertility ultimately produces more workers, and the problem is whether economies of scale in using resources tend to offset tendencies toward diminishing returns. There is no clear-cut answer except in the long run. Life expectancy having reached some seventy years, high fertility—even the modest sort of high fertility characteristic of the United States—implies quite rapid growth, to something like a billion persons in the United States in a century, six billion in two centuries, and one person per square foot in about seven hundred and fifty years. Ultimately, high fertility produces a population that overwhelms *any* finite resources, and diminishing returns must sometime become more important than economies of scale. But short-run predictions that larger populations would put a disastrous strain on resources have repeatedly proved wrong. Apparently there has been little rise in the cost of extracted products (farm products and minerals) relative to highly processed products. This fact does not *prove* that economies of scale have offset diminishing returns. After all, had population growth been less, raw materials might have become *cheaper* relative to other products. Also, the technological effort required to maintain the flow of useful resources at no higher relative cost might have been used to achieve greater productivity in other parts of the economy. But it nevertheless remains a tenable hypothesis that the real costs of using resources are fairly constant over a wide range of population size, and that high fertility would not on this account tend to produce lower per capita output for many years in the industrialized countries.

Two further points must be noted on the question of population size. Simon Kuznets emphasizes the crucial role of technical knowledge in raising productivity and speculates that if geniuses constitute a fixed proportion of the population, a larger population might contain more geniuses and attain faster scientific and technical progress. It was stated during the discussion of Kuznets' paper that because of the international transmission of information his argument applies to the population of the world rather than to a national population. Moreover, the extraordinary bursts of intellectual output in classic Greece, in Renaissance Italy, in the England of Elizabeth I, Bacon, and Newton, and in Budapest during the 1920's and 1930's bring into question the importance of numbers as such as a source of intellectual progress.

The second further point about size is that whatever the elasticity of resources as population grows there is one resource—living space—that inevitably becomes scarce. Harold Barnett recently quoted a passage from John Stuart Mill, who more than a century ago stated with typical eloquence the inevitable problem of space limitation:[9]

> There is room in the world, no doubt, and even in old countries, for a great increase in population, supposing the arts of life to go on improving, and capital to increase. But even if innocuous, I confess I see very little reason for desiring it. . . . It is not good for man to be kept perforce at all times in the presence of his species. A world from which solitude is extirpated, is a very poor ideal. . . . Nor is there much satisfaction in contemplating the world with nothing left to the spontaneous activity of nature; with every rood of land brought into cultivation, which is capable of growing food for human beings; every flowery waste or natural pasture ploughed up, all quadrupeds or birds which are not domesticated for man's use exterminated as his rivals for food, every hedgerow or superfluous tree rooted out, and scarcely a place left where a wild shrub or flower could grow without being eradicated as a weed in the name of improved agriculture.

The final question about the effect of demographic variables on per capita output relates to the availability of capital. High fertility, by increasing the ultimate rate of growth of the labor force, increases the need for current investment in order merely to keep output per worker constant. If the labor force grows by 3 per cent a year, an investment of perhaps 9 per cent of annual output is needed merely to equip new workers. In short, high fertility, by raising the rate of growth, greatly increases the proportion of national income that must be devoted to investment in order to achieve any specific rate of increase in per capita output. But high fertility exerts an upward pressure on the proportion of income devoted to consumption, and hence tends to *depress* the proportion diverted to investment. The pressure for consumption is the result of more dependents per earner.

High fertility leads to faster population growth and more dependents per earner. Faster growth means, of course, greater numbers; and while in the long run a constantly growing population swamps any finite resources, the only certain effect in the near future is greater crowding. But faster growth requires more investment, and the greater burden of dependency that high fertility entails implies both dividing the output of each producer with more consumers and diverting a smaller proportion to investment. High fertility stimulates demand, but tends to reduce productivity per capita.

The effects of *mortality* on productivity can be dismissed more summarily. Additional reductions in mortality would add very little to the growth of the population. Even the perpetual avoidance of all deaths beginning in 1950 would have yielded a lower long-range growth rate

[9] John Stuart Mill, *Principles of Political Economy*, Bk. 4, ch. 6.

than continuing the mortality risks then current, but adopting the fertility rates of 1957. If there are future major reductions in the risks of death, they must occur in what are now the later years of life and would tend to increase the proportion of the population beyond the now customary ages of retirement. But it is probable that health and vigor as well as life would be prolonged, and it is not certain that dependency burdens would be increased in the same proportion as the change in the age distribution.

When viewed in aggregate terms, the effects of demographic variables on the economy form a paradox of sorts: the growth arising from high fertility increases aggregate demand but reduces the full employment capability of the economy to increase its output per head.

MORE DETAILED INTERRELATIONS

The synopsis just presented treats only uniform fertility trends (high and low), distinguishes only very broad groups in the age distribution, and treats output very nearly as if it were a homogeneous commodity. A fuller analysis of population would consider such questions as the age composition within the ages of labor force participation, the number of persons annually passing the usual age of labor-force entry, and so forth. A fuller economic analysis would note that demographic factors affect the *composition* of output as well as helping determine its total value at constant prices. The conference papers could touch only fragments of these detailed issues, and this introduction ends without touching them at all.

The participants in the conference are indebted to the Universities-National Bureau Committee for Economic Research for sponsoring the meeting, and to Princeton University for making available the Social Science Lounge of the Firestone Library. Serving on the planning committee with the writer were Edgar M. Hoover, Richard Ruggles, J. J. Spengler, Warren G. Robinson, *Secretary*, and Margaret MacDonald, who succeeded Mr. Robinson. Irwin Friend of the University of Pennsylvania organized the papers for the last session of the conference.

Cornelius J. Dwyer of the National Bureau of Economic Research did an exceptional job in preparing the papers and comments for publication. Not only was he an unusually skillful editor, who improved the quality of the contributions while shortening them substantially, but because of his technical competence as an economist he helped a number of the authors in clarifying their arguments. H. Irving Forman of the National Bureau prepared the charts.

PART I
The Analysis of Population Change

An International Survey of Recent Fertility Trends

HALVOR GILLE

BUREAU OF SOCIAL AFFAIRS, UNITED NATIONS

THE disturbed period of fertility during the depression, the Second World War and the early postwar years seems to have ended in the economically developed countries. Economic conditions have, in recent years, been stable and hardly any changes have taken place in birth rates. The repercussions of the disturbed period may not have ended, and all adjustments made since the marriages which contributed largely to the war and postwar baby boom have not yet completed their reproductive history. But sufficient time has passed for an appraisal. The United Nations has recently published a survey of fertility trends in the industrialized countries up to 1954.[1] More recent data and a summary of some of the findings with regard to recent trends in countries in western Europe, North America, and Oceania are given below.

Trends in the Crude Birth Rate

The declining trend in the birth rate which began in most of the industrialized countries around the 1880's continued generally until the middle of the 1930's, only temporarily interrupted by a brief period of recuperation after the slump during the First World War. The downward trend in the birth rate was halted in northern Europe and Oceania in 1933–1935 and in most other countries in 1936–1937; only in Belgium, France, Portugal, and Spain did the birth rate continue to decline up to the outbreak of the Second World War or longer.

While the timing of the check in the birth-rate decline was fairly similar in the various countries, there were important differences in the levels of the birth rate at which the turn took place. Around the middle of the 1930's, the birth rate was 13–17 per 1,000 population in northwestern Europe and Oceania, except in Finland, Ireland, and the Netherlands where the lowest recorded birth rates were 18–20 per 1,000. In Canada and the United States, the minimum rates were 16 and 18, respectively. However, in the southern European countries the decline in the birth rate came to an end at a level of about 20 or more per 1,000.

[1] United Nations, *Recent Trends in Fertility in Industrialized Countries*, New York, 1958 (ST/SOA/Ser. A.27, October 1957).

17

These marked differences in the prewar level of the birth rate were not merely due to differences in the sociological backgrounds of the countries. The timing of the long-term fertility decline varied from country to country; in the southern European countries the decline did not reach major proportions until the middle of the 1920's. Furthermore, the depression, which contributed to the decline in the birth rate in the early 1930's by discouraging marriage and encouraging postponement of births, did not have the same impact in countries with different levels of development and industrialization.

After the decline was halted, the birth rates remained relatively stable or began to increase slightly in the late 1930's. Although in some countries the birth rate dropped in the early years of the Second World War there was no such substantial decline as that experienced during the First World War. The recovery began in most countries in 1942 or 1943 and the rise accelerated toward the end of the war and in the early postwar years. The average birth rate during the war years 1940–1944 generally exceeded the prewar level of 1935–1939 (Table 1).

The rise in the birth rate came to an end in most countries in 1946 or 1947, one or two years earlier in countries which had remained neutral during the war. Peak rates generally exceeded the prewar level by 20–50 per cent.

Subsequent declines in birth rates in the late 1940's were rather modest. In the majority of countries, the birth rate declined less than 25 per cent in the years following the postwar peak. The magnitude of the decline varied considerably from country to country, but, generally speaking, in countries where the war and postwar rise in the birth rate had been comparatively large, the subsequent decline was most pronounced. This seems to indicate that the recovery in the birth rate to a considerable extent was related to the postponement of births.

The decline in the birth rate after the recuperation was of only short duration. In most countries, it stopped around 1950. Since then, a remarkable stability in the birth rate has prevailed. In thirteen of the nineteen countries for which data are presented in Table 1, the birth rate has varied less than 1 point per 1,000 population during the years 1953–1957. A modest increase has taken place in Austria and the Federal Republic of Germany since 1953 amounting to around 2 points per 1,000. On the other hand, a slight decline amounting to 1–2 points per 1,000 has occurred in Denmark and Finland.

In a number of countries the present level of the birth rate is in the neighborhood of the low prewar level of 1935–1939 or has declined below

TABLE 1

Crude Birth Rates

Country	1930–1934	1935–1939	1940–1944	1945–1949	1950–1954	1953	1954	1955	1956	1957
Australia	17.6	17.3	19.5	23.1	23.0	22.9	22.5	22.6	22.5	22.9
Austria	15.1	14.7	19.1	16.7	15.0	14.8	14.9	15.6	16.6	16.8
Belgium	17.6	15.6	13.8	17.3	16.7	16.7	16.8	16.8	16.8	16.9
Canada	22.2	20.3	23.0	26.8	27.7	28.1	28.5	28.2	28.0	28.2
Denmark	17.9	17.9	20.3	21.6	17.9	17.9	17.3	17.3	17.2	16.7
Finland	20.0	20.2	20.1	27.0	22.8	21.9	21.4	21.2	20.7	20.1
France[a]	17.3	15.1	14.9	20.1	19.3	18.7	18.9	18.6	18.4	18.5
Germany[b]	16.3	19.4	—	16.6[c]	15.9	15.5	16.1	16.0	16.5	17.0
Great Britain:										
England and Wales	15.3	14.9	15.5	18.0	15.5	15.5	15.2	15.0	15.6	16.1
Scotland	18.6	17.7	17.7	19.3	17.9	17.8	18.0	18.0	18.5	19.0
Ireland	19.5	19.4	20.9	22.5	21.4	21.2	21.2	21.2	21.0	21.2
Italy	24.5	23.2	20.6	21.2	18.3	17.6	18.2	18.1	18.1	18.2
Netherlands	21.7	20.3	21.8	25.9	22.1	21.8	21.6	21.4	21.2	21.2
New Zealand	17.5	17.4	21.4	25.1	24.5	24.1	24.7	24.9	24.7	25.1
Norway	15.7	15.0	17.7	20.8	18.7	18.8	18.5	18.5	18.5	18.2
Portugal	29.3	27.1	25.0	25.4	24.0	23.5	22.7	23.9	22.9	23.7
Spain	27.7	22.0	22.0	22.2	20.3	20.6	20.0	20.6	20.7	21.7
Sweden	14.4	14.5	17.7	19.0	15.5	15.4	14.6	14.8	14.8	14.6
Switzerland	16.7	15.4	17.9	19.4	17.3	17.0	17.0	17.1	17.4	17.7
United States	19.7	18.8	21.2	24.1	24.9	25.0	25.3	25.0	25.3[d]	25.4[d]

[a] Data exclude infants born alive but dying before registration.
[b] Beginning 1946, data relate to the Federal Republic of Germany, excluding Berlin.
[c] 1946–1949 average.
[d] Provisional.
Source: For this and all subsequent tables, United Nations Statistical Office and official publications of the countries concerned.

it (in the three southern European countries). On the other hand, several countries have recorded a birth rate in recent years substantially above the prewar level (in Australia, Canada, New Zealand, and the United States the average birth rate in 1955–1957 was 34–43 per cent, and in France and Norway 23 per cent, above the prewar level).

Important changes have taken place within the last twenty years in the grouping of countries according to the level of the birth rate. Table 2 presents the countries listed in order of their birth rate before the war as well as their birth rate in recent years. The three Catholic countries in southern Europe which before the war had the highest prewar birth rates among the industrialized countries have been replaced in the top positions by Canada, New Zealand, and the United States. Little change, however, has taken place at the other end of the scale. Austria, England

TABLE 2

Ranking of Countries according to Average Birth Rates 1935–1939 and 1955–1957

1935–1939		*1955–1957*	
Position	Country	Country	Position
1	Portugal	Canada	1
2	*Italy*	UNITED STATES	2
3	*Spain*	NEW ZEALAND	3
4	Canada	Portugal	4
5	Netherlands	AUSTRALIA	5
6	Finland	Netherlands	6
7	Ireland	Ireland	7
8	UNITED STATES	*Spain*	8
9	*Denmark*	Finland	9
10	Scotland	Scotland	10
11	NEW ZEALAND	France	11
12	AUSTRALIA	Norway	12
13	Belgium	*Italy*	13
14	Switzerland	Switzerland	14
15	France	*Denmark*	15
16	Norway	Belgium	16
17	England, Wales	Austria	17
18	Austria	England, Wales	18
19	Sweden	Sweden	19

and Wales, and Sweden are still, as before the war, the three countries with the lowest birth rates.

Trends in the Gross Reproduction Rate

Birth rate trends are affected by factors such as the composition of the population by age and sex, the number of married persons, the proportion married at various ages, and the distribution of the married population according to number of years married, number of children born previously, and time elapsed since last birth. The effect, if any, of changes in the sex and age distribution upon fertility will become apparent by following the trend in the gross reproduction rate, which is independent of the sex and age composition of the population. The gross reproduction rates for recent years are presented in Table 3.

Trends in the gross reproduction rate have generally been fairly parallel to the trends in the crude birth rate. Gross reproduction rates increased from the middle of the 1930's to the early postwar period. In most countries, they followed closely the trend in birth rates, showing that the increase in the birth rate was not caused by changes in the sex and age composition of the population. In a few countries, the gross reproduction rate had a slightly higher incline, indicating that changes in the age and

to the birth
ge structure
mark which
scale, but,
t down one
tle ground

Rates

TABLE 3
Reproduction Rates

5–39	1940–1944	1945–1949	1950–1954	1953	1954	1955	1956
06	1.18	1.43	1.53	1.56	1.56	1.57	1.61
—	0.95	1.21	1.14	1.13	1.15	1.17	1.18
.30	1.42	1.64	1.77	1.82	1.87	1.83	1.83
.04	1.21	1.38	1.24	1.25	1.23	1.25	1.26
.18	1.17	1.61	1.46	1.44	1.39	1.42	1.40
1.02	0.99	1.39	1.34	1.30	1.31	1.31	1.30
0.87	0.94	1.15	1.06	1.08	1.07	1.08	1.14
—	1.10	1.31	1.20	1.18	1.21	1.23	1.28
1.46	1.30	1.32	1.16	1.12	1.15	1.15	1.16
1.26	1.37	1.68	1.49	1.47	1.46	1.48	1.48
1.07	1.28	1.59	1.69	1.70	1.76	1.81	1.70
0.89	1.03	1.25	1.25	1.28	1.30	1.34	1.30
1.70	1.55	1.58	1.50	1.50	1.40	1.32	1.41
0.87	1.07	1.22	1.09	1.10	1.05	1.08	1.11
0.88	1.08	1.24	1.23	1.25	1.17	1.13	1.16
1.09	1.22	1.45	1.62	1.67	1.72	1.73	1.79

lation tended rather to retard the increase in the

nd 1946 and 1947 the gross reproduction rates
tries at a much slower rate than the birth rate.
in the sex and age composition of the population
sponsible for the postwar decline in the birth rate.
decreasing proportion of women in the reproductive
lation tended to give an exaggerated picture of the
asured by the birth rate.

cline in
middle

l effect
repro-
h age
d the
at the
o age
stwar
tility
uent
ually
twar
has

countries show both a stable birth rate and a stable
te. On the other hand, a marked increase in the gross
as taken place in Australia, Canada, New Zealand,
tes; the gross reproduction rate in these countries is
recorded at the peak of the baby boom in the early

anges have also taken place in the ranking of the
of gross reproduction rate since before the war. Italy,
cond highest gross reproduction rate before the war,
h lowest, as shown in Table 4. Portugal, which had the
re the war, is now found on a considerably lower level
three countries with the lowest gross reproduction rates
and, England and Wales, and Sweden as before the war.

21

Some of the changes in the ranking of countries according
rate (Table 2) appear to be due to changes in the sex and a
of the population. This is the case, for example, in Den
dropped in rank by birth rate about one-third of the entire
ranked according to the gross reproduction rate, merely wer
place. On the other hand, Portugal, which lost only a li

TABLE 4

Ranking of Countries according to the Average Gross Reproduction
1936–1939 and 1955–1956

1936–1939		1955–1956	
Position	Country	Country	Position
1	*Portugal*	Canada	1
2	*Italy*	UNITED STATES	2
3	Canada	NEW ZEALAND	3
4	Netherlands	AUSTRALIA	4
5	Finland	Netherlands	5
6	UNITED STATES	Finland	6
7	NEW ZEALAND	*Portugal*	7
8	AUSTRALIA	Norway	8
9	Scotland	France	9
10	Denmark	Scotland	10
11	Belgium	Denmark	11
12	France	Belgium	12
13	Norway	*Italy*	13
14	Switzerland	Switzerland	14
15	England, Wales	England, Wales	15
16	Sweden	Sweden	16

according to ranking by the birth rate, showed a substantial de
the gross reproduction rate which moved it from the top to the
of the scale.

Trends in the gross reproduction rate merely indicate the over-al
of changes in fertility in the various age groups of women of all
ductive ages. A study of the recent trends in fertility within ea
group shows that the war and postwar recovery in fertility, an
subsequent decline, are recorded among women of most ages. B
magnitude of these changes varies considerably from age group t
group. The increase in fertility during the war and the early po
years was especially pronounced among younger women. Their fe
increased sharply during the period of recovery and the subse
decline was small; fertility among women aged 15–19 years act
continued to increase in a number of countries even after the po
peak in the birth rate. In most recent years, a considerable increase

22

taken place in fertility among women under 25 years of age. An all-time-high level of fertility among these women prevailed by 1957 in all countries except France, Portugal, and the Netherlands. On the other hand, women over 40 were affected only to a small extent by the recovery of the birth rate in the early postwar period. The level of fertility among these women has been declining rather steadily for a long period of time and this decline seems to have continued in recent years. Only in France did a marked increase in fertility occur among these women during the 1940's.

The recent trends in fertility at various ages have tended to increase the relative contribution of younger women to total fertility. Women under 25 years of age contribute now almost one-half of the total fertility in the United States and almost two-fifths in the Scandinavian countries. The lowest relative contribution of women in this age group is made in the Netherlands, where women under 25 years account for only one-fifth. An even lower ratio undoubtedly exists in Ireland, although age-specific fertility rates are not available.

Trends in Annual Marital Fertility

As the large majority of all births takes place in marriage, an important factor in the study of fertility is changes in the marriage rate. Changes in the annual number of marriages will affect the total number of married persons exposed to risk of childbearing in the future. Furthermore, such changes will alter the distribution of marriages according to duration of marriage at future dates.

Substantial variations have taken place in the marriage rate in recent decades. The depression caused a considerable decline in the marriage rate in the early 1930's, which was followed by a slow recovery until the outbreak of the Second World War brought about a marked rise. In a number of countries, it remained high during the war years as marriages which were postponed during the depression were contracted. At the end of the war, another pronounced rise in the marriage rate took place. After the peak in 1946 or 1947, it began to decline slowly—a decline which has continued up to the most recent years. The marriage rate by 1957 was below the prewar level in most countries.

The effect upon the birth rate of recent changes in the number of married persons and the distribution of married couples by duration of marriage becomes apparent by comparing the trend in the birth rate with the trend in the total marital fertility rate. The latter rate is the sum of fertility rates for successive durations of marriage per 100 marriages

23

observed in a given calendar year. In Table 5 the courses of these two rates since 1939 are outlined for six selected countries.

It appears that the rise in the birth rate which took place in several countries in the early 1940's was due to a large extent to the increase in marriages. Marital fertility lagged considerably behind the upward trend in the birth rate in Australia, England and Wales, New Zealand,

TABLE 5

Indexes of Total Marital Fertility Rates (A) and Crude Birth Rates (B)
(1939 = 100)

Year	Australia A	B	Belgium A	B	England and Wales A	B	Finland A	B	New Zealand A	B	Norway A	B
1939	100	100	100	100	100	100	100	100	100	100	100	100
1940	99	102	91	87	94	95	82	84	108	113	98	102
1941	99	107	84	79	85	94	112	114	112	122	89	97
1942	96	108	92	85	95	105	76	78	108	116	97	112
1943	101	117	105	97	101	109	94	96	98	105	104	120
1944	104	119	110	99	112	119	96	100	108	115	124	129
1945	107	123	110	101	99	108	111	120	118	124	117	127
1946	115	134	121	118	120	130	114	131	128	135	133	144
1947	116	136	112	115	129	138	111	132	130	141	123	136
1948	111	131	109	113	112	120	108	130	125	136	116	130
1949	111	130	106	111	105	113	104	123	121	133	110	124
1950	116	132	105	109	101	107	100	115	121	132	109	121
1951	116	130	102	106	98	104	96	108	120	130	104	117
1952	120	132	105	108	95	103	98	109	123	132	107	119
1953	120	130	106	107	98	105	96	103	122	129	107	119
1954	120	128	108	108	98	102	95	101	127	131	107	117
1955	123	128	108	108	98	101	96	100	130	133	109	117
1956	—	—	109	108	103	105	96	98	130	132	—	—

and Norway. For example, in Australia, the birth rate by 1943 exceeded the prewar level by 17 per cent but the marital fertility rate was merely 1 per cent above it. In other countries, marital fertility was rising but contributed only in part to the increase in the birth rate. On the other hand, in Belgium the slump in the marriage rate during the war years was so considerable that the birth rate was below the 1939 level in all war years although marital fertility was considerably above that level since 1943.

The rise in the birth rate towards the end of the war and in the early postwar period was mainly caused by an increase in marital fertility. This factor was responsible in New Zealand and Norway for three-quarters, in England and Wales for two-thirds, and in Australia for half of the rise in the birth rate above the prewar level by 1946. The remaining part of the rise was due to the increase in the number of newly-wed couples. Similarly, declining marital fertility was mainly responsible for the decline in the birth rate after the peak in the early postwar period as indicated by the fairly parallel downward trend in the two rates.

It is interesting to note that, since 1951, total marital fertility rates have shown an upward trend in all the selected countries (except Finland), particularly in Australia and New Zealand. In this period the birth rate has remained fairly stable in these countries. The increase in marital fertility has been sufficient to offset the tendency toward a decrease in the birth rate caused by the declining marriage rate in recent years.

The recent changes in the number of married women and their distribution by duration of marriage, which are responsible for a considerable part of the recent rise in the birth rate, are associated with important changes in marriage customs.

During the last 20 or 30 years, a substantial increase has taken place in the proportion of women married, particularly at the younger ages where fertility is comparatively high. In a number of countries, the median age at marriage among women who ultimately marry declined by two to three years from around 1930 to 1950. Furthermore, there has been a tendency toward a smaller proportion of women remaining single.[2] These changes are not necessarily temporary shifts related to the conditions that existed during and immediately after the Second World War; the evidence suggests a long-term change in marriage patterns in response to changing social conditions.

The recent change from one level of age at marriage to another, and from one proportion ultimately marrying to another, has been an important factor contributing to the recent rise and decline in the birth rate. During a period when age at marriage is declining and the proportion ultimately marrying is increasing, the number of marriages will be inflated and the birth rate will increase. A decline in marriages and births will take place as soon as the trend levels off, although the marriage rate and the birth rate will not necessarily return to their former levels.

But another question is the ultimate effect upon fertility of a shift in the marriage pattern. An increase in the proportion of ever-married women will undoubtedly tend to raise the birth rate as more women become exposed to risk. Whether a lower age at marriage means a higher number of births will depend upon the circumstances and the causes for the decline. Women who marry earlier may not necessarily adopt the

[2] J. Hajnal, "Age at Marriage and Proportions Marrying," *Population Studies*, Vol. 7, no. 2, 1953.

pattern of relatively large family size previously prevailing among women marrying young. They may have the same attitude toward family size as women who formerly married late, and be confident that they, in spite of earlier marriage, will be able to control the number of births efficiently. On the other hand, early marriage may be associated with a desire to have more children.

The ultimate effect upon the family size of the recent decline in age at marriage may be illustrated by the data available for England and Wales on family building in recent marriage cohorts. While the trend in family size has been the same at all ages of marriage for women married before the 1930's, the pattern of relationship between fertility and age at marriage has been subject to a change among women married since the middle of the 1930's. The difference in average family size of women marrying young and those marrying at older ages has declined substantially. For example, in the 1936–1940 cohorts, women married under 20 years of age had after ten years of marriage nearly 30 per cent more children than women married at 20–24 years, but in the 1946 cohort the difference was only 20 per cent. In the 1936–1940 cohorts the difference in family size between women married at 20–24 years and at 25–29 years amounted to 21 per cent, but in the 1946 cohort merely to 12 per cent. In view of the decline in age at marriage for recent marriage cohorts, it appears that women marrying younger have not accepted the pattern of relatively high fertility prevailing earlier in the group of women married at a young age.

Trends in Family Size

The discussion in the previous section showed that only a part of the recent changes in the birth rate can be explained by the changes in marriage patterns. The important question arises whether the recent trends in marital fertility are explained merely by changes in the timing of the family building in marriages or indicate changes in the ultimate size of the families. This requires a study of family building over the entire or at least the major part of the childbearing ages of cohorts of women married or born in the same period.

Information on the trend in family size for marriage or birth cohorts may be obtained from census data on the number of children ever born to women at the census date. In a number of countries, data of this kind are available in a recent census. They show a continued decline in ultimate family size. However, this information is limited to cohorts originating in the 1920's or earlier. Investigation of more recent developments requires the study of cohorts of incomplete fertility. To obtain information on reproductive behavior of these women, it is necessary to have data from two or more censuses to provide a basis for comparing the family size obtained in a certain period of a recent cohort with the family size accomplished in a similar period of an earlier cohort.

TABLE 6

Number of Children Born per 100 Marriages by Duration of Marriage
at the Dates of Recent Censuses

| Country | Year | Years of Marriage | | | |
		Under 5	5–9	10–14	15–19
Belgium	1930	72	150	198	—
	1947	69	146	182	—
Norway	1930	88	205	295	376
	1946	82	167	211	244
	1950	81	174	217	240
Switzerland	1941	67	158	208	245
	1950	81	182	221	237
United States	1940	63	114	181	250
	1950	79	168	220	253

Table 6 shows the number of children born to married women who had been married a certain length of time at a recent census compared with the number of children born to women within a similar duration of marriage at a previous census for Belgium, Norway, Switzerland, and the United States.

The evidence is inconclusive as to whether a reversal in the declining trend in family size is indicated by the information on incomplete fertility from recent censuses. In Norway, Switzerland, and the United States an increase in the number of children per 100 married women has taken place between the two recent censuses for durations of marriage of 5–9 years and 10–14 years. In particular, the increase in the United States is remarkable. In 1940, women who had been married 5–9 years had borne 114 children per 100 marriages, while women at the same duration in 1950 had 168 children. But the latter women spent a major part of their married life during the postwar period when the employment situation was favorable, while the former group spent the same part of their marriage during the period of economic distress. It might be more conclusive that women who had been married 15–19 years in 1950 had about the same family size as women married the same number of years in 1940, in spite of the fact that the former group of women spent their most fertile years of marriage during the depression while the latter group

27

were spending the similar period of married life under far more favorable economic conditions.

More revealing information is available for England and Wales by using the data available in the 1946 Family Census and 1951 Population Census on family size for marriage cohorts, not merely at the time of the census but also at any earlier date, and linking them with the vital statistics registration data on births which occurred to women in these cohorts in post-census years.[3] This material, which is limited to first marriages, seems to indicate that the decline in average completed family size has slackened considerably and for cohorts originating in the late 1930's and early 1940's the decline has been brought to an end.

After ten years of marriage, women who married in the year 1920 had borne 197 children per 100 marriages, women married in 1930 164 children, and women of the 1935 cohort 160 children. Women who married in the year 1940 had after ten years of marriage approximately the same live births as women who married in 1930. For the cohorts 1945 and 1946 the average family size was 180, which is a larger family size than recorded for any previous cohort of married women almost twenty-five years back. It should be noted, however, that the 1945 and 1946 cohorts may give an exaggerated impression of the level of fertility in the early years of marriage, which for these women coincided with the postwar years.

Instead of census data, current vital statistics may be used to obtain information on the behavior of fairly recent cohorts. In a number of countries, a series of annual statistics on births by duration of marriage or age of mother is available which makes it possible to reconstruct the family building in cohorts of married women or cohorts of women born in the same period by allocating all births occurring in a year to the year of marriage or year of birth of the mother. The number of births which occurred to women at various durations of marriage or ages within each cohort are related to the number of women at risk. In the case of birth cohorts, the population at risk is easily available through census data and intercensal estimates of the composition of the population by sex and age. But for marriage cohorts, annual data on the number of married women at various durations of marriage are seldom available and often difficult to construct. Instead, the birth data may be related to the number of women which constituted the original size of the marriage cohort. The fertility rates obtained in this way give the net fertility of marriages, as

---

[3] United Kingdom, *The Registrar General's Statistical Review of England and Wales*, 1955, part III, and 1956, part II.

no allowance is made for marriages which are dissolved owing to death, divorce, or separation.

Table 7 shows, for five selected countries, the total number of births which took place within a specified number of years of marriage, per 100 marriages of a cohort(s). For women married in the 1920's and 1930's, the cumulative rates are given for five-year groups of cohorts only. Information is given on fertility within the first twenty years of marriage (except in the case of France where information is only available for the first fourteen years of marriage). The cumulative fertility for women married at twenty years may be considered as a reasonably good indication of the ultimate family size as only a few births occur later in marriage.

It is brought out clearly in this table that the decline in the ultimate family size which has taken place during many decades has been brought to an end at least temporarily. The average family size after twenty years of marriage was about 5 to 10 per cent lower in marriages contracted in the late 1920's than in those contracted in the early 1920's. But the family size at this duration was about the same in marriages originating in the 1930's as in marriages from the late 1920's. Only in Norway did the decline seem also to continue for the cohorts originating in the early 1930's.

For later cohorts, no statistics are available on cumulative fertility at twenty years of marriage. But in view of the fact that the majority of births (around four-fifths of all births) takes place within the first ten years of marriage, the gap in information on reproduction at higher duration of marriage has been filled for some recent cohorts by estimates (shown in brackets in the table). The pattern of family building at the upper durations has been estimated by assuming that the proportionate additions to the ultimate family size experienced in the cohorts of the early 1920's will apply to later cohorts of incompleted fertility above duration of ten years.

The decline in ultimate family size for women married in the late 1920's may to some extent be associated with the depression. But the fact that this group since very early in marriage lagged behind the preceding cohorts seems to indicate that the main factor was a desire to have a smaller number of children.

As for women married in the 1930's, the depression continued to slow down the rate of family building in the earlier years of marriage. In these cohorts, the cumulative fertility rates at similar durations of marriage are considerably below the rates experienced among women

29

TABLE 7

Cumulative Fertility Rates in Selected Marriage Cohorts 1920–1950

Number of years after marriage	YEAR OF MARRIAGE											
	1920/21–1924/25	1925/26–1929/30	1930/31–1934/35	1935/36–1939/40	1940/1941	1942/1943	1944/1945	1945/1946	1946/1947	1947/1948	1948/1949	1949/1950
Australia												
3	119	114	109	103	95	95	104	110	118	119	120	120
5	158	147	142	137	133	133	143	153	161	164	165	165
7	185	171	167	166	161	161	172	185	193	197		
10	213	196	193	196	190	190	191					
15	237	219	221	218	211	(211)	(212)					
20	247	228	(231)	(227)	(220)	(220)	(221)					
New Zealand												
3	121	113	107	106	98	102	121	128	127	125	125	127
5	158	147	141	145	141	145	162	173	171	170	170	175
7	184	171	167	175	176	175	192	205	203	204	204	
10	210	195	196	209	208	204	220	238				
15	231	218	225	(230)	(229)	(224)	(242)	(262)				
20	240	230	(234)	(239)	(238)	(233)	(251)	(272)				
Norway												
3	115	107	96	92	109	110	113	103	102	99	101	104
5	151	141	127	126	146	146	150	136	135	133	135	141
7	178	165	150	155	175	171	176	161	160	158		
10	206	191	174	188	202	197	202					
15	230	214	203	(210)	(225)	(220)	(225)					
20	239	225	(211)	(218)	(234)	(229)	(234)					

(continued on next page)

TABLE 7 (cont.)

Number of years after marriage	YEAR OF MARRIAGE							
	1925	1938	1943	1945	1946	1947	1948	1949
Sweden								
3	107	88	86	98	97	96	96	94
5	133	112	114	126	122	121	122	
7	152	130	137	145	141	139		
10	171	152	160	162				
15	190	174	(178)	(180)				
20	198	(181)	(185)	(187)				
France								
3	100	87	114	113	115	114	114	115
5	127	112	147	145	148	146	147	149
7	148	136	173	169	171	170		
10	168	167	199					
14	181	180	214					

married early in the 1920's. Under more favorable economic conditions later on, the cohorts of the early 1930's stepped up family building, but the gap between fertility of these two groups of cohorts was never quite closed.

A substantial change in fertility in the earlier part of marriage appears to have taken place in cohorts of women married in the early 1940's. These women had, after five or ten years of marriage, a family size substantially above that of women married in the early 1920's. This was the case in all the selected countries except Australia. In France, the women married in 1943 had after five years of marriage borne 35 more children per 100 marriages, and after ten years of marriage 32 more children per 100 marriages, than women in the 1938 cohort. Fertility of the 1943 cohort in France even exceeded that of the 1925 cohort, which is the only cohort in the 1920's for which information is available. But, in the other countries, the family size in cohorts of the early 1940's generally fell short of the fertility pattern of the cohorts originating in the early 1920's.

As a large majority of births occurs within the first ten years of marriage, the increase shown in cumulative fertility for women married in the early 1940's might be interpreted as an indication of a beginning of an upward trend in ultimate family size, also indicated by the projected rates beyond ten years duration of marriage. However, women married in the early 1940's spent some of their most fertile years of marriage during the early postwar period when fertility was comparatively high for marriages of all durations. It is still difficult to say to what extent this increase is due to the advancement of births which normally would have occurred late in marriage, but in France and New Zealand the increase in family size at ten years of marriage is so substantial for recent cohorts that a rise in ultimate family size seems to be indicated.

The level of fertility at the earlier years of marriage increased further for the postwar cohorts in several countries. In Australia, New Zealand, and France more children had been born in these marriages after five or seven years of marriage than in all earlier cohorts since the First World War. In New Zealand, women married in 1945–1946 had after ten years of marriage given birth to approximately the same number of children as women married in the 1920's had borne after twenty years of marriage, and given birth to more children than women married in the 1930's had after fifteen years of marriage.

The previous discussion has been based upon the study of family building in groups of women married during specified years. The pattern of family building among groups of women born in the same period, that is, birth cohorts, is illustrated in Table 8. This line of analysis does not eliminate the influence of changes in the number of marriages and the distribution of marriages by duration, but it does give an indication of the reproductive capacity of the total population.

TABLE 8

Cumulative Fertility Rates at Selected Ages in Birth Cohorts:
Canada, Finland, New Zealand, and Sweden

Women born in:	Aged 15 in:	Live births per 100 women aged:						
		20	25	30	35	40	45	50
Canada								
1906/07	1922	16	86	163	223	266	281	283
1911/12	1927	15	73	146	212	255	270	(281)
1916/17	1932	13	75	159	229	271	(287)	(288)
1921/22	1937	15	92	194	271	(324)	(344)	(346)
1926/27	1942	17	107	208	(286)	(342)	(362)	(363)
1931/32	1947	23	129					
Finland								
1895/1896	1911	10	65	147	214	256	277	279
1900/1901	1916	8	65	138	193	232	253	255
1905/1906	1921	9	60	120	173	216	237	239
1910/1911	1926	8	53	117	180	231	249	(252)
1915/1916	1931	8	58	129	201	240	(259)	(262)
1920/1921	1936	9	64	160	224	(269)	(290)	(293)
1925/1926	1941	7	87	166	(239)	(287)	(310)	(313)
1930/1931	1946	13	88					
New Zealand								
1906/1907	1922	10	64	130	186	223	236	237
1911/1912	1927	10	57	132	200	241	252	(253)
1916/1917	1932	8	71	160	234	272	(288)	(289)
1921/1922	1937	11	76	186	260	(314)	(332)	(334)
1926/1927	1942	10	99	214	(308)	(372)	(394)	(396)
1931/1932	1947	15	122					
Sweden								
1895/1896	1911	10	62	129	176	204	215	216
1900/1901	1916	9	58	111	151	178	189	190
1905/1906	1921	9	50	96	137	170	182	183
1910/1911	1926	9	46	95	148	179	187	(188)
1915/1916	1931	8	50	117	169	193	(204)	(205)
1920/1921	1936	10	65	134	178	(206)	(218)	(219)
1925/1926	1941	14	76	142	(194)	(225)	(238)	(239)
1930/1931	1946	18	84					

Figures in parentheses are forecasts.

The average number of live births per 100 women up to selected ages are presented for Canada, Finland, New Zealand, and Sweden for selected cohorts beginning around the turn of the century. For cohorts of incomplete fertility, the number of children to be born within the reproductive period still remaining has been estimated by assuming that these women had completed the same proportion of their ultimate family size as women born around the turn of the century.

The cumulative fertility rates for birth cohorts show not merely that the decline in the average number of children born has been discontinued but indicate also that there is an upward trend under way. At the age of 35, women born in 1921–1922 in New Zealand had borne 260 children per 100 women, while women born in 1906–1907 had borne only 186 children at that age. The women born in 1921–1922 had at the age of 35 actually about ten per cent more children than the women born in 1906–1907 had at the end of the reproductive ages. A similar trend is found in Canada and Finland. In Sweden, also, the decline in the average number of children seems to have been brought to an end, but the upward trend is not so marked as for the other countries.

The projected figures indicate a pronounced rise in family size for cohorts of completed fertility. Women born early in the 1930's would according to these estimates end up with an average number of children much higher than that of any cohort of women born earlier in this century. But these calculations undoubtedly give an exaggerated picture of the increase in fertility as they do not make allowance for the tendency towards concentration of childbearing at younger ages, which is only partly due to the decline in age at marriage.

In considering the level of reproduction of the population it is necessary to take mortality into account. Owing to the continuous decline in mortality, the reproduction of the population has increased more than indicated by the recent rise in fertility. The populations in all countries considered above appear to be reproducing themselves. This is even the case in England and Wales which has one of the lowest levels of fertility at present.[4]

COMMENT

FRANK LORIMER

This paper is limited to a consideration of recent fertility trends in technically advanced countries. Even within this category, attention is

---

[4] Replacement rate calculated on the basis of cohort fertility rates of 1951–1955 and mortality experience 1950–1952 is 1.01 for females and 1.06 for males (*ibid.*).

restricted to western European and overseas British areas. This limitation seems arbitrary, though omission of the Soviet Union and some other countries may be attributed to paucity of relevant data. But why omit Japan from a list of industrial countries that includes Spain and Portugal? Surely we can no longer assume that we live in a European world.

A first over-all view of recent variations in current fertility is provided by crude birth rates. Such rates are generally useful for this purpose, in contrast to crude death rates which are worthless in comparing levels of mortality in different populations. The picture thus presented is only slightly modified by the use of other period indexes of fertility. A brief reference to some of these modifications might have sufficed in place of the rather extensive discussion of these alternative indexes. On the other hand, one wishes that the treatment of cohort indexes of fertility could have been expanded. This approach is essential to a satisfactory analysis of changing trends; but adequate information is not yet available for developing this sort of analysis in a general international survey. Other papers of this conference may contribute to the development of this approach.

One of the major implications of the information reviewed in this paper is that a movement toward the control of fertility induces a progressive decline of fertility toward a lower "asymptotic zone" in the vicinity of two births per woman of completed fertility—with the actual level varying, under different economic and social conditions, from about 1.5 to about 3 births per woman. All known industrial cultures seem to have stabilizing factors which prevent a decline in cohort fertility to a point much below the replacement level.

The countries considered in this paper seem to fall, as regards fertility, into three major groups: (1) the transition from largely uncontrolled to relatively controlled fertility was still in full swing during recent years in some countries, for example, Spain, Portugal, Italy (and Japan)—with consequent progressive declines in fertility; (2) in the European countries in which control of fertility has been largely achieved, economic and social constraints check motivations to parenthood so as to hold fertility at fairly constant levels; (3) among British populations in the more spacious overseas areas, there has been a significant rise in fertility. The major factor in this upward shift seems to have been a trend in these abundant economies toward juvenile precocity and early parenthood.

Differential Fertility in European Countries

GWENDOLYN Z. JOHNSON

EVIDENCE that traditional differentials in fertility are tending to diminish in a number of European countries has been disclosed by several recent studies and at least one earlier study. These investigations have also raised questions as to whether the differentials may not vanish entirely or perhaps in the long run be replaced by differentials of an opposite nature, that is, by a positive association of fertility with socio-economic status. It is the purpose of this paper to draw together findings of as many as possible of these studies and to supplement them with newly available data extracted from censuses and other sources. In what follows, attention is confined largely to the pattern of differentials in fertility between socio-economic groups and between urban and rural inhabitants in the industrialized countries of Europe.[1]

Before discussing differentials within the various countries, a brief review of the differences in fertility between countries at present and in the recent past may be desirable. Maps 1 and 2 depict the level of the gross reproduction rate in countries of Europe around 1930 and around 1955.[2] A comparison of the maps discloses two significant features: the decrease (1) in the number of countries with gross rates of 1.75 and above, and (2) in the number with rates below 1.00. Whereas the latter group contained seven countries around 1930, all countries had rates above unity around 1955. Around 1930 six countries had GRR's in excess of 1.75; in 1955 only Albania was in this class.

---

[1] Published data of the kind and quality required for an investigation of fertility differentials are not available for most nonindustrialized countries, nor for some of the important industrialized countries. Wherever possible the nonindustrialized countries are included, especially if the data for such countries show divergent patterns.

[2] The statistics are from the following sources: Dudley Kirk, *Europe's Population in the Interwar Years*, Princeton, Princeton University Press, 1946, p. 56; United Nations, *Recent Trends in Fertility in Industrialized Countries*, New York, United Nations Publications, 1958, pp. 142–143; and *Population Index*, Vol. 24, no. 2, April, 1958, pp. 190–196. The Foreign Manpower Research Office of the U.S. Bureau of the Census kindly supplied estimates for the U.S.S.R., Albania, and Bulgaria as of 1950–1955. The gross reproduction rates for the countries of Europe, excluding the U.S.S.R., around 1950–1955 have been published in the Bureau of the Census monograph. "The Population of Hungary," *International Population Statistics Reports*, Series P-90, no. 9. Rates in Map 2 for Greece, Iceland, Rumania, and Spain were estimated by a method similar to that used in indirect standardization.

The continued decline or unimportant increases in high fertility countries during this period and the substantial gains experienced in low fertility countries—mainly the industrialized countries—combined to effect a contraction of prewar differences, particularly between the less developed and the industrialized countries.[3] The region of lowest fertility in 1930, Northwest-Central Europe, maintained its prewar position in 1955, as did the other regions.

Differential Fertility Prior to 1900

Urban and rural inhabitants in European countries have had different levels of fertility for nearly a century. Indeed, crude birth rates for rural inhabitants exceeded those of the urban population in Sweden as early as the middle of the eighteenth century, and in England and Wales as far back as 1850.[4] The early differentiation of urban and rural inhabitants in Norway is illustrated in Chart 1. Here fertility is expressed as the average number of live births per woman after twenty years of marriage, for women married in 1880 to 1930 at age 24 or 25. Among couples married in 1880 there was little difference by residence in the completed family size. It varied from 5.98 per woman in Oslo, the capital, to 6.60 in rural areas. The subsequent widening of the differential was due to the more rapid declines in Oslo and the towns and to the relatively slow pace of the decline in completed family size among couples in rural areas. It will be noted later that the pattern which developed in the Netherlands (Chart 2) was almost identical with that observed for Norway.

Studies of the fertility characteristics of social and economic classes within European countries other than Sweden usually found fertility to be inversely associated with status, no matter what the definition of status or the measure used to describe the level of fertility. Although data that would give a comprehensive picture are lacking, there is some evidence that a fertility distinction between classes was rather widespread prior to 1900 in the now industrialized countries of Europe.[5]

In England and Wales, differences in fertility between classes developed among cohorts of marriages that began during the latter half of the nineteenth century. Stevenson shows that, in marriages contracted prior

---

[3] Demographic factors in the recovery of the birth rate in industrialized European countries are discussed in the paper by Halvor Gille in this volume. See also United Nations, *Recent Trends in Fertility in Industrialized Countries*, United Nations Publications, 1958, pp. xi, 182.

[4] A. J. Jaffe, "Urbanization and Fertility," *The American Journal of Sociology*, Vol. XLVIII, no. 1, July 1942, pp. 48–60.

[5] For a more detailed discussion see United Nations, *Determinants and Consequences of Population Trends*, United Nations Publications, 1953, pp. 86–89.

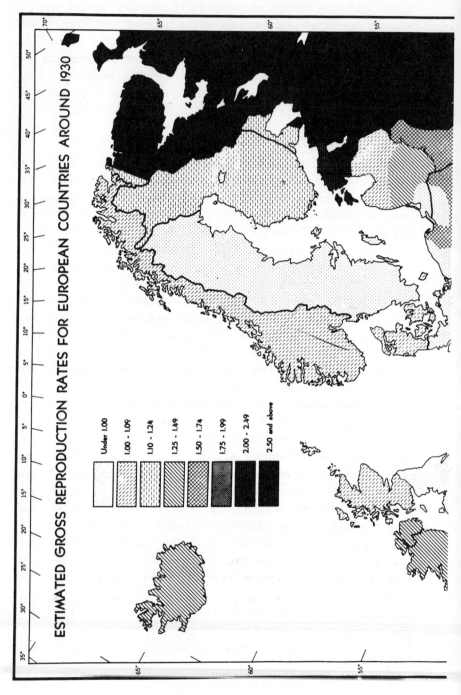

ESTIMATED GROSS REPRODUCTION RATES FOR EUROPEAN COUNTRIES AROUND 1930

Under 1.00
1.00 - 1.09
1.10 - 1.24
1.25 - 1.49
1.50 - 1.74
1.75 - 1.99
2.00 - 2.49
2.50 and above

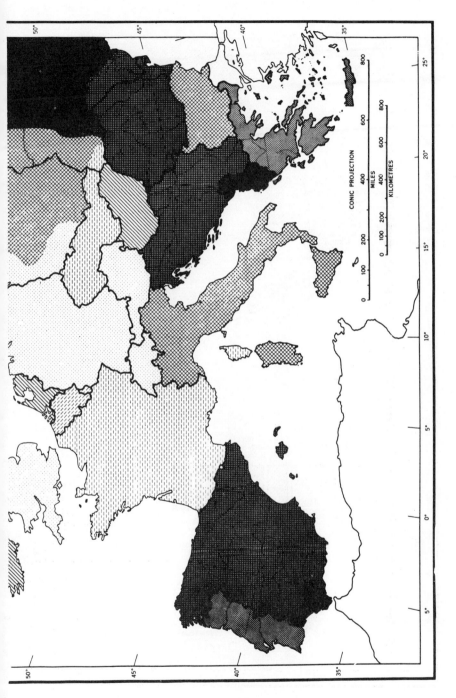

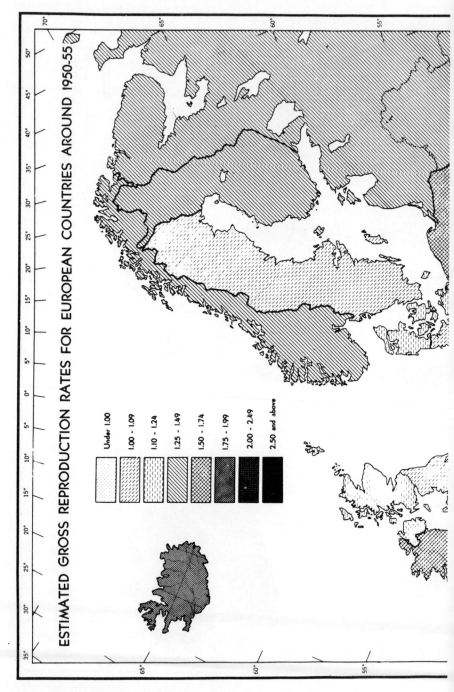

ESTIMATED GROSS REPRODUCTION RATES FOR EUROPEAN COUNTRIES AROUND 1950-55

Under 1.00
1.00 - 1.09
1.10 - 1.24
1.25 - 1.49
1.50 - 1.74
1.75 - 1.99
2.00 - 2.49
2.50 and above

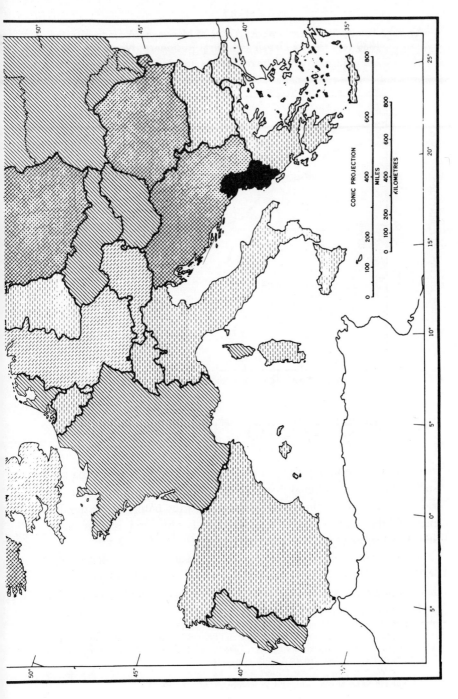

CHART 1

Average Family Size after Twenty Years of Marriage, Women Married
1880 to 1930, by Urban and Rural Residence, Norway
(age of wife at marriage, 24 and 25 years)

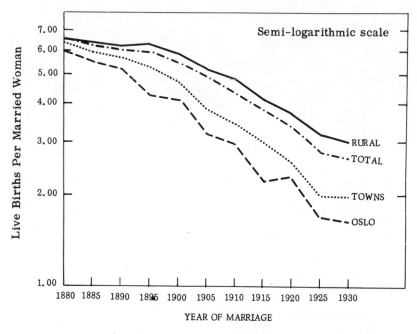

Source: L. Henry: "La fécondité des mariages en Norvège d'après les recensements",
Population (Paris), 13ᵉ, No. 1, January-March 1958, pp. 136-143.

to 1871, average family size did not vary consistently with occupational status of husband, although the general tendency was towards an inverse relationship.[6] Notestein has already analyzed the nature of the development of the inverse relationship between fertility and socio-economic status in England and Wales (Chart 3).[7]

The differentiation of broad occupational classes was also well developed in the Netherlands at the turn of the century, as may be observed from information on completed family size for marriages contracted from 1891 and earlier to 1922–1926. From the standpoint of cohort fertility, the

[6] T. H. C. Stevenson, "The Fertility of Social Classes in England and Wales from the Middle of the Nineteenth Century to 1911," *Journal of the Royal Statistical Society*, London, Vol. LXXXIII, Part III, May 1920, pp. 401–432.

[7] Frank W. Notestein, "Class Differences in Fertility," *Annals of the American Academy of Political and Social Science*, Vol. 188, November 1936, pp. 26–36.

CHART 2

Average Family Size after Twenty and More Years of Marriage, Women
Married 1891 to 1926, by Urban and Rural Residence, the Netherlands
(age of wife at marriage, 25 and under)

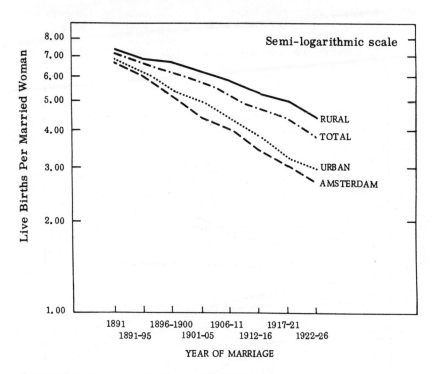

Source: Adapted from a chart by T. Van Den Brink: op. cit., p. 751.

development of the inverse relationship was not complete until the
termination of the reproductive span of couples married during 1896–
1900. Chart 4 illustrates the number of live births per marriage in existence more than 20 years at the census of 1947 and in which the wife
was under 25 years of age at marriage.[8]

Data are not available to show the early development of this relationship in other European countries. However, the results of a survey
carried out in Poland in 1948 (Chart 11, below) provide evidence of a
positive association of fertility with economic status among peasant Polish

[8] T. Van Den Brink, "Levelling of Differential Fertility Trends in the Netherlands,"
World Population Conference, 1954, *Papers*, Vol. 1, United Nations Publications, 1955,
pp. 743–752.

CHART 3

Development of Inverse Relation between Fertility and Socio-economic Status in England and Wales, during the Last Half of the Nineteenth Century

I. Upper and middle class
II. Intermediate between I & III
III. Skilled workers
IV. Intermediate between III & V

V. Unskilled laborers
VI. Textile workers
VII. Miners
VIII. Agricultural workers

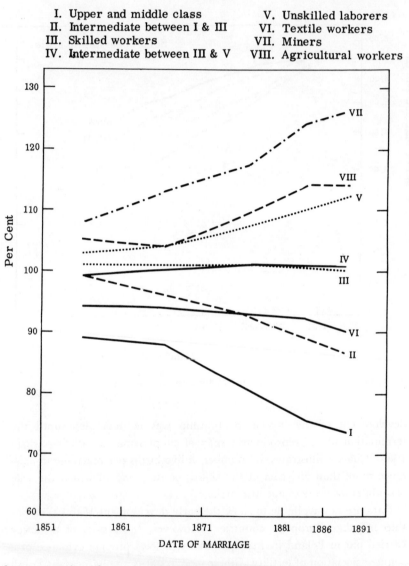

Source: Reproduced from a chart by Frank W. Notestein: "Class Differences In Fertility", Annals of the American Academy of Political and Social Science, Vol. 187, September, 1936, p. 27.

CHART 4

Number of Live Births per Hundred First Marriages, in Marriages of
Twenty and More Years Duration, by Occupation of Husband and
Year of Marriage, Netherlands, Census of 1947
(age of wife at marriage, under 25 years)

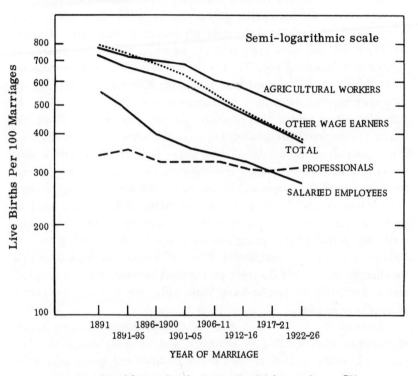

Source: Adapted from a chart by T. Van Den Brink: op. cit., p. 751.

women prior to 1900.[9] The finding of immediate interest was that,
among farm women born during the years 1855–1880 the average number
of children increased consistently with increased size of the farm.[10]

[9] W. Stys, "The Influence of Economic Conditions on the Fertility of Peasant
Women," *Population Studies*, London, Vol. XI, no. 2, November 1957, pp. 136–148. This
study was based upon a survey carried out in twenty villages in Southern Poland in 1948.
The data are shown in Chart 11, below.

[10] The author states that the number of women born between 1855 and 1880 and
surviving at the time of the survey was small and was combined in a single age-group, in
order to obtain numbers sufficiently large to permit subdivisions by size of family. He
claims that the use of such a broad age group does not distort the relation of family size to
size of farm, because older women did not practice birth control, and adds that, "The
difference in fertility between the richest and poorest women caused by age differences
amounted only to 2.74%" (*ibid.*, p. 138).

Patterns and Trends since 1900

URBAN-RURAL DIFFERENTIALS

The differentiation of urban and rural inhabitants by the level of their completed fertility was generally more pronounced after the turn of the century than previously (Charts 1 and 2). Throughout the period, the average completed family size of couples living in small towns more nearly approximated that of city residents than rural inhabitants. Current fertility is perhaps more aptly reflected by ratios of children under 5 to women of childbearing age. The trouble is that fertility ratios are affected by birth spacing and, as used here to describe differential fertility, by the difference between urban and rural areas in rates of child mortality. In addition, trends which they describe do not necessarily indicate the trends in completed family size. However, for what it is worth, Chart 5 shows the sharper decline in children under five per 1,000 women aged 20–24 in urban areas up to the mid-1930's in Denmark and Sweden and the constancy of the differential in England and Wales from 1890 to 1931.

In Denmark and Sweden, the downward trend is characterized by differing rates of decline resulting in a broadening of the differential, while the period of increasing fertility is marked by differing rates of increase resulting in a contraction of the differential. In both countries, the sharper decline and the more pronounced increase occurred in urban areas. This holds for England and Wales only with regard to the period of increasing fertility.

Trends in the urban-rural differential in Switzerland more nearly approximate the situation in Denmark and Sweden, except that the postwar increases in fertility were minor in cities and barely evident in the rest of Switzerland. However, the downward trend is marked by differing rates of rural and urban decline and, consequently, an expansion of the differential (Chart 6).

RELIGION

It is unfortunate that the recent censuses do not provide data adequate for a discussion of trends in fertility differences among language, nativity, and religious groups in the countries where important divisions exist, particularly Belgium, Germany, and Switzerland.[11]

[11] Most of the available data on recent patterns and trends in these countries are in the following sources: Switzerland: Kurt B. Mayer, *The Population of Switzerland*, Columbia University Press, 1952, 366 pp., and Mayer, "Cultural Pluralism and Linguistic Equilibrium in Switzerland," *American Sociological Review*, Vol. 16, no. 2, April 1951, pp. 157–163. Germany: Statistik der Bundsrepublik Deutschland, *Die Bevolkerung der Bunds-*

CHART 5

Number of Children under Five per Thousand Women Twenty to Twenty-Four Years Old, by Urban and Rural Residence, Denmark, Sweden, and England and Wales at Given Census Dates, 1890–1955

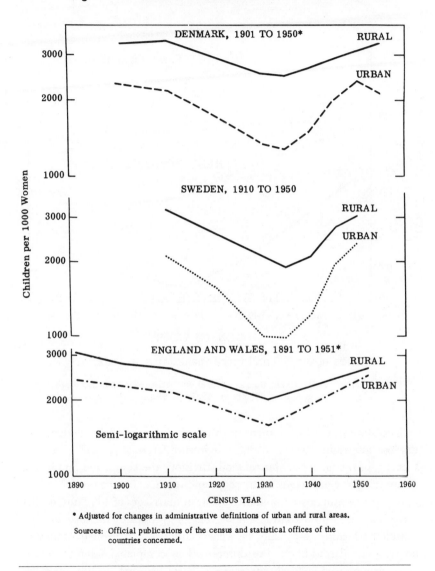

* Adjusted for changes in administrative definitions of urban and rural areas.

Sources: Official publications of the census and statistical offices of the countries concerned.

republik Deutschland Nach der Zahlung vom 13 Septembre 1950, Heft 9, Textheft, Stuttgart-Köln, 1956, 117 pp. Belgium: Institut National de Statistique, *Recensement général de la population, de l'industrie et du commerce au 31 décembre 1947*, Vol. 7, Recensement des familles, Brussels, 1951, 131 pp.

47

CHART 6

Number of Live Births per Thousand Married Women Aged Fifteen to
Forty-Four Years by Urban and Rural Residence in Switzerland, at Census
Periods, 1899–1902 to 1949–1952

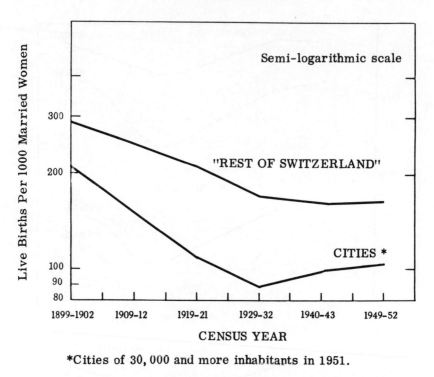

*Cities of 30,000 and more inhabitants in 1951.

Source: Switzerland. Bureau Fédéral de Statistique, Annuaire Statistique
de la Suisse 1955, Bern, 1956, p. 99.

Two studies based on returns from the 1947 census of the Netherlands
disclose interesting aspects of the religious differential in that country.[12]
Chart 7 shows for the major religious divisions the completed family size
of marriages contracted from 1891 and earlier to 1922–1926. Two
noteworthy features are apparent. First, in marriages of 1891 and earlier
there is a clear differentiation among religious groups by the level of their
completed fertility, especially between Catholics and women professing
no religion. In addition, the differences in completed family size are
more pronounced in each successive cohort; the net decline over the

[12] T. Van Den Brink, *op. cit.*, pp. 743–752 and P. de Wolfe and J. Meerdink, "La
fécondité des mariages à Amsterdam selon l'appartenance social et réligieuse," *Population*,
12e année, no. 2, Paris, April–June 1957, pp. 089–318.

CHART 7

Number of Live Births per Hundred First Marriages of Twenty and More Years Duration, by Religion of Wife and Year of Marriage, Netherlands, Census of 1947

(age of wife at marriage, under 25 years)

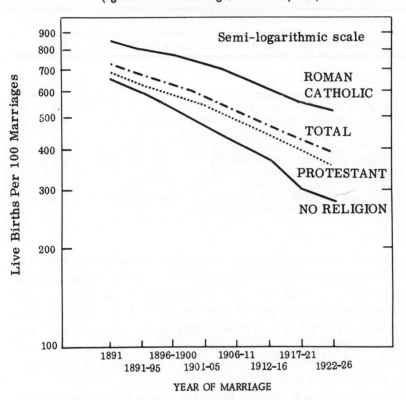

Source: Adapted from a chart by T. Van Den Brink: op. cit., p. 751.

period for Catholics, Protestants, and those "without religion" amounted to 39, 48, and 59 per cent, respectively.

For information on more recent trends, it is necessary to examine marriages of incomplete fertility, in this case, marriages of 9 to 18 years duration (Table 1). These data suggest that the differentials are decreasing. However, they may be somewhat misleading as to trends, for patterns of family building vary among religious groups.

De Wolfe and Meerdink show that during the period 1948–1955 Catholics tended to have their first children within a shorter period after marriage (excluding pre-marital conceptions) and subsequent births occurred at closer intervals than was the case with non-Catholics.[13]   On the other hand, the interval between marriage and births of first and second order increased among Catholics after 1948.   The behavior of Calvinists was similar, but their fertility appears to be falling more slowly than that of Catholics.

TABLE 1

Indexes of Live Births per 100 First Marriages in Cohorts of Incomplete Fertility by Religion and Year of Marriage in the Netherlands and the City of Amsterdam, 1947
(Catholic rate = 100)

Year of Marriage	The Netherlands			Amsterdam		
	Calvinist	Reformed	No Religion	Calvinist	Reformed	No Religion
1924–28	86	62	51	88	63	62
1929–33	88	64	52	99	68	64
1934–38	91	69	58	97	73	67

Fertility rates for Jewish marriages were not included in the source of information.
Source: de Wolfe and Meerdink, *op. cit.*, p. 299.

EDUCATIONAL STATUS

The level of fertility among the better educated classes is above that of the general population in England and Wales, and in Sweden.   This is not to say that among all married women or men in these countries reproduction is directly related to the extent of their education;   data that would yield information on the family size of each educational class are not available.   However, two recent studies make possible a comparison of the fertility of university graduates with that of the general population in these countries.

Table 2 compares the average family size in 1952 of a sample of women graduates of ten colleges and universities with that of the general population of Great Britain at the census of 1951.[14]   It clearly indicates the tendency of better-educated women to have larger families.   For example, where age at marriage was 25–29 years, the average family size among graduates after 5–6 years of marriage was equal to that of all British women in marriages of 15–24 years duration.   This particular example

[13] *Op. cit.*, pp. 301–315.

[14] Judith Hubback, "The Fertility of Graduate Women," *The Eugenics Review*, Vol. 27, no. 2, July, 1955, pp. 107–113.   This study of 1,165 graduates of 10 colleges and universities in Oxford, Cambridge, London, Durham, and Birmingham was carried out in 1952.   It was not originally intended as a demographic study, but considerable demographic information was obtained.   Questionnaires were used to render the original data suitable for fertility analysis   Three-fourths of these were sent to Oxford, Cambridge, and Durham.

may merely point up the proportionately greater contribution of the graduates to the recent increase in the birth rate, particularly those in marriages of less than ten years duration in 1952.[15] But it will be noted that their fertility is higher in marriages of all durations and for all ages at marriage. In her discussion of the material, Hubback pointed out

TABLE 2

Average Family Size of Graduate Women and of All British Women, by
Age at Marriage and Duration of Marriage, Great Britain

	Duration of Marriage in Years			
Groups	5–6	7–9	10–14	15–24
Age at marriage under 24				
Graduates	1.9	2.0	2.6	2.8
All British women	1.5	1.7	2.1	2.6
Age at marriage 25–29				
Graduates	1.7	2.4	2.3	2.6
All British women	1.3	1.5	1.7	1.7
Age at marriage 30–34				
Graduates	1.3	1.6	1.8	—
All British women	1.2	1.3	1.3	—

Data for the graduates related to the year 1952. Material for all British women was taken from the 1951 One Per Cent Sample Census of Great Britain.
Source: Judith Hubback, *op. cit.*, p. 110.

that in marriages of less than five years duration graduate fertility is below that of other marriages of comparable duration. Thereafter, as a result of the making up of births postponed during early years of marriage, the average family size of the better-educated women uniformly exceeds that of the general population.

A recent Swedish study provides information on the average family size of married males who reached at least matriculation standard and on certain occupational groups, subdivided according to level of education.[16] Among employers and officials living in towns in 1935–1936 and

[15] Of course, the relative contribution that each population subgroup makes to the level of a country's fertility depends not only upon "group-specific" fertility, but also upon proportions married among women of childbearing age in each group. However, this aspect of the problem is not discussed here in detail, as the aim of the study is to determine group differences in fertility levels and trends, rather than the factors responsible for levels and trends in the fertility of the different countries.

[16] Sven Moberg, "Marital Status and Family Size Among Matriculated Persons in Sweden," *Population Studies*, Vol. IV, no. 1, June 1950, pp. 115–127. The basic data on marital status, number of children, and income of males who matriculated as students in 1910 and 1920 were taken from official population and tax registers and questionnaires.

who had been married 0–20 years, average family size is lowest for those who had no more than elementary school education (1.16) and rises with increases in level of education, 1.26 for high school graduates and 1.35 children for those who reached at least matriculation standard.

Moberg found that the average family size of Swedish men who matriculated in 1920 was above that of the general married male population of comparable age and that, while the data for men who matriculated from 1910 to 1930 indicate an increase in fertility, a decline occurred among non-matriculated males of similar ages.[17]

A particularly interesting feature of the material from the last Netherlands' census (Table 3) is that, among all first marriages existing in 1947,

TABLE 3

Live Births per 100 First Marriages by Education of Husband and Year of Marriage in the Netherlands, 1947. Age of Wife at Marriage 25 to 29 Years

Year of Marriage	All First Marriages	Male University Graduates	Graduates as Percentage of Total
A. Complete Fertility			
Before 1914	434	297	68
1914–18	371	285	77
1919–23	338	277	82
1924–28	324	280	86
B. Incomplete Fertility			
1929–33	309	288	93
1934–38	266	263	99
1939–43	185	188	102

Source: The Netherlands: Central Bureau voor de Statistiek, *12e Volkstelling, annex woningtelling 31 Mei 1947*, Deel 4. Statistiek der bestaande huwelijken en van de vruchtbaarheid dezer huwelijken (Statistics of Existing Marriage and Marital Fertility), Utrecht, 1951, pp. 114, 138.

Background data for those who matriculated in 1930 were obtained from the census of 1935–1936. The range in the per cent distribution of all males matriculating as students from 1910 to 1943 according to social status of father was as follows: Upper class, 32–36 per cent; Middle class, 41–48 per cent; Lower class, 17–22 per cent; Unknown, 1–2 per cent. At the time of the investigation the percentage married among the former students was higher than among all urban males and, 16 years after matriculation, at an average age of 36, there was a higher percentage married among the students of 1920 and 1930 than among all Swedish males of comparable age.

According to Moberg, ". . . the matriculation examination is generally taken at the age of 18–20 after 12 or 13 years of regular school attendance." It is required for entrance into the universities. During the period 1941–1945, approximately 5.1 per cent of all males and 2.8 per cent of all females aged 20 years passed the examination annually.

[17] *ibid*, p 193 The findings from this study are, on the whole, in keeping with the patterns and trends outlined in an early work by Karl A. Edin and Edward P. Hutchinson. See their *Studies of Differential Fertility in Sweden*, P. S. King & Son, Ltd., London, 1935.

the ratio of the fertility of male university graduates to that of all Dutch marriages increases in each successive marriage cohort, beginning with marriages of 1914 and earlier. Finally, in the youngest cohort, the graduates achieved an average family size slightly *above* the average for the Netherlands; the figures are 1.88 and 1.85, respectively. In view of the general trend suggested by the comparative behavior of the two series of cohorts, it is not unreasonable to assume that the slight reversal of relationship observed in the 1939–1943 cohort is indicative of what may be a lasting change in the relationship between fertility and higher education, and that it is not merely a matter of differential spacing or making up of postponed births during the recent recovery of the Netherlands' birth rate.

In Sweden, England and Wales, and the Netherlands, fertility rates of the better-educated class are clearly above the average rates for these countries. The question remains, to what extent are the differentials between those with higher education and the remainder of the population due to differences in group composition as regards socio-economic status, religion, and so forth, and to fertility differences between these substrata? There are virtually no data on this subject. Moberg has given the most recent information for Sweden for the census period 1931–1935. Although it does not meet the specifications outlined above, it at least shows the combined effects of income and education for an urban occupational group upon the level of fertility.

Table 4 gives the average number of live births per marriage for employers and officials living in towns by their educational status and level of family income, Sweden 1935–1936. The rates are standardized

TABLE 4

Average Number of Live Births by Level of Education and Income for
an Urban Occupational Group in Sweden 1935–1936
(duration of marriage between 1 and 20 years)

Income Class (family income) *Thousands of Kroner per Year*	*Employers and Officials in Town Educational Group:*		
	A	B	C
0–3	1.44	1.24	1.18
3–5	1.30	1.26	1.22
5–10	0.91	1.19	1.38
10 and over	0.97	1.36	1.61
Standardized[a]	1.16	1.26	1.35

[a] Differences in distribution due to income and marriage duration eliminated.
Source: Moberg, *op. cit.*, p. 124.

for differences in distribution by income and marriage duration. Among the group with primary education or less (Group A), family size is inversely related to income. In the group of average education, that is, above elementary but below matriculation (Group B), there is no apparent relationship. However, among men who had reached at least matriculation standard (Group C), there is a clear-cut positive correlation of income with family size.[18]

Data for the latter group may be compared with information for men (of all occupations) who matriculated as students in 1910, 1920, and 1930 (Table 5). The patterns are identical, although at all income levels

TABLE 5

Average Number of Live Births and Indexes of the Average Number of Live Births by Income–Male Students Matriculated in Sweden in 1910, 1920, and 1930

Income Class (husband's income) Thousands of Kroner Per Year	Average Number of Live Births Year of Matriculation[a]		Indexes of the Average Number of Live Births (all classes = 100) Year of Matriculation		
	1910	1920	1910	1920	1930
0–9	1.61	1.91	83	90	90
10–14	2.06	2.07⎱			
15–19	2.11	2.23⎰	99	94	102
20–29	2.20	2.47	102	105⎱	
30–39	2.63	2.83	114	121⎰	117
40 and over	2.39	2.86	109	119	
All classes	2.12	2.28	100	100	100

[a] Rates for men who matriculated as students in 1930 were not given in the source.
Source: Moberg, *op. cit.*, p. 125.

fertility is higher among the former students. Upon further observation of Table 4, another striking feature may be observed; for the two lower income groups fertility is *inversely* associated with level of education. In the two upper income groups, the relationship is strongly in the opposite direction. Thus, for the poorer classes gains in education depress fertility,

[18] Findings from the Edin and Hutchinson material were contradictory: This study of family size among 6,629 Stockholm families in 1917–1922 showed a modest positive association of fertility with income in the lower educational group (A), a sharper one for the group of average education (B), and a somewhat erratic one for the group of higher education (C plus D). However, in Moberg's study employers and officials in towns were a select occupation group, and the Stockholm families were not. When Edin and Hutchinson controlled age of wife at marriage and used broad income classes, higher income was associated with larger families in all education groups (*ibid.*, pp. 78–80).

whereas, in middle-income and wealthier classes, educational advances have a positive effect. As these data relate to family income, differences between income classes in the employment of the wife must be taken into consideration.[19]

OCCUPATION STATUS

The changes in the magnitude of differences in fertility between occupation groups in England and Wales, France, the Netherlands, and Norway since 1900 have been rather dissimilar, although in each of these countries an *inverse* association of fertility with status has until recently been fairly clear. In the Netherlands, the general fertility decline was accompanied by a gradual reduction of differences in completed cohort fertility. There was a similar tendency in Great Britain, particularly England and Wales, although here the evidence is less conclusive. In France, on the other hand, occupational differences in paternity rates for males aged 45–54 in 1946 were slightly more pronounced than those for males aged 50–59 in 1911. A similar trend was observed in Norway, where status groups have become, on the whole, more strongly differentiated in terms of their completed marital fertility. (The details are in Tables 6, 7, and 8, and Charts 4 and 8.)

It is plain that limited comparability both as to measures of fertility and as to classifications of occupations considerably complicates the manipulation and the interpretation of the data; it may, in fact, conceal similarities as well as differences in actual trends. The material is perhaps best examined separately for each country.

Information provided by the British family census of 1946 (Chart 8) shows that, in post-1900 marriage cohorts of completed fertility in England and Wales the smallest proportionate declines occurred among professionals and laborers, occupational groups which among marriages of 1900–1909 exhibited the extremes of behavior with respect to ultimate family size.[20]

The more noteworthy features are the reversals in the relative positions of professionals and salaried employees and of workers on own account and nonmanual wage earners in the 1920–1924 cohort. When the nine status categories were grouped into nonmanual and manual workers it

---

[19] The earlier study of Swedish fertility by Edin and Hutchinson gave evidence that employment status of wife was not related to the direction of the relationship between family size and income of husband within education groups A, B, C, and D (*ibid.*).

[20] The Royal Population Commission, *Papers*, Vol. VI, The Trend and Pattern of Fertility in Great Britain: A Report on the Family Census of 1946, by D. V. Glass and E. Grebenik, Part I, Report, HMSO, London, 1954, chs. I–VII.

TABLE 6

Indexes of the Number of Live Births per Woman First Married
in 1900–1909 and 1920–1924 by Occupational Status of Husband,
Great Britain, 1946

| | | All Categories—100 | | |
| | | 1900–1909 Cohort | 1920–1924 Cohort | 1920–1924 as Per Cent of 1900–1909 |
Occupational Status of Husband				
Non-manual	I Professional	66	72	75
	II Employers	75	76	70
	III Own account	84	81	66
	IV Salaried employees	67	68	70
	V Non-manual wage earner	82	81	68
	VI Farmers and farm managers	99	95	66
Manual	VII Manual wage earners	112	112	68
	VIII Agricultural workers	110	112	70
	IX Laborers	126	138	75
Non-manual		80	79	68
Manual		116	112	69
All categories		100	100	69

Source: The Royal Population Commission: *Papers*, Vol. VI, The Trend and Pattern of Fertility in Great Britain: A Report on the Family Census of 1946, by D. V. Glass and E. Grebenik, Part I, Report, London, HMSO, 1954, p. 5.

TABLE 7

Indexes of the Average Number of Births per Married Male by
Occupational Group and Age at Census, France, 1911 and 1946

| | All Classes—100 | | |
Occupational Group	Males Aged 50–59 in 1911	Males Aged 45–54 in 1946	1946 as Per Cent of 1911
I Miners, transport workers, and agricultural laborers	118	136	95
II Farmers	108	126	95
III Independent artisans, minor employers	98	91	76
IV Subordinate employees in industry and transport	97	95	80
V Subordinate among soldiers, police, etc.	92	97	86
VI Managers and owners of small businesses, professionals, public officials	92	85	76
VII Shopkeepers	82	83	83
VIII Civil servants	79	81	84
IX Employees in business and commerce (white collar)	70	70	82
All Classes	100	100	82

Source: M. Febvay: "Y-a-t'il un nivellement graduel des écarts observé jusqu'ici dans la fécondité des groupes distincts de population," World Population Conference 1954, *Papers*, Vol. I, New York, United Nations Publications, 1955, p. 610.

TABLE 8

Indexes of the Number of Children in Marriages of 18 and More
Years Duration by Occupation of Husband.
Age of Wife at Marriage 24 and 25 years.
Norway Censuses of 1920, 1930, and 1950.

	All Classes—100			1950 as Per Cent of 1920
Occupation of Husband	1920	1930	1950	
A. *Agriculture*				
I. Workers in agriculture	107	114	116	64
II. Farmers	105	111	125	70
B. *Industry*				
III. Factory workers	101	94	82	48
IV. Owners of small businesses, retail dealers	90	84	83	54
V. Business and commercial clerks	82	75	69	49
VI. Factory owners, wholesale merchants, etc.	80	79	79	58
C. *Professions and Government*				
VII. Workers	94	86	70	44
VIII. Working on own account, officials in superior service, etc.	63	63	79	73
All Classes	100	100	100	59

Source: Norway, Statistiske Sentralbyrå, *Folketellingen 1 December 1950*, Femte hefte, Barnetallet i norske ekteskap, Vol. v, Fertility of Norwegian Marriages, Oslo, 1957, pp. 36–37.

was seen that the fertility differential between broad classes had been very stable; the completed fertility of the manual group ranged from 41 to 43 per cent above that of nonmanual workers in all marriages contracted from 1900–1909 to 1920–1924.

Evidence of a widening of differences in paternity rates between occupation groups in France in 1946 as compared with 1911 may be observed in Table 8. Actually, this is primarily a matter of the further separation of the high fertility groups I and II from the remainder. The percent decline in their rates was very small, while that of some other groups, including independents, small owners, artisans, professionals, public officials, and the like, amounted to as much as one quarter. The association of fertility with status is not clear-cut, at least not uniformly inverse, either in 1911 or in 1946, but this may arise at least in part from some of the rather refined distinctions between types of occupations. In view of this and of the small size of the average completed family in France in 1946 (2.00 live births per married male aged 45–54), it is remarkable that the differentiation is as pronounced as it is.

CHART 8

Number of Live Births per Woman, by Social Status of Husband and Year of First Marriage, Great Britain, Census of 1946
(age of wife at marriage, 20 to 24 years)

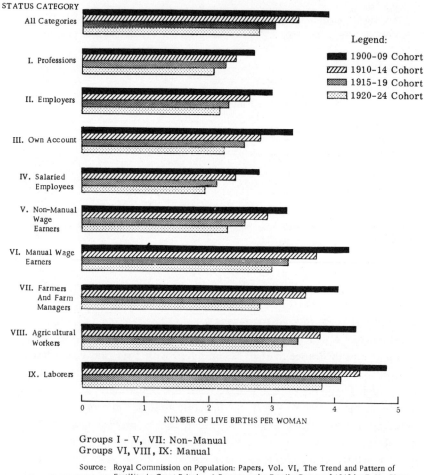

Groups I - V, VII: Non-Manual
Groups VI, VIII, IX: Manual

Source: Royal Commission on Population: Papers, Vol. VI, The Trend and Pattern of Fertility in Great Britain, A Report on the Family Census of 1946 by D. V. Glass and E. Grebenik, Part I: Report, London, HMSO, 1954, p. 115.

As for patterns and trends in completed family size in the Netherlands (Chart 4) since 1900, two facts are worth noting: (1) the increasing rate of decline among agricultural workers and other wage earners and the constancy of average completed family size among the professionals, of which the combined result is a contraction of the differentials, and (2) the reversals of the positions of professionals and salaried employees in the two youngest cohorts.

The increased differentiation since 1920 of occupation groups in Norway with respect to their completed family size was pointed out earlier. The principal features of this trend are the relatively slow rates of decline among groups in agriculture and the rapid decreases that took place among white collar workers, that is, business and commercial clerks and workers in the professions and government. The figures are given in Table 8. As in Great Britain, the range of variation in completed family size within the intermediate groups (III–VII) narrowed somewhat in 1950. Further, the completed fertility of higher professionals and government officials increased in proportion to the national average. However, groups at either extreme are more widely separated than previously. More important, perhaps, is the number of reversals in the positions of groups with respect to their completed fertility at the census of 1950. The number of changes is such that the previous negative association of family size with occupational status has been significantly modified.

It has been seen that in England and Wales, France, and Norway the range of variation in family size within the higher-status category has narrowed. From this standpoint, a contraction of the differentials has taken place. However, the rate of decline in fertility among agricultural groups, (and, in France and England and Wales, also among non-agricultural groups of low status) has been at so slow a pace that there is now a more pronounced differential between these groups and the remainder of the occupational classes.

In recent cohorts, the completed fertility of professionals has increased in relation to the average in each country, except France, and in all four countries this occupational group no longer has the fewest children per couple. The smallest families are now found among civil servants and other white collar workers. In fact, the available data suggest that the inverse association of completed fertility with occupational status in advanced European countries may no longer be regarded as the customary pattern.

As has often been noted, the decline in family size began among the well-to-do, the urban and the educated; these groups were the first to adopt the rational attitudes towards fertility needed to utilize means of fertility control and to offset the effects of the decline in mortality. The poorer, the less-urbanized, and less-educated elements of the population followed this lead, but apparently after a considerable time lag. It is possible, therefore, that the negative association of fertility with socio-economic status may be characteristic only of periods of demographic transition, from high to low fertility, from uncontrolled to controlled family size. It may be that when urban and upper class attitudes and practices have completely permeated all areas and all strata of society, differentials in fertility will either vanish or shift so that the relation of fertility to status will become a positive one.

Patterns and Trends During the Recovery of the Birth Rate

The recent recovery of the birth rate in the industrialized countries of Europe has given rise to much speculation as to its implications for fertility differences between socio-economic classes and between urban and rural inhabitants. Unfortunately, good data on the patterns and trends in the fertility differentials during this period are scant. The available material permits only a limited discussion of the situation in a few countries.

Differences in the trends in urban and rural fertility ratios during the recovery of the birth rate may be observed for four countries in Charts 5 and 6. The ratios suggest that the rise in fertility began in urban areas and that it was generally more pronounced among urban inhabitants.

The long-standing inverse association of fertility with size of community continues to prevail in France, Denmark, and Sweden. However, in Great Britain at the census of 1951 the relationship was rather weak, especially for younger marriages. In France, in the census year 1946 there was a pronounced inverse relation; gross reproduction rates were 1.23, 1.43, 1.56, and 1.66, respectively, for four classes of communities in descending order of size.[21] Bjerke found a similar pattern for Denmark and Sweden at the censuses of 1940, 1945, and 1950.[22] He observed differences in fertility between inhabitants of the capital cities and towns, and between the inhabitants of towns and rural areas. His data also showed that in Sweden the largest and second largest per cent increases in standardized birth rates per 1,000 married women of

---

[21] "Notes et Documents" in *Population*, 6e année, no. 2, Paris, Avril–Juin 1951, p. 352.

[22] Kjeld Bjerke, "The Birth Rate of the Rural and Urban Populations in Denmark, Finland, Norway and Sweden During the 1940's," World Population Conference 1954, *Papers*, Vol. I, United Nations Publications, 1955, pp. 563–584.

childbearing age during the baby boom (1940 compared with 1945) took place in the capital and the towns, respectively. In Denmark, the relative increase in standardized births per 1,000 women was greater in the towns than in Copenhagen. In Sweden and Denmark, the relative increase in rural fertility during this period was smaller than that for the urban localities. In both countries the rates for all areas were lower in 1950 than in 1945, with the most pronounced per cent decreases occurring in the urban localities. On the whole, rates for the different communities were somewhat more nearly equal in 1950 than previously.

Information on occupational differentials is available for the city of Copenhagen, Denmark, for England and Wales, and for Norway, and data on fertility by level of income or property value were located for Sweden, Copenhagen, England and Wales, the Netherlands, Ireland, and Poland. The Danish Statistical Office published data on the distribution at 31 December 1948 of couples married in Copenhagen in 1939 only, by number of live-born children, occupational status of husband, and employment status of wife. Duration of marriage was at least nine but less than ten years. The data are illustrated in Chart 9, from which the following may be observed:

1. The strongest and most consistent factor is employment status of wife. For each age-group at marriage and each occupational group, childlessness is far more pronounced among the fully employed wives than among those not fully employed.

2. The effect of the age of the woman at the time of her marriage is also a consistent factor, but this point is of minor interest in the present context.

3. The differences by socio-economic status of husband are not consistent. For women married at older ages there is a slight suggestion of an inverse relation of childlessness to husband's occupational status, but among fully employed women who married under age 25 the relationship tends to be in the opposite direction. The data also suggest a limited positive association of size of family with occupational status of husband in cases where the wife was married at a relatively early age.

In England and Wales there was a modest amount of leveling of fertility differences between Social Class I (non-manual workers) and Social Class II (manual workers) in more recent cohorts, particularly couples married in 1930–1934 and 1935–1939. This contraction of group differences was due largely to fertility declines in the lower status group although slight increases were observed for Social Class I.[23] However,

---

[23] For details see Glass and Grebenik, *op. cit.*, p. 212.

CHART 9

Distribution of Couples Married in Copenhagen in 1939 by Number of Children, Occupation Status of Husband, Employment Status of Wife, and Age of Wife at Marriage, December 31, 1948

A. WIFE NOT FULLY EMPLOYED

STATUS GROUP
OF HUSBAND *

1. Age At Marriage Under 25

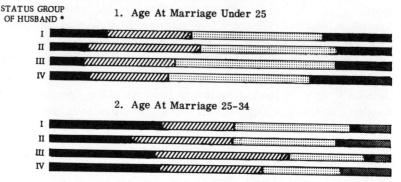

2. Age At Marriage 25-34

B. WIFE FULLY EMPLOYED

1. Age At Marriage Under 25

2. Age At Marriage 25-34

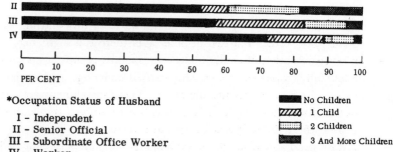

0   10   20   30   40   50   60   70   80   90   100
PER CENT

*Occupation Status of Husband

  I - Independent
  II - Senior Official
  III - Subordinate Office Worker
  IV - Worker

  ■ No Children
  ▨ 1 Child
  ▦ 2 Children
  ▩ 3 And More Children

* The number of cases in Status Group I in which the wife was fully employed was too small to permit a distribution by age at marriage and number of children.

Source: Denmark, Statistiske Departement, "Frugtbarheden i og Holdbarheden at Københavnske Aegteskaber Indgaet i 1939 i Relation til Aegtefaellernes Indkomst of Erhverv", Statistisk Manedsskrift, 1955, No. 2, p. 29.

reproduction among couples married during the later period was still largely incomplete at the Family Census of 1946.

During the last twenty years the pattern of the occupational differential in Norway has been considerably modified (Chart 10). The primary concern here is with family size after 10 years of marriage, and particularly at the censuses of 1946 and 1950. This does not pose too serious a problem for the interpretation of the data, inasmuch as the major portion of childbearing takes place within the first ten years of marriage.

The occupational groups have been classified by industry, primarily because the data suggested it, and by locality of residence. One of the interesting features disclosed in this chart is that, among several groups in Oslo in 1946 and 1950, particularly those in manufacturing and commerce (the bulk of the labor force), family size is larger for couples married 10 years than for those in marriages of 17 years duration. This suggests that the recovery of the birth rate was more pronounced in Oslo than elsewhere in Norway, and it is in keeping with findings based upon the fertility ratios for Denmark, England and Wales, Sweden, and Switzerland. To return to the occupational differential in Norway, it may be observed that, on the whole, within the various industries there is no longer an inverse association of family size with status, as was the general pattern outside of commerce, at the census of 1930. In the rural districts the relation of family size to class within agriculture and within commerce has been positive for some time. Within manufacturing and within the professional occupations and public administration the behavior of the groups since 1930 has been such that, within the latter "industry" the change has been from an inverse association to a situation in which fertility has no relation to status, and within manufacturing a differentiation of groups is now hardly noticeable.

Wives of men working in manufacturing and commerce, and living in Oslo and in other towns, showed a tendency in 1950 toward a larger completed family size, and this trend is most noticeable among groups of lower occupational status and of comparatively low fertility.[24]

At the census of 1930, family size did not vary consistently with occupational status within the professional occupations and public administration in Oslo and in towns, but at the 1946 and 1950 census the number of live births per marriage of 10 and more years duration was positively associated with social class within this broad group. It is significant that

[24] The social status of occupational groups often changes over a period of time, and it seems that this is the case with artisans and factory workers. According to a Norwegian informant, artisans now enjoy a higher status than most factory workers, some clerks, and, occasionally, small business men.

CHART 10

Average Number of Live Births per Marriage, by Occupation of Husband,
Type of Locality, and Duration of Marriage, Norway, Censuses of 1930,
1946, and 1950
(age of wife at marriage, 20 to 29 years)

I. RURAL DISTRICTS
A. AGRICULTURE

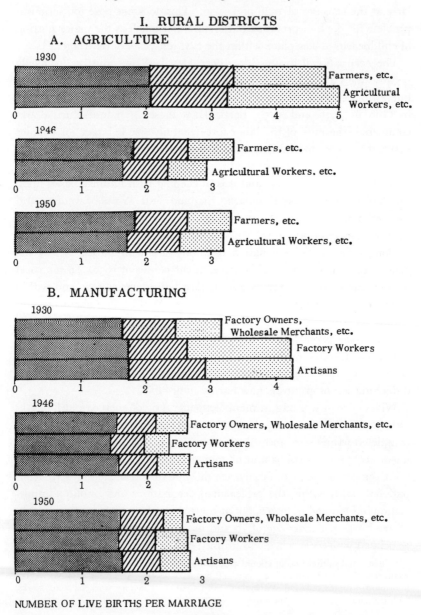

NUMBER OF LIVE BIRTHS PER MARRIAGE

64

CHART 10 continued

I. RURAL DISTRICTS
C. COMMERCIAL SERVICES

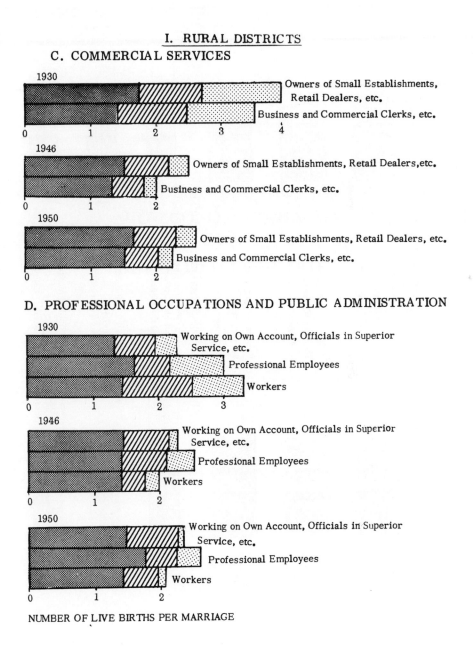

1930

Owners of Small Establishments, Retail Dealers, etc.

Business and Commercial Clerks, etc.

0   1   2   3   4

1946

Owners of Small Establishments, Retail Dealers,etc.

Business and Commercial Clerks, etc.

0   1   2

1950

Owners of Small Establishments, Retail Dealers, etc.

Business and Commercial Clerks, etc.

0   1   2

D. PROFESSIONAL OCCUPATIONS AND PUBLIC ADMINISTRATION

1930

Working on Own Account, Officials in Superior Service, etc.

Professional Employees

Workers

0   1   2   3

1946

Working on Own Account, Officials in Superior Service, etc.

Professional Employees

Workers

0   1   2

1950

Working on Own Account, Officials in Superior Service, etc.

Professional Employees

Workers

0   1   2

NUMBER OF LIVE BIRTHS PER MARRIAGE

65

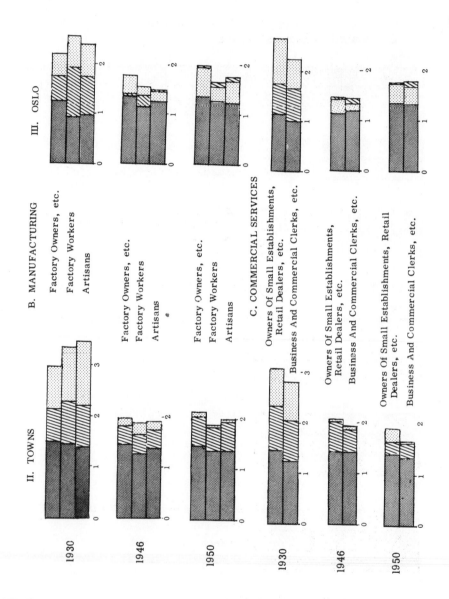

CHART 10 concluded

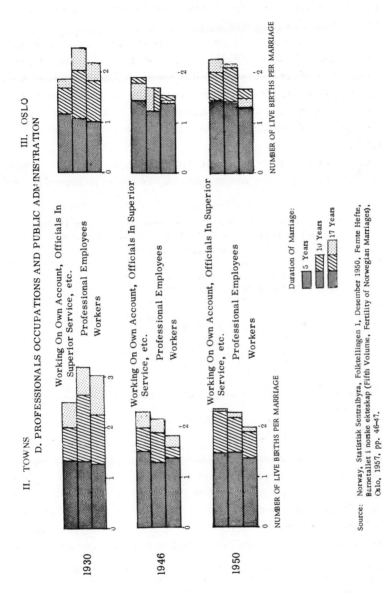

II. TOWNS.   III. OSLO

D. PROFESSIONALS OCCUPATIONS AND PUBLIC ADMINISTRATION

1930

1946

1950

Working On Own Account, Officials In Superior Service, etc.

Professional Employees

Workers

NUMBER OF LIVE BIRTHS PER MARRIAGE

Duration Of Marriage:

5 Years

10 Years

17 Years

Source: Norway, Statistisk Sentralbyra, Folketellingen 1, Desember 1950, Femte Hefte, Barnetallet i norske ekteskap (Fifth Volume, Fertility of Norwegian Marriages), Oslo, 1957, pp. 46–47.

67

the pattern of differential fertility within the professional occupations and public administration that existed in Oslo and the towns in 1930 is virtually identical with that in the rural areas in 1946 and 1950, and that the pattern in rural areas in 1930 is similar to the association of completed family size with status in towns in 1920.[25]

In four of the five industrialized countries for which data on fertility by income class or property value are available for fairly recent years, the evidence indicates that large families are more closely associated with wealth than with low income or property of low value. Unfortunately, the evidence for some of these countries is based upon fertility rates for which age of wife at marriage and/or duration of marriage are not controlled.

In urban Sweden in 1945, the average number of children per couple married during 1931–1935 was smallest for the lowest income class and

TABLE 9

Average Number of Live Births in 1945 per Marriage Contracted During
1931–1935 in Towns of Sweden by Annual Income of Husband
(duration of marriage 10–14 years[a])

Annual Income ('000 Kroner)	Live Births per Marriage	Per Cent Childless
0–2	1.44	30
2–4	1.53	24
4–6	1.54	20
6–10	1.34	25
10–15	1.53	26
15 and over	1.97	26

[a] Differences in distribution of income groups by age of wife at marriage eliminated by standardization.

Source: Carl-Erik Quensel, "Familjestorleken i Skelda befolkningsgrupper," *Försäkringstidningen*, no. 7, 1954, p. 3.

increased with status up to the middle-income group, where it dropped. However, family size then increased at each succeeding income level (Table 9). Childlessness was most prevalent in the lowest income group, although it was also widespread among couples with the largest incomes.

The same positive relationship between fertility and income appears in the sample of graduate women in England and Wales mentioned earlier.

[25] The average number of children in marriages of 18 and more years in towns in 1920 where age of wife at marriage was 24 and 25 years was as follows:

Working on own account and officials in superior service	3.65
Professional employees	5.17
Workers	5.41

Norway: Statistiske Sentralbyrå, *op. cit.*, p. *36.

Among them, higher income is clearly associated with larger families (Table 10). However, the value of the material is limited somewhat by the use of family income as the index of economic status; there are likely to be differences between the income classes with respect to the employment status of the wives. The relation of the latter factor to the level of fertility was noted earlier. It is not surprising that family size is positively

TABLE 10

Average Family Size Among a Sample of Graduate Women by Gross Family Income, Age at Marriage, and Duration of Marriage, England and Wales, 1952

Age at Marriage and Annual Income (in pounds)	Duration of Marriage in Years			
	5–6	7–9	10–14	15–24
Age at marriage under 24				
Under £1,000	1.4	2.1	2.4	2.6
£1,000 and more	2.5	1.9	2.7	2.8
Age at marriage 25–29				
Under £1,000	1.4	2.5	1.9	2.0
£1,000 and more	1.9	2.3	2.3	2.9

Source: Judith Hubback: "Fertility of Graduate Women," *The Eugenics Review*, Vol. 47, no. 2, July 1955, p. 113.

related to income within the professional class for, as Hubback points out, couples in the professions in England, as in most countries, generally plan their families.[26] If the number of children desired is related to the couples' financial ability to rear them, then the achievement of the desired family size would be expected to effect a positive relation between completed family size and economic status.

Recent studies of patterns of differential fertility in the Netherlands, Ireland, and Poland have found family size to be directly related to wealth. These studies do not relate specifically to differential reproduction during the baby boom; they are included here mainly because their findings are among the most recent. A sample survey of income tax returns in the Netherlands in 1949 yielded data on the number of births in relation to net income of the head of the house.[27] It was found that

[26] Judith Hubback, *op. cit.*, p. 113.
[27] The Netherlands: Centraal Bureau Voor de Statistiek, *Statistische en econometrische Onderzoeringer.* 4e Kw., 1956, pp. 157–177. The average number of children per couple by net income of family head in 1949 was as follows:

Net income ('000 guilders)	Under 1	1–2	2–3	3–4	4–5	5–6
Children per couple	3.1	3.1	3.6	4.0	4.4	4.6
Net income ('000 guilders)		6–7	7–8	8–10	10–20	20 plus
Children per couple		4.8	4.9	4.5	4.2	4.0

the average number of children per couple was lowest where income was lowest and that it increased uniformly, although modestly, with income up to a certain point, thereafter declining as income increased. The trouble is that the rates were not standardized for duration of marriage and age of wife at marriage. These factors are obviously correlated with income and are at the same time known to have considerable bearing upon fertility.

The Irish material also discloses a positive relationship between fertility and wealth, but its validity is limited in the same manner as the data just described for the Netherlands. The information relates to farmers and agricultural workers in Ireland at the census of 1951 and shows that except where farms were of lowest value, family size increased with size of farm.[28] These data are subject to the further limitation that they were taken from household schedules and relate to children living at home rather than to children ever born. Other research has shown that children of poor families migrate from the farm more frequently than do those of more prosperous parents.

An investigation of children ever born per married woman by her year of birth in twenty villages in Southern Poland in 1948 also revealed a positive association of family size with size of family farm.[29] The pattern and trends are illustrated in Chart 11. The author determined that the positive correlation of fertility with size of farm was due to the earlier marriage of the wealthier girls, who bear children sooner, more frequently, and over a longer period. The noticeable leveling of the differential in the younger generation was considered to have resulted from the parceling of land to offspring and to the consequent convergence of differences in economic status between families, rather than to class differences in the practice of birth control. Some of the leveling is probably due also to the fact that reproduction among the younger women was not complete at the time of the survey.

Summary

Fertility differences between the various population strata of the now industrialized countries of Europe have existed for at least a century and a half. The historical decline in the birth rate was characterized by a

---

[28] R. C. Geary, "The Family in Irish Census of Population," *Journal of the Statistical and Social Inquiry Society of Ireland*, Vol. XIX (1954–1955), pp. 1–27. Forty folios were selected at random from the 4,151 which contained the household schedules. The sampling unit was the folio rather than the schedule.

[29] W. Stys, *op. cit.*, pp. 136–148.

CHART 11

Average Number of Children per Married Woman, in Selected Birth
Cohorts, by Size of Family Farm in Poland

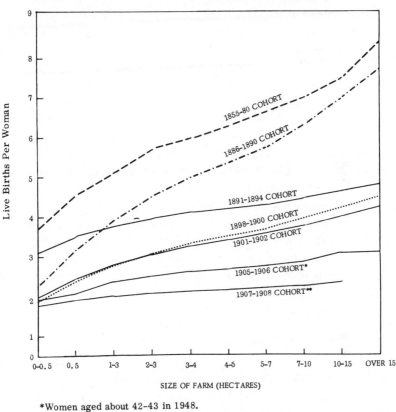

SIZE OF FARM (HECTARES)

*Women aged about 42-43 in 1948.
**Women aged about 40-41 in 1948.

Source: W. Stys, "The Influence of Economic Conditions on the Fertility of Peasant Women",
Population Studies (London), Vol. XI, No. 2, November 1957, p. 141.

gradual development of an inverse association of fertility with socio-
economic status and by a broadening of fertility differentials. Average
family size became increasingly smaller in urban communities than in
rural areas, and the differentiation of occupational groups became more
marked.

During the long-term decline in the birth rate, the increased differentiation of groups by residence and occupational status resulted largely
from differences between them in the rate of fertility decline; the contraction of group differentials that took place during the recent recovery

of the birth rate primarily reflected the higher rates of increase in fertility among groups of previously low fertility.

The often-observed inverse association of fertility with socio-economic status is still present in some, and possibly in the majority of the industrialized countries of Europe. But where it does exist, it has, with few exceptions, been significantly modified. In general, the higher professionals and the wealthier classes no longer have the smallest families; this position is now occupied by intermediate occupational groups and by married couples of average means.

Little is known directly of the relation of family size to the level of educational attainment in these countries, but according to such information as is now available, the fertility of individuals with higher education exceeds that of the general population. This pattern has existed for some years in England and Wales and in Sweden, and has recently become evident in the Netherlands.

More information of good quality is needed on the patterns and trends in residence and class differences in fertility during and since the recovery of the birth rate. It is hoped that the forthcoming censuses will provide such data so that future research and analysis may add to our knowledge of the complex relationships between socio-economic characteristics and fertility.

COMMENT

RONALD FREEDMAN, University of Michigan

In many respects fertility similarities may be more important than fertility differentials. The evidence in Miss Johnson's paper—as well as in the papers by Kiser, Goldberg, Becker, the Ruggles, and others—indicates that the long-heralded contraction of fertility differences is hard upon us. Analyses of fertility differentials sometimes underestimate the contraction of fertility differentials because they concentrate on percentage differences between classes, although it is clear that there is a greater contraction in the size of the absolute differences in family size. For many purposes such absolute contractions are the more important.

The range within which fertility variation is contained in Western Europe is a very small one, whether we take as our frame of reference the maximum physiological potential or the actual performance in Western Europe as recently as 75 years ago. In most of the Western European countries a large majority of families are now having 1, 2, or 3 children—with 1 or 2 as a modal size. For the most part, differentials between the kinds of groups Miss Johnson has considered involve different concentrations within this narrow range. The outstanding exceptions to this generalization are Ireland and the Netherlands, both of which present demographic paradoxes in which religion plays an important role. The over-all situation in Western Europe in the concentration of family-size distributions in a very narrow range is similar to that in the United States, except that in the United States the range is one child higher, with the concentration on 2, 3, or 4 children.

Whether we deal with Miss Johnson's data for Western Europe or Kiser's for the United States, it is clear that there must have developed a rather homogeneous and standardized set of values guiding behavior in the area of fertility-values that have very wide reference in the society, reaching into all of the major social- and economic-status groups.

The standardization of values would be even clearer if the data on actual behavior were supplemented by data on desires, intentions, and ideals. Many of the families without children want them but cannot have them because of fecundity impairments. At the other extreme, a good many families with large numbers of children have their large families involuntarily. This is undoubtedly linked to economic and social status in Western Europe, as it can be demonstrated to be in the United States. There are some data on attitudes toward ideal family size, desired family size, and expected family size for many of the countries of Western Europe and these generally indicate a very small range of values. Stoetzel presented a summary of surveys of ideal family size at the last World Population Conference. Other surveys have asked such questions since then. For example, a recent survey on expected, desired, and ideal family size in West Germany shows a strong concentration in a very small range of values from 1 to 3. We have every reason to expect that with the further spread of effective methods of contraception these attitudes will be more effectively realized in action, so that the actual fertility will also become more homogeneous, within a narrow range of variation.

Even if attitudes are not always effective in guiding fertility behavior, they may have an independent effect on economic decisions, because the couples may not know that their plans and expectations will not be fulfilled.

I think that a principal task of fertility analysis is to explain the reasons for the existence of the particular boundaries that now contain the range of fertility values. The classical sociological explanation for the secular decline in fertility is the transfer of functions from the family to other institutions. If this transfer of functions were assumed to continue indefinitely, the proportion of families with no children should become very large. Despite the existence of low fertility groups, this hasn't been the case in any country in Western Europe except under very limited and exceptional circumstances. Even when only specific groups that are highly urbanized and secular are considered, we rarely find a majority childless. The data from the Growth of American Families Study indicates that childlessness at present is largely involuntary in the United States in all social groups. But why is there such a strong repugnance to childlessness through Western society? To put the problem in another way, why do married couples have any children? The question we need to answer is this: what functions do children continue to play in the lives of adults in Western societies?

Even in the Western European countries where many families have only one child, there is a strong preference for two as the minimum number, as indicated by answers to questions about a desirable or ideal family size. The lower boundary may be two rather than one. Certainly this is true in the United States where there is a strong feeling that an only child is undesirable.

At the upper end of the range, it is clear that very few Western Europeans irrespective of social characteristics want more than four children, and most do not want more than three. This is clear not only in the actual family-size distributions, but in answers to questions about ideal family size, which typically give rather inflated values. In a recent survey in West Germany only six per cent of all respondents indicated a desire for more than four children, even when asked for the number they would want if economic and social conditions were very favorable. The lack of enthusiasm for larger families in almost all social strata probably can be explained in terms of the transfer of functions away from the family and the competition of non-familial activities with those located in the family context.

The fact that such a large part of all of the traditional social and economic strata agree in behavior and attitude on a moderate-size family is indicative, I believe, that the function of children has become very similar in the lives of these various groups. Without venturing into a complete statement, I suggest that with all its loss of functions, the family in a highly mobile, specialized society continues to have a unique set of core functions. It is, in the first place, the only continuing primary group that a man takes with him in his travels in space and in society. It is the unit which specializes in nonspecialized relationships in a highly specialized society. It is, therefore, the only social unit which can provide dependably the emotional support and stable orientation man needs in a kaleidoscopic, mobile, specialized world. A considerable literature has documented the fact that men develop primary groups to orient their behavior wherever they associate in large groups for any period of time —on the job, in schools, in the army, in formal organizations. But all of these relationships are transitory in a highly mobile society. The fundamental need their appearance represents is met most dependably for most people in the family. Since mobility tears people away from their parental families rather early, the early formation of their own families becomes important.

The family performs a correlated and equally important function in serving as the center which organizes the impersonal specialized services of the economy and the society for consumption on a personal basis by its members. This important function increases the family's strength as a source of nonspecialized orientation and emotional support.

The organizing function I have described and its emotional correlates have both production and consumption aspects. Insofar as they involve consumption aspects, they may lead to a positive correlation between economic status and fertility. This possibility is discussed in some detail in Becker's paper. There is some evidence to support his thesis in Miss Johnson's paper. However, I would expect such a positive correlation to be much smaller than the former negative correlation, for two reasons: (1) it will not be supported by differences in contraceptive practice. In fact, effectiveness in contraceptive practice will probably continue to have a positive correlation to economic and social status for a long time, and (2) insofar as the organizing function of the family has a production as well as a consumption function, the positive correlation need not follow. While the basic orienting and supportive function is probably equally important in all strata, it may be that, in a future situation where contraceptive effectiveness is not an important variable, those who are better off may be able to afford this important value more easily. I am more inclined to believe that this is a value which everyone wants so much that it will not be highly correlated to income.

I am proposing to interpret the trend to disappearance of the traditional fertility differentials as an indication that differences in family function as between social strata are also disappearing and that the remaining important central organizing and orienting functions of the family are equally relevant in all the strata defined on such traditional bases as occupation, income, education, and rural-urban background. We might cite as an example of a disappearing difference in family functions the former reliance of low-status groups on their children and other relatives as a source of social security. Social security measures and higher wage levels have greatly diminished this dependence and have thereby reduced the value for lower-status families of a large clan of relatives.

Some types of differentials are likely to be of continuing importance in the future as the differentials more traditionally studied narrow or disappear. One of the largest differences cited by Miss Johnson is in the set of data about the labor-force status of women in Copenhagen. While data were not available for other West European countries, it is most likely that this differential is large in other countries, too. It is one of the largest differentials found in the American data. It seems likely that this differential will become more important in the future. It has rather clear-cut relations to economic phenomena both as a cause and as an effect.

Another area of persistent differences is religion. Unfortunately, Miss Johnson only had data for the Netherlands. In this case, there is evidence of some convergence, but it is not very marked and it is much less than the convergence in other social characteristics. Unpublished data on expectations and desires for family growth in West Germany indicate a persistent difference between Catholics and Protestants that is larger than differences for any of the other standard social and economic characteristics. In the case of religion, children have the function of meeting, directly or indirectly, needs created by distinctive religious values. If American data are generally pertinent, the old notion that Catholic-Protestant differences were a temporary result of differences in status, urbanization, and contraceptive information is fallacious. Certainly in the Netherlands there is significant evidence that urbanization and education need not mean elimination of Catholic-Protestant fertility differentials.

While the traditional economic differentials may disappear or even be reversed, new differentials may appear under the influence of new principles of economic organization. For example, one of my colleagues, Guy Swanson, has suggested that in the present situation men who are involved occupationally in large bureaucratic enterprises with well-defined and secure career lines may be more inclined to early marriage and larger families than men who must face the uncertainties of occupations with a strong risk element either as professionals or entrepreneurs.

Differential Fertility in the United States

CLYDE V. KISER

MILBANK MEMORIAL FUND

DIFFERENTIAL fertility consists of the group differences in human fertility associated with such factors as nativity, color, residence, socio-economic status, and psychological characteristics. This paper briefly considers past trends in certain types of differential fertility, but it is concerned mainly with recent developments and patterns. It is restricted to the United States, but a companion article on certain countries of Europe has been prepared by Gwendolyn Z. Johnson of the United Nations.[1]

Development of Fertility Differentials

Various theories have been advanced in the past regarding the reasons for group differences in human fertility. Less than thirty years ago, there was a respectable body of opinion to the effect that group differences in fertility reflected differences in biological capacity to reproduce. Gini was a leading proponent of this interpretation,[2] and so was Pearl until the data from his own study convinced him that group differences in fertility could be accounted for in large measure by differences in the use of contraceptives.[3]

The development of differential fertility has often been explained somewhat as follows:

Contraceptive practice finds its first acceptance and extensive use among the so-called "upper" urban classes. It later spreads outward to

[1] Gwendolyn Z. Johnson, paper in this volume.

[2] C. Gini, "The Cyclical Rise and Fall of Population" in *Population*, Harris Foundation Lectures, University of Chicago Press, 1929, p. 25.

[3] The extent of the shift in Pearl's point of view may be seen by comparing two statements:

"It is probable that the very harshness and inadequacy of the human environment which is the inevitable and indeed necessary concomitant of real poverty, tends perhaps directly, and certainly indirectly through psychological reactions, to produce a high birth rate among human beings. And, on the other hand, it seems to me to be equally clear that the probably super-optimal environment, biologically speaking, which even moderate wealth is able to command, tends both directly and indirectly to low fertility and even a good deal of actual sterility." R. Pearl, *The Biology of Population Growth*, Knopf, 1925, p. 167. "*It is that if it were not for the effect of contraceptive efforts and the practice of criminal abortion, together with correlated habits as to postponement of marriage, there would apparently be little or no significant differential fertility as between economic, educational, or religious classes of urban American married couples.*" R. Pearl, *The Natural History of Population*, Oxford University Press, 1939, p. 244. (Italics Pearl's.)

77

the rural areas and downward to the "middle" and "lower" socio-economic classes. The process is accompanied first by an expansion and later by a contraction of class differences in fertility.

To what extent have actual trends in fertility differentials in the United States conformed to this model? What are the trends in differentials according to (a) urban-rural and other characteristics of residence, (b) nativity and color, (c) socio-economic status, and (d) religion?

Fertility Differentials by Residence

Urban-Rural Residence. Urban-rural differentials in fertility in this country probably existed even in Colonial times. According to Grabill, as early as 1703 the fertility ratios were substantially lower in New York County (at the Southern tip of Manhattan Island) than in the remainder of the Colony of New York (which was practically all rural).[4]

In his "Observations Concerning the Increase of Mankind, the Peopling of Countries &c", published in 1755, Benjamin Franklin was concerned mainly with the rapid increase of population in America as a whole. In explaining it, he likened Europe to the cities and America to the country and displayed a knowledge of the tendency for marriages to be earlier and more prolific in rural than in urban areas.[5]

It should be emphasized that the existence of differential fertility in Colonial times is in no way incompatible with the theory of the role of contraception. Some methods of contraception are very old and studies have repeatedly affirmed the effectiveness even of simple methods in reducing fertility. However, such factors as differences in age at marriage were probably responsible for a considerable part of the early differentials in fertility, such as the urban-rural differentials in New York in 1703.

Charts 1–3 adapted from Grabill's computations from Census data for the years 1800–1840 and 1910–1950 point up in general the similarity of urban and rural declines in fertility ratios during the period 1810–1940.[6] The absolute declines in fertility ratios during this period were somewhat more marked in rural than in urban areas. Hence, on an absolute basis, there was a little *narrowing* of the urban-rural differential in fertility ratios. Charts 1–3 were plotted on semi-logarithmic scales, however, and on a relative basis there was a little widening of the urban-rural differential in fertility ratios from 1810 to 1940.

[4] In 1703, the number of children under 16 years old per 1,000 white women 16 years old and over was 1,906 for New York County and 2,446 for the remainder of the Colony or State of New York. See W. H. Grabill, C. V. Kiser, and Pascal K. Whelpton, *The Fertility of American Women*, Wiley, p. 12.

[5] See Carl Van Doren, *Benjamin Franklin*, Viking, 1938, p. 210.

[6] Grabill, Kiser, and Whelpton, *op. cit.*, pp. 17–18.

CHART 1

Ratio of Children to Adult Females, by Urban-Rural Residence, United States, New England, and Middle Atlantic, 1800–1840 and 1910–1950

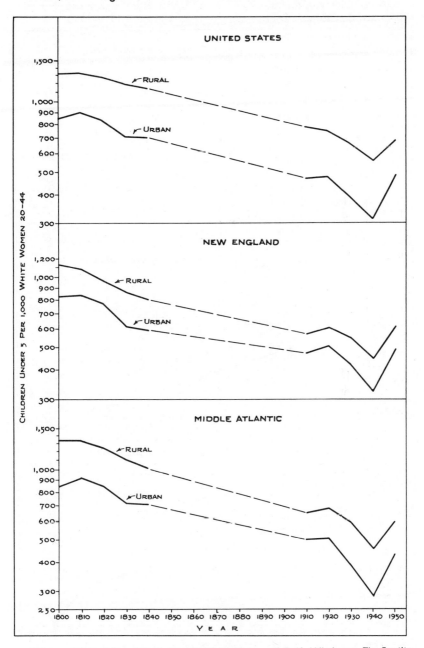

Source: Adapted from W. H. Grabill, C. V. Kiser, and P. K. Whelpton, *The Fertility of American Women*, for the Social Science Research Council in cooperation with the Census Bureau, 1958, p. 17.

79

CHART 2

Ratio of Children to Adult Females by Urban-Rural Residence, North Central and South Atlantic, 1800–1840 and 1910–1950

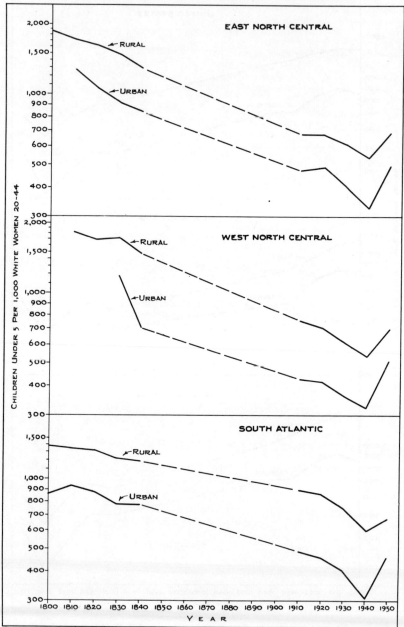

Source: Same as for Chart 1.

CHART 3

Ratio of Children to Adult Females by Urban-Rural Residence, South Central, Mountain, and Pacific, 1800–1840 and 1910–1950

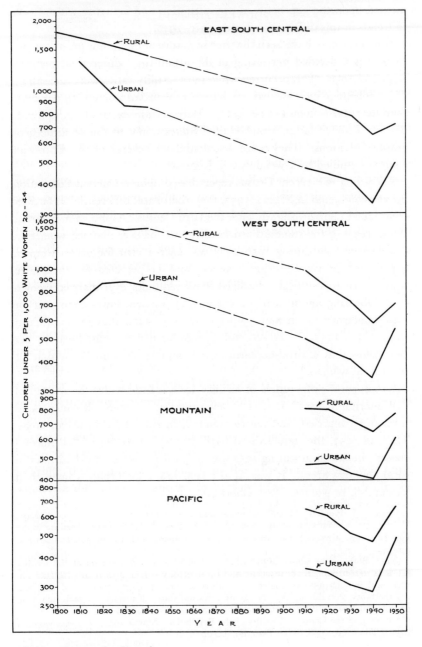

Source: Same as for Chart 1.

On the basis of the theory stated above, one might have expected some initial widening of the urban-rural differential followed by some narrowing thereafter. In their previous analyses, both Woofter and Westoff commented upon the gap between preconception and actuality with respect to trends in this differential during 1910–1940.[7]

Whatever may have been the precise nature of the trends prior to 1940, there was a decided narrowing of the urban-rural differential between 1940 and 1950. This occurred while most fertility ratios were increasing. The percentage increase was much higher for urban women (54 per cent) than for rural women (22 per cent). With certain exceptions, the trends described above for the total United States apply to the separate geographic divisions. They were also found for several of the European countries studied by Gwendolyn Z. Johnson.

According to a recent Census report based upon a Current Population Survey conducted in March, 1957, the urban-rural differential in fertility continued to narrow slightly after the 1950 Census. As shown in Chart 4, the increase in the standardized fertility rate for ever-married women of childbearing age during 1950–1957 was 24 per cent for urban women, 9 per cent for rural-nonfarm women, and 11 per cent for rural-farm women. In 1950, the standardized fertility rate for ever-married women of childbearing age in urban areas was 24 per cent lower than that for rural-nonfarm women and 39 per cent lower than that for rural-farm women. In 1957, the corresponding rate for urban women was 14 per cent below that of rural-nonfarm women and 31 per cent below that for rural-farm women.[8]

Urban-rural differentials in fertility were a little wider for women of "all marital classes" than for "ever-married women" because more women get married, and marry younger, in rural than in urban areas. Thus, in 1957, the standardized fertility rate for women of "all marital classes" in the childbearing ages was 20 per cent lower in urban than in rural-nonfarm areas. It was 34 per cent lower for urban women than for rural-farm women. (See Chart 4.)

[7] See T. J. Woofter, "Trends in Rural and Urban Fertility Rates," *Rural Sociology*, Vol. 13, no. 1, March 1948, pp. 3–9, also C. F. Westoff, "Differential Fertility in the United States: 1900 to 1952," *American Sociological Review*, Vol. 19, no. 5, October 1954, pp. 549–561.

Note: Both of the above authors have emphasized the deficiencies of the fertility ratios as measures of trends in urban and rural fertility. Among these are variations in time and by urban-rural residence of (a) completeness of enumeration of children, (b) mortality of children, and (c) age and marital status of women. Woofter has also described the complications introduced by urban-rural migration.

[8] Bureau of the Census, "Fertility of the Population: March 1957," *Current Population Reports*, August 8, 1958, Series P-20, no. 84, pp. 2, 10.

CHART 4

United States Fertility Rates, White and Nonwhite, by Residence,
1950 and 1957

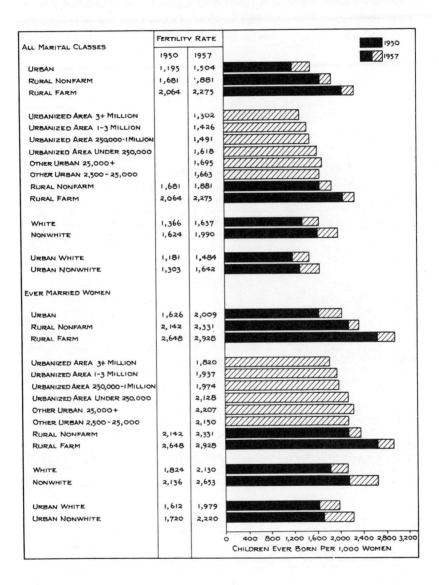

ALL MARITAL CLASSES	FERTILITY RATE		
	1950	1957	1950 ■ / 1957 ▨
URBAN	1,195	1,504	
RURAL NONFARM	1,681	1,881	
RURAL FARM	2,064	2,275	
URBANIZED AREA 3+ MILLION		1,302	
URBANIZED AREA 1-3 MILLION		1,426	
URBANIZED AREA 250,000-1 MILLION		1,491	
URBANIZED AREA UNDER 250,000		1,618	
OTHER URBAN 25,000+		1,695	
OTHER URBAN 2,500-25,000		1,663	
RURAL NONFARM	1,681	1,881	
RURAL FARM	2,064	2,275	
WHITE	1,366	1,637	
NONWHITE	1,624	1,990	
URBAN WHITE	1,181	1,484	
URBAN NONWHITE	1,303	1,642	
EVER MARRIED WOMEN			
URBAN	1,626	2,009	
RURAL NONFARM	2,142	2,331	
RURAL FARM	2,648	2,928	
URBANIZED AREA 3+ MILLION		1,820	
URBANIZED AREA 1-3 MILLION		1,937	
URBANIZED AREA 250,000-1 MILLION		1,974	
URBANIZED AREA UNDER 250,000		2,128	
OTHER URBAN 25,000+		2,207	
OTHER URBAN 2,500-25,000		2,150	
RURAL NONFARM	2,142	2,331	
RURAL FARM	2,648	2,928	
WHITE	1,824	2,130	
NONWHITE	2,136	2,653	
URBAN WHITE	1,612	1,979	
URBAN NONWHITE	1,720	2,220	

0   400   800 1,200 1,600 2,000 2,400 2,800 3,200
CHILDREN EVER BORN PER 1,000 WOMEN

(Rates given for women 15–44 years old, all marital classes, standardized for age.)
Source: *Current Population Reports*, Series P-20, No. 84, pp. 9–10.

Geographic Area. In general, fertility rates are highest in the South and lowest in the Northeast. However, much of the high fertility of the South is related to the fact that a high proportion of the population is rural and nonwhite. As indicated in Table 1 and Chart 5, regional differences in the fertility rates of urban white women in 1950 were not of much consequence although the rates were relatively low in the Northeast for

TABLE 1

Children Ever Born per 1,000 Women Ever-Married, by Age, Color, Region, and Urban-Rural Residence, United States, 1950

		WHITE					NONWHITE			
Age	United States	North East	North Central	South	West	United States	North East	North Central	South	West
					Regional Total					
15–19	548	554	515	550	594	917	893	928	929	726
20–24	1,028	855	1,010	1,130	1,108	1,473	1,270	1,377	1,561	1,274
25–29	1,620	1,423	1,632	1,758	1,672	1,932	1,415	1,653	2,177	1,643
30–34	2,034	1,862	2,084	2,180	1,988	2,272	1,730	1,690	2,623	1,983
35–39	2,218	2,049	2,231	2,459	2,069	2,476	1,677	1,827	2,873	2,145
40–44	2,329	2,147	2,331	2,631	2,130	2,660	1,843	2,054	3,063	2,189
45–49	2,456	2,237	2,423	2,873	2,211	2,803	2,217	2,226	3,107	2,619
					Urban					
15–19	502	503	490	493	539	901	879	950	903	741
10–24	910	775	914	977	1,019	1,320	1,251	1,346	1,348	1,221
25–29	1,454	1,336	1,488	1,502	1,547	1,632	1,390	1,599	1,774	1,474
30–34	1,821	1,762	1,885	1,819	1,824	1,806	1,674	1,562	1,991	1,735
35–39	1,943	1,959	1,977	1,942	1,846	1,879	1,619	1,721	2,063	1,809
40–44	2,022	2,035	2,044	2,053	1,906	2,057	1,789	1,941	2,259	1,715
45–49	2,141	2,141	2,153	2,257	1,963	2,263	2,159	2,122	2,370	2,210
					Rural Nonfarm					
15–19	612	628	582	599	686	946	—	—	964	—
20–24	1,218	1,098	1,175	1,272	1,305	1,687	—	—	1,693	1,498
25–29	1,857	1,674	1,809	1,962	1,950	2,469	—	2,579	2,482	2,395
30–34	2,325	2,149	2,344	2,423	2,315	2,930	—	—	2,923	2,861
35–39	2,543	2,311	2,477	2,773	2,461	3,255	—	—	3,219	3,642
40–44	2,661	2,458	2,589	2,886	2,599	3,328	2,739	—	3,318	—
45–49	2,776	2,479	2,691	3,075	2,727	3,166	—	—	3,108	—
					Rural Farm					
15–19	589	730	504	598	686	927	—	—	936	—
20–24	1,304	1,239	1,207	1,380	1,363	1,902	—	—	1,916	—
25–29	2,167	2,150	2,065	2,257	2,177	2,947	—	—	2,967	—
30–34	2,732	2,695	2,603	2,874	2,677	3,963	—	—	3,976	—
35–39	3,137	2,901	2,968	3,359	2,984	4,508	—	—	4,540	—
40–44	3,403	3,155	3,185	3,722	3,009	4,719	—	—	4,758	—
45–49	3,582	3,348	3,218	3,998	3,240	4,869	—	—	4,868	—

Source: 1950 Census of Population, Fertility, *Special Report*, P–E, no. 5C, Tables 1 and 32.

CHART 5

Ratio of Children to White Women Married at Least Once, by Age, Region, and Urban-Rural Residence, 1950

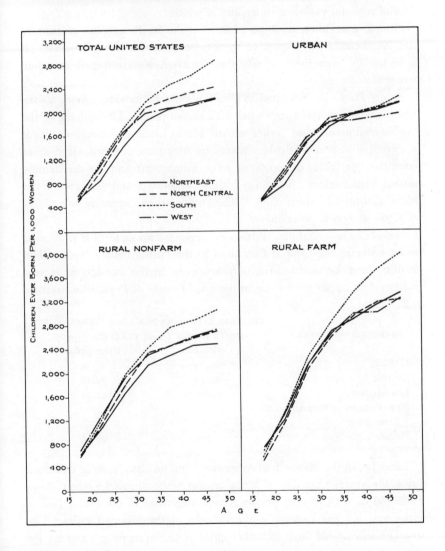

women 20–34 and in the West for women 35–49 years old. In rural-nonfarm areas, fertility rates were rather conspicuously high for the South among white women 30–49 years old and low for those in the Northeast. In rural-farm areas, fertility rates for the South were relatively high among women 25–49 years old but otherwise there was not much in the way of regional variation in fertility of whites.

Among nonwhites, the high position of the South and low position of the Northeast with respect to fertility was especially pronounced. It persisted in large measure when the analysis was restricted to urban women.

Size of Place. As indicated in Chart 4, the fertility rates among urban women were inversely associated with size of place. The splicing of the "urbanized areas" and "other urban" places in the classification affords a virtual continuum of urban places by size, since the urbanized areas comprise "(*a*) cities of 50,000 or more inhabitants and (*b*) the densely settled urban fringe, including both incorporated and unincorporated areas, surrounding these cities." The "other urban" areas include places of 2,500–49,999 population.

Central City versus Suburbs. Within metropolitan areas, fertility rates tend to be lower in the Central City than in the "other urban" areas. The fertility rates for ever-married white women in the five largest metropolitan districts set up for use in the 1940 Census of Population were as follows:[9]

METROPOLITAN DISTRICT	CHILDREN EVER BORN PER 1,000 EVER-MARRIED WHITE WOMEN 45–49 YEARS OLD (1940)	
	Central City	*Other Urban*
Chicago	2,473	2,574
Detroit	2,642	2,818
Los Angeles	1,820	2,220
New York—Northeastern New Jersey	2,535	2,608
Philadelphia	2,729	2,575

Likewise, in the "Growth of American Families" Study, to be discussed later, the average number of births among white married women 18–39 years old in 1955 was 1.7 per woman among those in the twelve largest cities and 2.1 per woman in the suburbs of those largest cities. The average was 1.9 for those in "other cities of 50,000 or more" and 2.1 for those in the suburbs of the "other cities."[10] The relatively high fertility

[9] From Grabill, Kiser, and Whelpton, *op. cit.*, p. 99.
[10] Ronald Freedman, Pascal K. Whelpton, and Arthur A. Campbell, *Fertility Planning, Sterility, and Population Growth*, McGraw-Hill, 1959, p. 310.

of the suburbs, of course, is partly selective. The suburbs tend to select as well as to encourage large families. Some of the suburban women had their first children in Central Cities.

Fertility by Type of Housing. Closely akin to the differences in fertility between the "Central Cities" and "Other Urban" parts of Metropolitan areas are those by type of dwelling unit. This is illustrated by data concerning number of children under five years old per 1,000 urban women 15 to 49 years old, standardized for age, as found in a Current Population Survey in April, 1947.[11]

TYPE OF HOUSING	FERTILITY RATIO
Structures without Business	483
1 dwelling unit	510
2 dwelling unit	474
3+ dwelling unit	435
Structures with Business	420

Again it is realized that selective factors help to account for the differentials in fertility by type of housing. Single-family houses may attract as well as stimulate larger families. Couples may move from apartments to houses when they have children.

Significance of Trends by Residence. In assessing the significance of trends in fertility by residence, the increasing urbanization of our population should be kept in mind. In 1810, only 7.3 per cent were urban; in 1950, the proportion urban was 59 per cent by the old definition and 64 per cent by the new definition. This trend reflects both rural to urban migration and the graduation of some areas from rural to urban status. Furthermore, it should be remembered that to some extent the recent narrowing of the urban-rural differential in fertility reflects the standardizing and leveling influences of the automobile, surfaced roads, movies, radio, television, and school consolidation. The sharp demarcation between city and country no longer exists. Instead, the suburban pattern of life has come to the fore.

Differentials by Nativity and Color

Nativity. Foreign-born white women in the United States now show relatively low fertility compared to the period around 1910 when immigration was large and heavily weighted by women from Southern and Eastern Europe. At that time the foreign born were much more fertile than native whites of comparable age and residence.[12] In 1950, in

---

[11] *Current Population Reports*, Series P-20, no. 18, Table 13.

[12] See Joseph A. Hill, "Fecundity of American Women," a section in *Reports of the Immigration Commission*, Vol. 28, 1911, pp. 731–826.

contrast, the fertility of the few foreign-born white women was much the same as that of native whites of comparable age and residence (see Table 2).

TABLE 2

Children Ever Born per 1,000 Women Ever-Married, by Age, Nativity, Color, and Urban-Rural Residence, United States, 1950

Age	Native-White	Foreign-Born White	Negro	Other Races	Native-White	Foreign-Born White	Negro	Other Races
	United States				*Urban*			
15–19	547	661	921	—	501	554	901	—
20–24	1,029	998	1,474	1,459	910	934	1,327	1,061
25–29	1,628	1,401	1,931	1,965	1,460	1,325	1,639	1,373
30–34	2,040	1,839	2,250	2,829	1,824	1,746	1,797	2,126
35–39	2,223	2,128	2,450	3,505	1,937	2,028	1,868	2,696
40–44	2,335	2,273	2,619	4,173	2,001	2,183	2,040	3,115
45–49	2,457	2,452	2,767	4,171	2,096	2,369	2,250	3,158
	Rural Nonfarm				*Rural Farm*			
15–19	610	—	967	—	586	—	931	—
20–24	1,218	1,247	1,678	1,806	1,305	1,222	1,906	—
25–29	1,860	1,730	2,472	2,433	2,171	1,831	2,950	2,892
30–34	2,327	2,190	2,895	3,375	2,734	2,573	3,977	3,760
35–39	2,542	2,569	3,202	3,960	3,136	3,251	4,530	—
40–44	2,661	2,665	3,236	4,699	3,408	3,259	4,701	—
45–49	2,773	2,808	3,093	—	3,587	3,460	4,840	—

Source: 1950 Census of Population, Fertility, *Special Report*, P–E, no. 5c, Table 12.

Color. In 1957, nonwhites in the United States numbered about 19 millions and constituted about 11 per cent of the population. Some 96 per cent of them are Negro. The others, in order of numerical importance, are American Indians, Japanese, Chinese, and "all other." The fertility rate of each of these groups probably is higher than that of the whites. In fact, as indicated in Table 2, the fertility rates of the "other races" combined surpassed those of the Negroes in 1950 except within rural-farm areas.

There are no adequate data on fertility differentials by color in the United States prior to 1850. However, the fertility ratios of nonwhites since then have been higher than those for whites. To some extent, this has been due to the greater concentration of nonwhites in the rural-farm areas of the South. However, even within those areas the fertility of nonwhites has tended to surpass that of whites.

In contrast to the recent narrowing of fertility differentials by nativity, there has been a widening of differentials by color. This has been the result of rather dramatic increases in the fertility of young nonwhite married women in urban areas since 1940. Thus the 1940–1950 increases in the fertility of urban ever-married women 15–19 years old was 33 per cent for nonwhites and 3 per cent for whites. At ages 20–24, the increase was 34 per cent for nonwhites and 15 per cent for whites. At ages 25–29 and 30–34, the percentage increases were larger for whites than for nonwhites. At ages 35–49, there were *decreases* in fertility during 1940–1950 for both whites and nonwhites. These changes reflect low birth rates during the economic depression of the 1930's and the relatively high birth rates of the postwar period. The women who were 35 to 49 years old in 1950 bore many of their children in the 1930's when birth rates were low.

During 1950–1957, the increase in the standardized fertility rate of urban ever-married women, 15–44 years old, was 23 per cent for whites and 29 per cent for nonwhites. The standardized rate for nonwhites surpassed that for whites by 7 per cent in 1950 and by 12 per cent in 1957. (See Chart 4.)

In the past, nonwhites in this country have been characterized by having both a relatively high proportion of childless families and a relatively high proportion of large families (4 or more children). Becau; of the high proportion with large families, the nonwhites have been able to overcome the handicap of the childless to exhibit higher average levels of fertility than the whites. The 1950 Census revealed a striking reduction in proportions childless among the nonwhites. Presumably, much of this reduction in childlessness was a sequel to the decrease in the prevalence of venereal disease that has taken place since 1940. There has also been a general betterment of the economic, social, and civil status of Negroes in this country since 1940.[13]

Differentials by Socio-Economic Status

Early Origin. Fertility differentials by socio-economic status are also of long duration. Jaffe found that a rather marked inverse relation of reproduction rates to "plane of living" existed among white women in selected urban and rural areas of the United States during 1800–1840. Writing in 1940, he stated, "it is likely that fertility differentials were as large at the beginning of the nineteenth century as they are today. Consequently, it may well be assumed that they had been in existence since the beginning of the eighteenth century, if not earlier. . . ."[14]

[13] See Clyde V. Kiser, "Fertility Trends and Differentials Among Nonwhites in the United States," *Milbank Memorial Fund Quarterly*, Vol. 36, no. 2, April 1958, pp. 149–197.
[14] A. J. Jaffe, "Differential Fertility in the White Population in Early America," *Journal of Heredity*, xxxi, no. 9, September 1940, p. 411.
Note: Jaffe's index of fertility was the standardized gross reproduction rate computed

Bash's recent study indicated the existence of certain types of fertility differentials in Madison County, New York, in 1865. Foreign-born wives and the wives of unskilled laborers had relatively high fertility. Among the farmers, fertility showed a slight inverse correlation to cash value of farm and to value of tools and machinery.[15]

Analyses of completed fertility rates in the 1911 Census of England and Wales, by age of wife and occupation group of husband, have yielded impressive indications of a widening of class differences in fertility in that country during the last quarter of the nineteenth century.[16] Analyses of similar materials from the 1910 Census of the United States have not yielded as impressive results as the British data. However, they do indicate steeper declines in the completed fertility of wives of professional and other white-collar workers during the period of about 1885–1910 than among wives of laboring men.

A study of age-specific fertility rates of a sample of northern native-white women 45 years of age and older in the 1910 Census led Sallume and Notestein to conclude that declines in size of completed families extended back well into the nineteenth century and that the declines probably had been somewhat more rapid in the "upper" than in the "lower" occupational groups.[17]

Trends 1900–1910. The writer's study of fertility among comparable groups of women of childbearing age in the 1900 and 1910 Censuses indicated some expansion of class differences in fertility during the first decade of the century among native-white women in the East North Central States.[18] However, since the 1900–1910 comparisons were

from census data by an indirect method. His "plane of living" index was based upon somewhat different criteria for the three cities and rural areas that were studied. For New York and Boston, wards were classified into three groups on the basis of ownership of real or personal property. For Providence, individual households were classified into three groups, according to amount of taxable property. For New York rural areas, counties were classified by amount of agricultural land and livestock per person 10 years old and over. For rural areas in Georgia, North Carolina, and South Carolina, the counties were classified by proportion of slaves in the population.

[15] Wendell H. Bash, "Differential Fertility in Madison County, New York, 1865," *Milbank Memorial Fund Quarterly*, Vol. 33, no. 2, April 1955, pp. 161–186.

[16] See J. W. Innes, *Class Fertility Trends in England and Wales, 1876–1934*, Princeton University Press, 1938, pp. 37–69.

F. W. Notestein, "Class Differences in Fertility," *Annals of the American Academy of Political and Social Science*, Vol. 188, November 1936, p. 27. A chart from Notestein's article has been reproduced as Chart 4 in Gwendolyn Johnson's paper in the present volume.

[17] Xarifa Sallume and Frank W. Notestein, "Trends in the Size of Families Completed Prior to 1910 in Various Social Classes," *American Journal of Sociology*, Vol. 38, no. 3, November 1932, p. 408.

[18] C. V. Kiser, "Trends in the Fertility of Social Classes from 1900 to 1910," *Human Biology*, Vol. 5, no. 2, May 1933, pp. 256–273.

restricted to one geographic division, we do not know certainly that similar trends existed in other areas of the country.

Trends since 1910. Because intercensal comparisons for the country as a whole are available for periods since 1910, we can talk with much more confidence about trends in class differentials since then. We can say with assurance that (*a*) a small net change toward contraction is revealed by comparison of 1910 and 1940 census data, (*b*) a marked narrowing of the differential occurred during 1940–1950 concerning fertility of women under 35 years old, (*c*) some widening may have occurred during 1940–1950 in class differences in completed fertility, that is, in the fertility of women 40–44 and 45–49 years of age.

Furthermore, whereas the earlier trend toward convergence arose mainly from differential declines in fertility (somewhat more rapid declines in the "lower" than in the "upper" socio-economic classes), the 1940–1950 convergence arose from differential *increases* in fertility (more pronounced increases in the "upper" than in the "lower" socio-economic classes).

Since the question on children ever born was not asked in the Censuses of 1920 and 1930, it is not possible to pinpoint the date of any possible change from enlargement of differentials during 1900–1910 to contraction during the 1910–1940 period. Possibly, a turning point came in the twenties.[19] However, there probably was no single point of change. The time that changes occurred might well have varied by characteristics considered, by age, by area, and by other factors.

The data in Tables 3–4 and Charts 6–10 regarding trends in fertility differentials by occupation and education are from the previously cited monograph *The Fertility of American Women*.[20] Two related measures or indexes of trends in fertility differentials by occupation and education are used, those of "average deviation" and "relative variation." These are respectively described as "(*a*) the average of the per cent deviations of the fertility rates of the seven nonagricultural occupational classes . . . from the base rate for the total age group, regardless of the direction of that deviation, and (*b*) the relative spread of the fertility rates by occupational class obtained by expressing the fertility rate of each occupational class within an age group as a per cent of the base rate for the total age group."[21]

[19] Notestein's analysis of 1930 Census data for the East North Central States on children under 10 years old per couple married 5–9 years, by monthly rental-value of the dwelling unit (and other factors) yielded the now-familiar reversal from "inverse" to "direct" relation of fertility ratios to rental-value within the brackets of highest rental value. See Frank W. Notestein, "Differential Fertility in the East North Central States," *Milbank Memorial Fund Quarterly*, Vol. 16, no. 2, April 1938, pp. 173–191.

[20] Grabill, Kiser, and Whelpton, *op. cit.*, pp. 173–179, pp. 253–261.

[21] *ibid.*, p. 173.

As indicated in Table 3, within urban areas, the average deviations for women under 45 years old tended to be *somewhat* lower in 1940 than in 1910. They tended to be *much* lower in 1950 than in 1940. By age, the most striking reductions in average deviations during 1940–1950 (that is, fertility differentials by occupation) occurred in age groups 25–39.

TABLE 3

Index of Average Deviation of Fertility Rates by Occupation of the Husband, Native-White Women in 1910 and 1940 and White Women in 1950, 15 to 49 Years Old, Married Once and Husband Present, by Residence and Age of the Woman

Residence and Age of Woman	1910	1940	1950
Urban			
15–19	11.1	13.3	12.8
20–24	16.3	16.8	12.7
25–29	17.7	16.0	9.6
30–34	16.3	15.2	7.4
35–39	16.2	15.2	9.5
40–44	16.7	15.0	13.5
45–49	15.7	15.1	17.1
Rural Nonfarm			
15–19	11.6	18.8	11.3
20–24	15.0	16.8	13.1
25–29	16.2	19.9	11.7
30–34	14.7	18.5	12.4
35–39	15.2	18.8	16.3
40–44	14.6	18.1	18.2
45–49	13.0	18.4	19.7

The figure for any specified age group is the average of the percentage deviations (regardless of direction) of the fertility rates of seven non-agricultural groups from the base rate for the total age group. The base rates for age groups were standardized for occupational composition. The standard used was the occupational distribution of the non-agricultural husbands of white women of given age in 1950.

Source: Grabill, Kiser, and Whelpton, *op. cit.*, p. 174.

Among urban women of completed fertility (45–49 years old) the average deviations in fertility by occupation were a little larger in 1950 than in 1940.[22]

The extent of the narrowing of fertility differentials by occupation during 1940–1950 was about the same among rural-nonfarm as among

[22] In his analysis of differential fertility in the United States since 1900, Westoff also found some enlargement in the occupational differentials in *completed fertility* during the 1910–1952 period. He found a contraction in fertility differentials during 1940–1952 among women of reproductive age. See C. F. Westoff, "Differential Fertility in the United States: 1900 to 1952," *American Sociological Review*, Vol. 19, no. 5, October 1954, pp. 549–561.

urban women. However, among the rural-nonfarm women there was slight enlargement rather than slight contraction of fertility differentials by occupational class during the earlier period, 1910–1940.

TABLE 4

Index of Average Deviation of Fertility Rates by Education of the Woman, Native-White Women in 1940 and White Women in 1950, 15 to 49 Years Old, Total Women and Ever-Married Women, by Residence and Age of Woman

Residence and Age of Woman	Total Women		Ever-Married Women	
	1940	1950	1940	1950
Urban				
15–19	59.5	42.9	31.1	30.5
20–24	64.5	50.1	39.2	33.3
25–29	39.4	24.4	28.4	19.2
30–34	29.7	14.9	21.8	11.3
35–39	26.0	15.8	19.1	11.6
40–44	24.5	20.1	18.4	16.0
45–49	24.2	25.8	18.0	22.2
Rural Nonfarm				
15–19	57.4	38.1	—	—
20–24	63.9	41.0	38.3	28.2
25–29	42.2	27.0	32.7	24.4
30–34	33.6	19.2	27.8	17.6
35–39	29.7	21.7	25.5	21.0
40–44	27.9	24.0	25.1	22.9
45–49	25.8	29.5	23.0	27.8
Rural Farm				
15–19	63.2	41.1	—	—
20–24	64.3	38.6	27.1	27.8
25–29	41.0	23.5	28.9	20.9
30–34	30.6	17.8	24.8	16.2
35–39	29.4	21.1	24.4	19.7
40–44	24.5	24.0	21.6	22.8
45–49	24.7	26.0	22.7	25.5

The figure for any specified age group is the average of the percentage deviations (regardless of direction) of the fertility rates for five educational groups from the base rate for the total age group. The base rates for age groups were standardized for educational composition. The standard used was the educational distribution of white women of given age in 1950.

Source: Grabill, Whelpton, and Kiser, *op. cit.*, p. 253.

Charts 6–7 exhibit the relative variations in fertility rates by occupation of the husband in 1910, 1940, and 1950. As already indicated, this device sacrifices the convenience of the average deviation but it portrays in detail the direction and relative range of the variations in the fertility rates by occupation. The use of "relative variations" permits comparison

CHART 6

Fertility Rates for Urban White Women by Occupation of Husband, 1910, 1940, and 1950

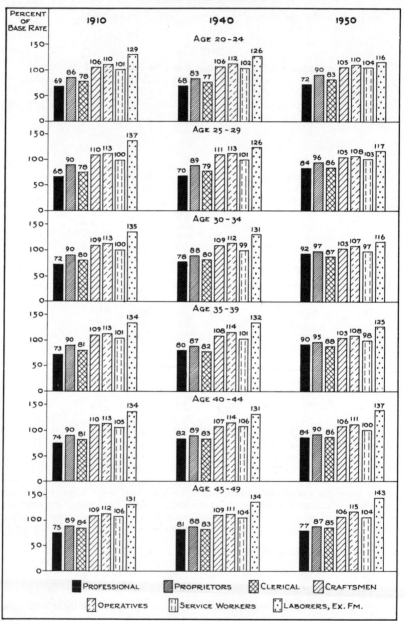

Cumulative rates for women of specified age (married once and husband present) in each occupational class, as per cent of base rate for total age group considered (base rate = 100).

Source: See Grabill, Kiser, and Whelpton, *op. cit.*, pp. 176–177.

CHART 7

Fertility Rates for Rural Nonfarm White Women by Occupation of Husband, 1910, 1940, and 1950

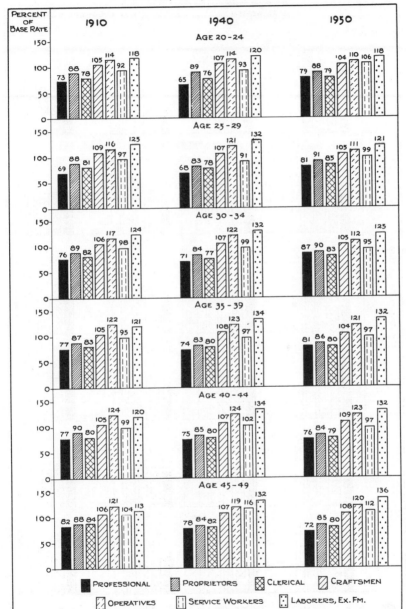

Cumulative rates for women of specified age (married once and husband present) in each occupational class, as per cent of base rate for total age group considered (base rate = 100).

Source: Same as for Chart 6.

CHART 8

Fertility Rates for Urban White Women by Education of Woman, 1940 and 1950

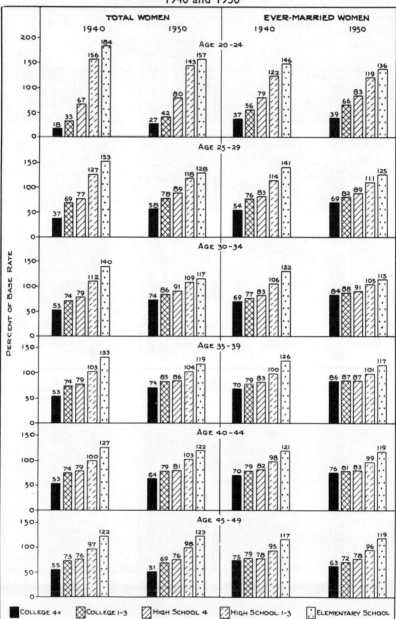

Cumulative rates for women of specified age and marital status in each educational class, as per cent of base rate for total age and marital status group considered (base rate = 100).

Source: See Grabill, Kiser, and Whelpton, *op. cit.*, pp. 256–257.

CHART 9

Fertility Rates for Rural Nonfarm White Women by Education of Woman, 1940 and 1950

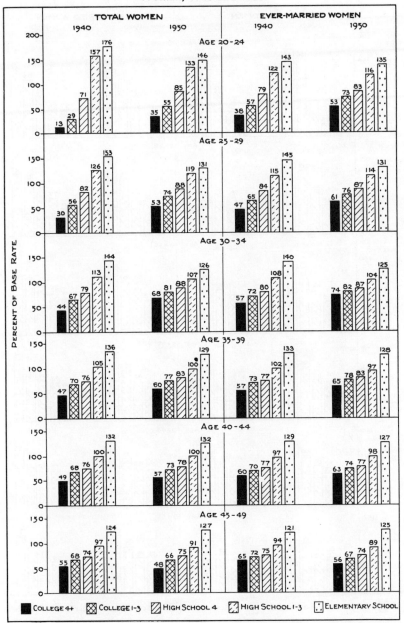

Cumulative rates for women of specified age and marital status in each educational class, as per cent of base rate for total age and marital status group considered (base rate = 100).

Source: Same as for Chart 8.

CHART 10

Fertility Rates for Rural Farm White Women by Education of Woman, 1940 and 1950

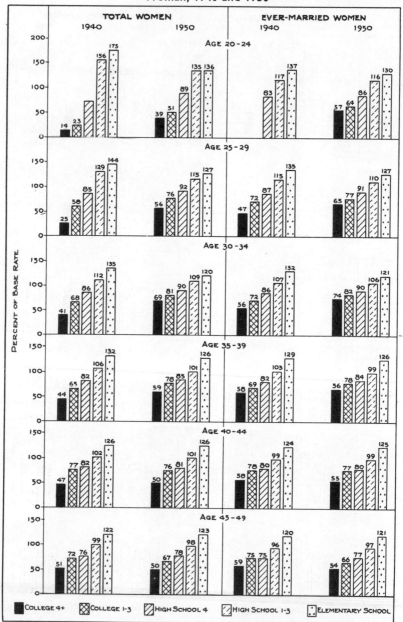

Cumulative rates for women of specified age and marital status in each educational class, as per cent of base rate for total age and marital status group considered (base rate = 100).

Source: Same as for Chart 8.

of the spread of the fertility rates at different times without the complications of secular trends in the general levels of absolute rates. Again, it will be noted that whereas the relative range of the fertility rates of urban women by occupation of the husband tends to be a little smaller in 1940 than in 1910, it tends to be much smaller in 1950 than in 1940 *except at oldest ages*. In other words, except among women of virtually completed fertility (40–44 and 45–49) the rates were much more homogeneous by occupational class in 1950 than in 1940. Among rural-nonfarm women under 45, the relative spread of the fertility rates by occupational class tended to be larger in 1940 than in 1910 but was smaller in 1950 than in 1940. Among rural-nonfarm and urban women 45–49, there was still a trend toward expansion of occupational differentials in fertility during 1940–1950.[23]

Table 4 and Charts 8–10 present the trends in fertility differentials by educational attainment of the women. The data are restricted to 1940 and 1950 because census questions on highest grade in school completed were not asked prior to 1940. However, data are given for "all women" as well as for ever-married women. Again, the average deviations and the relative variations of the fertility rates by educational attainment of the women tended to be much smaller in 1950 than in 1940.[24] The average deviations tended to be somewhat larger by education of the wife than by occupational group of the husband. The following factors may be involved: (*a*) education relates to wife and the wife may tend to be more concerned with family planning than is the husband, (*b*) educational attainment of the adult is, in the nature of the case, less changeable in time than is occupational group, (*c*) age of wife at marriage probably is more closely associated with her own educational attainment than with occupational group of the husband at time of the census, and (*d*) agricultural people in urban and rural-nonfarm areas are absent in the classifications by occupation but present in the classifications by education. The last-mentioned statement is important in that agricultural workers tend to be characterized at once by high fertility and low educational attainment.

Fertility Ratios in 1950

Owing to the recency of the increases in fertility rates, it is well to examine some materials less affected by past conditions than are the data relating to children ever born in 1950. Chart 11 shows number of own children under 5 per 1,000 urban white women of given age in comparison with

[23] *ibid.*, pp. 175–179.   [24] *ibid.*, pp. 253–261.

CHART 11

Ratio of Children to Urban White Women by Age of Wife and Occupation of Husband, 1940 and 1950

(women married once and husband present)

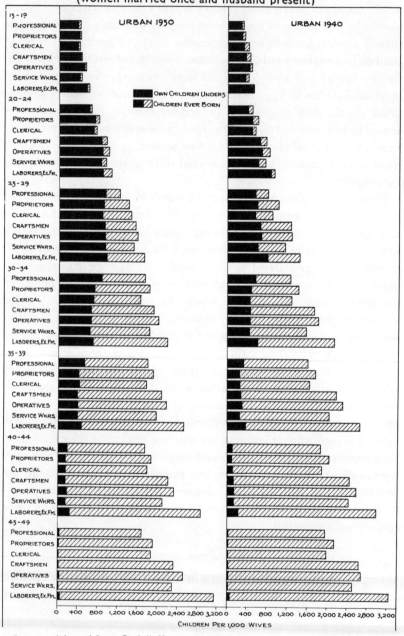

Source: Adapted from Grabill, Kiser, and Whelpton, *op cit.*, pp. 131–132, 156–157.

CHART 12

Ratio of Children to Urban White Women by Age and Education of Woman, 1940 and 1950
(women married at least once)

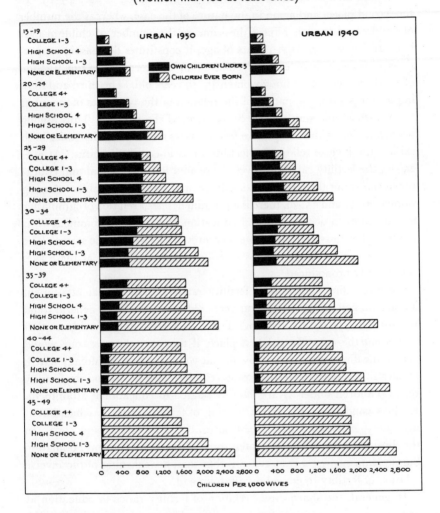

Source: Grabill, Kiser, and Whelpton, *op. cit.*, pp. 205–228.

number of children ever born to these same women, by occupation of husband. The data are shown for 1940 and 1950 and relate to urban white women classified as "married once and husband present." Chart 12 presents the same type of materials by educational attainment of the woman but this time the data relate to "ever-married" women.

Several situations are pointed up by the two charts. In the first place, whereas the rates based upon children ever born naturally increase with age, those based upon children under 5 tend to reach a maximum at ages 25–29 and then to decline; they reach very low levels at ages 45–49. In the second place, and again in the nature of the case, whereas the number of children under 5 is almost the same as the number of children ever born among women 15–19 years of age, it constitutes decreasing proportions at successively older ages; children under 5 form only a tiny fraction of children ever born among women 45–49 years old. The third and most important point is the nature of the relation of the two types of measures to socio-economic status at successive ages of the women. Thus among women under 25 the cumulative fertility rates and the fertility ratios both exhibit the inverse relation of fertility to socio-economic status. At ages 25–29, the fertility rates are inversely related to occupational and educational status but the fertility ratios differ little by these variables. Among women 30–34 and 35–39, there is a prominent *inverse* relation of cumulative fertility rates to occupation and education and a fairly prominent *direct* relation of fertility ratios to those measures of socio-economic status. The direct relation of fertility ratios to educational attainment at these ages is especially pronounced.

Does the direct relation of fertility ratios to educational attainment among women 30–34 and 35–39 years old portend a more general trend toward this type of relationship? There are several lines of evidence that this is not the case. In the first place, if this were the case, one would expect the direct relation to show first at younger ages. As already noted, at ages 20–24, both the fertility rates (children ever born) and the fertility ratios (children under 5) are *inversely* related to educational attainment. In the second place, the direct relation of fertility ratios to education at ages 30–39 existed in 1940, albeit not to the same extent as in 1950. In the third place, as will be seen later, some of the recent Current Population Survey data suggest a resurgence rather than a weakening of the inverse relation of fertility to educational attainment.

In general, the sharp direct relation of fertility ratios to education at ages 30–39 arises in large part from differences by education in duration of marriage. As indicated by skeleton figures in Table 5, duration of marriage is inversely related to educational attainment among the white women 30–34 years of age. The average number of children under 5 was higher among the college graduates than the elementary school group because a larger proportion of the former were just beginning their families. Among women 30–34 years old and married 0–5 years there

102

TABLE 5

Children Ever Born per 1,000 Women 30–34 Years Old by Duration of Marriage and Educational Attainment. White Women, Married Once and Husband Present, United States, 1950

Education of Woman	All Durations	Under 5 Years	Duration of Marriage 5–9 Years	10–14 Years	15–19 Years	20+ Years
			Per Cent Distribution of Women			
College 4+	100.0	16.4	52.9	28.2	2.2	0.3
College 1–3	100.0	12.9	43.3	38.9	4.7	0.3
High School 4	100.0	10.8	34.5	46.8	7.4	0.4
High School 1–3	100.0	7.6	22.1	50.8	18.7	0.7
Elementary	*100.0*	*7.8*	*19.9*	*47.6*	*23.2*	*1.4*
Elementary 7–8	100.0	8.4	20.3	48.8	21.3	1.1
Elementary < 7	100.0	6.2	18.8	44.5	28.3	2.3
			Fertility Rate			
College 4+	1,667	832	1,657	2,097	—	—
College 1–3	1,790	860	1,656	2,174	2,290	—
High School 4	1,841	744	1,574	2,181	2,399	—
High School 1–3	2,169	843	1,577	2,329	2,902	—
Elementary	*2,590*	*926*	*1,730*	*2,716*	*3,563*	—
Elementary 7–8	2,429	880	1,678	2,603	3,321	—
Elementary < 7	3,025	1,098	1,882	3,053	4,057	—

Source: adapted from Bureau of the Census, "Fertility by Duration of Marriage: 1950," *Special Report*, Series PC–14, no. 22, September 7, 1956, pp. 8–9.

TABLE 6

Children Ever Born, Children Under 5 Years Old, and Children Five Years of Age and Older, per 1,000 Ever-Married Women 30–34 Years Old, by Education of the Woman, White Women in Urban Areas of the United States, 1940 and 1950

Education of Woman	1940[a] Children Ever Born	Children Under 5	Other Children Ever Born	1950[b] Children Ever Born	Children Under 5	Other Children Ever Born
College 4+	1,070	555	515	1,559	861	698
College 1–3	1,192	481	711	1,626	755	871
High School 4	1,287	428	859	1,687	662	1,025
High School 1–3	1,639	400	1,239	1,933	562	1,371
Elementary	2,046	445	1,601	2,134	589	1,545

[a] 1940 Census of Population: Population, Differential Fertility 1940 and 1910: Women by Number of Children Ever Born, 1945, Table 49; *ibid.*: Women by Number of Children Under 5 Years Old, 1945, Table 25.

[b] 1950 Census of Population: Fertility, *Special Report*, P–E, no. 5c, Tables 20 and 44. The data for 1940 relate to native-white women and those for 1950 to white women. The urban areas are those defined by each Census. The numbers of "other children ever born" are derived by subtraction.

was an inverse relation of children ever born to educational status. As indicated in Table 6 there is a strong inverse relation indeed between educational attainment and number of children *5 years of age and over* among women 30–34 years of age.

The most recent comprehensive data on differential fertility in the United States are those collected in the March, 1957 Current Population Survey. The Current Population Survey periodically covers a sample of some 35,000 households. The sample is fractionally rotated at given intervals and it is designed to be fairly representative of the United States. In fact, the numbers in the published reports are generally inflated to the size of the estimated total population of the universe considered, although, of course, the computed sampling errors are based upon the actual numbers.

The March, 1957 Current Population Survey included questions on children ever born, occupation of the husband, income of the husband during the preceding year, and education of the wife. Chart 13, based upon comparable materials from 1957 and 1952 Current Population Surveys, presents fertility rates by husband's occupation group and by husband's income during the preceding year. The fertility rates relate to children ever born per 1,000 women (married and husband present) 15–44 years old (standardized for age).

On the basis of Chart 13, it would appear that the inverse relation of fertility to occupational and income status of the husband was a little stronger in 1957 than in 1952. The apparent enlargement of the differentials by income was quite pronounced. The *Current Population Reports* stated: "The first data tabulated by the Bureau of the Census on children ever born by income of the husband were those for 1952 (*Current Population Reports*, Series P-20, no. 46). At that time, it was noted that fertility rates for wives 15 to 44 years old, standardized for age, were fairly similar at different income levels. By 1957, there had been more increase in fertility of women whose husbands' incomes were below $5,000 than among wives whose husbands' incomes were $5,000 or more per year. . . . Accordingly, a strong pattern of relatively more children among people with little income than among people with more income has been at least temporarily re-established."[25] However, in view of the small size of the sample in the Current Population Survey and the lack of controls by color or urban-rural residence, the apparent absence of differentials in 1952 may not be real.

Some of the weakness mentioned above is absent in the data by education

---

[25] *Current Population Reports*, Series P-20, no. 84, August 8, 1958, p. 3.

CHART 13

United States Fertility Rates by Occupation and Income of Husband, April 1952 and March 1957

(rates for women 15–44 years old, standardized for age; husband's income for previous calendar year)

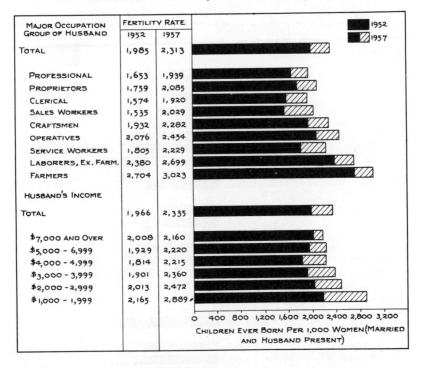

Major Occupation Group of Husband	Fertility Rate 1952	Fertility Rate 1957
Total	1,985	2,313
Professional	1,653	1,939
Proprietors	1,759	2,085
Clerical	1,574	1,920
Sales Workers	1,535	2,029
Craftsmen	1,932	2,282
Operatives	2,076	2,454
Service Workers	1,805	2,229
Laborers, Ex. Farm.	2,380	2,699
Farmers	2,704	3,023
Husband's Income		
Total	1,966	2,335
$7,000 and over	2,008	2,160
$5,000 – 6,999	1,929	2,220
$4,000 – 4,999	1,814	2,215
$3,000 – 3,999	1,901	2,360
$2,000 – 2,999	2,013	2,472
$1,000 – 1,999	2,165	2,889

Children Ever Born Per 1,000 Women (Married and Husband Present)

Source: *Current Population Reports*, Series P-20, No. 84, pp. 11–12.

in Chart 14. In this instance, the data are available for urban areas separately, as well as for the total country. Also in this instance, the 1957 Current Population Survey data are compared with a sound body of earlier materials, those from the 1950 Census. However, in this case, too, "fertility differentials by education tended to widen rather than narrow in the period from 1950 to 1957."[26]

It will be noted that the range of the variation is smaller within urban areas than within the United States as a whole because the groups with lowest education are more heavily weighted by rural people than are those of high education. It will also be noted that for both 1950 and 1957 the range of variations in general fertility rates relating to all marital

[26] *ibid.*, p. 2.

CHART 14

United States Fertility Rates by Woman's Marital Status and Education, April 1950 and March 1957

(women 15–44 years old, standardized for age)

	FERTILITY RATE		
	1950	1957	
ALL MARITAL CLASSES			■ 1950 ▨ 1957
TOTAL	1,395	1,677	
COLLEGE 4+	807	1,046	
COLLEGE 1-3	1,019	1,360	
HIGH SCHOOL 4	1,141	1,502	
HIGH SCHOOL 1-3	1,501	1,910	
ELEMENTARY 8	1,642	1,914	
ELEMENTARY UNDER 8	1,972	2,346	
URBAN	1,195	1,504	
COLLEGE 4+	770	984	
COLLEGE 1-3	937	1,272	
HIGH SCHOOL 4	1,041	1,384	
HIGH SCHOOL 1-3	1,351	1,790	
ELEMENTARY 8	1,402	1,592	
ELEMENTARY UNDER 8	1,598	2,085	
EVER MARRIED WOMEN			
TOTAL	1,859	2,188	
COLLEGE 4+	1,265	1,592	
COLLEGE 1-3	1,438	1,812	
HIGH SCHOOL 4	1,529	1,940	
HIGH SCHOOL 1-3	1,906	2,347	
ELEMENTARY 8	2,109	2,465	
ELEMENTARY UNDER 8	2,560	3,118	
URBAN	1,626	2,009	
COLLEGE 4+	1,236	1,601	
COLLEGE 1-3	1,350	1,727	
HIGH SCHOOL 4	1,423	1,833	
HIGH SCHOOL 1-3	1,738	2,217	
ELEMENTARY 8	1,827	2,127	
ELEMENTARY UNDER 8	2,094	2,792	

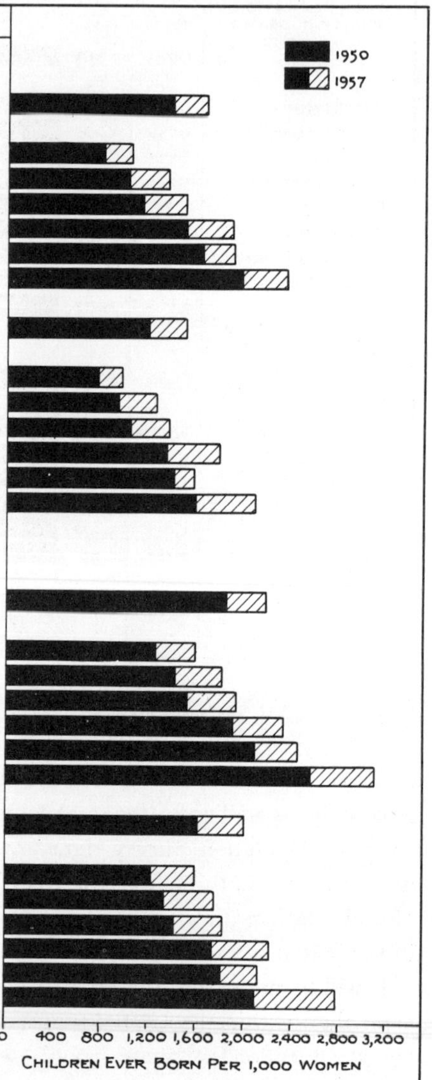

0   400   800   1,200   1,600   2,000   2,400   2,800   3,200
CHILDREN EVER BORN PER 1,000 WOMEN

Source: *Current Population Reports*, Series P-20, No. 84, p. 10.

classes was wider than that relating to ever-married women. As previously stated, the reason is that marriage still tends to be earlier and more likely in the lower than in the upper educational groups.

In Chart 15, fertility rates are presented according to status of the women with respect to all three of the criteria of socio-economic status in 1957, namely education, occupation, and income. Thus, Group A is

CHART 15

Fertility Rates for Urban and Rural Nonfarm Women by Combination of Woman's Education and Husband's Occupation and Income, 1957
(rates standardized for age of woman; husband's income, 1956)

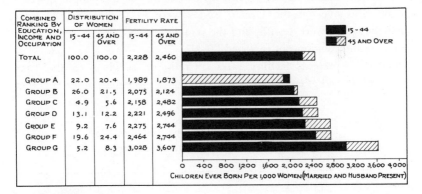

COMBINED RANKING BY EDUCATION, INCOME AND OCCUPATION	DISTRIBUTION OF WOMEN		FERTILITY RATE		
	15-44	45 AND OVER	15-44	45 AND OVER	
TOTAL	100.0	100.0	2,228	2,460	
GROUP A	22.0	20.4	1,989	1,873	
GROUP B	26.0	21.5	2,075	2,124	
GROUP C	4.9	5.6	2,158	2,482	
GROUP D	13.1	12.2	2,221	2,496	
GROUP E	9.2	7.6	2,275	2,744	
GROUP F	19.6	24.4	2,464	2,744	
GROUP G	5.2	8.3	3,028	3,607	

CHILDREN EVER BORN PER 1,000 WOMEN (MARRIED AND HUSBAND PRESENT)

Source: *Current Population Reports*, Series P-20, No. 84, p. 3.

composed of women who were "Status 1" in all three characteristics. The women were at least graduates of high school. Their husbands were in professional, managerial, or proprietary occupations in 1957, and earned $5,000 or more in 1956. At the other extreme, Group G is composed of women of "Status 3" in all three characteristics. Specifically, they are women with less than 8 years of schooling. Their husbands were operatives, service workers, or laborers in 1957, and earned under $3,500 in 1956. The standardized fertility rate for women 15-44 years old was only about two-thirds as high for Group A as for Group G.[27] However,

[27] The description of all groups in Chart 15 is as follows:
Group A: Status 1 in all three characteristics.
Group B: Status 2 in any one or two characteristics, status 1 in other(s), no status 3.
Group C: Status 2 in all three characteristics.
Group D: Status 3, status 2, and status 1.
Group E: Status 3 in any one or two characteristics, status 1 in other(s), no status 2.
Group F: Status 3 in any one or two characteristics, status 2 in other(s), no status 1.
Group G: Status 3 in all three characteristics.
See *ibid.*, p. 3.

the range of variations in the fertility rates is much reduced if the high fertility of Group G (comprising only 5 per cent of the total) is ignored. In general, the chart again emphasizes that the inverse relation of fertility to socio-economic status is still with us.

Differentials by Religion

Although a question regarding religious affiliation is asked in the censuses of many other countries, it has never been asked of individuals in the regular United States Census. However, the question was included in the above-mentioned Current Population Survey of March, 1957. According to that sample, about two-thirds (66.2%) of the people 14 years of age and over in the United States were Protestant, 25.7% were Catholic, 3.2% were Jewish, and the remainder were "other religion, no religion, and religion not reported."[28]

Chart 16 presents fertility rates by religion, as given in the 1958 *Statistical Abstract of the United States*. A point of immediate interest is that

CHART 16

United States Fertility Rates by Religion, 1957
(rates standardized for age of woman)

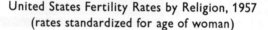
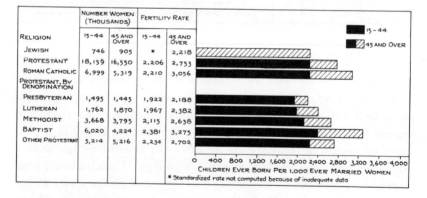

RELIGION	NUMBER WOMEN (THOUSANDS) 15-44	45 AND OVER	FERTILITY RATE 15-44	45 AND OVER
JEWISH	746	905	*	2,218
PROTESTANT	18,159	16,550	2,206	2,753
ROMAN CATHOLIC	6,999	5,319	2,210	3,056
PROTESTANT, BY DENOMINATION				
PRESBYTERIAN	1,495	1,445	1,922	2,188
LUTHERAN	1,762	1,870	1,967	2,382
METHODIST	3,668	3,795	2,115	2,638
BAPTIST	6,020	4,224	2,381	3,275
OTHER PROTESTANT	5,214	5,216	2,234	2,702

15 - 44
45 AND OVER

0 400 800 1,200 1,600 2,000 2,400 2,800 3,200 3,600 4,000
CHILDREN EVER BORN PER 1,000 EVER MARRIED WOMEN
* Standardized rate not computed because of inadequate data

Source: Sample from Current Population Survey of March, 1957; *Statistical Abstract of the United States*, Bureau of the Census, 1958, p. 41.

in the United States as a whole the standardized fertility rate for ever-married women under 45 years old was almost precisely the same for Protestants as for Catholics. However, two factors may tend to conceal a somewhat higher fertility of Catholics than of Protestants of similar residence and color. In the first place, the Catholics are more heavily

[28] *Current Population Reports*, Series P–20, no. 79, February 2, 1958, p. 6.

concentrated in urban areas than are the Protestants. In the second place, the Catholics are predominantly white, whereas the Protestants are both white and Negro.

As indicated, the fertility rate of women 45 years old and over was 3,056 for the Catholics, 2,753 for the Protestants, and 2,218 for the Jews. The wide Protestant–Catholic differential in fertility among the women past the childbearing age probably reflects former fertility differentials by nativity. The Indianapolis Study revealed that among native whites in that area the age-specific fertility rates for Catholic married women were about the same as those for Protestant married women under age 30. At later ages, the rates for Catholics became rather progressively higher than those of the Protestants. The present data are not restricted to natives, but the factor of nativity per se is no longer a source of fertility differentials among women of childbearing age.

As a group, the Jews are characterized by lower fertility than the Protestants and Catholics.[29] This group is more largely concentrated in the large cities than the others. It is also characterized by relatively high occupational and educational status and by relatively liberal attitudes toward contraception.

Within the Protestant group, the observed ranking of Presbyterians, Lutherans, Methodists, and Baptists in order named from low to high fertility may reflect in varying degrees fertility differentials by color, urban-rural, and socio-economic status.

Other studies have affirmed the relatively high fertility of the Catholics[30] and low fertility of the Jews, relative to that of urban white Protestants.[31] In the previously-mentioned Household Survey of Indianapolis, the fertility rate (standardized for age with wife 15–44) of native-white couples was 18 per cent higher for the Catholics than for the Protestants. The rate for Jewish couples was 25 per cent lower than that for Protestants. The Catholic–Protestant mixed marriages were 10 per cent less fertile than the Protestant couples.[32]

Kirk's analysis of Catholic populations and infant baptisms in 1953, as reported in the *Official Catholic Directory* yielded a crude birth rate of about

[29] Although the standardized fertility rate for the Jewish women of childbearing age is not shown, the unstandardized rates for ever-married women 15–44 years old in 1957 were Catholic 2,282, Protestant 2,220, and Jewish 1,749. *Statistical Abstract of the United States, 1958*, Bureau of the Census, 1958, p. 41.

[30] John L. Thomas, *The American Catholic Family*, Prentice-Hall, 1956, pp. 141–147.

[31] Ben B. Seligman, "Some Aspects of Jewish Demography," in *The Jews*, The Free Press, Marshall Sklare, ed., 1958, pp. 63–69.

[32] Pascal K. Whelpton and Clyde V. Kiser, *Social and Psychological Factors Affecting Fertility*, Vol. I. *The Household Survey in Indianapolis*, Milbank Memorial Fund, 1946, p. 7.

35 for Catholics in that year. Because of certain biases in the data, however, Kirk believed the computed rate was too high. Consequently, he estimated the actual rate for Catholics to be about 29 or 30 (as compared with a rate of about 25 for the United States as a whole in 1953). His estimate of a higher *crude birth rate* during 1953 for all Catholics than for áll Protestants is not necessarily at variance with the comparisons given in Chart 16, regarding *children ever born to ever-married women of childbearing age.* Kirk summarized his study as follows: "(1) the Catholic population of the United States continues to have a substantially higher birth rate than the non-Catholic population; (2) the narrowing of religious differentials predicted in the 1930's has not in fact occurred; (3) the Catholic population has contributed disproportionately to the sustained high birth rate in the United States since the Second World War."[33]

The first phase of the Study of the Future Fertility of Two-Child Families, has indicated that native-white Catholic couples had their first and second children more quickly after marriage than did the native-white non-Catholic two-child families. Furthermore, the Catholic couples expressed desires for and expectations of larger families than did the non-Catholic couples. In fact, differentials in "fertility desires" were much larger by religion than by socio-economic status.[34]

Special studies have documented the high fertility of other religious groups, such as the Mormons[35] and the Hutterites.[36]

Materials from Growth of American Families

Through the courtesy of Ronald Freedman, Pascal K. Whelpton, and Arthur A. Campbell, some unpublished tables on differential fertility

[33] Dudley Kirk, "Recent Trends of Catholic Fertility in the United States," in *Current Research in Human Fertility*, Milbank Memorial Fund, 1955, p. 104.

[34] The Study of the Future Fertility of Two-Child Families is a partially longitudinal study of 1,165 native-white couples in seven of the eight metropolitan areas of two million or more population in 1950 who had their second child in September, 1956. Initial interviews with these couples were held early in 1957. Second visits will be made in the spring of 1960. The study is under the technical direction of the Office of Population Research of Princeton University. It is sponsored by the Milbank Memorial Fund, with funds from the Carnegie Corporation of New York, the Population Council, and the Milbank Fund.

[35] E. Huntingdon and L. F. Whitney, *The Builders of America*, Morrow, 1927, p. 342. (Based chiefly on a study of persons listed in the 1926–1927 edition of *Who's Who in America.*)

[36] J. W. Eaton and A. J. Mayer, *Man's Capacity to Reproduce: The Demography of a Unique Population*, The Free Press, 1954, 59 pp. (Reprinted from *Human Biology*, September 1953, Vol. 25, no. 3, pp. 206–264.)

C. Tietze, "Reproductive Span and Rate of Reproduction among Hutterite Women," *Fertility and Sterility*, Vol. 8, no. 1, January–February 1957, pp. 89–97.

based upon the recent study "Growth of American Families"[37] were made available to the writer for this analysis.

The GAF materials include two indexes of fertility—"births by 1955" and "most likely expected total births." In both cases, the average numbers are given by birth cohort equivalent to cumulative rates for the age groups 18–24, 25–29, 30–34, and 35–39. They are given by religion, fertility-planning status, and a variety of socio-economic attributes such as education of the woman and occupation and income of the husband.

The GAF materials on religion in relation to fertility are of particular interest. In the first place, the average numbers of births by 1955 were virtually the same for the white Protestant and Catholic wives of specific age. A refinement of the cohort-specific rates by duration of marriage yielded somewhat higher averages of "births by 1955" for the Catholics than for the Protestants. This was due to the fact that the wife's age at marriage tended to be somewhat lower for the Protestants than for the Catholics.

The average numbers of "most likely expected total births" were consistently larger for the Catholic than for the Protestant wives. The Protestant–Catholic differential in expected total births was largest for the youngest couples and smallest for the oldest couples. Thus, if "expectations" are fulfilled, the Protestant–Catholic differentials in completed fertility will be wider than those in incompleted fertility. The authors believe, however, that the tendency to overstate expectations was somewhat greater for Catholics than for Protestants. The wives of "other" religions (mainly Jewish) were characterized by relatively low average numbers of "births by 1955" and "most likely expected total births."

The average number of "births by 1955" tended to be inversely related to wife's education. Wives of grade school status had, on the average, about one child more than did those of college status. This held true for each cohort for the combined religions. It held true for Protestants and Catholics for the combined cohorts.

Among the older cohorts, fertility expectations were also inversely related to education. Among the youngest cohorts, however, the wives

[37] "Growth of American Families" is a study of fertility and fertility expectations in relation to various characteristics and motivations among some 2,700 white married women 18–39 years of age in 1955, when the field work was done. The sample was designed to be representative of such women in the United States. The study is jointly sponsored by the Scripps Foundation for Research in Population Problems of Miami University and the Survey Research Center of the University of Michigan. It is supported by the Rockefeller Foundation.

The materials utilized in the present report are from a book now available: Ronald Freedman, Pascal K. Whelpton, and Arthur A. Campbell, *Family Planning, Sterility, and Population Growth*, McGraw-Hill, 1959.

who had gone to college expected more births than those with only a grade school education. Although the expectations of neither group may be realized, the data suggest the further narrowing of educational differences in fertility.

The differentials in births by husband's income were not of much consequence. The data for all cohorts combined suggest some positive relation of average number of "births by 1955" to husband's income. However, this reflects the correlation of income with age; the suggestions of a direct relation melt away in the cohort-specific analyses. Fertility expectations tend to be inversely related to husband's income within the two older cohorts and not systematically related to income among the two younger cohorts.

The differentials in fertility and fertility expectation tend to be somewhat sharper by husband's occupation than by husband's income. One reason may be the segregation of the "farmers," a group of characteristically high fertility, in the classification by occupation. Among the 1916–1920 cohort (wives aged 35–39) there was a sharp inverse relation of "births to 1955" and fertility expectations to husband's occupation. Among the younger women, the range of variation in fertility by occupation was narrow.

Summary

Of the various types of differentials discussed, perhaps those by nativity have most completely disappeared.

Except for women of virtually completed fertility, the decade of the forties was one of sharp contraction of differentials, owing to the tendency for the increases in fertility to be largest among groups previously characterized by lowest fertility.

Since 1950, there has been a further convergence of the urban-rural differentials but this is not the case with certain other types of differentials. According to data collected in the Current Population Survey in 1957 the fertility differentials by occupation have "persisted," those by income have become "re-established" since 1952, and those by education have "widened rather than narrowed" since 1950. The more adequate data from the 1960 Census may not confirm the trends indicated by the Current Population Survey data. On the other hand, in view of the very pronounced increases in the fertility, say, of college graduates during 1940–1950, it seems natural to expect a slackening of the trend toward convergence or a temporary period of widening. In the author's view, there will be still further convergence in the future. However, cyclical changes from convergence to divergence and back again probably will be more common in the future, as increasing proportions of people learn to control their fertility effectively.

C O M M E N T
ROBERT GUTMAN, Rutgers, The State University

Clyde V. Kiser's summary of the findings of research in the field of differential fertility is so comprehensive and his evaluation of the findings so judicious that I feel there is nothing that I can add of a substantive nature to what he has said in his paper. With your permission, I would like to turn my attention to some general methodological considerations in the field of differential fertility.

As I see research in the field, there appear to have been two distinct ways of approaching the phenomenon of group differences in fertility. In one approach, we tend to regard the groups whose fertility differences we are studying as discrete universes of facts, we compute summary measures to describe what is going on in each of these universes with regard to fertility, and we then compare these summary measures.

For instance, if we are studying the fertility of different occupational groups in the American population, we will compute the mean parity of each of the groups or the number of children born to one thousand women of a certain age in each of the groups. Then, as Kiser does for Table 3 of his paper, we will compute the number of children born per one thousand women for all the groups taken together, determine the amount of deviation of the rate for each of the groups from the average rate for all the groups, and express this deviation as a percentage of the average rate for all the groups. If then, in turn, we average these percentage deviations, and repeat the entire computation for a similar set of groups at another point in time, we are in a position to say whether group differences in fertility have been converging, diverging or whether they have remained at the same distance from one another.

No matter whether we proceed in the particular way that is reported in Kiser's paper or in some other way, and regardless of whether we are interested or not in the problem of converging rates, there is not anything about this procedure which indicates that we view the various occupational groups as other than distinct universes of fertility phenomena.

There is another approach, however, which is based on the assumption that the different subgroups of the population are really samples drawn from a single universe of phenomena. This approach is implicit in the kind of differential fertility analysis that one finds in the Indianapolis

Study, or in a variety of studies that are based on data obtained from sources other than census enumerations. It is expressed in numerous ways, two of the most obvious of which in the Indianapolis study are the use of correlation analysis, both simple and multiple correlation, and factor analysis. Although the question has rarely been raised in studies of differential fertility, the logical outcome of this approach would be to ask: what proportion of the variation in the fertility of the total population or the full set of groups can be attributed to the variation between the groups; and what proportion is to be ascribed to the variations within each of the occupational groups?

It would appear from Kiser's summary that the large majority of studies of differential fertility have been conducted with the first approach in mind. That is to say, there is nothing in the way in which most studies in the field are carried out which would suggest that the researchers necessarily think of the groups they are investigating as other than separate universes of facts.

There are several reasons for this situation, most of them of a historical kind. The definition of the groups as discrete universes was perfectly appropriate for considering questions about how fertility, along with other demographic characteristics and processes, varied by social group. The same assumption was probably adequate also for the earliest quasi-scientific investigations of differential fertility—the studies by researchers with interests in eugenics during the last century and the early decades of this century who wished to ascertain the relative reproductivity of the more and less talented segments of the population.

It is only when we come to regard the study of differential fertility as a means of approaching the larger question of the causes of fertility variation in the population as a whole that the assumption of samples drawn from a single universe becomes relevant. For in order to answer this question, it is essential to know not only that there *are* fertility differences by social group but also to know the magnitude of these differences and the direction in which they are moving. What is really crucial for understanding the role of occupational, educational, nativity, residential, and racial factors as determinants of fertility is to ask *what proportion* of the total variance of fertility is the result of the differences in fertility between particular groups.

As I have indicated, there are studies in which the importance of this question has been recognized. But there are also many in which it has not, especially studies based on census data. And even in the studies which have analyzed their groups as if they were samples drawn from the same universe, the implications of this approach have not been pursued to their logical conclusions. How often do we come across a statement which indicates the amount of the total variance which can be explained in terms of a particular coefficient of correlation? Seldom! How often do we find statements which tell us what proportion of the total variance in a population is the consequence of group differences along the dimensions studied and what proportion is the result of differences within these groups? Even less often, and in the case of the numerous studies based on census data, never at all! For census studies, perhaps it made sense once upon a time to excuse these deficiencies in statistical analysis by claiming that the data, at least the published data, were inadequate for this purpose. But given the excellent tables presented in the recent monograph, *The Fertility of American Women* (Wiley, 1958), such as those which show the distribution of parity in 1940 and 1950 in terms of educational attainment of the mother, this excuse is no longer tenable.

If we make it a habit to think of differential fertility in terms of the model of the analysis of variance, it will be helpful to us in several respects. In the first place, it may offer a convenient way of coping with the low correlation coefficients which regularly turn up in studies of fertility variation. These coefficients seem to be low regardless of the number of reasonable controls which are used in analyzing the data. As a consequence, there has been an unfortunate tendency among demographers—we are all guilty of this fault—to ascribe importance to the few factors which are not so low as most of the others, even though the factors which are more closely related to fertility are not high in absolute terms. This tendency deludes other demographers, other social scientists, and the lay reader. If we habitually indicated the small proportion of the total variance which can be attributed to each of the correlation coefficients, it would be harder for the demographer to confuse himself, and it is also less likely that the reader would be misled.

In the second place, the investigation of differential fertility in terms of the analysis of variance could develop some new information about the sources of fertility variation. Consider this question as an example: To what extent was the convergence in differential fertility by educational attainment that occurred between 1940 and 1950 produced by changes in the frequency distributions of parity within each of the educational groups? We have tended to assume that the convergence which took place in mean parity among the different groups during this period was accompanied by a similar convergence in the variances of the distributions within each group. But are we sure? May not the reduction in inter-group differences have been accompanied by a divergence of intra-group variances? If the intra-group variances did converge, did they converge for all the groups to the same degree? Then we must also admit the possibility that the variances remained the same or did not converge, while the area under the distribution curves taken up with mothers of two parity or three parity became similar. What I am suggesting, in other words, is that our understanding of the dynamics of the trends of differential fertility between 1940 and 1950 might well be considerably enhanced if we knew something about the role of inter-group and intra-group differences as factors which contribute to the changes in the total variance of the population.

Finally, the study of differential fertility as a problem in the analysis of variance might sensitize us to future changes in the factors affecting fertility. We seem to be entering a phase in the history of differential fertility where the traditional group differences are disappearing. This does not, of course, mean that fertility variation will disappear from the population considered as a whole. There will still be childless married women, mothers of one child, of two and three children, etc. What the disappearance of the traditional group differences probably does indicate is that occupational, residential, educational, nativity, and color groups are coming to account for a smaller proportion of the total variance of the population. If this is so, would it not be the path of wisdom to convince ourselves of the fact, to know how much the contribution of inter-group differences is being reduced and the rate at which this decline is taking place? Then, too, we will be in a position to keep our eyes open to the sources of intra-group differences; or perhaps better still, we will be able to revise in a systematic fashion the criteria we use in selecting the groups whose inter-group differences have been the historical concern of the study of differential fertility.

The Structure and Tempo of Current Fertility

NORMAN B. RYDER

UNIVERSITY OF WISCONSIN

1. Introduction

THE births occurring in any one year are contributed by parents who began their lives in many different years, while the births occurring to any group of parents identified by common time of birth (a so-called 'cohort') are experienced over an extended span of years. If we call any index of the fertility occurring in a particular year a period measure, and any index of a particular cohort's fertility a cohort measure, then we have available for analysis two time series of fertility indexes, one for successive periods, and the other for successive cohorts. Generally speaking, these time series will differ, despite the fact that it is the same flow of experience through time that is being summarized. The divergence of the two is a function of changes in the distribution through time of the childbearing of successive cohorts. Demographers prefer, all other things being equal, to analyze the determinants of fertility through use of a cohort time series, essentially because it is assumed that successive events in life histories are interdependent. But if attention is focused on the most recent experience, the only cohorts with complete records for summarization are those past the menopause, whose principal procreation occurred several decades before, whereas the cohorts which are currently the most important bearers of children have fertility records of a still unknown degree of incompleteness.

No such difficulty is present in summaries of experience in a period, but time series of this kind of index are unsatisfactory for direct analytic use because of the tendency of such a series to diverge from the desired sequence of cohort behavior. This paper presents a way of escaping from the dilemma of distorted period measures vs. incomplete cohort measures. The procedure is based on the observation that knowledge about the distribution through time of cohort fertility would permit us to translate cohort rates into period form, whereas knowledge about the distribution by age of period fertility would permit us to translate period rates into cohort form. Convenient formulae for these purposes are developed and used to estimate fertility indexes for currently incomplete cohorts by making assumptions about trends in the age distribution of period

117

fertility. This procedure provides an interpretation of the great depression in American fertility, as well as an assessment of the current situation, which uses less defective data than have heretofore been available.

2. The Data

This paper is based entirely on one type of fertility measure, the birth rate by age of mother by order of birth of child, for individual ages from fifteen through forty-six, for first through seventh births separately and for eighth and higher order births, and for individual years from 1920 through 1956. This rate is obtained by dividing the number of births of a given order to women of a given age in the year in question by the number of women in the age in that year.[1] The population is that of native white females in the United States. The data are taken from P. K. Whelpton's monograph, "Cohort Fertility," Tables A and G, from supplements to Table G for 1951–1954, and from supplements for 1955 and 1956 prepared by the writer. These statistics are the best currently available for American fertility analysis, in terms of accuracy and detail.[2]

The tables provide cumulative birth rates by exact age of mother by order of birth, arranged by birth cohorts.[3] The definition of birth cohort T was women between exact ages a and $a + 1$ in the calendar period bounded by exact years t and $t + 1$, where $T = t - a$. The birth rates computed by this definition are assumed to be identical with those for women born in the twelve-month period centered on exact year T, the so-called "fiscal" birth cohort of year T. In the present paper, individual birth rates for each age are used. These are the first differences by age of the cumulative birth rates of the order concerned, for each cohort. The rates for each order for successive cohorts may be visualized in the form of a surface, with time and age as axes of the horizontal plane, and fertility in the vertical dimension. Each cohort fertility-age function is a (diagonal) plane section of this surface for a particular value of $(t - a)$. Three summary measures of such a fertility-age function are used frequently through this paper: (1) The zero moment of the function, or sum of the birth rates over the fertile age span, indicating for a cohort

---

[1] The numerator of the birth rate for age 15 includes all births to age 16.0, and the numerator of the birth rate for age 46 includes all births beyond age 46.0.

[2] For a discussion of the reliability of these data, and the reasons for confining attention to native white women, see Pascal K. Whelpton, *Cohort Fertility, Native White Women in the United States*, Princeton University Press, 1954. Whelpton and the writer have recently prepared new estimates. See Appendix B, pp. 420–438, of Wilson H. Grabill, et al., *Fertility of American Women*, John Wiley and Sons, 1958.

[3] The cumulative nth order birth rate to exact age x gives the proportion of women who have had at least n births by that age, under the assumption of no mortality.

the proportion of women who eventually have at least n births, and called here the complete nth order birth rate; (2) the arithmetic mean of the distribution of birth rates by age; (3) the variance of the same distribution. The values for these measures, as computed for periods, are also utilized. Each period fertility-age function is derived from a plane section of the same fertility surface, for a particular value of t.

3. Comparison of Time Series of Period and Cohort Parameters

Some relevant characteristics of the time series of complete birth rates by order, period, and cohort, are presented in Table 1. Rates are provided

TABLE 1

Complete Birth Rates by Order of Birth, Quinquennial
Averages, Period, and Cohort

Order of Birth	1	2	3	4	5+	All
	A. Order-specific birth rates (per woman) period 1920–56					
Initial (1920–24)	0.82	0.64	0.45	0.32	0.82	3.05
Minimal (see below)	0.68	0.51	0.32	0.19	0.34	2.24[a]
Terminal (1952–56)	1.04	0.99	0.67	0.35	0.41	3.46
Minimal Years	1931–35	1933–37	1937–41	1938–42	1947–51	1936–40
	B. Order-specific birth rates (per woman) cohorts 1892–1918					
Initial (1892–96)	0.79	0.64	0.45	0.31	0.67	2.86
Minimal (see below)	0.77	0.58	0.36	0.21	0.34[b]	2.30[a]
Terminal	—	—	—	—	—	—
Minimal Cohorts	1901–05	1905–09	1907–11	1909–13	1913–17	1907–11

[a] This is the minimum quinquennium for the complete birth rate for all births and not the sum of the rates for separate orders in the row.

[b] A little projection was required for births occurring since 1957.

for three quinquennia of periods: the initial five years; the intervening quinquennium with the minimum rates for the series; and the terminal five years, covering the time span 1920–1956. This form of comparison was selected because the time series surveyed are all approximately U-shaped. In the lower portion of the table the same kind of information is presented for the cohorts of 1892–1896 and for the subsequent minimum quinquennium of cohorts. The choice of the initial cohort group was based on the fact that its childbearing experience was centered in the five years corresponding to the initial period group.[4] No terminal cohort group is presented because the appropriate cohorts have not yet completed their fertility.

[4] The problem of appropriate temporal juxtaposition of cohort and period parameters is discussed more fully below.

The table reveals: (1) Although the initial period group has similar rates to the initial cohort group, there are considerable differences apparent once the respective minima are considered. This is true despite the fact that the minimum rate for all births, for periods, is not much less than that for cohorts. (2) Although there is no terminal quinquennium of cohorts available for comparison with that for periods, it is apparent that there would have to be large divergences. The period average for first births, 1952–1956, is impossible for a cohort because it exceeds unity, and the average for second births is also impossibly high.

It is clear from these considerations that temporal variations in the fertility of cohorts, measured in various ways, cannot be inferred directly from the movements of the same indexes computed for contemporaneous period aggregations of birth rates, despite the fact that the same surface of fertility by age and time is being summarized in both period and cohort series. This is true of the magnitudes of decrease and increase, and also of their structure by order. If cohort behavior is given analytic priority, then an approach to fertility measurement other than period aggregation must be devised. Yet no direct summary of current cohort behavior is feasible, as the missing line in Table 1 bears witness. The cohorts which are the major contributors to current fertility are by the same token cohorts which are a long way from completing their childbearing. This is the crux of the methodological dilemma to which the next section is devoted.

4. Types of Interdependency among Period and Cohort Parameters

Among the various ways in which these two modes of temporal aggregation of birth rates may be distinguished, one approach is to consider the cohort sources of the fertility occurring during a year. Each of 32 cohorts (those in ages 15–46 inclusive) contributes a certain part of its total fertility to the annual output of children. This proportion is identical with the proportion of the cohort's childbearing which occurs in the age it passes through during the year in question. The complete birth rate for a year is from this viewpoint a weighted sum of the complete birth rates of the cohorts represented among the parents that year, the weights being the respective age-distributional components of each cohort's fertility. Now if all cohorts had the same age distribution of fertility, the complete birth rate for the period would simply be a special kind of moving average of cohort birth rates, since the weights would add up to unity. But if, as is generally the case, the age distribution of cohort fertility were changing from cohort to cohort, then these changes would be reflected in modifications of the sum of weights upward or downward, and the consequent period complete birth rate would manifest this condition.

As a way of coming to formal and quantitative grips with this phenomenon, a simple model has been designed which permits the expression of the complete birth rate for a period as a function of parameters of cohort fertility. The formula for distributional distortion derived from this model is $s = S(\mathrm{I} - M' + V'R)$, where S, M and V are the sum, mean, and variance of cohort birth rates by age, M' and V' are the first derivatives of M and V, R is the first derivative of S, divided by S, and s is the complete birth rate for the period which corresponds to the year in which the cohort concerned is at its mean age of fertility, M.[5]

Before proceeding to discuss this formula, a note is appropriate on the logic of cohort dating and period dating with respect to one another. Since thirty-two cohorts are represented in the fertility-age function of each year, and since each cohort is fertile for thirty-two years, there is no one cohort which is necessarily appropriate to compare with any one of these years, and vice versa. There does, however, seem to be an intuitive rationale for comparing the experience in a period with that for the cohort whose childbearing is centered in that year. For two reasons there is also a mathematical rationale for choosing the cohort which is at its mean age of fertility. If there is linear change in the cohort complete birth rate, and no distributional variation, then such a choice yields equality of period and cohort fertility. Thus in this simple model the temporal positioning of the cohort in the manner described permits an assessment of the extent to which distributional variation has caused divergence from equality. In the second place there is an obvious advantage for discussion in the circumstance that such a choice yields a relationship in terms of conventional analytic parameters, namely the mean and the variance.[6]

The formula $s = S[\mathrm{I} - M' + V'R]$ is useful for indicating, in a simple situation, the nature of the distributional distortion present in period fertility measures.[7] If, say, because of a depression, cohorts postpone their childbearing, and also reduce somewhat their eventual output, this

---

[5] The derivation of the formula is presented in Appendix I-A, below. For convenience, capital letters are used throughout to refer to cohort parameters, and lower-case letters for the same parameters for periods.

[6] The same is true of higher moments of period fertility, expressed as functions of moments of cohort fertility, in the same type of model, provided the present dating practice is followed. Thus $v = V[\mathrm{I} - Ra_3/\sigma + R^2V]$, where σ is the standard deviation and a_3 is the customary moment type of skew measure.

[7] This is true of all types of period measure of fertility, mortality, nuptiality, and any other processes using the synthetic cohort device for index formation.

means that the mean and the variance of the age distribution rise, (M' and V' are positive) while total fertility declines (R is negative). Thus the distortion factor is less than unity and period fertility is depressed below that for the mean constituent cohort. These conditions obtained during the 1930's in the United States. Conversely, if, in a prosperity period, more births occur, and sooner, then the distortion factor is positive and period fertility is too high.[8] This corresponds with the present situation in the United States. Distributional distortion has also occurred in the long run, because of a secular decline in the mean age of fertility.

At this juncture one issue should be made quite clear. The relationships discussed above are mathematical properties of a surface, expressing the interdependency of vertical plane sections of the surface at one angle to the time axis and vertical plane sections at another angle to the same axis. Cohort complete birth rates may be expressed as a function of the sum, age mean, and age variance of period fertility, rather than, as above, the other way around, and this circumstance is utilized in what follows. The argument for the direction of discussion which considers cohort fertility as intrinsic and period fertility as a distorted reflection of it is founded on considerations entirely outside the realm of the model. For present purposes the writer will simply assert that this seems to be the most fruitful conceptualization for time series analysis, as well as the one which virtually all demographers seem to be employing implicitly, although verbally rather than operationally in most cases.

5. Techniques for Completing Truncated Cohort Fertility-Age Functions

In the preceding sections, evidence has been presented for the proposition that time series of period fertility parameters sometimes fail to represent intrinsic cohort trends. The sources of distortion have been identified as distributional variations with time in cohort fertility-age functions. Now if all other things were equal, the message of this paper would simply be: "Accept no substitutes—if you want cohort measures, compute them directly." But all other things are far from equal. Cohort data are just not available in the same convenient sense as period data. The present series of birth records for 1920–1956 contains thirty-seven complete years of information, but there are complete procreative histories for only six cohorts.[9] This number may be increased somewhat with small risk

---

[8] This is strictly true only in an empirical sense, and that because $V'R$, being of the second order of smalls, tends to be smaller in absolute magnitude than M'.

[9] If it be assumed that the fertile age span is 15–46, then the number of complete cohort histories in 37 years is $(37 - 32 + 1) = 6$.

because of the growing tendency for American women to terminate childbearing well before the menopause. But there is no general procedure yet developed for completing these truncated cohort histories.

Here it seems that the model introduced in the preceding section to demonstrate the relationships among cohort and period fertility-age parameters may be useful. The basis for this impression is the gratifying success the writer has had with attempts to "predict" the time series of period complete birth rates for all births (total fertility rates) using the movements of cohort complete birth rates and cohort mean ages of fertility for Sweden, 1751–1950.[10] There are three important differences between the Swedish experiment and the present situation: (1) The Swedish series used a quinquennial unit for time and age. This would tend to smooth out the most extreme deviations and improve the efficacy of the "predictions." (2) The direction of translation or "prediction" in the Swedish experiment was from cohort parameters to period parameters, and not, as here, vice versa. Now there is no special obstacle to the derivation of a formula for this direction of translation. It is: $S = s(1 + m' + v'r)$, using the symbol system discussed in the previous section. The complete birth rate estimated by this formula is the one for that cohort which is at age m in the period for which the parameters have been computed. But the direction of translation may imply practical difficulties because of the well-known tendency for birth rates to move more erratically from period to period than from cohort to cohort. (3) The third important difference between the Swedish and the American situations is that the former was mostly a continuous development in one direction, whereas the time span for the latter encompasses the most extreme short-run variations in fertility observed in statistical history.

To test the formula $S = s(1 + m' + v'r)$, linear functions were derived for successive fifteen-term moving series of moments of the period fertility-age function for first births, complete first birth rates were derived from the formula on the basis of these values, and the results compared with actual cohort experience. These results are presented in Table 2. First births have been selected because complete rates for relatively recent cohorts can be more confidently estimated for this order than for higher orders (or for all births). The discrepancies between estimated and actual cohort complete birth rates are very small, and particularly in comparison with the period-cohort differences. The three estimates corresponding to

---

[10] The formula used in that work, $s = S(1 - M')$, was derived from an even more restricted model. See N. B. Ryder, "Problems of trend determination during a transition in fertility," *Milbank Memorial Fund Quarterly*, Vol. 34, No. 1, January 1956, pp. 5–21.

TABLE 2

Actual Cohort Complete First Birth Rates (S), and Estimates of Them (S*)
Based on Period Complete First Birth Rates (s), Multiplied by the Distributional Distortion Factor $(1 + m' + v'r)$. (See App. I-B)

(all rates per thousand)

Year	s	S*	S	Per Cent of Deviation	
				S* from S	s from S
1927	770	779	775	+1	−1
1928	744	774	772	0	−4
1929	732	766	772	−1	−5
1930	740	764	774	−1	−4
1931	698	764	779	−2	−10
1932	677	760	778	−2	−13
1933	647	753	780	−3	−17
1934	685	758	784	−3	−13
1935	707	769	786	−2	−10
1936	726	782	799	−2	−9
1937	749	785	808	−3	−7
1938	777	791	811	−2	−4
1939	773	818	813	+1	−5
1940	779	852	825	+3	−6
1941	887	875	841	+4	+5
1942	1,028	890	860	+3	+20
1943	954	896	898	0	+6
1944	817	905	891	+2	−8
1945	810	909	894	+2	−9
1946	1,077	905	909	0	+18
1947	1,310	909	916	−1	+43
1948	1,125	911	915	0	+23
1949	1,066	909	918	−1	+16

years 1940–1942 are in fact probably equally as good as the others. The actual complete birth rates for the cohorts concerned are in fact underestimates of true cohort fertility for reasons connected with defects of the estimating procedure used in construction of the original tables. These errors are suggested by the abrupt changes at that point in the actual cohort series. Concerning 1933–1934, the years for which the divergence is a little over 3 per cent, two comments are appropriate: (1) these are the years corresponding to the minimum in period fertility, i.e. that section of the time series for which the assumption of linear change in the period complete birth rate is least justified. This corresponds with the well-known property of simple moving averages at maxima and minima. (2) Even for these years the cohort estimates are much closer to the true cohort level than the basic period values.

The relevance in the present context of the departures of the model from reality is reduced by the consideration that the intention is to project cohort fertility on the basis of assumptions which encompass current types of temporal variation in fertility-age distributions. Provided this is achieved, there is no necessary proscription of a linearity assumption, particularly for the short run. Furthermore, it is both unwise and unnecessary to attempt a prediction of all births for a cohort without using the fertility records which have already been accumulated for it. The formula $S = s(1 + m' + v'r)$ is applicable not only to a distribution covering all ages, but also to the missing tail of a distribution. Thus the procedure developed to complete the truncated fertility-age function for a cohort which is exact age x at the end of 1956 consists of an application of the formula to fertility data for ages x to 46 inclusive, for the years up to and including 1956. An extrapolation of the linear function for cohort complete birth rate thus obtained provides the required estimate of the cohort's fertility beyond age x. Finally, a method has been devised for applying the procedure described separately to fertility within each parity. (See Appendix II.)

6. The Time Series of Cohort Parity-Specific Fertility

The procedure outlined in section 5 has been used to complete the records for cohorts up to 1930. The period selected to serve as a basis for determining current trends in period parameters of amount and age distribution was 1948–1956, because it is characterized by modest and approximately monotonic change in these parameters. The results are presented in Table 3, first in terms of parity mean and parity variance,

TABLE 3

Cohort Parity Distributions (Per Cent) and Parameters, 1891–1930

			Parity						
Cohorts	*Mean*	*Variance*	*0*	*1*	*2*	*3*	*4*	*5–6*	*7+*
1891–95	2.90	7.86	21	15	18	14	10	11	11
1896–00	2.70	6.99	22	16	19	14	10	10	9
1901–05	2.43	5.97	23	19	21	14	8	9	7
1906–10	2.31	5.20	22	19	23	14	8	8	6
1911–15	2.35	4.79	20	18	25	16	9	7	5
1916–20	2.59	4.53	14	15	27	19	11	8	5
1921–25	2.89	4.54	10	12	26	22	13	10	6
1926–30	3.21	4.57	8	9	23	24	18	13	6

and second in the form of the more detailed parity distribution. Before making some observations on the results, it is noteworthy that, despite the present youth of the later cohorts, most of the fertility presented has already occurred. Thus the first five quinquennial groups have completed their childbearing, cohorts 1916–1920 are 95 per cent complete, cohorts

1921–1925 are 83 per cent complete, and cohorts 1926–1930 are 64 per cent complete. The completeness varies inversely by parity, so that the most hypothetical entries in the table are those for the higher parities in the youngest cohort group.

The developments displayed in Table 3 fall conveniently into two twenty-year spans. In the earlier half of the experience both the mean and the variance of the parity distribution show large declines The changes in distributional components which yielded these results were decrease in the proportion with more than three births, and increase in the proportion with fewer than three births. In the latter half of the record the mean rises, although the variance remains steady.[11] Examination of the distributional components of this more recent experience reveals a large drop in the proportion with fewer than two births, and a considerable increase in the proportion with more than two births. The modal parity, which is located at zero for the cohorts of 1891–1905, moves to two for 1906–1925, and then to three for the most recent cohort group.[12] Insofar as any influence of the depression can be discerned in the variations of the parity distribution, it appears to be confined to a slight increase in the proportion with fewer than two children, for the cohorts of 1901–1910, whose childbearing was centered in the early thirties. It may be inferred that the principal effects of the depression were to change the time pattern of cohort fertility and perhaps also to retard temporarily a long-run transformation of the parity distribution. The outstanding fact revealed by these data is the reduction to minimal levels of the proportion who fail to bear at least two children. This is the principal reason for the recent rise in mean parity, and not a reversal of the trend away from large families.

For many analytic purposes the parity distribution is not as revealing as is a series of proportions which represent the component acts which go into the construction of the parity distribution. These proportions, which have been termed parity progression ratios, indicate the proportion who, having achieved a given parity, advance beyond that parity. Table 4 presents these ratios for the same cohort groups discussed in the last paragraph. The progression ratios for parities zero and one have risen throughout the past twenty cohorts, but biological considerations would

[11] The coefficient of variation (the ratio of the standard deviation to the mean) was approximately constant at about 100 per cent in the first half, and then declined to 67 per cent for the cohorts of 1926–1930.

[12] For the individual cohort of 1930, the mode is firmly placed at three, with the proportions in parities two and four markedly smaller than the proportion in parity three and approximately equal.

TABLE 4

Cohort Parity Progression Ratios (Per Cent), Parities 0-4, 5+, 1891-1930

Cohorts	0	1	2	3	4	5+
1891–95	79	81	72	70	69	68
1896–00	78	79	69	67	67	67
1901–05	77	76	65	64	65	66
1906–10	78	76	61	60	61	65
1911–15	80	78	60	57	58	64
1916–20	86	82	62	56	55	62
1921–25	90	86	66	57	54	61
1926–30	92	90	73	60	52	60

lead us to suspect that they must now be very close to an upper asymptote. The progression ratio for parity three has become relatively stable, while those for parities four and above have fallen throughout the whole series. Only in the parity two progression ratio is there evident a distinct reversal of direction. This would seem to be the decisive stage of procreation for measurement of the net impact of the depression on the amount of fertility, and also the principal problematic feature of the future development of parity patterns.[13]

To complete the analytic picture, reference may be made to another component of the present research which was reported more fully at the Milbank Memorial Fund Conference in October of 1958.[14] By use of translation formulae for higher moments developed in the same way as those outlined in Appendix I of this paper, estimates were prepared of the mean and standard deviation of the fertility-age function for first births, for currently incomplete cohorts. The mean age of first order fertility rose from 23.4 (1900 cohort) to 24.7 (1914 cohort) and then declined to 22.3 (1934 cohort) The standard deviation of the age distribution of first order fertility followed a similar path to that of the mean, rising to a peak during the depression and declining to a new low level in the postwar years. Thus, although the impact of the depression on the parity structure of cohort fertility may have been relatively small, it disturbed greatly the time pattern of that fertility.[15] In several respects, however, the observations on timing dovetail with those on amount: The

[13] It is of interest to note that there has been a distinct decline recently in the rate of increase of the parity two progression ratio.

[14] N. B. Ryder, "An appraisal of fertility trends in the United States," pp. 38–49 in *Thirty Years of Research in Human Fertility: Retrospect and Prospect*, Milbank Memorial Fund, 1959.

[15] Although the observations reported refer only to the timing of first births, it may be asserted rather confidently on the basis of other evidence that most of the variations in fertility timing are concentrated in this order.

postwar fertility pattern is a marked departure from previous experience, in both dimensions; there is a marked increase in the homogeneity of American fertility in both dimensions; and there are signs that temporal variations in both the structure and the tempo of American fertility are approaching an asymptote. Barring developments which have not yet manifested themselves, a decline in period fertility is implied, since the distributional distortion which is the source of the present spurious excess of period over cohort fertility will tend to disappear under conditions of stability of fertility time patterns. Although we may agree on the analytic priority of cohort behavior, problems are posed and policies formulated in terms of the consequences of this behavior period by period. Because of the central influence of variations in the time pattern of cohort child-bearing on period birth rates, as well as the status of the subject as an interesting but neglected area of human behavior, research on the determinants of fertility time patterns deserves high priority.

7. Conclusion

The confidence with which the assertions in the present paper have been made can be increased by further methodological improvements. These would include: (1) experimentation with models based on more realistic assumptions than those of linear change; (2) a more elegant solution than presented here of the problem of combining parity-specificity and additivity considerations in the translation formulae; (3) incorporation of marriage data in the parity sequence; (4) extension of the population considered to that of all women. These steps are feasible with currently available data and the writer hopes to implement such a program in the near future. Further methodological refinements will probably require data of types not yet provided by the birth registration process, in particular the dates of birth of previous children and of marriage. The position seems tenable, however, that investments in such purely demographic models are approaching a point of diminishing returns, and that it is now time to establish firm functional links between the vital processes and their socio-economic contexts. At best, the kind of research reported above yields a somewhat more precise statement of the variations to be explained by such analyses.

Appendix I

PERIOD-COHORT TRANSLATION FORMULAE

A. The problem is to determine the value of the complete birth rate for a period, given hypothetical functions of cohort behavior.

Assume that the complete birth rate for cohort T is a linear function of T. $S_T = a_0 + b_0 T$. Assume that the proportion of S_T in age i of the cohort's experience is also linear. $P_T(i) = c_i + d_i T$. Then the birth rate in age i, cohort T is $(c_i + d_i T)(a_0 + b_0 T)$. Let $M_T = a_1 + b_1 T$, the mean age, stand for $\Sigma i(c_i + d_i T) = [\Sigma i c_i] + [\Sigma i d_i] \cdot T$. (Note: all sums $[\Sigma]$ in this presentation are for the complete range of i.)

Let $N_T = a_2 + b_2 T$ stand for $\Sigma i^2(c_i + d_i T) = [\Sigma i^2 c_i] + [\Sigma i^2 d_i] \cdot T$. $V_T = M_T - N_T^2 = (a_2 + b_2 T) - (a_1 + b_1 T)^2$ is the age variance. The first derivative of $S = S' = b_0$; and of $M = M' = b_1$. The first derivative of V,

$$V' = b_2 - 2a_1 b_1 - 2b_1^2 T = b_2 - 2b_1(a_1 + b_1 T) = b_2 - 2b_1 M.$$

Now the birth rate in age i, for the period in which cohort T is in age x is $[a_0 + b_0(T + x - i)] [c_i + d_i(T + x - i)]$ and the complete birth rate for the period is the sum of products like this over all i's.

$$s = \Sigma[a_0 + b_0(T + x) - b_0 i] [c_i + d_i(T + x) - i d_i]$$
$$= [a_0 + b_0(T + x)] \cdot \Sigma[c_i + d_i(T + x)] - [a_0 + b_0(T + x)] \cdot \Sigma i d_i$$
$$- b_0 \Sigma i[c_i + d_i(T + x)] + b_0 \Sigma i^2 d_i$$
$$= S_{T+x}(1 - b_1) - b_0(M_{T+x} - b_2).$$

Now $S_{T+x} = S_T + b_0 x$ and $M_{T+x} = M_T + b_1 x$.

Let $x = M_T$. Then the complete birth rate for the period in which cohort T is at its mean age of fertility M_T equals

$$(S + b_0 M)(1 - b_1) - b_0(M + b_1 M - b_2) = S(1 - b_1) + b_0(b_2 - 2b_1 M)$$
$$= S(1 - M') + S'V'$$
$$= S(1 - M' + RV')$$

where $R = (S'/S)$. All parameter values in this statement are for cohort T.

Appendix I-B

By the same procedure, i.e., making assumptions about period fertility of the same type as those in Appendix I-A for cohort fertility, and deriving the complete birth rate for the cohort which is at the mean age of period fertility in period t, it is found that $S = s(1 + m' + rv')$ where the lower-case letters have the same meaning for periods as their capitalized counterparts had for cohorts, and the parameter values in the equation are for period t.

Appendix I-C

General formulae have been developed, for both directions of translation, using the assumption that the birth rate for age i is an n-order polynomial function of time. The solution has been generalized to encompass the rth moment of the period or cohort fertility-age function. The result, which involves at each step derivatives of various degree and moments of various order, is logically satisfying, but rapidly approaches the realm of impracticality because of the instability of higher derivatives and higher moments, particularly when the data betray such patterned irregularities as those produced by age misstatement. The general presentation and discussion will be included in a forthcoming monograph.

Appendix II

AN ADDITIVE FORM FOR PARITY-SPECIFIC FERTILITY

A. Zero Parity. If the central first birth rate in age x is $b(1, x)$ and the exposure to risk of a first birth in age x is defined operationally as the women who had not had a first birth by exact age x, i.e. $1 - \sum_{i=1}^{x-1} b(1, i)$, then the fertility rate for age x, parity o,

$$f(0, x) = [b(1, x)]/[1 - \sum_{i=1}^{x-1} b(1, i)].$$

By using $b(1, x) = [f(0, x)] [1 - \sum_{i=1}^{x-1} b(1, i)]$ as a recursion formula, it may be shown that $b(1, x) = f(0, x)$.

$$\prod_{i=1}^{x-1} [1 - f(0, i)] = \prod_{i=1}^{x-1} [1 - f(0, i)] - \prod_{i=1}^{x} [1 - f(0, i)].$$

Then

$$\sum_{x=1}^{a-1} b(1, x) = \sum_{x=1}^{a-1} \left\{ \prod_{i=1}^{x-1} [1 - f(0, i)] - \prod_{i=1}^{x} [1 - f(0, i)] \right\}$$

$$= 1 - \prod_{x=1}^{a-1} [1 - f(0, x)].$$

Thus the complete first birth rate

$$\sum_{x=1}^{w} b(1, x) = 1 - \text{antilog} \sum_{x=1}^{w} \log [1 - f(0, x)]$$

Accordingly, in anticipation of application of the cohort-period translation formulae, the surface of first birth rates by age and time is transformed into a surface in which the "vertical" variable is $\log [1 - f(0, x)]$.[16] The complement of the antilog of S, as yielded by application of the formula below, is the desired complete first birth rate.

B. Parity One. If $f(1, x)$ is defined as $[b(2, x)]/[1 - \sum\limits_{i=1}^{x-1} b(2, i)]$ then, as above,

$$[1 - \sum_{x=1}^{w} b(2, x)] = \text{antilog} \sum_{x=1}^{w} \log [1 - f(1, x)].$$

The dependency of $\sum\limits_{i=1}^{x} b(2, i)$ on $\sum\limits_{i=1}^{x-1} b(1, i)$ is operationalized by computing what may be called the relative change in the first parity nonprogression ratio. Symbolically:

$$\frac{1 - \sum\limits_{x=1}^{w} b(2, x)}{1 - \sum\limits_{x=1}^{w} b(1, x)} = \text{Antilog} \sum_{x=1}^{w} \log \left[\frac{1 - f(1, x)}{1 - f(0, x)}\right]$$

Thus once $\sum\limits_{x=1}^{w} b(1, x)$ is achieved by following Appendix II-A, this formula permits estimation of $\sum\limits_{x=1}^{w} b(2, x)$. Similarly the higher parity computations may be made sequentially.

COMMENT

EDWARD P. HUTCHINSON, University of Pennsylvania

As the author points out, this paper relates to two fundamental aspects of fertility study: first, the description or analysis of fertility patterns, and second, the formation of inferences about the course of fertility. It is to the latter aspect of the paper that the following remarks are addressed for the most part, but necessarily include some comment on the former.

The work described in this paper promises to be a significant further step in the development of techniques of fertility analysis and population projection. During the past several decades there has been large advance in the techniques of projection. In the 1920's we were generally satisfied to use a simple arithmetic extrapolation, at least for short run projections, or more elegantly, to use a geometric extrapolation that assumed a constant growth rate. Soon after there was a vogue of curve fitting, especially the logistic curve. On into the 1930's, however, demographers

---

[16] In practice, to avoid a negative surface, since the parity-specific rates have values between 0 and 1, cologs are used in place of logs.

came to prefer composite estimates derived from projection of the separate components of population change. Here it was the fertility projections that gave by far the most trouble, for fertility was the most variable and least predictable of the components of population change. It was the projection of the fertility trend of the 1920's and early 1930's that led to forecasts of an eventually stationary or declining population, which forecasts were refuted by the rebound of fertility that accompanied returning prosperity and World War II.

In 1936 Himes made the quotable remark that "The whole history of population thought shows that populations adjust to conditions more promptly than do writers on population." And by 1940 this remark had taken on a sharper edge than when it was written. It is worth re-emphasizing in this connection that populations do adjust, and that a large part of the adjustment is in fertility.

This paper well represents the direction recently taken by demographers faced with the limitations of their previous analysis of fertility. Whelpton's work has shown, and this paper demonstrates very neatly, that period fertility may diverge quite deceptively from cohort fertility. Or as Ryder puts it, distributional distortion may cause the two to diverge. The answer to the problem, we can believe, lies in more detailed analysis of the pattern of fertility as demonstrated here.

The paper also gets at several fundamental technical problems. If relative security in analysis and projection of fertility trends lies in the use of generation or cohort measures, then we face an impasse, for we have to wait some 30 years before a given cohort has passed through its childbearing period. Attacking this problem, the paper presents techniques for approximating the relation between period fertility and cohort fertility and for estimating completed fertility from incomplete cohort data. It thus goes to the heart of the methodological problem of getting at generation processes with data for briefer periods.

My reaction to this work, insofar as it related to the problem of projection, is one of admiration mixed with a small feeling of caution. The latter perhaps calls for a little explanation.

My feeling of caution arises from a strong conviction that fertility is a variable quantity, capable of adjusting itself, and rather quickly, to changes in the socio-economic environment, rather than being ruled wholly by its own internal dynamics. Here we can visualize several different types of adjustment bringing changes in the pattern of fertility. One is a temporary change, such as from war or depression, that may have little effect in the long run on the size of completed family. Second is secular change, such as toward earlier marriage or greater concentration of childbearing in the first years after marriage. Third are the periods of transition from one long time trend to another. The formulae have shown remarkable ability to adjust for distributional distortion when tested on past data; but the necessary data are not available for many cohorts of completed fertility in the United States, and we shall need to continue testing out the formulae in order to find out how well they operate under changing conditions from year to year.

A lesser question concerns the formula linking period and cohort fertility, which relates the fertility of a given year and the cohort whose mean age of childbearing falls on that year (if I follow the procedure correctly). At a time of changing fertility pattern, is it possible that no cohort or that more than one cohort centers its fertility on that year? And in any case the basis for the determination of distributional distortion seems a rather narrow one, cohort-wise, especially at a time of change in the distribution of fertility.

Finally, to omit other particular comments, there is a general point that bears not on this paper alone, that needs to be underlined strongly. That is that population and fertility are far from being independent variables. As other papers in this conference point out correctly enough, demographic change may affect labor supply, the volume of demand, the composition of demand, and so on. But at the same time population, especially in its reproductive behavior, is responsive to economic and other changes. So regarded, therefore, the projection of population trends cannot proceed from a purely demographic base, for there are unknowns that are more in the field of the economist than of the demographer.

I should not close, however, without pointing out that my comments on the problem of projecting fertility patterns and population trends do not acknowledge adequately the contributions of the work reported in this paper. It is based on the most detailed dissection of fertility that we have yet achieved with the aid of official data, and presents what seem to me important new tools for the analysis of fertility.

ANSLEY J. COALE, Office of Population Research, Princeton University

Since I feel that Ryder has made an important contribution to the understanding of fertility and its measurement, I have little in the way of comment or criticism to offer. Therefore I shall limit my remarks to a short non-technical exposition of what I conceive as the main point of his paper.

There are two major categories of fertility measurement that convey quite different sorts of information. One category of measures concerns the birth performance of persons at all ages during a specific interval of time. The other category concerns the childbearing performance through the whole reproductive span of persons starting life during a given interval. Measures of the first kind are *period* or *cross-sectional* measures of fertility, while measures of the second kind are *cohort* or *longitudinal* measures. Demographers use the term cohort (or birth cohort) to signify members of a population born in the same year (or quinquennium).

The common period measures are the *crude birth* rate (births in an interval divided by person-years lived), and *general fertility rate* (births divided by person-years lived by women in childbearing ages), and the *total fertility rate* (the sum over all ages of birth rates for each age of mother). The last measure is independent of the age-distribution of the population; it represents the total number of children at current childbearing rates that would be born this year if there were one woman at each age in the childbearing span.

There are more refined period measures of fertility, giving fertility rates for each order of birth, i.e., first births per person-year lived by women in the childbearing ages, second births per person-year, etc. Incidentally, the first order fertility rate in the United States reached a sharp peak in 1947, fell until 1950 and has been stable since. Second-birth fertility reached a new high plateau in 1950, while third and higher order fertility rates were still rising in 1956, the most recent year for which rates for the various orders are available.

Period measures of fertility are indispensable tools in analyzing (or estimating) the flow of births through time. It is by definition the fertility of a *period* and not of a *cohort* that determines the number of births in 1958 or 1965. Moreover, temporal variations in fertility in response to economic fluctuations can scarcely be fully analyzed without period measures. Thus to trace the relation in either direction between economic variations and variations in fertility or to construct population projections calls for the use of period measures of fertility.

The advantage of cohort measures over period measures arises from the greater stability of fertility from cohort to cohort than from period to period. A rise or fall in the total fertility of a period may connote no change in the total fertility of *any* of the cohorts currently in the fertile ages, but simply a temporary concentration or avoidance of birth experience during the period in question.

As an example of the effect of changes in timing among cohorts on period fertility, consider a change in age at marriage. With no change in fertility at each duration of marriage (and consequently no change in completed size of family), a sudden reduction by one year in the average age at marriage would, in effect, move forward by one year the whole childbearing cycle of all cohorts subsequently coming into marriageable ages. During the year of the change the number of marriages would be approximately doubled. During the following 20 years there would be extra births equal to the total offspring of one cohort. The "transient" surplus of births due to younger marriage would gradually disappear, but no offsetting birth deficit would ever appear, unless age at marriage rose at some later time. The extra crop of babies (and their offspring) would be a permanent addition to the population.

The so-called baby boom that began in the late thirties and reached a sustained high level after the war is complicated by just such a shift in timing. There has been an important decline in age at marriage as well as a rise in the fraction getting married, and marked reductions in the proportion of couples with no children, or with only one or two children. At the same time it appears that the tendency to move above four children (once having achieved four) has continued to decline.

It is obvious that the significance of fertility changes, and particularly the likelihood that high fertility rates will persist, can be better appreciated by an understanding of the changing fertility of *cohorts*. However, the basic weakness of measures of cohort fertility is that we have the full record only of cohorts that have passed age 40 or 45 and made their major contribution to total births 10 to 20 years ago. When one attempts to appraise fertility in the near future, it is disturbing to note that recent cohorts have been setting twentieth century records at each stage they pass. We have no apparent assurance that they won't continue to set records through the higher birth orders. In other words, cohort analysis indicates that the baby boom *may* connote only relatively moderate increases in completed size of family, but such an inference is permissive, not obligatory.

Ryder has constructed a method (*inter alia*) for inferring the likely complete fertility records of cohorts still in the childbearing span from period fertility data. The technique is basically simple and elegant, and somewhat fragmentary tests indicate that it is successful under quite difficult circumstances.

The problem can be visualized as follows:

Fertility is a function of time and age. We may visualize age on one axis of a horizontal plane, and time on the other, while the third dimension, fertility, forms a surface above this plane. The age-schedule of fertility (births per woman at each age) at any period is represented by a vertical section (perpendicular to the time axis) through this surface. The fertility schedule of a cohort is represented by a vertical section that bears off at 45° to the time axis, starting at the cohort's date of birth. We wish to estimate the remaining fertility of a cohort (the remaining surface along a 45° angle to the time axis), knowing only its fertility to date and the changing fertility distribution of slices perpendicular to the time axis.

Ryder shows that the completed fertility of cohorts only partly through childbearing may be estimated by a simple formula on the straightforward assumption that period completed fertility, period mean age of childbearing, and the second moment of the period fertility schedule by age all change linearly with time. The suitability of these assumptions is confirmed by the close estimates of first-order cohort fertility that Ryder derives from period data for 1927–1949.

His preliminary results indicate (among other interesting findings) that the cohort now at the middle of childbearing will have larger average completed fertility than any cohort within the preceding 40 years. However, current cohorts will have very few childless or one-child women, a sharp concentration of women with 2, 3, and 4 children, and sharply diminished proportions with very large numbers. In contrast, cohorts who bore children early in the century had large proportions childless and with only one or two children, but the distribution by birth order was flat, with high proportions of very large families also.

Limitations

Ryder's techniques permit us to make systematic allowance for the changing age pattern of period fertility as well as for changing total fertility in estimating the complete experience of cohorts not yet through with childbearing. However, it is a technique based on mechanical extrapolation (albeit of higher *moments* rather than a simple total) and can be accepted as reliable only in estimating the remaining fertility of cohorts well along in childbearing. His techniques can give us little guide to the fertility of cohorts not yet married, or not yet beyond the initial stages of family formation. But it is precisely these cohorts who will determine the size of future birth crops, even in the next few years. It is of course a tribute to the soundness of Ryder's techniques that it should not yield such prophecies, since purely internal analysis of demographic factors, no matter how ingenious, could not foretell future behavior of groups that have as yet compiled no fertility record.

Some Recent Developments in American Fertility Research

DAVID GOLDBERG

UNIVERSITY OF MICHIGAN

In 1952, with the analysis of the Indianapolis Study drawing to a close and with an apparent increase in American family size desires and behavior taking place, a Milbank Round Table was held to explore the possibilities for new studies of fertility.[1] Since that time, some of the proposed studies have been undertaken and are at various stages of completion. Three of the studies will be discussed in this paper.

Two of the three studies deal with rather restricted populations and focus on the social and psychological factors which presumably affect fertility behavior. One—the "Princeton Study"—is a sample of 1,165 two parity native-white women living in the seven largest metropolitan areas. Each of the women interviewed had given birth to her second child four to seven months prior to the time of interviewing. The second project—the "Detroit Study"—was undertaken in metropolitan Detroit as part of the general research program of the Detroit Area Study. This was a sample of 221 married fecund women under 33 years old.

The third study under consideration is called the "Growth of American Families." Its purpose is different from the others in that it seeks to provide a unique set of information concerning the fecundity and planning status of the nation's population and, also, data on fertility desires and expectations to be used in a set of national population projections. The GAF sample is made up of 2,713 white married women under 40 years of age.

The purpose of this paper is to report on the progress of these three surveys and to show how each of them fits into the findings, problems, and gaps created by the design and analysis of the Indianapolis materials.

The Indianapolis Study

The Indianapolis Study was specifically designed to look into future trends in American fertility through its emphasis on factors affecting

---

[1] A summary of the round table is reported by: Clyde Kiser, "Exploration of Possibilities for New Studies of Factors Affecting Size of Family," *Milbank Memorial Fund Quarterly*, Vol. 31, 1953, pp. 436–480.

Note: See introduction to this volume for a fuller description of the studies mentioned in this chapter.

planned fertility. Most of the 23 hypotheses dealt with planning status and size of planned family. An emphasis on planning status led to what was perhaps the most striking finding of the study. Fertility was inversely related to socio-economic status among the couples who were least successful in family planning while it was directly related to status among the couples who were most successful in planning the number and spacing of their children.[2] The study did not yield any strong relationships between psychological variables—such as feeling of personal inadequacy, ego-centered interest in children, or felt restriction of personal freedom— and fertility.[3]

In reviewing the major findings of the Indianapolis Study, it became apparent that there were a number of flaws in the design which made the analysis and interpretation of the data a difficult task.[4] One problem was the ex post facto nature of the study. The independent variables were measured after the birth of children. Thus, in a number of the analyses it became difficult to ascertain the direction of the relationship between the presumed independent variable and family size. In addition to the problem of selectivity, there is the problem of refining the dependent variable in fertility research. Completed size of family represents the cumulation of a series of births, each of which may be affected by a different set of variables. The small magnitude of relationships found in the study has been attributed to the possibility of there being distinct sets of conditions coming into prominence with each birth order.

If the Indianapolis materials were to serve as a guide to further research, it was apparent that future studies should focus on the dynamics of the relationship between fertility and socio-economic status and make some attempt at refining the dependent variable both in order to eliminate the ex post facto problem and to gain more precise knowledge of the factors affecting the decision to have children at each birth order. The three studies under discussion have met these objectives with some success.

The Princeton Study

The Princeton Study grew out of the work of a committee whose major purpose was to develop new schemes for the study of differential

[2] Clyde Kiser and P. K. Whelpton, "Social and Psychological Factors Affecting Fertility. IX. Fertility Planning and Fertility Rates by Socio-Economic Status," *Milbank Memorial Fund Quarterly*, Vol. 27, 1949, pp. 188–244.

[3] Charles Westoff and Clyde Kiser, "Social and Psychological Factors Affecting Fertility. XXI. An Empirical Re-Examination and Intercorrelation of Selected Hypothesis Factors," *Milbank Memorial Fund Quarterly*, Vol. 31, 1953, pp. 421–435.

[4] Clyde Kiser, "General Objectives and Broad Areas of Interest in a Proposed New Study in Fertility," in *Current Research in Human Fertility*, Milbank Memorial Fund, 1955, pp. 115–120.

fertility.[5] Various members of the committee presented working papers, of which the ones that seem to be most relevant to the final product were those of Freedman, Mishler, and Westoff and Bensman.

The central idea in Freedman's proposal is that family size is related to the degree of concentration of activities within the family unit. Differences in fertility among social strata, he says, are a reflection of differences in the extent to which activities are family oriented. Thus changes in fertility, over time, are linked to the relative concentration of activities in role systems within and outside the family unit. The cost of having a child is small in cases where a large proportion of the adult functions are already performed in the home or family. Freedman argues that the socio-economic variable has affected fertility not directly but by its impact on the location of such functions inside or outside the family.[6]

In the Mishler proposal, fertility is viewed as a social event which is dependent upon a system of psychologically meaningful relationships. His major assumption is that fertility will be depressed if raising children interferes with the needs of the husband or wife. The central hypothesis states that the probability of adding a child to the family is inversely related to the discrepancy between the desired social structure and the structure required for child rearing. As the number of desired statuses increases, the number of rights, obligations, and demands also increases. The addition of a child makes the maintenance of existing statuses more difficult. Mishler points out that high income and education have been accompanied by low fertility and argues that the variables income and education produce the opportunity for many distinct statuses which will be in competition with the parental role.[7]

In the Westoff and Bensman proposal, it is suggested that family size is but one value in a whole scale of values held by the couple. The scale of values is labeled "life plan" and it is assumed that fertility values must be consistent with the other values in the life plan. A work-mobility-success orientation is hypothesized as being incompatible with a family orientation. Thus, the person committed to upward mobility will spend his leisure time in matters related to self-improvement rather than in

[5] The Steering Committee on the Development of Plans for New Studies in Fertility is sponsored jointly by the Milbank Memorial Fund and the Population Council. The Committee consists of Frank Notestein, chairman; Ronald Freedman, Philip Hauser, Clyde Kiser, Frank Lorimer, Frederick Osborn, Lowell Reed, and P. K. Whelpton. Elliot Mishler, Robert Potter, Philip Sagi, and Charles Westoff are members of the staff.
[6] Ronald Freedman, "The Family Function Approach to Fertility Studies," Ann Arbor, 1954, mimeographed.
[7] Elliot Mishler, "Problems of Method and Theory in the Social Psychological Study of Fertility," Princeton, 1954, mimeographed.

consuming the benefits of his children. The authors suggest that differences in mobility orientations among the social classes have been at least partially responsible for the pattern of differential fertility observed in Western societies.[8]

Note that each of these proposals assumes that there is a systematic relationship between family structure and fertility. And each one attempts to show how differences in family structure, whether labeled "family activity ratio," "status field," or "life plan," have produced the pattern of differential fertility observed over the past hundred years or so. Each seemed to agree that family structure was the variable underlying socio-economic differences in fertility. This was in no way out of line with previous ideas about the subject. The most widely held but least researched hypothesis concerning the decline in family size had to do with the changing function of the family. Furthermore, while none of the original Indianapolis hypotheses were concerned with the relationship between extra-familial activity and family size, Pratt and Whelpton found that the amount of club and work activity was inversely associated with number of children.[9] This relationship held for all socio-economic groups.

The final product of these working papers was the Princeton Study proposal, developed by Mishler and Westoff. It includes some 40 hypotheses in an attempt to integrate the various proposals. These hypotheses were spelled out in considerable detail in a recent paper.[10] Let us mention only some of the themes and then get on to the preliminary findings.

Mishler and Westoff focus on two broad questions: What styles of life or family organization are compatible with child rearing? What factors of personality are relevant to family size decisions? The idea of using personality as a major independent variable had not appeared in the previous proposals, but had been discussed at some length at the 1952 Milbank Round Table. To me, one of the peculiar developments resulting from the Indianapolis Study was the fact that in spite of the weak and inconsistent relationship of psychological characteristics to

---

[8] Charles Westoff and Joseph Bensman, "The Social Mobility Model Restated with Some Research Implications and Suggestions," Oxford, Ohio, 1954, mimeographed.

[9] Lois Pratt and P. K. Whelpton, "Social and Psychological Factors Affecting Fertility. xxx. Extra-Familial Participation of Wives in Relation to Interest in and Liking for Children, Fertility Planning, and Actual and Desired Family Size," *Milbank Memorial Fund Quarterly*, Vol. 34, 1956, pp. 44–78.

[10] Elliot Mishler and Charles Westoff, "A Proposal for Research on Social Psychological Factors Affecting Fertility: Concepts and Hypotheses," in *Current Research in Human Fertility*, Milbank Memorial Fund, 1955, pp. 121–150.

family size, a number of the investigators felt that the next logical step in fertility research should emphasize personal motivations. Some of the personality variables included in the Princeton Study are ambiguity tolerance, manifest anxiety, impulse gratification, nurture needs, and compulsiveness. The hypothesis around which most of the personality variables are organized is that excessive and unsatisfied dependency needs are incompatible with desires for children.

Hypotheses at the family organization level are an extension of the working papers. They include not only hypotheses about the extent to which activities are located in the family or home, but hypotheses concerning aspects of the structure of the family such as marital adjustment, homogeneity in the characteristics of the marital partners, husband-wife dominance, and division of labor within the household. At both the individual level and the family group level the mobility theme of the Westoff–Bensman proposal is restated.

Another theme developed in the proposal, and incidentally one which may ultimately prove fruitful in cross-cultural studies, is a consideration of the relative benevolence of the environment in defraying the economic and social costs of having children. Here it is hypothesized that the greater the amount of help available from one's community or kinship system, the weaker the desire to prevent or postpone pregnancy.

In the study design it was felt that completed family size was too complex to deal with, given our present understanding of the problem. So the dependent variable is broken into its component parts. The design originally called for an examination of factors affecting the postponement of a first pregnancy among newly married couples and factors affecting the probability of occurrence or the timing of third pregnancies among two parity couples. However, the cost of carrying out both of the studies resulted in limiting the field work to women who had recently given birth to their second child. At present it is expected that the 1,165 women who were interviewed in the fall of 1956 will be reinterviewed in 1960.

Mishler and Westoff state that the hypotheses presented in their paper are not graded in order of priority for study. Some months ago, I received a copy of a code covering 81 variables in the study. While this does not exhaust all the variables from the study, it must reflect some of the major interests.

Of the 81 variables, 16 represent either the dependent or control variables. These include total fertility desires of husband and wife, expected third birth interval, contraceptive efficiency, age, and age at marriage. Of the remaining 65 independent variables, nearly half are devoted to mobility or personality measures. Mobility is measured in at least 16 ways, including intra- and inter-generation mobility plus scales of mobility drive or commitment. The standard socio-economic data are represented by ten variables. Six variables are given to a theme which concerns the degree of felt control over the social environment. For example, scales of achievement of life goals and feelings of economic security are included. Religious interest is measured by four scales. The remaining variables cover a wide range of topics and levels of abstraction —husband-wife dominance, I.Q., availability of help in child rearing, heterogeneity in the backgrounds of husband and wife, and so on.

Clearly, the central theme running through all the working papers has been slighted. The original papers as well as the final product by Mishler and Westoff stressed the relative participation in familial or extra-familial social roles as related to fertility desires. Granting that mobility aspirations are one part of this general theme, the schedule is barren with respect to other materials which could illuminate the division of labor between the family and other social institutions. There are virtually no data dealing with the locus of leisure activities, extra-familial involvement, or participation in the kinship network. We are left only with measures of the internal structure of the family unit such as marital adjustment, power relations, and homogamy.

The data collected on mobility in the Princeton Study represent the most thorough exploration of the topic until now. Demographers have frequently suggested that upward mobility and familism are incompatible. However, the few American studies showing consistent differences in fertility by mobility have been restricted to small segments of the population, usually elite groups.[11] In the present study each of the mobility measures is related, in the predicted direction, to the family size desires of the two parity women. That is, the greater the mobility experienced by the couple or the greater the drive to get ahead, the smaller the number of children desired. But the magnitudes of the relationships for the total sample are extremely small. The absolute values of the Pearsonian correlations between the sixteen measures of mobility and number of children desired by the wife range from 0.008 to 0.187. Only five of the 16 measures account for more than one per cent of the variance in the dependent variable. From the initial tabulations it would appear that many of our hunches concerning the impact of mobility on familism were grossly inaccurate, outdated, or, at best, inoperative at this stage of

[11] E. Digby Baltzell, "Social Mobility and Fertility Within an Elite Group," *Milbank Memorial Fund Quarterly*, Vol. 31, 1953, pp. 411–420.

family development. Of course, these are only preliminary runs. I am certain the investigators will make some attempt to isolate those elements of the population in which the mobility variable is operative and those in which it is not.

From the collection of 14 personality measures, five account for more than one per cent of the variance, the largest correlation being 0.136. My objection to the use of personality as a major independent variable in a fertility study has nothing to do with the size of the correlations. It is simply out of the mainstream of our knowledge about trends and differences in fertility. Any hypotheses about fertility which make up part of a theoretical scheme should give us a more comprehensive knowledge of relationships observed in the past. They should help us understand changes in fertility over time and differences among societies. In the working papers, hypotheses dealing with the performance of functions in the family or other social units were precisely an effort to close the gap between levels of fertility and degree of urbanization-industrialization or levels of fertility and position in the social system. Unless the personality hypotheses are linked to social system variables the size of the correlations makes little difference. A correlation between ambiguity tolerance and fertility desires of 0.80 instead of 0.11, as it actually stands, will contribute little if anything until we can demonstrate that changes in social organization are accompanied by changes in personality structure.

The correlations between the socio-economic variables and fertility desires are low and inconsistent. Desired family size has no relationship with prestige of occupation, has a slight negative relationship with income or positive changes in income, and a slight positive relationship with education of husband and wife. The strongest association is that between income change and desired number of children, − 0.169. These findings are consistent with some recent census data, in the sense that they are an extension of the convergence pattern and they are almost identical with the GAF and Detroit Studies. The data may reflect changes in our economic system which has witnessed a minimization of income and occupational differences through the leveling of pay, the mushrooming credit structure, and the rationalization of white collar jobs.

Among the other independent variables, none of those dealing with the internal family structure, such as husband-wife dominance and marital adjustment, or perceived control over environment, account for more than one per cent of the variance in number of children desired. Peculiarly, one item, a question dealing with the relevance of finances in having another child yields the strongest correlation in the study, 0.373.

Women who feel that finances have nothing to do with adding children to the family are the ones desiring the largest number of children.

One group of variables yields relatively high correlations. The association between the four religious interest variables and desired family size ranges from $+0.187$ to $+0.286$. Being closely related to one another, the multiple of the four items with fertility is 0.310. While religious groups differ in their ideas about the use of contraception, all of them place considerable emphasis on the values of family life. Religiosity may also be linked to certain aspects of family structure, particularly with respect to the role of women. It seems likely that participation in religious activities reinforces the traditional female role with its emphasis on home- or family-centered activities. I believe that the relatively high correlations between religious activity and fertility in the Princeton Study may be a rough index of the impact of family-oriented activities on desired number of children. Religiosity and traditionalism were among the better predictors of fertility in the Indianapolis Study as well. Using data from the Borgatta–Westoff articles,[12] I find that the two measures of traditionalism together with a measure of religious activity predict completed family size as well as or better than the combination of income, education, and occupation when fertility planning status is held constant. In the total Indianapolis sample we obtain the following results through the use of the multiple-partial correlation:

$$r_1 \, (3, 4, 5) \, .2, 6 = 0.204$$
$$r_1 \, (6, 7, 8) \, .2 \quad = 0.140$$

And in the "number and spacing planned" group we obtain the following:

$$r_1 \, (3, 4, 5) \, .6 = 0.242$$
$$R_{1.678} \quad\quad = 0.203$$

where: $1 =$ completed family size $5 =$ religious interest

$2 =$ fertility planning status $6 =$ income

$3 =$ traditionalism in female role $7 =$ education

$4 =$ general traditionalism $8 =$ occupational prestige

[12] Edgar Borgatta and Charles Westoff, "Social and Psychological Factors Affecting Fertility. xxv. The Prediction of Total Fertility," *Milbank Memorial Fund Quarterly*, Vol. 32, 1954, pp. 383–419.
Charles Westoff and Edgar Borgatta, "Social and Psychological Factors Affecting Fertility. xxvi. The Prediction of Planned Fertility," *Milbank Memorial Fund Quarterly*, Vol. 33, 1955, pp. 50–62.

Although some facets of family structure have been ignored in the Princeton Study, the schedule provides us with many opportunities to explore certain areas which up to now have been untapped. These include: (1) an analysis of differences in factors affecting fertility among those segments of the population within the large scale bureaucratic setting and those outside its boundaries, the purpose being to make use of cross-sectional data in order to reconstruct the effect of organizational changes on work-mobility ideology and family orientations;[13] (2) an analysis of differences in the variables that influence the family size desires of husband and wife.

The Detroit Study

I can elaborate on the factors affecting family size desires of husband and wife by reference to the findings of the Detroit Study. In contrast to the Princeton Study this one included young married women (17–32) of *all* parities. The dependent variable was expected number of children. The similarity of the Detroit Study to some of the working papers was not coincidental.[14] Emphasis was placed on the underlying differences in family activities which may have provided the basis for the differences in fertility associated with economic differences in the past.

Probably the most striking feature of the Detroit data is the demonstration that there are two distinctly different sets of conditions which influence men and women in their family size decisions.[15] Among wife-dominant couples, fertility norms and behavior are conditioned by the extent of the wife's participation in the kinship network and home-centered roles. Kin contact ($+ 0.165$), organizational participation of the wife ($- 0.183$), the production of goods and services in the home ($+ 0.136$), and a home-centered leisure pattern ($+ 0.318$) are all related in the expected direction to the decision to have additional children. Partialing out the influence of number of children already born and age of the wife, the combined influence of the above variables as measured by the multiple partial is 0.375.

In the husband-dominant families, the activity variables have no impact on expected family size. Instead, status considerations seem to play the most prominent part in the decision to add children to the family, high status being associated with relatively high fertility. A

---

[13] This theme is elaborated in the Westoff and Bensman proposal, *op. cit.*

[14] Ronald Freedman, author of one of the original working papers, was an active participant in the study.

[15] David Goldberg, "Family Role Structure and Fertility." Paper presented at the meetings of the Population Association of America, 1957.

combination of four socio-economic indicators yields a multiple correlation of 0.384 with expected number of children. Thus the number of children born to a family may represent a compromise between the desires of husband and wife since the pressures exerted by each have a tendency to cancel one another. As the socio-economic status of the family becomes higher, the wife is likely to be exposed to areas of consumption which shift the balance of roles away from home and family. Under these conditions the husband may want a relatively large family, as his status position will accommodate, while the wife may exert pressures in the opposite direction because a large family would put considerable strain on her role pattern. These divergent influence patterns help us to account for the relatively small social class differences in fertility found in the youngest cohorts.

Another set of data from the Detroit Study amplifies our understanding of the process of family building. In the Princeton Study, the decision to concentrate on the family size desires of a group of women all of the same parity was guided by the assumption that the reasons for adding children to the family vary with the number that are already in the family. Factors influencing the family size decisions of newly married couples are different from those involved in the decision to add a third child in a two child family. Since the Detroit sample includes couples at various stages in the family building process, we can explore the merits of the assumption.

For couples that have no children or one child, the variable that seems to have the most influence on number of children wanted or expected is the proportion of leisure activities of the wife that are home-centered. Also related to large family size desires or expectations are the variables that measure the amount of contact with the kin group. In general, the socio-economic standing of the family is inversely related to the dependent variable.

Among couples that already have three or more children, the decision to have additional children is influenced in a completely different manner. The syndrome of status characteristics is directly related to expectations, whereas home-centered leisure and kin contact either lose their importance or are negatively associated with expectations. Factors influencing families which now have two children lie somewhere between these polar types.

Although the correlation coefficients are rather small, the findings are fairly consistent. The data show an apparent shift in the kinds of variables that influence family size decisions during the process of family growth.

The partial correlations between the independent variables and expected number of children, holding constant age and number of children already born, for the 0–1 parity and 3+ parity couples are summarized below:

home centered leisure of wife . . .	from +0.351 to +0.036
frequency of family gatherings . . .	from +0.144 to −0.123
per cent of all visits with relatives . .	from +0.130 to −0.048
participation in formal organizations .	from −0.139 to +0.156
income	from −0.151 to +0.105
education	from +0.046 to +0.194

The multiple using leisure and kin contact to predict expected number of children for the zero and one parity couples is 0.382. The combination of income, education, and organizational participation on the expectations of the three-plus parity couples yields a multiple of 0.285. An overwhelming part of the variance remains unexplained. But I think we have enough information to tell us that a zero parity or n parity study will unfold only part of the story.

Why are young couples influenced by the leisure pursuits of the wife or kinship contact, whereas couples having two or three children add to the family on the basis of their socio-economic position? Or to put it another way, why are the female variables important early in marriage, while the male variables are important later in marriage? Much as I would like to believe that the balance of power shifts from wife to husband as the marriage matures, our data do not support the hypothesis. The change in the variables may result from the fact that a first child will grossly alter the activity pattern of a couple but that additional children necessitate only minor shifts in the already existing parental roles. Once the parent is committed to a home-centered role structure in order to provide the services for child care, adding children to the family becomes a type of luxury item rather than a revolution in daily activities.

The Detroit Study data fill some of the gaps in the more comprehensive Princeton Study. It raises some questions regarding types of variables affecting husbands' and wives' decisions about family size which may be examined more intensively in the larger sample of the Princeton Study. And it provides an all-parity sample base which may be used to evaluate some of the two parity findings. But like the Princeton Study, it fails to account for a large part of the variation in fertility.

Growth of American Families Study

In the same sense that the Princeton and Detroit Studies complement one another by their division of labor in the choice of independent variables, the Freedman–Whelpton–Campbell Growth of American Families Study complements the research efforts of the other two studies.[16]

One purpose of the GAF Study is to map the relationship between socio-economic or cultural variables and an extensive set of fertility data. The achievement of this objective provides us with national data which were previously available only from the Indianapolis sample. On a national basis our knowledge of differential fertility is extended both on the independent and dependent variable sides. In addition to the types of data available in census publications, GAF provides information about religion, occupational mobility, personal economic perspectives, rural-urban origin, and work history of the wife, and social class identification. The fertility data include the use, attitudes, and expectations about family limitation practices, actual, expected, and ideal family size, and fecundity information. A large part of these data are then used for a projection of births in the coming five-year periods.

The results of the investigation show that while fecundity impairments are widespread, their complete elimination would only lead to an increase in births by about 10 or 15 per cent. Most cases of subfecundity develop after the birth of children. Complete sterility exists in less than four per cent of the sample. A cross-section of married women under 40 indicates that 10 per cent are definitely sterile, most of them having had operations making additional live births impossible, and an additional 24 per cent have some type of fecundity impairment, ranging from cases in which conception may be possible but dangerous to the mother's health, to cases in which the only difficulty encountered was having children at a relatively slow rate when contraception was not used. Among the two out of three women for whom there is no evidence of fecundity impairment it seems likely that there is some hidden subfecundity which could not be tested because of the continual use of contraceptives. About half of the women aged 35–39 or married at least 15 years are subfecund.

The GAF data clearly demonstrate that the overwhelming majority of couples in all major socio-economic strata use family limitation practices. Differences in the proportion of users among the strata are fairly small. Nearly 95 per cent of the fecund couples are past or future users (including rhythm and douche "for cleanliness only" users). Alternative practices and effectiveness of use vary to a greater extent among the major strata than differences in the proportion of users.

Although nearly all couples in the sample use some form of contraception,

[16] All data in this section of the paper are taken from the forthcoming Freedman, Whelpton, and Campbell monograph, *Family Planning, Sterility, and Population Growth*, McGraw-Hill, 1959.

only a small proportion of couples have completely planned families. Nineteen per cent of the women conceived only at times when contraception was interrupted in order to have a child. Only one family in ten is completely planned after 15 years of marriage. The most common pattern is the partially planned family. Two-thirds of the couples fall into this heterogeneous category including some non-users who desired all their pregnancies. Excess fertility (most recent pregnancy was unwanted at that time or later by either marriage partner) was reported by 13 per cent of the women.

These data raise some questions about the meaning of the Indianapolis analysis of factors affecting fertility in the "number and spacing planned" group. An emphasis on size of planned family was important as a means of looking into future fertility patterns, but restriction of the analysis to number and spacing planned may have been drawing the line at the wrong point. Most American couples are able to plan their families in the sense of having the number of children they desire. The planned family, however, is not usually achieved by stopping the use of contraception for each pregnancy. The completed planned family is likely to be a minority pattern in American society for many years to come, particularly in an abundant economy.

Religion and education seem to be the most important variables in differentiating family limitation patterns. About 93 per cent of the fecund Protestant couples and 79 per cent of the fecund Catholic couples have used contraception. These differences become smaller with increasing age or duration of marriage. Many Catholic couples start late, not beginning the use of contraception until they have had at least one child. More than half of the Protestant users but less than one-third of the Catholic users began using contraception before the first pregnancy. Even Catholics who do not attend church are less likely to be users than Protestants, regardless of church attendance.

Among the socio-economic variables, education is the only one that consistently produces differences in planning practices. More than a third of the college women who are fecund and use contraception have completely planned families. The comparable proportion for grade school women is less than one in ten.

The authors assert that the widespread use of some form of family limitation could result in great variability in the birth rate for the coming years. If new members of the population are added in waves rather than in a continuous flow, the consequences for institutional growth and decline are considerable.

The American public has apparently reached consensus on families including two to four children. Three-fourths of the women interviewed expect to have two to four children, 85 per cent said they would have two to four if they could live their lives over again, and 94 per cent consider two to four children ideal for the average American family. Most of the women expecting less than two children are subfecund while a substantial number of those expecting five or more children don't want them.

The 1871–1875 cohort of native-white married women had an average of four children. Smallest family size was attained in the 1906–1915 cohorts, an average of 2.4 children. GAF data cover the cohorts of 1916–1937. The women report an average expected number of children of 3.0, having already produced about two children.

The study data are suggestive of a continuation of the narrowing socio-economic differences in fertility. Differences in expected family size by income and occupation are very small. Once more, education produces the largest differences in fertility behavior. Grade school women expect an average of 3.6 children, while all others expect an average of just less than three.

What does the likely increase in family size mean in terms of the future growth of the American population? The authors answer this question by a method that is unique in population projections. Forecasts of fertility rates are made by combining past rates with the future rates implied by the expectation data. In addition, adjustments are made to include the women who were not interviewed, the divorced, widowed, separated, and single women who will marry.

Expectations of future births are checked against the record of cohorts of women who have already completed their families. For example, women 30–34 expect an additional 578 children per 1,000 women. The minimum and maximum number of births from age 30–34 to the end of the child-bearing period as recorded in the actual cohorts tables, is 362 and 673. Additional expectations of women aged 20–24 and 25–29 are also in line with the experience of previous cohorts.

It is the anticipated timing of births which the authors doubt. They feel that the women who were interviewed overstated the number of children they would have in the five years after the interview. Using the example of the women aged 30–34 again, the 578 additional children per thousand were distributed as follows by the women themselves: 530 children per 1,000 in the next five years, which would be a record high in the cohort tables, and 48 per 1,000 from ages 35–39 to the end of the childbearing period, a record low. Because the stated patterns seem unlikely, the timing of future births has been adjusted to a distribution that takes into account the experience of previous cohorts. In addition to the "adjusted" projections that were made, I would like to have seen the women's expectations projected without adjustment for "reasonable" timing patterns. Since the projections are age-based rather than duration-based, a shift to younger marriage age (as has occurred) *can* result in record highs and lows for given age intervals even if the timing pattern of births by duration of marriage remains unchanged.

The survival rates used in the projections are those prepared by Greville and the migration rates are the ones developed by the Census Bureau. Neither mortality nor immigration will have much influence on the future growth of American population. Greater changes can result from small changes in family size, length of generation, and proportion marrying. A 10 per cent deviation in completed family size together with comparable changes in proportion marrying and median age at childbirth would produce about a 20 per cent difference in the medium projections by the latter part of the twentieth century.

The medium projections imply an average crude birth rate of about 21–22 and a crude death rate of 8 or 9. Results of the cohort projections are similar to the component projections of the Census Bureau. The cohort projections do, however, give us a much broader base for evaluating the results by spelling out in detail a larger number of assumptions, such as how many women marry, when they marry, how the children are distributed over time, and the resultant family size.

I have not been able to do justice to the research efforts involved in the three fertility studies. Clearly, they emphasize the need for research which will pinpoint the accuracy of expected family size data both on an individual and group basis and call for additional research into the family building process, perhaps with a zero parity study.

COMMENT

CHARLES F. WESTOFF, Department of Sociology, New York University, and Office of Population Research, Princeton University

Since much of this paper concentrates on the "Princeton Study," with which I have been connected for four years, I would like to reply to a number of specific criticisms.

Goldberg finds it strange, considering the lack of encouraging results in the Indianapolis Study, that personal motivations are stressed so in the follow-up Princeton Study. If his generalization is true that the three different proposals preceding the final formulation of this study are in fact saying the same thing, then the emphasis on "personal motivations" is simply the level at which a number of "family structure" variables are being measured. Thus, "psychological commitment to work" can be regarded either as measuring an individual interest in work or as an index of an extra-familial orientation.

Although I think there is some confusion here between theory and measurement, the basic criticism that the interview schedule is "barren with respect to other materials which could illuminate the division of labor between the family and other social institutions" is essentially accurate. Particularly is there a lack of attention paid to the locus of leisure activities or participation in the kinship network. The version of the schedule pretested on a probability sample of 100 couples focused much more than did the final version on the internal social structure of the family. However, the underlying theme stresses the capacity of the internal distribution of role responsibilities to absorb the strains resulting from the addition of another child rather than the "division of labor between the family and other social institutions." The former type of variable was minimized simply because there was little pay-off in the pretest; as conceptualized and measured the variable simply did not relate to the various fertility indicators. In view of Goldberg's reported success in the Detroit Study with such factors as extent of home-centered leisure of the wife, frequency of family gatherings, visits with relatives, and participation in extra-familial organizations, it is tempting to consider including at least some of these measures in the second interview with the same couples. However, his own results indicate their decreasing importance with increasing parity. If this is a reliable generalization, such factors would be of little value in our sample. Nor would they have paid off particularly in our original sample of two parity women if I may "interpolate" a little in the correlational values for the 0–1 and 3 + parities.

Goldberg concludes that the exploration of the social mobility hypothesis has produced correlations of only negligible value. This is basically correct but, as his own data on different variables indicate, correlations with family size desires seem to depend upon what stage in the family-building process is considered. It may very well be that mobility is irrelevant at this stage but that it was quite relevant in deterring some couples from ever having two children, or that it might affect future fertility. I think it would be fairer to conclude that mobility considerations seem unimportant at this stage of the process rather than that "many of our hunches concerning the impact of mobility on familism were grossly inaccurate." Although difficult problems of conceptualization and measurement remain, I would agree with Goldberg's alternative explanation that our hunches may have been outdated. The whole ideology of "getting ahead" has changed in the postwar period from one reflecting the competitive individualism of the small entrepreneur period of American history to one of association with the large organization's visible channels of mobility. And with the increased economic security and credit psychology of the postwar period, there seems to be little economic or career need for postponing a family. The fertility rates of graduate students at many university housing developments bear eloquent testimony to this new climate.

One of the most interesting but also perplexing sections of Goldberg's paper is introduced by the statement: "Probably the most striking feature of the Detroit data is the demonstration that there are two distinctly different sets of conditions which influence men and women in their family size decisions." In the Princeton Study, wives and husbands were asked independently for the total number of children they desired.[1] Each is treated as a dependent variable in the analysis so that each was correlated separately with 79 other variables on the total sample as well as within the religious and class subdivisions of the sample. A graphing of correlational values for these 79 "observations" reveals a very close correspondence; in fact, this correlation of correlations reaches 0.96. Even considering the questionable properties of such a statistic as, for example, the influence of low reliabilities, it seems safe to conclude, for this sample at least, that no new information is to be gained by utilizing both variables in the general correlational analysis.[2]

The confusing aspect of Goldberg's description lies in the implication that he is referring to analyses within two control groups of (1) wife-dominant families for whom familial interests correlate with the decision to have additional children, and (2) husband-dominant families among whom socio-economic considerations best predict expected fertility.

A little further elaboration by the author would clarify such questions as (a) does this dichotomy exhaust the sample? (b) if these are different couples, I do not understand how "the number of children born to a family may represent a compromise between the desires of husband and wife since the pressures exerted by each have a tendency to cancel one another." It would seem more likely that the fertility of different segments of the population is predictable from different variables much in the same

---

[1] The correlation between the two is 0.65 on a sample of 1,165 couples.
[2] The same high correspondence prevails in the subsamples.

way that we in the Princeton Study seem to be finding different factors operating for Protestants, Catholics, and Jews.

Perhaps the most fascinating analysis reported by Goldberg is that different factors seem to affect fertility decisions at different stages in the family building process. Thus, he reports that home-centered leisure and kinship contact of the wife with no children, or only one child, correlates positively with decisions to add another child, whereas income correlates negatively, and education not at all. However, among couples with three or more children, attitudes toward further enlarging the family relate positively both to income and education while the "female" variables diminish in importance or become negatively associated. Although further elaboration, if not analysis, is necessary to relate this to the earlier generalizations about factors affecting the fertility decisions of males and females, this finding is very exciting in theory and tends to confirm the strategy of the Princeton Study which controlled parity by design. I would prefer Goldberg's conclusion that "we have enough information to tell us that a zero parity or *n* parity will unfold only part of the story," if the word "only" were left out.

One of the chronic complaints about research in this area generally is that the correlations tend to be quite low. In fact, if the value of a zero-order correlation reaches 0.20, we tend to be pleased; if it reaches 0.30 or 0.40 there is jubilation; on the rare occasions when it exceeds this, the usual reaction is distrust. Either there has been a clerical error or the variables are in fact the same phenomenon. I have heard it only half-jokingly proposed that all correlations over 0.30 should be checked again on the assumption that they must be in error.

It is clearly possible that our theories may be simply invalid or that our measures contain too much unreliability, but I am inclined to believe rather that our expectations are simply naive. Why should a variable so complex even as number of children *desired* yield to single unidimensional predictors? Fertility is a complex variable, a fact that researchers dealing with individuals rather than aggregates must take into account in their expectations. I believe that we will be doing very well to achieve a 50 per cent control of the variance with a battery composed of perhaps 20 sociological and psychological predictors.

In conclusion, I would like to applaud the over-all objective of Goldberg's paper, which is to evaluate the theoretical implications of a few of the chief findings of the major fertility studies currently in process. He has made it dramatically clear that more integration of research efforts is desirable.

Differential Fertility in United States Census Data

RICHARD AND NANCY RUGGLES

YALE UNIVERSITY

Summary

THE rate of population growth in the United States has in the past been strongly influenced by three high fertility groups. These groups are farmers, the foreign born, and the urban native born of lower education. The rapidly falling birth rate since 1900 has been due in large part to the gradual attrition of these groups, and to a lesser extent to falling fertility within the groups themselves. Farmers and foreign born are now a much smaller proportion of the total population, and cannot be expected to have as much influence on the growth of the population in the future as they have had in the past. It is the fertility of the urban native born group which holds the key to future population growth.

This study, made possible by a grant of the Milbank Memorial Fund, analyzes a differential fertility sample of North Central United States obtained in conjunction with the 1940 population census. The study is restricted to urban native women of native parentage, married once to native men of native parentage, aged 40–70. For this group, the number of children ever born was examined in relation to (1) woman's education, (2) husband's education, (3) husband's wages, (4) husband's occupation, (5) size of city, (6) woman's marriage age, and (7) woman's age. The analytic procedure adopted involved the examination of differences between the average family size of different classifications of women, testing the statistical significance of this difference both for individual comparisons of cells and for groups of such comparisons.

It must be noted at the outset that this study is purely descriptive. It does not test any hypotheses; it merely describes the differences in family size observed in the data. Descriptive studies such as this, however, may be useful to investigators who are attempting to formulate hypotheses which they in turn will test against other bodies of data. Also, the data examined were obtained almost twenty years ago. This fact does not, of course, invalidate the observations, but it does mean that they may not be pertinent to women who are now of childbearing ages. On the other hand, it is entirely too cavalier to disregard the evidence of these data on this ground. The fact that the data were collected in 1940 is in itself of no particular significance; the childbearing years of the women covered extend from 1890 to 1940, and, by examining women of different ages, time trends in family size for different groups can be analyzed.

Examining the relation of family size to woman's education, the familiar inverse relationship was observed up to the four year high school level. In comparing women of four year high school education with women of one year college or more, however, the situation differed. The families of the high school women were larger in circumstances where the husband either had less education or was in a low wage or occupation group. Where the husbands had more education, or were in a high wage or occupation group, however, the college women had larger families.

Husband's education, like woman's education, was also inversely related to family size up to the four year high school level. When examined within woman's education or husband's occupation classes beyond this point, a positive relationship emerges. When examined within husband's wage classes, however, this positive relationship does not appear, strongly suggesting that income is the factor which produces it.

The strong inverse relationship also appears for the lower occupation classifications. When examined within some variables (such as woman's education and husband's education), a positive relationship again appears between the top two occupational groups. This positive relationship does not appear when the relation with occupation is examined within husband's wage groups, again strongly suggesting that the positive relationship is due to income.

In view of the manner in which these positive relationships of family size with the other variables at the higher socio-economic levels tend to disappear when examined within husband's wage groups, special attention was given to the analysis of husband's wages. There are some indications in the general tabulations of a positive relationship between family size and husband's wages at the higher wage levels when the examination is made within woman's education or husband's education, but the relationship is weak, and does not appear when wages are examined within occupational groups. To examine the question in greater detail, a special tabulation was made of the relation of family size to wages for women with four year high school education or more married to husbands of four year high school education or more, subdivided into three occupational groups. A separate special tabulation was also available for a sample of college graduates collected by Time Inc. These special tabulations did not bear out the contention that family size is positively related to income at higher socio-economic levels. However, the inverse relationship between husband's wages and family size characteristic of the lower groups also disappeared.

Thus, this examination seems to indicate that for lower socio-economic levels there is in fact a highly inverse relationship between family size and socio-economic status, no matter how this status is measured. However, for higher socio-economic levels this inverse relationship disappears, and seems to be replaced by a fairly weak positive relationship, which cannot be attributed specifically to any single factor. Woman's education, husband's education, income, and occupation all make some slight contribution, but the relationship for any one of them alone is so weak that it does not rise above the noise of the random disturbing factors.

In conclusion, therefore, it would seem that as the income and education of the general population increase, the differences in family size of different groups will become smaller and the population will become very much more homogeneous with respect to family size. It may then be that changes in the composition of the society will become less important in determining population change than changes in desired sizes of families. While it is still true that wars, depressions, and other unusual circumstances will affect the timing of births, and therefore family size for specific cohorts, there will nevertheless be greater stability in average family size in future years than there has been in the past.

The basic reason for studying population growth is of course in order to be able to throw some light upon the future development of our society. As far back as Malthus, fairly elaborate theories were formulated regarding the path which population growth might be expected to follow. At the present time interest in the subject of population growth is sufficient so that estimates of future developments are continually being made, by a number of different methods. Some of these estimates are direct extrapolations of general population growth trends, but others do try to take into account the interactions between population growth and various other facets of our society. Before any accurate—or any useful—extrapolations can be made, a clear understanding of these interactions is essential.

THE EFFECT OF POPULATION GROWTH UPON THE ECONOMY

To consider first the effect of population growth upon the economic development of the society, it is obvious that the pattern of population growth is a prime determinant of the pattern of both economic needs and economic resources. For example, a rapidly growing population will have a larger proportion of people in the younger age groups, and a declining population a larger proportion in the older age groups. This will affect not only the demand for housing and other consumer goods, but also the need for such things as education and old age assistance, and the nature of full employment policy. One of the prime requisites of city planning is to foresee what the future population will be, so that the present development of cities will meet future needs. An accurate estimate of future population size and composition is therefore basic to planning the type and magnitude of investment both by private enterprise and by government. It is important to know how many people will share the natural resources of the country, become consumers, and enter the labor market.

THE EFFECT OF SOCIAL CHANGE UPON POPULATION GROWTH

The relationship between population growth and other factors in the society is of course not one-sided. Population growth is in turn strongly influenced by social change. For instance, the influence of increasing industrialization is well recognized. When the majority of the population lived on farms the advantages of large families in farming strongly influenced family size. As urbanization progressed, the declining advantages of large families were reflected in a declining rate of population growth. Similarly, there are other social changes which it is possible to foresee. The standard of living will probably continue to increase, and there will be foreseeable changes in the distribution of income, of occupations, and of the level of education. Any realistic population projection must take such factors as these into account. In order to do so, it is necessary to make an evaluation of what their impact is likely to be.

In evaluating this impact, it is useful to consider two types of effect. First, the birth rate within relatively homogeneous groups may change. The term "homogeneous" as used here means people with similar social and economic characteristics. Second, the relative size of different groups may change, and therefore the weights to be attached to their birth rates may also change.

With respect to the first of these effects, it is of course reasonable to expect that groups of families with similar socio-economic status will have a similar distribution of numbers of children—or else there is no point to the analysis. At the same time, however, it is impossible as a practical matter so to specify the characteristics of the individual groups that their birth rates will not change over time. A great many factors which do influence the birth rate cannot be taken into account. A farmer, for instance, is not the same today as he was in 1900—among other reasons, because of the introduction of mechanization, which reduces the necessary labor supply and thereby changes the large family from an earning asset to an expense. It is therefore bound to reduce the pressure for large families in this group. If increasing farm mechanization is expected to reduce the need for labor still more in the future, the birth rate of farm families may be expected to fall further, but if mechanization is not expected to have much more effect, there should be no further influence upon the birth rate from this source. In this way, making allowance where possible for factors that are likely to have an influence but cannot be separated out, an estimate of the expected development of the birth rate for each group can be derived.

The second effect derives from factors which change the relative importance of the various groups in the population by some means other than changes in their birth rates. Such factors include industrialization, with its accompanying migration from the farms to the cities; the cessation of immigration, with the resulting smaller number of foreign born; and rising standards of education. The influence of each of these factors must be appraised, so that the composition of the population at some future date can be estimated. Combining these two elements, an estimate of aggregate population growth can be derived by applying the birth rates expected for each sector to the expected future composition of the population, and the total growth of the whole population estimated by adding together the growth in each sector.

Population estimates made by this method may differ markedly from estimates derived from a simple extrapolation of the general rate of population growth. Different groups in the population have widely different birth rates, and as the relative importance of these groups changes, so also will the average birth rate. The fact that the birth rate of a society has steadily decreased does not mean that it will continue to decrease even though the same general trends for individual groups continue. Suppose, for example, that the importance of certain high fertility groups, such as the foreign born or farmers, declines. The over-all rate of growth will decline even if birth rates within each sector of the economy do not change. As the trend continues, however, the decline in the average birth rate due to this cause will fade into insignificance as these groups become a smaller and smaller proportion of the total population.

This study is not intended to lead to any general population theory or to provide the tools necessary for forecasting population growth. Nevertheless, it is conceived within the framework discussed above. Its attention is focused on one aspect of the problem, specifically, the analysis of differential fertility in terms of education, income, and occupation, for a particular population group.

The origin of the present investigation goes back to work originally started just prior to World War II, and summarized in an unpublished report in 1947. This earlier study used as basic data a sample of 50,000 cases collected from maternity hospitals in Boston and New York, and a sample of 8,000 college graduates collected by Time Inc., in 1940. It focused on the relationship between income and family size.

In examining the samples obtained from the various hospitals, it was found that groups similarly defined derived from different hospitals had significantly different numbers of previous children per thousand women. This suggested that there were probably differences in the type of patient to whom the various hospitals catered. Although the study was confined to native born women, it is probable that some hospitals had a larger proportion of women whose parents were not native born than other hospitals. Furthermore, there were known to be religious differences among the hospitals. In any event, whatever the cause for the differences between hospitals, it was evident that adding all the cases together would yield conclusions dependent mainly on the size of the samples from the various hospitals, rather than on any true relations existing in the population as a whole. For this reason, the data for each hospital were examined separately.

Because the data were lacking in reliability and validity, they did not support any definitive answer with respect to the relationship between income and family size. There was no instance in which a reliable negative relationship between income and family size was found for groups homogeneous in other respects, and the few groups for which the data were most reliable and valid generally yielded positive relationships. On the other hand, a negative relationship may well have existed for the groups in which the reliability of the sample was too low to permit analysis. The best evidence, however, was in conflict with the traditional view of the relation between income and family size. The evidence in itself was far from conclusive, but it pointed to the desirability of further study of this question.

The differential fertility sample obtained by the Census Bureau as a part of the Census of 1940 offered a possible source of additional data. The experience with the hospital data pointed to the desirability of obtaining as much homogeneity in the groups analyzed as possible. One way to accomplish this was to omit from the analysis groups which in themselves were of marginal interest or which were too complex or of insufficient size to yield valid conclusions. In the context of the Census data, the foreign born constituted such a group, which seemed better eliminated. On the one hand, the variance among the foreign born themselves, in terms of family size, was very considerable. Previous studies had shown that immigrants born in northern Europe tended to behave quite differently from those born in southern Europe. By 1940, furthermore, the number of foreign born of childbearing ages was rapidly decreasing, and given the existing immigration restrictions it promised to be a factor of minor importance in the future. The farm population, similarly, has been a declining element in the picture, and the analysis could be considerably simplified by restricting it to urban families. Also, in order to reduce the complexity of the study, the analysis was restricted to one region of the country, since different regions might well differ in fertility patterns. Finally, in order to be able to deal with number of children ever born rather than with birth rates, the study was restricted to completed families. In this way, problems relating to differences among groups in such factors as marriage age and spacing of children could be avoided, and final family size used as an indicator of fertility over the childbearing age.

On this basis, an intensive analysis was undertaken, with the generous support of the Milbank Memorial Fund, of differential fertility of native-white women of native-white parents married to native-white men of native-white parents, urban, aged 40–70, married once and husband present, living in North Central United States. When these criteria were applied to the Census sample, the available number of cases came to 40,000. A breakdown of the total population in North Central United States and the sample is shown on p. 162.

The punchcards are for a 5 per cent sample in some areas and a $2\frac{1}{2}$ per cent sample in other areas; the punchcards for the $2\frac{1}{2}$ per cent sample were duplicated by Census to bring them to a level comparable with that for cards from other areas. Hence computed sampling variances will be too small in many cases, depending as they do on some duplicated punchcards.

Another source of bias is the exclusion of women with no report on children ever born. There is evidence that in 1940 a disproportionately

	TOTAL POPULATION (million)	5 PER CENT SAMPLE PUNCHCARDS (thousand)
A. All women aged 15–70	15.0	750
Minus: Single women	−4.3	−215
B. Equals: Women ever married	10.7	535
Minus: Husband not present	−3.2	−160
C. Equals: Women husband present	7.4	375
Minus: Women aged 15–40	−3.3	−165
D. Equals: Women aged 40–70	4.2	210
Minus: Rural women	−2.0	−100
E. Equals: Urban women	2.2	110
Minus: Women having either parent foreign born or husband with either parent foreign born	−1.4	−70
F. Final selection	0.8	40

large number of the women with no report on children ever born were childless. Evidently the enumerators sometimes left the item blank for childless women instead of entering zero. Approximately 11 per cent of the ever-married women sampled were recorded as not reporting on children.

At the time this study was undertaken, the only equipment available was a punchcard sorter and a hand calculator. As a result, the analysis proceeded slowly and painfully over a two-and-a-half-year period. The present paper is a discussion and analysis of the data which emerged.

GENERAL METHODOLOGY

The methodology employed in this study was conditioned both by these technological considerations and by the need to develop statistical procedures which did not entail unduly restrictive assumptions. Regression analysis might have seemed the logical approach. However, both the earlier study of hospital data and other available studies on this topic strongly suggested that the problems of lack of linearity in the regressions and co-variation among the major variables would seriously weaken the suitability of linear regression analysis. More complex forms of multivariate analysis were beyond the computational resources available at that time.

For these reasons, a simple and straightforward procedure was adopted. The sample data were classified into homogeneous groups according to the following characteristics: (1) age of woman, (2) education of woman, (3) education of husband, (4) husband's wages, (5) husband's occupation, (6) size of community, and (7) woman's marriage age. Tabulations of number of women and number of children ever born were then made showing cross-classifications of pairs of these variables and woman's age, such that differences over time in the relationships between these pairs of variables could be examined. Thus the following 15 cross-classifications of number of women and number of children ever born were developed, all of them additionally cross-classified by age.

1. Woman's Education and Husband's Education
2. Woman's Education and Husband's Wages
3. Woman's Education and Husband's Occupation
4. Woman's Education and Size of Community
5. Woman's Education and Woman's Marriage Age
6. Husband's Education and Husband's Wages
7. Husband's Education and Husband's Occupation
8. Husband's Education and Size of Community
9. Husband's Education and Woman's Marriage Age
10. Husband's Wages and Husband's Occupation
11. Husband's Wages and Size of Community
12. Husband's Wages and Woman's Marriage Age
13. Husband's Occupation and Size of Community
14. Husband's Occupation and Woman's Marriage Age
15. Size of Community and Woman's Marriage Age

These tabulations are presented in the Appendix.

The question could now be posed whether, within cross-classifications of this sort, family size differed significantly from group to group. The obvious approach to this question would have been through conventional variance analysis. But here again, the earlier studies suggested that this procedure would have serious limitations for the kinds of questions we were trying to answer. Variance analysis could only show whether a given cell differed significantly from the average of all other cells in a given group. It could not, for instance, adequately handle such questions as whether the relationships between variables were continuously increasing throughout the range of variation. For this reason, a somewhat different technique was resorted to. Differences in family size between *adjacent* cells in the tables shown in the Appendix were examined for significance and direction. Where a series of differences between adjacent

163

cells were significant and of the same sign, it suggested that a significant and consistent relationship existed between changes in the variables being examined and family size.

The number of possible comparisons between adjacent cells in the fifteen tables is very large. Since the tables in the Appendix are three-way cross-classifications, comparisons between adjacent cells can be made in three directions. This is shown in the diagram below; cell A can be compared with cells B, C, or D by altering each of the three variables in turn.

A. Woman aged 40–44;
Education grade 6;
Husband's education
grade 6

B. Woman aged 40–44;
Education grade 7–8;
Husband's education
grade 6

C. Woman *aged 45–49;*
Education grade 6;
Husband's education
grade 6

D. Woman aged 40–44;
Education grade 6;
Husband's education
grade 7–8

In all, about 8,500 comparisons would be possible in the fifteen tables. However, many of the cells are empty, and many others contain only a very small number of cases. In order to economize on computational effort, these cells where the sample was too small to be likely to yield significant results were omitted from the analysis. An arbitrary cut-off point of 100 cases was adopted; no comparisons were made for cells containing a smaller number of cases. In a few instances, comparisons were made between non-adjacent cells where the immediately adjacent cell had less than 100 cases but the next cell was larger. However, these non-adjacent comparisons do not enter into the final analysis. On this basis, about 3,000 comparisons were made.

For each pair of cells that were compared, the significance of the difference between the means of family size was computed. The results of these computations were expressed in standard error units. Hereafter this measure will be referred to as $\tilde{D}$. The size of $\tilde{D}$ is dependent upon three factors: (1) the variance within the cells being compared; (2) the number of cases in each of the cells being compared; and (3) the magnitude of the difference between the means of the cells. Thus a high value for $\tilde{D}$ may come about either through a large difference between means or through a much smaller difference between the means accompanied by smaller variances and larger sample sizes. It should be emphasized that $\tilde{D}$ does not measure the magnitude of the difference between means. What it does measure is the significance of a null hypothesis as the explanation for the observed difference between the means. The table below illustrates the probabilities that can be attached to various magnitudes of $\tilde{D}$, that is, the likelihood of a given $\tilde{D}$ occurring through chance if there is in fact no difference between the true means.[1]

PROBABILITIES ASSOCIATED WITH SPECIFIC MAGNITUDES OF
$\tilde{D}$ OR $\tilde{S}$ FOR DIFFERENCES BETWEEN MEANS OF A GIVEN SIGN

$\tilde{D}$ *or* $\tilde{S}$	*Probability*
0.10	0.4601
0.50	.3085
1.00	.1586
1.50	.0668
2.00	.0228
2.50	.0062
3.00	.0013
3.50	.0002
4.00	.00003

The tables in the Appendix are extremely useful in examining questions at a highly detailed level, but neither they nor the $\tilde{D}$'s directly computed from them readily lend themselves to summarization or generalization. The procedure finally adopted for summarizing the $\tilde{D}$'s is basically a simple one. It is based upon the principle that if for any group of comparisons the null hypothesis is valid, the sample $\tilde{D}$'s with signs attached should be normally distributed about the central value of zero. The means of the $\tilde{D}$'s for groups of comparisons were therefore computed, and the significance of their difference from zero in turn computed. This statistic, equal for any particular group of $\tilde{D}$'s to $\dfrac{\sqrt{N}\Sigma\tilde{D}}{N}$ where N equals the number of comparisons, will be referred to hereafter as $\tilde{S}$. It provides a measure to which the probability table shown above also relates, since it measures differences of the means of $\tilde{D}$ from zero in standard error units. Again it should be emphasized that the magnitude of $\tilde{S}$ is not a measure of the magnitude of the mean of the $\tilde{D}$'s, since consistent and reliable small values of $\tilde{D}$ will yield large $\tilde{S}$'s, just as consistent and reliable small differences between cell means will yield large $\tilde{D}$'s. As the probability table shows, differences in values of $\tilde{D}$ and $\tilde{S}$ above the level of 3 or 4 mean very little in terms of probability.

Table 1 below shows the $\tilde{D}$'s and $\tilde{S}$'s which result from comparing women of different educational levels within specific husband's educational levels. In addition to the $\tilde{D}$'s and $\tilde{S}$'s, the absolute difference in

[1] The biases resulting from (1) duplicated punchcards and (2) the erroneous classification of childless women will of course impair the validity of $\tilde{D}$ as a measure of significance.

TABLE 1

Differences in Woman's Education within Husband's Education

Wife's Education	Husband's Education									
	Grade 6		Grade 7-8		High School 1-3		High School 4		College 1 and more	
	$m_2 - m_1$	$\bar{D}$	$m_2 - m_1$	$\bar{D}$	$m_2 - m_1$	$\bar{D}$	$m_2 - m_1$	$\bar{D}$	$m_2 - m_1$	$\bar{D}$
A. Grade 6 to Grade 7-8										
1 40-44	117	0.66	−309	2.54						
2 45-49	−383	3.31	−525	4.00						
3 50-54	−454	2.86	−244	1.84						
4 55-59	−350	2.05	−272	1.75						
5 60-64	−475	2.28	164	0.86						
6 65-69	−296	1.02	−949	3.63						
7 Total §	−306	4.43	−356	5.27						
B. Grade 7-8 to High School 1-3										
1. 40-44	−217	0.99	−79	1.19	−59	0.55	62	0.49	−460	2.62
2. 45-49	283	2.03	−117	1.37	−349	2.59	318	1.99	−265	1.30
3. 50-54	−24	0.09	−314	3.48	−405	3.10	−26	0.16	−384	1.75
4. 55-59			−453	4.30	−290	1.84	−295	1.79		
5. 60-64			−186	1.10	−143	0.61				
6. 65-69			−283	1.41						
7. Total §	14	0.54	−239	5.24	−249	3.88	15	0.27	−369	3.27

C. High School 1–3 to High School 4

1. 40–44	−251	2.84	−321	2.97	−136	1.30	24	0.20
2. 45–49	−612	5.78	75	0.61	−458	3.22	−105	1.49
3. 50–54	6	0.03	81	0.49	10	0.07	−90	0.48
4. 55–59	333	2.79			−56	0.34		
5. 60–64	−544	3.35						
6. 65–69								
7. Total §	−213	4.08	−55	1.08	−165	2.47	−57	1.02

D. High School 4 to College 1 and more

1. 40–44	−83	0.62	236	1.73	−143	1.39	−79	1.00
2. 45–49	8	0.06	−503	3.33	35	0.28	−34	0.40
3. 50–54	−469	2.19			−204	1.52	−20	0.15
4. 55–59							−53	0.30
5. 60–64							351	1.80
6. 65–69								
7. Total §	−181	1.59	−133	1.13	−104	1.52	73	1.01

family size is also shown in the columns labeled $m_2 - m_1$. In this case m_2 refers to the women with higher education and m_1 refers to the women with lower education. It will be noted that many of the cells in this table are vacant. This results from the fact that there were too few cases of the given characteristics in the sample to yield reliable results. For example, women of sixth grade education married to husbands having more than three years of high school could not be compared with seventh to eighth grade women with similar husbands, because there were not enough cases. This, of course, has significance for the $\tilde{S}$'s. The $\tilde{S}$'s are an aggregation of $\tilde{D}$'s, and will reflect only those $\tilde{D}$'s which are available. In many instances this will mean that the $\tilde{S}$'s for a specific comparison will represent only the younger age groups where the number of women in the sample is larger. The same is also true in aggregating the $\tilde{S}$'s to combined relationships: only those $\tilde{S}$'s which are actually available can be combined. In Table 1, for instance, for the comparison between sixth grade and seventh to eighth grade women, only two $\tilde{S}$'s are available. These refer to women whose husbands have sixth grade education, and to women whose husbands have seventh to eighth grade education.

Tables similar to Table 1 could also be drawn up to show the relationship of family size to woman's education within each of the other variables, viz., husband's wages, husband's occupation, size of community, and woman's marriage age. In all, thus, five tables of the form of Table 1 would be required to describe the relationships found in the Appendix Tables relating to woman's education. Another set of five tables would be required to describe the comparisons of family size for husbands of different education, another set of five for husbands of different wages, and so on. In all, 30 tables of the form of Table 1 would be needed to show all the $\tilde{D}$'s. In order to condense the presentation, the $\tilde{S}$'s have been extracted from these tables and arranged in the set of six tables in the following text. The $\tilde{S}$'s in Table 1, for example, appear in section A of Table 2. Each section of Table 2 summarizes the comparison of family size of women of different education within one of the other variables; thus section A refers to comparisons of family size of women of different education within husband's education; section B, to comparisons of family size of women of different education within husband's wages, and so on. Table 3 summarizes all of the comparisons of family size of husbands of different education; Table 4, comparisons of family size of husbands of different wages, etc.

Although the comparisons in these tables take the age of woman into account insofar as they make comparisons only within one age group, the effect of age itself is not shown. For this purpose it is necessary to compare women of a given age with a specific set of characteristics with women of another age having the same characteristics in other respects. Thus, women of age 40–44 having sixth grade education married to men of sixth grade education can be compared with women of age 45–49 having sixth grade education and married to men of sixth grade education. These comparisons can be made between four adjacent age groups for each of the 15 tables in the Appendix. They can be summarized in much the same way that Table 1 was summarized in Table 2, by computing Š's for the combined relationship. This has been done in Table 8.

WOMAN'S EDUCATION

The familiar generalization that the higher the woman's education the smaller the family size is borne out by Table 2. Here the Š's for the combined relation are generally high, and the direction of the difference is usually negative, indicating an inverse relationship. This inverse relationship between woman's education and size of family is well known, but examination of the specific comparisons as shown in Table 2 provides considerably more information. The magnitude of the Š's and the signs of the differences indicate precisely where the inverse relationship holds.

Up to four years of high school, the inverse relationship between woman's education and family size is valid. However, in the comparison of four year high school women with women with one year or more of college, there are a number of instances where direct positive relationships between family size and education appear. To discuss this situation further, it will be useful to examine the different sections of Table 2 in greater detail.

Husband's education. Within husband's education, the inverse relation between the level of the wife's education and family size holds for all groups except four year high school and college women married to college men. In this instance a positive relation appears, suggesting that the more highly educated women have somewhat larger families. It should be noted, however, that the more highly educated women do not have very much larger families, and the Š is not highly significant.

Husband's wages. Within husband's wages, the inverse relation between the level of the wife's education and family size holds, except for four year high school and college women married to men having wages of $5,000 or more. Here a positive relation between education and family size appears, indicating that at the highest income and education levels the relation between family size and woman's education is direct.

TABLE 2

WOMAN'S EDUCATION

Significance and Direction of Differences in Number of Children Ever Born per 1,000 Women for Grouped Comparisons Expressed in Standard Error Units ($\tilde{S}$)

	Woman's Education							
	Grade 6 to Grade 7–8		Grade 7–8 to High School 1–3		High School 1–3 to High School 4		High School 4 to College 1	
Group	$m_2 - m_1$	$\tilde{S}$	$m_2 - m_1$	$\tilde{S}$	$m_2 - m_1$	$\tilde{S}$	$m_2 - m_1$	$\tilde{S}$
	(1)	(2)	(3)	(4)	(5)	(6)	(7)	(8)
A. *Husband's Education*								
1. Grade 6 and under	−306	4.43	14	0.54	−213	4.08	−181	1.59
2. Grades 7–8	−356	5.27	−239	5.24	−55	1.08	−133	1.13
3. High School 1–3			−249	3.88	−165	2.47	−104	1.52
4. High School 4			15	0.27	−57	1.02	73	1.01
5. College 1 and more			−369	3.27			−86	1.62
6. Combined relation	−331	6.88	−165	5.17	−122	4.33		
B. *Husband's Wages*								
1. $0–$999	−215	3.27	−93	1.45	−573	5.76	72	0.34
2. $1,000–$1,499	−635	6.52	−270	4.89	−143	1.54	−697	4.75
3. $1,500–$1,999	−744	4.31	−70	0.36	−209	2.77	−419	2.01
4. $2,000–$2,999			47	0.00	−232	3.42		
5. $3,000–$3,999			−53	0.24	−419	2.01		
6. $4,000–$4,999								
7. $5,000 and over							123	1.14
8. Combined relation	−531	8.15	−87	3.10	−315	6.91	−230	2.98

170

C. Husband's Occupation

	(1)	(2)	(3)	(4)	(5)	(6)	(7)	(8)
1. Laborers	-483	7.44	-266	5.26	-283	2.54	70	0.74
2. Service Workers	-444	5.91	-61	0.58	-305	4.26	194	2.12
3. Operatives	-177	1.89	-321	5.33	-270	4.02	98	1.74
4. Craftsmen			-55	0.62	-90	1.91	-107	1.57
5. Clerical Workers			-353	5.51	-265	1.51		
6. Proprietors			58	0.27				
7. Professional								
8. Combined relation	-368	8.81	-185	7.17	-252	6.35	64	1.52

D. Size of Community

	(1)	(2)	(3)	(4)	(5)	(6)	(7)	(8)
1. 2,500–5,000	-749	3.86	-483	3.82	-796	5.09	224	1.80
2. 5,000–10,000	-860	8.95	-368	3.93	-646	6.59	37	0.33
3. 10,000–25,000	-443	5.62	-407	5.57	-208	2.90	-142	1.42
4. 25,000–100,000	-822	3.20	-294	4.73	-337	5.51	-165	2.26
5. 100,000–250,000	-616	4.05	-100	1.23	-283	2.51	123	0.01
6. 250,000–500,000	-691	7.85	-345	4.42	-113	1.41	-40	0.09
7. 500,000 and over			-235	3.33	-141	2.20	-162	1.65
8. Combined relation	-597	12.65	-319	10.20	-360	9.89	-53	1.25

E. Woman's Marriage Age

	(1)	(2)	(3)	(4)	(5)	(6)	(7)	(8)
1. Under 18	-846	4.10	-175	0.75	-312	5.60	67	0.58
2. 18–20	-638	8.27	-506	7.82	-132	2.92	123	1.50
3. 21–23	-392	4.89	-124	1.27	-87	1.13	-54	1.02
4. 24–26	-249	1.63	-59	4.31	82	0.82	-119	1.18
5. 27–29			-493	4.65	-371	2.61	-205	2.24
6. 30–35			-141	0.28				
7. Combined relation	-531	9.45	-249	7.79	-164	5.10	-37	1.05

TABLE 3

HUSBAND'S EDUCATION

Significance and Direction of Differences in Number of Children Ever Born per 1,000 Women for Grouped Comparisons Expressed in Standard Error Units ($\tilde{S}$)

Group	Husband's Education							
	Grade 6 to Grade 7–8		Grade 7–8 to High School 1–3		High School 1–3 High School 4		High School 4 to College 1	
	$m_2 - m_1$	$\tilde{S}$	$m_2 - m_1$	$\tilde{S}$	$m_2 - m_1$	$\tilde{S}$	$m_2 - m_1$	$\tilde{S}$
	(1)	(2)	(3)	(4)	(5)	(6)	(7)	(8)
A. Wife's Education								
1. Grade 6 and under	−491	6.24	−274	4.59	−405	5.51	256	2.89
2. Grades 7–8	−553	9.50	−293	4.87	−113	2.20	−147	1.32
3. High School 1–3	−767	7.79	−150	1.23	−269	3.55	24	1.45
4. High School 4	−422	2.26	−48	0.38	−115	1.16	209	2.98
5. College 1 and more								
6. Combined relation	−558	12.89	−191	5.56	−278	4.51	85	3.00
B. Husband's Wages								
1. $0–$999	−651	9.08	−707	4.68	−475	4.12	−301	1.45
2. $1,000–$1,499	−343	4.32	−292	4.03	−312	3.05	161	1.24
3. $1,500–$1,999	−464	4.72	−343	5.13	−102	0.25	−134	1.44
4. $2,000–$2,999	−951	4.42	94	1.35	−229	2.00	−45	0.05
5. $3,000–$3,999			6	0.27	−376	2.64	233	1.89
6. $4,000–$4,999								
7. $5,000 and over								
8. Combined relation	−602	11.27	−286	6.66	−299	5.38	−81	1.03

C. Husband's Occupation

1. Laborers	—727	6.99	—154	0.65	—72	0.35	242	1.20
2. Service Workers	—550	5.99	123	0.60	—621	4.03	135	1.57
3. Operatives	—543	7.18	—157	2.44	—291	3.69	40	0.41
4. Craftsmen			—64	1.21	—253	3.97	—96	0.64
5. Clerical Workers			7	0.03	—292	4.17		
6. Proprietors							80	1.27
7. Professional								
8. Combined relation	—606	11.65	—49	1.64	—305	7.23		

D. Size of Community

1. 1,500–5,000	—1,050	5.68	—401	2.94	—433	2.74	158	1.12
2. 5,000–10,000	—713	4.87	—625	6.79	—148	1.36	31	0.46
3. 10,000–25,000	—854	8.78	—189	2.53	—426	5.30	126	1.59
4. 25,000–100,000	—668	8.63	—58	2.41	—364	4.95	—134	1.80
5. 100,000–250,000	—706	4.25	—92	1.29	—127	1.50	51	0.21
6. 250,000–500,000	—602	5.76	—228	2.95	—71	1.06	44	0.44
7. 500,000 and over	—669	8.37	—121	1.78	—215	2.80	52	0.65
8. Combined relation	—751	17.48	—245	7.81	—255	7.44	21	0.68

E. Woman's Marriage Age

1. Under 18	—803	4.65	—320	3.63	—513	6.47	130	1.42
2. 18–20	—763	9.72	—226	4.15	—254	4.27	129	2.22
3. 21–23	—408	5.81	—255	4.02	—24	0.10	132	2.45
4. 24–26	—432	5.39	—155	1.97	—20	0.60	214	2.04
5. 27–29							183	1.71
6. 30–35								
7. Combined relation	—601	12.79	—239	6.89	—190	5.02	157	4.34

TABLE 4
HUSBAND'S WAGES

Significance and Direction of Differences in Number of Children Ever Born per 1,000 Women for Grouped Comparisons Expressed in Standard Error Units (S̃)

Husband's Wages

Group	$0–999 to $1,000–1,499		$1,000–1,499 to $1,500–1,999		$1,500–1,999 to $2,000–2,999		$2,000–2,999 to $3,000–3,999		$3,000–3,999 to $4,000–4,999		$4,000–4,999 to $5,000 and over	
	$m_2 - m_1$	S̃	$m_2 - m_1$	S̃	$m_2 - m_1$	S̃	$m_2 - m_1$	S̃	$m_2 - m_1$	S̃	$m_2 - m_1$	S̃
	(1)	(2)	(3)	(4)	(5)	(6)	(7)	(8)	(9)	(10)	(11)	(12)
A. Wife's Education												
1. Grade 6 and under	−318	2.66	−176	1.17	−276	4.28	258	2.40				
2. Grade 7–8	−449	8.07	−136	2.52	−159	3.08	35	0.18				
3. High School 1–3	−687	7.33	38	1.35	−139	2.04	−203	0.05				
4. High School 4	−118	1.33	99	1.19	251	2.30	−19	0.33				
5. College 1 and more			−340	2.38					81	0.42	−115	0.57
6. Combined relation	−393	9.70	−103	1.58	−80	3.55	18	1.15	81	0.42	−115	0.57
B. Husband's Education												
1. Grade 6 and under	−679	7.11	−15	0.08	−22	0.08	−12	0.24				
2. Grade 7–8	−394	7.23	68	0.91	−332	5.51	22	0.18				
3. High School 1–3	−297	3.03	−139	1.42	−33	0.11	106	0.98				
4. High School 4	−198	1.84	156	1.71	45	0.73	−13	0.19				
5. College 1 and more	357	1.78	−179	1.42	159	1.57			218	1.66	−158	0.90
6. Combined relation	−242	7.78	−49	0.87	−54	2.17	25	0.62	218	1.66	−158	0.90

C. Husband's Occupation

1. Laborers	−580	4.48	−750	3.21	−341	3.52	−305	2.17				
2. Service Workers	−106	0.88	13	0.13	−7	0.43	−103	0.87				
3. Operatives	−269	3.25	−85	0.78	−26	0.24	98	1.14				
4. Craftsmen	−354	4.44	−147	1.84	−27	0.23	−129	0.81				
5. Clerical Workers	45	0.68	−268	1.60								
6. Proprietors												
7. Professional									187	0.96	90	0.49
8. Combined relation	−270	6.13	−252	3.38	−100	2.21	−106	1.36	187	0.96	90	0.49

D. Size of Community

1. 2,500–5,000	−717	4.28	−293	1.72	302	1.41	−467	2.82
2. 5,000–10,000	−434	3.86	−43	0.34	192	0.74	−53	0.68
3. 10,000–25,000	−363	3.64	−165	1.34	−269	2.87		
4. 25,000–100,000	−542	6.67	7	0.06	−294	4.05		
5. 100,000–250,000	−743	7.21	8	1.47	−79	1.06	52	0.30
6. 250,000–500,000	−137	1.21	−246	2.48	−116	1.48	178	1.52
7. 500,000 and over	−280	3.44	−39	0.18	−148	1.88	−72	0.84
8. Combined relation	−459	11.43	−128	2.87	−59	3.47		

E. Woman's Marriage Age

1. Under 18	−240	1.43	86	1.29	−278	3.88	133	1.00	150	0.75
2. 18–20	−508	7.63	−242	3.20	−112	1.80	83	0.42		
3. 21–23	−469	6.33	−161	1.70	154	2.04	−70	0.46		
4. 24–26	−222	2.82	−169	1.11	350	1.76				
5. 27–29	122	0.61	57	0.34	51	0.37	19	0.12		
6. 30–35	284	1.79	−109	2.26	34	2.57	34	0.58		
7. Combined relation	−172	6.45							150	0.75

Husband's occupation. Within husband's occupation, the inverse relationship between education and family size holds only below four year high school education. Comparing four year high school women with college women, a positive relationship between woman's education and family size was found for all groups except women married to professional men. Here an inverse relationship of some significance persists.

Size of community. Within size of community, a quite strong inverse relationship between woman's education and family size exists for woman's education levels below four year high school. In the higher educational levels, the situation is less clear, with both positive and negative relationships appearing. These relationships could be accounted for by causality running from number of children to size of community, rather than the reverse: more highly educated people of higher incomes who have large families may have more tendency to move away from large cities than do either people of similar family size in lower socio-economic groups, or people of similar socio-economic groups with small families.

Marriage age. Within marriage age, it appears that for early marriages (before age 24) college women have more children than high school women. If they marry after age 24, however, the high school women have more children.

In summary, it would appear that the inverse relationship between woman's education and family size holds generally up to four year high school education. In comparing women with sixth grade education or less with women of seventh to eighth grade education, the difference is quite large. Smaller differences appear when comparisons are made between women of seventh to eighth grade education and women with one to three years of high school, and between one to three years of high school and four years. In the comparison of four year high school women with college women, the inverse relationship is not always present.

HUSBAND'S EDUCATION

In broad outline, the observations made about the effect of changes in woman's education on family size hold also for changes in husband's education. As Table 3 shows, the relationship between husband's education and family size is generally quite significant, and the direction is inverse. As in the case of woman's education, however, it is also evident from Table 2 that the comparison of husbands of four year high school and college education exhibits characteristics different from those found at other levels of husband's education.

Within woman's education, the comparison of the family size of men with four year high school education with that of college men yields Š's which are positive and significant, for all but one level of the wife's education (one to three years of high school). In the discussion of the effect of differences in woman's education on family size above, it was noted that when four year high school and college women married husbands of lower education the high school women had larger families than the college women, but that when they married men of college education, college women tended to have larger families than the high school women. For husbands, it is found that even when the men are married to women of four year high school education the college men tend to have larger families than high school men.

Within husband's wages, no significant relationship emerges from the comparison of four year high school men with college men, even though in several instances the direction of the difference is negative. In contrast with the data shown in Table 2 for woman's education, these data exhibit somewhat stronger positive relationships and weaker negative relationships.

Within husband's occupation and within size of community, the Š's for the comparison of four year high school men with college men are positive but not highly significant. In the case of husband's occupation the differences were found to be positive in all cases except for professional men. This same result was found in the examination of woman's education within husband's occupation. Within size of community college men generally have larger families than four year high school men, but the relationship is mixed and rather weak. As was suggested above in the discussion of size of community and woman's education, there may be intercorrelations between family size and subsequent choice of community which affect the total relationship.

Within woman's marriage age a consistent positive relation appears in the comparison of four year high school and college men. Although this means that with a given wife's marriage age, college men have larger families than four year high school men, it does not follow, of course, that college men as a group have larger families. To the extent that men of four year high school education marry younger, and thus have younger wives, this effect may offset or more than offset the other tendencies.

HUSBAND'S WAGES

The combined relation between husband's wages and family size is generally inverse when measured within wife's education, husband's education, husband's occupation, size of community, or woman's marriage

TABLE 5
Special Tabulations of Income and Family Size for Specified Groups
(CEB = Children Ever Born)

| | Census Sample of Women with 4 Year High School Education and Above, Husbands 4 Year High School Education and Above | | | | | | Time Inc. Sample | |
| | Clerical | | Managerial | | Professional | | College Graduates | |
Group	Number of Cases	CEB: 1,000 Women	Number of Cases	CEB: 1,000 Women	Number of Cases	CEB: 1,000 Women	Number of Cases	CEB: 1,000 Women
Women Ages 40–44:								
Income:								
$0–$999	44	1,841						
$1,000–$1,999	209	1,373	90	1,811	81	1,839	67	1,492
$2,000–$2,999	218	1,670	123	1,740	192	1,797	140	1,621
$3,000–$4,999	133	1,939	300	1,705	198	1,787	203	1,507
$5,000 and above	46	1,630	206	1,937	78	1,846	154	1,688
Women Ages 45–49:								
Income:								
$0–$999	56	1,673						
$1,000–$1,999	162	1,882	84	1,392	73	1,986	46	1,826
$2,000–$2,999	213	2,009	105	1,800	125	2,112	81	1,393
$3,000–$4,999	112	1,642	147	1,762	157	2,267	165	1,357
$5,000 and over	*	*	186	1,806	79	2,000	163	1,730

Significance and Direction of
Difference Between Means ($\hat{D}$ and $\tilde{S}$):

	Clerical		Managerial		Professional		College Graduates		Average	
	$m_2 - m_1$†	$\hat{D}$	$m_2 - m_1$†	$\hat{D}$	$m_2 - m_1$†	$\hat{D}$	$m_2 - m_1$†	$\hat{D}$	$m_2 - m_1$†	$\tilde{S}$
Women Ages 40–44:										
$0–$999 to $1,000–$1,999	−468	1.79							−468	1.79
$1,000–$1,999 to $2,000–$2,999	297	2.11	−71	0.32	−42	0.20	129	0.59	78	1.09
$2,000–$2,999 to $3,000–$3,999	269	1.51	−35	0.21	−10	0.02	−114	0.69	27	0.30
$4,000–$4,999 to $5,000 and above	309	1.16	232	1.46	59	0.27	181	1.12	195	0.89
Women Ages 45–49:										
$0–$999 to $1,000–$1,999	209	0.92	408	1.88	126	0.50	−433	1.53	209	0.92
$1,000–$1,999 to $2,000–$2,999	127	0.73	−38	0.19	155	0.71	−36	0.18	57	0.90
$2,000–$2,999 to $3,000–$4,999	−367	1.98	44	0.25	−267	1.10	373	2.17	−75	0.82
$3,000–$4,999 to $5,000 and above									50	0.76
Average and $\tilde{S}$	54	0.13	90	1.17	4	0.07	17	0.60	9 / 41	0.80 / 0.98

* Less than 25 cases. † Number of children ever born per 1,000 women.

179

TABLE 6

HUSBAND'S OCCUPATION

Significance and Direction of Differences in Number of Children Ever Born per 1,000 Women for Grouped Comparisons Expressed in Standard Error Units ($\tilde{S}$)

	Husband's Occupation											
	Laborers–Service Workers		Service Workers–Operatives		Operatives–Craftsmen		Craftsmen–Clerical		Clerical–Proprietors		Proprietors–Professional	
Group	$m_2 - m_1$	$\tilde{S}$	$m_2 - m_1$	$\tilde{S}$	$m_2 - m_1$	$\tilde{S}$	$m_2 - m_1$	$\tilde{S}$	$m_2 - m_1$	$\tilde{S}$	$m_2 - m_1$	$\tilde{S}$
	(1)	(2)	(3)	(4)	(5)	(6)	(7)	(8)	(9)	(10)	(11)	(12)
A. Wife's Education												
1. Grade 6 and under	−808	5.87	−111	1.02	−54	1.21	−601	11.59	195	3.49	−58	0.34
2. Grades 7–8	−783	8.64	24	0.05	−140	1.61	−311	4.36	−71	1.10	−89	0.51
3. High School 1–3			276	1.44	−123	0.90	−175	2.73	113	1.13	196	2.74
4. High School 4							−243	2.28	61	0.24	61	0.92
5. College 1 and more												
6. Combined relation	−795	10.29	63	0.27	−105	2.15	−332	10.48	74	1.88	27	1.41
B. Husband's Education												
1. Grade 6 and under	−1,656	6.01	827	2.91	−83	0.43	−363	7.53	34	0.84		
2. Grade 7–8	−682	7.52	−9	0.22	−51	0.90	−286	3.94	38	0.35		
3. High School 1–3			−112	0.54	−216	2.34	−249	3.45	−2	0.03	97	0.04
4. High School 4					125	0.67	−595	3.08	−112	1.07	215	3.67
5. College 1 and more												
6. Combined relation	−1,169	9.59	−353	1.27	−56	1.50	−373	9.00	−27	0.08	151	2.63

C. Husband's Wages

1. $0–$999	−767	7.81	136	1.28	16	0.03	−698	8.22	82	0.56	242	1.18
2. $1,000–$1,499	−353	2.12	−631	0.30	−167	2.19	−390	4.92	−29	0.17	−50	0.25
3. $1,500–$1,999			392	2.26	−159	1.91	−451	6.99	44	0.37	9	0.32
4. $2,000–$2,999					185	1.94	−470	7.32	90	0.67	−256	1.53
5. $3,000–$3,999							−12	0.06				
6. $4,000–$4,999												
7. $5,000 and over											−149	0.82
8. Combined relation	−560	7.04	−34	1.87	−31	1.07	−404	12.28	6	0.16	−41	0.49

D. Size of Community

1. 2,500–5,000	−657	4.86	−269	1.65	234	1.33	−378	2.11	−461	3.05	−58	0.48
2. 5,000–10,000	−513	2.32	201	1.70	−266	1.99	−398	3.70	−185	1.26	61	0.65
3. 10,000–25,000					16	0.16	−554	6.49	−122	1.30	20	0.36
4. 25,000–100,000					−172	2.38	−417	6.87	65	0.73	113	0.78
5. 100,000–250,000					−105	0.94	−280	2.76	−121	1.00	−29	0.23
6. 250,000–500,000					−133	1.27	−421	4.92	−125	1.74	114	1.09
7. 500,000 and over					44	0.06	−515	8.28	231	3.28	16	0.06
8. Combined relation	−585	5.09	−34	0.03	65	0.93	−426	13.25	−102	1.64		

E. Woman's Marriage Age

1. Under 18	−975	8.08	110	1.21	−691	3.33	−569	8.31	12	0.15	104	0.84
2. 18–20	−659	4.95	150	1.31	2	0.29	−377	6.59	71	0.99	83	1.39
3. 21–23					−167	2.24	−184	2.59	64	0.56	244	2.78
4. 24–26					−98	1.00	−109	1.12	12	0.14	41	0.24
5. 27–29					237	1.44	57	0.36	−51	0.46	338	2.03
6. 30–35									21	0.62	162	3.24
7. Combined relation	−817	9.24	130	1.79	−143	2.16	−236	8.14				

age. The inverse relationship is most pronounced at lower income levels and for the lower socio-economic groups. At higher income levels or in higher socio-economic groups the inverse relationship may disappear, and in some cases a positive relationship between income and family size emerges. However, there is no distinct pattern, so that the most that can be said on the basis of the information in Table 4 is that at the higher income levels income does not appear to be an important element.

Because of the unevenness of the evidence with respect to the higher ranges of income, a special tabulation was made to obtain greater homogeneity in the educational and occupational classifications. To this end, a sub-sample of women of four year high school education or more with husbands of four year high school education or more was selected from the original sample. Within this sub-sample three occupational groups —clerical, proprietor, professional—was examined separately. Two ages of women were distinguished—forty to forty-four and forty-five to forty-nine. Within these highly specified groups, the relation between income and family size was examined. In addition, a special sample of college graduates was obtained from Time Inc. The special tabulation of the census sample contained about 3,400 cases and the Time sample about 1,000 cases. The result of these tabulations, with the corresponding $\tilde{D}$'s and $\tilde{S}$'s, is shown in Table 5. For these special tabulations as a group, $\tilde{S}$ comes out between 0.80 and 0.98, depending on how the $\tilde{D}$'s are aggregated. Although the sign of the difference between the means is positive, the $\tilde{S}$ is too small to be considered very significant. Of the 25 differences between the means that could be computed, 13 differences were positive and 12 were negative. For the 11 comparisons in which $\tilde{D}$ was greater than 1, six were positive and five were negative. Examination of the $\tilde{S}$'s for the individual rows or columns of $\tilde{D}$'s does not reveal any striking relationships. The Time sample does show more significant $\tilde{D}$'s at the highest income levels. However, it must be recognized that this sample is not as homogeneous as the census sample, and no such relationship emerges there. Such things as education of wife, occupation, region, and parentage of husband and wife are not specified in the Time sample, and they may well be different for different income levels.

HUSBAND'S OCCUPATION

Although the combined relationship between the occupational level of the husband and family size is generally inverse, this relationship does not hold between all pairs of occupations (see Table 6). It is strongest between craftsmen and clerical workers and highly significant between laborers and service workers. In the comparison of service workers with operatives and of operatives with craftsmen, direct relationships as well as inverse relationships appear in specific instances. Evidence of even stronger direct relationships appears for the comparisons of clerical workers with proprietors and proprietors with professionals. In a number of these instances, strong positive relationships can be found, and especially in the proprietor-professional comparison, the inverse relationships that do exist are not highly significant.

Thus the combined inverse relationship for occupation groups is mainly due to the comparisons of laborers with service workers and craftsmen with clerical workers. In comparing proprietors with professionals, it is generally found that professionals had the larger families.

SIZE OF COMMUNITY

As was suggested above, although the size of community in which one lives may affect the size of one's family, it is obvious that the size of one's family is also likely to influence the size of the community in which one lives. Because of the interdependence between these two factors, it is difficult to attach much analytic meaning to the observed differentials in Table 7. However, it may be useful to describe the relationships which are found. In general the relationship between size of community and family size is inverse and quite significant. There is one exception, however. There does not appear to be a significant difference in family size between communities of 2,500–5,000 and communities of 5,000–10,000. Other minor exceptions can be found that suggest that the effect is not as universal as some of the summary combined relationships would indicate.

MARRIAGE AGE

The expected inverse relationship between marriage age and family size appears in Table 8. $\tilde{S}$ is significant and negative for all groups. It is obvious that the effect which the difference in marriage age has upon family size is more important in the lower socio-economic groups than in the higher. Similarly, differences in marriage age are somewhat more important in absolute terms for women who marry young than for those who marry later.

WOMAN'S AGE

As a final step in the analysis, it is possible to examine comparisons of successive woman's age levels, within pairs of other variables, to see whether on average older women tended to have larger families than

183

TABLE 7

SIZE OF COMMUNITY

Significance and Direction of Differences in Number of Children Ever Born per 1,000 Women for Grouped Comparisons Expressed in Standard Error Units (S)

Group	2,500–5,000 to 5,000–10,000		5,000–10,000 to 10,000–25,000		10,000–25,000 to 25,000–100,000		25,000–100,000 to 100,000–250,000		100,000–250,000 to 250,000–500,000		250,000–500,000 to 500,000 and over	
	$m_2 - m_1$	S	$m_2 - m_1$	S	$m_2 - m_1$	S	$m_2 - m_1$	S	$m_2 - m_1$	S	$m_2 - m_1$	S
	(1)	(2)	(3)	(4)	(5)	(6)	(7)	(8)	(9)	(10)	(11)	(12)
A. Wife's Education												
1. Grade 6 and under	− 44	0.56	− 21	0.18	−704	5.70	150	0.53	−157	1.02	− 49	0.26
2. Grades 7–8	0	0.18	−306	4.25	− 62	1.50	−159	3.13	−219	3.11	−119	2.64
3. High School 1–3	86	1.38	−104	1.38	− 64	0.08	− 72	1.05	−412	3.97	− 48	0.69
4. High School 4			83	0.94	−135	2.00	− 46	0.73	−123	1.61	− 61	1.07
5. College 1 and more	−278	0.88	−160	1.77	− 95	1.17	200	1.59	−319	2.44	−169	1.28
6. Combined relation	− 59	0.04	−101	2.96	−212	4.92	14	1.25	−246	5.42	− 89	2.66
B. Husband's Education												
1. Grade 6 and under	− 69	0.28	−118	0.76	−270	2.38	− 96	0.53	−273	1.37	−165	0.93
2. Grades 7–8	− 3	0.26	−262	4.21	− 48	1.52	− 94	1.78	−239	3.33	− 4	1.47
3. High School 1–3	−177	1.31	121	1.01	− 34	0.40	−269	2.69	−317	2.92	− 64	0.82
4. High School 4	38	0.39	−117	1.30	96	1.29	− 72	1.01	−165	1.61	−209	2.39
5. College 1 and more	6	0.07	− 54	0.76	−168	2.08	19	0.34	−259	2.62	−112	1.25
6. Combined relation	− 51	0.69	− 86	2.69	− 85	2.26	−102	2.53	−250	5.29	− 99	3.06

C. Husband's Wages

	(1)		(2)		(3)		(4)		(5)		(6)	
1. $0–$999	0.14	−32	2.41	−249	0.87	−100	0.50	43	4.94	−591	1.27	−120
2. $1,000–$1,499	0.65	84	0.76	97	2.63	−231	1.74	−157	0.19	14	3.18	−263
3. $1,500–$1,999	2.31	482	0.34	49	1.02	−73	2.87	−246	1.39	−137	0.80	−56
4. $2,000–$2,999	1.73	416	3.27	−478	1.17	−97	1.08	−70	1.78	−187	0.79	−87
5. $3,000–$3,999					1.43	226			0.48	−211	2.12	451
6. $4,000–$4,999												
7. $5,000 and over												
8. Combined relation	2.28	237	3.05	−194	1.90	−55	2.60	−107	3.75	−222	1.75	−15

D. Husband's Occupation

	(1)		(2)		(3)		(4)		(5)		(6)	
1. Laborers	3.43	−1,229	0.20	63	0.13	−40	2.07	−219	4.02	−1,013	1.78	−168
2. Service Workers	2.41	414	3.33	−437	1.38	−140	0.29	3	3.04	−486	1.74	152
3. Operatives	0.60	−96	0.48	−39	1.39	138	1.30	132	0.63	119	4.12	−278
4. Craftsmen	1.81	−281	0.24	−6	1.04	79	0.09	−14	1.42	−125	1.05	84
5. Clerical	0.50	−74	0.79	−67	0.87	−47	0.11	−25	2.92	−251	1.12	151
6. Proprietors			0.67	−97	0.70	96			2.70	−241		
7. Professionals									2.24	−340		
8. Combined relation	1.76	−253	2.46	−117	0.39	25	0.56	−26	5.93	−368	0.88	−12

E. Wife's Marriage Age

	(1)		(2)		(3)		(4)		(5)		(6)	
1. Under 18	0.07	5	0.56	−39	2.13	−738	3.26	−248	1.19	−143	0.18	72
2. 18–20	2.89	−263	1.57	−96	1.93	−230	1.12	−83	2.11	−175	2.62	−193
3. 21–23	1.07	−137	0.37	−37	2.17	−137	1.53	−141	1.72	−121	0.17	1
4. 24–26					0.79	−21			2.15	−311	1.73	−196
5. 27–29					1.09	128			4.37	−440		
6. 30–35					0.94	154						
7. Combined relation	2.33	−131	1.44	−57	2.03	−141	3.41	−157	5.15	−238	2.17	−79

TABLE 8
WOMAN'S MARRIAGE AGE

Significance and Direction of Differences in Number of Children Ever Born per 1,000 Women for Grouped Comparisons Expressed in Standard Error Units ($\tilde{S}$)

Group	Under 18 to 18–20 $m_2 - m_1$ (1)	$\tilde{S}$ (2)	18–20 to 21–23 $m_2 - m_1$ (3)	$\tilde{S}$ (4)	21–23 to 24–26 $m_2 - m_1$ (5)	$\tilde{S}$ (6)	24–26 to 27–29 $m_2 - m_1$ (7)	$\tilde{S}$ (8)	27–29 to 30–35 $m_2 - m_1$ (9)	$\tilde{S}$ (10)
A. Wife's Education										
1. Grade 6 and under	−957	4.86	−724	7.16	−615	4.58	−141	2.74	−625	9.68
2. Grades 7–8	−718	7.99	−191	4.31	−375	9.18	−134	1.72	−438	3.49
3. High School 1–3	−26	0.12	−237	4.09	−411	6.59	−304	3.97	−494	5.21
4. High School 4			−178	3.06	−245	3.40	−203	2.04	−648	5.79
5. College 1 and more			−268	2.40	−296	4.10				
6. Combined relation	−567	7.49	−319	9.38	−388	12.41	−195	5.23	−551	12.08
B. Husband's Education										
1. Grade 6 and under	−1,177	7.57	−755	8.89	−531	5.33	−395	6.81	−449	6.96
2. Grades 7–8	−1,043	9.89	−462	8.92	−394	10.03	−395	4.01	−396	3.73
3. High School 1–3			−374	5.71	−579	8.35	−270	3.34	−427	4.17
4. High School 4			−248	3.86	−196	3.50	−339	4.03		
5. College 1 and more			−236	3.10	−233	3.89				
6. Combined relation	−1,110	12.38	−415	13.60	−386	13.88	−350	9.09	−424	8.58

C. Husband's Wages

1. $0–$999	−1,032	8.34	−488	6.74	−496	7.30	−669	3.75	367	2.19
2. $1,000–$1,499	−1,364	10.13	−469	5.94	−505	7.59	−199	1.79	−430	2.74
3. $1,500–$1,999			−621	8.57	−426	6.40	−79	0.59	−493	4.61
4. $2,000–$2,999			−36	1.73	−159	2.96	−304	3.11		
5. $3,000–$3,999			−391	2.87	−14	0.74				
6. $4,000–$4,999										
7. $5,000 and over					−316	2.19				
8. Combined relation	−1,193	13.09	−401	11.54	−319	11.09	−313	4.62	−185	2.98

D. Husband's Occupation

1. Laborers	−1,015	5.93	−730	5.99	−535	1.97				
2. Service Workers	−529	3.41	−414	3.15						
3. Operatives			−374	4.79	−532	6.17	−682	4.43	−603	4.81
4. Craftsmen			−542	8.97	−459	7.66	−373	4.32	−480	4.68
5. Clerical			−349	5.60	−245	4.34	−256	3.32	−552	4.99
6. Proprietors			−266	3.78	−342	5.48	−273	3.25		
7. Professional			−171	1.34	−195	2.62	−282	1.87	−197	1.12
8. Combined relation	−772	6.62	−406	12.68	−384	11.51	−372	7.67	−458	2.99

E. Size of Community

1. 2,500–5,000	−1,598	5.91	−421	4.55	−551	4.89	−604	5.37	−381	2.08
2. 5,000–10,000	−574	3.90	−519	6.06	−563	5.87	−337	4.75	−354	3.63
3. 10,000–25,000			−551	7.83	−443	6.21	−113	1.00		
4. 25,000–100,000			−428	9.33	−347	6.26	−277	3.86		
5. 100,000–250,000			−308	3.56	−586	6.46				
6. 250,000–500,000			−357	4.54	−462	7.08				
7. 500,000 and over			−556	7.53	−270	5.73			−478	4.95
8. Combined relation	−1,086	6.95	−448	16.37	−460	16.03	−332	7.49	−404	6.16

TABLE 9
WOMAN'S AGE

Significance and Direction of Differences in Number of Children Ever Born per 1,000 Women for Grouped Comparisons Expressed in Standard Error Units ($\check{S}$)

Group	Woman's Age									
	40–44 to 45–49		45–49 to 50–54		50–54 to 55–59		55–59 to 60–64		60–64 to 65–69	
	$m_2 - m_1$	$\check{S}$	$m_2 - m_1$	$\check{S}$	$m_2 - m_1$	$\check{S}$	$m_2 - m_1$	$\check{S}$	$m_2 - m_1$	$\check{S}$
	(1)	(2)	(3)	(4)	(5)	(6)	(7)	(8)	(9)	(10)
a. Woman's Education and Husband's Education	130	4.63	5	0.24	−28	0.95	104	3.13	252	1.81
b. Woman's Education and Husband's Wages	150	4.30	−33	0.15	17	0.35	46	0.49	−458	2.10
c. Woman's Education and Husband's Occupation	244	6.75	103	0.48	43	0.44	215	2.61	54	0.22
d. Woman's Education and Size of Community	198	6.22	−46	0.20	−15	0.48	251	3.13	149	1.36
e. Woman's Education and Woman's Marriage Age	214	7.88	119	3.80	29	0.95	61	1.38	324	4.73

f. Husband's Education and Husband's Wages	115	3.93	84	1.97	−90	1.60	179	2.16	384	2.36
g. Husband's Education and Husband's Occupation	155	4.84	61	2.09	−20	0.96	353	4.79	−499	3.92
h. Husband's Education and Size of Community	144	5.15	87	2.47	−29	0.58	423	6.25	−199	2.22
i. Husband's Education and Woman's Marriage Age	203	6.61	74	2.42	−21	0.48	63	1.70	432	3.26
j. Husband's Wages and Husband's Occupation	101	3.84	78	1.88	−48	1.50	166	0.98		
k. Husband's Wages and Size of Community	218	6.56	93	2.50	−90	2.64	−17	0.12		
l. Husband's Wages and Woman's Marriage Age	298	7.64	144	2.61	−112	1.99	54	0.22	59	0.20
m. Husband's Occupation and Size of Community	195	6.42	146	3.74	−119	2.41	434	1.96		
n. Husband's Occupation and Woman's Marriage Age	250	6.66	145	3.96	−63	1.62	79	1.93		
o. Size of Community and Woman's Marriage Age	193	6.52	145	4.30	−84	2.16	88	1.61	391	2.85

younger women. In general, Table 9 would lead to this conclusion. However, the smaller family size of women aged 40–44 may be partly due to the fact that these families are incomplete; some children are still born to women aged 40–44. At the next two age levels, the inverse relationship is not nearly so consistent. Thus, comparing women aged 45–49 with women aged 50–54, no significant difference in family size is found for comparisons within (1) woman's education and husband's education, (2) woman's education and husband's wages, (3) woman's education and husband's occupation, and (4) woman's education and size of community. Comparing women aged 50–54 with women aged 55–59, there is in addition no significant difference in family size for comparisons within (5) woman's education and marriage age, (6) husband's education and husband's occupation, (7) husband's education and size of community, and (8) husband's education and marriage age. There are also other comparisons in the table which are of doubtful significance because they involve a small number of cases. By and large, however, the standardization of data for woman's education seems to have the greatest effect on the comparisons between ages, which suggests that it is changing educational levels which are responsible for much of the difference in family size for women of different ages. As was suggested earlier, the differences among women of different ages become smaller when the lower educational levels are eliminated.

COMMENT

Pascal K. Whelpton, Director, Scripps Foundation for Research in Population Problems, Miami University

The main task which the authors undertook was to ascertain whether any one of seven chosen characteristics was independently related to the completed fertility rate of cohorts of women (the number of births per 1,000 women living to the end of the childbearing period), and, if so, the direction and strength of the relationship. I think that they developed an ingenious and useful procedure. They computed the statistical significance—$\tilde{D}$—of the difference in the mean fertility rate—F—of successive groups classified by a given characteristic—C—within various classes for the other characteristics. The values of $\tilde{D}$ for a given characteristic are then summarized by $\tilde{S}$. This procedure brings out the relationship between F and C at various places along a C continuum. For example, it shows a strong inverse relationship between fertility and education when education is low but not when education is high *within* various classes for each of the other five variables studied.

190

Because I consider myself a demographer rather than a statistician, I shall not try to evaluate from a statistical standpoint the measures which the authors developed, but shall merely say that I think S̃ is useful, but not ideal. It tells us much about the significance of the fertility differentials but not enough about their size. Perhaps we can't have everything.

I wish the authors would modify slightly their statement that "the magnitude of S̃ is not a measure of the magnitude of the mean of the Ď's." The formula they use to compute S̃ is $S̃ = \dfrac{\sqrt{N}\Sigma Ď}{N}$. It seems obvious that the magnitude of S̃ does vary with the magnitude of the mean of the Ď's, although not proportionally because of the effect of $\sqrt{N}$ as a multiplier in the numerator.

It may be well to point out that the usefulness of S̃ depends on the size of the sampling ratio. If the data being analyzed were for the universe instead of a sample, it seems to me that S̃ would be of little value.

The study was restricted to urban native-white women of native parentage, aged "40–70" (probably 40–69 inclusive), married once and to native born white men of native parentage. I sympathize with the reasons for the nativity and parentage restriction, namely, to rule out the influence of first and second generation immigrants on fertility trends and differentials. I am bothered, however, by the effect which it may have on the interpretation of the findings. As shown in the population breakdown the sample contained 110,000 women meeting all the requirements except nativity and parentage but only 40,000 after the nativity and parentage restrictions were applied.

One of the results of this reduction undoubtedly is to increase substantially the proportion of women who are Protestants. This occurs because Catholics were much more numerous relatively among the immigrants arriving between 1900 and 1940 than among the population of 1900. Another effect is to raise the proportion of women who are migrants from the southern hill areas, in which the proportion of the white population that is native born of native parentage is unusually high. It may well be that the nativity and parentage restrictions introduce other changes. Prior to 1940 there had been much intermarriage of immigrants (also of their children) on the one hand, and, on the other hand, intermarriage of the descendants of earlier generations of migrants who constituted the remainder of the white population. Consequently, the sample in question may be heavily weighted with somewhat isolated "pocket" groups.

The remainder of my comments relate in greater degree to the data that the authors used than to the use they made of these data. The information on children ever born that has been collected and published by the Bureau of the Census is very valuable; I am delighted to see it used in this and other studies. In interpreting the results, however, it may be desirable to think about the extent to which biases may be introduced because no report on births was obtained from many women (about 10 to 12 per cent of those in the age groups considered here). Investigations made by the Bureau of the Census indicate that the non-reporting women had borne fewer children than the others. If there is a relation between nonreporting and the characteristics being studied, this may bias the size of the observed fertility differentials. A similar statement may be made with respect to the tendency for the omission of some of the children borne by the reporting women. This and other biases probably affect the fertility differentials between successive birth cohorts.

The effect of no report for certain other items—especially husband's occupation and wages—may be more damaging. This may be illustrated by the data for women aged "65–70" in Tables A1 through A15. The tables relating to husband's occupation and/or wages include only 863 to 1,281 of the (approximately) 2,350 women aged "65–70" in the sample; the birth rate of these women is between 2,229 and 2,459. In contrast, the tables *not* relating to these variables contain between 2,033 and 2,316 women; their birth rate is between 2,646 and 2,883. (The explanation probably is that a relatively large proportion of the husbands for whom occupation and/or wages are not reported are in the upper socio-economic groups where fertility is relatively low.) An unfortunate result of this bias is that 10 of the tables in question place the fertility of women aged 65–70 *below* that of women aged 60–64 while the other 5 tables place it *higher*. How is it possible to analyze the relation between the fertility of one group of cohorts and that of a preceding group when the data used for certain characteristics show an upward trend in fertility over time and those used for other characteristics show a downward trend?

Migration undoubtedly influences the differentials being studied here. For example, the lower socio-economic groups probably contain a relatively high proportion of migrants from the southern Appalachians, who have a high fertility background. Part of the apparent relation between fertility and the measures of economic status employed in this study may reflect the cultural differences between these migrants and the couples that had lived longer in the North Central region.

One of the important differentials shown is that between educational groups. In considering the meaning of these differentials we need to keep in mind the increase from earlier to later cohorts in the proportion of women classified as high school graduates or as having some college education. It is probable that the rise in the relative size of these groups is associated with changes in the distribution of each group by socio-economic and cultural background—higher education has become less restricted to the upper groups of the population.

It is most unfortunate that the influence of religion on fertility could not have been considered. Religion undoubtedly affects some of the differentials in question, for example, those relating to size of community. Evidence from other studies shows that the fertility of Catholic wives exceeds that of Protestant wives, which in turn is above that of Jewish wives. It shows also that the proportion of Catholics varies directly with size of community and that the inverse relation between fertility and size of city is larger when religion is controlled than when it is uncontrolled.

Because of the need for data for religious groups I was very happy when I heard that the Bureau of the Census had asked a question on religious preference in the Current Population Survey of March 1957, and more pleased when I saw some of the tables prepared from these data. Later I was greatly shocked to hear that the Bureau had been forbidden to publish the data which had been collected and tabulated except those in the *Statistical Abstract* for 1958.

In closing I would like to call attention again to the difficulty in generalizing from the results for native-white women of native parentage when information is not available about religious differentials in fertility. The authors say, "In conclusion, therefore, it would seem that as the income and education of the general population increase, the differences in family size of different groups will become smaller, and the population will become very much more homogeneous with respect to family size." In evaluating this conclusion I remember that the Indianapolis Study (in 1941) and the nationwide study Growth of American Families (in 1955) show that the differences between the fertility of Catholic and Protestant wives are greater among upper than lower educational groups. It may be, therefore, that as larger proportions of our population go to college the Protestant–Catholic differentials in fertility will increase. This would partially balance, and might more than offset, the tendencies found by the authors for other differentials to diminish in the future.

TABLE A-1

Woman's Education by Husband's Education

Woman's Present Age	Woman's Education	6th Grade or less			7-8th Grade		
		No. Cases	No. CEB	CEB/1000 Women	No. Cases	No. CEB	CEB/1000 Women
40-44	6th Grade or less	283	845	2986	328	872	2659
	7-8th Grade	465	1443	3103	2659	6249	2350
	1-3 years High School	114	329	2886	1139	2587	2271
	4 years High School	59	111	1881	614	1240	2020
	1 year College or more	15	29	1933	207	401	1937
	Total	936	2757	2946	4947	11349	2294
45-49	6th Grade or less	480	1676	3492	358	1106	3089
	7-8th Grade	579	1800	3109	2768	7097	2564
	1-3 years High School	130	441	3392	665	1627	2447
	4 years High School	46	138	3000	485	888	1835
	1 year College or more	19	45	2368	172	317	1843
	Total	1254	4100	3270	4448	11035	2481
50-54	6th Grade or less	536	1890	3526	323	925	2864
	7-8th Grade	430	1321	3072	2274	5958	2620
	1-3 years High School	104	317	3048	572	1319	2306
	4 years High School	18	44	2444	141	326	2312
	1 year College or more	18	33	1833	127	234	1843
	Total	1106	3605	3259	3437	8762	2549
55-59	6th Grade or less	457	1593	3486	243	719	2959
	7-8th Grade	382	1198	3136	1662	4666	2687
	1-3 years High School	94	314	3340	398	889	2234
	4 years High School	184	550	2989	709	1820	2567
	1 year College or more	23	38	1652	79	180	2278
	Total	1140	3693	3239	3091	8274	2677
60-64	6th Grade or less	349	1246	3570	150	414	2760
	7-8th Grade	231	715	3095	968	2830	2924
	1-3 years High School	54	150	2778	195	534	2738
	4 years High School	33	87	2636	144	316	2194
	1 year College or more	6	29	4833	53	130	2453
	Total	673	2227	3309	1510	4224	2797
65-69	6th Grade or less	252	1014	4024	114	434	3807
	7-8th Grade	122	456	3738	673	1920	2853
	1-3 years High School	26	52	2000	127	327	2575
	4 years High School	20	44	2200	91	193	2121
	1 year College or more	5	12	2400	35	74	2114
	Total	425	1578	3713	1040	2948	2835

(CEB= Children Ever Born)

TABLE A-1

Husband's Education

1-3 years High School			4 years High School			1 yr, College or more			Total		
No. Cases	No. CEB	CEB/1000 Women	No. Cases	No. CEB	CEB/1000 Women	No. Cases	No. CEB	CEB/1000 Women	No. Cases	No. CEB	CEB/1000 Women
59	127	2153	22	46	2091	2	2	1000	694	1892	2726
633	1363	2153	345	654	1896	163	357	2190	4265	10066	2360
477	999	2094	343	668	1948	226	391	1730	2299	4974	2164
476	844	1773	964	1747	1812	630	1105	1754	2743	5047	1840
218	438	2009	317	529	1669	1116	2046	1833	1873	3443	1838
1863	3771	2024	1991	3644	1830	2137	3901	1825	11874	25422	2141
60	188	3133	23	44	1913	7	30	4286	928	3044	3280
329	807	2453	311	588	1891	158	350	2215	4145	10642	2567
490	1031	2104	191	422	2209	127	235	1850	1603	3756	2343
363	791	2179	744	1355	1751	731	1429	1955	2369	4601	1942
170	285	1676	215	384	1786	818	1571	1921	1394	2602	1867
1412	3102	2197	1484	2793	1882	1841	3615	1964	10439	24645	2361
57	154	2702	26	68	2615	9	12	1333	951	3049	3206
355	867	2442	231	447	1935	145	352	2428	3435	8945	2604
484	986	2037	186	355	1909	137	280	2044	1483	3257	2196
72	154	2139	316	600	1899	218	426	1954	765	1550	2026
74	142	1919	154	261	1695	545	1076	1974	918	1746	1902
1042	2303	2210	913	1731	1896	1054	2146	2036	7552	18547	2455
36	135	3750	14	52	3714	8	25	3125	758	2524	3330
253	602	2379	116	244	2103	115	232	2017	2528	6942	2746
304	635	2089	125	226	1808	80	186	2325	1001	2250	2248
188	408	2170	400	701	1752	355	641	1806	1836	4120	2244
48	117	2437	74	102	1378	401	703	1753	625	1140	1824
829	1897	2288	729	1325	1818	959	1787	1863	6748	16976	2516
23	101	4391	15	51	3400	3	3	1000	540	1815	3361
114	268	2351	75	159	2120	72	147	2042	1460	4119	2821
149	329	2208	54	115	2130	64	165	2578	516	1293	2506
79	174	2203	212	462	2179	172	352	2047	640	1391	2173
15	52	3467	38	83	2184	181	434	2398	293	728	2485
380	924	2432	394	870	2208	492	1101	2238	3449	9346	2710
12	30	2500	9	22	2444	3	15	5000	390	1515	3885
64	154	2406	55	105	1909	65	151	2323	979	2786	2846
68	138	2029	28	63	2250	29	59	2034	278	639	2299
46	93	2022	115	205	1783	99	225	2273	371	760	2049
6	10	1667	20	49	2450	56	141	2518	122	286	2344
196	425	2168	227	444	1956	252	591	2345	2140	5986	2797

TABLE A-2

Woman's Education by Husband's Wages

Woman's Present Age	Woman's Education	$1-$999			$1000-$1499			$1500-$1999		
		No. Cases	No. CEB	CEB/1000 Women	No. Cases	No. CEB	CEB/1000 Women	No. Cases	No. CEB	CEB/1000 Women
40-44	6th Grade or less	253	764	3020	172	480	2791	108	266	2463
	7-8th Grade	894	2445	2735	954	2191	2297	861	1985	2305
	1-3 years High School	250	685	2740	289	567	1962	358	802	2240
	4 years High School	217	420	1935	293	550	1877	466	918	1970
	1 year College or more	77	159	2065	159	278	1748	218	358	1642
	Total	1691	4473	2645	1867	4066	2178	2011	4329	2153
45-49	6th Grade or less	303	1036	3419	203	655	3347	149	484	3284
	7-8th Grade	976	2906	2977	832	2184	2628	736	1783	2423
	1-3 years High School	337	971	2881	272	576	2118	332	821	2473
	4 years High School	189	380	2011	247	488	1976	285	619	2172
	1 year College or more	90	167	1856	104	213	2048	122	180	1475
	Total	1895	5460	2881	1658	4116	2483	1624	3887	2393
50-54	6th Grade or less	324	1198	3698	157	495	3153	128	386	3016
	7-8th Grade	800	2500	3125	614	1575	2565	540	1290	2389
	1-3 years High School	240	623	2596	239	553	2314	229	526	2402
	4 years High School	15	41	2733	36	84	2333	0	0	-
	1 year College or more	80	178	2171	101	181	1792	76	148	1947
	Total	1459	4540	3112	1147	2888	2518	973	2350	2415
55-59	6th Grade or less	269	907	3160	143	397	2776	66	175	2652
	7-8th Grade	595	1881	3161	432	1177	2725	311	736	2367
	1-3 years High School	183	575	3506	155	400	2581	131	270	2093
	4 years High School	270	602	2230	261	514	1969	293	579	1976
	1 year College or more	33	62	1879	41	70	1707	44	97	2205
	Total	1350	4027	2983	1032	2558	2479	845	1857	2198
60-64	6th Grade or less	145	446	3076	83	259	3120	33	142	4302
	7-8th Grade	307	980	3192	211	576	2730	123	342	2780
	1-3 years High School	84	249	2964	75	205	2733	32	77	2406
	4 years High School	67	181	2701	42	89	2119	65	128	1969
	1 year College or more	30	89	2967	25	66	2640	24	63	2625
	Total	633	1945	3073	436	1195	2741	277	752	2715
65-69	6th Grade or less	73	296	4055	34	107	3147	20	76	3800
	7-8th Grade	158	432	2734	87	236	2713	56	133	2375
	1-3 years High School	43	85	1977	30	61	2033	22	36	1636
	4 years High School	40	79	1975	34	88	2588	24	24	1000
	1 year College or more	11	29	2636	8	13	1625	3	9	3000
	Total	325	921	2834	193	505	2617	125	278	2224

(CEB=Children Ever-Born)

TABLE A-2

Husband's Wages $2000-$2999			$3000-$3999			$4000-$4999			$5000 and over			Total		
No. Cases	No. CEB	CEB/1000 Women	No. Cases	No. CEB	CEB/1000 Women	No. Cases	No. CEB	CEB/1000 Women	No. Cases	No. CEB	CEB/1000 Women	No. Cases	No. CEB	CEB/1000 Women
73	160	2192	7	10	1429	2	5	2500	0	0		615	1685	2740
697	1474	2115	151	395	2616	23	46	2000	26	58	2231	3606	8594	2383
432	942	2281	98	175	1786	41	95	2317	32	59	1844	1500	3325	2217
594	1068	1798	223	413	1852	105	203	1933	187	340	1818	2085	3912	1876
369	659	1786	243	402	1654	81	162	2000	207	402	1942	1354	2420	1787
2165	4303	1988	722	1395	1932	252	511	2028	452	859	1900	9160	19936	2176
87	228	2621	10	17	1700	2	6	3000	2	3	1500	756	2429	3213
721	1583	2196	133	286	2150	26	65	2500	37	100	2703	3461	8907	2574
308	635	2062	103	216	2097	15	26	1733	52	87	1673	1419	3332	2348
447	891	1993	211	354	1678	71	152	2141	158	297	1880	1608	3181	1978
238	436	1832	162	312	1926	67	158	2358	178	333	1871	961	1799	1872
1801	3773	2095	619	1185	1914	181	407	2248	427	820	1920	8205	19648	2395
91	266	2923	16	42	2625	4	21	5250	1	3	3000	721	2411	3344
466	985	2114	122	297	2434	19	37	1947	46	80	1739	2607	6764	2595
216	480	2222	93	185	1989	26	39	1500	43	110	2750	1086	2516	2317
49	161	3286	27	10	370	7	18	2571	116	223	1922	250	537	2148
146	243	1664	76	109	1434	47	85	1809	119	259	2176	645	1203	1865
968	2135	2206	334	643	1925	103	200	1942	325	675	2077	5309	13431	2530
51	130	2549	14	19	1357	0	0		0	0	-	543	1628	2998
253	581	2296	99	225	2273	21	36	1714	23	40	1739	1734	4676	2697
159	332	2088	51	108	2118	15	33	2200	20	41	2050	714	1759	2464
431	823	1910	151	341	2258	77	127	1649	93	158	1699	1576	3144	1995
86	128	1488	46	94	2043	15	32	2133	68	143	2103	333	626	1880
980	1994	2035	361	787	2180	128	228	1781	204	382	1873	4900	11833	2415
11	10	909	3	17	5667	4	8	2000	1	2	2000	280	884	3157
124	268	2161	37	90	2432	2	10	5000	14	41	2929	818	2307	2820
58	130	2241	18	38	2111	3	5	1667	11	27	2455	281	731	2601
70	141	2014	25	49	1960	15	28	1867	31	73	2355	315	689	2187
31	75	2419	18	42	2333	5	16	3200	25	54	2160	158	405	2563
294	624	2122	101	236	2337	29	67	2310	82	197	2402	1852	5016	2708
5	15	3000	4	8	2000	1	0	0	0	0	-	137	502	2664
42	82	1952	15	24	1600	7	10	1429	8	16	2000	373	933	2501
18	23	1278	12	34	2833	2	0	0	1	2	2000	128	241	1883
42	120	2857	16	20	1250	8	11	1375	21	25	1190	185	367	1984
7	3	429	5	10	2000	0	0	-	6	14	2333	40	78	1950
114	243	2132	52	96	1846	18	21	1167	36	57	1583	863	2121	2458

TABLE A-3

Woman's Education by Husband's Occupation

Woman's Present Age	Woman's Education	Professional			Proprietors			Clerical and Sales		
		No. Cases	No. OEB	OEB/1000 Women	No. Cases	No. OEB	OEB/1000 Women	No. Cases	No. OEB	OEB/1000 Women
40-44	6th Grade or less	4	6	1500	33	64	1940	59	134	2271
	7-8th Grade	125	244	1952	457	925	2024	592	1206	2037
	1-3 years High School	113	214	1894	422	837	1983	466	953	2045
	4 years High School	318	518	1629	764	1393	1823	700	1237	1767
	1 year College or more	573	1067	1862	515	899	1746	410	674	1644
	Total	1133	2049	1808	2191	4118	1879	2227	4204	1888
45-49	6th Grade or less	9	37	4111	66	155	2348	64	160	2500
	7-8th Grade	101	225	2228	524	1191	2273	627	1319	2104
	1-3 years High School	83	171	2060	258	464	1798	295	594	2014
	4 years High School	343	747	2178	678	1163	1715	587	1082	1843
	1 year College or more	436	879	2016	363	651	1793	317	592	1868
	Total	972	2059	2118	1889	3624	1918	1890	3747	1983
50-54	6th Grade or less	9	48	5333	80	195	2437	72	192	2667
	7-8th Grade	88	200	2273	455	1077	2367	485	896	1847
	1-3 years High School	78	123	1527	312	564	1808	291	580	1993
	4 years High School	104	231	2221	235	470	2000	109	156	1431
	1 year College or more	272	557	2048	268	509	1899	181	343	1895
	Total	551	1159	2103	1350	2815	2085	1138	2167	1904
55-59	6th Grade or less	7	13	1857	36	97	2694	41	134	3268
	7-8th Grade	85	183	2153	336	804	2393	269	581	2160
	1-3 years High School	48	100	2083	196	403	2056	185	347	1876
	4 years High School	263	537	2042	458	801	1749	532	962	1808
	1 year College or more	180	309	1717	146	298	2041	94	154	1638
	Total	583	1142	1959	1172	2403	2050	1121	2178	1943
60-64	6th Grade or less	2	6	3000	40	103	2575	29	69	2379
	7-8th Grade	51	93	1824	175	397	2269	162	352	2173
	1-3 years High School	35	68	1943	85	213	2506	89	215	2416
	4 years High School	76	149	1961	148	327	2209	129	268	2078
	1 year College or more	79	202	2557	75	182	2427	61	150	2459
	Total	243	518	2132	523	1222	2337	470	1054	2243
65-69	6th Grade or less	4	10	2500	15	52	3467	16	44	2750
	7-8th Grade	33	78	2364	77	166	2156	73	159	2178
	1-3 years High School	14	32	2286	43	94	2186	34	59	1735
	4 years High School	40	103	2575	71	129	1817	74	147	1986
	1 year College or more	14	24	1714	28	52	1857	18	43	2839
	Total	105	247	2352	234	493	2107	215	452	2102

(OEB = Children Ever Born)

TABLE A-3

Husband's Occupation

Skilled			Operatives			Service Workers			Laborers			Total		
No. Cases	No. CEB	CEB/1000 Women	No. Cases	No. CEB	CEB/1000 Women	No. Cases	No. CEB	CEB/1000 Women	No. Cases	No. CEB	CEB/1000 Women	No. Cases	No. CEB	CEB/1000 Women
200	529	2645	185	519	2805	50	142	2840	124	378	3048	655	1772	2705
1236	3047	2465	986	2286	2318	312	761	2439	391	1157	2959	4099	9626	2348
582	1253	2153	404	930	2302	97	213	2196	133	343	2579	2217	4743	2139
459	860	1874	232	477	2056	109	194	1780	69	152	2203	2651	2631	1822
182	395	2170	84	175	2083	33	44	1333	20	42	2100	1817	3296	1814
2659	6084	2288	1891	4387	2320	601	1354	2253	737	2072	2611	11439	24268	2122
			240	800	3333	74	193	2608	175	726	4149	628	2071	3298
1264	3207	2537	849	2156	2539	274	702	2562	413	1422	3443	4052	10222	2523
435	1089	2503	256	641	2504	77	190	2468	106	349	3292	1510	3498	2317
389	771	1982	162	354	2185	89	176	1978	44	115	2614	2292	4408	1923
110	201	1827	61	106	1738	33	49	1485	15	35	2333	1335	2513	1882
2198	5268	2397	1568	4057	2587	547	1310	2395	753	2647	3515	9817	22712	2314
237	720	3038	179	563	3145	74	254	3432	173	673	3890	824	2645	3210
948	2612	2755	626	1717	2743	252	719	2853	293	1015	3464	3147	8236	2617
361	835	2313	168	434	2583	78	214	2744	80	233	2912	1368	2983	2181
67	122	2933	30	88	2933	14	28	2000	8	24	3000	567	1119	1974
76	99	1303	34	52	1529	26	40	1538	14	33	2357	871	1633	1875
1689	4388	2598	1037	2854	2752	444	1255	2827	568	1978	3482	6777	16616	2452
178	491	2758	120	339	2825	84	225	2679	166	706	4253	632	2005	3172
615	1660	2699	348	960	2759	200	480	2400	244	864	3541	2097	5532	2638
227	500	2203	98	252	2571	37	86	2324	73	210	2877	864	1898	2197
321	670	2087	182	377	2071	86	183	2168	60	160	2667	1902	3690	1940
48	96	2000	22	65	2955	12	12	1000	7	27	3857	509	961	1888
1389	3417	2460	770	1993	2588	419	986	2353	550	1967	3576	6004	4086	2346
76	249	3276	50	144	2880	47	167	3553	80	296	3700	324	1034	3191
298	855	2869	136	395	2904	103	295	2864	126	457	3627	1051	2844	2706
72	170	2361	34	113	3324	46	154	3348	18	47	2611	379	980	2586
68	147	2162	27	67	2481	54	132	2444	10	26	2600	512	1116	2180
14	26	1857	7	18	2571	9	24	2667	5	42	8400	250	644	2576
528	1447	2741	254	737	2902	259	772	2981	239	868	3632	2516	6618	2630
57	203	3561	23	76	3304	24	83	3458	50	190	3800	189	658	3481
119	335	2815	74	162	2189	52	155	2981	55	138	2509	483	1193	2470
39	72	1846	14	39	2786	15	22	1467	9	28	3111	168	346	2060
29	36	1241	11	32	2909	6	10	1667	11	18	1636	242	465	1921
6	9	1500	2	10	5000	3	4	1333				71	142	2000
250	655	2620	124	319	2573	100	274	2740	125	364	2912	1153	2804	2432

TABLE A-4

Woman's Education by Size of Community

Woman's Present Age	Woman's Education	2,500-5,000			5,000-10,000			10,000-25,000		
		No. Cases	No. CEB	CEB/1000 Women	No. Cases	No. CEB	CEB/1000 Women	No. Cases	No. CEB	CEB/1000 Women
40-44	6th Grade or less	47	137	2915	74	216	2919	102	319	3127
	7-8th Grade	317	808	2549	395	1173	2970	690	1770	2565
	1-3 years High School	151	335	2219	242	638	2636	363	834	2298
	4 years High School	237	445	1878	336	651	1937	440	854	1941
	1 year College or more	190	417	2195	259	509	1965	308	555	1802
	Total	942	2142	2274	1306	3187	2440	1903	4332	2276
45-49	6th Grade or less	61	261	4279	104	433	4163	150	554	3693
	7-8th Grade	371	1250	3369	490	1435	2929	620	1719	2773
	1-3 years High School	164	503	3067	210	500	2381	269	634	2357
	4 years High School	183	339	1852	240	491	2046	370	772	2086
	1 year College or more	120	238	1983	197	412	2091	233	427	1833
	Total	899	2591	2882	1241	3271	2636	1642	4106	2501
50-54	6th Grade or less	52	203	3904	135	445	3296	120	457	3808
	7-8th Grade	283	901	3184	383	1161	3031	511	1511	2957
	1-3 years High School	152	355	2336	205	534	2605	253	544	2150
	4 years High School	47	101	2149	87	160	1839	121	274	2264
	1 year College or more	108	236	2185	143	290	2028	163	321	1969
	Total	642	1796	2798	953	2590	2718	1168	3107	2660
55-59	6th Grade or less	82	346	4220	84	344	4095	107	402	3757
	7-8th Grade	243	818	3366	311	993	3193	410	1087	2651
	1-3 years High School	98	250	2551	128	270	2109	188	472	2511
	4 years High School	165	330	2000	213	427	2005	321	709	2209
	1 year College or more	43	54	1256	82	188	2293	100	205	2050
	Total	631	1798	2849	818	2222	2716	1126	2875	2553
60-64	6th Grade or less	67	282	4209	71	273	3845	98	355	3622
	7-8th Grade	167	521	3120	170	541	3182	265	758	2860
	1-3 years High School	50	141	2820	66	141	2136	64	165	2578
	4 years High School	86	191	2221	100	265	2650	89	230	2584
	1 year College or more	35	127	3629	45	129	2867	62	138	2226
	Total	405	1262	3116	452	1349	2985	578	1646	2848
65-69	6th Grade or less	46	219	4761	68	305	4485	61	237	3885
	7-8th Grade	127	408	3213	178	575	3230	154	445	2890
	1-3 years High School	37	114	3081	37	117	3162	46	109	2370
	4 years High School	27	72	2667	46	84	1826	54	130	2407
	1 year College or more	19	62	3263	20	54	2700	18	51	2833
	Total	256	875	3418	349	1135	3252	333	972	2919

(CEB = Children Ever Born)

TABLE A-4

Size of Community

25,000-100,000			100,000-250,000			250,000-500,000			Over 500,000			Total		
No. Cases	No. CEB	CEB/1000 Women	No. Cases	No. CEB	CEB/1000 Women	No. Cases	No. CEB	CEB/1000 Women	No. Cases	No. CEB	CEB/1000 Women	No. Cases	No. CEB	CEB/1000 Women
153	369	2412	64	192	3000	92	240	2609	168	422	2512	700	1895	2707
939	2412	2569	471	1044	2217	821	1672	2037	661	1276	1930	4294	10155	2365
522	1208	2314	289	589	2038	296	575	1943	443	790	1783	2306	4969	2155
611	1136	1859	294	550	1871	351	615	1752	489	779	1593	2758	5030	1824
440	788	1791	206	370	1796	226	369	1633	241	373	1548	1870	3381	1808
2665	5913	2219	1324	2745	2073	1786	3471	1943	2002	3640	1818	11928	25430	2132
218	655	3005	87	259	2977	131	373	2847	192	557	2901	943	3092	3279
992	2615	2636	439	1061	2417	506	1156	2285	899	1758	1956	4317	10994	2547
387	937	2421	183	414	2262	166	287	1729	217	421	1540	1596	3696	2316
593	1148	1936	264	492	1864	313	552	1764	440	804	1827	2403	4598	1913
353	633	1793	129	282	2186	180	310	1722	187	316	1690	1399	2618	1871
2543	5988	2355	1102	2508	2276	1296	2678	2066	1935	3856	1993	10658	24998	2345
231	710	3074	107	345	3224	137	416	3036	180	519	2883	962	3095	3217
871	2218	2546	356	855	2402	422	998	2365	629	1390	2210	3455	9034	2615
370	820	2216	168	409	2435	155	308	1987	187	329	1759	1490	3299	2214
151	319	2113	77	157	2039	101	186	1842	110	201	1827	694	1398	2014
210	361	1719	73	136	1863	120	250	2083	107	163	1523	924	1757	1902
1833	4428	2416	781	1902	2435	935	2158	2308	1213	2602	2145	7525	18583	2469
186	572	3075	65	186	2862	95	297	3126	163	439	2693	782	2586	3307
610	1668	2734	264	686	2598	290	642	2214	420	894	2129	2548	6788	2664
228	538	2360	96	225	2344	123	229	1862	137	253	1847	998	2237	2241
535	1100	2056	232	459	1978	299	512	1712	344	543	1578	2109	4080	1935
135	270	2000	53	97	1830	77	142	1844	68	112	1647	558	1068	1914
1694	4148	2449	710	1653	2328	884	1822	2061	1132	2241	1980	6995	16759	2396
120	403	3358	52	178	3423	72	200	2778	67	175	2612	547	1866	3411
318	891	2802	152	434	2855	204	509	2495	197	523	2655	1473	4177	2836
95	271	2853	42	86	2048	55	110	2000	69	159	2304	441	1073	2433
171	325	1912	81	198	2444	86	207	2407	95	193	2032	708	1609	2273
63	148	2349	15	23	1533	29	69	2379	42	82	1952	291	716	2460
767	2038	2657	342	919	2687	446	1095	2455	470	1132	2409	3460	9441	2729
101	410	4059	38	114	3000	48	163	3396	38	109	2868	400	1557	3892
208	632	3038	88	268	3045	117	275	2350	120	258	2150	992	2861	2884
64	129	2016	28	61	2179	36	70	1944	36	85	2361	284	685	2412
108	254	2352	34	70	2059	57	86	1509	48	64	1333	374	760	2032
24	42	1750	10	10	1000	22	48	2182	9	19	2111	122	286	2344
505	1467	2905	198	523	2641	280	642	2293	251	535	2131	2172	6149	2831

TABLE A-5

Woman's Education by Woman's Marriage Age

Woman's Present Age	Woman's Education	Under 18			18-20			21-23		
		No. Cases	No. CEB	CEB/1000 Women	No. Cases	No. CEB	CEB/1000 Women	No. Cases	No. CEB	CEB/1000 Women
40-44	6th Grade or less	73	264	3616	258	794	3078	192	520	2708
	7-8th Grade	287	813	2833	1664	4838	2907	1168	2770	2372
	1-3 years High School	117	311	2658	749	1971	2632	681	1546	2270
	4 years High School	47	111	2362	677	1435	2120	896	1849	2064
	1 year College or more	7	17	2429	209	489	2340	587	1246	2123
	Total	531	1516	2855	3557	9527	2678	3524	7931	2251
45-49	6th Grade or less	146	710	4863	352	1342	3812	229	632	2760
	7-8th Grade	322	1332	4137	1451	4385	3022	1254	3074	2451
	1-3 years High School	66	268	4061	483	1408	2915	461	1043	2262
	4 years High School	45	91	2022	589	1358	2306	725	1500	2069
	1 year College or more	5	18	3600	175	375	2143	410	877	2139
	Total	584	2419	4142	3050	8868	2908	3079	7126	2314
50-54	6th Grade or less	126	581	4611	357	1338	3748	218	686	3147
	7-8th Grade	203	740	3645	1044	3112	2981	959	2420	2523
	1-3 years High School	65	253	3892	414	984	2377	466	1189	2552
	4 years High School	13	51	3923	140	344	2457	187	430	2299
	1 year College or more	11	22	2000	118	307	2602	276	557	2018
	Total	418	1647	3940	2073	6085	2935	2106	5282	2508
55-59	6th Grade or less	96	491	5115	270	998	3696	181	548	3028
	7-8th Grade	198	832	4202	805	2612	3245	692	1815	2623
	1-3 years High School	32	107	3344	266	751	2823	309	744	2408
	4 years High School	41	125	3049	448	1034	2308	670	1405	2097
	1 year College or more	0	0	-	69	146	2116	138	340	2464
	Total	367	1555	3127	1858	5541	2982	1990	4852	2438
60-64	6th Grade or less	67	322	4806	225	867	3853	118	345	2924
	7-8th Grade	112	471	4205	518	1698	3278	462	1216	2632
	1-3 years High School	27	112	4148	132	318	2409	124	307	2476
	4 years High School	19	56	2947	194	466	2402	234	509	2175
	1 year College or more	4	4	1000	41	117	2854	101	260	2574
	Total	229	965	4214	1110	3466	3122	1039	2637	2538
65-69	6th Grade or less	64	382	5969	118	514	4356	98	382	3898
	7-8th Grade	83	394	4747	371	1218	3283	261	731	2801
	1-3 years High School	7	18	2571	102	257	2520	65	165	2538
	4 years High School	6	9	1500	85	174	2047	98	287	2929
	1 year College or more	0	0	-	35	98	2800	26	83	3192
	Total	160	803	5019	711	2261	3180	548	1648	3007

(CEB= Children Ever Born)

TABLE A-5

													Woman's Marriage Age		
24–26			27–29			30–35			36 and over			Total		
No. Cases	No. CEB	CEB/1000 Women	No. Cases	No. CEB	CEB/1000 Women	No. Cases	No. CEB	CEB/1000 Women	No. Cases	No. CEB	CEB/1000 Women	No. Cases	No. CEB	CEB/1000 Women
86	145	1686	24	40	1667	34	30	882	10	11	1100	677	1804	2665
551	960	1742	245	313	1278	179	136	760	62	10	161	4156	9840	2368
399	692	1734	140	170	1214	117	128	1094	27	9	333	2230	4827	2165
618	1041	1684	211	302	1431	166	120	723	57	12	211	2672	4870	1823
553	944	1707	256	397	1551	162	188	1160	42	4	95	1816	3285	1809
2207	3782	1714	876	1222	1395	658	602	915	198	46	232	11551	24626	2132
105	225	2143	48	72	1500	33	42	1273	9	0	0	922	3023	3279
625	1254	2006	281	495	1762	191	192	1005	70	9	129	4194	10741	2561
322	589	1829	122	187	1533	67	85	1269	34	15	441	1555	3595	2312
550	994	1807	204	302	1480	175	185	1057	38	14	368	2326	4444	1911
421	862	2048	167	267	1599	129	133	1031	45	12	267	1352	2544	1882
2023	3924	1940	822	1323	1609	595	637	1071	196	50	255	10349	24347	2353
134	304	2269	38	50	1316	50	65	1300	8	1	125	931	3025	3249
584	1334	2284	326	935	2868	172	230	1337	66	27	409	3354	8798	2623
241	448	1859	110	185	1682	124	115	927	18	1	56	1438	3175	2208
171	338	1977	69	123	1783	51	44	863	29	5	172	660	1335	2023
225	459	2040	110	224	2036	191	106	1050	43	9	209	884	1684	1905
1355	2883	2128	653	1517	2323	498	560	1124	164	43	262	7267	18017	2479
115	308	2678	29	65	2241	27	56	2074	44	65	1477	762	2531	3322
425	872	2052	150	242	1613	139	156	1122	47	7	149	2456	6536	2661
200	400	2000	69	105	1522	52	55	1058	23	5	217	951	2167	2279
474	890	1878	196	303	1546	149	178	1195	74	41	554	2052	3976	1938
170	300	1765	69	160	2319	57	74	1298	35	5	143	538	1025	1905
1384	2770	2001	513	875	1706	424	519	1224	223	123	552	6759	16235	2402
91	219	2407	30	60	2000	14	33	2357	0	0	–	545	1846	3387
264	560	2121	80	149	1862	37	83	2243	0	0	–	1473	4177	2836
108	269	2491	42	63	1500	10	20	2000	0	0	–	443	1089	2458
183	390	2131	59	124	2102	29	64	2207	0	0	–	718	1609	2241
95	217	2284	40	91	2275	10	27	2700	0	0	–	291	716	2460
741	1655	2233	251	487	1940	100	227	2270	0	0	–	3470	9437	2720
55	186	3382	13	12	923	15	4	267	14	8	571	377	1488	3947
129	381	2953	23	30	1304	35	20	571	46	16	348	948	2790	2943
36	99	2750	9	11	1222	20	18	900	19	11	579	258	579	2244
70	163	2329	25	57	2280	30	38	1267	33	3	91	347	731	2107
34	83	2441	3	6	2000	6	1	167	13	13	1000	117	284	2427
324	912	2815	73	116	1589	106	81	764	125	51	408	2047	5872	2869

TABLE A-6

Husband's Wages by Husband's Education

Woman's Present Age	Husband's Wages	6th Grade or less			7-8th Grade		
		No. Cases	No. CEB	CEB/1000 Women	No. Cases	No. CEB	CEB/1000 Women
40-44	$1-$999	301	1062	3528	959	2554	2663
	$1000-$1499	232	625	2694	1018	2297	2256
	$1500-$1999	155	441	2845	925	2181	2358
	$2000-$2999	86	197	2291	827	1737	2100
	$3000-$3999	16	54	3375	130	280	2154
	$4000-$4999	4	8	2000	34	72	2118
	$5000 and over	3	2	667	47	93	1979
	Total	797	2389	2977	3940	9214	2339
45-49	$1-$999	395	1375	3481	949	2597	2737
	$1000-$1499	233	630	2704	879	2180	2480
	$1500-$1999	196	607	3097	767	1940	2529
	$2000-$2999	133	409	3075	686	1457	2124
	$3000-$3999	17	36	2118	142	283	1993
	$4000-$4999	2	4	2000	31	80	2581
	$5000 and over	3	0	0	54	107	1981
	Total	979	3061	3127	3508	8644	2464
50-54	$1-$999	382	1458	3817	763	2341	3068
	$1000-$1499	185	600	3243	613	1486	2424
	$1500-$1999	151	424	3808	525	1296	2469
	$2000-$2999	82	254	3098	448	959	2141
	$3000-$3999	16	50	3125	121	240	1983
	$4000-$4999	2	4	2000	21	22	1048
	$5000 and over	4	10	2500	51	111	2176
	Total	822	2800	3406	2542	6455	2539
55-59	$1-$999	332	1249	3762	650	1866	2871
	$1000-$1499	174	487	2799	500	1371	2742
	$1500-$1999	103	274	2660	400	879	2197
	$2000-$2999	93	234	2516	331	710	2145
	$3000-$3999	16	39	2437	114	266	2333
	$4000-$4999	0	0	-	25	42	1680
	$5000 and over	3	6	2000	24	37	1542
	Total	721	2289	3175	2044	5171	2529
60-64	$1-$999	149	388	3275	323	1056	3269
	$1000-$1499	114	345	3026	213	607	2850
	$1500-$1999	37	174	4703	113	323	2858
	$2000-$2999	22	45	2045	113	253	2239
	$3000-$3999	4	15	3750	40	108	2700
	$4000-$4999	0	0	-	3	2	667
	$5000 and over	1	3	3000	18	44	2444
	Total	327	1070	3272	823	2393	2908
65-69	$1-$999	77	253	3286	182	534	2918
	$1000-$1499	38	93	2447	104	253	2433
	$1500-$1999	17	48	2824	63	138	2190
	$2000-$2999	9	20	2222	54	82	1519
	$3000-$3999	4	10	2500	21	39	1857
	$4000-$4999	0	0	-	9	4	444
	$5000 and over	2	8	4000	10	15	1500
	Total	147	432	2939	443	1065	2404

(CEB = Children Ever Born)

TABLE A-6

Husband's Education											
1-3 years High School			4 years High School			1 year College or more			Total		
No. Cases	No. CEB	CEB/1000 Women	No. Cases	No. CEB	CEB/1000 Women	No. Cases	No. CEB	CEB/1000 Women	No. Cases	No. CEB	CEB/1000 Women
244	524	2148	166	302	1819	78	173	2218	1748	4615	2640
352	689	1957	224	382	1705	121	215	1777	1947	4208	2161
432	830	1921	356	723	2031	221	375	1697	2089	4550	2178
474	964	2034	453	810	1788	441	827	1875	2281	4535	1988
126	276	2190	169	309	1828	240	431	1796	681	1350	1982
27	50	1852	59	132	2237	134	270	2015	258	532	2062
43	79	1837	119	206	1731	294	546	1857	506	926	1830
1698	3412	2009	1546	2864	1853	1529	2837	1855	9510	20716	2178
249	615	2470	169	352	2083	101	180	1782	1863	5119	2748
270	638	2363	235	444	1889	209	447	2139	1826	4339	2376
298	674	2262	203	364	1793	157	292	1860	1621	3877	2392
345	710	2058	362	656	1812	281	562	2000	1807	3794	2100
111	216	1946	142	221	1556	205	421	2054	617	1177	1908
20	39	1950	35	80	2286	93	204	2194	181	407	2249
42	105	2500	94	168	1787	236	455	1928	429	835	1946
1335	2997	2245	1240	2265	1843	1282	2561	1998	8344	19548	2343
183	464	2536	78	133	1705	57	113	1982	1463	4509	3082
142	345	2430	78	186	2385	77	153	1987	1095	2770	2530
133	271	2038	85	128	1506	71	159	2239	965	2278	2361
148	307	2074	150	311	2073	17	49	2882	845	1880	2225
71	163	2296	50	78	1560	79	108	1367	337	639	1896
18	36	2000	20	49	2450	45	91	2022	106	202	1906
32	60	1875	73	125	1712	170	358	2106	330	664	2012
727	1646	2264	534	1010	1891	516	1031	1998	5141	12942	2517
175	485	2771	113	233	2062	71	169	2380	1341	4002	2984
145	288	1986	143	254	1776	62	130	2097	1024	2530	2471
131	257	1962	137	276	2015	76	168	2211	847	1854	2189
157	309	1968	233	467	2004	173	282	1630	987	2002	2028
62	126	2032	83	200	2410	84	157	1869	359	788	2195
21	42	2000	30	41	1367	52	103	1981	128	228	1781
22	52	2364	50	88	1760	112	207	1848	211	390	1848
713	1559	2187	789	1559	1976	630	1216	1930	4897	11794	2408
67	214	3194	54	110	2037	20	42	2100	613	1910	3116
44	103	2341	17	39	2294	43	98	2279	431	1192	2766
22	50	2273	31	68	2194	49	127	2592	252	742	2944
47	116	2468	46	101	2196	51	100	1961	279	615	2204
17	36	2118	10	19	1900	22	52	2364	93	230	2473
2	2	1000	9	26	2889	13	35	2692	27	65	2407
5	11	2200	22	55	2500	28	80	2857	74	193	2608
204	532	2608	189	418	2212	226	534	2372	1769	4947	2796
35	52	1486	29	52	1793	21	50	2381	344	941	2735
17	21	1235	17	39	2294	23	56	2435	199	462	2322
26	53	2038	22	19	864	17	28	1647	145	286	1972
17	27	1588	28	51	1821	15	36	2400	123	216	1756
10	18	1800	14	22	1571	11	11	1000	60	100	1667
3	8	2667	6	7	1167	2	2	1000	20	21	1050
4	9	2250	15	22	1467	14	11	786	45	65	1444
112	188	1679	131	212	1618	103	194	1883	936	2091	2234

TABLE A-7

Husband's Education by Husband's Occupation

Woman's Present Age	Husband's Education	Professional			Proprietors			Clerical and Sales		
		No. Cases	No. CEB	CEB/1000 Women	No. Cases	No. CEB	CEB/1000 Women	No. Cases	No. CEB	CEB/1000 Women
40-44	6th Grade or less	2	7	3500	74	176	2378	46	90	1957
	7-8th Grade	79	117	1481	544	1098	2018	645	1396	2164
	1-3 years High School	77	145	1883	401	763	1903	486	916	1885
	4 years High School	143	273	1909	597	1082	1812	618	1094	1770
	1 year College or more	833	1510	1813	584	1077	1844	434	716	1650
	Total	1134	2052	1810	2200	4196	1907	2229	4212	1890
45-49	6th Grade or less	13	36	2769	77	225	2922	78	187	2397
	7-8th Grade	85	150	1765	602	1198	1990	661	1350	2042
	1-3 years High School	43	91	2116	327	663	2028	312	707	2266
	4 years High School	99	196	1980	419	711	1697	514	893	1737
	1 year College or more	735	1584	2155	439	772	1759	336	620	1845
	Total	975	2057	2110	1864	3569	1915	1901	3757	1976
50-54	6th Grade or less	6	18	3000	92	257	2793	62	171	2758
	7-8th Grade	47	96	2043	443	880	1986	632	1339	2119
	1-3 years High School	66	124	1879	256	540	2109	240	471	1962
	4 years High School	43	94	2186	254	459	1607	270	490	1815
	1 year College or more	420	884	2105	276	506	1833	176	353	2006
	Total	582	1216	2089	1321	2642	2000	1380	2824	2046
55-59	6th Grade or less	12	35	2917	75	203	2707	48	89	1854
	7-8th Grade	50	93	1860	386	859	2225	340	689	2026
	1-3 years High School	34	69	2029	188	415	2207	206	408	1981
	4 years High School	78	134	1718	278	490	1763	352	619	1759
	1 year College or more	402	782	1945	235	405	1723	170	360	2118
	Total	576	1113	1932	1162	2372	2041	1116	2165	1940
60-64	6th Grade or less	3	9	3000	49	169	3449	24	51	2125
	7-8th Grade	37	64	1730	172	415	2413	169	445	2633
	1-3 years High School	14	37	2643	82	170	2073	90	187	2078
	4 years High School	16	42	2625	85	204	2400	72	152	2111
	1 year College or more	155	352	2271	91	209	2297	88	201	2284
	Total	225	504	2240	479	1167	2436	443	1036	2339
65-69	6th Grade or less	6	18	3000	16	55	3437	11	30	2727
	7-8th Grade	11	16	1455	109	211	1936	100	179	1790
	1-3 years High School	4	10	2500	35	66	1886	42	74	1762
	4 years High School	26	47	1808	57	94	1649	56	101	1804
	1 year College or more	74	172	2324	51	80	1569	32	68	2125
	Total	121	263	2174	268	506	1888	241	452	1876

(CEB = Children Ever Born)

TABLE A-7

Husband's Occupation

Skilled			Operatives			Service Workers			Laborers			Total		
No. Cases	No. CEB	CEB/1000 Women	No. Cases	No. CEB	CEB/1000 Women	No. Cases	No. CEB	CEB/1000 Women	No. Cases	No. CEB	CEB/1000 Women	No. Cases	No. CEB	CEB/1000 Women
247	763	3089	272	762	2801	71	161	2268	178	651	3657	890	2610	2933
1417	3202	2260	1102	2594	2354	343	790	2303	411	1116	2715	4541	10313	2271
553	1193	2157	293	621	2119	104	232	2231	85	189	2224	1999	4059	2031
320	64?	2003	161	298	1851	66	102	1545	42	73	1738	1947	3563	1830
106	238	2245	55	105	1909	16	56	3500	15	31	2067	2043	3733	1627
2643	6037	2284	1883	4380	2326	600	1341	2235	731	2060	2818	11420	24278	2126
337	1046	3104	315	932	2959	90	235	2611	239	960	4017	1149	3621	3151
1449	3531	2437	951	2382	2505	311	796	2559	731	2197	3005	4790	11604	2423
305	725	2377	145	423	2917	63	130	2063	44	137	3114	1239	2876	2321
240	466	1942	124	241	1944	54	85	1574	33	87	2636	1483	2679	1806
80	154	1925	33	83	2515	29	53	1828	9	30	3333	1661	3296	1964
2411	5922	2456	1568	4061	2590	547	1299	2375	1056	3411	3230	10322	24076	2332
259	817	3154	235	779	3315	72	255	3542	189	671	3550	915	2968	3244
716	1865	2605	602	1545	2566	232	665	2866	294	1041	3541	2966	7431	2505
290	682	2352	133	367	2759	56	155	2768	50	151	3020	1091	2490	2282
128	262	2047	35	84	2400	25	43	1720	20	48	2400	775	1480	1910
51	123	2412	25	33	1320	16	35	2187	11	32	2909	975	1966	2016
1444	3749	2596	1030	2808	2726	401	1153	2875	564	1943	3445	6722	16335	2430
245	681	2780	151	511	3384	106	271	2557	197	830	4213	834	2620	3141
707	1810	2560	425	1054	2480	216	519	2403	281	918	3267	2405	5942	2470
204	480	2353	96	204	2125	43	76	1767	38	144	3789	809	1796	2220
156	325	2083	68	171	2515	33	59	1788	23	44	1913	988	1842	1864
65	98	1508	20	35	1750	17	50	2941	5	10	2000	914	1740	1904
1377	3394	2465	760	1975	2599	415	975	2349	544	1946	3577	5950	13940	2343
100	309	3090	66	210	3182	62	227	3661	81	268	3309	385	1243	3229
287	776	2704	142	414	2915	113	309	2735	131	491	3748	1051	2914	2773
60	155	2583	15	57	3800	27	61	2259	7	31	4429	295	698	2366
33	83	2515	4	4	1000	15	39	2600	12	26	2167	237	550	2321
23	62	2696	10	33	3300	7	16	2286	1	1	1000	375	874	2331
503	1385	2753	237	718	3030	224	652	2911	232	817	3522	2343	6279	2680
61	221	3623	31	79	2548	29	92	3172	46	158	3435	200	653	3265
150	379	2527	79	180	2278	53	151	2849	66	195	2955	568	1311	2308
25	47	1880	16	27	1687	10	16	1600	10	12	1200	142	252	1775
20	24	1200	4	7	1750	14	31	2214	5	13	2600	182	317	1742
14	18	1286	9	31	3444	0	0	-	2	0	0	182	369	2027
270	689	2552	139	324	2331	106	290	2736	129	378	2930	1274	2902	2278

TABLE A-8

Husband's Education by Size of Community

Woman's Present Age	Husband's Education	2,500-5,000			5,000-10,000			10,000-25,000		
		No. Cases	No. CEB	CEB/1000 Women	No. Cases	No. CEB	CEB/1000 Women	No. Cases	No. CEB	CEB/1000 Women
40-44	6th Grade or less	66	188	2848	96	372	3875	162	495	3056
	7-8th Grade	385	961	2496	484	1327	2742	777	1867	2405
	1-3 years High School	183	391	2137	201	438	2179	308	692	2247
	4 years High School	138	251	1819	236	475	2013	306	583	1905
	1 year College or more	173	353	2040	262	545	2080	342	669	1956
	Total	945	2144	2269	1279	3157	2468	1895	4308	2273
45-49	6th Grade or less	128	502	3922	142	555	3908	219	730	3333
	7-8th Grade	398	1219	3063	574	1601	2789	724	1974	2727
	1-3 years High School	124	325	2621	151	336	2225	185	426	2303
	4 years High School	109	226	2073	156	305	1955	234	393	1679
	1 year College or more	132	286	2167	208	445	2139	274	544	1985
	Total	891	2558	2871	1231	3242	2634	1636	4067	2486
50-54	6th Grade or less	89	334	3753	147	464	3156	141	567	4021
	7-8th Grade	296	854	2885	379	1199	3164	517	1408	2723
	1-3 years High School	85	218	2565	161	395	2453	191	468	2450
	4 years High School	77	155	2013	88	148	1682	137	250	1825
	1 year College or more	89	228	2562	168	353	2101	161	376	2335
	Total	636	1789	2813	943	2559	2714	1147	3069	2677
55-59	6th Grade or less	111	456	4108	124	494	3984	188	628	3340
	7-8th Grade	285	817	2867	341	1008	2956	476	1207	2536
	1-3 years High School	81	211	2605	135	310	2296	123	324	2634
	4 years High School	79	178	2253	104	238	2288	178	413	2320
	1 year College or more	75	142	1893	123	262	2130	155	303	1955
	Total	631	1804	2859	827	2312	2796	1120	2875	2567
60-64	6th Grade or less	81	336	4148	90	328	3644	114	420	3684
	7-8th Grade	180	566	3144	196	599	3056	255	707	2773
	1-3 years High School	47	127	2702	57	137	2404	62	172	2774
	4 years High School	32	72	2250	28	103	2679	60	163	2717
	1 year College or more	55	145	2636	70	169	2414	69	139	2014
	Total	395	1246	3152	441	1336	3029	560	1601	2859
65-69	6th Grade or less	57	261	4579	68	305	4485	82	276	3366
	7-8th Grade	152	472	3105	204	578	2833	163	457	2804
	1-3 years High School	17	48	2824	12	24	2000	36	84	2333
	4 years High School	25	48	1920	24	60	2500	29	60	2069
	1 year College or more	21	75	3571	31	71	2290	46	108	2348
	Total	272	904	3324	339	1038	3062	356	985	2767

(CEB = Children Ever Born)

TABLE A-8

25,000-100,000			100,000-250,000			250,000-500,000			Over 500,000			Total		
No. Cases	No. CEB	CEB/1000 Women	No. Cases	No. CEB	CEB/1000 Women	No. Cases	No. CEB	CEB/1000 Women	No. Cases	No. CEB	CEB/1000 Women	No. Cases	No. CEB	CEB/1000 Women
216	677	3134	79	237	3000	141	365	2589	187	452	2417	947	2786	2942
1055	2558	2425	510	1132	2220	525	1104	2103	1009	1926	1909	4745	10877	2292
458	956	2087	279	555	1989	282	529	1876	377	664	1761	2088	4225	2023
430	832	1935	226	403	1783	277	479	1729	378	607	1606	1991	3630	1823
851	1559	1832	231	436	1887	256	428	1672	340	534	1571	2455	4524	1843
3010	6582	2187	1325	2763	2085	1481	2905	1962	2291	4183	1826	12226	26042	2130
318	1009	3173	119	364	3059	142	399	2810	227	577	2542	1295	4136	3194
1100	2533	2303	498	1174	2357	541	1178	2177	913	1838	2013	4748	11517	2426
318	856	2692	132	304	2303	156	318	2038	236	480	2034	1302	3045	2339
375	714	1904	194	344	1773	222	352	1586	263	437	1662	1553	2771	1784
431	881	2044	162	347	2142	228	406	1781	291	523	1797	1726	3432	1988
2542	5993	2358	1105	2533	2292	1289	2653	2058	1930	3855	1997	10624	24901	2344
271	859	3170	120	371	3092	141	394	2794	177	511	2887	1086	3500	3223
810	2032	2509	348	829	2382	383	891	2326	590	1224	2075	3323	8437	2539
302	704	2331	115	306	2661	145	298	2055	158	334	2114	1157	2723	2354
177	326	1842	99	220	2222	131	260	1985	131	226	1725	840	1585	1887
262	441	1683	90	169	1878	140	307	2193	146	266	1822	1056	2140	2027
1822	4362	2394	772	1895	2455	940	2150	2287	1202	2561	2131	7462	18385	2464
264	782	2962	96	228	2375	115	338	2939	177	507	2864	1075	3433	3193
668	1813	2714	293	728	2485	333	705	2117	474	965	2036	2870	7243	2524
212	506	2387	112	238	2125	132	243	1841	117	192	1641	912	2024	2219
331	799	2414	133	330	2481	177	394	2226	208	353	1697	1210	2705	2236
233	466	2000	106	202	1906	145	247	1703	148	253	1709	985	1875	1904
1708	4366	2556	740	1726	2332	902	1927	2136	1124	2270	2020	7052	17280	2450
127	463	3646	75	245	3267	84	256	3048	83	196	2361	654	2244	3431
315	907	2879	151	440	2914	182	444	2440	177	531	3000	1456	4194	2880
73	159	2178	38	105	2763	64	161	2516	52	98	1885	393	959	2440
68	163	2397	31	57	1839	50	100	2000	59	114	1932	328	772	2354
103	279	2709	32	69	2156	50	118	2360	77	163	2117	456	1082	2373
686	1971	2873	327	916	2801	430	1079	2509	448	1102	2460	3287	9251	2814
112	403	3598	46	139	3022	55	170	3091	38	74	1947	458	1628	3555
242	689	2847	99	260	2626	121	261	2157	119	269	2261	1100	2986	2715
57	87	1526	27	52	1926	32	59	1844	27	81	3000	208	435	2091
66	124	1879	25	48	1920	49	84	1714	44	45	1023	262	469	1791
87	164	1885	19	31	1632	44	88	2000	40	73	1825	288	610	2118
564	1467	2601	216	530	2454	301	662	2199	268	542	2022	2316	6128	2646

TABLE A-9

Woman's Marriage Age by Husband's Education

Woman's Present Age	Woman's Marriage Age	6th Grade or less			7-8th Grade		
		No. Cases	No. CEB	CEB/1000 Women	No. Cases	No. CEB	CEB/1000 Women
40-44	Under 18	96	328	3417	275	773	2811
	18-20	398	1386	3482			
	21-23	220	638	2900	1348	3266	2423
	24-26	106	232	2128	706	1208	1711
	27-29	33	47	1424	254	350	1378
	30-35	45	46	1022	242	214	884
	36 and over	12	3	250	82	23	280
	Total	910	2680	2945	2907	5834	2007
45-49	Under 18	152	719	4730	306	1311	4284
	18-20	483	1815	3758	1435	4169	2905
	21-23	329	906	2754	1233	3018	2448
	24-26	140	326	2329	617	1294	2097
	27-29	74	164	2216	309	531	1718
	30-35	60	69	1150	199	221	1111
	36 and over	20	10	500	88	11	125
	Total	1258	4009	3187	4187	10555	2521
50-54	Under 18	133	622	4677	248	990	3992
	18-20	413	1506	3646	1088	3350	3079
	21-23	268	860	3209	960	2456	2558
	24-26	136	327	2404	564	1177	2087
	27-29	45	95	2111	219	361	1648
	30-35	60	81	1350	187	238	1273
	36 and over	14	2	143	79	32	405
	Total	1069	3493	3268	3345	8604	2572
55-59	Under 18	127	662	5213	168	662	3940
	18-20	316	1164	3684	860	2668	3102
	21-23	269	789	2933	822	2113	2571
	24-26	182	488	2681	494	1020	2065
	27-29	48	96	2000	197	323	1640
	30-35	51	112	2196	170	224	1318
	36 and over	32	16	500	66	15	227
	Total	1025	3327	3246	2777	7025	2530
60-64	Under 18	80	361	4512	98	428	4367
	18-20	265	1033	3898	531	1645	3098
	21-23	182	494	2714	442	1166	2638
	24-26	102	236	2314	294	688	2340
	27-29	32	79	2469	116	225	1940
	30-35	17	40	2353	33	75	2273
	36 and over	0	0	-	0	0	-
	Total	678	2243	3308	1514	4227	2792
65-69	Under 18	55	341	6200	84	388	4619
	18-20	140	583	4164	362	1140	3149
	21-23	117	420	3590	278	830	2986
	24-26	56	174	3107	133	394	2962
	27-29	10	10	1000	24	36	1500
	30-35	13	8	615	46	41	891
	36 and over	23	6	261	53	19	355
	Total	414	1542	3725	980	2848	2906

(CEB = Children Ever Born)

TABLE A-9

Husband's Education											
1-3 years High School			4 years High School			1 yr, College or more			Total		
No. Cases	No. CEB	CEB/1000 Women	No. Cases	No. CEB	CEB/1000 Women	No. Cases	No. CEB	CEB/1000 Women	No. Cases	No. CEB	CEB/1000 Women
83	238	2867	39	78	2000	33	87	2636	526	1504	2859
619	1545	2496	508	1160	2283	336	769	2289	1861	4860	2611
644	1394	2099	629	1282	2038	654	1331	2035	3495	7911	2264
388	681	1755	414	664	1604	589	997	1693	2203	3782	1717
152	190	1250	196	264	1347	237	369	1557	872	1220	1399
98	70	714	120	117	975	151	155	1026	656	602	918
'28	8	286	30	4	133	51	12	235	203	50	246
2012	4126	2051	1936	3569	1843	2051	3720	1814	9816	19929	2030
60	218	3633	47	124	2638	19	57	3000	584	2429	4159
437	1287	2945	378	858	2270	306	711	2324	3039	8840	2909
538	1216	2260	460	850	1848	501	1097	2190	3061	7087	2315
316	544	1722	351	599	1707	496	1021	2058	1920	3784	1971
135	194	1437	136	177	1301	170	258	1518	824	1324	1607
69	67	971	126	111	881	133	159	1195	587	627	1068
36	16	444	19	7	368	40	13	325	203	57	281
1591	3542	2226	1517	2726	1797	1665	3316	1992	10218	24148	2363
41	150	3659	23	83	3609	18	49	2722	463	1894	4091
278	729	2622	188	421	2239	173	426	2462	2140	6432	3006
301	772	2565	242	485	2004	314	674	2146	2085	5247	2517
212	383	1807	179	344	1922	255	559	2192	1346	2790	2073
81	121	1512	85	149	1753	122	226	1852	551	952	1728
80	61	762	64	55	859	91	110	1209	482	545	1130
19	11	579	34	1	29	36	8	222	182	54	297
1011	2227	2203	815	1538	1887	1009	2052	2034	7249	17914	2471
36	160	4444	24	75	3125	17	51	3000	372	1610	4328
241	699	2900	241	511	2120	179	422	2358	1837	5464	2974
253	591	2336	323	657	2034	300	635	2117	1967	4785	2433
199	330	1658	257	464	1805	249	460	1847	1381	2762	2000
67	122	1821	108	179	1657	94	162	1723	514	882	1716
54	50	926	80	93	1162	79	96	1215	434	575	1325
31	12	387	33	25	758	38	12	316	200	80	400
881	1964	2229	1066	2004	1880	956	1838	1923	6705	16158	2410
26	103	3962	10	36	3600	14	27	1929	228	955	4189
117	285	2436	96	199	2073	92	232	2522	1101	3394	3083
123	279	2268	132	308	2333	157	379	2414	1036	2626	2535
73	181	2479	116	248	2138	149	290	1946	734	1643	2238
29	44	1517	25	50	2000	52	104	2000	254	502	1976
6	12	2000	15	29	1933	27	67	2481	98	223	2276
0	0	-	0	0	-	0	0	-	0	0	-
374	904	2417	394	870	2208	491	1099	3348	3451	9343	2707
7	13	1857	4	11	2750	10	62	6200	160	815	5094
65	159	2446	51	125	2451	83	245	2952	701	2252	3213
44	129	2932	55	138	2509	53	122	2302	547	1639	2996
28	78	2786	54	117	2074	52	131	2519	323	894	2768
15	20	1333	9	19	2111	16	32	2000	74	117	1581
14	10	714	24	16	667	10	7	700	107	82	766
13	5	385	18	3	167	14	10	714	121	43	355
186	414	2226	215	429	1995	238	609	2559	2033	5842	2874

TABLE A-10

Husband's Wages by Husband's Occupation

Women's Present Age	Husband's Wages	Professional			Proprietors			Clerical and Sales		
		No. Cases	No. CEB	CEB/1000 Women	No. Cases	No. CEB	CEB/1000 Women	No. Cases	No. CEB	CEB/1000 Women
40-44	$1-$999	41	88	2146	51	95	1863	321	676	2106
	$1000-$1499	40	74	1850	87	143	1644	355	660	1859
	$1500-$1999	103	192	1864	198	379	1914	673	1237	1838
	$2000-$2999	258	481	1864	363	699	1926	634	1185	1869
	$3000-$3999	162	281	1735	222	442	1991	167	335	2006
	$4000-$4999	84	225	2679	102	183	1794	56	129	2304
	$5000 and over	102	177	1735	294	554	1884	99	170	1717
	Total	790	1518	1922	1317	2495	1894	2305	4392	1905
45-49	$1-$999	49	110	2245	91	159	1747	264	534	2023
	$1000-$1499	112	262	2339	318	667	2097	279	608	2179
	$1500-$1999	84	156	1857	140	256	1829	308	605	1964
	$2000-$2999	216	471	2181	294	518	1762	581	1158	1993
	$3000-$3999	90	182	2022	185	341	1843	114	188	1649
	$4000-$4999	58	137	2362	71	175	2465	38	76	2000
	$5000 and over	87	196	2253	258	466	1806	63	136	2159
	Total	696	1514	2175	1357	2582	1903	1647	3305	2007
50-54	$1-$999	17	45	2647	41	94	2293	176	362	2057
	$1000-$1499	20	32	1600	52	98	1885	177	349	1972
	$1500-$1999	41	112	2732	64	97	1516	190	379	1995
	$2000-$2999	76	188	2474	194	400	2062	268	500	1866
	$3000-$3999	47	73	1553	104	210	2019	76	116	1526
	$4000-$4999	22	33	1500	46	76	1652	25	60	2400
	$5000 and over	80	196	2450	197	366	1858	47	90	1915
	Total	303	679	2241	698	1341	1921	959	1856	1935
55-59	$1-$999	36	99	2750	26	41	1577	206	462	2243
	$1000-$1499	37	59	1595	74	147	1986	208	466	2240
	$1500-$1999	42	99	2357	68	121	1779	180	336	1867
	$2000-$2999	104	172	1654	191	379	1984	271	496	1830
	$3000-$3999	51	84	1647	148	326	2203	49	103	2102
	$4000-$4999	28	59	2107	51	93	1824	34	55	1618
	$5000 and over	42	107	2548	130	232	1785	32	42	1312
	Total	340	679	1997	688	1339	1946	980	1960	2000
60-64	$1-$999	20	34	1700	30	76	2533	81	190	2346
	$1000-$1499	14	24	1714	26	68	2615	90	222	2467
	$1500-$1999	19	41	2158	32	75	2344	66	144	2182
	$2000-$2999	23	35	1522	66	157	2379	75	176	2347
	$3000-$3999	15	30	2000	35	92	2629	19	51	2684
	$4000-$4999	6	19	3167	17	43	2529	4	7	1750
	$5000 and over	17	40	2353	37	96	2595	16	49	3062
	Total	114	223	1956	243	607	2498	351	839	2390
65-69	$1-$999	5	8	1600	12	34	2833	49	84	1714
	$1000-$1499	7	26	3714	7	13	1857	47	105	2234
	$1500-$1999	7	6	857	9	21	2333	36	51	1417
	$2000-$2999	12	24	2000	29	33	1138	33	57	1727
	$3000-$3999	6	12	2000	28	51	1821	11	14	1273
	$4000-$4999	6	12	2000	9	4	444	4	7	1750
	$5000 and over	10	13	1300	25	30	1200	5	9	1800
	Total	53	101	1906	119	186	1563	185	327	1768

(CEB = Children Ever Born)

TABLE A-10

Husband's Occupation

Skilled			Operatives			Service Workers			Laborers			Total		
No. Cases	No. CEB	CEB/1000 Women	No. Cases	No. CEB	CEB/1000 Women	No. Cases	No. CEB	CEB/1000 Women	No. Cases	No. CEB	CEB/1000 Women	No. Cases	No. CEB	CEB/1000 Women
405	1089	2689	403	1033	2563	141	337	2390	430	1327	3086	1792	4645	2592
526	1141	2169	567	1301	2295	150	404	2693	189	464	2455	1914	4187	2100
629	1433	2278	489	1142	2335	122	237	1943	67	174	2597	2281	4794	2102
622	1373	2207	295	614	2081	85	177	2082	9	5	556	2266	4534	2001
111	224	2018	17	55	3235	4	11	2750	1	0	0	684	1348	1971
18	48	2667	3	6	2000				0	0	-	263	591	2247
9	17	1889	2	2	1000	0	0	-	0	0	-	506	920	1818
2320	5325	2295	1776	4153	2338	502	1166	2323	696	1970	2830	9706	21019	2166
423	1076	2544	408	1152	2824	178	503	2826	400	1410	3525	1813	4944	2727
441	1096	2485	363	952	2623	112	236	2107	126	390	3095	1751	4211	2405
560	1447	2584	390	1023	2623	88	212	2409	44	146	3318	1614	3845	2382
548	1286	2347	216	470	2176	67	108	1612	10	38	3800	1932	4049	2096
82	158	1927	10	23	2300	1	0	-	1	0	0	483	892	1847
12	20	1667	1	1	1000	0	0	-	0	0	-	180	409	2272
11	17	1545	0	0	-	5	13	2600	0	0	-	424	828	1953
2077	5100	2455	1388	3621	2609	451	1072	2377	581	1984	3415	8197	19178	2340
289	893	3090	300	888	2960	149	418	2805	414	1554	3754	1386	4254	3069
306	784	2562	298	825	2768	124	343	2766	106	326	3075	1083	2757	2546
367	890	2425	225	590	2622	59	211	3576	15	25	1667	961	2304	2398
304	777	2556	104	239	2298	31	69	2226	2	5	2500	979	2178	2225
104	222	2135	5	19	3800	4	8	2000	0	0	-	340	648	1906
20	63	3150	2	0	0	0	0	-	0	0	-	115	232	2017
3	1	333	2	10	5000	1	4	4000	0	0	-	330	667	2021
1393	3630	2606	936	2571	2747	368	1053	2861	537	1910	3557	5194	13040	2511
242	702	2901	192	540	2812	160	415	2594	399	1485	3722	1261	3744	2969
256	664	2594	229	549	2397	123	325	2642	92	314	3413	1019	2524	2477
291	635	2182	180	455	2528	64	149	2328	20	54	2700	845	1849	2188
296	689	2328	81	187	2309	17	22	1294	5	3	600	965	1948	2019
93	206	2215	11	43	3909	2	1	500	1	1	1000	355	764	2152
13	15	1154	0	0	-	0	0	-	0	0	-	126	222	1762
2	4	2000	1	0	0	0	0	-	0	0	-	207	385	1860
1193	2915	2443	694	1774	2556	366	912	2491	517	1857	3592	4776	11436	2393
118	363	3076	69	234	3391	107	339	3168	144	500	3472	569	1736	3051
86	206	2395	77	253	3286	64	167	2609	57	208	3649	414	1148	2773
60	229	3817	42	133	3167	15	53	3533	12	47	3917	246	722	2935
91	203	2231	15	31	2067	2	1	500	1	2	2000	273	605	2216
23	62	2696	3	1	333	0	0	-	0	0	-	95	236	2484
1	1	1000	0	0	-	0	0	-	0	0	-	28	70	2500
3	5	1667	0	0	-	0	0	-	0	0	-	73	190	2603
382	1069	2798	206	652	3165	188	560	2979	214	757	3537	1698	4707	2772
58	155	2672	50	126	2520	57	165	2895	72	248	3444	303	820	2706
53	136	2566	35	95	2714	24	55	2292	18	45	2500	191	475	2487
52	138	2654	24	47	1958	5	7	1400	5	1	200	138	271	1964
26	42	1615	10	19	1900	3	4	1333	4	12	3000	117	191	1632
12	20	1667	0	0	-	1	1	1000	0	0	-	58	98	1690
0	0	-	0	0	-	0	0	-	0	0	-	19	23	1210
0	0	-	0	0	-	0	0	-	0	0	-	40	52	1300
201	491	2443	119	287	2412	90	232	2578	99	306	3091	866	1930	2229

TABLE A-11

Size of Community by Husband's Wages

Women's Present Age	Size of Community	$1-$999			$1000-$1499			$1500-$1999		
		No. Cases	No. CEB	CEB/1000 Women	No. Cases	No. CEB	CEB/1000 Women	No. Cases	No. CEB	CEB/1000 Women
40-44	2,500-5,000	176	477	2710	159	350	2201	129	255	1977
	5,000-10,000	244	710	2910	189	467	2471	183	450	2459
	10,000-25,000	314	867	2761	357	827	2317	299	730	2441
	25,000-100,000	373	1041	2791	476	1090	2290	488	1113	2281
	100,000-250,000	151	447	2960	228	493	2162	316	625	1978
	250,000-500,000	228	516	2263	225	494	2196	252	519	2060
	Over 500,000	292	594	2034	323	521	1613	441	786	1782
	Total	1778	4652	2616	1957	4242	2168	2108	4478	2124
45-49	2,500-5,000	245	908	3706	132	367	2780	95	286	3011
	5,000-10,000	273	921	3374	193	517	2679	149	385	2584
	10,000-25,000	364	1040	2857	261	826	2940	221	597	2701
	25,000-100,000	426	1162	2723	452	1092	2416	436	1075	2466
	100,000-250,000	152	470	3092	164	369	2250	216	507	2347
	250,000-500,000	168	371	2203	180	419	2328	191	370	1937
	Over 500,000	281	625	2224	264	555	2102	323	668	2068
	Total	1909	5497	2880	1666	4145	2488	1631	3888	2384
50-54	2,500-5,000	156	524	3359	73	223	3055	61	173	2836
	5,000-10,000	253	840	3320	137	396	2891	85	239	2812
	10,000-25,000	258	876	3395	175	459	2623	136	320	2353
	25,000-100,000	331	1063	3211	281	739	2630	240	574	2392
	100,000-250,000	136	415	3051	130	301	2315	122	273	2238
	250,000-500,000	156	426	2731	133	323	2429	137	316	2307
	Over 500,000	188	446	2372	173	364	2104	192	422	2198
	Total	1478	4590	3105	1102	2805	2545	973	2317	2381
55-59	2,500-5,000	164	555	3384	81	260	3210	50	136	2720
	5,000-10,000	178	610	3427	112	329	2937	90	205	2278
	10,000-25,000	258	782	3031	159	431	2711	108	263	2435
	25,000-100,000	297	922	3104	292	680	2329	182	455	2500
	100,000-250,000	113	328	2903	104	240	2308	121	253	2091
	250,000-500,000	185	451	2433	117	250	2137	111	200	1802
	Over 500,000	168	425	2530	177	393	2220	187	343	1834
	Total	1363	4070	2980	1042	2583	2478	849	1855	2185
60-64	2,500-5,000	75	258	3440	50	165	3300	20	70	3500
	5,000-10,000	94	361	3840	50	135	2700	24	70	2917
	10,000-25,000	118	377	3195	68	189	2779	31	89	2871
	25,000-100,000	117	340	2906	90	261	2900	54	149	2759
	100,000-250,000	59	182	3085	52	137	2635	36	131	3639
	250,000-500,000	82	218	2659	65	158	2431	44	120	2727
	Over 500,000	73	196	2685	58	152	2621	47	115	2447
	Total	618	1932	3126	433	1197	2764	256	744	2906
65-69	2,500-5,000	44	177	4023	8	25	3125	9	25	2778
	5,000-10,000	44	110	2500	25	59	2360	12	42	3500
	10,000-25,000	74	223	3014	30	82	2733	17	51	3000
	25,000-100,000	80	187	2337	65	171	2631	33	24	727
	100,000-250,000	27	60	2222	18	40	2222	17	34	2000
	250,000-500,000	45	109	2422	30	65	2167	31	66	2129
	Over 500,000	33	91	2753	27	56	2074	27	44	1630
	Total	347	957	2753	203	498	2453	146	286	1958

(CEB = Children Ever Born)

TABLE A-11

Husband's Wages

\$2000-\$2999			\$3000-\$3999			\$4000-\$4999			\$5000 and over			Total		
No. Cases	No. CEB	CEB/1000 Women	No. Cases	No. CEB	CEB/1000 Women	No. Cases	No. CEB	CEB/1000 Women	No. Cases	No. CEB	CEB/1000 Women	No. Cases	No. CEB	CEB/1000 Women
147	335	2279	38	85	2237	13	13	1000	22	52	2364	684	1567	2291
185	441	2364	60	131	2183	16	32	2000	71	145	2042	948	2376	2506
300	647	2157	142	240	1690	35	77	2200	80	157	1962	1527	3545	2322
532	1079	2028	159	311	1956	63	130	2063	107	202	1888	2196	4966	2259
273	513	1879	95	172	1811	27	50	1852	31	60	1935	1121	2360	2105
277	269	1693	110	192	1745	38	85	2237	62	121	1952	1192	2396	2010
564	1035	1835	143	314	2196	66	136	2061	91	152	1670	1920	3538	1843
2278	4519	1984	747	1445	1934	258	523	2027	464	889	1916	9590	20748	2164
103	249	2417	19	35	1842	7	14	2000	13	14	1077	614	1673	3050
144	424	2944	53	91	1717	18	40	2222	51	85	1667	881	2463	2796
224	492	2196	80	143	1787	25	54	2160	74	156	2108	1269	3308	2607
436	953	2186	138	283	2051	47	114	2426	120	269	2242	2055	4948	2408
228	458	2009	67	140	2090	17	41	2412	38	80	2105	882	2065	2341
182	359	1973	73	133	1822	25	42	1680	49	71	1449	868	1765	2033
485	929	1915	190	363	1911	42	102	2429	86	162	1884	1671	3404	2036
1602	3864	2144	620	1188	1916	181	407	2249	431	837	1942	8240	19826	2406
72	178	2472	16	22	1375	4	8	2000	10	21	2100	392	1149	2931
91	225	2473	26	56	2154	11	41	3727	26	51	1821	631	1648	2929
129	299	2318	61	134	2197	12	31	2583	51	110	2157	822	2229	2712
254	526	2071	82	135	1646	32	52	1625	106	220	2075	1326	3309	2495
96	267	2781	25	45	1800	16	27	1687	15	27	1800	548	1355	2509
135	273	2022	46	93	2022	19	36	1895	53	126	2377	679	1593	2346
212	429	2024	83	162	1952	14	19	1357	69	116	1681	931	1956	2103
989	2197	2221	339	647	1909	108	214	1981	332	671	2021	5321	13441	2526
64	129	2016	13	34	2615	6	6	1000	13	12	923	391	1132	2895
86	201	2337	35	61	1743	11	31	2818	16	43	2687	528	1480	2803
133	290	2180	62	150	2419	22	48	2182	47	97	2064	789	2061	2612
255	555	2176	102	227	2225	39	68	1744	54	93	1722	1221	3000	2497
120	275	2292	32	95	2969	6	8	1333	27	61	2259	523	1266	2409
129	252	1953	49	92	1878	16	25	1562	23	27	1174	630	1267	2059
203	308	1517	67	127	1896	28	42	1500	31	57	1839	861	1695	1969
990	2010	2030	360	786	2163	128	228	1781	211	390	1848	4943	11925	2413
25	72	2880	2	10	5000	5	15	3000	1	1	1000	178	591	3320
22	34	1545	6	20	3333	3	4	1333	8	32	4000	207	656	3169
39	80	2051	17	41	2412	3	9	3000	7	16	2286	263	801	2830
65	141	2169	22	68	3091	10	21	2100	16	45	2812	374	1025	2741
30	66	2200	8	15	1875	2	1	500	5	15	3000	192	547	2849
45	102	2267	16	31	1937	4	12	3000	14	38	2714	270	679	2515
54	120	2222	24	51	2125	1	8	8000	23	45	1957	280	687	2453
280	615	2196	95	236	2484	28	70	2500	74	192	2595	1784	4986	2795
10	18	1800	2	6	3000	0	0	-	2	4	2000	75	255	3400
7	18	2571	4	2	500	3	2	667	2	2	1000	97	235	2423
19	31	1632	3	2	667	5	8	1600	8	14	1750	156	411	2635
36	45	1250	13	22	1692	5	2	400	16	19	1187	248	470	1695
13	33	2538	4	3	750	0	0	-	2	3	1500	81	173	2136
18	34	1889	13	22	1692	2	1	500	7	8	1143	146	305	2089
21	27	1429	21	43	2048	5	10	2000	7	11	1571	141	282	2000
124	206	1661	60	100	1667	20	23	1150	44	61	1386	944	2131	2257

TABLE A-12

Woman's Marriage Age by Husband's Wages

Woman's Present Age	Woman's Marriage Age	$1-$999			$1000-$1499			$1500-$1999		
		No. Cases	No. CEB	CEB/1000 Women	No. Cases	No. CEB	CEB/1000 Women	No. Cases	No. CEB	CEB/1000 Women
40-44	Under 18	126	448	3556	117	328	2803	93	253	2720
	18-20	699	2242	3207	641	1699	2651	710	1898	2673
	21-23	461	1233	2675	539	1211	2247	581	1329	2267
	24-26	213	379	1779	331	521	1574	376	603	1604
	27-29	77	116	1506	142	197	1387	163	214	1393
	30-35	106	78	736	101	103	1020	109	105	963
	36 and over	37	18	486	26	12	462	27	8	296
	Total	1719	4514	2626	1897	4071	2146	2059	4410	2142
45-49	Under 18	181	820	4530	116	550	4741	91	351	3857
	18-20	653	2154	3299	532	1534	2883	480	1537	3202
	21-23	510	1484	2910	493	1190	2414	470	1002	2132
	24-26	278	622	2237	259	492	1900	308	582	1890
	27-29	111	174	1568	116	196	1690	134	271	2022
	30-35	95	106	1116	82	81	988	83	76	916
	36 and over	33	14	424	21	11	524	31	12	387
	Total	1861	5374	2888	1619	4054	2504	1597	3831	2399
50-54	Under 18	169	835	4941	235	1119	4762	53	191	3604
	18-20	488	1747	3580	364	975	2679	299	888	2970
	21-23	363	1158	3190	316	857	2712	295	672	2278
	24-26	203	474	2335	175	404	2309	168	330	1964
	27-29	89	129	1449	70	129	1843	58	110	1897
	30-35	73	112	1534	71	93	1310	53	79	1491
	36 and over	27	0	0	14	7	500	23	5	217
	Total	1412	4455	3155	1245	3584	2879	949	2275	2397
55-59	Under 18	107	509	4757	62	268	4323	35	141	4029
	18-20	437	1559	3568	285	831	2916	218	573	2628
	21-23	382	1079	2825	275	711	2585	259	594	2293
	24-26	226	558	2469	195	419	2149	175	320	1829
	27-29	73	150	2055	74	130	1757	75	141	1880
	30-35	59	92	1559	69	99	1435	52	47	904
	36 and over	33	17	515	36	17	472	28	27	964
	Total	1317	3964	3010	996	2475	2485	842	1843	2189
60-64	Under 18	52	234	4500	22	74	3364	15	62	4133
	18-20	230	751	3265	171	573	3351	80	301	3762
	21-23	165	475	2879	109	237	2174	85	196	2306
	24-26	106	338	3189	74	161	2446	54	129	2389
	27-29	50	103	2060	38	87	2289	14	35	2500
	30-35	15	31	2067	20	48	2400	8	21	2625
	36 and over	0	0	-	0	0	-	0	0	-
	Total	618	1932	3126	434	1200	2765	256	744	2906
65-69	Under 18	27	128	4741	6	29	4833	5	35	7000
	18-20	111	369	3324	63	187	2968	37	84	2270
	21-23	99	257	2596	64	151	2359	47	92	1957
	24-26	37	107	2892	29	87	3000	19	44	2316
	27-29	9	15	1667	9	5	556	3	4	1333
	30-35	21	10	476	5	7	1400	12	8	667
	36 and over	18	16	889	18	10	556	11	0	0
	Total	322	902	2801	194	476	2454	134	267	1993

(CEB = Children Ever Born)

TABLE A-12

Husband's Wages														
$2000-$2999			$3000-$3999			$4000-$4999			$5000 and over			Total		
No. Cases	No. CEB	CEB/1000 Women	No. Cases	No. CEB	CEB/1000 Women	No. Cases	No. CEB	CEB/1000 Women	No. Cases	No. CEB	CEB/1000 Women	No. Cases	No. CEB	CEB/1000 Women
83	207	2494	23	56	2435	9	16	1778	10	20	2000	461	1328	2881
621	1537	2475	170	426	2506	50	122	2440	81	163	2012	2972	8087	2721
734	1523	2075	238	463	2029	97	207	2134	160	329	2056	2810	6315	2247
463	820	1771	178	300	1685	61	131	2148	114	210	1842	1736	2964	1707
173	241	1393	62	90	1452	19	24	1263	38	61	1605	674	943	1399
227	207	912	52	73	1404	14	20	1429	25	35	1400	634	621	979
59	13	220	15	2	133	3	0	0	10	1	100	177	54	305
2360	4548	1927	738	1430	1938	253	520	2055	438	819	1870	9464	20312	2146
73	194	2658	14	38	2714	1	3	3000	7	19	2714	483	1975	4089
509	1280	2515	124	275	2218	36	70	1944	82	192	2341	2416	7042	2915
529	1157	2187	219	419	1913	49	138	2816	133	289	2173	2403	5679	2363
367	698	1902	132	281	2129	50	128	2560	139	244	1755	1533	3047	1988
134	224	1672	58	80	1379	25	41	1640	37	56	1514	615	1042	1694
114	133	1167	162	186	1148	8	12	1500	17	15	882	561	609	1086
39	5	128	8	4	500	3	2	667	3	2	667	138	50	362
1765	3691	2091	717	1283	1789	172	394	2291	418	817	1955	8149	19444	2386
52	192	3692	9	35	3889	0	0	-	3	4	1333	521	2376	4560
227	652	2872	59	172	2915	26	67	2577	61	134	2197	1524	4635	3041
305	620	2033	92	194	2109	18	38	2111	109	238	2183	1498	3777	2521
203	465	2291	85	136	1600	41	79	1927	81	174	2148	956	2062	2156
67	120	1791	31	42	1355	6	12	2000	44	80	1818	365	622	1704
73	82	1123	34	28	824	13	7	538	19	29	1526	336	430	1280
31	14	452	15	8	533	2	2	1000	5	0	0	117	36	308
958	2145	2239	325	615	1892	106	205	1934	322	659	2047	5317	13938	2621
27	95	3519	11	29	2636	6	24	4000	4	7	1750	252	1073	4258
231	577	2498	78	208	2667	24	65	2708	28	67	2393	1301	3880	2982
319	716	2245	122	284	2328	29	55	1897	56	134	2393	1442	3573	2478
198	384	1939	73	135	1849	33	40	1212	78	139	1782	978	1995	2040
78	115	1474	42	78	1857	14	21	1500	20	24	1200	376	659	1753
79	81	1025	27	44	1630	15	21	1400	14	13	929	315	397	1260
33	13	394	3	0	0	4	0	0	6	0	0	143	74	517
965	1981	2053	356	778	2185	125	226	1808	206	384	1864	4807	11651	2424
13	37	2646	1	9	9000	0	0	-	1	3	3000	104	419	4029
55	127	2309	31	83	2677	7	15	2143	19	66	3474	593	1916	3231
102	212	2078	34	84	2471	6	17	2833	21	51	2429	522	1272	2437
74	179	2419	13	33	2538	11	27	2455	14	34	2429	346	921	2662
23	36	1565	9	15	1667	3	6	2000	14	27	1929	151	309	2046
12	24	2000	7	12	1714	1	5	5000	5	12	2400	68	153	2250
0	0	-	0	0	-	0	0	-	0	0	-	0	0	-
279	615	2204	95	236	2484	28	70	2500	74	193	2608	1784	4990	2797
4	16	4000	1	1	1000	0	0	-	1	2	2000	44	211	4795
15	31	2067	13	27	2077	2	2	1000	7	14	2000	248	714	2879
36	61	1694	18	32	1778	3	2	667	16	23	1437	283	618	2184
27	58	2148	12	24	2000	5	7	1400	7	23	3286	136	350	2574
6	10	1667	4	0	0	2	6	3000	3	2	667	36	42	1167
10	8	800	6	9	1500	4	2	500	8	1	125	66	45	681
25	6	240	2	0	0	2	0	0	3	0	0	79	32	405
123	190	1545	56	93	1661	18	19	1056	45	65	1444	892	2012	2256

TABLE A-13

Size of Community by Husband's Occupation

Woman's Present Age	Size of Community	Professional			Proprietors			Clerical and Sales		
		No. Cases	No. CEB	CEB/1000 Women	No. Cases	No. CEB	CEB/1000 Women	No. Cases	No. CEB	CEB/1000 Women
40-44	2,500-5,000	95	206	2168	209	413	1976	135	312	2311
	5,000-10,000	140	264	1886	261	526	2015	213	430	2091
	10,000-25,000	182	331	1819	415	832	2005	300	574	1913
	25,000-100,000	286	512	1790	474	910	1920	487	997	2047
	100,000-250,000	114	220	1930	221	418	1891	262	509	1943
	250,000-500,000	127	205	1614	264	464	1634	323	601	1861
	Over 500,000	194	326	1680	336	577	1717	516	799	1548
	Total	1138	2064	1614	2200	4140	1882	2236	4222	1888
45-49	2,500-5,000	56	121	2161	216	424	1963	111	283	2550
	5,000-10,000	117	260	2222	220	486	2209	188	415	2207
	10,000-25,000	151	316	2093	289	586	2028	286	626	2189
	25,000-100,000	239	553	2314	444	814	1833	453	891	1967
	100,000-250,000	113	240	2124	172	333	1936	189	370	1958
	250,000-500,000	108	190	1759	207	372	1797	250	456	1824
	Over 500,000	191	381	1996	329	594	1805	426	718	1686
	Total	975	2061	2114	1877	3609	1923	1903	3759	1975
50-54	2,500-5,000	47	110	2340	132	321	2432	71	142	2000
	5,000-10,000	74	142	1919	197	395	2005	109	254	2330
	10,000-25,000	91	210	2308	215	450	2093	171	383	2040
	25,000-100,000	147	281	1912	327	658	2012	273	465	1703
	100,000-250,000	51	115	2255	117	235	2009	127	292	2299
	250,000-500,000	64	130	2031	174	349	2006	183	355	1940
	Over 500,000	80	177	2213	186	356	1914	234	372	1590
	Total	554	1165	2103	1348	2764	2050	1168	2263	1938
55-59	2,500-5,000	64	143	2234	115	270	2348	68	132	1941
	5,000-10,000	74	149	2014	155	340	2194	106	249	2349
	10,000-25,000	77	152	1974	209	424	2029	156	359	2301
	25,000-100,000	135	274	2030	286	630	2203	254	506	1992
	100,000-250,000	61	99	1623	104	216	2077	124	251	2024
	250,000-500,000	79	152	1924	162	245	1512	182	332	1824
	Over 500,000	87	139	1598	139	257	1849	234	360	1538
	Total	577	1108	1920	1170	2382	2036	1124	2189	1948
60-64	2,500-5,000	35	85	2429	76	191	2513	31	82	2645
	5,000-10,000	24	58	2417	56	141	2518	66	152	2303
	10,000-25,000	39	91	2333	91	239	2626	49	123	2510
	25,000-100,000	50	125	2500	88	216	2455	103	260	2524
	100,000-250,000	20	27	1350	45	121	2689	38	89	2342
	250,000-500,000	19	44	2316	64	137	2141	68	148	2176
	Over 500,000	45	86	1911	62	130	2097	87	183	2103
	Total	232	516	2224	482	1175	2438	442	1037	2346
65-69	2,500-5,000	7	27	3857	18	55	3056	12	33	2750
	5,000-10,000	8	22	2750	36	77	2139	33	69	2091
	10,000-25,000	16	25	1563	51	87	1706	38	92	2421
	25,000-100,000	36	76	2111	72	142	1972	59	86	1458
	100,000-250,000	4	8	2000	21	32	1524	24	32	1333
	250,000-500,000	19	36	1895	38	57	1500	37	83	2243
	Over 500,000	29	61	2103	38	70	1842	40	69	1725
	Total	119	255	2143	274	520	1898	243	464	1909

(CEB = Children Ever Born)

TABLE A-13

Husband's Occupation

Skilled			Operatives			Service Workers			Laborers			Total		
No. Cases	No. CEB	CEB/1000 Women	No. Cases	No. CEB	CEB/1000 Women	No. Cases	No. CEB	CEB/1000 Women	No. Cases	No. CEB	CEB/1000 Women	No. Cases	No. CEB	CEB/1000 Women
200	485	2425	124	281	2266	41	123	3000	87	229	2432	891	2049	2300
259	728	2811	189	528	2794	68	187	2750	93	275	2957	1223	2938	2402
395	1001	2534	320	796	2487	92	238	2587	135	406	3007	1839	4178	2272
620	1396	2252	418	1024	2450	106	245	2311	184	572	3109	2575	5656	2197
302	625	2070	260	583	2242	68	180	2647	68	166	2441	1295	2701	2086
319	660	2069	202	458	2267	86	146	1698	84	242	2881	1425	2776	1948
568	1184	2085	382	729	1908	142	239	1683	102	224	2196	2240	4076	1821
2663	6079	2283	1895	4399	2321	603	1358	2252	753	2114	2807	11488	24376	2122
182	581	3192	121	349	2684	50	142	2840	101	468	4634	837	2368	2829
265	682	2574	173	551	3185	65	191	2938	116	395	3405	1144	2980	2605
339	908	2678	245	676	2759	73	177	2425	158	548	3466	1541	3637	2490
606	1511	2493	393	1037	2639	121	288	2360	168	600	3571	2424	5694	2349
284	689	2426	168	414	2464	67	165	2463	60	198	3300	1053	2409	2288
241	525	2178	168	379	2256	54	106	1963	66	189	2864	1094	2217	2027
512	1056	2063	311	687	2209	121	246	2033	92	276	3000	1982	3958	1997
2429	5952	2450	1579	4093	2592	551	1315	2387	761	2674	3513	10075	23463	2329
127	389	3063	84	276	3286	41	121	2951	59	219	3712	561	1578	2813
169	508	3006	156	501	3212	50	143	2660	107	395	3692	862	2338	2712
242	692	2860	196	547	2791	63	144	2266	90	337	3744	1068	2763	2587
422	998	2365	223	577	2587	112	422	3768	160	576	3600	1664	3977	2390
195	496	2544	122	282	2311	43	98	2279	51	188	3686	706	1706	2416
223	559	2507	102	291	2853	60	138	2300	55	178	3236	861	2000	2497
321	768	2393	164	421	2567	76	160	2105	58	127	2190	1119	2381	2128
1699	4410	2596	1047	2895	2765	445	1226	2755	580	2020	3483	6841	16743	2447
91	274	3017	69	219	3174	27	67	2481	106	366	3453	540	1471	2724
156	410	2628	68	210	3088	28	74	2643	98	406	4143	665	1638	2683
218	608	2789	133	367	2759	63	162	2571	100	365	3650	956	2437	2549
358	872	2436	182	466	2560	102	291	2853	139	462	3324	1456	3501	2405
162	404	2494	98	235	2398	34	67	1971	40	161	4025	623	1433	2300
158	376	2380	241	552	2290	71	151	2127	41	135	3293	934	1943	2080
242	480	1983	139	321	2309	96	186	1938	58	158	2724	995	1901	1911
1385	3424	2472	930	2370	2548	421	996	2371	582	2053	3527	6189	14524	2347
34	73	2147	13	28	2154	23	69	3000	39	202	5179	251	730	2908
59	212	3593	33	95	2879	19	64	3368	45	174	3867	302	896	2967
84	222	2643	41	151	3683	45	136	3022	40	135	3375	389	1097	2820
101	280	2772	40	111	2775	61	150	2458	50	171	3420	493	1313	2663
72	212	2944	43	132	3070	18	61	3389	26	80	3077	262	722	2756
86	202	2349	32	85	2656	28	93	3321	16	43	2688	313	752	2403
68	185	2721	38	124	3263	31	82	2645	22	59	2682	353	849	2405
504	1386	2750	240	726	3021	225	655	2911	238	864	3630	2363	6359	2691
24	77	3208	12	34	2833	9	21	2333	24	66	2750	106	313	2953
27	74	2741	9	19	2111	15	56	3733	13	53	4077	141	370	2624
33	97	2939	25	54	2160	17	81	4765	29	80	2759	209	516	2469
74	194	2622	40	103	2575	22	38	1727	40	114	2850	343	753	2195
29	66	2276	17	45	2647	12	27	2250	7	28	4000	114	238	2088
46	105	2283	19	41	2158	12	24	2000	9	22	2444	180	368	2045
37	59	1595	18	34	1889	19	42	2211	7	13	1857	188	348	1851
270	672	2489	140	330	2357	106	289	2726	129	376	2915	1281	2906	2269

TABLE A-14

Woman's Marriage Age by Husband's Occupation

Woman's Present Age	Woman's Marriage Age	Professional			Proprietors			Clerical and Sales		
		No. Cases	No. CEB	CEB/1000 Women	No. Cases	No. CEB	CEB/1000 Women	No. Cases	No. CEB	CEB/1000 Women
40-44	Under 18	7	17	2429	59	132	2237	53	105	1981
	18-20	162	361	2228	548	1217	2221	559	1326	2372
	21-23	389	822	2113	713	1476	2070	687	1407	2048
	24-26	281	483	1719	518	897	1732	485	785	1619
	27-29	142	204	1437	139	194	1396	226	348	1540
	30-35	104	129	1240	122	110	902	122	106	869
	36 and over	31	2	65	39	3	77	30	11	367
	Total	1116	2018	1808	2138	4029	1884	2162	4088	1891
45-49	Under 18	12	45	3750	48	145	3021	52	156	3000
	18-20	176	450	2557	486	1145	2356	433	1090	2517
	21-23	275	641	2331	597	1225	2052	585	1162	1986
	24-26	274	589	2150	377	650	1724	443	855	1930
	27-29	99	154	1556	169	257	1521	169	226	1337
	30-35	85	114	1341	115	105	913	124	130	1048
	36 and over	26	11	423	36	0	0	36	9	250
	Total	947	2004	2116	1328	3527	1929	1842	3628	1970
50-54	Under 18	6	17	2833	41	138	3366	38	140	3684
	18-20	86	220	2558	309	805	2605	267	652	2442
	21-23	164	368	2244	439	919	2093	334	698	2090
	24-26	141	315	2234	294	563	1915	248	430	1734
	27-29	52	108	2077	126	206	1635	119	195	1639
	30-35	58	78	1345	74	72	973	91	89	978
	36 and over	20	6	300	27	2	74	37	11	297
	Total	527	1112	2110	1310	2705	2065	1134	2215	1953
55-59	Under 18	12	43	3583	32	89	2781	26	87	3346
	18-20	96	252	2625	286	662	2315	253	594	2348
	21-23	181	394	2177	363	842	2320	325	705	2169
	24-26	80	134	1675	195	319	1636	184	360	1957
	27-29	69	135	1957	98	162	1653	99	138	1394
	30-35	53	54	1019	64	72	1125	80	90	1125
	36 and over	27	2	74	24	22	917	37	20	541
	Total	518	1014	1958	1062	2168	2041	1004	1994	1986
60-64	Under 18	5	6	1200	23	71	3087	10	34	3400
	18-20	39	91	2333	132	327	2477	129	330	2558
	21-23	75	158	2107	165	381	2309	152	334	2197
	24-26	74	148	2000	149	317	2128	119	241	2025
	27-29	37	82	2216	38	74	1947	46	85	1848
	30-35	17	40	2353	13	28	2154	16	27	1687
	36 and over									
	Total	247	525	2126	520	1198	2304	472	1051	2227
65-69	Under 18	3	3	1000	7	31	4429	1	7	7000
	18-20	20	62	3100	59	128	2169	68	175	2574
	21-23	23	47	2043	75	192	2560	45	121	2689
	24-26	29	73	2517	43	102	2372	38	91	2395
	27-29	7	42	6000	10	5	500	14	16	1143
	30-35	8	2	250	12	3	250	20	22	1100
	36 and over	7	2	286	15	4	267	15	1	67
	Total	97	231	2381	221	465	2104	201	433	2154

(CEB = Children Ever Born)

TABLE A-14

Husband's Occupation

Skilled			Operatives			Service Workers			Laborers			Total		
No. Cases	No. CEB	CEB/1000 Women	No. Cases	No. CEB	CEB/1000 Women	No. Cases	No. CEB	CEB/1000 Women	No. Cases	No. CEB	CEB/1000 Women	No. Cases	No. CEB	CEB/1000 Women
150	391	2607	138	441	3196	33	122	3697	70	232	3314	510	1440	2824
950	2723	2866	702	1915	2728	213	525	2465	290	1052	3628	3424	9119	2663
768	1775	2311	482	1201	2492	163	413	2534	193	481	2492	3395	7575	2231
440	758	1723	266	488	1835	77	134	1740	81	141	1741	2148	3686	1716
146	203	1390	118	136	1153	29	31	1069	40	58	1450	840	1174	1398
99	89	899	97	89	918	47	30	638	35	33	943	626	586	*936
43	10	233	34	9	265	7	1	143	12	13	1083	196	49	250
2596	5949	2292	1837	4279	2329	569	1256	2207	721	2010	2788	11139	23629	2121
142	530	3732	139	629	4525	47	177	3766	89	472	5303	529	2154	4072
819	2460	3004	558	1653	2962	165	496	3006	277	1094	3949	2914	8388	2879
700	1695	2421	418	1010	2416	156	361	2314	204	668	3295	2935	6762	2304
414	787	1901	245	455	1857	81	144	1778	104	285	2740	1938	3765	1943
164	299	1823	90	178	1978	51	79	1549	33	64	1939	775	1257	1622
109	108	991	72	85	1181	28	33	1179	23	30	1304	556	605	1088
33	14	424	19	3	158	11	10	909	11	4	364	172	51	297
2381	5893	2475	1541	4013	2604	539	1300	2412	741	2617	3532	9819	22982	2341
117	480	4103	81	321	3963	41	192	4683	89	469	5270	413	1757	4254
557	1662	2984	371	1156	3116	141	468	3319	199	751	3774	1930	5714	2961
465	1222	2628	286	813	2843	102	273	2676	133	449	3376	1923	4742	2466
278	622	2237	151	372	2464	69	169	2449	74	201	2716	1255	2672	2129
108	176	1630	49	103	2102	31	54	1742	21	31	1476	506	873	1725
101	127	1257	48	62	1292	26	30	1154	35	61	1743	433	519	1198
34	16	471	22	0	0	15	8	533	7	0	0	162	43	265
1660	4305	2593	1008	2827	2806	425	1194	2809	558	1962	3516	6622	16320	2465
66	254	3848	36	155	4306	35	122	3486	69	387	5609	276	1137	4120
376	1175	3125	248	785	3165	139	381	2741	177	722	4079	1575	4571	2902
410	1004	2449	223	608	2726	105	247	2352	139	468	3367	1746	4268	2444
175	370	2114	84	131	1560	44	109	2477	62	189	3048	824	1612	1956
103	169	1641	45	70	1556	25	40	1600	25	83	3320	464	797	1718
75	141	1880	52	80	1538	20	32	1600	28	20	714	372	469	1315
33	17	515	15	2	133	21	5	238	13	4	308	170	72	424
1238	3130	2528	703	1831	2605	389	936	2406	513	1873	3651	5427	12946	2386
42	153	3643	13	69	5308	11	36	3273	25	107	4280	129	476	3690
181	562	3105	82	277	3378	93	301	3237	88	367	4170	744	2255	3031
175	449	2566	58	136	2345	58	156	2638	67	218	3254	750	1834	2445
82	152	1854	68	174	2559	46	126	2739	37	122	3297	575	1280	2226
28	58	2071	22	41	1864	18	36	2000	15	32	2133	204	468	2000
14	23	1648	13	40	3077	2	6	3000	9	20	2222	84	184	2191
522	1397	2676	256	737	2879	228	663	2907	241	866	3593	2486	6437	2589
14	65	4643	4	29	7250	10	40	4000	11	48	4364	50	223	4460
66	232	3515	49	121	2469	42	142	3381	24	71	2958	328	931	2838
71	212	2986	31	89	2871	19	53	2789	35	130	3714	299	844	2823
30	78	2600	14	37	2643	14	31	2214	20	68	3400	188	480	2553
6	5	833	5	6	1200	2	2	1000	13	13	1000	57	89	1561
20	23	1150	4	5	1250	5	3	600	6	3	500	75	61	813
24	5	208	6	4	667	8	8	1000	8	4	500	83	28	337
231	620	2684	113	291	2575	100	279	2790	117	337	2880	1080	2656	2459

TABLE A-15

Woman's Marriage by Size of Community

Woman's Present Age	Woman's Marriage Age	2,500-5,000			5,000-10,000			10,000-25,000		
		No. Cases	No. CEB	CEB/1000 Women	No. Cases	No. CEB	CEB/1000 Women	No. Cases	No. CEB	CEB/1000 Women
40-44	Under 18	45	140	3111	67	212	3164	87	292	3356
	18-20	284	781	2750	387	1174	3034	619	1726	2788
	21-23	300	707	2357	388	1005	2590	546	1258	2304
	24-26	178	329	1848	226	424	1876	364	678	1863
	27-29	53	82	1547	99	169	1707	107	152	1421
	30-35	50	60	1200	80	104	1300	101	105	1040
	36 and over	15	4	267	18	6	333	37	8	216
	Total	925	2103	2274	1265	3094	2446	1861	4219	2267
45-49	Under 18	56	305	5446	95	446	4695	117	535	4573
	18-20	304	1033	3398	400	1215	3037	521	1550	2975
	21-23	238	660	2773	358	892	2492	427	1063	2489
	24-26	155	330	2129	205	422	2059	318	645	2028
	27-29	67	149	2224	95	190	2000	111	140	1261
	30-35	42	39	929	29	31	1069	73	66	904
	36 and over	13	0	0	24	14	583	26	4	154
	Total	875	2516	2875	1206	3210	2662	1593	4003	2513
50-54	Under 18	48	231	4812	60	258	4300	64	350	5469
	18-20	206	664	3223	333	996	2991	352	1182	3358
	21-23	177	523	2955	253	657	2597	313	793	2534
	24-26	88	202	2295	164	416	2537	220	469	2132
	27-29	53	98	1849	61	104	1705	73	137	1877
	30-35	41	35	854	49	92	1878	65	78	1200
	36 and over	13	4	308	14	3	214	32	7	219
	Total	626	1757	2807	934	2526	2704	1119	3016	2695
55-59	Under 18	48	268	5583	61	287	4705	57	210	3684
	18-20	180	594	3300	250	822	3288	325	1055	3246
	21-23	180	506	2811	235	645	2745	316	772	2443
	24-26	126	291	2310	133	258	1940	220	493	2241
	27-29	39	71	1821	55	102	1855	69	93	1348
	30-35	25	38	1520	50	94	1880	63	90	1429
	36 and over	16	3	188	22	5	227	26	8	308
	Total	614	1771	2834	806	2213	2746	1076	2721	2529
60-64	Under 18	43	223	5186	28	100	3571	44	207	4705
	18-20	139	432	3108	164	539	3287	202	596	2950
	21-23	122	365	2992	130	340	2615	177	494	2791
	24-26	59	149	2525	84	247	2940	122	254	2082
	27-29	29	59	2034	37	84	2270	40	101	2525
	30-35	11	32	2909	13	39	3000	9	28	3111
	36 and over									
	Total	403	1260	3127	456	1349	2958	594	1680	2828
65-69	Under 18	29	123	4241	28	110	3929	19	93	4895
	18-20	103	366	3553	146	544	3726	107	407	3804
	21-23	71	250	3521	69	175	2536	99	282	2848
	24-26	25	95	3800	61	199	3262	59	163	2763
	27-29	3	21	7000	5	7	1400	5	3	600
	30-35	9	12	1333	8	8	1000	6	6	1000
	36 and over	11	0	0	6	2	333	20	14	700
	Total	251	867	3454	323	1045	3235	315	968	3073

(CEB = Children Ever Born)

TABLE A-15

Size of Community

25,000-100,000			100,000-250,000			250,000-500,000			Over 500,000			Total		
No. Cases	No. CEB	CEB/1000 Women	No. Cases	No. CEB	CEB/1000 Women	No. Cases	No. CEB	CEB/1000 Women	No. Cases	No. CEB	CEB/1000 Women	No. Cases	No. CEB	CEB/1000 Women
110	329	2991	72	181	2514	57	143	2509	94	220	2340	532	1517	2851
816	2361	2893	427	1022	2393	396	1022	2581	641	1474	2300	3570	9560	2678
796	1779	2235	370	836	2259	463	1021	2205	676	1374	2033	3539	7980	2255
468	831	1776	220	380	1727	304	471	1549	460	694	1509	2220	3807	1715
224	316	1411	85	102	1200	130	193	1485	181	209	1155	879	1223	1391
144	172	1194	61	51	836	94	64	681	162	116	716	692	672	971
49	18	367	18	1	56	23	6	261	46	9	196	206	52	252
2607	5806	2227	1253	2573	2053	1467	2920	1590	2260	4096	1812	11638	24811	2132
121	464	3835	57	198	3474	65	254	3508	83	269	3241	594	2471	4160
734	2232	3041	335	923	2755	293	730	2491	488	1268	2598	3075	8951	2911
735	1707	2322	329	717	2179	398	862	2166	591	1226	2074	3076	7127	2317
505	976	1933	210	454	2162	260	444	1708	376	661	1758	2029	3932	1938
188	287	1527	77	124	1610	128	198	1547	165	245	1485	831	1333	1604
140	192	1371	64	60	937	88	92	1045	155	150	968	591	630	1066
54	11	204	27	14	519	18	11	611	41	3	73	203	57	281
2477	5869	2369	1099	2490	2266	1250	2591	2073	1899	3822	2014	10399	24501	2356
129	502	3891	47	185	3936	63	226	3587				411	1752	4263
451	1380	3060	190	604	3179	248	735	2964	285	768	2695	2065	6329	3065
515	1234	2396	257	685	2665	241	598	2461	354	806	2277	2110	5296	2510
305	674	2210	118	199	1686	200	380	1900	256	473	1848	1351	2813	2082
135	243	1800	55	98	1782	74	121	1635	102	155	1520	553	956	1729
109	121	1110	73	73	1000	59	56	949	89	96	1079	485	551	1136
49	19	388	10	1	100	27	6	222	36	12	333	181	52	287
1693	4173	2465	750	1845	2460	912	2122	2327	1122	2310	2059	7156	17749	2480
95	428	4505	29	109	3759	42	195	4643	47	161	3426	379	1658	4375
452	1374	3044	197	535	2716	208	485	2332	253	644	2545	1865	5509	2953
497	1145	2304	205	555	2707	227	493	2172	323	710	2198	1983	4626	2434
332	701	2111	138	261	1891	219	399	1822	226	396	1752	1394	2799	2008
121	235	1942	52	100	1923	75	111	1480	110	176	1600	521	888	1704
98	130	1327	53	61	1151	62	73	1177	86	93	1081	437	579	1325
46	37	804	29	15	517	19	4	211	45	17	378	203	89	438
1641	4050	2468	703	1636	2327	852	1760	2066	1090	2197	2016	6782	16348	2410
50	185	3700	23	103	4478	23	82	3565	21	94	4476	232	994	4264
249	772	3100	93	343	3688	141	399	2830	128	396	3094	1116	3477	3116
227	594	2617	112	278	2482	128	306	2391	152	284	1868	1048	2661	2539
169	356	2107	85	165	1941	105	223	2124	117	261	2231	741	1655	2233
54	94	1741	24	37	1542	33	61	1846	37	66	1784	254	502	1976
21	45	2143	13	19	1462	16	37	2312	19	38	2000	102	238	2333
770	2046	2657	350	945	2700	446	1108	2484	474	1139	2403	3493	9527	2727
47	285	6064	10	49	4900	15	59	3933	19	116	6105	167	835	5000
153	398	2601	70	201	2871	74	202	2730	65	198	3046	718	2316	3226
147	490	3333	48	151	3146	72	193	2681	45	110	2444	551	1651	2996
67	188	2806	35	80	2286	48	105	2187	31	86	2774	326	916	2810
28	41	1464	4	8	2000	14	24	1714	15	12	800	74	116	1568
22	13	591	12	6	500	20	15	750	30	22	733	107	82	766
28	15	536	11	2	182	19	1	53	30	13	433	125	47	376
492	1430	2906	190	497	2616	262	599	2286	235	557	2370	2068	5963	2883

An Economic Analysis of Fertility

GARY S. BECKER

COLUMBIA UNIVERSITY

AND

NATIONAL BUREAU OF ECONOMIC RESEARCH

THE inability of demographers to predict western birth rates accurately in the postwar period has had a saiutary influence on demographic research. Most predictions had been based either on simple extrapolations of past trends or on extrapolations that adjusted for changes in the age-sex-marital composition of the population. Socio-economic considerations are entirely absent from the former and are primitive and largely implicit in the latter. As long as even crude extrapolations continued to give fairly reliable predictions, as they did during the previous half century, there was little call for complicated analyses of the interrelation between socio-economic variables and fertility. However, the sharp decline in birth rates during the thirties coupled with the sharp rise in rates during the postwar period swept away confidence in the view that future rates could be predicted from a secularly declining function of population compositions.

Malthus could with some justification assume that fertility was determined primarily by two primitive variables, age at marriage and the frequency of coition during marriage. The development and spread of knowledge about contraceptives during the last century greatly widened the scope of family size decision-making, and contemporary researchers have been forced to pay greater attention to decision-making than either Malthus or the forecasters did. Psychologists have tried to place these decisions within a framework suggested by psychological theory; sociologists have tried one suggested by sociological theory, but most persons would admit that neither framework has been particularly successful in organizing the information on fertility.

Two considerations encouraged me to analyze family size decisions within an economic framework. The first is that Malthus' famous discussion was built upon a strongly economic framework; mine can be viewed as a generalization and development of his. Second, although no

Note: I am indebted to Richard A. Easterlin and Eugenia Scandrett for helpful comments, and to many others, especially Cornelius J. Dwyer, who commented on the draft prepared for the conference.

single variable in the Indianapolis survey[1] explained more than a small fraction of the variation in fertility, economic variables did better than others. Section I develops this framework and sets out some of its implications. Section II uses this framework to analyze the actual effects of income on fertility. Section III speculates about some further implications of the discussion in I and II.

I. The Economic Framework

GENERAL CONSIDERATIONS

In societies lacking knowledge of contraception, control over the number of births can be achieved either through abortion or abstinence, the latter taking the form of delayed marriage and reduced frequency of coition during marriage. Since each person maintains some control over these variables, there is room for decision-making even in such societies. Other things the same, couples desiring small families would marry later and have more abortions than the average couple. Yet the room for decision-making would be uncomfortably small, given the taboos against abortion, the strong social forces determining the age of marriage, and the relative inefficiency of reductions in the frequency of coition. Chance would bulk large in determining the distribution of births among families.[2]

The growth of knowledge about contraception has greatly widened the scope of decision-making, for it has separated the decision to control births from the decision to engage in coition. Presumably, such a widening of the scope of decision-making has increased the importance of environmental factors, but which of the numerous environmental factors are most important? To simplify the analysis of this problem I assume initially that each family has perfect control over both the number and spacing of its births.

For most parents, children are a source of psychic income or satisfaction, and, in the economist's terminology, children would be considered a consumption good. Children may sometimes provide money income and are then a production good as well. Moreover, neither the outlays on children nor the income yielded by them are fixed but vary in amount with the child's age, making children a durable consumption and production good. It may seem strained, artificial, and perhaps even immoral to classify children with cars, houses, and machinery. This classification does not imply, however, that the satisfactions or costs associated with

---

[1] *Social and Psychological Factors Affecting Fertility*, ed. by P. K. Whelpton and C. V. Kiser, Milbank Memorial Fund, Vols. 1–4.

[2] The effect of chance will be fully discussed in a subsequent paper.

children are morally the same as those associated with other durables. The satisfaction provided by housing, a "necessity," is often distinguished from that provided by cars, a "luxury," yet both are treated as consumer durables in demand analysis. Abstracting from the kind of satisfaction provided by children makes it possible to relate the "demand" for children to a well-developed body of economic theory. I will try to show that the theory of the demand for consumer durables is a useful framework in analyzing the demand for children.

TASTES

As consumer durables, children are assumed to provide "utility." The utility from children is compared with that from other goods via a utility function or a set of indifference curves. The shape of the indifference curves is determined by the relative preference for children, or, in other words, by "tastes." These tastes may, in turn, be determined by a family's religion, race, age, and the like. This framework permits, although it does not predict, fertility differences that are unrelated to "economic" factors.

QUALITY OF CHILDREN

A family must determine not only how many children it has but also the amount spent on them—whether it should provide separate bedrooms, send them to nursery school and private colleges, give them dance or music lessons, and so forth. I will call more expensive children "higher quality" children, just as Cadillacs are called higher quality cars than Chevrolets. To avoid any misunderstanding, let me hasten to add that "higher quality" does not mean morally better. If more is voluntarily spent on one child than on another, it is because the parents obtain additional utility from the additional expenditure and it is this additional utility which we call higher "quality."

INCOME

An increase in income must increase the amount spent on the average good, but not necessarily that spent on each good. The major exceptions are goods that are inferior members of a broader class, as a Chevrolet is considered an inferior car, margarine an inferior spread, and black bread an inferior bread. Since children do not appear to be inferior members of any broader class, it is likely that a rise in long-run income would increase the amount spent on children.[3]

[3] This is also suggested by another line of reasoning. It is known that $\Sigma k_i n_i \equiv 1$, where k_i is the fraction of income spent on the ith commodity, and n_i is the income

For almost all other consumer durables, such as cars, houses, or refrigerators, families purchase more units as well as better quality units at higher income levels, with the quantity income elasticity usually being small compared to the quality elasticity.[4] If expenditures on children responded in a similar way, most of the increased expenditures on children would consist of an increase in the quality of children. Economic theory does not guarantee that the quantity of children would increase at all, although a decrease in quantity would be an exception to the usual case. Thus an increase in income should increase both the quantity and quality of children, but the quantity elasticity should be small compared to the quality elasticity.

Malthus, on the other hand, concluded that an increase in income would lead to a relatively large increase in family size. His argument has two major components. First, an increase in income would cause a decline in child mortality, enabling more children to survive childhood. If a decrease in births did not offset the decrease in child mortality, the number of children in the average family would increase. His second argument is less mechanical and takes greater account of motivation. An increase in income increases fertility by inducing people to marry earlier and abstain less while married.

My analysis has generalized that of Malthus by relating the quantity of children to the quality of children and by permitting small (even negative) quantity income elasticities as well as large ones. My conclusion that in modern society the quantity elasticity is probably positive but small differs from his for the following reasons. First, child mortality has fallen so low that the ordinary changes in income have little effect on the number of survivors out of a given birth cohort. Moreover, it is doubtful that even a large decline in child mortality would have much effect on family size, for parents are primarily interested in survivors, not in births per se. Therefore, a decline in child mortality would induce a corresponding decline in births.[5] Second, births can now be controlled without abstinence and this has greatly reduced the psychic costs of birth

---

elasticity of the amount spent on the ith commodity. Other things the same, the larger k_i is, the less likely it is that n_i is either very small or very large. In particular, the less likely it is that n_i is negative. In most families the fraction of income spent on children is quite large and this decreases the likelihood that the income elasticity for children is negative.

[4] Chow estimated the total income elasticity for automobiles at about $+2$. Cf. G. C. Chow, *Demand for Automobiles in the United States*, North Holland Publishing Co., Amsterdam, 1957; however, the quantity elasticity is only about $+0.31$. Cf. *Federal Reserve Bulletin*, August, 1956, p. 820.

[5] This will be discussed more fully in a future publication.

control. "Human nature" no longer guarantees that a growth in income appreciably above the subsistence level results in a large inadvertent increase in fertility.

COST

In principle the net cost of children can be easily computed. It equals the present value of expected outlays plus the imputed value of the parents' services, minus the present value of the expected money return plus the imputed value of the child's services. If net costs were positive, children would be on balance a consumer durable and it would be necessary to assume that psychic income or utility was received from them. If net costs were negative, children would be a producer durable and pecuniary income would be received from them. Children of many qualities are usually available, and the quality selected by any family is determined by tastes, income, and price. For most families in recent years the net expenditure on children has been very large.[6]

Real incomes per capita in the United States have increased more than threefold in the last 100 years, which must have increased the net expenditure on children. It is possible that in the mid-nineteenth century children were a net producer's good, providing rather than using income. However, the marginal cost of children must have been positive in families receiving marginal psychic income from children; otherwise, they would have had additional children. Even in 1850, the typical family in the United States was producing fewer children than was physically possible. Some more direct inferences can be drawn from the data on Negro slaves, an extreme example of a human producer's good. These data indicate a positive net expenditure on male slaves during their first eighteen years.[7] Slave raising was profitable because the high price that an eighteen-year-old could bring more than offset the net cost during the first eighteen years. Presumably, in most families expenditures on white children during their first eighteen years were greater than those on slaves. Moreover, after eighteen, white children became free agents and could decide

---

[6] See J. D. Tarver, "Costs of Rearing and Educating Farm Children," *Journal of Farm Economics*, February, 1956, pp. 144–153, and L. I. Dublin and A. J. Lotka, *The Money Value of a Man*, Ronald Press, 1946, ch. 4. Most studies consider only the costs and returns before age eighteen. It is possible that returns bulk larger than costs at later ages; but because these ages are heavily discounted and because costs are so large before age eighteen, there is little chance that a correction of this bias would substantially reduce the net cost of children.

[7] See A. H. Conrad and J. R. Meyer, "The Economics of Slavery in the Ante Bellum South," *Journal of Political Economy*, April, 1958, p. 108. At an 8 per cent discount rate (about the estimated rate of return on slaves), the present value of the net costs is +$35, or about one-third of the present value of gross costs. The data are subject to considerable error and are at best a rough indication of the magnitudes involved.

213

whether to keep their income or give it to their parents. The amount given to parents may have been larger than the costs before eighteen, but it is more likely that costs before eighteen dominated returns after eighteen. This conclusion does not imply that monetary returns from children were unimportant, and indeed, they are stressed at several points in this paper. It does imply, however, that a basic framework which treats children as a consumer's good is relevant not only for the present, but also for some time in the past.

A change in the cost of children is a change in the cost of children of *given quality*, perhaps due to a change in the price of food or education. It is well to dwell a little on this definition for it is widely misunderstood. One would not say that the price of cars has risen over time merely because more people now buy Cadillacs and other expensive cars. A change in price has to be estimated from indexes of the price of a given quality. Secular changes in real income and other variables have induced a secular increase in expenditures on children, often interpreted as a rise in the cost of children. The cost of children may well have risen (see pp. 227–28) but the increase in expenditure on children is no evidence of such rise since the quality of children has risen. Today children are better fed, housed, and clothed, and in increasing numbers are sent to nursery schools, camps, high schools, and colleges. For the same reason, the price of children to rich parents is the same as that to poor parents even though rich parents spend more on children.[8] The rich simply choose higher quality children as well as higher qualities of other goods.[9]

It is sometimes argued that social pressures "force" richer families to

[8] One qualification is needed because the rich may impute a higher value than the poor to the time spent on children. The same qualification is needed in analyzing the demand for other goods.

[9] As an example of how prevalent this error is, even among able economists, we refer to a recent discussion by H. Leibenstein in *Economic Backwardness and Economic Growth*, John Wiley, 1957, pp. 161–170. He tries to relate cost of children to level of income, arguing, among other things, that "The relation between the value of a child as a contributor to family income and changes in per capita income is fairly clear. As per capita income increases, there is less need to utilize children as sources of income. At the same time the level of education and the general quality of the population implied by a higher income per head mean that more time must be spent on child training, education, and development, and, therefore, less time is available to utilize the child as a productive agent. Therefore, the higher the income, the less the utility to be derived from a prospective child as a productive agent" and "The conventional costs of child maintenance increase as per capita income increases. The style in which a child is maintained depends on the position and income of the parents; therefore, we expect such costs to rise as incomes rise. . . ." (*ibid.*, pp. 163–164.)

By trying to relate cost to income Leibenstein confused cost and quality, and succeeded only in inadvertently relating quality to income. His technique would imply that the relative price of almost every group of goods rose over time because the quality chosen spend more on children, and that this increases the cost of children to the rich. This higher cost is supposed to explain why richer families have fewer children than others and why richer societies have fewer children than poorer ones. However, since the cost of different goods is given in the market place, social pressures cannot change this, but can only change the basket of goods selected. That is, social pressures influence behavior by affecting the indifference curve structure, not by affecting costs. To put this differently, social pressures may affect the income elasticity of demand for children by rich (and poor) families, but not the price elasticity of demand. Therefore, the well known negative relationship between cost (or price) and quantity purchased cannot explain why richer families have had relatively few children. Moreover, nothing in economic analysis implies that social pressures would make the quantity income elasticity of demand for children negative. Thus my conclusion that the quantity income elasticity is relatively small but positive and the quality elasticity relatively large is entirely consistent with an analysis which emphasizes social pressures.

Suppose there was an equal percentage decline in the price of all qualities of children, real income remaining constant. Although economic theory suggests that the "amount" of children consumed would increase, it does not say whether the amount would increase because of an increase in quantity, quality, or both—the last, however, being most likely. It also has little to say about the quantitative relationship between price and amount. There are no good substitutes for children, but there may be many poor ones.[10]

---

rose, an obvious impossibility. This flaw in his procedure greatly weakens his analysis of the secular decline in birth rates.

Bernard Okun also applied economic analysis to the population area, and explicitly assumed that the cost of children is higher to rich people because they spend more on children (see *A Rational Economic Model Approach to the Birth Rate*, Rand Corp. Series, P1458, August, 1958). His argument, like Leibenstein's, would imply that the cost of many (if not most) goods is greater to richer families than to poorer ones. Also see S. H. Coontz, *Population Theories and the Economic Interpretation*, Routledge, London, 1957, Part II.

[10] Let x be the quantity of children, p an expenditure measure of the quality of x, y an index of other goods, I money income, U a utility function, α a parameter shifting the cost of each quality of x by the same percentage, and π the price of y. A consumer maximizes $U(x, y, p)$ subject to the constraint $\alpha px + \pi y = I$. This leads to the equilibrium conditions

$$\frac{Ux}{\alpha p} = \frac{Up}{\alpha x} = \frac{Uy}{\pi}$$

The marginal utility from spending a dollar more on the quantity of children must equal the marginal utility from spending a dollar more on their quality.

After a draft of this paper was written I came across an article by H. Theil, "Qualities, Prices, and Budget Inquiries," *The Review of Economic Studies*, XIX, pp. 129–147, which

SUPPLY

By and large, children cannot be purchased on the open market but must be produced at home. Most families are no longer self-sufficient in any major commodity other than children. Because children are produced at home, each uncertainty in production is transferred into a corresponding uncertainty in consumption, even when there is no uncertainty for all families taken together. Although parents cannot accurately predict the sex, intelligence, and height of their children, the distribution of these qualities is relatively constant for the country as a whole. This uncertainty makes it necessary to distinguish between actual and expected utility. Thus suppose a group of parents received marginal utility equal to U_m from a male child and U_f from a female child. The expected utility from an additional child equals $EU = PU_m + (1 - P)U_f \cong \dfrac{U_m + U_f}{2}$, where P, the probability of a male is approximately equal to $1/2$. They would have additional children whenever the expected utility per dollar of expected cost from an additional child were greater than that from expenditures elsewhere. The actual utility is either U_f or U_m, which differs from EU as long as $U_f \neq U_m$. In fact, if U_f (or U_m) were negative, some parents would receive negative utility.

A second important consequence of uniting consumption and production is that the number of children available to a family is determined not only by its income and prices but also by its ability to produce children. One family can desire three children and be unable to produce more than two, while another can desire three and be unable to produce fewer than five.[11] The average number of live births produced by married women in societies with little knowledge of contraception is very high. For example, in nineteenth-century Ireland, women marrying at ages 20–24 averaged more than 8 live births.[12] This suggests that the average family more frequently had excess rather than too few children.

---

treats the interaction of quality and quantity in an elegant manner. Also see, in the same issue, H. S. Houthhakker, "Compensated Changes in Quantities and Qualities Consumed," pp. 155–164. Theil differentiates equations like these and shows that a compensated decrease in the price of a good of given quality must increase either the quantity of goods or the quality, or both.

[11] There is some ambiguity in the last part of this sentence since abstinence enables a family to produce as few children as desired. The terms "unplanned," "excess," or "unwanted" children refer to children that would not be conceived if there were perfect mechanical control over conception. No children are unplanned in terms of the contraceptive knowledge and techniques actually known.

[12] See D. V. Glass and E. Grebenik, *The Trend and Pattern of Fertility in Great Britain*, Paper of the Royal Commission on Population, Vol. vi, p. 271.

Relatively effective contraceptive techniques have been available for at least the last 100 years, but knowledge of such techniques did not spread rapidly. Religious and other objections prevented the rapid spread of knowledge that is common to other technological innovations in advanced countries. Most families in the nineteenth century, even in advanced Western countries, did not have effective contraceptive information. This information spread slowly from upper socio-economic groups to lower ones.[13]

Each family tries to come as close as possible to its desired number of children. If three children are desired and no more than two are available, two are produced; if three are desired and no fewer than five are available, five are produced. The marginal equilibrium conditions would not be satisfied for children but would be satisfied for other goods, so the theory of consumer's choice is not basically affected.[14] Families with excess children consume less of other goods, especially of goods that are close substitutes for the quantity of children. Because quality seems like a relatively close substitute for quantity, families with excess children would spend less on each child than other families with equal income and tastes. Accordingly, an increase in contraceptive knowledge would raise the quality of children as well as reduce their quantity.

II. An Empirical Application

Having set out the formal analysis and framework suggested by economic theory, we now investigate its usefulness in the analysis of fertility patterns. It suggests that a rise in income would increase both the quality and quantity of children desired; the increase in quality being large and the increase in quantity small. The difficulties in separating expenditures on children from general family expenditures notwithstanding, it is evident that wealthier families and countries spend much more per child than do poorer families and countries. The implication with respect to quantity is not so readily confirmed by the raw data. Indeed,

---

[13] For evidence supporting the statements in this paragraph see the definitive work by N. A. Himes, *Medical History of Contraception*, The Williams and Wilkins Company, Baltimore, 1936.

[14] A consumer maximizes a utility function $U = u(x_1, \ldots x_n)$ (neglecting quality considerations) subject to the constraints $\sum_{i=1}^{n} p_i x_i \equiv Y$, and $x_1 \geq$ or $\leq c$, where p_i is the price of the ith commodity, Y is money income, and x_1 refers to children. If the second constraint were effective, x_1 would equal c. Then the consumer would maximize $U = U(c, x_2, \ldots x_n)$ subject only to $\sum_{i=2}^{n} p_i x_i \equiv Y' \equiv Y - p_1 c$, and this gives the usual marginal conditions for $x_2, \ldots, x_n$.

217

most data tend to show a negative relationship between income and fertility. This is true of the Census data for 1910, 1940, and 1950, where income is represented by father's occupation, mother's education, or monthly rental; the data from the Indianapolis survey, the data for nineteenth century Providence families, and several other studies as well.[15] It is tempting to conclude from this evidence either that tastes vary systematically with income, perhaps being related to relative income, or that the number of children is an inferior good. Ultimately, systematic variations in tastes may have to be recognized; but for the present it seems possible to explain the available data within the framework outlined in section I, without assuming that the number of children is an inferior good. First, it is well to point out that not all the raw evidence is one way. In some studies, the curve relating fertility and income flattens out and even rises at the higher income classes, while in other studies the curve is positive throughout.[16] Second, tastes are not the only variable that may have varied systematically with income, for there is a good deal of general evidence that contraceptive knowledge has been positively related to income. Himes, in his history of contraception, indicates that the upper classes acquired this knowledge relatively early.[17] If such knowledge spread gradually from the upper classes to the rest of society, fertility differentials between classes should have first increased and then narrowed. This was clearly the pattern in England and was probably the pattern in the United States.[18]

Such evidence does little more than suggest that differential knowledge of contraceptive techniques might explain the negative relationship between fertility and income. Fortunately, the Indianapolis survey makes it possible, at least for 1941, to assess its quantitative importance. Table 1 presents some data from this study. In column (1) the native-white Protestant couples in the sample are classified by the husband's income, and column (2) gives the number of children born per 100 couples in each income class. The lowest income class was most fertile (2.3 children per couple) and a relatively high class least fertile (1.5

[15] U.S. Bureau of the Census, Census of Population, 1940; *Differential Fertility 1910 and 1940*, Government Printing Office, Washington, 1945; U.S. Bureau of the Census, Census of Population, 1950; *Fertility*, Government Printing Office, Washington, 1955; *Social and Psychological Factors Affecting Fertility*, by P. K. Whelpton and C. V. Kiser, eds., Milbank Memorial Fund, 1951; A. J. Jaffe, "Differential Fertility in the White Population in Early America," *Journal of Heredity*, August, 1940, pp. 407–411.

[16] K. A. Edin and E. P. Hutchinson, *Studies of Differential Fertility*, London, 1935; W. H. Banks, "Differential Fertility in Madison County, New York, 1865," *Milbank Memorial Fund Quarterly*, Vol. 33, April, 1955, pp. 161–186.

[17] Himes, *op. cit.*

[18] See the papers by C. V. Kiser and G. Z. Johnson in this volume.

children per couple), but the highest class averaged slightly more children than the next highest. This relationship between economic level and fertility was about the same as that shown by the 1940 Census.[19] Sterility did not vary systematically with income, so column (3), which is restricted to relatively fecund families, differs only slightly from column (2).

TABLE 1

Children Ever Born per 100 Couples in Indianapolis Classified by
Husband's Income and Planning Status
(native-white Protestants)

Income (1)	All Couples (2)	Relatively Fecund (3)	Number and Spacing Planners (4)	All Planners (5)	Desires of Relatively Fecund (6)
$3,000+	159	180	149	175	171
2,000–2,999	149	176	182	161	170
1,600–1,999	163	194	91	126	153
1,200–1,599	189	229	97	144	175
1,200 and less	227	266	68	146	193

Source: *Social and Psychological Factors Affecting Fertility*, P. K. Whelpton and C. V. Kiser, eds., N.Y., Milbank Memorial Fund, 1951, Vol. 2, part 9. Columns (2) and (3) from Table 4; columns (4) and (5) computed from Figure 8; column (6) computed from Figures 8 and 21.

It is well known that rich families use contraception earlier and more frequently than poor families. It has been difficult to determine whether poor families are ignorant of contraceptive methods or whether they desire more children than richer ones. The Indianapolis survey tried to separate ignorance from tastes by classifying couples not only by use of contraception but also by control over births. Column (4) gives the average number of children for "number and spacing planning" couples, including only couples who had planned all their children. A positive pattern now emerges, with the richest families averaging more than twice as many children as the poorest families. The income elasticity is about +0.42. Column (5) presents data for "number planned" couples, including all couples that planned their last child. These data also show a positive pattern, with an elasticity of +0.09, lower than that for number and spacing planners.

Fecund couples having excess children were asked questions about the number of such children. Column (6) uses this information and that in column (5) to relate income to the number of children desired by all

[19] Whelpton and Kiser, eds., *op. cit.*, Vol. 2, p. 364.

fecund couples. The elasticity is negative, being about −0.07.[20] After an intensive study, however, Potter found evidence that the number of desired children was overestimated; his own estimates of desired fertility show a positive relationship with income.[21] Thus evidence from the Indianapolis survey indicates that differential knowledge of contraception does convert a positive relation between income and *desired* fertility into a negative relation between income and *actual* fertility.[22]

Several other surveys provide information on desired fertility. For example, in 1954 a group at Michigan asked Detroit area families; "In your opinion what would be the ideal number of children for a young couple to have, if their standard of living is about like yours?" There was a distinct positive relationship between the ideal number of children and income of the family head.[23]

If knowledge of contraceptive techniques did not vary with income, the relation between actual fertility and income would equal that between desired fertility and income. Contraceptive knowledge is said to be diffused among all income classes in Stockholm, and the fertility of Stockholm families from 1917–1930 was positively related to income.[24] Contraceptive knowledge was said to be very primitive in *all* income

[20] These elasticities are estimates of the slope of the regression of the logarithm of fertility on the logarithm of income. The mean of the open end income class is assumed to be $4,000, and the mean of the other classes is assumed to be at their mid-points.

[21] R. G. Potter, *The Influence of Primary Groups on Fertility*, unpublished Ph.D. dissertation, Department of Social Relations, Harvard University, 1955, Appendix A, pp. 277–304.

[22] This conclusion must be qualified to allow for the possibility that tastes and costs also varied with income. Since all couples lived in the same city the cost of children was presumably the same. Age, religion, color, and nativity were held constant in an attempt to limit the systematic variation in tastes. Education did vary with income, but for number and spacing planners it was possible to separate the effect of income from the effect of education. The simple correlation coefficient between fertility and income is +0.24 and between fertility and education +0.17, with both significant at the 1 per cent level. The partial correlation coefficient between fertility and income, holding education constant is +0.23, about the same as the simple coefficient, and is also significant at the 1 per cent level. The partial correlation between fertility and education is only +0.04, not significant even at the 10 per cent level. (For these correlations see Whelpton and Kiser, eds., *op. cit.*, Vol. 3.) Holding education constant has little effect on the relationship between income and fertility.

[23] See R. Freedman, D. Goldberg, and H. Sharp, " 'Ideals' about Family Size in the Detroit Metropolitan Area, 1954," *Milbank Memorial Fund Quarterly*, Vol. 33, April, 1955, pp. 187–197. An earlier survey asked about the ideal family size for the average American couple, and found a negative relationship between ideal size and income of the head. But ideal size should be related to the income *assumed* by a respondent, rather than to his own income; and there is no way to do this. R. G. Potter has criticized both surveys because of their tendency to show larger ideal than realized families. See his "A Critique of the Glass-Grebenik Model for Indirectly Estimating Desired Family Size," *Population Studies*, March, 1956, pp. 251–270. It is not possible to determine whether this bias is systematically related to income.

[24] See Edin and Hutchinson, *op. cit.*

classes of prewar China, and a positive relation between fertility and income also seemed to prevail there.[25] Graduates in the same college class are probably relatively homogeneous in contraceptive knowledge and values as well as in formal education. I have the impression that income and fertility of these graduates tend to be positively related, but I have been able to examine only one sample. Some graduates from Harvard and Yale were classified by occupation and "degree of success." Within each occupation, the more successful graduates usually had more children.[26]

Information has been obtained on the family income, education, earners, and dependent children of a sample of the subscribers to Consumers Union.[27] This sample is particularly valuable for our purposes since it primarily consists of families with a keen interest in rational, informed consumption. If my analysis is at all relevant, fertility and income should be more positively related in this group than in the U.S. population as a whole. Table 2 presents the average number of dependent

TABLE 2

Average Number of Dependent Children for Single Earner Families with Head Age 35–44 in a Sample of Subscribers to Consumers Union, April, 1958

	Average Number of Dependent Children by Education Class of Head			
Income Class	High School Graduate or Less	Some College	Graduate of Four Year College	Graduate Degree
Less than $3,000	2.43	1.61	2.50	2.17
$ 3,000–3,999	2.15	2.47	2.18	2.23
4,000–4,999	2.70	2.40	2.04	2.18
5,000–7,499	2.68	2.73	2.88	2.67
7,500–9,999	2.80	2.94	3.00	3.03
10,000–14,999	2.89	3.03	3.12	3.23
15,000–24,999	2.85	3.04	3.04	3.31
25,000 and over	3.12	3.23	3.28	3.60

Source: Unpublished data from consumer purchases study by Thomas Juster at National Bureau of Economic Research.

[25] See H. D. Lamson, "Differential Reproductivity in China," *The Quarterly Review of Biology*, Vol. 10, no. 3, September, 1933, pp. 308–321. Abstinence, which is equally available to lower and upper classes, is the major form of birth control when contraceptive knowledge is limited.

[26] See E. Huntington and L. F. Whitney, *The Builders of America*, New York, Morrow, 1927, ch. xv. Although they did not clearly define "success," it appears that income was a major factor in ranking persons within an occupation and a less important factor in ranking occupations.

[27] This is part of a study by Thomas Juster on buying plans, and I am indebted to him for making the data available to me.

children for single earner families with the head aged 35–44, each family classified by its income and by the education of the head. There is a substantial positive relationship between income and children within each educational class; education *per se* has relatively little effect on the number of children. The income elasticity is about 0.09 and 0.14 for graduates of a four year college and of a graduate school respectively. These data, then, are very consistent with my analysis, and indicate that well-informed families do have more children when their income increases.

Contraceptive knowledge in the United States spread rapidly during the War, largely fostered by the military in its effort to limit venereal disease and illegitimacy. We would expect this to have reduced the relative fertility of low income classes, and Census Bureau studies in 1952 and 1957 confirm this expectation. Table 3 presents the data for urban and rural nonfarm families for 1952 and all families for 1957 with column (1) giving husband's income, column (2) the age-standardized number

TABLE 3

Fertility by Husband's Income

Husband's Income (1)	Children Under 5 per 100 Married Men 20–59 (age standardized) (2)	Children Born per 100 Wives 15–44 Years Old (age standardized) (3)	Children Born per 100 Wives over 45 (4)
Part 1: In Urban and Rural Nonfarm Areas in the United States in 1952			
$7 000+	53	189	194
6,000–6,999	52	188	210
5,000–5,999	50	188	210
4,000–4,999	52	177	217
3,000–3,999	52	184	240
2,000–2,999	51	189	256
1,000–1,999	40	181	279
1,000 and less	40	211	334
Part II: For the United States in 1957			
$7,000+	—	216	213
5,000–6,999	—	220	230
4,000–4,999	—	221	240
3,000–3,999	—	236	279
2,000–2,999	—	247	304
1,000–1,999	—	289	341
1,000 and less	—	—	383

Source 1. U.S. Bureau of the Census, *Current Population Reports*, Wash., Government Printing Office, 1953, no. 46, p. 20.

II. U.S. Bureau of the Census, *Current Population Reports*, Wash., Government Printing Office, 1958, no. 84, p. 12.

of children under 5 per 100 men aged 20 to 59, column (3) the age-standardized number of children ever born per 100 wives aged 15 to 44, and column (4) the number ever born per 100 wives aged 45 and older. Columns (2) and (3) deal primarily with childbearing since 1940 and show a much weaker negative relationship between fertility and income than does column (4), which deals primarily with childbearing before 1940.

The relationship between fertility and income can be investigated not only with cross-sectional income differences but also with time series differences. Cyclical fluctuations in income have regularly occurred in Western nations, and, if our analysis is correct, a change in income would induce a change in fertility in the same direction. For our purpose cyclical fluctuations in fertility can be measured by the cyclical fluctuations in births (although see p. 227). Some earlier studies presented evidence that births do conform positively to the business cycle, even when adjusted for fluctuations in the marriage rate.[28]

I have related some annual figures since 1920 on first and higher order birth rates—brought forward one year—to the National Bureau annual business cycle dates. Column (3) of Table 4 gives the percentage change per year in first and higher order birth rates from the beginning of one phase to the beginning of the next phase. The strong secular decline in births before World War II makes most of these entries negative before that time and hence obscures the effect of cyclical fluctuations in economic conditions. If economic conditions affected births they should have declined more rapidly (or risen less rapidly) during a downswing than during an upswing. This can be detected from the first differences of the entries in column (3), which are shown in column (4). Aside from the wartime period, 1938–1948, second and higher order births conform perfectly in direction to the reference dates and first births conform almost as well. So reference cycle analysis strongly indicates that business conditions affect birth rates. This effect is not entirely dependent on cyclical fluctuations in the marriage rate since second and higher order births conform exceedingly well.

The next step is to relate the magnitude of the movement in births to that in general business, and to compare this with corresponding figures for other consumer durables. Time series giving net national product and purchases of consumer durables were analyzed in the same way as birth

---

[28] V. L. Galbraith and D. S. Thomas, "Birth Rates and the Interwar Business Cycles," and D. Kirk, "The Relation of Employment Levels to Births in Germany," both in *Demographic Analysis*, J. J. Spengler and O. D. Duncan, eds., Free Press, Glencoe, 1956.

TABLE 4

Reference Cycle Pattern of Birth Rates for U.S. Since 1920

FIRST BIRTHS

REFERENCE CYCLE DATES[1]		Birth Rates per 1,000 Women 15–44 Years of Age, Brought Forward One Year at Reference Cycle Dates[2]		Annual Percentage Change During a Business (3)		Excess of Annual Percentage Change During Business Expansion Over (4)	
Peak	Trough	At Peak	At Trough	Expansion	Contraction	Preceding Contraction	Succeeding Contraction
1920		39					
	1921		34		−12.82		
1923		34		0.00		+12.82	
	1924		34		0.00		0.00
1926		32		−2.94		−2.94	
	1927		30		−6.25		−3.31
1929		30		0.00		+6.25	
	1932		25		−5.57		−5.57
1937		31		4.80		+10.37	
	1938		31		0.00		−4.80
1944		29		−1.06		−1.06	
	1946		46		28.33		+29.39
1948		36		−10.87		−39.20	
	1949		33		−8.33		+2.54
1953		34		0.76		+9.09	
	1954		33		−2.94		−3.70
1957		33*		0.00		+2.94	

HIGHER ORDER BIRTHS

Peak	Trough	At Peak	At Trough	Expansion	Contraction	Preceding Contraction	Succeeding Contraction
1920		82					
	1921		78		−4.88		
1923		78		0.00		+4.88	
	1924		74		−5.13		−5.13
1926		68		−4.05		+1.08	
	1927		64		−5.88		−1.83
1929		60		−3.12		+2.76	
	1932		52		−4.45		−1.33
1937		48		−1.53		+2.92	
	1938		47		−2.08		−0.55
1944		57		3.46		+5.54	
	1946		67		8.47		+5.01
1948		71		2.98		−5.49	
	1949		73		2.81		−0.17
1953		84		3.77		+0.96	
	1954		85		1.19		−2.58
1957		88*		3.53		+2.34	

* Last figure is for 1956.

Source: [1] See National Bureau of Economic Research Standard Reference Dates for Business Cycles.

[2] See Dudley Kirk, Appendix to "The Influence of Business Cycles on Marriage and Birth Rates," this volume.

rates were. The figures for birth rates in column (4) of Table 4 and corresponding figures for purchases of consumer durables were divided by corresponding figures for national product to obtain cyclical income elasticities for births and consumer durables. These figures, shown in Table 5, are positive for almost all phases, and this indicates that cyclical

TABLE 5

Cyclical Income Elasticities for Births and Consumer Durable
Purchases During Reference Cycle Phases

Reference Cycle Phases (1)		First Births (2)	Higher Order Births (3)	Purchases of Consumer Durables (4)
1920–1921	Down	0.81	0.31	2.48
1921–1923	Up	0.00	.58	2.96
1923–1924	Down	−1.55	.57	6.63
1924–1926	Up	.87	.48	5.26
1926–1927	Down	2.05	.90	4.05
1927–1929	Up	.37	.09	1.40
1929–1932	Down	.47	.13	1.51
1932–1937	Up	.26	.03	1.96
1937–1938	Down	− .09	.46	1.38
1938–1944	Up	4.26	.73	9.20
1944–1946	Down	3.89	.54	5.33
1946–1948	Up	− .44	.03	0.11
1948–1949	Down	.88	.09	0.01
1949–1953	Up	.78	.54	1.78
1953–1954	Down	1.19	.95	3.23
1954–1957	Up			
Simple Average excluding				
1938–1948		.56	.42	2.84
and negative figures		.77	.42	2.84

Source: Birth rates from column (4) of Table 4; similar figures were computed for consumer durable purchases and net national product. The durable figures were from Raymond W. Goldsmith, *A Study of Savings in the United States*, Vol. 1, Tables Q-6 and A-25 for 1920–1949 and from U.S. Dept. of Commerce, *Survey of Current Business*, July, 1958, Table 2, for 1949–1957. Net National Product figures were from Simon Kuznets, Technical Tables (mimeo), T-5, underlying series in *Supplement to Summary Volume on Capital Formation and Financing* for 1920–1955 and from U.S. Dept. of Commerce, *Survey of Current Business*, July, 1958, Table 4, for 1955–1957.

changes in births and purchases of consumer durables have been in the same direction as those in national output. The cyclical change in first births was usually greater than that in higher order births, and both were usually less than the change in output. Changes in first and higher order births were, however, far from insignificant, averaging 74 and 42 per cent of the corresponding change in output.

Cyclical changes in births are small compared to those in consumer durables. The latter averaged about 2.84 times the change in output, or about 4 and 7 times the change in first and higher order births respectively. This is consistent with our emphasis on inadequate knowledge of birth control; inadequate knowledge seems to explain much but not all of the difference between the average cyclical change in higher order births and in purchases of durables.[29] Some would be explained by the fact that the data for children include only fluctuations in numbers, while those for durables include both fluctuations in numbers and in quality. The rest may be explained by other differences between children and consumer durables.

For example, to purchase a consumer durable it is necessary to make a down payment with one's own resources and to finance the remainder either with one's own or with borrowed resources. The economic uncertainty generated by a depression increases the reluctance to use own or borrowed resources and induces creditors to raise standards and screen applicants more carefully.[30] Therefore some purchases of durables would be postponed until economic conditions improved. The "purchase" of children, however, is less apt to be postponed than the purchase of other durables. The initial cost of children (physician and delivery charges, nursery furniture, expenses, and so on) is a smaller fraction of its total cost than is the initial cost of most other durables because expenditures on children are more naturally spread over time. Hence children can be "purchased" with a smaller down payment and with less use of borrowed funds than can most other durables.

There is still another reason why the "purchase" of children is less apt to be postponed. *Ceteris paribus*, the demand for a good with a lengthy construction period is less sensitive to a temporary economic movement than the demand for more readily constructed goods, since delivery is likely to occur when this movement has passed. The construction and delivery period is very short for durables like cars and quite long for

[29] An estimate of the desired change in births of planned families can be readily obtained if we assume that the distribution of contraceptive knowledge among U.S. whites is the same as among families in the Indianapolis study, that for planned families the actual change in births equals the desired change, and that for other families the actual change is nil. Then the desired change equals the actual change (averaging 42 per cent of the change in output) divided by the fraction of all births in planned families (31 per cent), or about 136 per cent of output. This is about half of the change for consumer durables.

[30] For evidence relating credit conditions to cyclical fluctuations in the demand for housing, see J. Guttentag, *Some Studies of the Post-World War II Residential Construction and Mortgage Markets*, unpublished Ph.D. dissertation, Department of Economics, Columbia University, 1958.

children. It takes about 10 months on the average to produce a pregnancy and this period combined with a nine-month pregnancy period gives a total average construction period of nineteen months. This period is sufficiently long to reduce the impact on the demand for children of temporary movements in income.

There are also some reasons why the "purchase" of children is more apt to be postponed. For example, since children cannot be bought and sold they are a less "liquid" asset than ordinary durables, and the economic uncertainty accompanying a depression would increase the community's preference for liquid assets. A more complete analysis would also have to take account of other factors, such as the accelerator and the permanent income concept, which may have produced different cyclical responses in fertility and consumer durables. Our aim here, therefore, is not to present a definitive explanation of the relative cyclical movement in fertility but only to suggest that economic analysis can be useful in arriving at such an explanation.

Although the data on cyclical movements in fertility appears consistent with our analysis, another piece of time series data is in apparent conflict with it. Over time per capita incomes in the United States have risen while fertility has declined, suggesting a negative relationship between income and fertility. Of course, many other variables have changed drastically over time and this apparent conflict in the secular movements of fertility and income should not be taken too seriously until it can be demonstrated that these other changes were not responsible for the decline in fertility. Three changes seem especially important: a decline in child mortality; an increase in contraceptive knowledge; and a rise in the cost of children.

The number of children in the average completed urban white family declined by about 56 per cent from 1870 to 1940. The decline in child mortality explains about 14 percentage points or 25 per cent of this decline.[31] Some evidence already presented indicates that a large secular increase in contraceptive knowledge occurred in the United States. It is not possible, however, to estimate its magnitude precisely enough to compare it to the decline in fertility.

I have emphasized that the increase over time in expenditures on children is not evidence that the cost of children has increased since the quality of children has also increased. Changes in the relative cost of children have to be assessed from indexes of the relative cost of given

[31] Taken from my unpublished paper "Child Mortality, Fertility, and Population Growth."

quality children. There are several reasons why the relative cost of a given quality child may have changed over time. The decline in child mortality decreased the cost of a given quality child, although it may have only a small effect. The growth of legislation prohibiting child labor and requiring education may have raised the cost of children, but largely made compulsory only what was being done voluntarily by most parents.[32] This is another aspect of the increase in quality of children and does not imply any increase in their cost. If such legislation raised costs at all, it did so primarily for the poorest families since they would be less apt to give their children much education. Therefore, legislation may have been partly responsible for the narrowing of fertility differentials by income class in the last fifty years.[33] The movement from farm to urban communities raised the average cost of children to the population as a whole since it is cheaper to raise children on a farm, but did not appreciably affect the cost within urban communities. Because technological advance has probably been more rapid in the market place than in the home, the imputed cost of time and effort spent on children probably rose, perhaps by a substantial amount. This discussion suggests that there was a secular rise in the cost of children which also contributed to the secular decline in fertility.

Secular changes in educational attainment, religious attachment, discrimination against women, and so on, may also have decreased fertility, and presumably there were changes other than the growth of income which increased fertility. It would take a major study—and even that might be inconclusive—to determine whether the factors decreasing fertility were sufficiently strong to produce a secular decline in fertility in spite of the secular rise in income. At present, it seems that the negative correlation between the secular changes in fertility and income is not strong evidence against the hypothesis that an increase in income would cause an increase in fertility—tastes, costs, and knowledge remaining constant.

III. Some Further Implications

Section II tries to show that the economic analysis of section I is very useful in understanding the effect of income on fertility. This section sketches some additional implications. Our understanding of temporal

---

[32] See G. J. Stigler, *Employment and Compensation in Education*, National Bureau of Economic Research, Occasional Paper 33, 1950, Appendix B.

[33] This analysis casts doubt on the view that the sharp decline in British fertility during the 1870's and 1880's resulted from the introduction of compulsory education. The decline was greatest in the upper classes which were least affected by this legislation.

fluctuations in births would be deepened if it were more widely recognized that births are "flows" to the "stock" of children, just as new car purchases are flows to the stock of cars. Flows are determined not only by variables determining stocks, but also by depreciation rates, acceleration, savings, and, as shown in our discussion of cyclical movements in births, by considerations of timing. The recent work relating births to parity shows that demographers as well as economists are beginning to stress the interaction between stocks and flows.[34] This work needs to be extended in a systematic fashion.

The discussion in section I made it clear that the quantity and quality of children are intimately related. An increase in income or a decline in the cost of children would affect both the quantity and quality of children, usually increasing both. An increase in contraceptive knowledge would also affect both, but would increase quality while decreasing quantity. The quality of children is very important in its own right, for it determines the education, health, and motivation of the future labor force. It is a major contribution of an economic framework to bring out the mutual interaction of quantity and quality—an interaction that has been neglected all too often in writings both on population and on the quality of the labor force.

It is often said that farm families are larger than urban families because of a difference in tastes. Since farmers have a comparative cost advantage in raising children as well as in raising foodstuffs, they would tend to be more fertile even without any difference in tastes. The rural advantage may not be the same at all qualities and, indeed, presumably is less at higher qualities where child labor and food are less important. Over time, rural as well as urban families have moved to higher quality children, and this may have contributed to the narrowing of urban-rural fertility differentials in recent decades. The influence of differences in the cost of children deserves much more systematic study, for it may partly explain not only these urban-rural fertility differences but also the secular decline in fertility up to World War II and the apparent secular narrowing of fertility differentials among urban economic classes.

In the Western World, birth rates in the early postwar period were well above rates of the thirties. In some countries, including the United States and Canada, they have remained at about the early postwar level; in others, including Great Britain and Sweden, they have drifted down to about their 1940 level; in still others, including France, they have

---

[34] Both economists and demographers found that wartime effects on stocks had important consequences for postwar flows.

drifted down to a position intermediate between their immediate pre- and postwar levels. The analysis in this paper does not readily explain these differences, but it does explain why birth rates in all these countries are well above levels predicted from their secular trends. The secular decline in child mortality and the secular increase in contraceptive knowledge were important causes of the secular decline in births. By 1945 the level of child mortality was so low that little room remained for a further improvement. Although contraceptive knowledge was not well spread throughout every layer of society, the room for its further improvement was also more limited than it had been. With the weakening of these forces, much of the steam behind the secular decline in birth rates has been removed. Positive forces like the growth in income are now opposed by weaker negative forces, and it is not too surprising that fertility has ceased to decline and even has risen in some countries.

Several recent studies of consumption have used a measure of family size as an independent variable along with measures of income and price.[35] This procedure is justifiable if family size were a random variable or completely determined by "non-economic" factors.[36] If, on the other hand, family size were partly determined by economic factors, this procedure would result in misleading estimates of the regression coefficients for the other independent variables. Thus, suppose family size were positively related to income, and food consumption varied with income only because family size did. The regression coefficient between food consumption and income, holding family size constant, would be zero, an incorrect estimate of the long-run effect of an increase in income on food consumption. One would not estimate the effect of income on gasoline consumption by finding the regression coefficient between gasoline consumption and income, holding the number of cars constant. For gasoline consumption might increase with income largely because the number of cars does, just as food consumption might increase because family size does. This discussion, brief as it is, should be sufficient to demonstrate that students of consumption economics need to pay more attention to the determinants of family size than they have in the past.

[35] See, for example, Theil, *op. cit.*, S. J. Prais and H. S. Houthhakker, *The Analysis of Family Budgets*, Cambridge, Cambridge University Press, 1955. Measures of family size often include not only the inner core of parents and their children but also other relatives living in the same household. My discussion refers only to the inner core; a somewhat different discussion is required for "other relatives."

[36] Prais and Houthhakker appear to believe that family size is determined by non-economic factors when they say "It might be thought that since household size is, in a sense, a noneconomic factor. . . ." *ibid.*, p. 88.

IV. Summary

This paper employs an economic framework to analyze the factors determining fertility. Children are viewed as a durable good, primarily a consumer's durable, which yields income, primarily psychic income, to parents. Fertility is determined by income, child costs, knowledge, uncertainty, and tastes. An increase in income and a decline in price would increase the demand for children, although it is necessary to distinguish between the quantity and quality of children demanded. The quality of children is directly related to the amount spent on them.

Each family must produce its own children since children cannot be bought or sold in the market place. This is why every uncertainty in the production of children (such as their sex) creates a corresponding uncertainty in consumption. It is also why the number of children in a family depends not only on its demand but also on its ability to produce or supply them. Some families are unable to produce as many children as they desire and some have to produce more than they desire. Therefore, actual fertility may diverge considerably from desired fertility.

I briefly explored some implications of this theory. For example, it may largely explain the postwar rise in fertility in Western nations, the relatively small cyclical fluctuation in fertility compared to that in other durables, some observed relations between the quantity and quality of children, and why rural women are more fertile than urban women.

I tested in more detail one important implication, namely that the number of children desired is directly related to income. Crude cross-sectional data show a negative relationship with income, but the crude data do not hold contraceptive knowledge constant. When it is held constant, a positive relationship appears. This view is supported by the positive correspondence between cyclical movements in income and fertility. The secular decline in fertility may also be consistent with a positive relationship since the secular decline in child mortality and the secular rise in both contraceptive knowledge and child costs could easily have offset the secular rise in income.

COMMENT

JAMES S. DUESENBERRY, Harvard University

I. For many years economists have taken variations in rates of population growth, and in family size, as *data* which help to explain various economic phenomena but which cannot themselves be explained in terms of economic theory. Becker has done us a real service in bringing economic analysis to bear on the problem once more. He has not only worked out the implications of traditional economic theory for demographic theory but has also gone some distance in testing those implications against the empirical data.

Becker argues that those couples with sufficient contraceptive knowledge to control births have to decide how many children to have. For most people, children produce certain satisfactions and have a net cost. In those circumstances we expect (with some qualifications) that the number of children per family will rise with income just as we expect the number of cars or chairs or cubic feet of housing space per family to rise with income. But just as in those cases we expect the quality of cars or chairs or houses to rise with income as well as the number, we also expect the quality of children to rise with income as well as the number. That is, we expect the children of the rich to be better housed, fed, and educated than those of the poor.

Becker then qualifies the argument by taking into account the fact that in some circumstances children may yield their parents a net income instead of having a net cost. In that case the theory of investment is relevant as well as the theory of consumption. He has brought in a number of other considerations which I need not review but which lead to only minor qualifications of his main arguments.

After reviewing the implications of economic theory, Becker then faces the fact that for many years the raw data on differential fertility have shown a fairly strong negative relationship between variations in income and variations in numbers of children per family. Moreover, until recently the average number of children per completed family has been declining although average family income has been rising secularly.

Becker maintains that the negative correlation between income and family size is due to the negative association between income and knowledge of contraceptive methods. I think that most of us would agree that differential knowledge does explain a large part of the apparent negative relation between income and family size.

The evidence of the Indianapolis study certainly supports that conclusion. Becker, however, tries to use the study to support his conclusion that there should be a positive association between income and family size. I must say that the evidence he cites did not strike me as exactly overwhelming.

The empirical evidence offers, I would say, rather ambiguous support for Becker's hypothesis. That may be because we have only a limited amount of the right kind of data but there are, I think, some reasons for thinking that Becker's theoretical case may not be so open and shut as appears. Those reasons have to do with the nature of the "cost" of children and with the limitations on the possibility of substitution between quantity and quality of children.

II. Becker has taken the occasion to correct the simple-minded who fail to distinguish between the cost of children of given quality and expenditure per child. Now, of course, it is correct to regard changes in prices (or relative prices) of a given quality of a good as changes in the cost of that good and changes in amount or quality of the good purchased (at a given price schedule) as changes in expenditure not involving changes in cost. But not all of those who say that the cost of children rises with income are so simple-minded as Becker suggests, though their language may not be exact. What Leibenstein, for example, appears to mean is that the expenditure per child which the parents consider to be necessary rises with income.

Questions of semantics aside, there is an important substantive difference between Becker's approach and that taken by economists whose approach is, if he will excuse the expression, more sociological.

I used to tell my students that the difference between economics and sociology is very simple. Economics is all about how people make choices. Sociology is all about why they don't have any choices to make.

Becker assumes that any couple considers itself free to choose any combination it wishes of numbers of children and expenditure per child (prices of particular goods and services being given). I submit that a sociologist would take the view that given the educational level, occupation, region, and a few other factors, most couples would consider that they have a very narrow range of choice. To take only one example, I suggest that there is no one in the room, not even Becker, who considers himself free to choose either two children who go to university or four children who stop their education after high school. It may be said that that still leaves lots of room for variation, but I think it can be said that no one in this room considers seriously having, say, four children who attend third-rate colleges at low cost per head or three who attend better ones.

For this audience I need not go through the whole routine about roles, goals, values, and so on. It will be sufficient to remark that there is no area in which the sociological limitations of freedom of choice apply more strongly than to behavior in regard to bringing up children.

Effective freedom of choice between quantity and quality of children is also limited by more mundane and mechanical considerations. The principle of substitution which is at the basis of Becker's argument suggests that if the parents have low quality children, as he puts it, they can spend more of their income on something else. Quality of children means, in Becker's terminology, nothing more than expenditure per child (with a given price schedule). But in many respects the standard of living of the children is mechanically linked to that of the parents. Is it possible to have crowded housing conditions for the children and un-crowded conditions for the parents? As the father of four I am in a position to answer with an unqualified negative. Children may eat a different menu from their parents, but if so, it is because they *like* peanut-butter sandwiches. I could go on but I am sure it's unnecessary. A final point in this connection is the non-cash cost of improving quality in children. Becker has used the term quality as though it were just another expression for expenditure at constant prices. But in the more ordinary sense of the term, quality has to be bought with time as well as money. Most parents think (probably mistakenly) that their children are better off if the parents spend time with them. Now time can be bought in the sense that domestic help and appliances can be bought to free time for other things. But even if one had nothing else to do, the marginal disutility of Cub Scout and PTA meetings rises rapidly. These non-cash costs must certainly be of some importance in determining family size.

Becker will say that this is merely an aspect of the diminishing marginal utility of numbers of children. He is correct, of course, but the investment of time in children is not a matter of individual choice any more than the investment of money. The time which parents spend on children is largely determined by social conventions. Those conventions differ among social classes. Since social class is often associated with income, the non-cash costs I have mentioned will influence the apparent relation between income and family size in many cross-sections.

Those considerations lead me to the following conclusions: (1) the effect of income on family size which Becker expects will be greatly weakened by the tendency for the standard of living for children to advance more or less proportionately with that of the parents, and (2) standards of education and of expenditure of time on children will vary with social class. Social class in turn will be associated with income but not in a unique way. In some societies it may turn out that the "cost" of children rises faster than income, in others more slowly.

To put it more generally, economic factors are certainly likely to influence the number of children born to those who are able to plan births. But I do not feel that we are likely to find out much about their influence by simply drawing an analogy between children and durable goods.

BERNARD OKUN, Princeton University

Rupert Vance, in his Presidential address before the Population Association of America at Princeton in 1952, prescribed for demographers "a good stiff dosage of theory, adequately compounded."[1] Gary Becker has heeded Vance's prescription, and in addition has presented us with an interesting and challenging paper.

The essence of Becker's theory of the demand for children can be reduced to two propositions. First, as family income increases, parents will provide their children with a higher level of living. Second, as income increases, parents will probably increase the number of children which they demand. My comments will strongly concur with the first proposition, but will question the second.

In his economic theory, Becker treats children like consumer durables. His justification for treating children in this fashion is that, like automobiles, children are a source of utility and require a considerable outlay of expenditures. It is then contended that the nature of the demand for children is similar to that for automobiles—higher income families demand more automobiles and better quality automobiles; similarly, they demand more children and spend more per child.

In his analysis, Becker distinguishes two components in the expenditures on a child. The first relates to the size and nature of the basket of goods and services which the child consumes. The second relates to the prices of the goods and services which the child consumes. Expenditures per child can change either because of a change in the composition of the child's consumption basket, or because of a change in the prices of the components of the basket. Becker equates the additional utility received by the parents resulting from an increase in expenditures of the first kind, i.e., expenditures directed toward an improvement in the composition of the basket, with the increase in the "quality" of the child. Such expenditures shall be referred to as quality expenditures. Becker defines a change in expenditures per child resulting simply from a change in the prices of one or more components of the basket, that is, the second kind of change, as a change in the "*cost*" of a child. Thus, in Becker's framework, the concept of a change in the cost of a child is a very narrow one. It refers only to a change in expenditures per child, where the child continues to consume a fixed basket of goods and services.

A word of caution is necessary here. Becker has related quality expenditures to the amount of utility that children provide for their parents. This relation, however, is valid only within a given family unit. One

[1] Rupert B. Vance, "Is Theory for Demographers?", *Social Forces*, Vol. 31, 1952, p. 13.

cannot conclude that the family which purchases less for their child derives less total utility from him in comparison with the family which purchases more. Such a conclusion implies an unwarranted inter-personal comparison of utility. If the Jones boy is paying for dancing lessons while the Smith boy is reading a borrowed copy of Marshall's *Principles*, one cannot conclude that the Joneses are deriving more utility than the Smiths with regard to these alternative pursuits of their respective sons.

Becker has imputed much theoretical significance to his distinction between the concepts of quality expenditures and cost expenditures. For example, in his conclusion, it is suggested that a secular increase in the "cost" component contributed to a secular decline in fertility. Nothing is said about the effect of a secular change in the "quality" component. We shall return to this point shortly.

Becker's paper suggests a second distinction between the quality and cost components. The cost of a child, which depends on the prices of commodities and services, is determined by the market forces of supply and demand. Cost, therefore, is not a family decision variable, and is independent of family income. On the other hand, quality expenditures are a family decision variable and are positively related to income. Becker stresses that higher income families have higher quality children (spend more per child), and that this is a voluntary decision. According to Becker, "The rich simply choose higher quality children."

Is the quality expenditure component purely a decision variable? Do the rich really have a choice? To a large extent, I submit that they do not. It is almost impossible to conceive of a child who is raised at a much lower level of living than that of his parents. He lives where they live, tends to eat what they eat, and in general, as a matter of course, shares about the same standard of living that they do, by virtue of his living with them. Surely, the child cannot be sent to live in the slums of the Lower East Side while his parents dwell in a penthouse on Park Avenue. Thus, automatically, when parents raise their own level of living, their child's is also raised, and quality expenditures per child *must* rise.

When demographers, economists, or anybody, for that matter, speak of a decline in the birth rate, they are referring to a decline in the number of children born divided by either total population or some component of population (for example, women of childbearing age). The total number of children born is not weighted by a quality index—every child is given a weight of unity. Thus, if we are to turn to economic theory for an explanation of the decline in the birth rate, one must argue that *expenditures* (as opposed to "cost") per child have risen over time. It is theoretically irrelevant to distinguish between quality expenditures and "cost" expenditures. Becker's conclusion that an increase in "cost" expenditures per child contributed to the decline in the birth rate is useful only if he is referring to a decline in the birth rate of children of homogeneous quality. But since quality expenditures per child have increased over time, this is not the case. Therefore, in explaining birth-rate trends or fertility differences by income, where quality expenditures per child vary in a systematic way, although not reflected in the measurement of the birth rate, Becker's distinction between quality and "cost" expenditures is not useful. The relevant economic variable is simply expenditures per child.

It is for the reasons cited above that I wish to defend Harvey Leibenstein against Becker's criticism. I might add that I have a vested interest in doing so since an argument similar to Leibenstein's appears in one of my own writings.[2] Becker quotes Leibenstein as follows: "The conventional costs of child maintenance increase as per capita income increases. The style in which a child is maintained depends on the position and income of the parents; therefore, we expect such costs to rise as incomes rise. . . ."[3]

Although Becker is correct in noting that Leibenstein failed to make the statistical distinction between quality and "cost" expenditures, this is not the relevant distinction that should be made in a theory of the demand for children which attempts to link income and fertility. The relevant distinction, if any, is voluntary expenditures versus involuntary expenditures. To a large extent, the higher income and social position of the family *require* that it spend more per child. In this sense, a rise in income necessarily results in a relative increase in expenditures per child. This, economic theory suggests, would have a depressing effect on the quantity of children demanded. Consequently, the quantity income elasticity of demand for children is quite low. Indeed, for most of the income range, the quality income elasticity may be so high that it contributes to a negative quantity income elasticity of demand.

On the other hand, the quantity income elasticity for consumer durables is generally much higher. Several distinctions between children and consumer durables account for this. One distinction has already been alluded to in the preceding discussion. The quality of a child as a function of income is less of a decision variable than, for example, the

[2] See Bernard Okun, *Trends in Birth Rates in the United States Since 1870*, The Johns Hopkins Press, Baltimore, 1958, pp. 177–180.
[3] Harvey Leibenstein, *Economic Backwardness and Economic Growth*, John Wiley, 1957, pp. 163–164.

quality of an automobile. This may tend to cause the quality income elasticity of consumer goods to be less than that for children, and this would allow a higher quantity income elasticity for consumer goods.

For consumer goods, quantity appears to be a closer substitute for quality than in the case of children. Two lower-price cars may be considered equivalent to one high-priced car for the high income family. But is it just as likely that this family would be indifferent toward having two children who are untrained or not well-educated, or having one well-educated child? Probably not. In fact some parents may derive disutility if their children fall below their quality standards.

Probably a more common occurrence among higher income two-car families is that they will own one high-priced car, and also own a lower quality second car. Are they apt to follow a similar policy with regard to children—that is, we already have one son who is a Princeton graduate, so we can plan to finance our second son only through high school? I think not. This unwillingness to diminish the quality of successive children tends to diminish the quantity income elasticity of demand for children, relative to that for commodities.

For reasons cited above, it is suggested here that unlike the typical case for consumer durables, the quantity income elasticity of demand for children may well be negative, or if positive, be very low. Briefly restated, our main point is that as income increases, quality expenditures per child do—and in a large measure must—increase to such an extent that parents tend to reduce their demand for children. Note, however, an exception to this proposition—in the very high income families, where family size tends to be larger than in the middle income families, it seems evident that parents can satisfy their quality requirements without having to restrict the quantity of children by the same degree as the somewhat lower income families.

The weight of the empirical evidence presented at this National Bureau conference as well as that of other studies supports the proposition that, for most of the income range, fertility varies inversely with income. Becker contends that these data do not apply to his theory because lower income people have inadequate knowledge of birth control. If all families had perfect control over family size, Becker contends that the relationship would be reversed. In this fashion, he defends the position that the quantity income elasticity is positive.

Becker notes correctly that knowledge of birth control is ever-increasing. If the quantity income elasticity of the demand for children is positive, one would expect the inverse birth-rate differentials by income to be ever-narrowing as birth-control knowledge continuously spreads. While a narrowing trend has occurred, it has been far from persistent. For example, Clyde Kiser found, in comparing family size and income in the United States in 1952 and 1957 that "the apparent enlargement of the differentials by income was quite pronounced."[4] This is a finding which clearly weakens Becker's point that differentials in birth-control knowledge are the factor accounting for the inverse relation between income and family size.

There is also strong evidence to suggest that where social or economic forces prevail which tend to diminish the size of family desired, the lack of knowledge of modern birth-control techniques is not an obstacle in the path of declining family size. For example, according to Whelpton's figures, in the Southern United States, which was largely rural in 1800 as well as in 1870, the fertility rate declined by more than 50 per cent from 1800 to 1870—a period long before modern birth-control methods were known.[5] A similar experience occurred in France after 1800. This evidence tends to weaken the contention that an improvement in birth-control knowledge explained a significant share in the secular decline in fertility.

Becker also attempts to support his thesis that income and the demand for children are positively related by pointing to the positive conformity of the birth rate to fluctuation in the business cycle. I feel that during a business cycle, the time period may be too short for parents' views and standards regarding quality of children to change significantly as a result of a change in income. During the downswing, parents will strive to maintain their standard of living and the quality of their children. Faced with this economic pressure, they will postpone having more children. During the peak stages, income may be rising faster than child-quality standards, and couples can think in terms of having more children without encroaching on their accustomed level of living and their child-quality standards.

The well-known "making-up" theory may partly account for the positive association between fluctuations in income and fertility over the business cycle. This theory holds that the business cycle mainly affects the timing of the arrival of children, but has no or but negligible effect on completed family size. For all these reasons, a positive association between changes in income and the birth rate over the cycle is readily explained.

[4] Clyde V. Kiser, "Differential Fertility in the United States," in this volume.

[5] P. K. Whelpton, *Forecasts of the Population of the United States 1945–1975*, Bureau of the Census, 1947, p. 16.

In the long run, however, standards of living and child quality standards adjust to a secular rise in income. The secular rise in income causes an increase in the quality of children, and therefore expenditures per child rise. This tends to diminish the quantity of children demanded, and the well-known empirical inverse relation between income and the birth rate reasserts itself.

The Influence of Business Cycles on Marriage and Birth Rates

DUDLEY KIRK

THE POPULATION COUNCIL

Both popular thinking and scholarly literature generally assume that there is a meaningful relation between business cycles and vital events. Marriage and birth rates were low during the great depression and high during the recent period of postwar prosperity. There have been predictions that the recession of 1957–1958 would be followed by a significant and perhaps precipitous recession in births.[1]

Despite widespread interest in the subject, efforts to measure this relationship and make it more precise have been relatively few. Early attempts at investigation were greatly hampered by defects in the basic data. While these have greatly improved, there remain quite difficult logical and methodological problems both in measuring and in interpreting the degree of covariance between economic data and vital statistics. The purpose of the present paper is to review this relationship for the period since the First World War.

The most authoritative study of the subject is that of V. L. Galbraith and D. S. Thomas on "Birth Rates and the Interwar Business Cycles." Using deviations from trends, these authors found a correlation of 0.80 between employment levels (that is, the Bureau of Labor Statistics adjusted index of factory employment) and total births for the period 1919–1937, with births lagged one year.[2] More detailed analysis of the relation between employment levels and successive orders of birth suggested that the influence of employment conditions was effective both indirectly through its influence on marriages and first births, and directly

---

[1] Population Reference Bureau, "Recession in Births?", *Population Bulletin*, Vol. xiv, no. 6, October, 1958, p. 110.

[2] Virginia L. Galbraith and Dorothy S. Thomas, "Birth Rates and the Interwar Business Cycles," *Journal of the American Statistical Association*, Vol. 36, no. 216, December, 1941, pp. 465–476. This correlation was higher than found by Thomas for earlier periods, a finding consistent with the diffusion of the practice of family limitation to larger segments of the population. Cf. William F. Ogburn and Dorothy S. Thomas, "The Influence of the Business Cycle on Certain Social Conditions," *Quarterly Publications of the American Statistical Association*, Vol. 18, 1922, pp. 324–340; Dorothy S. Thomas, *Social Aspects of the Business Cycle*, Knopf, 1927, pp. 97–103; Dorothy S. Thomas, *Social and Economic Aspects of Swedish Population Movements, 1750–1933*, Macmillan, 1941, pp. 161–166.

241

on the numbers of second and higher orders of birth. However, the results of multiple correlation analysis were inconclusive as to the comparative importance of these two channels of influence.

Yule, Thomas, Hexter, and others have found that marriages respond more sensitively to fluctuations in economic conditions than births, although as early as 1925 Thomas reported that the connection between birth rates and business cycles was becoming stronger while that between marriage rates and business cycles was becoming weaker, suggesting the "interesting hypothesis that whereas a business depression formerly led to prudential restraint through abstention from marriage, it now leads to a more widespread and deliberate use of birth control."[3]

The present study follows the basic method, used by Galbraith and Thomas, in correlating trend deviations of economic measures (as independent variables) to measures of nuptiality and natality (as dependent variables). This method greatly reduces the "auto-" or serial correlation that often inflates the apparent covariance in time series, for example, when this covariance is measured by absolutes, by annual per cent change, or by deviations from moving averages.[4]

[3] Dorothy S. Thomas, *Social Aspects*, etc., *op. cit.*, pp. 99–100. Cf. G. U. Yule, "Changes in Marriage and Birth Rates in England and Wales during the Past Half Century," *Journal of the Royal Statistical Society*, Vol. LXIX, March, 1906, pp. 100–132; M. B. Hexter, *Social Consequences of Business Cycles*, Houghton Mifflin Co., 1925.

[4] The validity of inferences based on correlation coefficients of time series is open to question because of the internal auto-correlation inherent in such series. This inherent quality arises from the circumstance that time series observations are not independent of each other, that they are not randomly chosen, that the value at any one time is strongly conditioned by the magnitude at time $t - 1$. Thus time series correlations tend to be highly correlated, either positively or negatively, not only for aggregate data but also for unit rates.

Even time series of deviations from respective trends do not fully meet the statistical requirements of random, normally distributed, independent observations, but inasmuch as the secular trend has been removed, such series are freer of auto-correlative properties than the original data from which they are derived. Thus it was found that the first lead auto-correlation coefficient for fertility rates for the period 1947 through 1958 (i.e. fertility rates correlated with itself lagged one year) is 0.87, but only 0.42 for the auto-correlation of the series representing deviations from a linear least squares trend line. Similarly, the first lag auto-correlation of the index of industrial production was 0.88 for the 1947–1957 period, compared with −0.20 for its deviations from trend.

In another test developed by Bartlett, the confidence limits of the coefficient of correlation are reinterpreted on the basis of Bartlett's calculation of the number of terms involved in the correlation. Cf. Orcutt and James, "Testing the Significance of Correlation between Time Series," *Biometrika*, December, 1948, pp. 397–413. In applying this test it was found that the correlation coefficient between trend deviations of the index of industrial production and fertility rates (the latter lagged one year) for the 1947–1957 period was unaffected by any auto-correlation. These tests suggest that the methods used in this paper greatly reduce, where they do not eliminate, the influence of auto-correlation.

An alternative method for investigating the relation between economic fluctuations and marriage and fertility rates is the National Bureau of Economic Research reference cycle technique. This involves an examination of the directional movement of the various

Theoretically, several economic indicators may be selected to examine the relationship between business conditions and marriage and fertility rates. In a previous study, I assumed that employment indexes would be a sensitive measure of the impact of business cycles on the birth rate.[5] Similarly Galbraith and Thomas did not think it necessary to explain the use of an employment index as synonymous with the business cycle. Perhaps for a period of massive unemployment such as was experienced in the 1930's, the supposition of employment as the decisive factor is valid. But in "normal" or prosperous periods a relatively small segment of the population is directly affected by unemployment. At such times the population as a whole may well be more influenced by the general level of economic activity or by the level of income and prices than by unemployment per se.

The economic indicators selected for this study are (*a*) real per capita personal income, (*b*) the Federal Reserve Board index of industrial production, and (*c*) nonagricultural employment and unemployment as a per cent of the civilian labor force. Each of these has been related for the period 1920–1958 (omitting years most directly affected by World War II) with measures of nuptiality and natality. The measures of the latter used here are marriage rates per 1,000 *unmarried* women at ages 15–44 and general fertility rates, that is, births per 1,000 women at ages 15–44. These measures of marriage and birth rates are used to reduce the variability arising from the effects of changes in the marital status and age structure of the population. The basic data are presented in Appendix A.

Using real per capita personal income as representative of the economic indicators, Chart 1 shows its relationship with the absolute numbers of births and marriages, and Chart 2 its relationship with nuptiality and fertility.

Four separate periods are discernible:

(1) *The prosperous 1920's*, characterized by rising levels of production and per capita income, but by a marked downward drift in marriage and birth rates, the last usually identified with the spread of birth control.

---

series under consideration at crucial reference dates predetermined by the National Bureau of Economic Research to represent the initial troughs, peaks, and terminal troughs of cycles of economic activity. This method is designed to analyze monthly and other short-interval data, and assumes a series of cycles. It is therefore not readily applicable to the annual data used in the present paper, and to the period under consideration, which includes only one major economic cycle. Cf. Arthur F. Burns and Wesley C. Mitchell, *Measuring Business Cycles*, National Bureau of Economic Research, Studies in Business Cycles, no. 2, 1946.

[5] Dudley Kirk, "The Relation of Employment Levels to Births in Germany," *Milbank Memorial Fund Quarterly*, Vol. 20, no. 2, April, 1942, pp. 126–138.

CHART 1

Real Per Capita Personal Income, Marriages and Births, 1920–1957

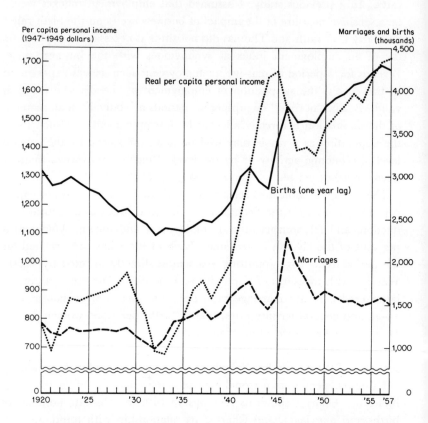

(2) *The depression 1930's,* which shows a trough in all three indexes but of quite different character. Marriage rates had already regained their 1929 level by 1934; personal income and the index of industrial production began to recover in 1935 but for the most part remained substantially below their historical secular trends, while the downward fertility curve of the 1920's seems to have leveled off to an asymptote reached in the middle 1930's.

(3) *The war years,* which introduced new factors strongly affecting the economic indexes and the marriage rates. Because of the influences of the draft, of demobilization, and of other special circumstances of the war extraneous to the present discussion, the data for the war and immediate postwar years have been omitted from the analysis.

CHART 2

Real Per Capita Personal Income, Nuptiality, Fertility, and
Respective Trends, 1920–1958

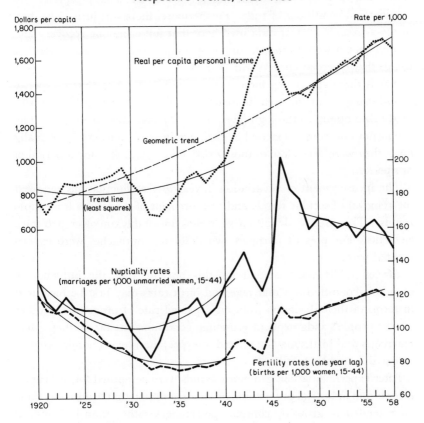

(4) *The postwar decade*, in which the economy resumed its historical trend of upward growth, this trend accompanied by an upward trend in birth rates but not marriage rates, which fell from high wartime levels early in the decade and have been relatively stable since 1952.

Descriptively, the variables are highly correlated in their absolute amounts but owing to the existence of internal serial correlation such evidence is unsuitable for inferential analysis. There is only a general correspondence between the longer-range secular trends in fertility, nuptiality, and economic conditions.

The decline of fertility during the 1920's occurred in the face of economic prosperity and its downward course was not markedly accentuated by the depression. In fact, the downward drift of fertility so evident in the 1920's was actually checked and stabilized in the depths of the depression. At its low point in 1933, the fertility rate was only 14 per cent below its 1930 level, a year which reflected the peak prosperity and employment conditions of 1929. Furthermore, there was little indication in the aggregate prewar data used here that full economic recovery and reemployment would produce anything comparable to the actual fertility trends that emerged after World War II.

Nor is there any strong indication in the prewar data that prosperity would bring about the great increase in marriage rates that has contributed substantially to the high level of fertility since World War II. The proportions of women married at each age in 1940 were not abnormally low; they were very close to those existing in 1930, following a period of prosperity.

The measurement of covariation in year-to-year fluctuations required the removal of secular trends and measurement of deviations from those trends. The precise definition of trends inevitably involves arbitrary elements. For present purposes two different approaches were experimented with.

Method 1. It was assumed for this purpose that the influence of economic conditions on marriage and birth rates may best be measured in terms of their deviation from an expected rate of progress. In other words, people's judgments of economic conditions insofar as they affect marriages and births may be related to expectations of economic progress rather than to absolute levels.

After experimentation, geometric trends were computed for per capita income and industrial production, on the assumption that historically these have tended to grow by constant percentages rather than by constant amounts. Points of origin were found by averaging the figures for 1920–1922 and 1955–1957, a procedure that provided an average annual rise of 2.3 per cent for real per capita income and of 3.9 per cent for industrial production. Data on unemployment as per cent of civilian labor force was assumed to represent deviations from the secular trend in employment potential, defined as the growing size of the civilian labor force.

While economic indexes have shown consistent historical growth, it would be unreasonable, of course, to make such assumptions about marriage and birth rates. After experimentation a second degree parabola was fitted by least squares to the natality data for 1921–1942, and a linear trend was computed for the postwar period. A linear trend was computed for the marriage rates for the entire period 1920–1957, excluding the war and immediate postwar years.

246

CHART 3

Percentage Deviations from Computed Trends of Economic Indexes, Nuptiality and Fertility, 1920–1958

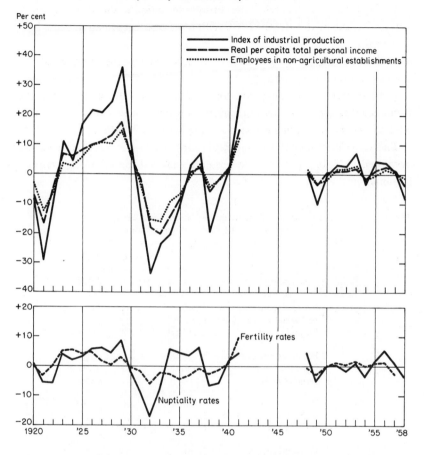

Method 2. In the second method least squares lines were fitted for all series. In each case parabolas were fitted to the data for the period 1920–1941 (1921–1942 for birth rates) and linear least squares lines for the postwar materials.

The second method assumes that marriage and birth rates might be expected to react more closely to the *absolute* changes in the economic indexes, rather than to the relation of existing economic conditions to a historical trend of economic progress. In the second method nonagricultural employment (Bureau of Labor Statistics) instead of unemployment was used as the third economic indicator.

247

The data and trends determined by the two methods are shown in Chart 2 and the trend deviations (for method 2 only) are presented in Chart 3. The data suggest the following generalizations:

1. Over the whole series the economic indexes show the greatest variability, the birth rates the least, with marriage rates in an intermediate position.

2. There was greater variability in all series during the interwar period than in the postwar period.

3. In most years marriage and birth rates are on the same side of the trend lines as the economic indicators, but are not so closely correlated with the economic indicators as these are with each other.

The correlations of the trend deviations under the two methods are presented in Table 1. The data presented suggest the following generalizations:

TABLE 1

Correlations of Percentage Deviations from Trends of
Fertility, Nuptiality, and Economic Indexes

Period	Independent Variable	Dependent Variable	Correlation Coefficient[a]	
			Method I	Method II
1920–41	Per capita income	Fertility[b]	0.74	0.77
	Industrial production	Fertility[b]	.73	.76
	Employment[c]	Fertility[b]	− .73	.76
	Per capita income	Nuptiality	.76	.68
	Industrial production	Nuptiality	.74	.76
	Employment[c]	Nuptiality	− .72	.72
1948–57[d]	Per capita income	Fertility[b]	.86	.66*
	Industrial production	Fertility[b]	.79	.78
	Employment[c]	Fertility[b]	− .65*	.57†
	Per capita income	Nuptiality	.79	.79
	Industrial production	Nuptiality	.66*	.66*
	Employment[c]	Nuptiality	− .45‡	.63*
1920–41	Nuptiality	Fertility[b]	.49*	.55
1948–57	Nuptiality	Fertility[b]	.30‡	.41‡

Note: Unless otherwise indicated, all values significant at 0.01 level.
* Significant at 0.05 level.
† Significant at 0.10 level.
‡ Not statistically significant.
[a] Methods as described in text.
[b] Fertility data related to economic indexes of preceding year.
[c] For Method 1, employment measured by unemployment as per cent of civilian labor force.
[d] 1947–1956 for Method 1.

1. The relationship between the economic indicators and natality was very stable in the interwar period, the coefficients falling within a very narrow range of 0.73–0.77, with no important difference where different independent variables or methods were employed. The coefficients in this series not unexpectedly approximate the figure of 0.80 obtained by Galbraith and Thomas for the period 1917–1937.

2. The relationship between economic indicators and nuptiality for the interwar period is also quite stable, with a range of coefficients from 0.68–0.76. The results give confidence that the method of determining the trend lines is not a decisive factor in the measure of the inter-relationships in the interwar period.

3. There is much greater variability in the coefficients for the past decade, probably owing to the shorter series. The selection of years makes an important difference in the results. There is some suggestion that the relation of employment (or unemployment) to nuptiality and fertility is lower in the postwar than in the interwar period, as might be expected on a priori grounds. Otherwise, the relationships seem to be of the same general order of magnitude as in the interwar period.

4. The coefficients of correlation between nuptiality and fertility are the lowest in the series both for the interwar and postwar periods though the figures for the latter are not statistically significant.

The results of partial and multiple correlation analysis are shown in Table 2. The coefficients of multiple correlation indicate a joint effect of economic factors and nuptiality that explains 50–60 per cent of the variability in fertility in the interwar period. The coefficients for the postwar period are of questionable significance, but suggest a similar level of influence for per capita income and industrial production, though not for employment.

Partial correlation analysis indicates that the entire influence of nuptiality on trend deviations in fertility is a secondary effect of economic fluctuations. When economic factors are held constant there is effectively no correlation between nuptiality and fertility.

The level of simple correlations between economic indicators and fertility using Method 2 is 0.76–0.77, and the simple correlation between nuptiality and fertility is 0.55 (cf. Table 1). The interrelationships of these figures suggest that the economic indicators explain some 58–59 per cent of the variance in the fertility series, of which 30 per cent or about one-half is exercised through nuptiality and the remainder through the direct influence of economic conditions on fertility.

The influence of marriages on fertility is of course most observable in connection with first births. The correlation of numbers of marriages and first births in the following year is very high. But the correlation of trend deviations for nuptiality and natality in the postwar period was lower than in the interwar period (cf. Table 1), a finding consistent with the declining percentage of first births among total births. In 1947 the

TABLE 2

Partial and Multiple Correlations among Trend Deviations of
Economic Indexes, Nuptiality, and Fertility[a]

		Correlation Coefficient	
Period	Variable	Method I[b]	Method II[b]
	Nuptiality constant	*Partial Coefficient*	
1920–41	Per capita income and Fertility	0.65	0.65
	Industrial production and Fertility	.64	.64
	Employment[c] and Fertility	− .61	.62
1948–57[d]	Per capita income and Fertility	.59*	.59*
	Industrial production and Fertility	.74*	.74*
	Employment[c] and Fertility	− .53*	.44*
	Per capita income constant		
1920–41	Fertility and Nuptiality		.06*
1948–57	Fertility and Nuptiality		− .22*
	Industrial production constant		
1920 41	Fertility and Nuptiality		− .08*
1948–57	Fertility and Nuptiality		− .21*
	Employment constant		
1920–41	Fertility and Nuptiality		.004*
1948–57	Fertility and Nuptiality		.08*
	Fertility and Nuptiality with:	*Multiple Coefficient*	
1920–41	Per capita income		.77
	Industrial production		.76
	Employment		.76
1948–57	Per capita income		.68*
	Industrial production		.79*
	Employment		.58*

* Not statistically significant in the postwar period because of lack of significance in correlation between nuptiality and fertility for that period (cf. Table 1).

[a] Fertility data related in all cases to economic indexes and nuptiality of preceding year.

[b] Methods as described in text.

[c] For Method 1, employment measured by unemployment as per cent of civilian labor force.

[d] 1947–1956 for Method 1.

250

rate of first births was 46.7 per thousand women 15–44, but had fallen by 1950 to about 33. Since 1952, it has been stable at this figure. By contrast, the rate of second and higher orders of birth has continued to rise, and is responsible for the rise in fertility and births since 1950.

General fertility rates by parity, presented in Chart 4, illustrate (a) the relation between marriage rates and first births and (b) the extent to

CHART 4

Real Per Capita Personal Income, Nuptiality Rates, and Fertility Rates by First, Second, and Third, and Higher Order Parity, 1920–1958

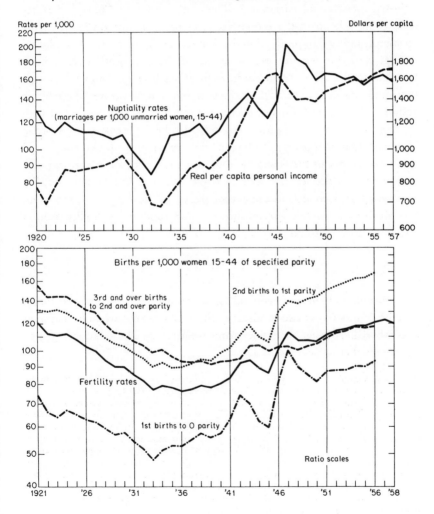

251

which total fertility reflects fluctuations in the rate of first births.[6] By contrast, the rates of second births, and particularly the rates for third and higher order births, show rather little year-to-year fluctuation. When the more immediate influence of marriages is removed, as in parity rates for higher order births, there is a clear secular trend, modified only slightly in its annual variation by economic fluctuations and even by World War II.

Further light on the relationships between economic factors and fertility may be obtained by an examination of the monthly data for the economic series as related to monthly data for fertility when both are adjusted for seasonal variation.[7] These are shown in Chart 5, fertility data being related to the economic series nine months earlier (i.e., the series for industrial production beginning in January 1948 is plotted against data for fertility beginning as of nine months later, namely October 1948). The variability in fertility has been very much less than that in the index of industrial production and other measures of economic activity. The effects of major events are reflected in both series but with different intensity. Both series responded to the outbreak of the Korean War in the summer of 1950. The recessions of 1949, 1954, and 1957–1958 stand out boldly in the economic data but their effects are not nearly so pronounced in the fertility series. There was a recent drop in fertility apparently associated with the earlier phases of the 1957–1958 recession. But much of the natality series shows almost random variability around a smooth upward trend.

General Conclusions

The possible influence of economic fluctuations on marriages and births may be considered at two levels: (1) The degree of covariation in annual and other short-range deviations from trends; (2) The relation between the trends themselves.

[6] The general fertility rates by parity were computed from data kindly supplied by the Scripps Foundation for Research on Population Problems. The level of marriages in a given year of course affects fertility not only in the following year but in subsequent years, and the number of women available to have second births is a function of the number who have already had their first child. These secondary effects are too diffuse to show in the aggregate data used here, but undoubtedly contribute to the stability of fertility trends. It should be noted that P. K. Whelpton, Director of the Scripps Foundation, who has pioneered in the analysis of fertility by age and parity, is now engaged in an extensive study of the relation of economic fluctuations to age-parity specific birth rates.

[7] The monthly fertility series adjusted for seasonal variation, was supplied to the author through the courtesy of Mr. Joseph Schachter from unpublished computations made under his direction in the National Office of Vital Statistics.

CHART 5

Index of Industrial Production and General Fertility Rates (Nine Months Lag), Both Series Adjusted for Seasonal Variation, by Month, 1948–1958

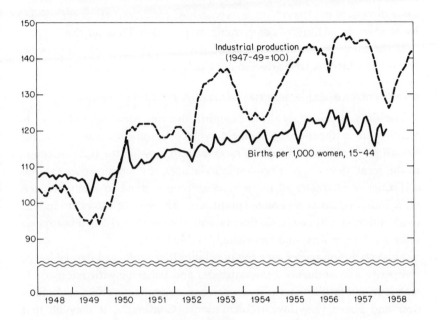

I. DEGREE OF COVARIATION IN DEVIATIONS FROM TRENDS

The results confirm the generally held view that marriages and births respond sensitively to changes in economic conditions. The correlation coefficients of trend deviations for fertility with economic indexes are generally high. They suggest that economic conditions control about one-half of the annual variance of fertility from its trend, the degree of control differing relatively little with the economic index, the choice of trend, and the period covered. A possible exception is the relatively low correlation of employment and unemployment with fertility in the postwar period.

Correlations of nuptiality with fertility are relatively low. When economic indexes are held constant, there is no correlation between the two, suggesting that nuptiality is not an independent factor affecting trend deviations in fertility but is a channel through which economic conditions influence annual variations in fertility. The results indicate that in the interwar period about half of the control exercised by economic conditions operates through nuptiality and the other half is exercised directly on fertility. For the postwar period the findings are too inconclusive to make such an apportionment.

It must be pointed out that the high correlation coefficients merely indicate that deviations from the respective trends are generally in the same direction, not that changes in economic conditions are accompanied by changes in fertility of comparable magnitude. Thus on the average over the whole period studied a trend deviation of 4 per cent in personal income produced a trend deviation of only 1 per cent in fertility.

2. RELATION OF MAJOR BUSINESS CYCLES TO FERTILITY TRENDS

The data of this study do not confirm the view that *major* changes in fertility are a function of business cycles. In other words, while the deviations from trend of fertility rates seem to move in the same direction as the trend deviations of economic indicators, the former series exhibits a distinctive character of its own, describing a trend in many respects quite independent of economic conditions. The surface waves are indeed much influenced by economic fluctuations, but the underlying tide appears to be an independent and surprisingly stable force.

This conclusion passes over the possibility that prolonged depression or prosperity may influence basic attitudes and behavior with reference to marriage and fertility and thereby exercise a cumulative effect on fertility over and above year-to-year fluctuations. Conversely, it may be that fertility would be much more responsive than previously to the onset of a major depression, especially in view of its present relatively high level and the present widespread knowledge of methods of family limitation. Such considerations argue for great caution in attempting to predict the future influence of business cycles on births.

Finally, the above analysis strengthens the view of the author that economic fluctuations in themselves should not be regarded as primary *causes* of fertility trends, but as important conditioning influences. It is highly questionable that many people in a modern industrial society produce children for their economic or market value, though they certainly do limit family size because of concern about the economic costs of an additional child. Economic costs associated with parenthood presumably bear less heavily in times of prosperity and more heavily in times of depression, but in both cases as a check on motivations and behavior of non-economic origin. Changes in the social and psychological forces affecting the latter may be quite independent of economic cycles.

Appendix A

TABLE A-1

Economic Data

Year	Index of Industrial Production (1947–49 = 100)	Real Per Capita Personal Income (1947–49 dollars)	Per Cent Unemployed of Civilian Labor Force	Number of Employees in Non-agricultural Establishments (millions)
1920	41	779	4.0	27.1
21	31	691	11.9	24.1
22	39	782	7.6	25.6
23	47	872	3.2	28.1
24	44	863	5.5	27.8
25	49	875	4.0	28.5
26	51	888	1.9	29.5
27	51	898	4.1	29.7
28	53	918	4.4	29.7
29	59	960	3.2	31.0
1930	49	874	8.7	29.1
31	40	814	15.9	26.4
32	31	687	23.6	23.4
33	37	678	24.9	23.5
34	40	740	21.7	25.7
35	47	804	20.1	26.8
36	56	901	16.9	28.8
37	61	933	14.3	30.7
38	48	874	19.0	28.9
39	58	936	17.2	30.3
1940	67	995	14.6	32.0
41	87	1,148	9.9	36.2
42	106	1,314	4.7	39.8
43	127	1,518	1.9	42.1
44	125	1,644	1.2	41.5
45	107	1,668	1.9	40.0
46	90	1,529	3.9	41.3
47	100	1,396	3.5	43.5
48	104	1,401	3.3	44.4
49	97	1,376	5.4	43.3
1950	112	1,470	4.9	44.7
51	120	1,507	3.0	47.3
52	124	1,544	2.6	48.3
53	134	1,592	2.5	49.7
54	125	1,566	5.0	48.4
55	139	1,649	4.0	50.0
56	143	1,700	3.8	51.9
57	143	1,712	4.3	52.2

TABLE A-2

Demographic Data

| Year | U.S. Live Births (Millions) | Birth Rates Per 1,000 Women 15–44 Years of Age | | Marriages Per 1,000 Unmarried Women 15–44 Years of Age |
		Total	Second and Higher Order	
1920	3.0	119	81	130
21	3.0	121	82	117
22	2.9	112	78	112
23	2.9	111	78	120
24	3.0	112	78	114
25	2.9	108	74	112
26	2.8	103	71	112
27	2.8	100	68	110
28	2.7	94	64	107
29	2.6	90	61	110
1930	2.6	90	60	99
31	2.5	85	57	92
32	2.4	82	55	84
33	2.3	77	52	94
34	2.4	79	52	110
35	2.4	78	49	111
36	2.4	76	47	113
37	2.4	77	47	119
38	2.5	79	48	108
39	2.5	78	47	113
1940	2.6	80	51	127
41	2.7	83	51	136
42	3.0	92	54	146
43	3.1	94	60	132
44	2.9	89	59	123
45	2.8	86	57	138
46	3.4	102	63	202
47	3.8	113	67	183
48	3.6	107	68	177
49	3.6	107	71	159
1950	3.6	106	73	166
51	3.8	111	77	165
52	3.9	114	80	160
53	4.0	115	81	163
54	4.1	118	84	154
55	4.1	118	85	161
56	4.2	121	88	165
57	4.3	123	—	157
58	4.2 est.	120 est.	—	—

Appendix B

I—*Economic Data*

(1) Federal Reserve Board Index of Industrial Production from U.S. Department of Commerce, *Survey of Current Business*, December 1953 and July 1958.

(2) U.S. Per Capita Personal Income in 1947–1949 Dollars: obtained by dividing U.S. Per Capita Personal Income by corresponding Consumer Price Index. Income data are from U.S. Department of Commerce, *Survey of Current Business* for the period 1929–1957; from National Bureau of Economic Research, *Personal Income During Business Cycles*, Business Cycles Studies no. 6, 1956, for the period 1920–1929, with adjustment to link with the Department of Commerce series. Consumer Price Index data are from U.S. Department of Labor, Bureau of Labor Statistics.

(3) Unemployment data: U.S. Department of Commerce, Bureau of the Census, for period 1929–1957; National Bureau of Economic Research, *Special Conference Series No. 8*, "Annual Estimates of Unemployment in U.S., 1900–1954," for period 1920–1928.

(4) Number of employees in non-agricultural establishments: U.S. Department of Labor, Bureau of Labor Statistics.

II—*Demographic Data*

Compiled and adapted from the several series of *Special Reports* published by the National Office of Vital Statistics. Births and birth rates corrected for under-registration. Data on second and higher order births for years prior to 1940 estimated from data published for native-white women.

COMMENT

DOROTHY SWAINE THOMAS, University of Pennsylvania

Dudley Kirk's paper on "The Influence of Business Cycles on Marriage and Birth Rates" throws new light on an old problem and makes ingenious use of improved basic data for analysis of interrelationships in recent years in the United States.

The close positive relationship between fluctuations in economic well-being and fluctuations in the marriage rate has been observed for long periods of time in almost all countries for which even rudimentary historical statistics exist; first, the concomitance of upswings and down-swings in various indexes of the adequacy of the harvest with marriage frequencies; later, the concomitance of various measures of business cycles and crude or refined marriage rates. The correspondence was, and has continued to be, so close that Farr suggested in 1885 that "it is a fair deduction from the facts that the marriage returns in England point out periods of prosperity little less distinctly than the funds measure the hopes and fears of the money market. If the one is the barometer of credit, the other is the barometer of prosperity, present in part, but future, expected, anticipated in still greater part."[1] Beveridge, in 1912, in his classic treatise on unemployment included a time series on marriage rates, along with various other cyclical series as a measure of "the pulse of the nation";[2] and Joseph S. Davis in a memorandum in the spring of 1958 proposes using "marriages as a current economic indicator" of consumer confidence or caution with respect to major commitments for the future in the United States.[3] With cycles as well-defined as they are in marriage series; with the longer term trends in the basic population "exposed to the risk of marrying," and in the age-specific propensities to marry so slow-moving and regular, in general no great refinement of technique is needed to demonstrate the direction and strength of correlations with economic cycles. When, as has become customary, secular trends are removed by moving averages or some other smoothing process and years of major war disturbances eliminated, the correlation coefficients rarely fall below 0.70 and often approach 0.90. The persistence of correlations of this magnitude, over time, and among different areas is, perhaps, one of the most firmly based empirical findings in any of the social sciences.

The situation with regard to the birth rate is not so simple. The relationships with economic fluctuations noted in England, in Sweden, and elsewhere during early industrializing or pre-industrial periods undoubtedly reflect in large part, the operation of the Malthusian positive check, as suggested by Sundbärg's observation that "when the harvest failed, marriage and birth rates declined and death devastated the land, bearing witness to need and privation and at times even to starvation."[4] Each famine was accompanied by an immediate rise in the death rate, and a fall, without lag (on an annual basis) in the birth rate, whether the latter was measured on a crude basis or in terms of legitimate and illegitimate fertility rates; each period of abundance by an equally quick response in falling death rates and rising birth and fertility rates. With a more rapid pace of industrialization, improved transportation and communication, and urbanization, the sharp secular decline that occurred in birth or fertility rates reflects primarily the operation of the neo-Malthusian preventive check. There is, moreover, evidence that the spread of the small-family system, through effective use of contraception or other means of birth control, proceeded until very recent years from

---

[1] William Farr, *Vital Statistics*, London, 1885, p. 68.

[2] William H. Beveridge, *Unemployment: A Problem of Industry*, London, 1912, p. 44.

[3] Mimeographed, Council of Economic Advisers, Washington, 1958.

[4] Translated and cited by Dorothy S. Thomas, in *Social and Economic Aspects of Swedish Population Movements, 1750–1933*, New York, 1941, p. 82.

the more favored economic and social classes through the middle classes and penetrated much more slowly into the lower economic and social ranges of the population. Thus, both secularly and structurally there has been a negative relationship between married fertility (or size of family) and income or level of living. At the same time, however, in most highly industrialized areas, positive relationships between business cycles and birth or general fertility rates have been observed, with a lag of a year or more. Compared with the correlations found for marriage rates, over long periods, birth-or-fertility rate correlations with various indexes of business cycles have been rather unstable, with the coefficients showing a pronounced upward trend; from little more than 0.30 to 0.40 during the late 19th and early decades of the 20th century to values clustering around 0.70 to 0.80, and therefore approximating those found for marriage rates during the interwar and postwar years, at least for the United States.

Intervening between the positive relationship of business cycles and fluctuations in birth or fertility measures is the demonstrated positive relationship of business cycles and marriage rates for, in general, if the marriage rate rises or falls there will, with an appropriate lag, be a secondary rise or fall in the birth rate. And, as Kirk points out, "the influence of marriage on fertility is of course most observable in connection with first births." With the spread of the small-family system, first births have, over a long period, had increasingly heavy weights in series representing aggregate births; and from the long-term view this may account for the strengthening of the correlation between business cycles and fluctuations in birth-fertility series. Kirk's slightly higher correlations for the last ten years, in spite of a short-term decrease in the weight of first births, is interesting, inasmuch as the correlation for this period between nuptiality and general fertility rates was only of the order of 0.50, a value much lower than that observed for the interwar period and suggesting that the impact of business cycles may be increasingly felt in the higher orders of births.

Kirk's findings and interpretations raise a number of questions about the most profitable procedures for future research in this important field:

(1) He questions the use of unemployment–employment indexes as measures of business cycles on the ground that "the direct effects of unemployment" would except in periods of "massive unemployment" be felt "by a relatively small part of the total population." I am in complete agreement with this point, as with his further statement that "it seems reasonable to suppose that persons are susceptible in the mass to the influence of economic factors that may not necessarily bear very heavily

or directly on all, but may shade, both consciously or unconsciously, decisions and behavior affecting the birth rate." Rather than taking, as he does "several economic series" that "might theoretically be·expected to influence the level of marriages and births," however, I suggest the use of highly generalized "reference cycles," prepared by the National Bureau of Economic Research.

(2) He computes various complicated trends, from geometric growth curves to the second degree parabolas to straight lines. My own experience with historical series suggests that all of these are open to question, on theoretical grounds, and that the "cutting" of the cycles is often very ineffectively done by these procedures. Some of the observed interperiod variations are unquestionably to be attributed to the vagaries of trend fitting rather than or in addition to substantive changes in the behavior under observation.

(3) Questions may also be raised about the propriety of computing correlation coefficients for periods covering only ten years, and as to the suitability of the correlation technique for demonstrating the nature and extent of cyclical covariation. If the cycle, rather than the year, the quarter, or the month, is the valid time unit for measurement, fruitful use can, again, be made of the National Bureau techniques of defining turning points and phases of cycles for both specific and reference series. In this connection I suggest that the long historical series that have been perhaps inappropriately analyzed by many investigators (including myself) for many areas be reexamined with new techniques.

(4) Kirk's final section on the relation of major business cycles to fertility trends is limited to very recent experience and does not take account of the fact that "the underlying tide" may not only be an independent force but also, as indicated above, has been negatively rather than positively correlated with trends in the general well-being of the population.

Mortality, Fertility, the Size–Age Distribution, and the Growth Rate

FRANK W. NOTESTEIN

OFFICE OF POPULATION RESEARCH, PRINCETON UNIVERSITY

THIS study deals with the ways in which the components of population change are related to growth and age composition. In general all of these relations and their sources are sufficiently obvious. They turn on a few basic facts of life. Birth is the beginning of life and death its termination, but death occurs at every age, whereas all births occur at age zero. It follows that a rise in the birth rate tends both to lift the rate of growth and to increase the proportion of children in the population. On the other hand, whereas falling death rates also tend to increase growth, their effect on the age composition of the population depends on the age incidence of the change in the risks of dying. In the past, peace-time reductions in mortality have had an age incidence that affected the age composition of the surviving populations rather little, tending to increase slightly the proportions in the youngest and oldest ages in a manner that on balance generally somewhat *reduced* the average age of the population.[1]

Basic Patterns in Population Change

Another basic element is the fact that vital events have rather definite age patterns. The human female seldom gives birth before 15 or after

[1] There is a considerable literature on this subject, including:

J. Bourgeois-Pichat, "Charges de la Population Active," *Journal de la Société Statistique de Paris*, Vol. 91, nos. 3-4, March–April, 1950, pp. 94–114.

Ansley J. Coale, "The Effects of Changes in Mortality and Fertility on Age Composition," *Milbank Memorial Fund Quarterly*, January, 1956, Vol. 34, no. 1, pp. 79–114.

F. Lorimer, "Dynamics of Age Structure in a Population with Initially High Fertility and Mortality," *Population Bulletin of the United Nations*, December, 1951, no. 1, pp. 31–41.

A. Sauvy, "Le Vieillissement des Populations et l'Allongement de la Vie," *Population*, October–December, 1954, Vol. 9, no. 4, pp. 675–682.

G. Stolnitz, "Mortality Declines and Age Distributions," *Milbank Memorial Fund Quarterly*, Vol. 34, no. 2, April, 1956, pp. 178–215.

United Nations Population Division, "The Cause of the Aging of Populations: Declining Mortality or Declining Fertility?", *Population Bulletin of the United Nations*, December, 1954, no. 4, pp. 30–38.

V. G. Valaoras, "Patterns of Aging of Human Populations," in the report of the Eastern States Health Education Conference, *The Social and Biological Challenge of our Aging Population*, Columbia University Press, 1950, pp. 67–85.

Note: The assistance of Mrs. Erna Härm in carrying through the population projections is gratefully acknowledged.

50 years of age, and, within these ages, the rate of childbearing rises rapidly to its maximum between 20 and 30 and thereafter falls off sharply. There is also a typical pattern in the risks of death, which are high in infancy and early childhood, decline to a minimum between 10 and 15 years, rise at first rather gradually and then with progressive speed. Migration, like death, can occur at any age, but has, in fact, a typical pattern of heavy concentration between ages 15 and 35. Obviously, the effect of migration on the growth and age of a particular population depends on the direction, magnitude, and duration of the movement.

In addition to these specific components of growth, there are their interrelations. From the point of view of a particular population, all persons born must eventually emigrate or die, and, before doing either, may have one or more offspring. Those who immigrate may also produce offspring before they emigrate or die. By contrast, death has no subsequent direct relation to the other vital processes. The secondary consequences, however, may be quite important, as, for example, when a shortage of males produced by war casualties increases the proportion of spinsters and reduces the number of births.

Finally, it is evident that the rates of birth, death, and natural increase are sharply influenced by the age composition of the population, as well as by the age specific risks of bearing and dying. At any given instant, the size and age composition of the population is the resultant of the fluctuating rates of birth, death, and migration during its past history.

With so many determinants of growth, each possessing substantial possibilities for variation in direction, magnitude, and age incidence, the number of possible combinations becomes indefinitely large. In principle, the range of possibilities presents formidable barriers to systematic analysis. In fact, however, the problem is more manageable than it appears to be because of the ways in which the variables have operated.

In many countries, emigration has been negligible. In most of the underdeveloped countries fertility has been both high and relatively invariant. Throughout most of the world, mortality has been falling, and in many instances during recent decades it has been falling very rapidly. In many of the underdeveloped countries, therefore, the combination of negligible emigration, high fertility, and falling mortality is producing progressively rapid population growth. Moreover, for reasons already noted, these mounting rates of population growth have been coupled with rising proportions of the population in the ages of young dependency.

The situation in the developed areas stand in sharp contrast with that of the underdeveloped areas. In the latter, mortality has been the principal variable. Its trend is almost universally downward in a fashion that has a marked effect on the rates of increase but slight effect on the age composition. In the developed countries, on the other hand, fertility is the principal variable. During recent decades, in some countries, it has moved more or less steadily down; in others, it has moved down and then sharply up. In still others, it has moved down, then sharply up, and then down again. Moreover, these movements, affecting as they do inputs at the beginning of the age span, sharply modify both the rate of growth and the age composition of the population. It would require a variety of models, therefore, to illustrate the interaction of vital trends, growth and age structure in the developed countries during recent decades.

Developments in the United States between 1930 and 1955

In the face of this complexity, the simplest approach to the interaction of vital rates and population growth and structure in the developed countries is by means of specific illustrations. In what follows we shall be concerned with developments between 1930 and 1955 in the female population of the United States. The female population is selected instead of the total, both to save computation and to avoid the complexities of dealing with troops overseas and with war casualties. A similar analysis for the male or the total population would give essentially similar results.

The influence of each element of change between 1930 and 1955 may be shown by comparing the actual trends of population with successive projections of hypothetical trends that depart from the actual situation by the alteration of specific components of change. In this manner we can illustrate the effect of the 1930 age distribution on subsequent growth, and show the effect of migration, changes in mortality, and changes in fertility on both the trends between 1930 and 1955, and the size and composition of the population in 1955.

This system of projections has been carried out by rough and ready methods which are sufficiently precise to serve present purposes. The initial 1930 population, for example, has been adjusted for the under-enumeration of children from birth to age 5, but left otherwise uncorrected for even obvious deficiencies. Similarly, fertility rates between 1930 and 1955 have been adjusted for underregistration of births, but fertility rates that run from January to January have been used, although the census figures run from April 1930 to April 1955. Moreover, instead of using annual age specific fertility rates, births have been estimated from general fertility rates for successive quinquennial periods. Surviving populations have been moved forward in quinquennial age groups five years at a time by means of survival ratios interpolated from available life tables, so that annual variations in mortality have been left out of account. It has been assumed, without serious violation to the facts, that there was no migration between 1930 and 1940. Thereafter, the estimates of migration used by the Bureau of the Census have been used, often with rather drastic interpolation to fit the necessary time periods.

The projected estimates yielded by such procedures are not closely calibrated, but neither are they grossly in error in ways that distort the comparisons needed for present purposes. There has been no attempt to close with the censuses of 1940 and 1950 or with the official estimates for 1955. Chart 1 permits the comparison of the female population, as

CHART 1

U.S. Female Population, 1955

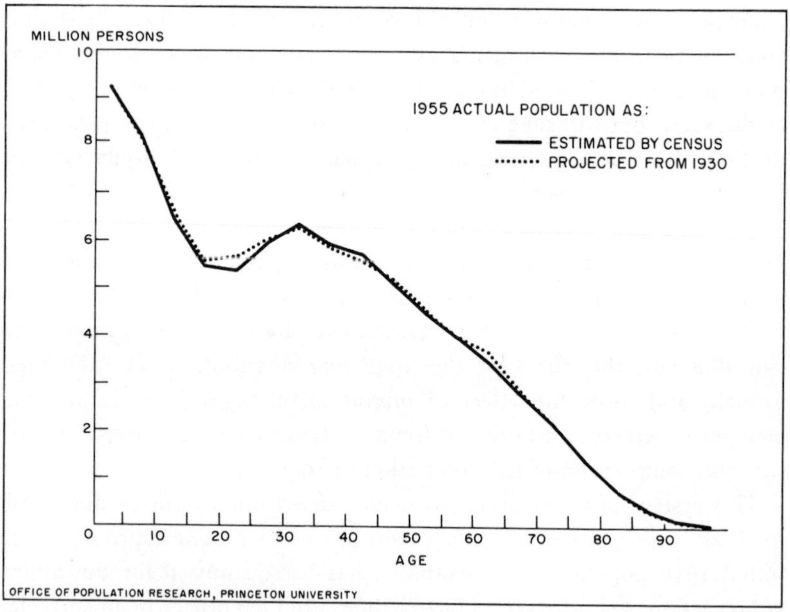

interpolated to April 1955 from the census estimates, with our estimate of the population for that date obtained by projecting the 1930 population with actual migration and fertility and mortality rates for 1930–1955. Panel A of Chart 3 permits analogous comparison for the total female population between 1930 and 1955.

The projected estimates of the actual situation are a trifle high, but it would be difficult to say which of the two results depart further from the truth. The most conspicuous disagreement between the projected figures and the census estimates falls in the group aged 20–25 in 1955, hence that born between 1930 and 1935. This is the least reliable period of birth registration with which we are concerned. A considerable part of the excess population projected for that group may well come from an over-generous allowance for incomplete registration in those years. There is a bump in the projected figures between ages 60 and 65 which is clearly the attenuated reflection of the corresponding bump between ages 35 and 40 in the 1930 census. The projected figures for the ages over 80 in 1955 fall below those of the census, which are almost certainly inflated by exaggeration of age.

Whatever the sources of the discrepancies between the census estimates and the estimates projected from 1930 for the actual population in 1955, it is clear that both series tell the same story. In the remainder of the paper, for consistency's sake, the "actual" population will be represented by the values obtained by projecting the actual course of events from the 1930 census.

Before turning to an examination of the components of change between 1930 and 1955, it should be noted that the results reflect the events of a specific period. Had we dealt with the first thirty years of the century the answers would have been sharply different. Both migration and the decline of mortality tended to increase the speed of growth. Their influence, however, was more than canceled by the steady decline of the birth rate, which was also the source of the rapid aging of the population. Between 1930 and 1955, by contrast, migration was very small and the birth rates moved first down, then up. The gains from rising birth rates canceled the losses of the earlier fall. If the study had closed with 1958 instead of 1955 the gains due to the rise of the birth rate would have been considerably larger than those presented below. In short, this analysis illustrates the principles of change, but the specific results relate only to the period under study.

The object of Chart 2 is to illustrate the extent to which the size and age composition of the 1955 population depended on the age composition of the population in 1930. Panel A shows the 1955 distribution and that for 1930, from which it developed. The relatively small number aged 0–4 in 1930 reflects the fact that births were less numerous between 1925 and 1930 than in the preceding five years. The survivors of this smaller group, born in the years 1925–1930, plus a few immigrants, appear between ages 25 and 30 in 1955. The deeper trough for the younger ages in the 1955 curve reflects the still smaller birth classes of the years 1930 to 1940. The very much larger numbers below age 15 in 1955 are

265

CHART 2

Effect of 1930 U.S. Age Structure on 1955 Female Population

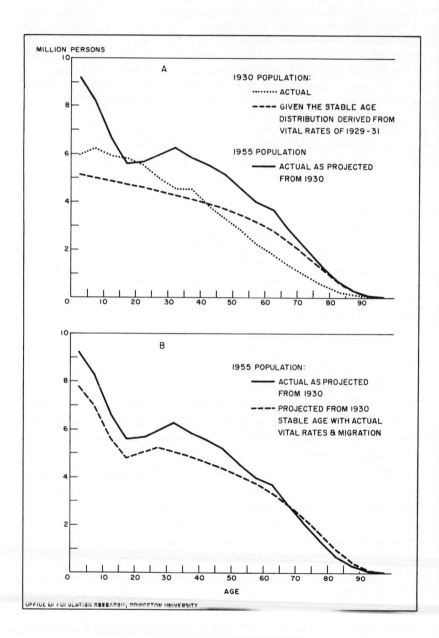

MILLION PERSONS

A

1930 POPULATION:
.... ACTUAL
- - - - GIVEN THE STABLE AGE
DISTRIBUTION DERIVED FROM
VITAL RATES OF 1929-31

1955 POPULATION
——— ACTUAL AS PROJECTED
FROM 1930

B

1955 POPULATION:
——— ACTUAL AS PROJECTED
FROM 1930
- - - - PROJECTED FROM 1930
STABLE AGE WITH ACTUAL
VITAL RATES & MIGRATION

AGE

OFFICE OF POPULATION RESEARCH, PRINCETON UNIVERSITY

CHART 3

Effect of 1930 U.S. Age Structure on 1930–1955 Female Population Size

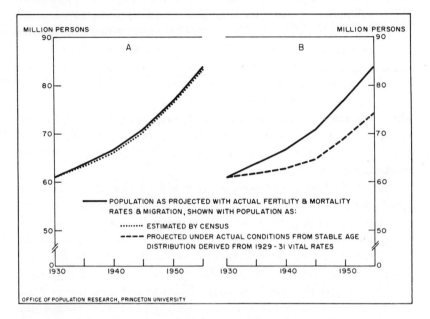

OFFICE OF POPULATION RESEARCH, PRINCETON UNIVERSITY

the result of the sharp war and postwar recovery of the birth rate. Clearly below age 25 the distribution of the 1955 population has been primarily determined by the drastic changes in the course of the birth rate between 1930 and 1955. The actual course of vital rates from 1930 on would have yielded something of the same general pattern in 1955 had it started from any plausible age distribution in 1930.

How much then would the course of events have differed if the actual trends had started from a 1930 population of the same size but a different age composition? Since there is an infinite number of possibilities there is an infinite number of answers. There is no population that is the most reasonable alternative to the actual one. To gain some insight into the influence of the initial age distribution, the stable age distribution obtained from the vital rates of 1929–1931 has been selected as a standard of comparison. This amounts to the age distribution that U.S. females would have had in 1930 if, prior to 1930, the age specific risks of bearing and dying had been fixed at the levels that characterized the years 1929–1931, and there had been no migration. This hypothetical population for 1930 was then projected to 1955 with actual migration and fertility and mortality rates. The difference between the hypothetical course of events for 1930 to 1955 and the actual one shows the lingering consequences of pre-1930 variations in fertility and migration, which had given the 1930 age distribution its particular structure. Panel B of Chart 2 shows that under these circumstances the 1955 population would have been considerably older than it actually was. Panel B of Chart 3 shows that growth would have been much slower and the 1955 total female population would have been some 10 million smaller than it actually was in 1955. In short, the general shape of the 1955 population under 25 years of age was mainly determined by the course of events after 1930, but both the rate of growth between 1930 and 1955 and the youth of the population in 1955 are due in part to the fact that events prior to 1930 had left the population with rather large proportions in the childbearing ages.

Panel A of Chart 4 permits comparison of the actual trend of the total female population between 1930 and 1955 with the hypothetical trend that results from projecting the 1930 population without migration or change in vital rates from the levels characterizing 1929–1931. Successive panels permit tracing the differences shown in Panel A to their source. Each shows the actual trend and the trend as projected under actual conditions except for a single variable. In the hypothetical case of Panel B there is no migration between 1930 and 1955, in that of Panel C the mortality rates are constantly those of 1929–1931, and in that of Panel D the fertility rates are constantly those of the same base period. Migration and changes in vital rates made rather little difference in the size of the population until 1945, but a growing difference thereafter. By 1955 they had given us some 9 million additional females. It is evident that the effect of migration was rather small, and that the principal gain from changes after 1930 was from the decline of mortality. This decline in the risks of death after 1930 had added some 5 million females to the population by 1955. Changes in fertility were more complicated, since birth rates dropped below the 1929–1931 level during the 1930's and rose sharply in the 1940's and 1950's. A maintenance of the fertility of 1929–1931 throughout the period would have given us a larger female population each year up to 1950.

The net change in the female population from 1930 to 1955 and its sources are shown in Chart 5 for all ages and for each of four broad age groups.[2] Between these two dates the female population grew by about

[2] It is to be noted that the sum of the individual effects of migration, changes in mortality, and changes in fertility as measured here should exceed the total departures from the actual situation from all sources combined which are obtained from the difference between the projection for the actual situation and that which assumed no migration and

CHART 4

Effect of Vital Rates and Migration on U.S. Female Population Size, 1930–1955

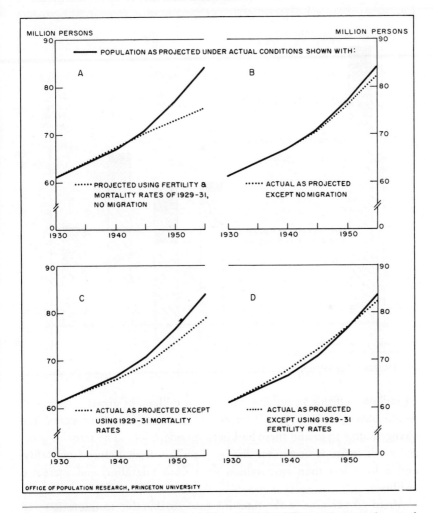

OFFICE OF POPULATION RESEARCH, PRINCETON UNIVERSITY

the maintenance of 1929–31 vital rates. The sum of the differences between the actual population and the projections in which only single factors depart from the actual situation incorporates too much allowance for the interaction of change. The results show the expected discrepancies which, however, are trivial above age 45, where only the interactions of migration and changes in mortality were involved. The discrepancies have been proportionately distributed to equal the total from all factors combined. The required adjustments are not large. The opposite difficulty would have been encountered if the influence of each factor had been measured by the difference between the projection incorporating the changes in that factor and that which provided for no change in any factor. In that case there would have been no allowance for the interaction of change.

CHART 5

Components of Change in U.S. Female Population, by Age, 1930–1955

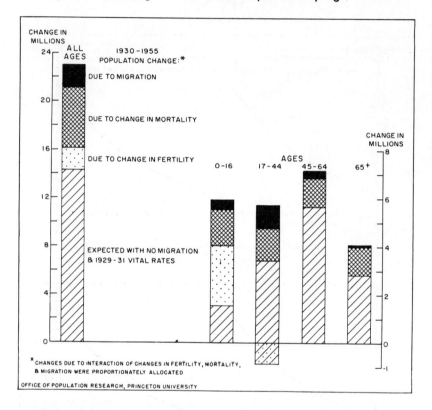

23 million. Of this 23 million increase, 14 million, or about 60 per cent, would have occurred even if fertility and mortality had remained unchanged after 1930 and there had been no migration. The remaining 8.7 million increase is accounted for by 5 million from reduced mortality, and a little less than two million each from migration and increased fertility.

About 50 per cent of the total increase attributable to migration and changes in vital rates falls in the group under 17 years of age in 1955. Indeed, just the rise in fertility accounted for an additional 2.5 million in that group, whereas the earlier decline in fertility below the 1929–1931 level reduced the number of persons aged 17–44 by about 0.8 million. On the other hand, half of the increase due to migration fell in the age group 17–45 years. The numerical gains due to declining death rates were a little larger in the two groups under age 45 than in the two older groups, but increases from this source were much the most evenly distributed of all.

Chart 6 presents the same series of projections for the age distributions of 1955. Panel A shows the distribution of the actual female population of 1955, and the hypothetical distribution derived from the assumption of no migration or change in vital rates after 1930. The successive panels permit the comparison of the actual distribution with hypothetical distributions obtained from projections of the actual course of events except for a single variable. The hypothetical population of Panel B assumes no migration after 1930, that of Panel C assumes a continuation of 1929–1931 mortality rates, and that of Panel D the continuation of 1929–1931 fertility rates.

Migration and changes in vital rates after 1930 produced marked changes in both the size and the age composition of the 1955 population. The influence of migration was small and concentrated under age 55. Under age 20, the differences in the two lines represent births to migrants as well as migrants themselves. Panel C brings out clearly the fact that reductions in the risk of death since 1930 have saved many lives, and that these changes have had very little effect on the age distribution. It is changes in fertility that have brought the major shifts in the age structure of the population. With the fertility rates of 1929-1931 we would have had some two million fewer girls under 5 years of age than were present in 1955.

For purposes of economic analysis, the shifts in the age structure of the population may be generalized in terms of the ratio of the population in the ages of dependency to the population in the working years of life. Without too much violation of the facts we may classify the population under age 17 and over age 65 as dependents, and that between ages 17 and 65 as workers. Chart 7 presents this "ratio of dependents to workers" over the period 1930 to 1955 for the array of actual and hypothetical populations with which we have been dealing.

In the actual population, the ratio dropped sharply from 1930 to 1940, was steady during the war, and rose even more sharply to 1955, when it was well above the 1930 level at 68 per cent. The trend was sharply downward during the great depression, and even more sharply upward during the postwar inflationary years. Panel A shows that, if we had had neither migration nor change in vital rates after 1930, the dependency ratio would have been higher through 1945, but substantially lower by 1955.

The influence of migration on the ratio is too small to be shown

CHART 6

U.S. 1955 Female Population Under Various Assumptions, by Age

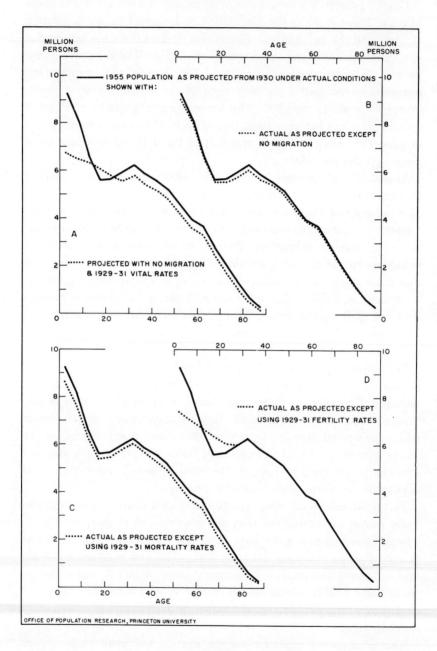

OFFICE OF POPULATION RESEARCH, PRINCETON UNIVERSITY

CHART 7

Effect of Changing Vital Rates and Initial Age Structure on Ratio of Females in Dependent Ages to Females in Working Ages, U.S., 1930–1955

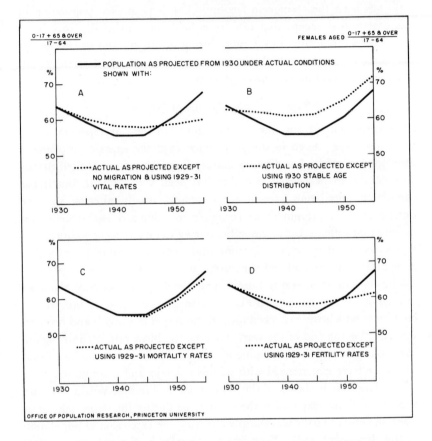

graphically. Panel B presents the comparison of the actual trend with the hypothetical trend that comes from projecting the stable age distribution of 1929–1931 with actual migration and vital rates from 1930 on. Much of the decline in the ratio to 1940 was locked up in the 1930 age distribution, as a product of the vital trends and migration before that date. The dependency load from 1935 on has been substantially lighter than would have been the case if our population had had a stable age structure in 1930.

In Panel C the hypothetical population is real except that the mortality is held to the level of 1929–1931. The reduction of death rates since 1930 has tended to expand the population at each extreme of life a little more rapidly than in the middle years. Lower risks of death have somewhat increased the dependency load.

Panel D shows clearly that a major source of the dip and rise in the ratio has been the change in fertility. The hypothetical population in this case is real except that fertility is held constant at the 1929–1931 level. Both the decline in the ratio during the 1930's and its rise during the postwar years would have been much less sharp if fertility had remained constant at the 1929–1931 level.

Trends in Other Developed Countries·

As already pointed out, the trends considered here are specific to the time and place. Even in the years since 1930 the experience of many developed countries has differed sharply from that of the United States. The decline in peacetime mortality has been very general, but it has stimulated population growth without substantially altering the age distribution. A prominent exception is the changed age structure in nations that suffered heavy casualties during the war. Some nations have also experienced heavy immigration and some emigration in ways that alter both numbers and age structures.

The nations of Western Europe and the English-speaking countries outside of Europe have generally experienced prolonged declines in the birth rates which were checked toward the end of the 1930's and reversed sharply after the end of the war. In some the birth rate declined again, but the usual result is a changing age structure somewhat similar to that which we have experienced with different details and magnitudes.

The large birth classes of the years prior to the first World War are often to be found expanding the labor force during the depression years when the ebb of births was sharply checking the expansion of population in the dependent ages. Even more generally in the prosperous years following World War II the small birth classes of the depression years were yielding only a slow expansion of the population in the working ages, precisely when numbers in the childhood ages were mounting rapidly.

It is not the purpose of this paper to allocate cause and effect relations among demographic and economic factors. Here we need only point out the fact that the depression came at the same time as the sharp decline in dependency ratios, and that the postwar prosperity came at the same time as the sharp rise in that ratio. Indeed, since fertility is under widespread voluntary control, the same perverse association of economic and demographic variables might be expected again if we were to undergo a prolonged and deep depression, followed in fifteen or twenty years by high levels of prosperity. That is about the time required for the births of the ebb to enter the labor force of the flow.

For the developed economies, about the only safe generalizations are the obvious ones:

1. The size and age composition of a population are heavily influenced by its size and age composition a quarter of a century earlier.

2. The rate of growth can be sharply modified by changes in the course of migration, mortality and fertility in a twenty-five year period.

3. The age composition has been little affected by changes in mortality, but with death rates as close to zero as they now are at ages under 45, the period for which this proposition can be confidently stated is drawing to a close.

4. In countries of low mortality, barring major catastrophe and major migration, changes in fertility provide the most important source of change in both the rate of growth and the age composition.

5. The continuation of a very low mortality and medium fertility, such as that which characterizes the United States at present, yields both rapid growth and high burdens of dependency as conventionally defined.

C O M M E N T
JOHN V. GRAUMAN, United Nations

Notestein's presentation is so effective and so self-contained that I can add very little while staying within its scope. If my comments are to contribute to discussion, I have no choice but to range beyond the subject treated in the paper.

Within the space allotted to me, I hope to be able to make four points:

1. Developments in other industrialized countries have been quite diverse;

2. Much use can be derived from the observation that age structures are very little affected by ordinary changes in mortality;

3. The age structure of the United States population provides good material for the study of causal relationships between economic and demographic trends;

4. For the further progress of demographic science, it is becoming desirable to study the structural dynamics of population also in terms other than age.

First Point: Other Countries

Notestein's paper makes it very clear that changes in fertility, mortality, and migration all have their effects on the rate of population growth, but that changes in fertility alone have major effects on population age structure. In industrialized countries, mortality is now so low that its further decline cannot be very rapid, but fertility is apt to fluctuate substantially. In a population of large size, migration is unlikely to have large effects.

The forces which have determined population growth and structure in the United States have also been at work, with varying intensity, in other industrialized countries. The effects, however, have been quite diverse, as illustrated in Chart 1. In this chart, the female population of various countries is shown by five-year age segments as percentages of total female population. Two graphs are superimposed wherever the comparison seemed to be particularly interesting.

The first panel shows the populations of the United States and Australia, which are at opposite poles of the earth. Despite the geographical distance, the structures are so similar that one population can be easily mistaken for the other. Australia has been more affected by immigration than the United States, but the birth rate trends in the two countries have been very similar.

The second panel shows the age structures of two close neighbors: Austria and Yugoslavia. They diverge conspicuously. Birth rates in Austria have long been very low and fluctuating. Yugoslavia's birth rate, though declining, is still comparatively high. One might attribute the difference to the fact that Austria has been more industrialized than Yugoslavia. But this is not the only reason.

France and Italy are compared in the next panel. The size of the age group 0–4 shows that both countries have now about the same crude birth rate. But this birth rate results in France from a smaller proportion of women in childbearing ages than in Italy. French women are now more fertile than Italian women. But France has long been more industrialized than Italy. Because of its larger proportion of aged persons, France has a higher death rate than Italy, though specific death risks are no lower in Italy than they are in France.

The last panel compared the populations of Sweden and Japan. Sweden, relatively little affected by wars, shows perhaps the most typical trend for a Western population. Here, a recovery of the birth rate around 1940 has now definitely ebbed away, and fertility is again very low. In Japan, since quite recently, fertility is now as low as in Sweden. Because of age structure, Japan has a higher birth rate and a lower death rate than Sweden.

CHART 1
Per Cent Age Distributions

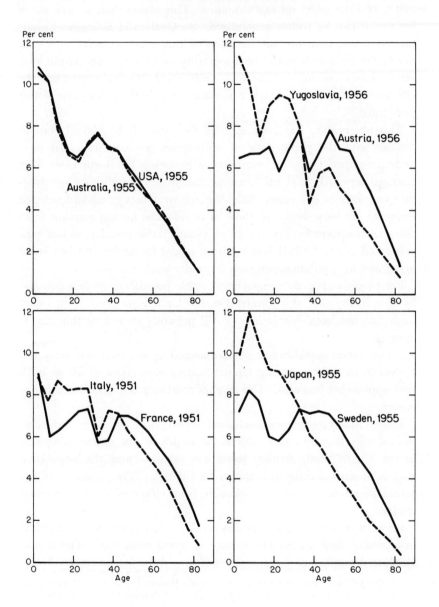

Second Point: Mortality Hardly Affects Age Structure

Notestein's paper shows that the decline of United States mortality has had very little effect on age structure. This observation is very useful because it can be widely generalized. As Coale and Bourgeois-Pichat[1] have demonstrated, the age structure of almost any population is very nearly the same as it would be if mortality had always been at the level attained most recently.[2] Therefore, under most practical conditions, the effects on age structure of higher mortality rates in the past can be almost discounted.

This observation has been used in the work of the United Nations dealing with the populations of underdeveloped countries. In most underdeveloped countries, mortality is declining but birth rates have changed very little, if at all. Since mortality has little effect on age structure and fertility has varied little, the age structures in underdeveloped countries are very similar to those of populations having constant mortality and constant fertility. A system of such stable populations has been calculated at the United Nations from model life tables and has found many uses in population estimates for underdeveloped countries.

For rough-and-ready comparisons, stable population models can also be used in the case of a country like the United States in 1955, whose birth rate has been fluctuating. I will presently show how this can be done.

A population model can be selected according to a level of fertility and a level of mortality. In the United States, expectation of life at birth now approaches 70 years. This level of mortality is also assumed in the model.

United States fertility has fluctuated recently from a gross reproduction rate of only slightly above 1.00 in the 1930's to one approaching 1.75 in the 1950's. Both fertility levels are relevant and the population models of such fertility are shown in Chart 2. The structure of the actual population differs considerably from either of the two extreme models.

Between these extremes, a fertility level can also be selected for a model to represent some reasonable average of recent conditions. The sum of absolute deviations of the actual population from the model was found

[1] Ansley J. Coale, "How the Age Distribution of a Human Population is Determined," *Cold Spring Harbor Symposia on Quantitative Biology*, 1957, J. Bourgeois-Pichat, International Statistical Institute, Stockholm, 1957.

[2] The coincidence of actual age structure with that which would have resulted had current mortality also prevailed in the past is not perfect, but discrepancies are seldom large, except at the most advanced ages.

CHART 2
U.S. Females and Stable Populations

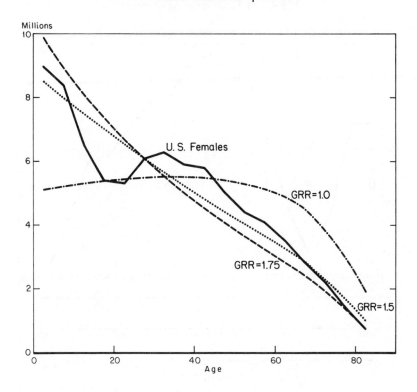

to be least when the gross reproduction rate in the model is assumed to be 1.50. This model is also shown in Chart 2.[3]

The age structures of the actual population and of the average model intersect in three points, near the ages of 10, 30, and 65 years, respectively. Compared to the stable average, the United States, in 1955, had a rather high proportion of small children, rather low proportion of adolescents and young adults, and so far, still a low proportion of aged persons. With time, these relative excesses and deficiencies will move farther up the age scale.

In Chart 3, the sizes of actual age groups are expressed as percentages relative to numbers in the average population model. In a sense, this is a chart of the history of United States fertility relative to that in the average model. Fertility, as a ratio of children to women of childbearing

[3] This, like any other averaging procedure, is only an arbitrary device which may have some practical uses.

CHART 3

U.S. Females in Each Age Group as Per Cent of Stable Population
(GRR = 1.5) in Same Age Groups

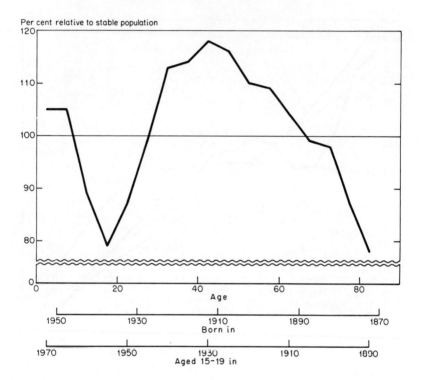

ages, is roughly indicated by the broken arrows in the chart. Recently, this ratio has been somewhat higher than the assumed average. In the 1930's, it was considerably lower. In a still earlier period, it was considerably higher.

Chart 3 has three scales: the age of each group of the population in 1955; the date when each of these groups were born; and the date when they attain ages 15–19 years and, therefore, become candidates for entry into the labor force.

There was a rising trend in birth numbers around the turn of the century, reaching a peak in 1910–1915. Then there was a sharp slowdown until the early 1930's, followed by a renewed steep rise to a plateau which has been maintained for the past ten years.

The rate of growth in potential labor force is mainly determined by numbers reaching ages 15–19. Entrants into the labor force constituted

280

a rising tide until about 1930. Then, they fell off sharply to a low point which was reached about 1955. From here on, labor force can be expected to grow very rapidly again.

It is possible that the two trends are interrelated. It can be noted for the past 30 years that *when entrants into labor force were many, births were few, and when entrants into labor force were few, births were many.* In fact, there may be a negative correlation between the supply of labor and the birth rate. And this brings me to my third point, namely that a contemplation of the age structure is useful in the study of economic and demographic relationships.

Third Point: Population and the Economy

This possibility is strongly suggested in Notestein's paper, especially in his last chart. It is shown there that everything seems to have conspired to accentuate the change in the ratio of dependents to workers that would otherwise have occurred. The fertility trend, in particular, has contributed greatly to this sharp change in the dependency ratio.

Elsewhere in this Conference it is suggested that a high dependency ratio stimulates demands for goods and services, and that these demands generate a high level of employment. Little consideration, however, has been given at this Conference to the effects of *a changing supply of the labor force itself.*

As a matter of primitive economics, it would seem that when there is a rapid influx of entrants into working ages, the marginal value of each entrant will be low relative to the value of other factors of production, for example, land and machinery. When the supply of labor is reduced, on the other hand, the entrants into labor force will command a relatively high price.

It may be presumed that, early in this century, the economy was geared to a situation in which the ranks of the labor force were swelling rapidly. Eventually, the continued absorption of growing numbers of entrants encountered difficulties. Around that time, fertility came increasingly under deliberate control and declined, at first slowly, and later more rapidly.

After 1930, the rate of entry into labor force slowed down. The economy underwent a reorganization in the depression. It can be presumed that eventually the economy became geared to a situation in which the supply of the labor force was a dwindling one. This situation has prevailed until now and has been associated with prosperity.

During this period of small labor supply and prosperity, persons in the labor force enjoyed considerable job security and prospects for economic advancement. This period had a high birth rate.

By 1955, the labor supply reached rock bottom. From now until the early 1970's, it will increase greatly. Workers may encounter greater difficulties of employment unless the economy can make a flexible adjustment to this changing situation. With marginal value of entrants into labor force on the decline, it is possible that the birth rate will drop again in the near future. A decline in the marriage rate has already been noted this year.

If this view has any validity, then it can be presumed that the labor market and the birth rate will tend to move in alternating cycles. This may already be the case in Sweden where a relatively early recovery of the birth rate has given way to a renewed decline.

Fourth Point: Population Structure in Terms Other than Age

Notestein has wisely refrained from drawing any inferences of the type which I have just outlined. The truth is that, so long as demography is confined to sex-and-age groups of the population, we are still far from coming to grips with the mechanism by which population trends influence the economy, and vice versa.

As is convincingly pointed out in another paper of this Conference, decisions which affect both the economy and population trends are usually taken within the family, the household, the spending unit, or some other primary groupings of this type.

Demography remains the child of actuarial science so long as it confines its analysis to individuals of varying sex and age. True, the dynamics of age structure and of age specific risks has become a powerful tool of demographic analysis and has been carried to a very high degree of refinement. But demographic analysis must not stop here. Its further progress will depend on the way in which it can meet a new challenge.

We are now being challenged to regard a population as composed of families or households of varying structure. In this population, we must examine the rates at which families of one type are replaced by families of another type. The definitions are still obscure, and the dynamics of a population in terms of family structure are likely to become very complex. Great efforts will be needed to meet this new challenge with as much success as has been attained in the demographic analysis of age structure. When the dynamics of family structure are being explored, great progress in our still limited understanding of demographic, economic and social interrelations is to be expected.

CONRAD TAEUBER, Assistant Director, Bureau of the Census

Notestein makes the point that the size and age of a population are heavily influenced by the size and age composition of that population a generation earlier. Individual units are added to a population at age zero and move through that population in well-defined steps. A few individuals are added at adult ages through migration and they move by similar steps. In our society, since relatively few individuals are removed by migration, virtually all of the losses are the result of deaths. These are distributed over the entire age range, although concentrated in the very young and the older ages. While the United States has not felt the effects of war in the form of deep gashes in its age pyramid, it does have some irregularities. The irregularities in the number of births in some past years are reflected in age groups which today are unusually large or unusually small. The small number of twenty-five-year-olds and the large number of eleven-year-olds in the population in 1958 clearly reflect past developments in fertility.

Rates of growth are subject to sharp changes in a short space of time. Here again the changes that have taken place in the number of births in the last twenty-five years amply illustrate the point.

Notestein has worked out an illustrative computation for a particular time period. Had he chosen another time period, the results would have been somewhat different but the method would have been equally applicable. During the period which he considers, as throughout our national history, the difference between the number of births and the number of deaths has been more important numerically than the difference between the number of immigrants and the number of emigrants. During each decade for which census figures are available, the excess of births over deaths has contributed a larger share of the total increase than the excess of immigration.

An advantage of presenting the computations for this particular period is that they bring into focus the importance of changes in mortality in recent years. The changes in fertility have been so dramatic that attention has generally been focused on them. The period includes the years of small numbers of births in the early 1930's, as well as the years with large numbers of births since World War II. Notestein measures increases against those which would have occurred had there been no immigration and had the vital rates of 1929–1931 prevailed. On that basis, reductions in mortality have contributed 5 million persons to the population increase. This is more than the contributions of increased fertility, 2 million, and increased immigration, about 2 million. Obviously, the relative position of these three factors would have been different if the selected time period were different.

However, I would like to stress the fact that reductions in mortality are continually being made. There have been very substantial reductions in infant mortality during the twenty-five-year period under consideration, and there have also been reductions in the mortality of persons in the older ages. Some of us spend a good deal of time explaining to laymen that the increase in the average expectation of life does not mean the total span has been increased, or that older persons are living longer. We may have tended to give too small a role to the decreases in mortality that have been taking place at the older ages.

In evaluating the prospects for the future, it would not be appropriate to underrate further improvements in mortality which are possible. Our infant mortality can be further reduced, and there exists the possibility of very significant developments in the control of the degenerative diseases. We do not need to envision the possibilities that travel in space may make time stand still for the few individuals who are likely to be involved in that undertaking in our lifetime. While advances may be slow in coming, improvements in mortality are likely to continue to make significant contributions to the size of our population.

We need not concern ourselves at the moment with whether the period chosen, or the vital rates which are applied, are the best suited ones. The method does permit the isolation of factors, and thus helps to identify the contribution to population growth which is made by the several components.

PART II

The Economic Effects of Population Change

An Economic and Demographic Model of the Household Sector: A Progress Report

GUY H. ORCUTT   ALICE M. RIVLIN

HARVARD UNIVERSITY   THE BROOKINGS INSTITUTION

IN general, previous quantitative studies of demographic-economic interrelationships have concentrated on unidirectional relationships. Demographers have sometimes attempted to measure the influence of economic change on the vital rates, and economists have sometimes studied the impact of population growth or family size on economic variables, but the mutual interaction of economic and demographic factors has received more verbal than statistical acknowledgment.

Although the relevant data are still highly inadequate, we believe it is not too soon to try to construct a model of the household sector of the United States economy in which the interaction of economic and demographic variables is represented. The most promising approach to the problem lies in estimating the interrelations of economic and demographic variables at the level at which decisions to spend, save, work, and have children are actually made—that is, at the individual or household level. Certainly, we are also interested in the relationships between aggregates —total population, personal income, consumption, and so on—but it seems more feasible to obtain estimates of these relationships by simulating the behavior of a large number of individuals or households and aggregating the results of such behavior than it does to estimate relationships between aggregate time series directly.

Hence we have attempted to construct a model of the household sector formulated in terms of the demographic (birth, death, marriage, divorce) and economic (spending and saving) behavior of individual "decision units" and designed to be solved by computer simulation. The first

Note: The authors are heavily indebted to John Korbel, who programmed the calculations reported in Part III of this paper for the IBM 704, and to Fred Raines for his assistance in getting the basic survey data on magnetic tape. We are also deeply indebted to the Survey Research Center of the University of Michigan and the Board of Governors of the Federal Reserve Board for use of the 1956 Survey of Consumer Finances, and to the Ford Foundation, the Computation Center at M.I.T., the Brookings Institution, the Littauer Statistical Laboratory at Harvard, and the Wisconsin Alumni Research Foundation, for financial support, computational assistance and fellowships making possible the study of which this paper is one result. However, the conclusions and opinions in this article are those of the authors and not necessarily those of these institutions or individuals who have been helpful.

section of this paper will discuss the principal features of this type of model and its solution; the second will contain a brief description of the way in which we have estimated the demographic "outputs" of the household, and the last major section will give a more detailed discussion of the determination of mortgage debt, personal debt, liquid assets, and expenditures on selected durables.

The model presented is a far from finished product, and this paper should be regarded as a status report on research in progress, designed to explain the direction in which we are working, to illustrate what has been accomplished so far and the problems encountered, and to stimulate discussion and constructive criticism of the project. We believe, however, that our results thus far amply support the position that demographic and economic phenomena should be jointly considered, and we are prepared to offer the hypothesis that the interaction of economic and demographic variables at the household level provides a partial explanation of the business cycle.

Decision Unit Models and their Solution[1]

The most important feature of this type of model is that its units are decision-making units of the real economy—individuals, households, firms, financial institutions, and so forth. In the household sector, the units are individuals and combinations of individuals such as married couples, families, and spending units. These units have several kinds of possible behavior or "outputs." Individuals die, marry, set up new households; married couples have children and get divorced; spending units make purchases and acquire debts and assets.

Each unit has certain characteristics or "inputs." Inputs to individuals include sex, age, race, marital status; inputs to married couples include duration of marriage and the number of children born to the wife; inputs to spending units include their composition, asset, and debt position.

In addition to specific unit inputs, there are certain inputs to the system which are common to all units. These include the season and the calendar year and may include such aggregates as national income or employment. When a complete model of the economic system is constructed, these aggregates will be generated by the model, but we are obliged to "plug in" to our model of the consumer sector assumed values of some of the economic variables generated by other sectors.

[1] The general features of this type of model were more fully described in an earlier paper. See. Guy H. Orcutt, Martin Greenberger, and Alice M. Rivlin, "Decision-Unit Models and Simulation of the United States Economy," paper presented to the meetings of the Econometric Society in Philadelphia, December, 1957, mimeographed.

The outputs of a unit in a given time period depend on the inputs at the beginning of the period. This relationship between inputs and outputs is stochastic in nature; that is, it is the *probabilities* of occurrence of certain outputs, rather than the outputs themselves, which are regarded as functions of the inputs. The probability distributions which related inputs to outputs are called the "operating characteristics" of the units. For example, if the probability that a man will marry in a given period is taken to depend on his age and marital status, then the table (or function) which specifies the probabilities of marriage for males of various ages and marital conditions would be one of the operating characteristics of male units.

This stochastic feature of the model will be no surprise to demographers, who are quite used to estimating the probabilities of vital events happening to individuals of given characteristics and to using these probabilities together with the characteristics of the current population to predict the total number of such events one or more periods into the future. Birth, death, marriage, and divorce of individuals depend on such a myriad of factors that it is impossible to predict what will happen in individual cases. No one can say whether or not a particular individual will be alive a year from now, but, when large populations are "at risk," the vital events exhibit considerable regularity. An experienced life insurance company can determine within narrow limits and with a high degree of confidence the number that will survive for the next twelve months out of ten thousand insured persons of a given age.

The probabilistic approach seems similarly appropriate to analyzing the economic behavior of households. Here again, the actions of an individual household are influenced by hundreds of factors which we can neither ascertain nor measure. It is impossible to predict whether a particular household will or will not buy a house in the next month, but the probabilities of house purchase for various types of households can be estimated and these estimates used to predict aggregate house-buying in a large group of households with given characteristics.

Quite obviously, our model will be useful only if operating characteristics can be estimated which will prove to be stable or to change in a predictable way. The main research job of the project, in fact, is that of estimating these characteristics. It is a vast and challenging job, on which we have just got a good start.

The model is recursive, that is, the outputs of a unit in any period depend on its prior inputs, so that there is no simultaneous interaction between units and, hence, there are no simultaneous equations to be solved. This does not mean that units are conceived of as acting independently of each other, since the prior outputs or other units may be inputs to the unit in question; but it does mean that all interaction of units in the model is sequential rather than simultaneous. This recursive feature of the model necessitates the use of a rather short period of analysis, since many reactions, such as the response of marriage probabilities to changes in income, which may be sequential in fact, will appear simultaneous if a long period such as a year is considered. The period used in this model is the month. In most cases when monthly data were not available, annual data were converted to a monthly basis by applying a seasonal index.

Solution of the model is to be obtained by simulation on a large electronic computing machine. A population of several thousand units will be specified, the units being assigned ages, marriage durations, liquid assets, and other inputs in the proportions in which these characteristics appear in the base population. The simulation proceeds in one-month steps. In each month, each individual unit is considered in turn. For each possible output of the unit a probability of occurrence is specified by the relevant operating characteristics and the inputs to the unit at the beginning of the month. Whether the output occurs or not is determined by a random drawing from this probability distribution.

For example, suppose the simulation is started with the month of January, 1958, and the first individual considered is a single white male, age 34. We have already estimated the probability that a male with these characteristics will die in this month at, say, 0.0002; that is, this is the probability of death specified by the relevant operating characteristic. Then, in essence, we make a random drawing from a bag containing 10,000 balls, two of which are marked "die" and 9,998 of which are marked "not die." The man either dies and is eliminated from the population (and from his spending unit) or he lives through his month —depending on the outcome of the draw.

Random numbers generated by the computing machine provide us with a less cumbersome method of making the random drawings than balls in a bag. There may, of course, be more than two possible outcomes of the draw. The output "amount spent on durables," for example, might have four possible values—for example, $0, $0–100, $100–500, and over $500—or it might have many more.

When each possible output for each unit has been considered in this way, the first "pass" or month is complete. We enter the second month with a population of units which is slightly different both in size and composition from the initial one, since some individuals have died, or married, some couples have divorced, some babies have been born, some spending units have been created or destroyed, many have altered their asset and debt positions, and all surviving individuals are one month older. The whole procedure is then repeated for the second month and for as many more as desired.

In sum, the distinctive features of this model are its formulation in terms of decision units, the stochastic relation between inputs and outputs of units, and the solution by computer simulation. Bearing in mind the general outlines of the model, we turn now to a consideration of specific outputs and to the estimation of the operating characteristics associated with these outputs.

The Household Sector: Demographic Behavior

Estimating all the operating characteristics necessary for a decision unit model of the United States economy, or even of the consumer sector, is a rather formidable task. Fortunately, it can be broken down into manageable pieces. A logical place to start the work seemed to be to formulate a process by which the units in the consumer sector would be created and destroyed in the model in the proportions in which this creation and destruction takes place in the real world. Hence, our first efforts involved estimating the operating characteristics associated with birth, death, marriage, and divorce.

A model containing only these four outputs is of considerable interest in itself, since it is, in effect, a population projection model. As such, it differs from the population models in current use (such as the "cohort survival" method used by the Bureau of the Census, and others) in that: (1) it includes marriage and divorce (as well as birth and death) among the events to be projected, thus enabling us to project the number of married couples as well as the total population, and to make birth and marriage projections which are consistent with each other; (2) several new variables are included in predicting birth, marriage, and divorce probabilities. In particular, the probabilities of these outputs are made to depend in part on an income variable, which will ultimately be generated by the larger model when it is completed. Even in working with the four-output model, however, it is interesting to "plug in" various alternative values of this economic variable in order to generate alternative population projections.

A model limited to the four outputs of birth, death, marriage, and divorce is in the last stages of programming, and the results of actual runs should be available in the near future. The way in which the operating characteristics for this model were estimated has been described elsewhere and will be outlined only briefly here.[2]

DEATH

In the model, death is a possible output for all individuals, and when it occurs it simply eliminates the individual from the population. The operating characteristic associated with death gives the probability that an individual will die in a particular month—expressed as a function of his characteristics at the beginning of the month and any other relevant inputs such as the season of the year.

We projected probabilities of death by the simple expedient of fitting a trend to age-sex-race-specific mortality rates and extrapolating it into the future. A straight line was fitted to the logarithms of mortality rates in each age-sex-race group for the years 1933–1954, and the fit seemed quite good. Thus, we effectively assumed that the average annual rates of decrease in mortality rates in all groups observed in the past twenty years would continue for the next decade or so. Predicted annual mortality rates were converted to monthly rates by applying a seasonal multiplier computed from monthly mortality rates for 1946–1954 and assumed to remain constant.

MARRIAGE

Marriage is much more difficult to handle in a simulation model than is death, because marriage involves two individuals who will form a single new unit, a married couple. In order to accomplish this matching of individuals, the marriage process has been broken into two stages. In the first stage, it is decided whether or not a given individual will marry in the month. If marriage *is* predicted, then the characteristics of his mate are selected in the second stage. A mate with the requisite characteristics is then picked out of the model population and the two are united to form a married couple.

For the first stage, we needed an operating characteristic giving the probability that an individual with given characteristics will marry in the month. Marriage probabilities by sex, age, and marital status (that is, single and previously married) were estimated from census and vital statistics data for 1950. The relationship between marriage probabilities and economic conditions in the last three decades was then investigated. An index of the level of marriage probabilities for the years 1920 to 1955

[2] *ibid.*

was estimated and plotted against an index of economic conditions (personal disposable income per capita in constant prices). If the war years are omitted, the two series show remarkably similar movements over time.

In estimating the operating characteristic associated with the first stage of the marriage simulation, the historical relationship between the level of marriage rates and per capita income was taken into account. The operating characteristic estimated was of this form:

P (individual i will marry in month)

$$= F_a \text{ (sex, age, marital status of } i) \cdot R \cdot F_b \text{ (month)}.$$

Here F_a is simply a table giving the marriage probabilities computed for 1950 by age, sex, and marital status, and F_b is a seasonal index computed for recent years and assumed to remain constant. R is a multiplicative factor which serves to raise and lower marriage probabilities in accordance with changes in the income variable. Actually R was of this form:

$R = a + b$ (change in income)

$$- c \text{ (moving average of } R \text{ minus "normal" } R).$$

Here the final term serves to dampen the income effect by tending to return marriage rates to a level at which about 5 per cent of all women never marry, although a different "normal" could be substituted.

Incidentally, our model would have predicted the marriage down-turn associated with the 1957–1958 recession if we had got it running in time. Recent experience suggests, however, that marriage rates may be more sensitive to changes in employment than to changes in personal income.

The matching of marriage partners (stage two of the marriage process) was carried out on the basis of age and previous marital status only. The probability that a person of given age and marital status would pick a partner of a given age and marital status (and opposite sex, of course), were computed from data on marriages in 1955 and these probabilities were assumed to remain constant.

DIVORCE

Divorce is an output which dissolves the unit created by marriage into two separate units again. In our model, it is a possible output for any married couple in any month. At the same time, it is assumed that all married couples live together.

In estimating the operating characteristic associated with divorce we were severely hampered by lack of data, since, of all the vital events, divorce is the one about which we have least information. To get our divorce probabilities we took an approach similar to that used in estimating probabilities of marriage; that is, we first computed estimates of the probability of divorce (by duration of marriage) for a single year, but instead of holding these probabilities constant we introduced a multiplicative factor designed to raise and lower our divorce probabilities proportionately in response to changes in our income variable. The relationship between income and divorce rates was estimated from data for the period 1921–1955. However, although there appears to have been a positive correlation between divorce rates and economic conditions in the interwar period, this relationship is not very strong, nor has it persisted in the postwar period. Hence, while we have considerable confidence that the introduction of economic variables will improve marriage projections, we do not have the same confidence in this approach to divorce.

BIRTH

In our model, birth is an output of married couples only. Someone particularly interested in illegitimate birth rates might wish to introduce them into the model, but we did not feel that the present state of the data justified this refinement.

For our first model, we started by estimating age-parity specific birth rates for married women for a single year (1950). The data here are still inadequate, but the work of P. K. Whelpton and others is steadily filling the remaining gaps. We then investigated the relationship between income and age-parity-specific birth rates over the last three decades (to the extent that the data permitted) and made several alternative assumptions about the future course of this relationship. One such assumption is the following: (a) that first birth rates for zero-parity married women will remain constant, (b) that changes in birth rates for first through fourth parity women will exhibit the same relationships to changes of income that they did in the period 1920–1955 and (c) that rates for fifth and higher parity women will show a slow but steady decline. Our plan is to experiment with several such sets of assumptions in order to see what they imply with respect to completed family sizes with various patterns of income change. It should be noted that even if we hold age-parity specific birth rates for married women constant, our model will generate birth series which fluctuate in response to the business cycle especially in the lower birth orders, because our marriage rates depend on an income variable.

Future Work with the Four-Output Model

One obvious gap in our population model is that we have not yet introduced immigration and emigration, although this would not be difficult. The possibilities of introducing more refinements into the estimation of birth, death, marriage, and divorce probabilities are almost limitless. In particular, we have not yet made any use of the growing body of information on differential vital rates, for example, data on the birth or mortality rates of different socio-economic groups. We plan to introduce these differential rates into our model as soon as possible, so as to avoid running into serious distortions in predicting economic outputs.

FAMILY AND SPENDING UNIT GENERATION

The model containing only birth, death, marriage, and divorce requires modification before it can be extended to include economic outputs such as spending and saving, because it generates only two kinds of units; namely, individuals and married couples (with their associated unmarried children). It is not clear that these are the units which make economic decisions.

Which units are relevant to the analysis of spending and saving decisions? This question seems to have no single answer. The logical unit of analysis for housing expenditures seems to be the household (that is, the person or persons occupying a dwelling). But for minor personal expenditures, it is probably the individual.

The most extensive and useful source of data on spending and saving behavior currently available to us is the Survey of Consumer Finances. These data relate to "spending units," which are defined as groups of one or more persons living together, related by blood, marriage, or adoption, and pooling their incomes for major expenditures. A grown child or other relative living in the family is counted as a separate ("secondary") spending unit if he earns as much as fifteen dollars a week and keeps more than half of it for his own purposes. The SCF data can also be tabulated by "family units" (that is, related persons living together, irrespective of financial arrangements). For our purposes, the family unit of the SCF is a particularly useful one, since it corresponds to the "family" as defined by the Census Bureau—a fact which gives us an additional source of information about the composition and demographic characteristics of such units.

We will eventually want to use households, families, spending units, and perhaps other units in our model of the consumer sector. For the present, however, we will concentrate first on family units and then on spending units in order to use the SCF data to the maximum extent possible.

There are several ways in which family formation might be simulated in the model. Perhaps the most obvious approach would be the introduction of a new matching process analogous to marriage. The marriage process itself would first have to be altered so that a new unit was *not* automatically created by every marriage—the newly married couple would remain associated with one set of parents. Then two new outputs would be introduced, "leaving a family" (analogous to divorce) and "joining a family" (analogous to marriage). Like marriage, the latter would involve two stages; that is, deciding whether or not a family would unite with another family in the period, and picking the other family which the first one would join.

However, it will be difficult to estimate the operating characteristics of families without collecting new information or at least making new tabulations. The basic problem is that statistics simply are not collected on movements of persons in and out of families. Birth, death, marriage, and divorce are well-defined events which are reported to "the authorities." By contrast, changes in family status (for example, a grown son moving out of the parental family) are not reported to anyone, and the probabilities of such events can only be inferred from cross-sectional data.

Although simulation of family formation by means of a matching and unmatching process seems feasible, an even simpler approach appears preferable as a first approximation. Since most children live with their parents and most "other adults" in families are either grown sons and daughters of the head or parents of the head or his wife,[3] it seems possible to generate family units of appropriate size by controlling the rate at which children leave the parental family without introducing any process other than marriage by which units are amalgamated.

The proportions of married and unmarried persons by age who were *not* living in families headed by a parent or other relative in 1950 can be estimated from the census (see Table 1). Can we use the changes in these proportions to measure the rate at which sons and daughters move out of the parental family as they marry and/or grow older? There are two difficulties with this interpretation. One is that children may become heads of families because the parents die, rather than because the children have left the family. This effect may be small at the younger ages (say, under 35) but it is certainly important as the "children" reach middle

[3] Paul C. Glick, *American Families*, Wiley, 1957, pp. 8, 36.

TABLE I

Proportions Not Living in Families Headed by Parent or
Other Relative, by Age, Sex, Marital Status, 1950

Age	Single Male	Single Female	Married Male	Married Female
14–17	3.6	2.6	33.0	60.2
18–19	21.0	19.1	59.4	73.2
20–24	27.8	24.0	80.1	84.3
25–29	29.7	26.3	88.9	90.7
30–34	32.2	29.7	93.0	94.4
35–44	38.8	33.8	95.7	96.4
45–54	52.1	42.2	97.7	98.1

Source: Estimated from U.S. Bureau of the Census, *U.S. Census of Population: 1950*, Vol. IV, *Special Reports*, Part 2, ch. D, Table I.

age. As a first approximation we will simply assume that no "children" leave the parental family after age 35. This arbitrary cut-off age can be raised or lowered after the results of the first few runs are examined. A second difficulty is that a substantial number of family heads have persons living with them who are reported as "parents of head or wife." These families cannot be ignored without distorting the size distribution of families in the model. Hence, we must introduce a new output which may be called "losing status as head of family." This is an output which as far as the model is concerned is possible only for parents whose children have not yet formed separate families. When it occurs, it involves no change in family composition, but merely a shift in the designation "head of household" from parent to child. The operating characteristic associated with this output can be only roughly estimated from census data and likewise may have to be adjusted in the light of preliminary results.

Once we have families in the model, the creation of spending units is not conceptually difficult. A new output is introduced which may be called "becoming a separate spending unit." This output is possible for any married couple or person over 18 except heads of families, and the operating characteristic may be estimated from the Survey of Consumer Finances.

Debt, Liquid Asset, and Spending Behavior of Spending Units

Up to this point we have been concerned with the demographic outputs of units—birth, death, marriage, divorce, family and spending unit formation—that is, those aspects of individual and family behavior

297

which serve to determine and continually modify the size, composition, and groupings of the population of individuals. It seems clear that it will be useful to regard these probabilities as determined in part by prior demographic inputs to the units and in part by economic inputs. The specific inclusion of economic inputs shows promise of improving our ability to predict demographic events.

Now we turn the telescope around and focus on economic variables regarded as outputs of units. We will be concerned here with the determination of the probabilities associated with certain types of economic behavior of spending units. Of special interest is the extent to which the demographic variables generated by the model will prove to be useful in predicting these economic outputs.

OUTPUTS AND INPUTS

A list of all the spending unit outputs whose determination we would like to include in the model would be quite lengthy. It would certainly include the following fifteen variables and might well include some others: (1) mortgage debt incurred during month, (2) mortgage debt repaid during month, (3) personal debt incurred during month, (4) personal debt repaid during month, (5) change in liquid assets during month, (6) change in other financial assets during month, (7) expenditure on purchase of house during month, (8) expenditure on purchase of automobile during month, (9) expenditure on other durables during month, (10) expenditure on clothing during month, (11) expenditure on food during month, (12) expenditure on services during month, (13) receipts from sale of automobile during month, (14) receipts from sale of house during month, and (15) receipts from sale of other non-financial assets during month.

So far we have been able to make only very limited inroads on this list. In fact, the operating characteristics estimated in this paper refer only to the following four outputs, three of which are not even on our "desirable" list: (1) mortgage debt held, (2) personal debt held, (3) liquid assets held, and (4) expenditure on selected durables. The first three are stock variables, that is, the amounts of debt or liquid assets held by the spending unit on the survey date, *not* the changes in these amounts in the preceding period. We worked with them only because data on the corresponding flow variables were not gathered in the survey we were using. The last variable, however, is a flow variable covering expenditures by the spending unit on a selected list of durables during 1955.

Our work on these four output variables should be regarded mainly as illustrative of the estimation techniques with which we have been experimenting and which we would like to apply to other outputs as time, money, and data become available. The probabilities associated with many of the variables on our "desirable" list (such as automobile purchases) can be estimated from existing bodies of data, but some of the others may have to wait for bigger and better surveys.

A complete list of input variables which we eventually want to include would also be quite long. The following sets of demographic and economic inputs seem to merit testing and one could think of others.

Demographic input variables: marital status of head of spending unit*, interval since marriage if married couple*, age of head*, race of head*, sex of head*, number of adults*, number of children*, age of youngest*, age of oldest under 18*, education of head, veteran status of head, region, city type, household type, and number of dependents outside of spending unit.

Economic input variables: income of spending unit in current and previous years, employment status, occupation of head, mortgage debt at start of period, personal debt at start of period, liquid assets at start of period, other financial assets at start of period, stock of housing at start of period, stock of automobiles at beginning of period, and stock of other durables at beginning of period.

The starred demographic variables are of particular interest to us at the moment, because they can be generated by the demographic model described in the previous section. Partly for this reason and partly because of the limitations of the survey data, we concentrated on estimating the effect of these demographic inputs on the four economic outputs available. The survey data on the economic inputs were quite inadequate for our purposes. The spending unit's stock of a particular durable at the beginning of the period is undoubtedly an important determinant of probability that it will purchase that durable in the period. Unfortunately, the data necessary to estimate this were not available nor were adequate income histories of the spending units. Hence, our strategy is to explain as much as possible of the variation in outputs on the basis of the available demographic variables and then to rely on the use of aggregative time series data about incomes, prices, and credit terms to explain part of the residual variation.

AN APPROACH TO THE PROBLEM OF JOINT OUTPUTS

Use of a short time period does facilitate handling interactions between units, but it does not remove the need for regarding several outputs of each individual unit as simultaneously and jointly determined. One could, for example, estimate the parameters of a single equation giving the amount a unit will spend on an automobile in a month as a function of income, family size, duration of marriage, and a random variable, and also the parameters of a separate equation giving the amount of personal debt the unit will incur in the month as a function of the same three variables and another random variable. However, it would not be valid to consider that the two random variables are distributed independently.

In general terms our approach to this problem may be described as follows. Let the output variables which are to be simultaneously determined at the household level be $X_1, \ldots X_K$. The specification of values of these K variables may then be regarded as specifying a point in a K-dimensional space in which there are K orthogonal axes, with X_1 measured along the first, X_2 along the second, and so on. It is assumed that each combination of the relevant input variables determines a probability distribution defined over this output space for the point or vector of output variables. In simulation studies the output of a particular unit in a particular time period is to be obtained by a random drawing of a point from the multivariable probability distribution determined for that unit at that particular time.

The practical problems involved are how the joint probability distribution shall be specified and estimated and how a point shall be randomly drawn from the probability distribution.

Let the probability of any point in the output space for a given unit at a given point in time be represented by $P(X_1, \ldots X_K)$. We are assuming that this probability is a function of R input variables denoted by $Z_1, \ldots, Z_R$ and the coordinates of the point. That is, we are assuming that

(1) $$P(X_1, \ldots X_K) = F(Z_1, \ldots Z_R, X_1, \ldots X_K)$$

Now by the usual laws of probability we know that $P(X_1, \ldots X_K)$ can be expressed as the product of a marginal probability and a number of conditional probabilities as follows:

(2) $$P(X_1, \ldots X_K) = P(X_1) \cdot P(X_2 | X_1) \cdot P(X_3 | X_1, X_2) \ldots$$

$P(X_K | X_1, \ldots, X_{K-1})$. Which of the K output variables happens to be labeled X_1, which X_2, and so on, is immaterial except for small sample estimation problems.

The probabilities into which we have factored $P(X_1, \ldots X_K)$ will then be related to input variables $Z_1, \ldots, Z_R$ as follows:

$$(3) \qquad P(X_1) = F_1{}^*(Z_1, \ldots Z_R, X_1)$$
$$P(X_2|X_1) = F_2{}^*(Z_1, \ldots Z_R, X_1, X_2)$$
$$\begin{array}{ccc} \text{''} & \text{''} & \text{''} \\ \text{''} & \text{''} & \text{''} \\ \text{''} & \text{''} & \text{''} \end{array}$$
$$P(X_K|X_1, \ldots X_{K-1}) = F_K{}^*(Z_1, \ldots Z_R, X_1, \ldots X_K)$$

The corresponding mean or expected values of $X_1, \ldots, X_K$, denoted by $E(X_1), \ldots, E(X_K|X_1, \ldots X_{K-1})$ will then be given as follows.

$$(4) \qquad E(X_1) = F_1(Z_1, \ldots, Z_R)$$
$$E(X_2|X_1) = F_2(Z_1, \ldots, Z_R, X_1)$$
$$\begin{array}{ccc} \text{''} & \text{''} & \text{''} \\ \text{''} & \text{''} & \text{''} \\ \text{''} & \text{''} & \text{''} \end{array}$$
$$E(X_K|X_1, \ldots X_{K-1}) = F_K(Z_1, \ldots, Z_R, X_1, \ldots X_{K-1})$$

In this study we approximated functions F_1 through F_K by either the sum or product of essentially free functions of the variables involved. At a later date, we hope to use the residual differences between expected values and observed values to explore additional features of the marginal and conditional probability distributions expressed in equation set 3.

ESTIMATION PROCEDURE

The basic estimation procedures used in this study may be characterized as a sequential application of single equation, least square techniques. The choice of a least square rather than a maximum likelihood criterion for the selection of appropriate parameter values has computational advantages. Moreover, it is our belief that it would be a preferable criterion even without these computational attractions. The primary justification for use of a least squares criterion is that its use does not require assumptions about the shape of the error term distribution function, whereas use of a maximum likelihood criterion does. Since we know very little about the shapes of error term distributions, if indeed stable and well defined error distributions are actually present, it seems advantageous to use estimation techniques which do not require assumptions about their shapes.

To estimate our parameters, we used a computer program designed to handle a wide variety of standard regression computations.[4] But since

[4] A preliminary write-up of this program is contained in "Description of General Correlation Package," by M. E. Callaghan, K. E. Kavanagh, and J. R. Steinberg, mimeographed distribution by M.I.T. Computation Center, CC-107, August 1, 1958.

we adapted this program to our particular needs by a device which is still somewhat unfamiliar, we will give an illustrative example.

Let the output or dependent variable be denoted by Y, its predicted value by Y^*, and the input or independent variables by X, Z, and W. Only three are used in this example, but the procedure is the same for more. The input variables are either classificatory by nature or are converted into such variables by scaling. For concreteness let us suppose that X may fall into any one of five categories numbered 0 through 4, and Z may fall into any one of eight categories numbered 0 through 7, and W may fall into any one of three categories numbered 0 through 2.

We selected the parameters in the following relations so as to minimize the sum of squares of the differences between Y and Y^* for the sample of spending units being used.

(5) $$Y^* = a + F_1(X) + F_2(Z) + F_3(W)$$

where for each spending unit $F_1(X)$, $F_2(Z)$, and $F_3(W)$ are the appropriate values of these functions obtained by entering the following tables with the value of X, Z, and W that applies for the particular spending unit.

TABLE FOR $F_1(X)$		TABLE FOR $F_2(Z)$		TABLE FOR $F_3(W)$	
X	$F_1(X)$	Z	F_2	W	F_3
0	0	0	0	0	0
1	b_1	1	c_1	1	d_1
2	b_2	2	c_2	2	d_2
3	b_3	3	c_3		
4	b_4	4	c_4		
		5	c_5		
		6	c_6		
		7	c_7		

The parameters to be estimated are thus seen to be a, b_1 through b_4, c_1 through c_7, and d_1 and d_2. If a particular spending unit has an X of 2, a Z of 6, and a W of 0, then the predicted value of Y, Y^*, will be $a + b_2 + c_6 + 0$. If X, Z, and W are all zero then the predicted value will be the intercept term, that is, a.

The above estimation problem could have been treated as an analysis of variance problem with three classificatory variables, unequal number of observations per cell, and with additivity being assumed. However, since an effective computer program for such a problem did not seem to be available, we sought to use the well developed programs which are available for linear regression problems. It should perhaps be added at this point that the only issue at stake here is computational ease, since the procedure we used does in fact yield mathematically identical estimates of the parameters involved.

To convert the above problem into a linear regression problem let us create a number of new variables $X_1, \ldots, X_4, Z_1, \ldots Z_7, W_1,$ and W_2. These twelve new variables are defined as follows.

$$X_1 = 1 \quad \text{if } X = 1$$
$$= 0 \quad \text{if } X \neq 1$$
$$X_2 = 1 \quad \text{if } X = 2$$
$$= 0 \quad \text{if } X \neq 2$$

and so on until we have

$$W_2 = 1 \quad \text{if } W = 2$$
$$= 0 \quad \text{if } W \neq 2$$

Then it will be seen that the following linear regression equation will always yield exactly the same value of Y^* as did equation 5.

$$(6) \quad Y^* = a + b_1 X_1 + \ldots + b_4 X_4 + c_1 Z_1 + \ldots c_7 Z_7 + d_1 W_1 + d_2 W_2$$

Since the way in which the a, b, c, and d parameters enter into any computed value of Y^* is unchanged, and since it is these parameters in both cases which are being selected to minimize $(Y - Y^*)^2$, it is, of course, evident why the same results are achieved by estimating the parameters in equation 6 as by estimating them in equation 5. All that has been done is to translate the estimation problem into a form for which a good computer program exists.[5]

Summary of Results

The four basic variables used as dependent or output variables were mortgage debt held, personal debt held, liquid assets held, and annual expenditure on selected durables.

The study of each basic variable was broken down into two parts. In the first of these, a prediction equation for the probability that the dependent variable would be greater than zero was derived. In the second of these, attention was limited to spending units having a greater than zero value of the dependent variable, and a prediction equation, for the value of the dependent variable, was derived. Our results thus fall naturally into eight sections.

In each of these eight parts of our study, the independent or input variables included marital status and duration of marriage if married,

[5] The essential idea of the "dummy variable" approach may be found in Daniel B. Suits, "Use of Dummy Variables in Regression Equations," *Journal of the American Statistical Association*, Vol. 52, December, 1957, pp. 548–551.

age of head, education of head, and race of head. In the study of personal debt held, mortgage debt held also was used as an input variable. In the study of liquid assets held, both mortgage debt held and personal debt held were used as input variables in addition to the four input variables common to all eight parts. In the study of expenditure on durables, mortgage debt held, personal debt held, and liquid assets held were all used as input variables in addition to the basic four input variables.

In each of these eight parts, we computed successive regressions, adding in the input variables one at a time until all the input variables used in that part were included. Only these eight final multiple regressions are reported in this paper. A summary of these results is presented in the following eight sections. In each case a brief verbal statement is followed by results of the final multiple regression.

PROBABILITY SPENDING UNIT HOLDS MORTGAGE DEBT

Marital status is highly significant and exerts a substantial effect. Marriage increases the probability. The probability increases as duration of marriage increases up to between five and nine years and then decreases for longer durations.

Age of head is highly significant and exerts a substantial effect. The probability increases with age up to between 45 and 49 years of age and then decreases.

Education of head may be significant and appears to exert a modest effect. The probability increases with educational level attained by head.

Race is highly significant and exerts a modest effect. The probability is lower for Negroes.

The residuals were found to be significantly related to income, occupation, role of the spending unit in the dwelling unit, and to the predicted value of the dependent variable. This last result indicates that in this case a correction introduced to weaken the additivity assumption would be an improvement.

The residuals also were found to exhibit what may be a significant relation to number of adults, number of children, and veteran status of the spending unit.

If Y_1^* is used to designate the predicted probability a spending unit will hold mortgage debt, our equation for Y_1^* is

$$(7) \qquad Y_1^* = -0.08 + F_{1.1} + F_{1.2} + F_{1.3} + F_{1.4}$$

Correlation coefficient $= 0.39$; Standard error of estimate $= 0.41$; Standard error of constant $= 0.09$

The values of functions $F_{1.1}$, $F_{1.2}$, $F_{1.3}$, and $F_{1.4}$ are to be obtained by using the following function tables. The bracketed figure to the right of each estimated value is the standard error of the estimated parameter.

$F_{1.1}$ (marital status)			$F_{1.2}$ (age of head)	
Marital Status	$F_{1.1}$		*Age of Head*	$F_{1.2}$
Unmarried	o		18–20	o
1 year	0.07 (0.06)		21–24	—0.02 (0.06)
2 years	.15 (.05)		25–29	.09 (.06)
3 years	.19 (.06)		30–34	.16 (.06)
4 years	.27 (.06)		35–39	.25 (.06)
5–9 years	.31 (.03)		40–44	.22 (.06)
10–20 years	.25 (.03)		45–49	.24 (.06)
Over 20 years	.14 (.02)		50–54	.16 (.06)
			55–59	.15 (.06)
			60–64	.12 (.06)
			65 and over	.07 (.06)

$F_{1.3}$ (education)			$F_{1.4}$ (race)	
Education	$F_{1.3}$		*Race*	$F_{1.4}$
None	o		White	o
Grammar	0.02 (0.07)		Negro	—0.10 (0.03)
Some H.S.	.05 (.07)		Other	— .14 (.09)
H.S. Degree	.08 (.07)			
Some College	.12 (.08)			
College Degree	.13 (.08)			

AMOUNT OF MORTGAGE DEBT HELD BY SPENDING UNIT

Marital status may be significant and seems to exert a substantial effect. Marriage increases the expected amount of mortgage debt, but the effect dwindles very rapidly as duration of marriage increases.

Age of head may be significant and may have a modest effect. The expected amount of mortgage debt seems to increase with increasing age until about thirty-four years of age and then it decreases.

Education of head is significant and exerts a large effect. The expected amount increases with the educational level achieved by the head.

Race does not seem very significant, although the expected amount is less for Negroes.

The residuals were found to be significantly related to income, occupation, and city type.

If $Y_2{}^*$ is used to designate the predicted amount in dollars of mortgage debt for spending units having mortgage debt, our equation for $Y_2{}^*$ is

(8) $$Y_2{}^* = 3040 + F_{2.1} + F_{2.2} + F_{2.3} + F_{2.4}$$

Correlation coefficient = 0.432; Standard error of estimate = 4311; Standard error of constant = 5160.

The values of the functions $F_{2.1}$, $F_{2.2}$, $F_{2.3}$, and $F_{2.4}$ are to be obtained by use of the following function tables. The figure in brackets to the right of each estimated value of a function is the standard error of the estimated parameter.

$F_{2.1}$ (marital status)

Marital Status	$F_{2.1}$
Unmarried	0
1 year	4,550 (1,740)
2 years	1,380 (1,300)
3 years	1,530 (1,300)
4 years	167 (1,130)
5–9 years	49 (700)
10–20 years	744 (628)
Over 20 years	215 (625)

$F_{2.2}$ (age of head)

Age of Head	$F_{2.2}$
18–20	0
21–24	526 (4,620)
25–29	1,290 (4,490)
30–34	1,560 (4,480)
35–39	1,200 (4,480)
40–44	964 (4,480)
45–49	134 (4,490)
50–54	166 (4,510)
55–59	−1,270 (4,520)
60–64	−1,140 (4,540)
65 and over	−1,000 (4,530)

$F_{2.3}$ (education)

Education	$F_{2.3}$
None	0
Gr. School	835 (2,570)
Some H.S.	1,190 (2,590)
H.S. Degree	1,980 (2,580)
Some College	3,610 (2,600)
College Degree	4,930 (2,600)

$F_{2.4}$ (race)

Race	$F_{2.4}$
White	0
Negro	−1,040 (891)
Other	−1,010 (2,510)

PROBABILITY SPENDING UNIT HOLDS PERSONAL DEBT

Marital status is significant and exerts a large effect. Marriage increases the probability. The probability increases with duration of marriage up to about three years and then drops off.

Age of head of spending unit is significant and plays a large role. The probability decreases with age after about twenty-four and is very low if the head is over sixty-five years of age.

Educational status of head is probably significant and exerts a modest effect. The probability decreases with increasing education of head.

Race is significant and exerts a substantial effect. Negroes are more likely to have personal debt than whites.

Mortgage debt held by spending unit is significant and plays a modest role. Mortgage debt holders are more likely to have personal debt except for very large mortgage holders.

The residuals were found to be significantly related to income, occupation, number of children, age of eldest child, and region. The residuals exhibited what may be a significant relation to city type and to the predicted value of the dependent variable.

If Y_3^* is used to designate the predicted probability that the spending unit will have personal debt, our equation for Y_3^* is

$$(9) \qquad Y_3^* = 0.63 + F_{3.1} + F_{3.2} + F_{3.3} + F_{3.4} + F_{3.5}$$

Correlation coefficient $= 0.426$; Standard error of estimate $= 0.454$; Standard error of constant $= 0.098$.

The values of the functions $F_{3.1}$, $F_{3.2}$, $F_{3.3}$, $F_{3.4}$ are to be obtained by use of the following function tables. Standard errors of the estimated parameters are given in brackets.

$F_{3.1}$ (marital status)		$F_{3.2}$ (age of head)	
Marital Status	$F_{3.1}$	Age of Head	$F_{3.2}$
Unmarried	0	18–20	0
1 year	0.11 (0.06)	21–24	—0.03 (0.07)
2 years	.22 (.06)	25–29	.00 (.06)
3 years	.29 (.07)	30–34	— .05 (.06)
4 years	.16 (.06)	35–39	— .14 (.06)
5–9 years	.17 (.03)	40–44	— .24 (.06)
10–20 years	.18 (.03)	45–49	— .18 (.06)
Over 20 years	.12 (.03)	50–54	— .27 (.07)
		55–59	— .30 (.07)
		60–64	— .38 (.07)
		65 and over	— .51 (.06)

$F_{3.3}$ (education)		$F_{3.4}$ (race)	
Education	$F_{3.3}$	Race	$F_{3.4}$
None	o	White	o
Gr. School	0.00 (0.08)	Negro	0.18 (0.03)
Some H.S.	.oo (.08)	Other	.o6 (.10)
H.S. Degree	— .10 (.08)		
Some College	— .10 (.08)		
College Degree	— .14 (.08)		

The value of $F_{3.5}$ (mortgage debt) is zero if the unit does not have mortgage debt. If the unit has mortgage debt,

$$F_{3.5} = 0.14 - 0.000007 \text{ (mortgage debt of unit in dollars).}$$
$$(0.03) \quad (0.000004)$$

AMOUNT OF PERSONAL DEBT HELD BY SPENDING UNIT

Marital status does not appear to be very significant. The expected value of personal debt may be larger for units married over twenty years.

Age of head does not seem very significant. The expected value may reach a peak at about forty or forty-five years of age.

Education may be significant and seems to exert a large effect. The expected value increases with the educational level of the head.

Race is probably significant and the expected value is less for Negroes than for whites.

The level of mortgage debt is significant and the expected amount of personal debt increases with the amount of mortgage debt held. The mere holding of mortgage debt is not significant.

The residuals were found to be significantly related to income and occupation. They also appear to be related to number of adults and region.

If $Y_4{}^*$ designates the predicted amount in dollars of personal debt for spending units having personal debt, our equation for $Y_4{}^*$ is

(10) $\qquad Y_4{}^* = 361 + F_{4.1} + F_{4.2} + F_{4.3} + F_{4.4} + F_{4.5}$

Correlation coefficient = 0.280; Standard error of estimate = 1133; Standard error of constant = 382.

The values of $F_{4.1}$, $F_{4.2}$, $F_{4.3}$, and $F_{4.4}$ are to be obtained by use of the following function tables. Standard errors of the estimated parameters are given in brackets.

$F_{4.1}$ (marital status)

Marital Status	$F_{4.1}$
Unmarried	0
1 year	310 (192)
2 years	59 (173)
3 years	−110 (194)
4 years	87 (188)
5–9 years	81 (110)
10–20 years	97 (101)
Over 20 years	266 (109)

$F_{4.2}$ (age of head)

Age of Head	$F_{4.2}$
18–20	0
21–24	67 (211)
25–29	127 (204)
30–34	99 (205)
35–39	119 (207)
40–44	420 (210)
45–49	140 (210)
50–54	−37 (222)
55–59	2 (230)
60–64	−51 (240)
65 and over	55 (233)

$F_{4.3}$ (education)

Education	$F_{4.3}$
None	0
Gr. School	−57 (336)
Some H.S.	93 (340)
H.S. Degree	210 (340)
Some College	329 (347)
College Degree	543 (347)

$F_{4.4}$ (race)

Race	$F_{4.4}$
White	0
Negro	−223 (106)
Other	−178 (297)

The value of $F_{4.5}$ (mortgage debt) is zero if the unit does not have mortgage debt. If the unit has mortgage debt,

$$F_{4.5} = -41 + 0.0421 \text{ (the amount of mortgage debt of unit in dollars).}$$
$$(105) \quad (0.0134)$$

PROBABILITY SPENDING UNIT HOLDS LIQUID ASSETS

Marital status is significant and exerts a modest effect. The probability increases with marriage and with marriage durations of over twenty years.

Age of head is significant and exerts a substantial effect. The probability increases with age of head up to about fifty-five to sixty years of age and then decreases.

Education of head is significant and exerts a very great effect. The probability increases with educational level achieved by head.

Race of head is significant and exerts a large effect. Negroes are less likely to have liquid asset holdings.

Mortgage debt of spending unit may be significant and appears to exert a modest effect. The amount of mortgage debt does not appear to

309

be very significant, but units with mortgage debt are more likely to have liquid assets.

Personal debt is significant and exerts a modest effect. Units with personal debt are less likely to have liquid assets unless personal debt is very large.

The residuals were found to be significantly related to income, occupation, number of children, city type, region, and the predicted value of the dependent variable. They also may be related to age of eldest child and role of spending unit in its dwelling unit.

If $Y_5{}^*$ designates the predicted probability that the spending unit holds liquid assets, our equation for $Y_5{}^*$ is

$$(11) \qquad Y_5{}^* = 0.20 + F_{5.1} + F_{5.2} + F_{5.3} + F_{5.4} + F_{5.5} + F_{5.6}$$

Correlation coefficient $= 0.508$; Standard error of estimate $= 0.364$; Standard error of constant $= 0.08$

The values of the functions $F_{5.1}$, $F_{5.2}$, $F_{5.3}$, and $F_{5.4}$ are to be obtained by use of the following function tables. Standard errors of the estimated parameters are given in brackets.

$F_{5.1}$ (marital status)

Marital Status	$F_{5.1}$
Unmarried	0
1 year	0.03 (0.05)
2 years	.06 (.05)
3 years	.04 (.05)
4 years	.07 (.05)
5–9 years	.05 (.03)
10–20 years	.01 (.02)
Over 20 years	.09 (.02)

$F_{5.2}$ (age of head)

Age of Head	$F_{5.2}$
18–20	0
21–24	0.01 (0.05)
25–29	.10 (.05)
30–34	.14 (.05)
35–39	.17 (.05)
40–44	.18 (.05)
45–49	.15 (.05)
50–54	.16 (.05)
55–59	.23 (.05)
60–64	.20 (.05)
65 and over	.16 (.05)

$F_{5.3}$ (education)

Education	$F_{5.3}$
None	0
Gr. School	0.28 (0.06)
Some H.S.	.44 (.07)
H.S. Degree	.54 (.07)
Some College	.61 (.07)
College Degree	.61 (.07)

$F_{5.4}$ (race)

Race	$F_{5.4}$
White	0
Negro	−0.40 (0.03)
Other	.04 (.08)

The value of $F_{5.5}$ (mortgage debt) is equal to zero if the unit does not have mortgage debt. If the unit has mortgage debt,

$$F_{5.5} = 0.04 + 0.000002 \quad \text{(mortgage debt of unit in dollars)}.$$
$$(0.02) \quad (0.000003)$$

The value of $F_{6.6}$ (personal debt) is equal to zero if the unit does not have personal debt. If the unit has personal debt,

$$F_{5.6} = -0.13 + 0.000019 \quad \text{(personal debt of unit in dollars)}.$$
$$(0.02) \quad (0.000008)$$

AMOUNT OF LIQUID ASSETS HELD BY SPENDING UNIT

Marital status was found to be fairly significant and to exert a substantial effect. The expected value increases with marriage and is particularly high for marriages of ten- to twenty-year duration.

Age of head was significant and exerts a large effect. The expected amount of liquid assets increases with age up to about sixty-five years of age and then drops off.

Education level of head is significant and exerts a large effect. The expected amount increases with the educational level achieved by the head.

Race is not significant.

Mortgage debt presence or absence is significant, but its level is not. The expected amount of liquid assets is much less for mortgage debt holders.

The amount of personal debt is not significant, but its presence or absence is. Spending units holding personal debt have substantially smaller liquid asset holdings.

The residuals were found to be significantly related to income, occupation, and to the predicted value of the dependent variable. They also may be related to number of children, age of eldest child, city type, and role of spending unit in its dwelling unit.

If Y_6^* designates the predicted amount in dollars of liquid assets for units holding liquid assets, our equation for Y_6^* is

$$(12) \quad Y_6^* = -4870 + F_{6.1} + F_{6.2} + F_{6.3} + F_{6.4} + F_{6.5} + F_{6.6}$$

Correlation coefficient $= 0.251$; Standard error of estimate $= 12566$; Standard error of coefficient $= 4660$.

311

The values of the function $F_{6.1}$, $F_{6.2}$, $F_{6.3}$, and $F_{6.4}$ are to be obtained by use of the following function tables. Standard errors of the estimated parameters are given in brackets.

$F_{6.1}$ (marital status)

Marital Status	$F_{6.1}$
Unmarried	0
1 year	463 (2,070)
2 years	1,380 (1,890)
3 years	492 (2,180)
4 years	928 (1,960)
5–9 years	1,540 (1,040)
10–20 years	2,970 (930)
Over 20 years	1,730 (833)

$F_{6.2}$ (age of head)

Age of Head	$F_{6.2}$
18–20	0
21–24	249 (2,280)
25–29	735 (2,180)
30–34	534 (2,150)
35–39	1,320 (2,160)
40–44	1,440 (2,160)
45–49	5,530 (2,170)
50–54	4,410 (2,210)
55–59	4,100 (2,220)
60–64	7,440 (2,240)
65 and over	5,220 (2,140)

$F_{6.3}$ (education)

Education	$F_{6.3}$
None	0
Gr. School	3,100 (4,250)
Some H.S.	5,260 (4,270)
H.S. Degree	6,270 (4,260)
Some College	7,280 (4,290)
College Degree	8,240 (4,290)

$F_{6.4}$ (race)

Race	$F_{6.4}$
White	0
Negro	−1,330 (1,800)
Other	12 (3,090)

The value of $F_{6.5}$ (mortgage debt) is equal to zero if the unit does not have mortgage debt. If the unit has mortgage debt,

$$F_{6.5} = -2590 + 0.107 \quad \text{(mortgage debt of unit in dollars)}.$$
$$(930) \quad (0.104)$$

The value of $F_{6.6}$ (personal debt) is equal to zero if the unit does not have personal debt. If the unit has personal debt,

$$F_{6.6} = -2340 - 0.119 \quad \text{(personal debt of unit in dollars)}.$$
$$(658) \quad (0.307)$$

PROBABILITY SPENDING UNIT MAKES EXPENDITURES ON CONSUMER DURABLES

Marital status is significant and exerts a large effect. Marriage increases the probability substantially. The probability increases until the second or third year of marriage and then decreases rapidly.

Age of head is significant and exerts a moderate effect. The probability increases with age until about fifty or fifty-five and then declines.

Educational status and race of head are not significant.

Presence or absence of mortgage debt is not in itself significant, but the amount of mortgage debt is significant. The probability increases with the amount of mortgage debt held.

The amount of personal debt does not appear to be significant; however, the presence or absence of personal debt is significant, and the probability of consumer durable expenditure is higher for spending units having personal debt.

The amount of liquid assets does not appear to be significant. However, the presence of liquid assets does not appear to be significant and increases the probability of expenditure on consumer durables.

The residuals were found to be significantly related to income, number of children, age of eldest child, role of spending unit in its dwelling unit, and to the predicted value of the dependent variable. They also may be related to number of adults, city type, and region.

If $Y_7{}^*$ designates the predicted probability that the spending unit purchases consumer durables during year, our equation for $Y_7{}^*$ is

$$(13) \quad Y_7{}^* = -0.048 + F_{7.1} + F_{7.2} + F_{7.3} + F_{7.4} + F_{7.5} + F_{7.6} + F_{7.7}$$

Correlation coefficient = 0.353; Standard error of estimate = 0.47; Standard error of constant = 0.10.

The values of the functions $F_{7.1}$, $F_{7.2}$, $F_{7.3}$, and $F_{7.4}$ are given in the following function tables. Standard error of the estimated parameters are given in brackets.

$F_{7.1}$ (marital status)		$F_{7.2}$ (age of head)	
Marital Status	$F_{7.1}$	Age of Head	$F_{7.2}$
Unmarried	0	18–20	0
1 year	0.34 (0.06)	21–24	0.07 (0.07)
2 years	.46 (.06)	25–29	.14 (.07)
3 years	.45 (.07)	30–34	.17 (.07)
4 years	.24 (.07)	35–39	.17 (.07)
5–9 years	.18 (.03)	40–44	.18 (.07)
10–20 years	.13 (.03)	45–49	.16 (.07)
Over 20 years	.15 (.03)	50–54	.21 (.07)
		55–59	.12 (.07)
		60–64	.05 (.07)
		65 and over	.10 (.07)

313

$F_{7.3}$ (education)

Education	$F_{7.3}$
None	0
Gr. School	0.07 (0.08)
Some H.S.	.14 (.09)
H.S. Degree	.05 (.09)
Some College	.06 (.09)
College Degree	.14 (.09)

$F_{7.4}$ (race)

Race	$F_{7.4}$
White	0
Negro	—0.02 (0.04)
Other	.05 (.10)

The value of $F_{7.5}$ (mortgage debt) is zero if the unit holds no mortgage debt. If the unit has mortgage debt,

$$F_{7.5} = -0.021 + 0.00011 \quad \text{(mortgage debt of unit in dollars)}.$$
$$(0.032) \quad (0.000004)$$

The value of $F_{7.6}$ (personal debt) is zero if the unit has no personal debt. If the unit has personal debt,

$$F_{7.6} = 0.149 - 0.000016 \quad \text{(personal debt of unit in dollars)}.$$
$$(0.022) \quad (0.000011)$$

The value of $F_{7.7}$ (liquid assets) is zero if the unit has no liquid assets. If the unit has liquid assets,

$$F_{7.7} = 0.087 + 0.0000001 \quad \text{(liquid assets of unit in dollars)}.$$
$$(0.025) \quad (0.0000008)$$

AMOUNT OF CONSUMER DURABLES EXPENDITURE IN A YEAR

Marital status, age of head, education of head, and race all failed to contribute significantly to explaining the amount of consumer durables expenditures.

The presence or absence of mortgage debt was not significant but the amount may be and appears to be positively related to the amount of expenditure on consumer durables.

Personal debt does not appear to be significant.

The presence or absence of liquid assets does not appear to be significant, but the amount of liquid assets does appear to be significant. The effect is modest, but the amount of liquid assets is positively related to the amount of expenditures on consumer durables.

The residuals were found to be significantly related to income. They also may be significantly related to occupation and role of the spending unit in its dwelling unit.

314

If $Y_8{}^*$ designates the predicted amount in dollars of consumer durables purchases for spending units having made any amount of such purchases, our equation for $Y_8{}^*$ is

$$(14) \quad Y_8{}^* = 145 + F_{8.1} + F_{8.2} + F_{8.3} + F_{8.4} + F_{8.5}$$
$$+ F_{8.6} + F_{8.7} + F_{8.8}$$

Correlation coefficient = 0.219; Standard error of estimate = 468; Standard error of constant = 216.

The values of $F_{8.1}$, $F_{8.2}$, $F_{8.3}$, and $F_{8.4}$ are to be obtained by use of the following function tables. Standard errors of the estimated parameters are given in brackets.

$F_{8.1}$ (marital status)		$F_{8.2}$ (age of head)	
Marital Status	$F_{8.1}$	*Age of Head*	$F_{8.2}$
Unmarried	0	18–20	0
1 year	128 (89)	21–24	118 (127)
2 years	41 (77)	25–29	167 (122)
3 years	57 (87)	30–34	110 (122)
4 years	−23 (90)	35–39	120 (123)
5–9 years	31 (54)	40–44	145 (124)
10–20 years	7 (48)	45–49	93 (124)
Over 20 years	−3 (47)	50–54	101 (127)
		55–59	70 (132)
		60–64	0 (134)
		65 and over	14 (127)

$F_{8.3}$ (education)		$F_{8.4}$ (race)	
Education	$F_{8.3}$	*Race*	$F_{8.4}$
None	0	White	0
Gr. School	61 (180)	Negro	2 (61)
Some H.S.	69 (182)	Other	112 (137)
H.S. Degree	107 (182)		
Some College	83 (185)		
College Degree	108 (184)		

The value of $F_{8.5}$ (mortgage debt) is zero if the unit has no mortgage debt. If the unit has mortgage debt,

$$F_{8.5} = -18 + 0.01 \text{ (mortgage debt of unit in dollars)}.$$
$$(45) \quad (0.005)$$

The value of $F_{8.6}$ (personal debt) is zero if the unit has no personal debt. If the unit has personal debt,

$$F_{8.6} = -50 + 0.01 \ \text{(personal debt of unit in dollars)}.$$
$$(35) \quad (0.02)$$

The value of $F_{8.7}$ (liquid assets) is zero if the unit has no liquid assets. If the unit has liquid assets,

$$F_{8.7} = 48 + 0.005 \ \text{(liquid assets of unit in dollars)}.$$
$$(40) \quad (0.002)$$

Prospective Use of Aggregative Time Series

Decision-unit models are ideally set up to use data and relationships that apply at a micro-level. This is one of the major advantages of this type of model and should be fully exploited. Nevertheless, certain things should be kept in mind. In some cases data needed to determine appropriate micro-operating characteristics may not be available. In other cases the data may be available, but the particular need may not justify the added complexity or computing effort required fully to utilize the micro-information. However, there is nothing about decision-unit models or their simulation that restricts the model builder to the use of micro-data or micro-relations. He has the added opportunity to build at the micro level, but he retains an equal facility to incorporate the use of aggregative data and relations.

Our strategy is to build and test as completely as possible at the micro-level, but then to use aggregative data and relationships to complete our models and to bring them into alignment with historical aggregative data. This puts as much of the burden of testing and formulation as is feasible at the micro-level where it belongs. It retains the use of aggregative data as fully as possible for final testing and alignment of the over-all model. As data availability improves, and as our knowledge grows, decision-unit type models of the economic system may, and in fact should, place less and less reliance on aggregative data and relationships.

However, this should be a gradual evolution, and, since the final "payoff" of these models will usually be in predicting things about aggregates, it follows that final testing against aggregative data will always be necessary. Hopefully such testing will not require extensive gross adjustments aimed at bringing the model into line with the aggregative data used in testing.

We expect to conduct further studies at the micro-level aimed at predicting household behavior with respect to a more adequate set of output variables. We also hope to use, as inputs at the micro-level, some additional variables such as income and employment. We realize that this present study leaves an unduly heavy burden for aggregative data, particularly income and employment series. Nevertheless, a point will inevitably come at which it seems necessary to accept and use whatever results are available at the micro-level. How then should we proceed?

In the absence of further studies at the micro-level, our procedure will be to use the obtained household operating characteristics, such as they are. An initial population appropriate to a convenient historical date will be used, and the behavior of components of the over-all model, such as the household sector, will be simulated. The discrepancies between the aggregative time series generated and the actual historical pattern would be ascertained and related to other appropriate aggregative monthly time series. Results obtained would then be incorporated into the model in preparation for additional studies and eventual prediction.

Conclusion

While the major substantive findings of this study have already been presented, a few of their implications need to be stressed.

1. Life cycle changes are of great importance in predicting the economic and demographic behavior of households. However, it is not possible to describe the life cycle position of a spending unit by the value of a single variable. Such variables as marital status of heads of spending units, duration of marriage, age of heads, and number of children all exert an independent and significant effect on economic behavior.

2. Since duration of marriage plays an important role with respect to several economic outputs of spending units, household surveys ought to include a question on this point.

3. The effects of demographic variables such as duration of marriage and age of head are not linear in either the original or logarithmic forms. In many cases, they are not even monotonically increasing or decreasing functions of these variables. This fact points up the need to estimate and test relationships which are flexible enough to approximate the role played by such variables. Completely flexible relationships cannot be determined from finite amounts of data. However, in specifying functional forms we have assumed only a weakened sort of additivity and a variety of local continuity. While we would like to move in the direction of doing without an additivity assumption, we feel that the approach used

by us is far more satisfactory than approaches based on assumptions of linearity, cumulative normal, or other rigid and pre-specified functional forms. It should go without saying, by now, that single variable approaches to multivariate problems are completely unsatisfactory.

4. The interdependence problem does arise with respect to some outputs even at the spending unit level and even if very short time periods are used. Treatment of such outputs as change in personal debt, change in liquid assets, and expenditures on durables as independently determined is clearly inadmissible. We have presented one approach to this problem which is both acceptable and relatively simple to use.

COMMENT

ROBERT SOLOW, Massachusetts Institute of Technology

I have been trying for weeks without success to remember the source, but somewhere Maxim Gorki tells the story of a man who is walking through a Russian village showing off some remarkable machine. It does all sorts of things: peels potatoes, fixes shoes, fits multiple regressions for all I know. Finally one old peasant silently watches the gadget perform and asks: "Yes, but will it whistle?" The owner scornfully replies that it won't, and starts to recite the list of the machine's accomplishments, but all the peasant says is: "What good is it if it can't whistle." Of course this is the big question about Guy Orcutt's grandiose "decision-unit" model of the household sector: will it whistle? Will it tell us what we really want to know? It is still too early to say. Even the bulky document presented here is only a beginning, and it will be a few years before we can even hope for a genuine, loud, clear, piercing whistle.

In one way, at least, the Orcutt-Rivlin model appeals to one of the deep-seated prejudices of the economics profession—the belief in disaggregation. J. K. Galbraith has claimed that the most common cliché in economics is the one about the baby and the bathwater. I would also settle for a nickel every time someone tells someone else that he should disaggregate. Now I do think the micro-economic instinct, in part, is sound. We probably ought to theorize in terms of the actual decision-making units of the economic system. Even purely macro-economic theories probably ought to be capable of being rationalized in terms of the behavior of households and firms. But it is a *non sequitur* to draw from this the implication that empirical relationships based on or derived from micro-economic data will be more reliable than those based squarely on aggregates. That depends on many subtle statistical properties of the system being observed and it is not hard to construct examples, or find them in reality, in which the balance goes either way.[1] So one cannot be sure without evidence that decision-unit models will predict better or produce more insight than more aggregative approaches to the data. The only way to get some evidence is to try, and so far nobody but Orcutt has had the tenacity to try.

Since I have no special competence or experience in demography, I will confine my comments to the last two-thirds of the paper. There some experiments are described on the interaction of demographic and economic factors in determining the behavior of households with respect to mortgage and personal debt, liquid asset ownership, and expenditures on durable consumer goods. The estimation procedure was carried out in a rather peculiar way, but one which does shed some oblique light on the significance of the demographic inputs. Each of the four dependent variables was studied in two stages: first a regression analysis with the probability that a spending unit will have mortgage debt, or personal debt or liquid assets, or that it will spend on durables as dependent variable; followed by a conditional regression analysis to predict the amount of debt, assets, or expenditure for those units which had any. Initially the regressions were carried out with the four major demographic variables as the only independent variables: marital status, education, age of head, and race. Then one by one a whole list of additional demographic and economic inputs were tested as possible independent variables. It is this last step that I find peculiar, not so much because of the information it gives as because of what it conceals. There is no way of telling how much weight ought to be attributed to each of the possible independent variables since the outcome of this asymmetric procedure will depend on the order in which additional variables are tried. Nor is there any way at the end to assess how successful the whole estimation procedure has been.

One conclusion does stand out. The amount of predictive power contributed by the four original demographic inputs is pitifully small. The multiple correlations run around 0.4 with only one of the eight as high as 0.5 and several others as low as 0.2. It is true that one rarely gets good fits from cross-sectional survey data but this fact in no way increases the percentage of variance explained. A more dramatic indication of how little help one gets from the first four variables comes from the standard errors of estimate. In the four regressions which are supposed to predict probabilities, the standard errors of estimate range from 0.36

---

[1] This point is well made in an unpublished paper, "Is Aggregation Necessarily Bad?", by Zvi Griliches and Yehuda Grunfeld of the Department of Economics, University of Chicago, September, 1958.

to 0.47. Thus a 90 per cent two-sided prediction interval would in all cases have a length greater than unity. Of course in many cases a shorter interval would be given by the necessary bounds zero and one to the size of a probability. But even then in nearly all cases, two standard errors on the free side of the best estimate will carry almost to zero or to one.

Among the additional variables tested for influence on the predictands are several other demographic inputs mainly having to do with location and family structure, and some of them appear to add something to the explanation. But the inputs which seem consistently to have the most work to do are income and occupation, the only truly socio-economic variables which make an appearance in the model. This leads me to believe that it would be much more enlightening to do the estimation just the reverse of the way it was actually performed. Not only ought the socio-economic inputs to be introduced at the very start, but the additivity assumption ought to be abandoned from the beginning. My complaint is not that the *ad hoc* method actually used to deal with non-additivity won't work, but rather that whether it works or not it effectively masks the most interesting aspect of the final results: the way in which demographic variables *interact* (in the analysis of variance sense) with economic variables in the determination of household behavior. I would be happy to trade a little predictive accuracy for this bit of insight if it were necessary. But I don't think it is.

This brings me to a related point. I notice that the list of desirable output variables includes changes in various categories of debt, expenditures on various categories of commodities, and receipts from sales. But the list of economic input variables is limited to income, employment and occupational status, and initial conditions. Not a single price or interest rate or price expectation appears on the list. I would be happier if the system being simulated looked a little more like a collection of markets and a little less like a collection of mice. It is true that survey data taken at one point of time rarely gives information on supply and demand responses to price changes. But although the data may be collected statistically the application is to a process continuing over time, and over time prices change. And even if prices do not change much, I would guess that there are significant interactions among price variables and the demographic and socio-economic determinants of household spending behavior.

Let me conclude with a few comments on a more technical level. I have already mentioned what seems to me to be a real difficulty with the device used to cope with non-additivity. The same remark goes for the quite similar way of dealing with additional independent variables. Whether or not the two procedures lead to improved fits or good fits, they seem to me to be makeshift substitutes for structural estimation.

Finally there is the matter of interdependence and simultaneous equations in the estimation procedure. I do not pretend to know how important this complication is likely to be in models of this kind. I do not even know how important it is in econometric models in general. But if the difficulty bulks large in the present context, I am not certain that the authors have avoided it by the device of taking a short time period. They say: "If we take income as one of the variables determining the probability that a unit will purchase an automobile in the month, we feel we can assume that the purchase itself does not affect the income of that unit in the same month. This is all that is necessary to avoid simultaneous equation difficulties at the system level." I'm not sure that it is. What is required is that the *residuals* from the "true" structural automobile demand function be uncorrelated with the family's income. And it does not seem at all unlikely to me that economic events should create differential effects within a month which might tend, say, to push high-income families below the normal relation and low-income families above. Moreover, the choice of a short time period could also have the side effect of straining the Markovian character of the process, so that even given prices, incomes, and the like, the probabilities for any given month might depend on the remoter past, and not only on the conditions at the beginning of that month.

I have used my time for carping, because I presume that is what I am expected to do. But the truth of the matter is that decades of conventional econometric effort have not added much to our stock of reliable empirical knowledge. Maybe the newer methods of digital and analog simulation are on the right track. At least we can guarantee ourselves reliable "empirical" knowledge about artificial economic systems and maybe that is half the battle. Maybe they will even whistle.

REPLY

That micro-economic data contains more information than the same data aggregated is obvious. In general, one might expect some of this extra information to be useful for purposes of testing and prediction. In any case, one always has the option of throwing away the extra information. Given the availability of the appropriate micro-data and the correct model underlying the behavior and interaction of micro-units, then the predictive power of this model will necessarily exceed, or at the very worst, match that of any model based on aggregates of the micro-data. If some data is available at an aggregative level but not at a micro-level or if account is taken of the fact that all models about the real world undoubtedly involve misspecifications, then it seems obvious that some models based in part or entirely on highly aggregative data will work better than some models based solely on micro-economic data. Our position is that some types of economic and demographic phenomena require the use of micro-data and relationships, and that it is important to develop models of socio-economic systems and methods of analysis that are appropriate for micro-data and relationships. Such models will be able to use aggregative data and aggregative relationships to the extent desired.

Solow errs in judging predictive power on the basis of correlation coefficients and standard errors of estimate derived from relationships pertaining to the behavior of micro-units. Correlation coefficients are seldom appropriate for such purposes for a variety of well-known reasons. The use of standard errors of estimate is frequently appropriate but only if the dependent variables in the estimated relationships are what one is actually trying to predict. The dependent variables in our relationships relate to the behavior of micro-units and in many cases can only assume the values zero or one. What we were estimating in these cases were *probabilities* and these probabilities are the *expected* or *average* values of the dependent variables. The standard errors of estimate refer to the standard deviation of the zeros and ones of the micro-units from the estimated probabilities of getting a one. To judge predictive ability with regard to the aggregates to be predicted, one would have to pay attention to the standard errors of the estimated *probabilities*. Judging from our study of residuals classified according to predicted probabilities, the standard errors of the estimated probabilities seldom exceed 0.03 in any range of probabilities that occurs frequently enough to be of much significance in terms of aggregative behavior. It might be noted also that many of our parameter estimates deviate from zero by between five and ten times their standard errors.

We agree with Solow that it would be better to introduce income at the start and thus at a micro-level. We hope to do so, but have not done so yet for two reasons. (1) Current income does not seem to be a reasonable variable for a causal explanation of something like present mortgage debt position. Income expectations at the time the debt was incurred would be relevant but were not available. Part of the idea in using such variables as education, race, and age was that they would be better proxies for the appropriate long-run income expectations than current income would be. (2) Before one can effectively utilize relationships making use of incomes of micro-units it is necessary to generate these micro-incomes. We hope to do this in a reasonable way, but we have not yet reached that stage. Therefore, we chose to use aggregate income in the way projected in our paper. Current micro-incomes as well as other variables were related to residuals out of curiosity, since it seemed that something might be learned and the added cost of doing so was minor.

Much the same comments could be made about our failure to include prices, interest rates, and expectations of these and other variables. We are as anxious as Solow that this should be done. The general framework of decision-unit or micro-analytic models and the methods available for studying such models are adequate. What is lacking is a proper knowledge of the role of such variables. Since existing bodies of cross-sectional data do not seem a promising base for estimating price and interest rate effects, our present strategy is to do what can be done with existing bodies of data and then use more or less aggregative time series to fill in some of the gaps.

We would be curious to see what kind of an operational definition Solow would give to the notion of, "the 'true' structural automobile demand function." We see no objection to micro-analytic models in which the random components appearing in different relationships are not treated as independent. Nor do we see any reason why probabilities for any given month should not be made to depend on conditions or events prior to the beginning of that month. We do this in making use of date of birth and marriage and might equally well do it in other respects. Why this should strain the Markovian character of the process is not exactly clear, since prior events can be interpreted as part of the conditions at the beginning of the month. In any case, we would not regard straining the Markovian character of the process as identical with original sin.

Population Change and Aggregate Output

SIMON KUZNETS

THE JOHNS HOPKINS UNIVERSITY

1. Introduction

FOR the modern period, that is, since the end of the 18th century, the available statistical records reveal no cases in which the prevalent substantial rises in population were accompanied by secular declines in per capita product. To be sure, there were sharp drops in total and per capita output—occasioned in the underdeveloped countries by crop failures and in the developed countries by cyclical recessions. In the underdeveloped countries population increase, occurring under conditions of pre-modern agriculture and primitive transportation and industry, can be viewed as a factor in the persistence of a low per capita standard of living, and hence in the catastrophic impact of famines. Yet the long-term statistical records, error-prone as they are for such countries as India and Egypt over the first half of the 20th century, give no clear indication of a long-term decline, althougĥ they do show failure of the low per capita income to rise. The evidence thus suggests that in modern times secular rises in population have been accompanied by secular rises in aggregate output—for many countries so large that there was also a marked secular rise in per capita product.[1]

It appears that population growth, despite pressure on the limited stock of natural resources and man-made capital, has permitted substantial rises in product per capita, particularly in countries with a social framework attuned to modern technology. However, the empirical evidence, at least in its present state, is insufficient for a detailed analysis of the impact of population growth on the growth of aggregate output. While it reveals marked contrasts among countries with respect to growth of income per capita, it does not suggest that differences in the rate of population increase are an important variable in accounting for these contrasts. In the discussion that follows, we must, therefore, resort to speculation.

[1] In Table 1 of my paper "Quantitative Aspects of the Economic Growth of Nations: I," *Economic Development and Cultural Change*, Vol. v, no. 1, October, 1956, p. 10, eighteen countries that show secular growth of population show also a substantial rise in per capita product. Ireland, in the nineteenth century, shows a decline in population and a rise in per capita income.

The theme is a broad one—the impact of secular growth of population on per capita output. I speak of growth rather than decline because it has been, and is likely to be, far the more prevalent pattern; and I focus on per capita output, because any conclusion concerning the contribution of population growth to the rise in per capita output leads to obvious inferences for aggregate output. Finally, a word about the drift of the speculations that follow. My impression is that recent professional (and popular) literature has emphasized the disadvantages and dangers of population growth—the drain upon irreproducible resources, upon capital accumulation, upon the organizing capacity of societies, and so on. Little can be added to these arguments. But as a matter of balance, I propose to dwell upon the positive contributions of population growth —admitting that they must eventually be weighed against the negative effects.

2. Population as Producers

An increase in population means, other conditions being equal, an increase in the labor force. The precise contribution to the labor force will differ depending upon whether population growth is caused by a decline in the death rate, by net immigration, or by an increase in the birth rate. The differences are of great importance, since reduction in the death rate of the working population or net immigration (usually of persons in the prime working years of life) minimizes the cost of investment in bringing infants to the age of effective participation in the labor force. We recognize these important differences but prefer not to complicate the discussion by treating them separately.

Let us assume that the labor force increases at the same rate as total population (or somewhat less if there is an increase in the birth rate). This increased labor force will be able to turn out as much or more product per worker (and hence per capita of total population) if it is equipped with the same amount of capital as, or greater amount than, was previously available per worker; and if the reproducible capital-output ratio remains the same or decreases. The latter "if" takes account of the possible effect of pressure upon the limited supply of irreproducible resources: if such pressure develops, there may be need for more man-made capital per unit of output, or for some chain of substitution and technological innovation.

I shall deal with the supply of capital in the section below. Here, the point to be stressed is that capital investment must include not only material goods, but the even more important input into education and training of the population—a factor of particular relevance if population growth stems from the birth rate rather than from the death and immigration rates. Obviously, the productive contribution of these additional numbers is as dependent upon their education and skills as upon the material capital equipment with which they are provided.

Let us assume further that capital investment, thus broadly conceived to include the raising and training of the new generations, is at least as large per capita for the additions to the labor force (B) as for the already existing labor force (A). What are the reasons for assuming that the per worker productivity of $A + B$ would be greater than that of A and, that, therefore, under the conditions given (constant proportions of labor force to population), per capita income would also be higher? Three somewhat different reasons can be advanced.

The first is connected with the distinctive assumption that there exists in the country a variety of unexploited natural resources and that additions to the labor force would permit greater utilization of these resources. This utilization, combined with a more specialized division of labor would, in all probability, lead to a greater product per worker. The crux of this argument lies in two points: (a) an increasing density of population spreading to formerly uninhabited parts of the country brings into use resources previously inaccessible, and the wider base of natural resources warrants the expectation of a higher per worker productivity; (b) a larger labor force permits a more intensive division of labor with whatever higher productivity benefits attach thereto. This is certainly a special case, but it should be kept in mind in view of the experience of several countries in the Western hemisphere. For example, the history of Brazil and even of Canada suggests that the diverting of most of the available immigration from Europe to the United States deprived these countries of an influx of immigrants before World War I (and perhaps even after) that could have contributed to a greater rise not only in aggregate output but even in output per capita. There may be countries in the world today in which a more intelligent and liberal immigration policy would mean an impetus to the growth of both aggregate and per capita product.

Second, there is the argument concerning the greater mobility of a growing than of a stagnant labor force, advanced by J. M. Keynes when the specter of stagnant or declining population haunted the advanced Western economies.[2] It is the younger groups in the labor force who are most mobile—in space and within the productive system—since, unlike

[2] See his "Some Economic Consequences of a Declining Population," *The Eugenics Review*, Vol. XXIX, no. 1, April, 1937, pp. 13–17.

older workers, they are not committed to family and housing or to established positions. This greater mobility is particularly true of new entrants into the labor force, who naturally veer toward those sectors that are likely to spearhead the country's economic growth, and who are oriented toward these sectors even in their training within the educational system.

There is an important related aspect. Population growth may be due either to immigration, or to a substantial rate of natural increase (or to both). In the latter case, there are likely to be sizable differences among various social groups and various parts of the country (for example, between the lower and upper income groups, and between the countryside and the cities) in the rates of their natural increase. Such differences are usually negatively correlated with differences in economic growth opportunities: while the transition to industrialization is occurring, the countryside and smaller cities with their lesser economic growth opportunities are likely to have higher rates of natural increase than the larger cities with their greater growth potentials; similarly, the rates of natural increase of low income groups are likely to be higher than those of high income groups with their greater economic opportunities. It follows that the realization of economic growth potentials is contingent upon a vast internal migration—movement of people from the country to the cities, and within the cities from places of lesser to those of greater economic promise. A substantial rate of population growth means, then, either a greater rate of immigration from abroad or a greater rate of internal migration, or both. This migration may be supplementary to the special mobility propensities of the young entrants into the labor force.

The importance of mobility in the distribution of human resources in response to the differential growth possibilities in the economy can easily be underestimated. Modern economic growth is characterized by rapid structural changes, shifts in importance among industries, and in their location within the country's economy. Stickiness in the response of the labor force to such potential changes can be a serious obstacle to economic growth and greater per capita product. If insufficient labor flows to rising economic opportunities, the relative cost of labor and the relative price of the product remain too high to permit expansion of output to the full potential. Conversely, if the labor force in relatively deteriorating economic opportunities remains attached to them, the national level of product per worker and per capita is not likely to rise. A young or otherwise mobile group within the labor force is therefore strategically important. Moreover, a migrant who has severed familial and other

327

noneconomic ties is a more adaptable economic agent than a person who, like a stationary stone, is overgrown with the moss of his habitual patterns of life. It follows that population growth, in contrast to population stability, may, because of the greater mobility and adjustability of human resources, be conducive to higher per worker (and hence per capita) levels of output; and this may be true, within limits, of greater vs. lesser population increase.

The third argument is perhaps the most far-reaching. The greatest factor in growth of output per capita is, of course, the increasing stock of tested, useful knowledge. The producers of this stock are the scientists, inventors, engineers, managers, and explorers of various description—all members of that population whose growth we are considering. Assume now that, judged by native capacities (and they do differ), 0.05 per cent of a given population are geniuses, another 2.0 per cent are possessors of gifts that may be described as talent, and another 10.0 per cent have distinctly higher than average capacity for fruitful search for facts, principles, and inventions. (The grades of native ability and percentages are, of course, purely illustrative, and would probably be changed by an expert in this field.) Since we have assumed the education, training, and other capital investment necessary to assure that the additions to the population will be at least as well equipped as the population already existing, the proportion of mute Miltons and unfulfilled Newtons will be no higher than previously. Population growth, under the assumptions stated, would, therefore, produce an absolutely larger number of geniuses, talented men, and generally gifted contributors to new knowledge—whose native ability would be permitted to mature to effective levels when they join the labor force.

We now face the question whether an increase in the absolute number of these contributors to new knowledge is likely to produce increasing, constant, or diminishing returns per head. Returns in this case mean potentially useful knowledge in the form in which it can have major effects on economic production—as has been the case in the modern period. My answer inclines strongly toward increasing returns—for two reasons. The first lies in the interdependence of knowledge of the various parts of the universe in which we human beings operate—in the sense that greater knowledge of chemistry contributes to greater knowledge of physics, and progress in both of these contributes to greater knowledge of physiological and biological functions. In the same sense, discoveries and inventions in the field of tensile strength of metals contribute to discoveries and inventions in the field of electric currents; and even new devices in social engineering in one field (for example, corporate organization) facilitate new organizational devices in other fields (for example, credit instruments). A greater supply of people who can contribute to new knowledge may therefore mean a better coverage of a variety of inter-related fields, and where discoveries so complement one another, econo-mies achieved are likely to make for a higher output per worker than would be possible for a smaller group whose coverage of these different but related fields is, perforce, spotty. Second, creative effort flourishes in a dense intellectual atmosphere, and it is hardly an accident that the locus of intellectual progress (including that of the arts) has been pre-ponderantly in the larger cities, not in the bucolic surroundings of the thinly settled countryside. The existence of adequately numerous groups in all fields of creative work is one prerequisite; and the possibility of more intensive intellectual contact, as well as of specialization, afforded by greater numbers may be an important factor in stepping up the rate of additions to useful knowledge. While, for obvious reasons, no simple measure of the stock or flow of new knowledge is available, the course of development of science, technology, and the useful arts suggests acceler-ation rather than retardation, with no diminishing returns, even taking account of the large increase in the human resources flowing into this particular area of activity. Compared with the two factors mentioned above as likely to make for greater per capita productivity of larger numbers of creators of new knowledge, the possibility of diminishing returns is remote: the universe is far too vast relatively to the size of our planet and what we know about it. Recent spectacular changes in the means of exploring the universe and the wide possibility of new, and eventually usable, knowledge that they suggest, only serve to strengthen this point.

Growth of economic output is a function of the growth of the stock of tested knowledge. Since, on the assumptions stated, population increase adds proportionately to the number of creators of new knowledge, it should result in at least a proportional addition to the stock of tested knowledge, and, therefore, to growth of product per capita at least as large as that in the past. If, for reasons suggested just above, we also assume increasing returns on output of new knowledge, per head of knowledge-creator and hence per head of population, we may infer that, *ceteris paribus*, population growth will contribute to *greater* growth of per capita product.[3] The argument is clearly venturesome; for example, it

[3] I am indebted to Professor Moses Abramovitz for a comment that led me to restate this argument in a form different from the original.

implies a theory of production of knowledge such that a smaller number of humans could not be compensated for by more intensive training. And I am sure that other objections could be raised, but for the present let me advance this argument as a plausible hypothesis which merits attention if only because of the far-reaching importance of the issues it poses.

Two final comments in this connection may be relevant. First, the argument stresses the importance of human beings not as producers of commodities and services, but as producers of new knowledge—as the only carriers of the learning and creative ability that provide the basis for our economical and social progress. This concept is quite close, of course, to the idea of the divine spark in human beings, which is at the core of much religious resistance to policies aimed at limitation of population. Passing over these matters, which are beyond my ken and interest, let me just point out that there is an element of sound instinct behind such resistance: insofar as it is possible to give the new generations the education and other requisites of *Homo sapiens*, failure to increase means failure to add to the possible carriers of light and knowledge—and the implicit losses may be far larger than the costs avoided.

Second, we should recognize that the creative and educated groups in the developed economies—and they are the central reference point here —serve partly, and should serve more fully, the economic needs of the whole world, not merely of their own countries. Knowledge is transnational in its application, and the returns on the input of effort into new discoveries, inventions, improvements, and so on, should be measured in terms of increased output per worker not only in the country of origin but elsewhere. In that sense, greater population growth that leads to a substantial increase in the cadres of creative workers at various levels— and this is likely to occur in developed economies alone, although there have been striking isolated instances elsewhere—may produce a *greater* rise in product per worker both in those countries *and* elsewhere than would result from lesser or no population growth.

3. Population as Savers

All the arguments above claiming that population increase may contribute to a higher per capita product are contingent upon the provision of sufficient capital to educate and train the additional workers, equip them with adequate tools, and implement the inventions and innovations they may introduce. We should now consider whether population growth impedes capital formation. A family with ten children is not likely to be able to spend as much on the education and training of each as a family with two, nor is it likely to contribute as much to the savings that finance material capital formation. Generalizing this case, we could argue that population growth, in and of itself, reduces the resources for investment in training and reproducible capital per head of new additions to population. If this argument were valid it would severely limit all those advanced above because the assumption of adequate capital would be removed.

The contention just set forth may be unchallengeable for under-developed countries, but in the advanced economies the situation is not that simple and determinate. There are reasons to assume that any *private* failure to make the proper investment in education and training can easily be corrected (and in many cases has been so corrected) by public action, and that the very process of population growth contributes to an increased flow of savings to finance additional material capital formation.

We begin with the case where population growth, stemming from natural increase, may result in inadequate investment in the education and training of the younger generation (I include all expenditures needed to develop an effective member of society, over and above bare sustenance). Such inadequacies may result either from inability of the family unit to cover the necessary costs; or, despite such ability, failure to appreciate the need. In either case, the shortfall, relative to the economic output of the advanced economies, is likely to be small; and in the past many countries have instituted free primary education, subsidies for higher education, etc. We are positing here limits to the birth rate: naturally, if every family unit attempts to raise twenty children, the problem assumes different dimensions. But we shall deal with this qualification toward the end of the paper, since it is relevant to most of the arguments here.

The effects of population increase on the possible shortage of savings to finance material capital formation pose a more serious problem. Indeed, it is the central problem in this section because we are assuming now that investment in raising and educating the younger generation is adequate. Consequently, the additional drain upon resources represented by population increase affects material capital formation alone. Can we assume that in the very process of population growth some forces emerge that tend to augment savings and hence capital formation? Several such forces can be suggested.

First, there is little ground for supposing that where population grows by natural increase, the added outlay by either parents or society is all at the expense of otherwise proportionately larger savings. So far as private spending-saving units are concerned, it is not clear that expenditures on children are a substitute for savings (particularly in the advanced economies) rather than for more consumer goods or for more leisure. While correlations are often deceptive, one may point to the fact that the birth rate is higher in those areas where the per capita consumer expenditures are lower; and in the big cities the choice is largely between children and a relatively more costly mode of living. Inasmuch as children provide an incentive to work and to save, it is not certain that the savings per child (or per future member of the labor force) generated in a family unit with a large number of children would not be at least as high as in the same family if it had fewer or no children. Nor is it certain that funds allocated by governments for education mean a reduction in governmental capital formation, or in the savings of the economic units who pay for public education in taxes.

Second, some major components of aggregate savings tend to be raised when population is growing. One of these, discussed in some detail in an earlier paper, may be briefly noted here.[4] Assume that part of savings is for retirement, to be completely offset by dissavings of the individual or family during post-retirement years. If the labor force is constant, then, given a fixed age at which withdrawal from the labor force occurs, and perfect foresight in estimating the amount of post-retirement expenses, it follows that, all other conditions being equal, positive savings in the process of accumulation for retirement will balance post-retirement dissavings and the net contribution to aggregate savings will be zero. By contrast, if population and the labor force are growing, the number of active members of the labor force who are saving for retirement is that much larger than the number of the retired; and their positive savings are larger than the dissavings of those retired. The resultant positive contribution to aggregate savings will reflect the past rate of growth of the labor force, and hence the past rate of population increase stemming from the birth rate or immigration. (An increase in population resulting from a decline in the death rates of the retired has an opposite effect, serving to diminish savings.)

This argument can be applied to all future-expense oriented savings. If savings are being accumulated to finance future outlays—for a house, a family, and so forth—the net contribution to the countrywide pool of savings is the excess of their flow into stock over their outflow at the end

---

[4] See the author's "International Differences in Capital Formation and Financing," in *Capital Formation and Economic Growth*, edited by Moses Abramovitz, National Bureau of Economic Research, Princeton University Press, 1955, particularly Appendix D, pp. 98–103.

of the period of accumulation and waiting. For the total body of individuals, the net balance of such future-expense oriented savings will be zero if the population is constant, assuming no indebtedness to the business or government sector, and assuming also that the calculations are correct. On these assumptions, growth in population will produce an excess of accumulation over disbursements, or positive net savings.

Third, there is an indirect and somewhat elusive effect of population increase on the consumption and savings patterns of the *upper* income groups, which may be worth noting. I argued above that in a developed country children may be a substitute for higher levels of consumption or for more leisure. Insofar as they are a substitute for the former, greater population growth means for those groups whose birth rate is higher than elsewhere, a lower per capita consumption level than would otherwise be enjoyed. This usually pertains to groups at the bottom rather than the top half of the economic scale. There tends to be a definite gradation of consumption expenditure through the whole structure of economic and social groups: we find no sharp break as we move along the scale—the consumption-savings pattern of the multimillionaires at the top is linked with that of the mere millionaires on the next lower rung, the latter is linked with that of the recipients of a $100,000 annual income, and so on for the entire array. The point is that, all other conditions being equal, particularly the size distribution of income, lower per capita consumption expenditures at the bottom, necessitated by population increase, will make for lower per capita expenditures and hence higher savings proportions for all groups—of *those* savings that are not oriented to any necessities, etc., but are a kind of automatic excess of large incomes over limited consumption expenditures. The argument is not that the greater impact of higher birth rates at lower income levels results in a wider inequality in the size distribution of income (on a per capita basis), and hence, other conditions being equal, in a greater proportion of savings. It is rather that, with a given size distribution of income on a per capita basis, greater population increase due to higher birth rates keeps down the per capita consumption levels of those in the lower and intermediate brackets who are in the childbearing and rearing ages; and that, because of the interconnection of consumption levels in the income pyramid, it also keeps down the consumption levels of those groups high enough in the array to save "automatically" and thus raises the savings of these upper income groups.

Finally, it has been assumed throughout that the reproducible capital-output ratio is constant, an assumption contrary to historical experience.

The marginal capital-output ratios, and it is with these that we are particularly concerned, have varied considerably over both the short-run business cycle and longer periods. In the early phases of the development of the advanced economies these ratios showed a secular rise, as in the United States from the 1870's to World War I; in the later phases they showed a marked decline, in the United States since the 1920's. The problem therefore assumes different aspects in the different secular phases of the movement of the capital-output ratios. Particularly in the declining phase, such as that in the United States since the 1920's, the presumed pressure of population increase on the supply of savings to finance capital formation would have been much less than during the period prior to World War I. Yet the changes in the capital-output ratios are not independent of the supply of savings or of the absolute level of the ratios at any given time. Greater pressure on the supply of savings, other conditions being equal, induces more capital-saving inventions, innovations, and improvements; and a high capital-output ratio provides greater incentive and more room for such capital-saving changes. The bearing upon the present discussion is obvious: if population increase does create greater pressure upon savings and the available stock of material capital, inventive and managerial ability forced in the appropriate direction may result in a greater emphasis on and success with capital-economizing innovations than would otherwise be the case. While this argument may seem like the resolution of a problem by a *deus ex machina*, it does seem plausible for developed economies with a variety of resources responsive to the task.

4. Population as Consumers

The arguments advanced in the two preceding sections, if valid, justify the expectation that population increase would lead to a higher per capita product than would failure to increase. They implicitly assume the adequacy of final demand, or, more precisely, a distribution between expenditures and savings that assures full employment of resources and the greatest growth possible with these resources, technological changes, related social innovations, and the demand of ultimate consumers. While consideration of the behavior of the population as consumers is implicit in the discussion of their behavior as savers, some specific aspects of consumption lend additional support to the suggestion that population increase may be a positive factor in making for higher per capita product.

The first of these aspects of consumption is related to its impact on the size of the domestic market. I argued above that population growth may be partly at the expense of greater leisure. On that score alone, without considering any of the other arguments in the preceding sections, the demand of a rapidly growing population for consumer goods would be greater than that of a constant or slowly growing population—since even the larger per capita demand of the latter would not be sufficient to compensate for their smaller numbers. If the other arguments in the preceding sections are granted, the total demand (output), including that for producers' goods, of a rapidly growing population can be expected to exceed that of a constant or slowly growing population. Once this is admitted—and the larger demand would be assured *even* if the per capita product of the rapidly growing population were equal to or less than the per capita product of the slowly growing or constant population—it will affect productivity and product per worker in ways not explicitly considered above. A larger domestic market will permit greater economies of scale; the development of industries that, because of the larger optimum size of their plants, are not feasible in countries with small domestic markets unless unwarranted reliance is placed upon foreign markets; and a more diversified productive structure providing more varied opportunities to the population. A smaller population and a smaller domestic market would make certain industries economically unfeasible, that is, too expensive; might limit the economies of scale for such industries as are indispensable within the country's boundaries; and would result in a domestic industrial structure which, because of its limited size, would tend to be more concentrated in fewer sectors. It is reasonable, I believe, to argue that since reliance on foreign trade is, perforce, limited, particularly in these times of international strain and strife, a large domestic market is an important prerequisite to the economies of scale of many modern industries and to the diversification of the domestic productive structure that provides varied opportunities for the growing population. A higher per capita product is more likely under such conditions than under conditions where no growth or only slight growth of population limits the size of the domestic market. To be sure, larger size poses other dangers, particularly the possibilities of greater disunity among the various parts of a large and regionally diversified population and the consequent difficulties of making promptly and without great cost the secular decisions essential in setting and adjusting conditions for a country's economic growth.[5] But let me limit myself at this point to the positive aspects of population increase.

[5] See discussion of this topic in my paper, "Economic Growth of Small Nations," in *Challenge of Development*, Alfred Borné, ed., The Hebrew University, Jerusalem, 1958, pp. 9–23.

Second, it is not only the size of the domestic market but its responsiveness to new products that is important. The technological changes that constitute the basis of modern economic growth affect consumer goods as much as they do the productive processes; and in a free market economy, lack of responsiveness by individuals and families to such new products would be a major obstacle to the growth of total and per capita output. It may be argued that the younger individuals and families are more responsive to new products than the older ones. The latter have more firmly established habits, which are largely a carryover from the past, and they have many more commitments, e.g., most of their durable consumer goods have already been acquired and they may find it more difficult to incorporate many new products. Comparable differences in responsiveness to new products may exist, at a given age and income level, between the migrant and the settled unit: the former, uprooted from his customary surroundings, may be freer in his choice of the new products, and may perhaps be psychologically more disposed toward them. It follows that population increase, accompanied as it usually is by a higher proportion of young and migrating units, may also be associated with greater responsiveness of the body of ultimate consumers to new goods—which in turn facilitates modern economic growth and may contribute to a higher product per capita.

We have dealt here, and in the preceding sections, with the direct effects of population increase on productivity, savings, and consumption, and with the effects of the latter two on productivity. There are some indirect effects of population increase, or rather effects of the general atmosphere accompanying it. Allowing substantial immigration reflects a faith in the country's power to absorb the immigrants and put them to productive use, a faith in the country's future. Having children is also evidence of faith in the future—not in the underdeveloped countries where the motivation may be a desire for support in old age, but in the developed countries where children are not expected to support their parents, where family planning is an accepted pattern, and where the social level of the majority of parents warrants the assumption of intelligent choice in the matter. Granted, in recent decades this faith has an apocalyptic tinge, colored by visions of atomic holocausts and Armageddons. It is a faith, nevertheless, in the country's future, unless or until terminated by such calamities as transcend the limits of planning of a household, a firm, or even a country. Contrariwise, a constant or slowly growing population is implicit evidence of lack of faith in the future.

This being the case, it can be argued that the climate of belief in the future within which population increase occurs, as compared with the atmosphere within which no increase or very limited increase occurs, is itself conducive to greater economic growth and greater growth of product per capita. For it presumably encourages forward-looking ventures by individuals planning their careers and by entrepreneurs planning their investments. The expectation of a future in which larger markets and wider opportunities will prevail encourages extension of capacity, both personal and material, and it discourages the stagnation which results when individuals cling to unsatisfactory but "safe" routine jobs or when entrepreneurs, bankers, the labor force, and other important agents of economic enterprise hesitate to commit themselves to ventures that depart from the "tried and true." It is naturally difficult to assign weights to this factor of buoyancy accompanying population increase, when the latter is a matter of choice rather than of obsolescent patterns of individual behavior under changed conditions. But the effect of the implicit view of the future on decisions by entrepreneurs and households can hardly be denied—particularly for entrepreneurs, for whom there is an economic rationale in being more venturesome, more forward-looking, under such conditions than when the view of the future is pessimistic. Greater venturesomeness, greater willingness to build for the future, is likely to contribute to more vigorous growth of both total and per capita product.

5. Concluding Comments

The preceding discussion has dwelt, by design, on the positive contributions that population growth may make to the increase in per capita product; and it has been pursued largely against the background of advanced, developed countries. The concluding remarks are addressed primarily to qualifications, to avoid dismissal of this discussion as an expression of exuberant, but unfounded optimism.

First, few if any of the points made are relevant to the underdeveloped countries. By definition, the latter suffer from an acute shortage of capital, not only for material investment but also for adequate raising and education of their younger generations; and the whole structure of their society is unfavorable to the adoption of many potentials of modern technology, since it necessitates major changes that no living society can absorb within a short period. It is, therefore, unrealistic to assume that population increase in an underdeveloped country is followed by the adequate investment in both human beings and material capital, by the advantages of greater mobility, and by the stimulus of a wider and more responsive market associated with population increase in developed countries and which contribute to greater product per capita. This is particularly true in view of the actual (or threatening) acceleration of rates of natural increase in the underdeveloped countries resulting from the maintenance of, or even slight rise in, the already high birth rates combined with the remarkably rapid reduction in death rates made possible by recent revolutionary changes in public health and control of diseases.

Second, even in the advanced and developed economies, population increase means further pressure upon limited natural resources, upon the supply of material capital, and above all, upon the capacity of the social and economic structure to adapt itself to it. All the factors cited in the current (and past) literature that make for the increased burden or larger populations—if higher per capita product is to be attained—are relevant here. In particular, an acceleration of population increase from a previously lower rate (like a marked retardation from a previously high rate), may mean a lag in the adjustment of economic and social institutions, with painful consequences resulting from delaying the kind of response that maximizes the advantages of a growing (or retarding) population and minimizes its disadvantages. The recent delay in this country, particularly on the part of the public sector, in responding to the obviously increasing educational needs of our growing population is a clear case in point, as are some of the lags in response to the reduction of immigration and to the retardation of population growth in the 1920's.

Third, for a single developed country, the impact of growth of its population, compared with the growth of the population of its partners in the concert of nations, should be considered. The contribution to new knowledge and technological change that its increased population may make would most likely become common property, after a short period of initial, pioneering advantage; but if a country's population grows proportionately more than that of its partners in international trade, it runs the risk of greater disadvantages—pressure for more imports, without a fully compensating reduction in cost of export goods and hence of exports. This problem of external balance has not been considered at all in the previous discussion, and yet it may impose limits upon the contribution of population growth to the economic performance in any single country.[6]

Hence, even in the advanced economies, there is the question whether the positive advantages of population increase outweigh its cost in terms of greater pressure upon limited resources, slowly changing organizational

[6] I am indebted to Dr. Hans Singer for calling my attention to this point after the paper was presented at the conference.

facilities, and external balance. It is at this point that the major qualification of our discussion, and indeed of most of the analysis in the field of relations between demographic and economic processes, becomes patent. Obviously, there can be in any country, no matter how advanced, too much population growth in that its contribution to increased productivity per head is outweighed by the costs. But how much is too much we cannot tell in general terms and often cannot fully ascertain in specific instances. Conversely, there can be too little growth of population in that the various undesirable corollaries in the way of increasing rigidities, the lag in shifting from extensive to intensive investment opportunities, the failure to add to numbers of creators of new knowledge, and the general pessimism about the future, are likely to outweigh the advantages of lesser pressure upon limited resources. But, again, we do not know how little is too little. To put it somewhat differently, we have no tested, or even approximate, empirical coefficients with which to weight the various positive and negative aspects of population growth. While we may be able to distinguish the advantages and disadvantages, we rarely know the character of the function that relates them to different magnitudes of population growth.

This is, of course, no excuse for not trying to secure a complete and balanced view, and provide, if policy needs compel it, the most considered answer to a specific problem. In particular, it is no excuse for the consistent bias in the literature in the field, in which the clearly observable limits of *existing* resources tend to overshadow completely the dimly discernible potentials of the new discoveries, inventions, and innovations that the future may bring. Perhaps only those who are alarmed rush into print whereas those who are less concerned with the would-be dangers are likely to be mute. And, to be sure, what exists can be observed; what is yet to come can only be surmised; and scholars naturally tend to dwell on the observable and tangible, and are wary of pies in the skies. Yet it must be recognized that we are concerned here with processes which have been vitally affected by additions to knowledge, unforeseen and undreamed of (except by Jules Verne, H. G. Wells, and others of their ilk); and that scientific caution should not extend to the exclusion of a dominant factor because it is difficult to grasp and fit into a model with a determinate, and hence limit-bound, outcome.

Finally, we should note that increase in per capita product has been a central reference point because it permitted me to handle conveniently the assigned topic of the relation between population change and aggregate product. It is not necessarily a superior, desirable criterion for guidance in population policy, nor is it a dominant criterion in population policy as currently practiced (implicitly or explicitly). For example, in an authoritarian society managed by a power-hungry political elite, no real concern is shown for per capita product. The aim there is to accumulate the maximum surplus of resources, material and human, compatible with internal stability of the party elite, for the purpose, however ideologically motivated, of extending its power elsewhere. Assume that of the labor force in such a country 5 per cent are the political elite; 15 per cent are its policemen, administrators, propagandists, and favored professionals; and the remaining 80 per cent are its workers—exploited to yield the surplus, either in labor camps, or by bamboozling propaganda concerning the coming millennium and the threats of the rest of the world. Now, if X of these exploited workers yields Y of power-orientable surplus, $X + a$ might yield $Y + b$; and the underlying population increase would be desired by the political elite even if b/a were a lower ratio than Y/X, that is, even if, with constant per head consumption levels of the exploited workers, product per head declined as population increased.

But even in free societies, where the consumer is sovereign, maximization of per capita income may not be the paramount or even an important aim; and population change will not be judged in these terms. A society may prefer a smaller population, even if it means smaller aggregate and per capita product; or, what is more likely, it may prefer a larger population, even if it means a lower per capita product than would smaller numbers—if the population feels itself to be in danger and considers that there is greater safety in greater numbers. Many other criteria than per capita income can be used for evaluating population change and formulating population policy in the free countries, but they are outside the scope of this paper. The only reason for raising this question is that any discussion, even if it is only an attempt to interpret the past or speculate upon the possible relations, inevitably carries policy connotations. And it is well to emphasize that concentration of the discussion here on the relation between population growth and per capita product does not mean that maximizing the latter is a dominant, or even important, criterion in policy evaluation of population change.

COMMENT

RICHARD E. QUANDT, Princeton University

Simon Kuznets has observed that substantial rises in population are usually accompanied by increases in per capita output. He poses himself the problem of finding causal relationships between an increase in population and an increase in per capita output. If I understand his argument correctly, it rests basically on the following three points: (1) If the increase in population is not accompanied by a reduction in the amount of available per worker capital (and if the capital-output ratio remains unaltered), a certain train of events will be set in motion which will result in an increased per capita output; (2) An increase in population will affect the savings behavior of the population in such a manner that per capita or per laborer capital remains the same or increases; (3) The receptivity of an increasing population to more products and new products is sufficiently high to create a favorable climate for expansion and economic growth and thus also for achieving higher per capita rates of output.

First of all, I would like to discuss the condition under which, given Kuznets' assumptions, an increase in population leads to an increase in per capita output. Assume an aggregate production function

$$X = f(L, K) \tag{1}$$

where X denotes output, L the amount of labor, and K the amount of capital. I shall assume, as does Kuznets, that the total population and the labor force differ only by a constant factor of proportionality, that is,

$$L = bP \tag{2}$$

where P denotes the population and where b is positive but less than one. Per capita output is X/P, and we wish to find the rate of change of this quantity with respect to time. We obtain

$$\frac{d\left[\frac{f(L, K)}{P}\right]}{dt} = \frac{\left(f_L \dfrac{dL}{dt} + f_K \dfrac{dK}{dt}\right) P - f(L, K) \dfrac{dP}{dt}}{P^2} \tag{3}$$

where f_L and f_K are the partial derivatives of the production function. In order to make certain that the amount of capital per worker is not decreasing and is perhaps increasing, we must require that the marginal increase in capital per unit addition to the labor force be no less than the average amount of capital per worker, that is, that

$$\frac{dK}{dL} = a\frac{K}{L} \qquad \text{where } a \geqq 1 \tag{4}$$

341

From (4) we obtain that

$$\frac{1}{K}\frac{dK}{dt} = a\frac{1}{L}\frac{dL}{dt} \tag{5}$$

that is, the percentage rate of increase in the capital stock must not be less than the percentage rate of increase in the labor force. Substituting in (3) for dK/dt from (5) and also for dL/dt which equals bdP/dt by (2), we have

$$\frac{d[f(L, K)/P]}{dt} = \frac{(bf_L P + af_K K - f)\dfrac{dP}{dt}}{P^2} \tag{6}$$

$$\frac{d[f(L, K)/P]}{dt} = \frac{(f_L L + af_K K - f)\dfrac{dP}{dt}}{P^2} \tag{7}$$

Since P^2 is always positive, an increase in the population $[dP/dt > 0]$ leads to an increase in per capita output if and only if

$$f_L L + af_K K - f(L, K) > 0 \tag{8}$$

Now the following possibilities exist. If $a = 1$, that is, if the amount of capital per worker remains unchanged, (8) becomes $f_L L + f_K K - f(L, K) > 0$. This cannot occur if the production function is homogeneous of the first degree. In order for (8) to be true with $a = 1$ we must assume that increasing returns to scale prevail in some fashion. If, for example, the production function is homogeneous of the second degree, it is easy to show that (8) will be satisfied. If $a > 1$, it is no longer necessary to assume that there are increasing returns to scale. Returns to scale may be constant or diminishing so long as they do not diminish too rapidly. The argument to the effect that an increase in population tends to raise per capita output must therefore rest on some combination of the following factors: (1) That the aggregate production function shows increasing returns to scale; (2) that a given percentage increase in population results in a greater percentage increase of the stock of capital; (3) that the form of the production function itself changes when population increases.

Kuznets mentions each of these points in one place or another. In support of the first proposition he advances two arguments which seem open to some doubt. He assumes that "the reproducible capital-output ratio remains the same or decreases" in order to "take account of the possible effects of pressure upon a limited supply of irreproducible resources." However, if the increase in population (and capital) resulted in a shortage of land and other natural resources, it would not be reasonable to assume that the production function, expressed as a function of labor and capital, would exhibit constant or increasing returns. It seems that his argument might be more applicable to under-developed economies which, however, he specifically rules out in his discussion. He suggests that increasing population will bring into use yet unexploited resources. Although it is difficult to debate the truth of this assertion, the yet unexploited resources may be of inferior quality. To use a simplified example, one may think that in a developed economy all the highest grade coal deposits are already being mined intensively; additional coal production could take place only by resorting to mines which are less efficient to operate, either because of the inferior heating quality of the coal or because of the greater labor effort required for the extraction of a ton of coal.

Kuznets' second point is that a greater population will allow greater specialization in production and therefore a higher output per capita. It is unquestionably true that one can subdivide a certain specified number of tasks among more men in such a fashion that greater speciali-zation results. It is not clear, however, whether there might not prevail counteracting tendencies in developed economies. I am referring to the increasing bureaucratization of life which seems to accompany growth in size in the developed economies. If the increase in the size of a firm results in a more than proportionate increase in the "non-producing" administrative staff, the economy's potential ability to achieve a higher degree of specialization may be effectively counteracted.

A third argument is intended to show that the production function itself may change its form in response to an increase in population. Assuming that the percentage of people born with given native capacities is constant, a larger population implies, other things being equal, that more geniuses and other talented people are born in absolute terms. Kuznets conjectures that useful knowledge increases more than in pro-portion to the number of people engaged in creating knowledge, that is, that knowledge exhibits increasing returns to scale (of scholarship). Finally, it is plausible to argue than an increase in the amount of know-ledge per capita will tend to increase output per worker. This conjecture is a very important and highly imaginative one. It must be emphasized that the truth of the conjecture and the magnitude of this "Kuznets effect" are purely empirical questions. It is tempting to say that the interrelatedness of knowledge strongly suggests that the per capita amount of knowledge will increase with population. However, on an a priori basis a contrary argument can also be made. The counterargument is certainly not as persuasive as Kuznets' own and I am inclined to accept his. However, the possibility of arguing rather fruitlessly on a priori grounds about the conjecture leads me to suggest that an empirical test of the proposition is necessary.

To turn to another point, we must examine the implications of the requirement that a given percentage increase in the population result in a greater (or at least not smaller) percentage increase in the stock of capital. Starting again from Equation (5) and substituting from (2) we have

$$S = dK = aK \frac{dP}{P} \tag{9}$$

Equation (9) shows that if the population is increasing at all, savings must be positive and that the faster population is growing in percentage terms, the higher must be aggregate savings. In other words, if the percentage rate of growth of the population increased, aggregate savings would have to increase too. Kuznets advances some reasons for aggregate savings to increase, yet one cannot help feeling a certain degree of scepticism. He believes that, as far as private spending units are concerned, it is not clear that expenditures on children are a substitute for savings rather than for more consumer goods or for more leisure. Nor is it clear, I feel, that the opposite is not the case. In fact, it is very plausible that an increase in the size of the family will make some inroads on the family's ability to save. Consider a population which is growing at 2 per cent per annum. If the capital/output ratio is three, savings would have to be 6 per cent of national product. If this population were growing at 4 per cent, savings amounting to 12 per cent of output would be required in order to provide labor with the same amount of per worker capital as before. If, in addition, we require that the coefficient a be greater than unity, the discrepancy between the respective savings percentages would be greater still. But even if we allow a to equal unity, it is not sufficient for the population to continue to save the same amount that they did before. As more children are born, not only must the parents deny themselves certain consumer goods in order to provide for the children, but they must deny themselves additional consumer goods if savings are to increase. Whether such behavior is plausible in a system where individuals are free to make their savings decisions is doubtful. It is also suggested that, as the population increases, the savings of those at the beginning of their earning life will exceed the dissavings of the retired and that thus aggregate savings will increase. This proposition must be reevaluated in the light of the possibility that young people may begin to save for retirement at a later date in their lives than they used to.

It seems that the last major point of Kuznets reinforces the conclusion that a developed economy may have difficulties in providing sufficient savings to allow for an increase in per capita output. Granted that a growing population is favorable for an extension of old markets and the creation of new ones, such an expansion is basically consumption oriented. The more adventurous the young population is in trying out new products, the less willing they will be to withhold an appropriate part of their income for the purpose of capital formation. If we posit that the governmental machinery operates to keep aggregate demand at a full employment level, the aggregate volume of savings may not be sufficient to increase the stock of capital to the point where the collaboration of labor with capital results in higher output per capita. When Kuznets mentions, albeit with a warning, that the birth rate tends to be higher in places where per capita consumer expenditures are lower, one cannot help wondering about the direction of the causation. Perhaps we should examine this problem still further to see (1) whether it is not the low per capita consumption which is responsible for the higher birth rate, (2) whether the places where the birth rate is high are not also the places where per capita savings are low, in other words, where per capita income or output is low.

I do not know the answers to many of these questions. Kuznets has provided a useful framework and has raised numerous tantalizing questions. Many of these relate to empirical propositions, and I feel that Kuznets' framework will be most useful when these empirical questions are answered.

MILTON FRIEDMAN, University of Chicago and National Bureau of Economic Research

The historical covariation of population growth and per capita output is, of course, susceptible of a number of interpretations—it may be historical coincidence, population growth may be the result of the growth in per capita output, the growth in per capita output may be the result of the population growth, or both may be the common result of other historical forces. As Simon Kuznets notes, professional and popular discussion has in the main tended to be unfavorable to the possibility that population growth is on net favorable to growth in per capita output.

Yet the uniformity of the historical covariation inevitably leaves a nagging doubt whether this interpretation can so blithely be dismissed and whether in our analysis we may not have neglected some effects of population growth favorable for per capita output.

The economic literature bearing on the relation between changes in population and in output has two main themes. One is the limitation of resources which together with the law of diminishing returns or law of variable proportions makes population growth a factor unfavorable to growth in per capita output. The other is the possibility of "external economies" as the size of an industry or an economy or a trading world grows which can have the opposite effect.

In this stimulating and imaginative paper, Kuznets attempts to render this analysis more explicit and to extend its scope particularly with respect to forces other than traditional external economies that might render population growth favorable to per capita output. In the process, he certainly puts flesh on well-worn bones and offers much food for thought. He does not, however, seem to me to add any additional categories of favorable effects to those implicit in the literature.

The favorable effects Kuznets lists are of two very different kinds. There are, first, those which are favorable in the sense that they are reasons why population growth would on net mean a higher rate of growth in per capita output than otherwise. These all seem to me special manifestations of "external economies." There are, second, effects which are favorable only in the very different sense that they tend to offset some unfavorable effects of population growth. They are brought into play only by virtue of the existence of these unfavorable effects and can never counter them in full. They are not reasons why population growth is a stimulant to economic growth but only why it may be somewhat less of a depressant than one might at first think. They are like a long-run rise in output along a positively sloping supply curve that can make the long-run price rise in response to an increase in demand less than the initial price rise but can never convert a short-run price rise into a long-run price decline.

The first category of effects includes three items: the first and third listed by Kuznets under the heading "population as producers," and the first under the heading "population as consumers."

(1) In Kuznets' words, "The first is connected with the distinctive assumption that there exists , . . a variety of unexploited natural resources, and that . . . greater utilization of these resources . . . combined with a more specialized division of labor would, in all probability, lead

to a greater product per worker." This itself is a combination of the two categories of effects distinguished. The "more specialized division of labor" is an external economy, a positively favorable effect of a larger population. The "variety of unexploited natural resources" simply reduces the rate at which diminishing returns occur; it limits the unfavorable effects of the expansion of population but does not render such expansion favorable.

(2) The third item listed by Kuznets under the heading "population as producers" is the existence of external economies in the production of knowledge arising mainly out of the greater division of labor and specialization of function in intellectual activity permitted by the larger size of the industry of creating and maintaining knowledge. This favorable effect is further intensified by the fact that insofar as knowledge accumulates, it is available to all and is not consumed in the process of being used, an external effect of a more subtle kind.

(3) The first item under "population as consumers" is the "impact on the size of the domestic market." This is simply a different face of (1) above—external economies arising out of the more extensive division of labor permitted by the greater size of the market.

All of the other items listed by Kuznets seem to me at best to fall into the second category of effects distinguished—those that partly offset unfavorable effects. Let us consider each in turn.

(1) A growing labor force imposes a need for the reshuffling of the economy to adapt to the new conditions. Similarly, the disproportionate growth of population in rural areas requires an additional reshuffling. In both cases, movement of resources is required by the very factors that give rise to "the greater mobility of a growing than of a stagnant labor force" cited by Kuznets as the second item under "population as producers." And this movement of resources is required simply to hold to a minimum the reduction in initial levels of per capita income that would occur in the absence of external economies. Kuznets gives no reason, and it is hard to see any, why the increased mobility produced by higher population growth is not only enough to permit the new resources to be organized as efficiently as the old but to increase the efficiency with which the old resources are organized.

(2) In considering "population as savers," Kuznets' first item is that added expenditure on training and education of children is not necessarily "all at the expense of otherwise proportionately larger savings." True enough, but so long as any such added expenditure is at the expense of savings, the faster population growth reduces on this ground the aggregate

savings available for capital formation and even more the amount available per capita. Thus the need to educate and train the younger generation is a factor that on net renders population growth unfavorable to maintenance let alone growth in per capita output.

(3) His forth item under this head, that "greater pressure on the supply of savings . . . may result in a greater emphasis on and success with capital-economizing innovations" is of the same kind. At most this can make the deleterious effect of capital shortage less than otherwise; it cannot convert capital shortage into a positive good—for of course if it did, there would then be no capital shortage to act as an additional incentive.

(4) It is explicit in Kuznets' analysis that more rapid population growth requires a higher fraction of income to be saved than otherwise in order to keep capital per head constant or increasing. The second item on savings he lists, the stimulation of all "future-expense oriented savings" can at best be only a partial offset to this need. If the capital-output ratio, to take a figure relatively favorable to Kuznets' position, were as low as 2 to 1, then each one percentage point increase in the annual rate of growth of population would require additional savings of 2 per cent of annual income to keep capital per head constant. But this would absorb an amount equal to twice the growth in aggregate income from the faster growth in population, with constant per capita income.

(5) The third item on savings, a possible effect of a higher rate of population growth on the "automatic" savings of higher income groups, is in a somewhat different category. It seems to me simply wishful thinking, derived from a theory of savings that is not only untested empirically, but has never even been fully and carefully elaborated theoretically. On this level, one can as plausibly argue that there is emulation of savings behavior as of consumption behavior, in which case the "automatic" consumption of upper income classes would have the opposite effect. And neither the one theory nor the other seems to me to derive any support from the large amount of empirical evidence and the fairly well elaborated theoretical analyses that we have.

(6) The greater responsiveness of a rapidly growing population to new products, Kuznets' second item under "population as consumers" is in a still different category. This implies a difference in tastes that makes it hard to compare per capita output under the alternative conditions or, alternatively, to attach economic meaning to a mechanical comparison —this is the kind of problem that Kuznets in some of his other writings has taught us so much about and has trained us to be wary of. The example that has always impressed me is the difficulty of comparing

Swiss and U.S. per capita incomes that arises out of the difference in attitude to new products. Casual observation suggests that the Swiss put far less emphasis than we on having the very "newest" and "latest" and much more emphasis on serviceability. By their standards, much of our so-called "production" is simply waste, involving the destruction of perfectly serviceable houses, electrical wiring, furniture, and so on indefinitely, in order to replace them by only moderately better items.

(7) The final item cited by Kuznets is "climate of belief in the future within which population increase occurs," a climate conducive to "forward-looking ventures." But this climate is not produced by the population increase. Rather the population increase is a result of the climate. The climate would, so far as this point alone is concerned, be even more favorable to increased output per capita if population did not increase. Hence the population increase is, in and of itself, an unfavorable factor, tending to offset any favorable effect of the general "faith in the future."

This examination of Kuznets' arguments does not of course justify any substantive conclusion about the effect of population change on per capita output, any more than Kuznets would claim that his own analysis does. It does suggest that classical "external economies" are the only category of effects we have yet found that can render population growth positively favorable to per capita output, and that Kuznets' contribution is, on the one hand, to spell out in more imaginative detail how these manifest themselves, and, on the other, to force us to be somewhat more sophisticated in evaluating the unfavorable effects of population growth.

In closing, I should like to note a point about external economies that seems to me to be of the utmost importance and yet frequently neglected because of our tendency to speak about a single country or a closed economy. An extension of the market giving rise to external economies can be achieved through more extensive international trade as well as through a growth in the national market. And external economies produced in this way are likely to give rise to none of the unfavorable effects accompanying external economies produced by population growth.

A striking illustration bearing on external economies in the production of knowledge is provided by recent Indian developments. There is a movement under way, backed by legislation, to eliminate the English language as the primary medium of higher education and to foster the use of native languages, with each region using its own major language though with some emphasis also on a common language other than English. If this movement is carried through, the effect will be in large measure to fragment intellectual activity and greatly to reduce inter-communication not only between India and the rest of the world but also among the different regions of India itself. Along the lines of Kuznets' analysis, it is conceivable that a greater rate of population growth in each region separately would produce external economies in the production of knowledge, but it is ludicrous to suppose that it could do more than offset a tiny part of the external diseconomy arising from subdividing the economy into language areas or that it is relevant to regard the one line of development as a meaningful substitute for the other. Yet, on a less extreme level, this is just what is implied by our tendency to concentrate on intra-national expansions of the market and our relative neglect of international extension.

REPLY

I find it difficult to deal with the comments by Milton Friedman and Richard Quandt because I agree with the substance of much of what they say, but not with the implicit emphasis or weight. My paper was written in an intellectual uneasiness concerning the conflict between the pessimistic tenor of most literature on population growth and the historical records that reveal association in time, in many countries, between large increases in population and high rates of growth of per capita product. The paper was not intended to provide an explanation of this association: this would require far-reaching empirical analysis, most of which has yet to be undertaken. It was, rather, a series of speculative probings into the possible positive contributions of population growth to the rise in per capita product—probings that could not, under the circumstances, be accompanied by tested weights.

Within this framework, it does not seem to me to matter whether the positive contributions suggested are, to refer to Friedman's comments, (a) offsets to the additional burden of larger population, (b) types of external economies, or (c) results of the wider complex of circumstances of which population growth is a corollary not in itself favorable. In the case of (a), offsets are welcome and significant since they leave so much more room for net contributions of other positive effects. In the case of (b), I am quite content to see the positive contributions classified as external economies, if cognizance is taken of the fact that they embrace the production of basic knowledge and of social innovations—processes not included in traditional economic analysis. In the case of (c), popula-tion growth is one way of *realizing* the wider complex (that is, a favorable climate of belief in the future), and without it such a climate would not come into being. In such case, it seems to me artificial to argue that population increase is a pure cost, to which no credit for the effects of the favorable climate is assigned.

Two more observations on Friedman's comments are appropriate. First, offsets may have a dynamism of their own which carry them far beyond the initial cost or burden that they are intended to counteract— as has been the case with many need-provoked innovations, both technological and social. Second, it is difficult for me to entertain the proposition that social imitation—internal demonstration effect—applies to savings patterns as effectively as it does to consumption patterns; and I am probably less willing than Friedman to accept the conclusions of the existing theoretical analysis.

I am in essential agreement with Quandt's comments on the implications of my discussion for the production function, while, for obvious reasons, it is difficult to counter his scepticism over some substantive points, for lack of empirical evidence. It is relatively easy to find both positive and negative effects of any trend within the complex process of economic growth—even of such an apparently wholly favorable movement as growth of the stock of material capital per worker. Thus, one could argue that if there is too much capital relative to other factors, the resulting inefficiency could depress our per capita product appreciably. We could in fact apply Parkinson's law to any and all productive factors. We are rescued from the bewildering conflict of the possible effects by a combination of empirical constraints and realistically guided reasoning. And in the light of both, it does seem to me that in the competition between geniuses and incompetents, the triumph of the former, in adding to the stock of useful (vs. worthless) knowledge, is clearly manifest; that continuous innovations permit an increasingly effective specialization and division of labor among larger numbers that more than offsets the effects of Parkinson's law; and that with the increasing substitutability between investment in human beings and knowledge and in material capital the deleterious effects of population growth on the supply of savings (in the traditional sense of funds available for investment in material capital) can be quite limited.

Let me conclude by stating that the aim of the paper is to suggest problems for further research, and that the claim of validity for any of the speculative suggestions, if made, is intended as an irritant, not a sedative. My purpose is to call attention to the interrelations between population growth and economic growth, which have been studied much less than their apparent importance in the field warrants.

Population Change and Demand, Prices, and the Level of Employment

ANSLEY J. COALE

OFFICE OF POPULATION RESEARCH, PRINCETON UNIVERSITY

EVER since Keynes set forth his theory of income determination, demographic variables have been discussed as possible determinants of effective demand, and consequently of the level of unemployment. Declining population growth was one of the major features of the secular stagnation thesis in the late 1930's, and its present rapid growth in the United States is often cited as a basis for optimism about the future of business in the 1950's.

This paper will be a reexamination of the effect of population change on aggregate demand. Its scope is deliberately restricted to demand, and effects on the capacity of the economy to produce will be intentionally neglected. We shall be concerned with how fully productive factors are used rather than with their capacity when used; with unemployment and inflation rather than with the level of living that an economy could provide at full employment. The most primitive Keynesian model of income determination will be used. It will be assumed that when alternative levels of national income are visualized, consumption expenditures will be a rising function of income; that net private investment is not directly dependent on current income, or perhaps is higher at higher alternative national income; and that government expenditures for goods and services are (with exceptions to be noted later) to be considered an independent variable. National income settles at a level where the three major components equal the total, or where (in the familiar diagram of Samuelson's *Economics* or other introductory texts) C plus I plus G intersects the 45° line. As part of this theory, it is assumed that for ranges of income implying substantial unemployment, higher national income usually takes the form of increased output and employment, while with full or nearly full employment a higher equilibrium national income implies merely higher prices.

Demographic variables affect aggregate demand (and thereby national income and employment or prices, or both) by having an effect on (a) the consumption function; (b) net private investment; or (c) government expenditures on goods and services. In considering the effect of population on each of these components I shall attempt, where possible, to estimate the magnitude as well as the direction of the relationship. An estimate will also be made of how much difference there would have been in income and employment in years prior to 1957 had certain demographic features of 1957 been present.

The basic technique of analysis that will be employed is simple. A schedule relating one of the principal components of national income to alternative levels of the total will be assumed *with a given population*. Our question will be: How would the schedule be changed if the population differed in various ways?

A word must be said about the demographic variables that will be considered. These will be various measures relating to the *age composition* of the population, and the *growth rate* of the population. It will frequently be convenient to treat age composition and growth independently, despite the fact that variations in the growth rate typically cause changes in age composition—and that the growth rate in turn is powerfully affected by age composition.[1]

When age distribution is the variable, the comparison will be among populations with the same number of persons in the ages of most intense labor force participation (roughly ages 17 to 69 for males), but with different numbers above and below these ages. We shall ask, for example: How would the consumption function be changed if the given number of persons aged 17–69 had more persons under 17 and over 70 dependent on them?

When growth is the variable, the basic comparison will be of populations the same in size, but differing in growth rate. We shall ask, for example: How would the levels of investment be affected if a given population were and had been growing steadily at a higher rate than the actual one?

Age Distribution and the Consumption Function

The consumption function defines the consumption expenditures that would take place at all relevant levels of national income. If it is to be a determinate function, forces other than national income (distribution of personal income among spending units, retention of earnings by corporations, tax rates, anticipated price changes, and so on) that might affect consumption must be either trifling, or must themselves vary in a predictable way with national income. One of the forces that might affect

[1] Cf. Frank W. Notestein's paper herein; A. J. Coale, "How the Age Distribution of a Human Population is Determined," *Cold Spring Harbor Symposia on Quantitative Biology*, Vol. xxii, pp. 83–88, and the references cited there.

consumption is the number of dependents that income recipients support. The number of dependents differs at different levels of national income, even if the population itself is assumed identical. At lower levels of employment, formerly self-supporting persons become dependent. Such differences in dependency status at different national income levels are, however, allowed for within the consumption function. The question we want answered is this: Would consumption expenditure at each alternative national income be different if, because of more persons under 17 and over 70, income recipients had more dependents to support? The answer, both from common sense and from empirical evidence, is yes.

Suppose a larger population is compared with the given population, the extra persons all being under 17 or over 70. Suppose further that the additional dependents are pictured as belonging to existing households. The most likely effect upon household budgets at any given disposable income would be an increase in expenditures. True, there might be an offsetting tendency to save specifically for the future welfare of children. Thus a family with an additional dependent child might save more (out of a given income) with the aim of establishing a fund for the child's college expenses. On balance, however, most households would find their consumption enlarged and their saving reduced by an extra member.

Analysis of the results of surveys of consumers' expenditures supports this conclusion. After examining some half a dozen surveys conducted between 1888 and 1948 in the United States, Dorothy Brady has estimated that at a given income level consumption expenditures increase at the 6th root of family size.[2] On this basis, one would expect a consumption function nearly one per cent higher at every point if extra dependents made a population 6 per cent larger.

The consumption function, it appears, is sensibly affected by demographic variables. The upward shift of the consumption function arising from a 6 per cent greater population if the increase consisted entirely of dependents would yield a national income nearly k per cent higher, where k is the multiplier. The effect on national income might be some 2 or 3 per cent.[3]

[2] Raymond Goldsmith, Dorothy Brady, and Horst Mendershausen, *A Study of Saving in the United States*, Vol. III, Princeton University Press, 1956, p. 211.

[3] If the extra dependents are visualized as constituting in part *additional households* it seems clear that the effect on the aggregate consumption function would be enlarged, since there are economies of scale in consuming while "doubled up"; and with separate households, aggregate consumption (for a given total income) would tend to be higher still.

Population Growth and the Consumption Function

An implication of the 6th root relationship estimated by Brady is that an x per cent annual growth of population raises the consumption function annually by something like $x/6$ per cent.[4] If non-consumption expenditures $(I + G)$ were unchanged, equilibrium national income would increase annually by $kx/6$ per cent.

Population Growth and Investment (Other than Housing)

The most discussed effect of population on aggregate demand is the effect of population *growth* on net *investment*. The belief that population growth serves to stimulate investment gave population growth a prominent part in the theory of secular stagnation. Most formulations of this doctrine merely pointed out that investment is needed if a growing population is to have even a constant level of living, and did not show in detail how this need is translated into decisions to invest more.[5] Some elaboration of this question is justified.

The Keynesian view is that additional investment occurs as long as the marginal efficiency of capital exceeds the interest rate, or, alternatively, as long as the net receipts expected as the consequence of the purchase of capital equipment exceed its cost. Why should expected returns from capital equipment be greater with a faster growth of population?

The principal element making expected returns more promising is an expected higher demand for the product. As a general proposition, expected total demand for products can be taken to depend on the expected course of national income. Total national income can rise without population growth, provided there is an increase in per capita income. In fact, with no growth at all, it takes only a sufficient expected increase in per capita income to yield *any* specified rise in expected total sales. This was a point made repeatedly by opponents of the stagnation thesis—that "investment outlets" exist so long as per capita incomes can be raised.

While rising individual incomes can provide greater prospective sales

---

[4] This conclusion is somewhat compromised by an implicit assumption that a given income would be distributed to the same earners in both years, and spent on a larger number of consumers in the second year. If we permit income redistribution as a concomitant of growth, the applicability of Mrs. Brady's rule is not so clear.

[5] Keynes did say on this score that investors are predominantly influenced by past experience. Past experience in turn would show that population growth tended eventually to rectify mistakes of overinvestment. However, as a general proposition it is growth of *income* (not population) that makes demand overtake any given potential supply. J. M. Keynes, "Some Economic Consequences of a Declining Population," *The Eugenics Review*, Vol. 29, no. 1, April, 1937, pp. 13–17.

to justify investment, the question remains: *ceteris paribus*, does faster population growth make the growth of total income more likely or more rapid? There are two reasons for supposing it would. First, a faster growing labor force can be expected eventually to cause a higher level of future employment and (with a positive marginal product of labor) a larger national income. Next year's increment to the labor force might simply be added to the unemployed. However, it is surely a reasonable expectation that in, say, fifteen years a steady annual increase in the labor force would add to the number employed. To assume that employment would *not* increase with growth even during the life of very durable equipment is to postulate a very inflexible economy indeed. Second, growth tends to raise the consumption function, as was shown earlier.

Finally, some forms of investment involve less risk when population is growing, even though the expected course of total income is considered independent of population growth. Such investment is in industries where the demand is particularly responsive to numbers and relatively insensitive to average incomes. Food consumption, the purchases of certain consumers' durable goods (household "necessities" such as refrigerators), or of semi-durables (such as children's clothing) might be expected to increase with a *constant* total national income but a growing population. Investment in these industries would take place more readily with rapid than with slow population growth, even with no assumed relation between growth of total income and numbers of persons.

Aside from these rather abstract arguments, there is ample testimony that investors are reassured by rising numbers. A few citations will document what most newspaper readers have noticed: business analysts and spokesmen consider population growth a favorable factor of major importance. *Business Week* ran an article entitled: "The Why behind the Dynamic 1950's. Overall Population Growth is One of the Mainsprings of Prosperity. . . .", (November 10, 1956), and *U.S. News and World Report* carried another entitled: "A Bonanza for Industry—Babies. 60 Million More U.S. Consumers in the Next 19 Years." (January 4, 1957).

I suspect that the basis for the confidence that the business community derives from the prospect of population growth is partly psychological. The future of human events (especially of business trends) is so opaque that an element whose future appears relatively assured is given grateful attention.[6] An investor who must decide the likely course of public

---

[6] Any great confidence in the validity of forecasts of future births and future population growth is misplaced. See Harold F. Dorn, "Pitfalls in Population Forecasts and Projections," *Journal of the American Statistical Association*, 45, 1950, pp. 311–334; John Hajnal,

tastes, of government tax policies, of competitors' behavior, of wages, and the prices of materials is gratified to find that the Census Bureau publishes a set of estimates of future population growth.[7] When the investor finds a variable projected convincingly and apparently competently by experts, it is not surprising that he gives it great weight.

While it is clear enough that population growth influences investment, there is no very satisfactory basis for expressing the relation in quantitative terms. All that can be asserted with confidence is that the prospect of faster growth leads to more investment. Any numerical formulation of investment as a function of simple demographic variables is more specific and invariant than is warranted. On the other hand, to omit such an important demographic force from our quantitative estimates would be more misleading still.

In the absence of a formula that can be accepted as truly representative, the best choice is a simple one. The simplest assumptions are that investors expect the indefinite continuation of current growth rates, and that extra people are expected to have the average income that would prevail in their absence. These assumptions lead to the following expression:

$$(1) \qquad I = (r' - r)(NI)m$$

where I is the increment in non-housing investment that results from an annual growth rate of r' rather than r, NI is the national income expected (next year) with the growth rate r, and m is the non-housing capital/output ratio. NI may (as a further simplification) be taken as approximately equal to current national income.

Demographic Factors and Investment in Housing

This section might logically be devoted to a discussion of investment by households. The usual convention followed by national income accountants is to consider only additions to the stock of houses for owner occupancy as the only investment made by households, and to count

---

"The Prospects for Population Forecasts," World Population Conference, Rome, 1954, Proceedings, *Papers*, Vol. 3, United Nations Publications, 1955, pp. 43–53; Robert J. Myers, "Comparison of Population Projections with Actual Data," World Population Conference, Rome, 1954, Proceedings, *Papers*, Vol. 3, United Nations Publications, 1955, pp. 101–112; Joseph S. Davis, *The Population Upsurge in the United States*, War-Peace Pamphlet no. 12, Food Research Institute, Stanford University, 1949, 92 pp.

[7] The Bureau is under continual pressure by business users to reduce the apparent uncertainty of population projections by publishing a *single* projection rather than a range of estimates of future population growth.

expenditures on other durable consumers' goods as consumption.[8] In other words, a new house is considered as an addition to wealth, while a new automobile or rug is considered as consumed when purchased.

This convention is clearly arbitrary but, fortunately, it has little effect on our analysis. If purchases of durable consumers' goods were considered as household investment, the schedule of total investment would be higher, would slope upward more steeply as a function of national income, and would be more responsive to demographic factors; while the consumption function would be lower, less steep, and less responsive to demographic factors. But the sum of investment plus consumption would not be altered.

However investment by households is defined, it has not been included in the consumption function or the forms of investment discussed earlier; expenditures on new housing (the conventional definition of investment by households) surely depend on demographic variables; and a separate discussion is required.

Expenditures for residential construction can be fitted into our general scheme by imagining a housing investment schedule that has different values for alternative national incomes. The question is: How would such a schedule be affected by demographic variables?[9]

The demographic factor most clearly related to expenditures for new houses is population growth. More people mean more shelter space needed; and the simplest assumption is that expenditures on new housing are such as to increase the stock of housing in the same proportion as population grows.

This simple assumption can be made more precise by noting that additions to the stock of housing take two forms: (1) new dwelling units (formed by construction from the ground up, or by subdivision of existing large units); (2) additions (or alterations) to existing dwelling units. The significance of these two forms is that an increase in the number of

---

[8] An exception occurs in Goldsmith's monumental study, where only depreciation and upkeep of durable goods are considered as consumption expenditures. Raymond W. Goldsmith, *A Study of Saving in the United States*, Princeton University Press, 1956, 3 volumes.

[9] The housing investment schedule for a stationary population would be positively inclined with national income, though not markedly or dependably so. Louis Winnick has calculated a regression equation with proportionate changes in the number of persons per room as the dependent variable, and changes in the average number of persons per household, in median income, and in average rent per room as the independent variables. The changes were from 1940 to 1950. The data (from the decennial censuses of housing) related to 89 cities with a population in 1950 of over 100,000. His analysis shows a small multiple regression coefficient with the income variable, and also a small partial correlation coefficient between persons per room and income. See Louis Winnick, *American Housing and Its Use*, John Wiley and Sons, 1957, pp.117–126.

households implies increase in the number of dwelling units, while a rise in the number of persons in existing households tends to cause additions to existing units.

Winnick's analysis indicates that, with income constant, households with more members occupy much less than proportionately more space; and the effect of income on space per person (or more precisely rooms per person) in households of a given size is relatively slight. Consequently, we may infer that if the *average size of household* remains constant (and hence the proportionate increase in the number of households and persons is the same), the stock of housing would tend to grow nearly in proportion to population; while if the *number of households* remained constant (and growth took the form of an increase in the average size of households), the amount of occupied dwelling space would tend to increase substantially *less* than in proportion to population.[10]

Thus population growth can be factored into two components having different implications for house construction: growth in the number of households, and growth in their average size. Until very recently there has been in the United States a nearly continuous *reduction* in household size, combined with a growth in the number of households that was more rapid than that of population.[11]

At any given level of national income there is associated with an annual growth in the number of households (at a rate of *s* per year) an expenditure on housing construction of α times *s* times (value of the stock of houses), where α is a number slightly less than one; and, associated with an annual growth in the size of household (at a rate of *u* per year), is an expenditure of β times *u* times (value of the stock of houses), where β is substantially less than one.

If there is an annual proportional increase in households (*s*), and in average size of household (*u*), the expenditure on housing construction *at a given level of national income* will equal the expenditure at that level with no population change, plus $(\alpha s + \beta u)S$ where S is the value of the housing stock. From Winnick's data, α can be crudely estimated as 0.95

---

[10] It is here assumed that "stock of housing" means the value of houses at constant prices, and that this value changes about in proportion to the total number of rooms.

[11] If $\quad P_t = P_{t-1}(1 + r), \quad H_t = H_{t-1}(1 + s), \quad$ and $\quad L_t = L_{t-1}(1 + u)$

where P_t = population at time t, and r is annual rate of growth of population; H_t = number of households at time t, and s is the annual rate of growth of the number of households; L_t = average number of persons per household and u is the annual rate of growth of household size.

Then $\quad\quad\quad\quad\quad 1 + r = (1 + s)(1 + u) \quad$ and $\quad r = s + u.$

and β as o.6.[12] In other words, an increase of s in the number of households and u in their average size would raise the schedule of housing investment by approximately $(0.95\,s + 0.6\,u)S$.

This formulation raises a further question—what determines changes in average household size and the rate of household formation? National income is a factor, because at higher incomes young people more readily marry and set up separate households, and also "doubled up" families undouble if income increases. Changes in custom—in age at marriage, in the proportion ever marrying, in the strength and extent of family ties —are also important determinants of size of household.

Even though these factors help to determine the size distribution of households, the *age distribution* of the population has played a dominant role in the United States. From 1890 to 1950, factors that changed the proportion of persons at each age heading a separate household accounted for 1/6 of the decline in average household size, while changes in age composition—especially the decline in the proportion of children— accounted for 5/6.[13] Age-specific "headship rates"—the proportion by age who are heads of households—can be used to factor a given change in population into growth in the number of households and growth in size. Apply the age-specific "headship rates" of the given population to the population one year later. The resultant number of household heads represents the number of households that would exist next year with unchanged nondemographic conditioning factors. If growth were of a form that involved no change in age composition, the number of households would increase as fast as population. If the number in dependent ages grew more rapidly than the rest of the population, the increase in number of households would be less than population growth, and average size of households would increase.

---

[12] Winnick derives an equation for the proportionate change in persons per room as a linear function of proportionate changes in median income, average rent, and size of household. The regression coefficients are -0.045, $+0.073$, and $+0.395$ respectively. If the size of households were constant, a larger population would necessarily be accompanied (at a given total national income) by a smaller income per household. For an $x\%$ smaller average income per household there would be approximately an $0.05x\%$ increase in persons per room, or an $0.05x\%$ *decrease* in rooms per person. The over-all increase in rooms occupied would be about $(x - 0.05x)\%$ or $0.95x\%$; thus $\alpha = 0.95$. By a similar argument, the coefficient of about 0.4 applying to the proportionate increase in household size in Winnick's equation implies a β of about o.6. The data are (as stated earlier) really not suited to drawing accurate inferences about population change, and there are a number of questionable statistical procedures involved in arriving at the above estimates of α and β. However, a general range of 0.9 to 1.0 for α, and of 0.4 to 0.8 for β is plausible on common-sense grounds, and these values will serve at least illustrative purposes.

[13] Winnick, *op. cit.*, p. 82.

The effect of a given change in population on housing investment can now be expressed in formulae. Suppose a population at time $t - 1$ with a specified number of males at each age $M(a, t - 1)$, and of females at each age $F(a, t - 1)$. Suppose the observed proportion at each age and sex who are heads of households is $H_m(a, t - 1)$ and $H_f(a, t - 1)$ for males and females respectively. Then the number of households at $t - 1$ would be given by:

(2) $H(t - 1) = \sum_a [H_m(a, t - 1) M(a, t - 1) + H_f(a, t - 1)F(a, t - 1)]$

The number of households at time t would be given by:

(3) $H(t) = \sum_a [H_m(a, t - 1) M(a, t) + H_f(a, t - 1)F(a, t)]$

The growth rate in the number of households would be:

(4) $$s = \frac{H(t) - H(t - 1)}{H(t - 1)}$$

and the growth rate of household size would be:

(5) $$u = r - s = \frac{P(t) - P(t - 1)}{P(t - 1)} - s$$

Finally, the effect of the given growth on housing investment would be an increase in the housing investment schedule by an amount:

(6) $$I' = (0.95\, u + 0.6\, s)S(t)$$

where $S(t)$ is the value of the stock of houses at time t.[14]

Demographic Variables and Government Expenditures

The response of households to demographic variables is to attempt to maintain living standards under the strain of more members, with a consequent upward shift in both the consumption function and the housing investment schedule. These shifts represent a diminution in savings for a given income, and a reallocation of some of the savings to housing rather than other forms of wealth.

The response of businesses is to increase investment in anticipation of higher demand as an expected consequence of population growth.

[14] This formulation is based on the assumption that this year's housing expenditures are affected by population changes since last year. Actually, the effect of growth would be felt with various lags and leads. Some construction may be in response to growth that has been pent up for several years; in other instances households might invest in larger houses in anticipation of additions to the population yet to come.

Government expenditures would undoubtedly respond in ways analogous to these private responses—increased expenditures on current account made to provide the same standards of government services to more people; expanded capital expenditure both on service facilities and on government-provided productive equipment (such as highways) in anticipation of higher demand in the future. If so, the degree to which a hypothetical schedule (listing government expenditures as a function of alternative levels of national income) would be shifted by a different number of dependents or a different rate of growth could be estimated.

The difficulty with a completely parallel treatment of government expenditures is that two important forces in government finance must be allowed for—the necessity (or desire) to balance budgets, and the possibility of deliberate compensatory fiscal policies. In particular, balanced budgets are the aim of state and local governments because of the limited credit they command. It is considered sound for these governments to finance all expenditures on current account out of current revenues, and to incur indebtedness only for capital expenditures. Thus (to oversimplify somewhat) only *expenditures on capital account* of governments below the federal level should be considered as simple changes in the schedule of total government expenditures. Expenditures on current account should be considered as also causing a reduction in the consumption and investment functions (because of the effects of increased taxes on disposable income).

In the federal government there is always an articulate group advocating a balanced budget per se, and other advisers advocating the use of fiscal measures to avoid severe unemployment or inflation. If such considerations prevail, the effect of demographic variables on federal expenditures (as well as non-federal) may be mitigated by compensating changes in taxes (or otherwise).

As a consequence of these complications, no serious quantitative estimate of how demographic variables affect over-all government expenditures will be attempted. The implications of population variables for government expenditure are somewhat clarified by a list of the government activities that would be most directly affected (most of which are responsibilities of state and local governments, to which balanced budgets are almost a necessity).

Perhaps the most obvious activity is education. With a given national income, the current operating expenses of public education are more or less proportional to the number of children of school age, and educational expenditures on capital account have a component proportional to the *growth* of the school-age population.

Services demanding support in proportion to the size of population (at a given level of national income) include police and fire protection, health, and postal service. Expenditures on new highways, hospitals, streets, sewers, and water facilities would tend to vary more or less in proportion to population *growth*.

At the other end of the spectrum, expenditures on defense, veterans' benefits, interest on the national debt, and foreign assistance—all in the federal sphere—would be affected only indirectly (if at all) by differences in dependency and the current rate of growth.

The pressure to spend more could be met by a reduction in the standards of service provided by the government, or offset in part by a change in the tax structure. A reduction in standards has been the response of many areas to the educational needs of the rapidly increasing school population of the past few years. If increased tax revenues were equal to additional expenditures, the enlarged budget would leave disposable incomes essentially unchanged. Furthermore, there are special obstacles to a reduction in disposable income when there is a greater proportion of dependents in the population. First, with no change in the tax structure, income tax payments would decrease because of more exemptions. Second, transfer payments for the various social security programs would increase.

The range of possible influence of greater population growth and more dependents on effective demand *via* government expenditures thus extends from minor increases in budgets financed by increased taxes to substantial increases in budgets with somewhat *reduced* revenues. The smallest effect would result if increased needs arising from more dependents and faster growth were met by reduced standards of service, and if a firm policy of budget balancing were followed. The greatest effect would arise from maintaining fixed standards of service and unchanged tax schedules.

The conclusion that emerges from this survey of demographic influences on government expenditures is that those demographic forces that tend to increase private components of effective demand also tend to add to effective demand on the part of the government. The government may, as a matter of deliberate policy, resist such a tendency. But the ease with which compensatory fiscal policy can be implemented is affected by demographic variables. If the government tries to exercise a restraining influence on effective demand in a period of inflation, it would find this course more difficult in the presence of many dependents and rapid growth. Conversely, it would be easier with many dependents and rapid growth for the government to assume a stimulating role during a period of heavy unemployment.

A Quantitative Estimate of the Effect of Demographic Variables on Aggregate Demand

As we have seen, an increase in the proportion of persons under 17 and over 70 increases private (and possibly public) expenditures on consumption, while an increase in the rate of population growth creates pressure for households, businesses, and governments to enlarge their expenditures on capital. More dependents raise the consumption function (C); growth raises the level of investment (I); and both exert upward pressure on government expenditures (G). The next issue is the magnitude of the over-all effect of a shift from an observed demographic situation to a reasonable alternative.

I shall first compare the United States population of 1940 with the population there would have been had the 1957 proportion of dependents/working-age population, and the 1957 growth rate prevailed in 1940.

Chart 1 shows the age distribution in the two years. Note that the proportions at both ends of the age distributions—young children and persons above the age of retirement—were higher in 1957. The ratio $\frac{\text{total population}}{\text{persons } 17\text{–}69}$ was about 1.63 in 1957, and only 1.485 in 1940. Had the dependency burden of 1957 existed in 1940, the population 17–69 would have had to support a total nearly 10 per cent bigger. If it is assumed that the extra dependents would be added to existing households, and if Dorothy Brady's 6th root rule is accepted, consumption expenditures at each alternative level of national income would be multiplied by $\sqrt[6]{1.097}$, or increased by 1.55 per cent.

The application of 1940 "headship rates" to the 1939 and 1940 age-sex distributions yields an expected increase in the number of households on account of demographic factors of 1.46 per cent, and a *decrease* in the average size of household by 0.51 per cent. If 1940 headship rates had applied to 1956–1957, the number of households would have increased by 1.13 per cent, and the average size by 0.69 per cent.[15] It was argued

---

[15] The relatively small increase (in 1956–1957) in number of households reflects the small numbers passing through the ages (10–15) of most frequent household establishment. These small numbers, in turn, are a consequence of low birth rates from 1932 to 1939. On the other hand, the increase in average household size (in contrast to the

CHART 1

Age Distribution for United States, 1940 and 1957

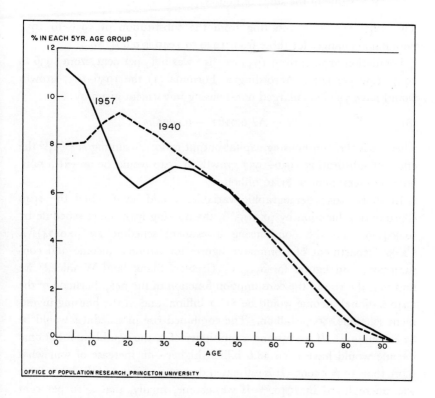

% IN EACH 5YR. AGE GROUP

OFFICE OF POPULATION RESEARCH, PRINCETON UNIVERSITY

decrease in 1939–1940) resulted from the sustained "baby boom" in the 1940's and 1950's. It must be noted that the changes in number and size of households are hypothetical changes that would occur with fixed "headship" rates. During the interval 1940–1957 there were two major changes in marriage patterns: an increase in the proportion ever marrying, and a decline in average age at marriage. As a consequence of these changes (and slightly decreasing proportions of married couples at given ages "doubled up"), the number of households increased much more than the hypothetical increase with constant age-sex-specific "headship" rates. The changes in married status by age could certainly be considered as demographic, but they are not so considered here. Only variations in growth and age distribution are analyzed.

above that investment in new house construction in excess of investment with a stationary population would be approximately:

$$(7) \qquad\qquad I' = (0.95s + 6u)S$$

where s = proportionate increase in the number of households

u = proportionate increase in the average size of household

S = value of the stock of houses.

The difference in I' resulting from the substitution of 1956 to 1957 population changes for those from 1939 to 1940 is $0.0041 S_{1940}$.

Population growth from 1939 to 1940 was 0.95 per cent, from 1956 to 1957, 1.82 per cent. According to Formula (1) the 1956–1957 growth would have yielded enlarged non-housing investment given by:

$$(8) \qquad\qquad I = NI(0.0182 - 0.0095)m$$

where m is the non-housing capital-output ratio. Assuming $m = 2$,[16] the effect of substituting 1956–1957 growth in 1940 would be an extra non-housing investment of $1.40 billion.

In short, 1957 demographic variables would have raised the 1940 consumption function by $(0.0155)C$, the housing investment schedule by $(0.0041)S$, and the non-housing investment schedule by $(0.0174)NI$. Using Department of Commerce figures for national income and consumption, and figures for S_{1940} by Grebler, Blank, and Winnick,[17] we find that the rise in the consumption function in the neighborhood of the 1940 national income would be $1.11 billion, and in the housing investment schedule, $0.35 billion. The combined rise in schedules would be $2.86 billion.[18] If we assume a multiplier of 3, the equilibrium national income would have been $8.6 billion higher—an increase of somewhat more than 10 per cent. It is estimated that 14.6 per cent of the labor force was unemployed in 1940.[19] If we assume, finally, that a 10 per cent increase in aggregate demand would have increased employment by 10 per cent, it appears that the dependency burden and growth rate of 1957 would have absorbed more than 60 per cent of the unemployed in 1940.

[16] R. A. Gordon, "Population Growth, Housing, and the Capital Coefficient," *American Economic Review*, Vol. 46, no. 3, June, 1956, pp. 307–322.

[17] Leo Grebler, David M. Blank, and Louis Winnick, *Capital Formation in Residential Real Estate*, published for the National Bureau of Economic Research by Princeton University Press, Princeton, 1956, pp. 360–361.

[18] It is interesting that only 18 per cent of this rise is attributed to business response to population growth.

[19] Stanley Lebergott, "Annual Estimates of Unemployment in the United States," in *The Measurement and Behavior of Unemployment*, published for the National Bureau of Economic Research by Princeton University Press, Princeton, 1956, p. 216.

No allowance has been made in these calculations for the effect of demographic variables on government expenditures, because of uncertainty about how budgets would be altered in the presence of greater needs. However, to show that the adjustment in government expenditure needed to maintain unchanged quality of service is not trivial, I shall present some estimates of the extra expenditures on education that the 1957 age distribution would require. The ratio $\dfrac{\text{Children } 5\text{--}14}{\text{Population } 17\text{--}69}$ was nearly 25 per cent larger in 1957 than in 1940. Moreover, the number of children 5–14 rose 3.8 per cent between 1956 and 1957, while the number fell 1.5 per cent between 1939 and 1940. Current expenditures on education in 1940 were about $2 billion;[20] 25 per cent more children of school age would have required about $0.50 billion additional spending on school operation. A growth of 3.8 per cent in the school population (instead of a reduction of 1.5 per cent) would take an extra investment at least equal to 3.8 per cent of the value of school buildings, or about $0.28 billion.[21] If current expenditures were met by increased taxes, the additional aggregate demand would be ($0.50 + $0.78) = $1.28 billion,[22] or 1.6 per cent of the national income. Further possible additions to demand would be uncovered by examining other government sectors. Even when a conservative view is taken of how the government would respond to needs generated by demographic circumstances, a further substantial reduction in unemployment caused by government expenditures is plausible. With a multiplier of three, it seems a reasonable conjecture that the demographic features of 1957 would—if transferred to 1940—have averted 75–90 per cent of 1940's unemployment.

Conversely, had the slow growth and light dependency burdens of the end of the thirties characterized the 1950's, inflationary pressure would have been much less, and in the absence of compensatory forces, unemployment rates of 7 to 12 per cent instead of 3 to 5 per cent might have prevailed.

The results of a further quantitative exercise are shown in Charts 2 and 3. Chart 2 shows the variations from 1921 to 1957 in rate of growth and in dependency. Note that growth provided the least stimulus during the early and middle 1930's, while dependency continued to decline

[20] U.S. Bureau of the Census, *Statistical Abstract of the United States, 1957*, p. 14.

[21] Value of school buildings taken as 90 per cent of the value of school property. U.S. Department of Health, Education, and Welfare, Office of Education, *Biennial Survey of Education in the United States, 1950–1952*, ch. 1, p. 18.

[22] Assuming a multiplier of one for balanced-budget extra expenditures, and of three for deficit-financed expenditures.

CHART 2

Annual Percentage Increase in Population, and Ratio of Total Population
to Persons Aged 17–69, United States, 1921–1957

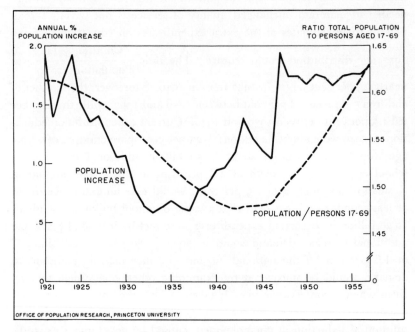

OFFICE OF POPULATION RESEARCH, PRINCETON UNIVERSITY

until the early 1940's. In Chart 3 the extra employment (as a per cent of the labor force) that would result from substituting 1957 dependency and growth rates for those of the given year is shown in conjunction with the unemployed (also as a per cent of the labor force). No allowance is made in Chart 3 for government expenditures. Their effect would be to amplify the variations shown.

The demographic features of 1957 would scarcely have been sufficient to prevent unemployment during the great depression, nor were changes in population sufficient to account for the substantial boom since the early 1940's. I am not proposing a demographic theory of business fluctuation, however, but merely suggesting that age distribution and growth are quantitatively significant elements in effective demand.

Amendments, Extensions, and Qualifications

A major weakness of the foregoing analysis is the coarse definition of the variables it treats. If the "fine structure" of the economy were taken into account, the conclusions would doubtless be modified. For example, the

CHART 3

Proportion of Labor Force Unemployed, 1921–1956, and Estimated Added
Proportion with Population Growth and Dependency of 1957

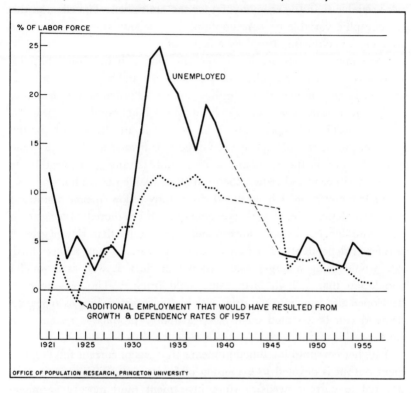

% OF LABOR FORCE

UNEMPLOYED

ADDITIONAL EMPLOYMENT THAT WOULD HAVE RESULTED FROM
GROWTH & DEPENDENCY RATES OF 1957

OFFICE OF POPULATION RESEARCH, PRINCETON UNIVERSITY

combination of the "sixth root" rule of household expenditure and
variations in age composition makes no allowance for variant trends of
household size among groups with different incomes. If the decreases in
fertility during the twenties and thirties were confined primarily to
upper-income families, the effect on saving would be greater than if the
decrease were uniform.

Similarly, the recognition of only three age groups (under 17, 17–69,
and 70 plus), and the failure to differentiate products beyond a division
into consumers' goods, houses, and producers' goods conceal the effects,
inter alia, of shifting demand (for example, from baby buggies to false
teeth) as age composition changes.

Finally, the numerical calculations summarized in Charts 2 and 3 can
scarcely be considered as precise. The estimate of 3 for the multiplier
cannot be defended. If the reader has another estimate he can easily

alter the results shown in Chart 3—raising or lowering them according to whether he believes the multiplier higher or lower than 3. Much of the other material used in constructing quantitative estimates is not much more reliable than the estimate of 3 for the multiplier. The effect of the demographic variable on consumption, housing investment, or business investment could easily be off by a factor of 2.

These imperfections are less important than a major issue that the analysis does not treat at all: many dependents and rapid growth are a stimulus largely because they constitute an extra burden on the economy. A high birth rate, which ultimately produces both rapid growth and a large proportion of dependents, is an economic advantage only in the sense that an excess of exports over imports is favorable. Both promote demand; but if the economy were already straining its productive capacity, either would reduce the product available per capita.

Edgar Hoover and I have stated (in a study of low-income countries) that when deficiencies of aggregate demand can be ignored, faster growth and more dependents yield lower income per capita than slower growth and fewer dependents. For at least 25 or 30 years, in fact, a lower birth rate would bring a larger *total* national product as well as a smaller population than a high birth rate would bring.[23] The reasoning we developed also applies to countries with high incomes, so long as aggregate demand can be counted on to keep available productive resources at work.

A higher consumption function means that less of current full employment output is devoted to expansion of future output (because more is devoted to current needs). More investment (and more government expenditures) inspired by population growth means more equipment and shelter diverted to put additional population on the same terms as the current population, and less available for increasing the per capita stock of equipment and housing.

In other words, the demographic features that stimulate effective demand are also features that can keep the economy from achieving the maximum growth in output per capita. A striking instance of the favorable effect of *low* dependency and growth is during World War II. Dependency was at its all time minimum during the war, a fact that in the absence of war might have continued to retard recovery from the great depression. But in wartime the small number of dependents made it easier to divert more resources to the military effort. In a similar

---

[23] Ansley J. Coale and Edgar M. Hoover, *Population Growth and Economic Development in Low Income Areas*, Princeton University Press, 1958.

fashion, under some peaceful circumstances, fewer dependents would permit more resources to be used for growth.

A final word about demographic and economic prospects in the United States. Population projections prepared by the Census Bureau indicate that if fertility remains at present levels, dependency will steadily increase and rapid growth continue during the next twenty years; while if fertility were to resume its historic downward trend, dependency and growth would again start to fall. Thus a continued secular economic boom could gain partial support from a continued baby boom. But after a century this trend would produce about a billion Americans, and after two centuries some six billion. There must be a better way to stimulate employment.

COMMENT

MARGARET G. REID, University of Chicago

Ansley J. Coale based his estimate of the relation of demographic changes to investment in housing on the assumption that the "effect of income on space per person is relatively slight." This seems a little surprising in view of the widespread notion that room-crowding is a characteristic of poverty.

Available evidence in the U.S. Census of Housing, as I read it, indicates that demand for space rises sharply with income. Such evidence comes from a comparison among census tracts.[1] One estimate shows the following correlation:

$$X_{pr} = 10.70 - 2.922X_i + 0.256X_p \qquad \begin{matrix} R^2 \\ 0.85 \end{matrix}$$

(1)

where X_{pr} is the percentage of households with more than one person per room, X_i is the median income of families and unrelated individuals, and X_p is the mean number of persons per household, with variables X_{pr} and X_i expressed in log form.[2] Thus two variables explain 85 per cent of the variation among tracts in the percentage of households with 1.01 persons per room. In this relationship, income is the dominant factor. Among

[1] The tracts were selected in order to maximize the likelihood that income reported by census tracts approximated that of primary units of households. The set includes all tracts in the Chicago metropolitan area in which at least 99 per cent of the population was living in households, and in which there were at least 99 families per 100 families and unrelated individuals. There were 144 census tracts with these characteristics. The data come from *Census of Population, 1950*, Vol. III, *Census Tract Statistics*, ch. 10, Tables 1 and 3. Various analyses which I have made indicate that Chicago is fairly representative of metropolitan areas in the relationships here described.

[2] Each tract has a weight of one.

the set of 144 tracts X_{pr} ranged from 1.4 to 42.4 per cent. Median income of these two tracts was \$8,325 and \$2,657, respectively. Income alone explains 76 per cent of the variation in X_{pr}.

Thus estimates based on data aggregated by census tracts indicate that income has a powerful effect on demand for space. On the other hand many sets of disaggregated data indicate that increase in income increases only slightly the demand for space. Coale's assumption rests on such evidence. A comprehensive comparison between these two types of evidence has yet to be made. In my opinion, comparison among census tracts provides more reliable evidence of basic tendencies related to income than does comparison among families. Data aggregated by census tracts are less affected by random reporting error in income and by income variation related to the age of the head and the number of persons currently employed in families. Both of these conditions account for much of the variation in income among families and they seem unlikely to have much effect on demand for space.[3]

Coale in addition cites an intertemporal demand for space based on certain changes between 1940 and 1950. He noted that "the evidence . . . indicates only a slight tendency to demand more rooms with higher income, size of household, and rent held constant." Coale recognizes that the data may be very crude, hence that this evidence may not be especially useful. He does not, however, note (a) that the estimates were undoubtedly affected by variation in the effect of rent control among the cities involved in the comparison, (b) that rent paid was assumed to represent price and that important changes had occurred in the stock of tenant-occupied dwellings, (c) that the income related to wage and salary workers irrespective of tenure, and (d) that the importance of owner occupancy had changed appreciably between 1940 and 1950. Thus I would like to underscore Coale's word of caution about using these data as indication of the nature of demand for space in relation to income.

In estimating the effect of change in number of dependents on aggregate demand Coale again relied on estimates derived from expenditure-income regressions among families. Such regressions for total expenditure

---

[3] It is of some interest that the fertility rate tends to be higher and doubling up in households of relatives in addition to those of the nuclear family more frequent among the poor than the rich. Thus it is not surprising that among the selected set of census tracts for which income is probably a fairly good measure of economic status, the number of persons per household is negatively related to average income. On the other hand, among consumer units, number of persons tends to rise with income. This tendency provides further reason for questioning the validity as to consumption-income relation observed among families as evidence of basic tendencies for products such as housing that are little affected by household size.

as well as for housing seems likely to be biased by random components in income. Average income and total expenditure are directly related to number of persons per consumer unit. Because of random components in income, the level of expenditure at a given income tends to be correlated with average expenditure of the respective groups of units. Such expenditure will hence be directly related to the number of persons[4] among groups stratified by number of persons. This difference tends to disappear when comparison is made at a given income position in the respective income distributions.[5]

Nevertheless a tendency for expenditure to increase with number of persons in a family experiencing no increase in income would not be surprising. Increase in funds can come from drawing on reserves, from a reduction of savings, or from an increase in debt. Such changes would not be surprising in the stage of family formation when persons are increasing but earners are not. Reserves used at this time may, however, be rebuilt and debts incurred may be paid off later when the ratio of earners to persons tends to increase or need declines.

Among types of units, that is, those differing in relationship among members and in number of persons, there is a tendency for expenditure per $100 of average income to be directly related to the number of persons.[6] The correlation[7] is, however, very low. It is increased markedly if the number of earners[8] is held constant. The correlations of these variables are as follows:

$$R^2$$

$$(2) \qquad X_{Reti} = \$102.06 + 0.154 X_p \qquad\qquad 0.0025$$

$$(3) \qquad X_{Reti} = \$107.73 + 1.426 X_p - 10.425 X_{ea} \qquad 0.26$$

[4] For interpretation of this characteristic of the data see Milton Friedman, *A Theory of the Consumption Function*, published for the National Bureau of Economic Research by Princeton University Press, 1957, pp. 121–122.

[5] This characteristic of relative levels of expenditure-income curves has been investigated systematically by Dorothy S. Brady and Rose D. Friedman, using data for families differing in average income. See "Savings and the Income Distribution," *Studies in Income and Wealth*, National Bureau of Economic Research, Vol. 10, 1947, pp. 247–265.

[6] The data used in this analysis are those for 1950 for consumer units reporting for the large cities in the north, a total of 3,853 units. The estimate is confined to this set because data for the urban set in general are not summarized. The report distinguishes 37 types. For many of these the number reporting is low. Hence some combinations are made of units differing in number of persons. The estimates relate to 24 subgroups with at least 30 consumer units in each group. The observations are weighted by the number of the reports. The data come from *Study of Consumer Expenditures, Incomes and Savings* (tabulated by the Bureau of Labor Statistics for the Wharton School of Finance and Commerce), University of Pennsylvania, 1956, Vols. I and II, Table 14.

[7] For this set of subgroups average expenditure and average income are highly correlated. With the variables expressed in the logs the elasticity of expenditure with respect to average income is 0.90 and r^2 is 0.92.

where X_{Reti} is total expenditure[9] per \$100 of disposable income, X_p is average persons per consumer unit, and X_{ea} is average earners per consumer unit, for 24 subgroups of units differing in relationship among members and in number of persons. Thus the higher the number of persons, the higher tends to be expenditure per \$100 of income; the higher the number of earners per unit, the lower tends to be such expenditure.

This equation predicts with number of earners equal to the average of units in general, i.e. 0.90 earners that increase from three to four persons would increase R_{eti} from \$102.59 to \$104.01, an increase of 1.4 per cent. This is much less than that predicted by the ratio of the sixth root of the family sizes, a coefficient that may well have been much influenced by the random components in income.

Even though there is some tendency for expenditure to rise with number of persons, one cannot assume that expenditure as a percentage of income will rise with increase in fertility rates and consequent tendency for the peak size of consumer units to rise. The tendencies observed above relate to a life cycle adjustment. The projection would have to take into account behavior over the entire life cycle.

WILLIAM J. BAUMOL, Princeton University

We must all be grateful to Coale for performing an ingenious and highly relevant calculation. The effect of employment on the level of income is one of those things which every economist talks about but few indeed have attempted to do anything about. In light of such discussions as those of the stagnation thesis, the relevance and the importance of Coale's conclusions are clear and they are best left to speak for themselves.

As a parochial theorist, there is relatively little I can say about the statistical calculations which lie behind the paper. I wish only to raise the omnipresent question of identification. For Coale leans heavily on other writers' correlations and it may well be asked whether a correlation which involves population growth and income shows the effect of demographic change on the economic variable or the reverse (or, for that matter, some mongrel combination of the two).

Coale's model suggests some further lines of theoretical investigation. It is easy to extend his construction into one which is completely analogous with the Harrod growth model. Coale's basic conclusion for this purpose

---

[8] The correlation of R_{eti} and average number of earners, among the 24 subgroups, is significant at the 10 per cent probability level.

[9] Expenditure as here defined includes outlays for gifts and contributions.

is that effective demand (and hence demand for labor) is an increasing function of the rate of growth of population. If, for simplicity, we assume that the relationship is linear, this may be written:

(1) $$L_{Dt} = k(P_t - P_{t-1}) + A$$

where L_{Dt} is the demand for labor during period t, P_t is the level of population during that period, and A is the "autonomous" (nondemographically determined) demand for labor. For simplicity, k and A are taken to be constants, in accord with our linearity assumption.

Suppose now that the age distribution of population is more or less fixed and that the supply of labor is a roughly constant proportion of population, that is, that we have

(2) $$L_{St} = cP_t$$

where L_S is the supply of labor.

Then by (1) and (2), if labor supply is to be equal to the demand we must have

$$cP_t = k(P_t - P_{t-1}) + A,$$

that is,

(3) $$P_t = (k/k - c)P_{t-1} - A/(k - c)$$

This first order difference equation has the well known solution

(4) $$P_t = (k/k - c)^t P_0 + K$$

where K is constant and P_0 is the level of population during some arbitrarily selected "initial" period. We may draw the following conclusions:

(*a*) The time path of P_t which is given by equation (3) represents a sort of equilibrating population growth pattern, for if and only if population grows at this rate will labor supply equal labor demand.[1]

(*b*) If $k > c$, the equilibrating population level will grow at a roughly constant geometric rate [cf. equation (4)].

(*c*) Paradoxically, if in these circumstances the growth of population falls short of its equilibrating rate, there will tend to be excess labor supplies and vice versa (equation 1).

(*d*) There is reason to suspect that the equilibrating time path will be unstable. For if the population growth exceeds its equilibrating rate, it

---

[1] Instead of a model which determines the equilibrating population growth it is easy to formalize one which purports to predict actual population growth. To do this we substitute demand for income in place of demand for labor in equation (1) and set up instead of (2) a second equation describing how population is affected by income. The criticisms of such a second relationship are, however, obvious.

follows from equation (1) that there will be "over-full" employment, that is, the excess demand for labor and the high standards of living which result may cause population growth to increase even further above its equilibrating level. A similar argument applies to the downward side of the equilibrating time path. However, it is clear that this conclusion rests on a rather tenuous assumption about the connection between income levels and population levels.

There is little point in extending the argument further. It is easy to revise equations (1) and (2) to take account of age distribution and some of the other complications which characterize the connection between population growth and demands. Much of this can be accomplished just by a careful retracing of Coale's calculations. However, the nature of the conclusions would not be affected materially.

Certainly the concept of an equilibrating population growth rate must not be asked to bear too much weight. As a normative concept it is subject to objections which have been raised against "optimum population" concepts. Moreover, the amount of demand for labor which must be induced by population growth in order to achieve full employment will vary with the level of the "autonomous demand," that is, that which results from the behavior of the strictly economic variables. I want only to indicate with the aid of this concept how demographic variables can once again be fitted comfortably into some of our economic analysis as Leibenstein has been at such pains to point out.

Population Change and the Supply of Labor

STANLEY LEBERGOTT

OFFICE OF STATISTICAL STANDARDS, BUREAU OF THE BUDGET

It goes without saying that the most authoritative and succinct review of the links between population growth and labor force change appears in the Book of Genesis.[1] It is difficult to decide how much more can usefully be said on the subject. But there has been a welter of secular experience since that report. And there have been some excellent recent studies of that experience.[2]

To an economist, the most interesting question may well concern how population growth affects the extent of the market and the division of labor. Certainly from the time that Smith emphasized the link between the extent of the market and the division of labor, and Hodgskin fitfully exorcised the Malthusian devil by insisting that population gains forced further division of labor,[3] these subjects have been worked over many times—though not always to advantage.[4] Fortunately, this vital topic is in the competent hands of Coale and Kuznets. I shall therefore deal with other aspects.

The essential and necessary relationship that links short-run population and labor force change is simple to describe: there is none. A country's population may rise, with no corresponding gains in its labor force. When Chadwick and others brought sanitation to London in the nineteenth

---

[1] "Unto the woman he said . . . in pain thou shalt bring forth children . . . And unto Adam he said . . . cursed is the ground for thy sake; in toil shalt thou eat of it all the days of thy life."

[2] The most lucid and comprehensive contemporary study that emphasizes population-labor force relationships appears as Chapter xi in the United Nations, Population Studies, no. 17, *The Determinants and Consequences of Population Trends*, 1953. Essential contributions appear in the well-known studies by Durand, Jaffe, Wolfbein, Stewart, and Douglas as well as less directly in the labor force analyses by Palmer, Miller, and others.

[3] Scott Gordon, "The London Economist and the High Tide of Laissez-Faire," *Journal of Political Economy*, December, 1955, p. 473, quotes Hodgskin as demonstrating: "an increase in population provides a larger market, permits a more extensive division of labor." Hodgskin actually emphasized the euphoric impact of population gains on technological changes.

[4] Young's tautology is deservedly famous: "The division of labour depends upon the extent of the market, but the extent of the market also depends upon the division of labour." Allyn Young, "Increasing Returns and Economic Progress," *Economic Journal*, December, 1928, p. 539.

Note: This paper was prepared while the writer was on leave from, and has no connection with the work of, the Budget Bureau.

century, when a more complex bureaucratic organization brought DDT to Ceylon after World War II, sharp changes in mortality and in population occurred, but without corresponding gains in the labor force. It is equally clear that the labor force can rise without the population gaining correspondingly: thus the enormous jump in our labor force during the war took place with only limited change in the population totals.[5]

But while there may be no necessary tie, the size of the labor force does in fact tend to be limited by the size of the population in an era of nationalism and xenophobia.[6] (It is difficult, for example, to imagine foreign sailors continuing to comprise the bulk of America's seamen, as they did in the nineteenth century.)[7] And in the longer term population, surges and declines do imply changes in the labor force—granting merely the useful assumptions that man must earn his daily bread and that a high level of inertia in human behavior is confidently to be counted upon. The most challenging aspects of the population-labor force link, however, are to be found in the study of how changes in population and the labor force are related to their causes. For such causes encompass the major social, economic, and political factors at work in a society.

In the present paper we will consider first some effects of immigration on U.S. labor force gains over the past century. Second, we shall consider how changing social goals for child and women workers affected the labor force, and population-labor force relationships.

Immigration and Labor Supply

Birth and death take place without special reference to the labor force requirements of given geographic areas. The transfer of population from place to place has therefore long been an integral mechanism in adjusting labor supply and demand.[8]

The nature of this transfer is of considerable importance. Folk migrations in historic time have tended to involve entire families. When the

---

[5] A completely different view appears in Sydney H. Coontz, *Population Theories and the Economic Interpretation*, 1957, ch. 8. Coontz concludes, "In summary, the economic analysis proceeds on the assumption that population is the dependent variable reflecting both long- and short-run changes in the demand for labour," p. 183, referring back to Young, Smith, and Malthus, pp. 88–89.

[6] This generalization is less true where such qualifications do not apply—say, for the regular movement of laborers from Ruanda-Urandi to Kenya, or Java to Malaya.

[7] *Remarks on the Scarcity of American Seamen and the Remedy, by a Gentleman Connected with the New York Press*, printed at the Herald Office, New York, 1845, p. 17. Chairman Reed of the Committee on Naval Affairs is quoted as saying that 100,000 of the 100,000 men in the Navy and Merchant Marine were foreigners. It is to be doubted that this estimate was finically precise, but it does at least suggest that a majority were foreigners.

[8] It need not be, of course. Trade alone could fairly well bring the adjustment.

Marcomanni moved to the uplands of Bohemia, when the Athenians settled the islands of Asia Minor, a balanced population change and labor force change occurred: dependents as well as working adults moved.

The key characteristic of migration to the United States in the past century, however, has been that adults in the prime labor force ages tended to dominate migration. The labor force increased by a far greater proportion than did the population. Thus, despite higher birth rates among the foreign born, less than 7 per cent of this group were under 15 years of age in 1880—as compared to 42 per cent for native whites.[9]

In addition to the dominance of adults in the migration, there was a disproportionate tendency for men to migrate even if married. Thus, an extensive survey by the Immigration Commission as late as 1910 reported that 23 per cent of the married immigrants in their survey had wives still living in the old country.[10]

While this particular pattern tended to reflect the dominance of four nativity groups (Magyar, Slovak, Italian, and Russian) in the later migration, males also composed the larger share in the earlier migration of Irish and Germans, though the latter were mostly unmarried.

The causes of this movement were twofold. The first was a vision of America as a land, perhaps not of milk and honey, but at least of veal cutlets and gooseberry pie—at reasonable prices.[11] Where conditions in Europe were intolerable, the migration push was as critical as the pull.

What converted a dream castle into steerage space and what produced selective migration of males, was sponsored migration by American firms.

In a labor-scarce country, without limits on immigration, substantial attempts to attract labor were perhaps to be expected. When heavy, bunched demands for labor were created by such projects as canal construction, a choice appeared to be posed between bidding up wages to attract labor from other pursuits—or importing it.[12]

"I wish to reduce the price of labor on the Canal to ten dollars per month of 26 working days. It is now 12 and 13 dollars a month," wrote

[9] 1880 Census, *Statistics of the Population of the United States*, p. 549. These figures seem basically inconsistent with the age distribution of immigrants. Reports in this and other Censuses are consistent, would appear to rest on more reliable procedures than the *pro forma* queries of immigration officers on a mere statistical point.

[10] U.S. Immigration Commission, *Immigration Reports*, Part 23, Vol. II, *Immigrants in Industry*, p. 383. The reports covered 145,354 immigrants.

[11] Morris Birkbeck, *Notes on a Journey in America*, Severn and Co., London, 1819, p. 64, "coffee, rolls, biscuits, dry toast, waffles . . . pickerill salted . . . veal cutlets, boiled ham, gooseberry pie, stewed currants, preserved cranberries, butter and cheese—for all this for myself and three children" plus fodder for 4 horses—the charge was "6 shillings and nine pence sterling."

[12] In principle productivity gains could moderate the dilemma—and did over the course of time.

the President of the Chesapeake and Ohio Canal Company to his emigration agent.[13]

The advantages to foreign labor seemed clear enough., "Meat, three times a day," he wrote to the American Consul in Liverpool, "a plenty of bread and vegetables, with a reasonable allowance of liquor, and eight, ten or twelve dollars a month for wages would, we have supposed, prove a powerful attraction to those who, narrowed down in the circle of their employments have at this moment, a year of scarcity presented to them."[14] And such early recruiting attempts in Dublin, Belfast, and Cork did help to initiate a stream of migration "beneficial to both England and the United States."[15]

When gold was discovered in California, wrote a contemporary, "workers were dear . . . and slavery was prohibited. This directed the attention of moneyed men to the great proletariat of China: they sent many ships there and imported within a few years 40,000 Chinamen."[16]

In some instances a highly local situation constituted the incentive for directed migration. Demands for high wages were made against the Delaware and Hudson Canal in 1832. The Directors found that "Against this evil the only effectual remedy was the introduction of additional miners from abroad. This was done as promptly as possible and to such an extent that it is believed a recurrence of the evil will not be experienced."[17]

A cotton planter in 1866, trying to reestablish a Sea Island plantation and finding the local labor easy and unreliable, reported that "I have sent to the Ionian Islands to get fifteen Greeks at an expense of $2,000 and I hope they are on their way now."[18]

Whether the canals of Maryland or Louisiana were involved, or the plantations of South Carolina or Texas, sponsored migration emphasized the importation of single males. Time, to some extent, and rising wage rates for females, tended to correct the resulting imbalance in the sex ratio. Thus, one writer's tongue-in-cheek comment on the frontier's

[13] Mercer to Richards, July 8, 1829. C. and O. Letterbook, U.S. National Archives, p. 84.

[14] Mercer to Maury, November 28, 1828. C. and O. Letterbook, pp. 38–39.

[15] Mercer to Barbour, November 18, 1828: "I will write to Canning directly for it would be beneficial to both England and the United States to relieve the dominions of the former of a wretched surplus population."

[16] Janos Zantus, May 5, 1857, writing from San Francisco, quoted in "California for Hungarian Readers," *California Historical Society Quarterly*, June, 1949.

[17] *Annual Report* of the Board of Managers of the Delaware and Hudson Canal Company for the year 1890, New York, 1899, p. 95.

[18] Edward S. Philbrick in *Report of the United States Revenue Commission on Cotton*, Special Report no. 3, Appendix, U.S. Treasury Department, 1866.

shortage of women for housework: "The supply is not equal to the demand as girls who come to Minnesota always have numerous advantageous offers of marriages, some one *or more* (sic) of which they are generally sensible enough to accept."[19]

Specifying the orders of magnitude involved is a difficult matter. We can, however, see them somewhat darkly through the Census data on the sex ratio in pioneer states and territories:[20]

	Free white males per 100 females	
	1820	1840
	Age 26–45	Age 30–40
Alabama	137	128
Mississippi	164	153
Louisiana	197	206
Indiana	117	115
Illinois	138	139
Missouri	155	138
Michigan	179	135
Arkansas	156	155
Florida	—	230
Wisconsin	—	235
Iowa	—	105
U.S.	104	111

The limitations of such ratios as measures of migrant characteristics are well known.[21] Yet it seems reasonable to infer that men constituted a disproportionately great share of the migrants who pioneered the midwestern and southeastern states.

It was not until the railroad building period began that the migration of single males diminished in relative importance. Beginning perhaps as early as 1851, when the Erie ran its first emigrant train, the emphasis changed to importing families who would settle on the railroad lands and provide a continuing source of traffic.[22] This shift meant that the supply of labor, once provided with a minimum of population increase, now was associated with greater gains in population as women and children entered these lands in increasing proportions.

[19] *The Immigrants' Guide to Minnesota in 1856*, by an Old Resident, W. W. Wales, St. Anthony, 1856, p. 67.

[20] Computed from 1820 Population Census, p. 1, and 1840 Census, p. 474.

[21] Cf. the pointed discussion in Dorothy Thomas, *Research Memorandum on Migration during the Depression*, Social Science Research Council, 1937.

[22] Frank Andrew, *Railroads and Farming*, U.S. Department of Agriculture, Bureau of Statistics, Bulletin 100, 1912, pp. 8, 18.

To this point comments have related primarily to white migration. What of the major migrant stream from Africa? Several pieces of evidence suggest a no less substantial tendency for males to predominate among the nonwhite group. The "uniform practice of dealers in selecting cargoes of negroes on the African coast, (was) to purchase a considerably larger proportion of males than females. All witnesses agree on the fact, though they differ as to the motive."[23] Confirmation is suggested by the practice in supplying other systems of plantation agriculture. According to an American physician who dealt extensively in slaves prior to 1830 "the proportion of sexes of Africans who are brought to Brazil (is) about 1 to 10," women being taken only when the captains put 1 or 2 in a lot of 10 and insisted on a sale en bloc.[24]

The migration pattern after 1865, of course, was quite different. As General John A. Wagener of South Carolina wrote in 1867, "South Carolina has never heretofore taken steps, officially, to induce immigration because of her peculiar institution of African slavery, which enabled her inhabitants to prosper and live in patriarchal peace and contentedness. . . . Slavery is now, however, with her own consent, forever abolished."[25] The labor force ceased to meet local demand requirements. Although the population totals were as high as ever, and although the South continued to have population exports for many decades, widespread attempts were made to sponsor labor force replacements. Thus, General Wagener was made Commissioner of Education for South Carolina about this time and similar positions were established in other states. The work of such commissions, however, does not appear to have had any great impact on either the labor force or population totals.[26]

The migration process involved in the peopling of the American states reflected, in sum, concentrated demands for labor, sometimes taking the form of directed migration. Such demands, in the early decades, were primarily for labor, not for population. As a result, a disproportionately great share of all migrants were males in the prime age groups. With

---

[23] Report of the Freedmen's Commission, in U.S. Congress, *The War of the Rebellion*, Series 3, Volume 4, p. 324.

[24] Jose Clifford testimony in Great Britain, Parliamentary Papers, Session January 31–August 15, 1850, Vol. IX, p. 154. Clifford stated that he had extensive slave trading experience until the trade was outlawed in Brazil in 1830. Cf. R. B. Sheridan, "The Commercial and Financial Organization of the British Slave Trade," *Economic History Review*, August, 1958, p. 259, for a similar conclusion based on trade with the West Indies.

[25] South Carolina, *A Home for the Industrious Immigrant*, Charleston, 1867, p. 5.

[26] Data in the 1880 Census, *Population*, p. 426, indicates that several southern states showed declines in the number of foreign born after 1860, most had no significant change, while Missouri and Texas had significant gains. These gains are readily explicable by other factors.

the ending of canal construction, of slavery, and of the opulent opportunities in Mississippi and Alabama during the flush days, a more settled type of migration began. The slave coffle and the single horse were replaced as symbols of movement by the covered wagon, transferring the lares and penates of entire households. In recent years, of course, population change has been almost solely a matter of working out permutations in the parent population of native Americans.

Child Labor and Fertility Change

Where is the man with soul so dead that he interests himself only in the economic aspects of children? But these are the ones on which the economist—who is by profession neither bachelor nor married man—can most usefully comment. It has long been noted by economists that an increase in the number of children will eventually increase the labor supply and therefore tend to drive down wages. How many poor law administrators since Malthus have counseled the working class against the folly of seeking higher living standards without also limiting philo-progenitiveness. Yet while an abstract "working class" may suffer, any specific family may benefit. It must take the labor market as it finds it; in past centuries more children per family have usually meant more income per family. "Considerations of the economic and social advantages to be derived from children were once powerful motives in encouraging large families. Of patriarchal society it was said 'Happy is he who has his quiver full of them'; in agricultural communities, especially new ones, the farmer literally produces his own farm hands."[27] The contribution that children can make in their parents' old age is, of course, a second, highly important economic factor.[28]

In a labor-scarce country, such as the United States in the nineteenth century, the natural desire for children would, to say the least, not run contrary to what a calculation of their mere economic value would indicate. In the U.S. today, with fewer farmers than Chicagoans, it is difficult to credit an 1819 report that the population of the mid-West was "so thinly scattered" that "there were but twelve human habitations in two hundred square miles, and these occupied principally by hunters."[29]

[27] James A. Field, *Essays on Population and Other Papers*, 1931, pp. 278f. Cf. Isaiah Bowman, *The Pioneer Fringe*, 1931, p. 251, on children in other pioneering societies.

[28] Speaking to another way of life, but not a wholly different one, is the finding of a recent survey of Japanese opinion, in which the proportion of adult males expecting to depend on their children in their old age was 25% in the major cities and more than double—57%—in rural areas. Quoted in Horace Belshaw, *Population Growth and Levels of Consumption*, 1956, p. 33.

[29] John Lorain, *Hints to Emigrants*, 1819, p. 78.

But, given these conditions, one writer warned potential immigrants, "no assistance worthy of notice can be obtained from others outside the family."[30] Under such circumstances a high birth rate was not wholly unexpected. A late nineteenth century publication of the Department of Agriculture, noting an 1846 record of "a family of 26 strong healthy boys," adds that "Today a family of five children is a rarity. This, of course, affects the amount of help."[31]

When U.S. factories began to proliferate, the economic value of children became still greater. Cotton factories became a new source of demand for child labor. "It is well known," remarked a writer in 1815, "that in this country . . . children, from their birth until they are of an age to go into apprenticeship (say 14 or 16) render little service to their parents; this is more especially the case in towns. But it is this description of persons who are required in cotton and woolen workers."[32]

In Rhode Island, where the mills began, 42 per cent of those who staffed the cotton mills in 1832 were in fact boys under 12. The average for New England and the country as a whole was about 20 per cent.[33] These children provided a substantial supplement to family income, being paid a quarter as much as adult males.[34]

How the growing demand for labor in the mills may have affected population growth is not altogether clear. The English Census for 1821 asserted that the manufacturing population was, in part, increasing rapidly because, "in many Manufactures, Children are able to maintain themselves at an early age, and so entail little expense on their Parents, to the obvious encouragement of marriage."[35]

However, no similar encouragement is apparent in the United States with its long-term decline in fertility rates. And a priori one can surmise that in a labor-scarce country such as the United States at this early date, children had been sufficiently valuable on farms so that the mere growth of the manufacturing system would not increase supply. At most, it would divert population increase to nonfarm pursuits.

[30] ibid.
[31] U.S. Department of Agriculture, Miscellaneous Series, Report no. 4, *Wages of Farm Labor in the United States*, 1892.
[32] *Niles Magazine*, October 7, 1815, p. 96.
[33] These figures are weighted averages of reports appearing in U.S. Congress Serial Set 222,229, *Documents Relative to the Statistics of Manufactures in the United States*, 1833, Duff Green, Washington, Vols. I and II. The definition of "boys" as being those under 12 is indicated by the Report of the New York Convention of Friends of the Manufacturing Interest appearing in *Niles Register*, XLII, Addendum, 1832, March–August, p. 7.
[34] Ratio computed from data in Serial Set 222,223.
[35] Quoted by T. H. Marshall in E. M. Carus-Wilson, *Essays in Economic History*, 1955, p. 330.

Children were no less valuable under slavery. As a great Southern architect and engineer noted, "It may indeed be justly considered one of the excellencies of the cultivation of cotton, that in its collection no manual labour is lost. Neither age nor childhood, if in health, is prevented from giving its aid in this innocent and useful pursuit. Children from eight years old can be employed to advantage."[36]

This "excellency" was not lost sight of on most plantations. Even after the heavy discounting for future mortality, the sales value of children was great enough to suggest the nontrivial value of their labor. About 1820 the average sales value of girls aged 5–10 was set at $175 by the Maryland Orphans court—or perhaps half the value of an adult male.[37] Even in 1865, $400 and more was paid in New Mexico for "a likely girl of not more than eight years old, healthy and intelligent."[38] Considering how uncertain the continuation of slavery was in 1865, most of the latter price must have reflected advantages expected to be realized in the very near future.

Given the distinct contribution that child labor made to the family or plantation exchequer throughout the nineteenth century, its decline in the twentieth century hardly reflects any inability of the economy to continue utilizing such labor efficiently. Instead, the change would seem to stem from concurrent changes in family values and social attitudes.

Was such a factor the ever-increasing level of education? The spread of free public schools is, of course, a matter of history. From 1850 to 1950 the following rise took place:[39]

Year	Children Aged 5–14	Enrollment in public schools	Ratio
1850	6,132	3,354	55%
1950	24,329	20,242	83%

Some parents had repeated the calculation made by John Stuart Mill, if not by Horace Mann, of the advantage to the individual of forgoing an immediate income to assure an eventual higher one.[40] Many had been

---

[36] Robert Mills, *Statistics of South Carolina*, Hurlburt and Lloyd, Charleston, 1826, p. 153.

[37] *American Historical Review*, Vol. 19, 1914, p. 817.

[38] According to Kirby Benedict, Chief Justice of the New Mexico Supreme Court, quoted in LeRoy R. Hafen and Ann W. Hafen, *The Old Spanish Trail*, 1954, p. 280.

[39] The 1850 data are from *The Seventh Census of the United States: 1850*, 1854, pp. xl, xlii–xliv. They are based on school reports and were used as being more reliable than the population census count. The 1950 data are from the 1950 Census, Vol. ii, *Characteristics of the Population*, Part 1, Tables 38, 111, and relate only to those age 5–14.

[40] Entering school in 1807, Sophia Simpson was unable to pronounce the letter H. "Do try," said her teacher, "for it will be a thousand pounds in your pocket." Sophia S. Simpson, *Two Hundred Years Ago*, Otis Clapp, Boston, 1859, p. 47.

moved by other factors. The rise in educational horizons, however, seems to have had no discernible impact before 1900 in reducing the child labor force.[41]

The decisive factor in reducing the nineteenth century child labor force was the steady decline in birth rates, from roughly 55 per thousand population in 1820 to 20 by 1940.[42]

We can compare the contribution of fertility declines and the drop in the proportion of children working, using data from Table 1:[43]

TABLE 1

Number of Children Ever Born
(per 1,000 women, by color)

Mothers' Year of Birth	Adjusted		Native White		Negro	
	Native White	Negro	as reported in Census of			
			1910	1940	1910	1940
1835–44	5,172	7,433	4,863		7,000	
1845–54	5,034	7,216	4,805		6,897	
1855–59	4,729	6,783	4,583		6,580	
1860–64	4,408	6,257	4,339		6,162	
1865–69	4,050	5,484	4,050	3,544	5,484	4,678
1870–74	3,538	4,515	3,538		4,515	
1875–84	3,375	4,169		3,221		3,985
1885–89	3,118	3,802		3,022		3,688
1890–94	2,966	3,391		2,920		3,340
1895–99	2,738	3,091		2,738		3,091

Source. See footnote 45, p. 387.

The number of child workers is estimated simply as the product of the worker rate and the number of children ever born.[44] It measures the

[41] The proportion of children working shows no signs of decline in any of the scanty indications we possess for the nineteenth century. In fact the Census figures for 1870–1900 suggest a possible rise near the end of the period as new mills opened in the South.

[42] Conrad Taeuber and Irene Taeuber, *The Changing Population of the United States,* 1958, p. 249.

[43] Fertility data from above table. Worker rate data from Alba M. Edwards, Census of 1940, *Comparative Occupation Statistics for the United States, 1870 to 1940,* p. 92. This assumes, for arithmetic convenience, that the first child is born when the mother is aged 20. Other assumptions would make little difference. More important, the 1870 worker rate seems unreasonably low, the adjustment made by Edwards for the 1870 undercount perhaps being insufficient. The 1880 rate is therefore used for 1870, being more meaningful for a longer view even if the 1870 figure properly reflects the immediate postwar disturbances.

[44] Because the worker rate relates to all children the absolute levels are meaningless and therefore not shown.

average number of children, of those born to each group of mothers, that worked between the ages of 10 and 15. Its decline from the first to the second period derives solely from the fertility decline—since worker rates actually rose. The subsequent drop in child workers from the period around 1900 (mothers born 1865–1869) to the depression years, reflects primarily the fall in worker rates. For even if the number of children ever born had not changed, the number of child workers would still have fallen by 74 per cent—nearly as much as their actual 85 per cent decline.[45]

	Indices of		
Mothers' year of birth	Number of children (ever born per 1,000 native-white females)	Child worker rate in year 1st child becomes 10 years of age	Number of child workers
1835–44	100.0	100.0	100
1865–69	78.3	108.3	85
1895–99	52.9	28.0	15

From the earliest period of settlement, therefore, children's work made a significant contribution to our national product. Despite the continued monetization of such work, however, fertility rates fell over the course of the entire nineteenth century. Other values than the incomes potentially provided by their young children became increasingly important to American families. The proportion of the children sent to work did not decline until the vague dawn of the twentieth century. Since World War I it has been the significant decline in child worker rates which accounts for the diminishing share of children in the labor force. The fruits of philosophy and of education alike led to a decline in child labor.

[45] 1940 Census, *Differential Fertility, 1940 and 1910: Women by Number of Children Ever Born*, Table III. This report gives differing figures from the 1940 and from the 1910 Census on the number of children born to the same groups of women. The causes of these differences are discussed lucidly in Taeuber and Taeuber, *op. cit.*, p. 255.

The method of adjusting the Census data used here was as follows: In the 1910 Census, 3,128 women born in 1865–1874 reported an average of 3.769 children; in the 1940 Census, 1,771 women born in the same period reported an average of 3.544 children. The two averages would be quite consistent if we could assume that 2,357 women (3,128 minus 1,771) had died by the latter date and had had an average of 4.030 children. Neither assumption seems grossly unreasonable. The 6.35% excess between the 1910 and 1940 reports would then be taken to reflect the steady toll of selective female mortality, and assumed to have developed at a steady rate. The contemporary 1910 report was therefore taken as standard, the rate of excess interpolated for the group born in 1865–1874 through the 1895–1899 group.

A parallel mortality bias would of course have appeared in the 1910 reports. Lacking a better measure, the same 6.35% excess was applied to the 1835–1844 group (which stands in the same relation to the 1910 Census as the 1865–1874 one does to the 1940), with interpolation to give the excess for the other years. This implicitly assumes a stable trend in selective mortality.

Women in the Labor Force

The link between population and labor force change is most evident when the role of women is studied, for women constitute part of this generation's population and labor force and produce the next generation of each. Relatively little information, unfortunately, is available on women's work when their work in factory and store was uncommon. This probably reflects the basic convention of our society (like most nonmatriarchal ones) that women do not work unless they work outside the home. Thus, the 1820 Census schedules, taken in the days of John Adams and John Randolph, report virtually no women in the labor force, although a large number undoubtedly did farm chores, worked in domestic service, and the like.

No factor changed the composition of the female labor force more than did the introduction of the cotton gin and the cotton mill. Let us review the longer term development, first for white and then for nonwhite females.

White females. After the recession of 1819, jobs under factory discipline opened up in the new centers of Great Falls, Waltham, York, and Lowell. Offering incomes larger than the imputed value of work on the family farm,[46] and usually paying in cash, the new factory system transformed existing labor force patterns for women.[47] By 1831, one of the founding fathers of Lowell could pridefully note that "No less than thirty-nine thousand females find employment in the cotton factories of the United States." Yet before "the establishment of these and other domestic manufactures this labor was almost without employment." His inference?

Daughters are now emphatically a blessing to the farmer. Many instances have come within the personal knowledge of individuals of this committee, in which the earnings of daughters have been scrupulously hoarded to enable them to pay off mortgages on the paternal farm.[48]

In addition to freeing the paternal homestead, daughters working in textile mills undoubtedly also provided their own dowries (as they do today in Japan)—thus linking labor force increase to subsequent population change.

[46] One may set the imputed value of farm female labor at something near the $1 a week then paid to domestic servants.

[47] This shift may have involved only a slight increase in hours worked by the male labor force. A recent study of industrialization in a rural county found that a new factory drew female workers mostly from marginal farms, with little change in farm labor inputs. Cf. Paul H. Price *et al.*, *The Effects of Industrialization on Rural Louisiana*, January, 1958, Louisiana Agricultural Experiment Station and U.S. Department of Agriculture, Table 13, p. 42.

[48] P. T. Jackson in *Journal of the Proceedings of the Friends of Domestic Industry*, Baltimore, 1831, p. 111.

It would be helpful in contemplating this interesting course of consequences if we could get a bearing on the extent to which women did enter the labor force as the factory system developed and urbanization spread. The figures in Table 2 are an attempt to provide this, indicating the change over two sixty-year periods.

TABLE 2

Working Women: 1830–1957

Worker Rates by Marital Status, Color, and Age

	All Ages						Age 35–44			
	White			Nonwhite			Native White		Nonwhite	
Year	Total	Single	Married	Total	Single	Married	Single	Married	Single	Married
1830[a]	(8)	—	—	(90)	(90)	(90)	—	—	(95)	(95)
1890 (Durand)[b]	13.1	30.0	2.2	37.6	52.5	21.9	37.7	2.3	75.6	21.5
1940 (Durand)[b]	23.0	45.6	13.9	37.1	42.3	32.2	73.4	14.5	71.8	36.0
1940 Census	24.5	45.9	12.5	37.6	41.9	27.3	73.6	13.8	71.1	30.5
1950 Census	28.1	47.5	20.7	37.1	36.1	31.8	76.5	25.3	65.8	38.7
1951 CPS[c]	31.5	50.5	24.3	41.1	41.3	36.0	—	—	—	—
1957 CPS	33.9	48.0	28.7	42.5	37.9	40.2	—	—	—	—

[a] See Appendix A.
[b] Durand data for whites relate to native white.
[c] Current Population Survey, Census Bureau.

A variety of problems in definition and measurement besets the comparison of data from such different sources.[49] But reasonable adjustments for them would not change the key inference from the table: the gain between 1830 and 1890 was small as compared with that between 1890 and 1950. It is clearly impossible to measure each of the separate factors at work in creating this difference—the move to the city, the changing tide of immigration, the varying marriage and birth rates, and so on. But a summary reckoning would suggest that the dominant factor was almost certainly the changing pattern of work for women. For the proportion working rose sharply as time went on, even apart from changes in the age, nativity, marital status, rurality composition of the group.

For the period since 1890 the proof is reasonably clear. A study by Wolfbein and Jaffe of the 1890–1930 changes shows that shifts in the distribution of the female population as between various demographic

[49] Many of these are canvassed in Durand's basic study. Since the time that was published, further incomparabilities have occurred even within the Current Population Su..vey reporting. Adjustments in the 1890 data to make them comparable with the 1940 Census labor force concept have not been adopted because it is not clear whether the result would be more comparable with the actual 1950 Census figures. However, only 0.2 points are involved in Durand's adjustment.

categories (sex, color, nativity, marital status) made a trivial contribution to the great gains in female worker rates over these four decades.[50] A more precise review made by Durand of our 1920–1940 experience ingeniously measures the contribution of each factor to worker rate changes, including the farm-nonfarm move.[51] His conclusions on this point are similar.

It should be particularly noted that the 1950 rates, high as these are, tell us only of labor force participation at a point in time. The proportion of women who work at some time during the year is far greater. For 1956 we have the following data which, though relating to both white and nonwhite married females, may fairly be taken as demonstrating for white females the greater participation during the year.[52]

	Wives, husband present	
	with	without
	children under 6	
Census		
Per cent in the labor force (3/57)	17.0	36.0
Per cent working in 1956	30.7	46.2
Survey of Consumer Finances		
Per cent employed in 1956	27.5	32.7

The Census data report a very substantial margin of part-year employment—both for women with young children and those without. (The data from the Survey of Consumer Finances that appear to contradict this point for those without young children are not wholly comparable. And unfortunately any of the variations in definition and enumerative approach that come to mind as explanations for these Census-SCF differences are too convincing: they explain equally well differences for women with young children—a group for which differences do not exist!)[53]

[50] S. L. Wolfbein and A. J. Jaffe, "Demographic Factors in Labor Force Growth," *American Sociological Review*, August, 1946.

[51] Durand, *op. cit.*, ch. 3, Table 10 and passim.

[52] Census: Current Population Reports, Series P-50, no. 81, *Family Characteristics of Working Wives: March 1957*, Tables 9, 10, and unpublished Census data. Survey of Consumer Finances: unpublished data kindly provided by Professor James Morgan from Study 650, Economic Behavior Program, relative to the 1957 Survey of Consumer Finances. Comparisons were made for 1955 (using Census reports P-50, nos. 62 and 73, and unpublished SCF data), which show similar, but less extreme, differences.

[53] These results are particularly puzzling since no reference, say, to differences in interviewing approach, seems to explain (a) the essentially same results for women with young children, and (b) the striking difference for those without young children. James N. Morgan notes in a private communication that "question sequences in the SCF are directed toward more complete income reports rather than employment detail," and that reports on employment status are "highly sensitive to the question asked."

In summary, while worker rates for white females rose markedly during the nineteenth century, their gain 1900–1950 appears to have been considerably greater. The rise during a long period of national growth and expansion was nowhere nearly equal to that during the latter decades. One factor may have been the supply of slave labor, a topic to which we now turn.

Nonwhite females. The system of slavery, which had been faltering in the tobacco and hemp fields, took on renewed strength with the spread of the cotton gin. Female Negroes began to be used throughout the South in substantial numbers not merely as domestics but as field hands. It would appear that as early as 1820 the proportion of female slaves in the labor force was probably as great as that of males.

The broad sweep that appears if the suggested orders of magnitude (from the Appendix) are correct is shown in the following table:

Per Cent of Nonwhite Females in the Labor Force[54]

	All Nonwhites 14 and over			Age 35–44	
Year	*Total*	*Single*	*Married*	*Single*	*Married*
Estimated 1830	(90)	(90)	(90)	(95)	(95)
1890	37.7	52.5	21.9	75.6	21.5
1950	37.1	36.1	31.8	65.8	38.7

Surely the enormous decline over the sixty-year span beginning in 1830 is the most striking aspect of this table. It is even more striking if we assume, as seems not unreasonable, a precipitous fall between 1860 and 1865. The substance of the decline appears to have been a fall in rates for married women: the rates for single women changed much more moderately. Nearly a century has passed since that time but the over-all rate in 1950 appears to be much as it was in 1865. Mild declines in the rate for single women, and mild changes in the ratio of single to married women offset the moderate rise in rates for married women.

Population-Labor Force Trends

Given this pattern of change in worker rates for women in the century and a quarter between the days of the first Lowell operatives and the

[54] 1830 figures for the 35–44 age group estimated, given the review noted in the text of 1820 Census data, at 95%—or a rate similar to that reported for males in this age group in any Census providing such data—i.e., from 1850 on. For the 10 and over category, an arbitrary reduction is made to allow for the aged and sick who, on the average, did not work 1 hour or more a week. 1890: derived from data in John Durand, *The Labor Force in the United States, 1890–1960*, 1948, pp. 216f. 1950: 1950 Census, *Employment and Personal Characteristics*, Table 11.

women who assemble missile components, what can we say of some of the associated population changes?

In part, the far greater 1890–1950 rise in female worker rates than the 1830–1890 rise was produced by the changing demographic composition of the population. A still more significant force, however, must have been the falling immigration tide. Kuznets and Rubin have pointed out that nearly a fifth of the population gain in the decades from 1860 to 1890 consisted of immigrants, and about the same proportion for the labor force, with the figures dwindling rapidly in subsequent decades.[55] But immigrants competed disproportionately in the low wage markets where women were actual and potential employees. Especially after 1920, therefore, when immigration was drastically cut, demand shifted and an increasing proportion of women were hired.

Turning to another facet of this change, how did changing fertility rates (with their impact on the population totals) affect worker rates for females, and vice versa? To speculate on possible answers to this question, we require first a measure of fertility trends. For whites, the Census data on the number of children under 5 provide us with rough but useful indications for 1850ff.[56]

The level of nonwhite fertility prior to 1850, however, is a highly uncertain matter. Under conditions of slavery, a high fertility rate was a desideratum to be commended and encouraged. Testimony on this point ranges from the horrified specificity of Mrs. Kemble to the consoling skepticism of Ulrich Phillips. Both imply such a conclusion.[57]

Many leading Southern analysts concluded, in the words of General Jubal Early, that a "rapid multiplication of the slaves by natural increase" took place; whereas "premature emancipation" (in the words of the Reverend Robert L. Dabney) was "leading to ultimate extermination" as fertility rates fell.[58]

---

[55] Simon Kuznets and Ernest Rubin, *Immigration and the Foreign Born*, 1954, p. 45. The valuable discussion on pp. 43–49 deals generally with the contribution of immigration to the population and labor force increase.

[56] Summarized in Taeuber and Taeuber, *op. cit.*, p. 25.

[57] Cf. William Gilmore Simms, *The Geography of South Carolina*, Babcock and Co., Charleston, 1843, p. 21: "The slaves are very prolific, increasing in greater proportion than the whites; a sufficient proof of the mildness of their servitude and labor."

[58] Jubal E. Early, *The Heritage of the South*, 1915, pp. 113–114. The full quotation reads: "Let anyone compare the condition of the African in his native land with the slaves of the South before the violent abolition of slavery, and then say whether that institution, which had produced such a vast improvement in his condition was so great a wrong after all. The most conclusive answer to the slanders against Southern slave owners is to be found in the rapid multiplication of the slaves by natural increase, which could not have taken place if such barbarities had been practiced or such immorality had existed as has been represented." Robert L. Dabney, D.D., in *A Defence of Virginia*,

"As a factor in the increase of population" the Negro "must of necessity decline in ratio to the whole" concluded the Commissioner of Agriculture for Georgia, in his discussion of postwar labor supply.[59]

But did a high absolute birth rate result among nonwhites before 1861 —a higher one, say, than for whites? These various pressures may only have kept the nonwhite rate above the level it would have otherwise reached. Indeed, both the 1850 and 1860 Census results suggests that fertility was approximately the same among whites and nonwhites in the South, whatever the basic fecundity trends.[60]

More striking still is the rise in the proportion of children that took place among the nonwhite population from 1860 to 1880. The 1900 Census report—presumably prepared by Walter Willcox—suggested that "a greatly increased birth rate . . . was one of the first results of emancipation. If that be admitted, the parallel between the emancipated Negroes in the South, and the emancipated serfs in Russia, the rate of increase among whom since emancipation has been extraordinary, is a striking one."[61]

Putting these elements together, we may deduce that a variety of factors led to Negro family limitation under slavery. Such factors should have been somewhat more important in 1830 than 1850, given the increased volume of transfers from the breeding states to Missouri, Texas, and the Gulf States. On the other hand, a much greater proportion of the 1830 female slave population had been transported from Africa than of the 1850 population. Setting one factor off against the other, we return to the simpler hypothesis—namely, that the level of nonwhite fertility under slavery was much the same in 1830 as in 1850 and 1860. We will

---

and through Her, of the South in Recent and Pending Contests against the Sectional Party, 1867, p. 90, wrote of changes 1865–1867 in Virginia: ". . . facts already evince the doom of ultimate extermination which Southern Philanthropists have ever predicted as the result of premature emancipation is already overtaking the negro with giant strides . . . the population of blacks in 1860 being 531,000" reduced by 1867 to "340,500." Dabney was no casual observer but had been ecclesiastical professor of history and polity and systematic and polemic theology at a leading seminary, as well as adjutant general to Stonewall Jackson.

[59] Thomas P. Jones, Commissioner of Agriculture for the State of Georgia, Handbook of the State of Georgia, 1876, p. 152. "The future of the Negro in America . . . as an element in politics, his career is virtually at an end. As a factor in the increase of population, his race must of necessity decline in ratio to the whole. . . ."

[60] 1900 Census, Supplementary Analysis, p. 418, shows for 1850, 695 white and 705 nonwhite children under 5 years of age per 1,000 females 15–49. For 1860, the rates were 682 and 688, respectively.

[61] ibid., p. 417. To get over the difficulty of the 1870 undercount, one may simply look to the 1860–1880 change, which was a slight decline for southern whites, a substantial increase for southern nonwhites, p. 418.

therefore assume that the average of the rates reported by the Census for 1850 and 1860 applied equally well in 1830 (Table 3).[62]

TABLE 3

Children under 5: 1830–1950
(per 1,000 women aged 20–44)

Year	Native White	Negro
1830 est.	1,145	988
1850 est.	892	1,010
1860 est.	905	965
1890	685	930
1900	666	845
1910	631	736
1920	604	608
1930	506	554
1940	419	513
1950	587	706

Sources: 1830–60.   See text.
1890–1950.   Taeuber and Taeuber, *op. cit.*

Population-Labor Force Relationships

Given this background of worker rate and fertility change, what conclusions can we draw from the data summarized below:

	Native-White Women		Nonwhite Women	
Year	Worker rate	Number of children under 5 years of age per 100 women 20–44	Worker rate	Number of children under 5 years of age per 100 women 20–44
1830	8	114	90	99
1890	13.3	69	37.7	93
1950	28.1	59	37.1	71

It would be hard to find a set of figures that shows less of a simple relationship between long-run trends in worker rates and in fertility.

[62] These figures differ from the adjusted estimates shown in Taeuber and Taeuber, p. 251, for nonwhites. The latter writers assume a 13% understatement in reported Census totals for 1850 and 1860—the percentage found in a study covering 1925–1930. It is here assumed, however, that the true percentage for these particular years would be the same 5% as that used by Taeuber and Taeuber for whites. Because of the great monetary importance of slaves, there is no reason to believe that the underenumeration among nonwhites was greater than among whites. Reporting by planters for their slaves may in fact have produced more precise figures than did the endeavors of Census enumerators to find marginal white inhabitants. Therefore we have no basis for assuming differential underenumeration rates for the slave period.

The 1830 figure was estimated as the average of the 1850 and 1860 figures as revised on this 5% basis.

For native whites, the worker-rate rise over the first sixty years was far less than over the second—but the fertility-rate fall over the first period was enormously greater than over the second. For nonwhites, the contrast is even more extreme. Worker rates fell precipitously over the first period, not at all over the second; fertility fell only slightly over the first period but largely over the second.

A decline in fertility must surely facilitate a rise in worker rates, yet the overriding impact of factors other than fertility change was clearly much greater. One would hardly conclude from such data that major changes in fertility are sufficient, or even necessary, conditions for major changes in worker rates. The data, of course, are chancy, and they are limited to particular Census years. Yet reasonable shifts of the worker rates, or shifts in our reference dates to a Census ten years earlier or later, would make little difference in this basic conclusion. Social and economic factors other than fertility change must have dominated the change in the female labor force.

Let us now go on to the period since 1890, for which the Census data and the basic study by John Durand make possible a review of such vital

TABLE 4

Female Labor Force and Fertility Trends: Changes 1890–1940
(by nativity, color, and age)

	Age Groups	Children Ever Born Per 1,000 Women	Worker Rates		
			Single	Married	Excess Married Over Single Rates
Native	14–24	− 299	+ 8.7	+13.8	+ 5.1
	25–34	− 707	+34.9	+15.5	−19.4
	35–44	−1,195	+35.7	+12.2	−23.5
	45–54	−1,477	+30.6	+ 9.0	−21.6
	55–64	−1,584	+22.0	+ 5.9	−16.1
	65+	−1,319	+ 3.4	+ 2.2	− 1.2
Foreign	14–24	− 280	− 8.6	− 0.8	+ 7.8
	25–34	− 966	+ 8.5	+15.6	+ 7.1
	35–44	−1,831	+24.9	+14.8	−10.1
	45–54	−1,851	+32.1	+ 8.9	−23.2
	55–64	−1,966	+13.1	+ 3.7	− 9.4
	65+	−1,818	− 1.0	− 0.3	+ 0.7
Nonwhite	14–24	− 362	−15.3	+ 5.1	+20.4
	25–34	− 968	+ 0.1	+14.2	+14.3
	35–44	−2,036	− 3.8	+14.5	+18.3
	45–54	−2,843	−12.7	+ 9.2	+21.9
	55–64	−2,912	−25.2	+ 0.5	+25.7
	65+	−2,322	−22.9	− 3.7	+19.2

factors as the changing age and marital composition of the female population. Data for the 1890–1940 change are presented in Table 4. Here we are concentrating not on the data for the entire female group—nor even for the married group per se. Now it is obvious that nativity change, migration, urbanization, and so on, all affected worker rates. How can we adjust for their influence in trying to measure the relationship between changing fertility and changing worker rates?

One method of approximate allowance is to assume that the changes in worker rates for single women will measure the changes—age for age —that would have occurred for married women apart from the factors associated with their marital status For measuring these influences we therefore consider single women to be an enormous sample of the population. The sample may well have some biases for this measurement. But its great size, and lack of any obvious important bias, make it worthy of consideration. We therefore take the differential between the worker rates for single and married women as measuring the factors associated with marriage.

WHITE: the worker rates for married women gained *less* than did those for single women. Despite sharp declines in fertility—measured either in terms of number of children in the Census year or long-term cohort fertility—worker rates for this group did not gain relatively.

NONWHITE: the opposite pattern appears—fertility falling substantially and worker rates rising substantially.

What seems to be at work in producing these contrasting responses? An analytic tradition reaching to Malthus and beyond makes children and material acquisitions alternative goods: "we are familiar with the notion that a man's standard of living is defined by the wants he insists upon satisfying before he is willing to enlarge his family."[63] We might, therefore, emphasize how the decline in fertility facilitated the rise in worker rates, thereby providing a basis for increased income and acquisition.

But while some such interactions undoubtedly occurred, they are no very simple ones. Had a single-minded preference for income been the major force at work, it would have been simpler to satisfy such a preference in the traditional manner by sending children to work early and often.

We can more plausibly link the decline in fertility to a conscious

---

[63] J. A. Field, *op. cit.*, p. 231. For Malthus, as for others, "hope of bettering one's conditions was the great inducement from which restriction of numbers was to "result," p. 54. Field quotes Ely's *Principles*, 1893: "The number and character of the wants which a man considers more important than marriage and family constitute his 'standard of living,' " p. 389.

attempt to reduce the dangers and burdens of childbearing, to a desire to achieve greater comfort for mothers and greater well-being for children. As men increasingly achieved a shorter work day it was only to be expected that women too would seek equal rights. The hope might reasonably be entertained that both halves of the old jingle—"Man's work is from sun to sun; women's work is never done"—were becoming obsolete.

But given the shortened period of childbearing and responsibility that followed upon fertility declines, the time thus freed was utilized quite differently by each group. Nonwhite married women increased their worker rates more than single women; the white group did not (Table 4) and by 1940 substantially more nonwhite than white women of the prime ages and in detailed categories were in the labor force (Table 5).[64]

TABLE 5

Proportion of Married Women Aged 35–44
in the Labor Force: 1940

	Family Income $600–$999		All Incomes	
Area	Without Children under 10	With Children under 10	Without Children under 10	With Children under 10
Metropolitan areas				
Total	29.6	12.0	21.8	8.0
Nonwhite	36.5	21.5	38.2	20.1
Urban places 25,000–100,000				
Total	34.3	15.9	24.9	11.0
Nonwhite	54.0	—	52.1	39.8
Urban places 2,500–25,000				
Total	31.6	15.0	24.4	11.5
Nonwhite	44.9	29.1	50.0	37.8
Rural nonfarm				
Total	21.2	8.8	18.9	8.6
Nonwhite	23.0	16.4	33.2	22.8
Rural farm				
Total	—	—	7.5	4.2
Nonwhite	—	—	16.4	13.2
U.S.				
Total	—	—	19.7	7.5
Nonwhite	—	—	34.5	19.4

[64] 1940 Census, *Employment and Family Characteristics of Women*, Table 23. Unfortunately statistical progress has not provided data for later years.

The plantation heritage was surely a major factor in producing this differential. What about the income insurance that a second earner provided—surely no mean consideration in a group that appears disproportionately in those industries and occupations that are hit first by unemployment?[65] The influence of low and unstable income, however, was surely at work among the foreign born too—employed as they were in domestic service, in basement cigar factories or rag picking, in piecework at home, or in sweat shops. Yet the trend for foreign-born whites largely paralleled that for native whites. They adopted American standards of family size despite the high fertility traditions in which most of them were raised. And they followed prevailing American standards as to the propriety and desirability of women working outside the home; despite low and unstable incomes they did not adopt worker rates similar to those of the nonwhite group.

If we combine all the color and nativity groups (taking each of the age-nativity-color groups with complete or near-complete fertility shown in Table 4 as an independent observation) and chart worker rate change against fertility change, a broad pattern of relationship can be seen.[66]

Within the nonwhite group there seems to be a clear inverse relationship—the greater the decline in fertility, the greater the relative rise in worker rates. There is clearly no relationship within the foreign-born group. There may be one for native whites. But when all are considered together a moderately high correlation appears. This correlation reflects, it is believed, a tendency for gross differences in fertility levels to diminish as a national pattern developed. Greater than proportionate decreases in the initially high rates for Negroes, smaller ones for whites, brought the two sets of rates together. Over the 1830–1940 period differentials between native, foreign-born, and nonwhite worker rates and fertility rates diminished. The decline in fertility rates, while undoubtedly facilitating a rise in worker rates, hardly seems to have produced any such rise. For major portions of the female population, worker rates actually fell; for others the change bore no reasonable proportion to the change in fertility rates.

[65] The inverse relationship between income of husband and worker rate for wife is discussed at length in Clarence D. Long, *The Labor Force under Changing Income and Employment*, published for the National Bureau of Economic Research by Princeton University Press, 1958. Cf. also Paul Douglas, *The Theory of Wages*, 1934, ch. xi and Nedra Belloc, "Labor-Force Participation and Employment Opportunities for Women" in *Journal of the American Statistical Association*, September, 1950, especially p. 405.

[66] Rates for the under 35 group are ignored. The "number of children ever born" is an inadequate measure of completed fertility for the younger age groups, while the number of children under 5 is a shorter term measure, grossly affected by short term variations in economic activity and other elements.

Our experience since 1940 is a striking supplement. I have referred above to "the" American standard of living. But that standard refused to stay still—and the income goal for all Americans rose at an accelerated pace as prices jumped and a multitude of new jobs opened. Not only were opportunities for women's work increasing at a great rate—but they were taken up. Thus, the proportion of women with young children who worked nearly tripled from 1940 to 1957 (Table 6).[67] Not only did

TABLE 6

Working Wives, 1940–1957
(per cent in labor force by age and by presence of young children)

	Under 65	18–24	25–34	35–44	45–64
U.S. WHITE AND NONWHITE					
Without children under 6					
1940	16.5	26.7	26.9	17.0	9.0
1950	27.5	45.5	39.8	31.5	18.4
1954	34.4	—	—	—	—
1957	38.2	—	—	—	—
With children under 6					
1940	6.1	5.8	6.5	5.6	5.5
1950	10.6	9.9	10.5	11.2	11.7
1954	14.9	—	—	—	—
1957	17.0	—	—	—	—
U.S. NONWHITE					
Without children under 6					
1940	31.5	32.6	38.9	32.7	22.7
1950	37.8	36.5	46.3	43.6	27.9
1954	46.4	—	—	—	—
1957	50.7	—	—	—	—
With children under 6					
1940	14.9	13.6	14.9	16.4	16.5
1950	17.3	12.8	18.2	20.6	20.0
1954	21.8	—	—	—	—
1957	24.0	—	—	—	—

[67] 1940: computed from 1940 Census, *Employment and Family Characteristics of Women*, Tables 4 and 5. The overall total relates to women 18–64. Durand, *op. cit.*, p. 207, gives adjustment factors to make the 1940 Census data comparable with the CPS data for 1945ff. These suggest that limited increases in the estimates shown above are necessary for strict comparability with more recent data.

1950: 1950 Census, *General Characteristics of Families*, Tables 12 and 13.

1954: Current Population Reports, no. 62, *Marital and Family Characteristics of the Labor Force in the United States, April 1955 and 1954*, Table 3, p. 50. This source reports data for married women of all ages. These were adjusted to apply to those under 65 by the difference between these groups that can be computed from the 1950 data. For those with children under 6, no adjustment is required. For those without children under 6, worker rates increase when the responsibilities of child rearing declined; they rose even when such responsibilities increased.

The rise in second and third births would certainly have tended to keep women with children under 6 from working. The rise in first births would have tended to reduce the over-all worker rate for newly-married women. The sharp decline in domestic servants since the war, also the shift in population to the suburbs (to houses from apartments), would also have exercised a restraining effect.

What appear to be the major factors that offset these forces and made worker rates for females rise more, and faster, than ever before in our history? A minor contribution was certainly made by the move from farm to city.[68] Another small factor was the change in composition of the female population.[69] But the major factors lie elsewhere—two on the supply side, and two on the demand.

(1) On the supply side the major incentive is to be found in the dazzling array of material goods now incorporated into the American standard of living. Some may define this as the means to an easier life; others, as the desire to keep up with the Joneses (as they keep up with the Smiths); still others, as the crass materialism characteristic of the postwar Byzantine periods in world history. But however such interpretations are decided, the result is the same. In recent years in the United States, the consumer in "consumer durables" has proved to be the working wife.[70]

A recent study, made for quite different purposes, throws a brilliant light on one side of this problem. If we look at Table 7, we see a clear tendency at each income level for a greater proportion of families with working wives to have debts than families with only the husband working.[71] (Rosett's study, using 1952 Survey of Consumer Finances

---

the 1950 data showed 25.3 for all ages and 27.5 for under 64, and a 36.1 to 37.8 contrast for nonwhites. These absolute differences in 1950 were assumed to apply in 1954 as well.

1957: Current Population Reports, P-50, no. 81, *Family Characteristics of Working Wives*, March, 1957, Table 9, and unpublished Census data. The reported all-age data were adjusted to under-65 levels by the same procedure as used above for 1954.

[68] For the 1920–1940 period this contribution was minor for the over-30 year group, significant for the 20–24 group. Cf. John Durand, "Married Women in the Labor Force," *American Journal of Sociology*, November, 1946, pp. 220–221.

[69] But not much. A trivial increase in the proportion of nonwhite females to total 14 and over works in the opposite direction.

[70] It does not, of course, have to follow that these causes and consequences were without parallel in other countries. The rising worker rate for women, especially married women, in other countries is discussed in UN, *Determinants*, p. 200f. and in Long's forthcoming monograph.

[71] These data are based on a supplement to the Census Bureau's Current Population Survey for August, 1956, and appear in Federal Reserve Board, *Consumer Instalment Credit*, Part I, Vol. 2, *Growth and Import*, 1957, Table D-1.

TABLE 7

| Family Income | Families with Debts as a Per Cent of all Families (1956) | | Excess |
	With Husband Only Working (1)	With Wife and Husband Working (2)	(2) − (1) (3)
Under $3,000	57	65	+8
$3,000–$4,999	71	72	+1
$5,000–$7,499	74	78	+4
$7,500 and over	67	74	+7

data, suggests the same conclusion.[72]) The excess for the families with working wives would be still greater if we classified the families by their husband's income alone—as is essentially done in the above table for the other families. (For families with working wives almost by definition have come from lower levels of income if classified by husbands' income.)

In summary, families with working wives not merely have higher incomes but more commonly acquire debts, despite, or because of, the wife's work. It is doubtful, on the latter alternative, whether it is possible to know, or particularly useful to assert, the priority of the chicken or the egg. Work by the wife *and* the incurring of debts are interrelated means to the prompt acquisition of consumer durables.

We can proceed a bit further by examining the type of debt involved (Table 8).[73] A priori one might not expect any significant differences by type of debt, but the figures do in fact show sharp contrasts. Families with working wives, far more than those without, go into debt for cars and household equipment—at every income level. This excess does not appear where mortgage debt and car debt are both present. And where *only* mortgages are involved, or mortgages and household equipment debt, the pattern is actually reversed.[74] A steadily widening gap appears in Table 8 between families with working wives and those without, as one proceeds across from the figures for auto purchase, through auto purchase in combination with houses, to data for house purchase.

Today's wife will enter the labor force to work for a car, washing machine, a refrigerator. Such durable items can be delivered at once,

[72] *Econometrica*, March, 1958, p. 326.

[73] Federal Reserve Board, *Consumer Instalment Credit . . .*, p. 237f. It has been assumed that the husband worked both in those families reporting one paid worker and in those where 2 or more workers were reported, one being the wife.

[74] In explaining this contrast one must make due allowance for the role of FHA regulations, and the stipulations of the capital market, as not counting the income of the wife as a sufficiently solid source for buttressing mortgage loans. This element, however, does not preclude the wife's working.

TABLE 8

Debtors by Type of Debt, August, 1956

| Income | All Debtors | Debtors for | | |
		Cars Alone or With Household Equipment	Mortgages and Cars	Mortgages Alone or With Household Equipment
Under $3,000				
Husband working	100	20	2	26
Wife and husband working	100	23	2	19
		+3	0	−7
$3,000–$4,999				
Husband working	100	21	7	39
Wife and husband working	100	24	7	34
		+3	0	−5
$5,000–$7,499				
Husband working	100	14	12	49
Wife and husband working	100	23	10	36
		+9	−2	−13
$7,500 and over				
Husband working	100	11	15	58
Wife and husband working	100	18	12	47
		+7	−3	−11

and title acquired within a finite time. They require only temporary labor force participation by the wife.[75] The purchase of a home, on the other hand, is a long-range affair. Its final acquisition is necessarily obscured in the indefinite future.[76] A further influence that one might assume to be at work in producing this result is the tendency for house acquisition to operate as a surrogate variable for the presence of young

[75] Cf. Federal Reserve Board, *Consumer Instalment Credit* . . ., p. 186, in which Murray Wernick states ". . . both the increased seeking of employment by married women and the incurrence of debt may be influenced by the desire for the ownership of additional durable goods." The "very high incidence of credit use and indebtedness among families in which the head is employed and the wife is unemployed and looking for work" suggest that "financial pressures are a factor influencing the wife to enter and remain in the labor market, when employment opportunities and incomes are at high levels."

[76] Morgan's comment on spurious correlation is not a contradiction of this point but an apexegesis. He does not disagree with the point that at every family income level today's wife is more likely to enter the labor force to help purchase a car or other durable than to help buy a house. He is asking whether this is equally true within given age and parity groups. The implication that young married women without children must per se prefer to buy durables rather than houses does not follow, of course, and need not. But the point is an interesting one and it is to be hoped that the Survey of Consumer Finances will enlighten us on this point in future surveys. Since income advances with age, Table 7 gives us a crude indication that at higher ages there is no growing inclination to work for mortgage payments rather than cars and other durables. If anything, the reverse may be indicated by the table.

children. However, the over-all relationship between age and mortgage debt is not negative, as it should be to make this factor real and substantial.[77]

(2) A second factor in getting more women to enter the work force has been the reduction in family income receipt from once customary sources, such as, as already noted, the decline in working children, and such as the decline in family income from boarders and lodgers—for urban families a source once second only to earnings by the family head (see Table 9).[78]

TABLE 9

Proportion of Urban Families

| | With Lodgers | | | With Income |
Year	Native White	Foreign Born	All Families	from Lodgers or Boarders
1901	—	—	—	23
1910	10.0	32.9	(17.6)	—
1930	9.0	10.2	9.8	—
1941	—	—	—	12
1950	—	—	(5.0)	8

On the demand side, where the increasing opportunities for work by women appear, two factors may be briefly mentioned. One is particularly associated with the rise in female worker rates that followed after the

[77] The proportion with mortgage debt rises steadily with age. The proportion with mortgage debt alone or in combination with household equipment or miscellaneous debt also shows a tendency to rise with age. FRB, *Consumer Instalment Credit . . .*, p. 236. Most important, for present purposes, no decline with age is apparent for mortgage debt.

[78] 1901: *Eighteenth Annual Report of the Commissioner of Labor, 1903*, 1904, p. 363.

1910: U.S. Immigration Commission, *Reports*, Part 23, I, 1911, Vol. 19, p. 128. The Commission only reports rates for native white and for foreign-born white. The Negro rate was assumed as equal to the foreign born. All three were then weighted together by the number of married males in each nativity-color group. 1910 Census, *Population*, p. 522. The number of married males was equal to 90% of the number of families, *ibid.*, p. 1285.

1930: Census of Population, *Families*, Vol. VI, p. 24.

1941: Bureau of Labor Statistics Bulletin no. 822, *Family Spending and Saving in Wartime*, 1945, pp. 33, 95.

1950: Census of Housing, *Nonfarm Housing Characteristics*, Vol. II, Part I, Table A-10. Of 35.9 million occupied dwelling units 2.2. had nonrelatives living in the household. This ratio of about 6% was reduced to 5% to allow for servants living in.

1950: BLS Wharton School of Finance and Commerce, *Study of Consumer Expenditures Incomes and Savings*, 1956, XI, p. 4.

Data in the 1901 report on the proportion with lodgers—running to about 2% for natives and for foreign born—were ignored as unreasonably low. They must reflect a confusion in reporting between lodgers and boarders and/or the special characteristics of the sample. It is suggestive that one-third of the reporting families paid union dues (including one-half of the sample families from Pennsylvania). *ibid.*, p. 501.

closing off of immigration—namely, the significant gap between prevailing male and female wages. A second, of slight importance during World War I and of major importance during World War II, was the removal of a large share of the experienced labor force at the time that increased demands for production were being made. The combination brought dramatic changes in the tables of organization traditional in many industries, and increased the opportunities for female employment.

In sum, the very substantial 1830–1865, and 1890–1950 rises in the proportion of women in the labor force may be attributed to a variety of supply and demand factors, few of which are closely associated with population changes. Fertility declines helped make it possible for an increasing number of women to work. But they were hardly essential: in some periods the trend was actually opposite to what an a priori analysis might have indicated. And conversely, while the increasing participation of women in the labor force may have limited birth rates over "what they would have been otherwise," the rapid rise in birth rates since 1940 suggests that it did not produce any absolute decline in rates.

Convergence

The outstanding development in the United States labor force–population relationships over the past century has been that of convergence: differentials between social groups, nativity groups, and regions have tended to diminish and (in some instances) to dwindle away. Fertility rates have risen for certain groups while for others they have plummeted. Worker rates have stayed rigidly fixed at levels established many years ago for some categories, and have shifted rapidly for others. The one uniformity at work throughout these phenomena is that the spread between the rates for the different social, age, and nativity groups tended to diminish. This tendency is related to the economist's equalizing of marginal factor returns, to the anthropologist's acculturation, to the statistician's regression to the mean. But it is not quite the same as any of these. The process is dynamic, the goal is perpetually in motion, and noneconomic factors, as well as economic advantage, are being maximized. Let us consider some instances of such convergence.

In Table 2 we can review the trend of United States worker rates for females over a century and a quarter.[79] Because of obvious

[79] 1820: data estimated as outlined in text above. 1890, 1940: Durand, *op. cit.*, pp. 49, 216–217. These Census data have been made as comparable as possible by Durand. The data used relate to native whites and to nonwhites, to single and to married women. 1940, 1950: 1950 Census, *Employment and Personal Characteristics*, Table 11. The data relate to all whites, to nonwhites; to married women, spouse present, and to single

incomparabilities in the data over time,[80] the table is set up to permit rough generalizations with respect to change over overlapping periods.

What, then, do these data indicate on the convergence of worker rates? First, white-nonwhite comparisons. The nonwhite rate was 16 times as great as the white rate when the Napoleonic wars closed. It was only 3 times as great by 1890; not quite twice as much in 1940; and only half again as great by 1957. The nonwhite rate for married women in 1890 was 10 times that for whites. By 1940 it was less than 3 times as great. Over the same period the nonwhite rate for single women fell from a rate nearly double the white rate to one virtually the same.

Since 1940, white and nonwhite married women's rates have further converged, but rates for nonwhite single women have decreased, producing divergence rather than convergence for this group.[81]

Second, we can look at the contrast between the rates for single and married women. The proportion of unmarried white women working, in ratio to married white women, in 1890 was 14 times as great; in 1940 was less than 4 times as great; in 1957 was less than twice as great. For nonwhite women the ending of slavery increased the spread between rates for single and married females: married women no longer worked

women. 1951, 1957: Census Bureau, Current Population Reports, Series P-50, no. 39, *Marital and Family Characteristics of the Labor Force: April 1951*, Table 2 and P-50, no. 76, *Marital Status of Workers: March 1957*, Table 3.

[80] (1) The crudeness of the 1820 data has been emphasized above. (2) We may note that the 1890 and 1940 Durand data represent the most informed and careful attempt to provide comparability between these Census reports. (3) The 1940 and 1950 data marked "Census" are published as comparable by the Census. (4) Two major empirical differences separate the two sets of 1940 figures: the Durand data used here relate to native whites, and to all married women, while the Census data relate to all whites, and to married women–spouse present. (The omission of spouse–absent in the latter group accounts for the major incomparability in the table—for nonwhites.) Unfortunately progress has made it impossible to show separate figures for 1950ff. for native whites, leading to some incomparability with the earlier data. Data in Table 5 of *Employment and Personal Characteristics*, however, show over-all worker rates for foreign born and native whites by age. The two are within 10% of each other and, given the small weight for foreign born by 1950, the incomparability is probably not significant. (5) The Current Population Survey appears to secure more comprehensive reporting than does the census, and this factor accounts for most of the 1950–1951 difference, rather than the impact of Korea. Thus for March, 1950, the Census reports a worker rate of 31.8 for married nonwhites, while the Current Population Survey, P-50, no. 29, Table 6, reports 37.0. For whites the comparison was 20.7 and 22.8.

[81] The precision of Consumer Population Survey worker rates for the small group of nonwhite single females is not great but the downward drift seems unquestionable for the years 1951–1957: 41.3; 40.8; 38.6; 43.4; 35.9; 35.6; 37.9. One cause of this drift (the 1953–1954 rise probably reflects the energetic control and enumerative efforts associated with the new sample introduced in that period) was the rise in school attendance rates for nonwhite females, these rates rising toward the levels for whites. School enrollment of nonwhite females 14–17 rose from 71.9 to 81.1% between 1950 and 1956. Cf. Census Bureau, Current Population Reports, P-20, nos. 34 and 74.

in as great numbers as single women. Beginning from the first date of a free market shown in Table 2, however, the differential declined sharply from 1890 to 1940, and continued to decline thereafter.

For the native-white versus foreign-born white comparison, the initial contrast was far smaller and the convergence far less. For the foreign group as a whole, rates were almost half again above the native in 1890, were about a quarter below the native by 1940.[82] This narrowing occurred primarily in the younger age groups. Durand suggests that selective immigration was a significant factor at work in the 14–19 age groups.[83] In any event, the spread for each of the age groups under 44 diminished markedly, whereas those for the older ages changed little or increased somewhat. This contrast suggests the greater flexibility, the prompter adoption of American standards by the younger groups, and the contrasting reluctance to change on the part of those whose work patterns tended to be formed abroad or in large foreign-born enclaves in this country.

Third, we can note that white male-female worker rate differentials narrowed considerably: over-all male rates changed very little, while female rates rose greatly. For nonwhites, however, no narrowing since 1865 can be demonstrated.

The trend in fertility rates was also toward a reduction in differentials.[84] We are fortunate here in having two different time dimensions, unlike the worker rate area where our measure only describes activity in a limited period. And in these data it is clear that the phenomenon of convergence also occurs, not as anything inevitable or mystical, but simply as an aspect of human adjustment in a free social and economic market.

Table 1 indicates that the differential between white and nonwhite women born in the most recent period was markedly under that for those born in earlier years. By referring to Table 3, we can go on to see the impact of the free market. For 1850 and 1860 the white and nonwhite fertility rates (measured in terms of number of children under 5 at the Census date) were much the same.[85] With the end of slavery a dramatic change occurred: fertility rates among nonwhites ranged from 20 to 30

[82] These and related data are summarized conveniently in Durand, *op. cit.*, p. 49 and pp. 216f.

[83] *ibid.*, p. 49.

[84] The subject is discussed in fuller detail in Charles Westoff, "Differential Fertility in the United States: 1900 to 1952," *American Sociological Review*, October, 1954.

[85] We assume that the Census need not be corrected any more for the omission of slaves than of whites. The wisdom of this assumption, as noted earlier, in preference to the procedure of using the higher rate indicated by the 1915 1930 study, is that masters would rarely be ignorant of the total count of slaves, and, in addition, would be seriously interested in a full count for purposes of Congressional representation.

per cent above those for whites in the next two or three Censuses.[86] The rates then began to converge toward virtual identity in 1920. The subsequent impact of the depression is well known and here we can contrast (a) the short-term impact that made birth rates for the two groups diverge markedly, from (b) the longer-run tendency (indicated by data on completed fertility) toward a reduced differential.

Within the white group differentials between regions and states diminished. A single indication is given by the relationship between two regional averages. The East South Central average for children under 5 per 1,000 women was one of the highest in the nation in 1800, and was still one of the highest in 1950. New England ranked among the lowest at each date. But while the former rate was about 60 per cent above that for New England in 1800 it ran only about 20 per cent more in 1950. More generally, one may note that a very clear inverse correlation exists between the state-by-state averages of fertility rates in 1870–1910 and the declines from that level to the 1910–1940 levels.[87]

The causes of such convergence were primarily social and economic. In the social area we are dealing with the steady endeavor of marginal groups to adopt the dominant American standards—migrants forsaking their work patterns[88] as well as food intake patterns, changing the desired dimensions of their family and of their clothes. In the economic area, the endeavors of the employer to secure low-cost labor, and of the migrant and woman worker to secure higher incomes, joined to equalize marginal returns by severely reducing wage differentials, affecting family incomes and eventually family patterns of labor force participation.

Some Conclusions

This brief review of United States labor force trends in past decades has begun from certain premises and has suggested certain inferences. Labor-force change has been sometimes a slow, sometimes a startling, process. In other countries and other climes there may well have been a quasi-automatic link between population change and labor-force change. But changing economic and social goals have precluded any such simple

[86] Because of the undercount in 1870, the testimony of this Census cannot be firmly accepted. Hence we must look to the next two Censuses for confirmation.

[87] State fertility data for the two dates appear in an unpublished thesis by Bernard Okun. If one simply charts his data (a) for the initial period against (b) the changes from one period to the next, a marked inverse correlation appears. It is to be hoped that these or similar data will become available as part of the major study on population redistribution and economic growth being made under the direction of Simon Kuznets and Dorothy Thomas.

[88] A fascinating discussion of the occupational ladder has recently been completed by E. P. Hutchinson in *Immigrants and Their Children*, Wiley, 1957.

linkage in the United States. These changing goals have evidenced themselves in migration, fertility, and mortality shifts that affected both our population and our labor force.

The expansive mood of the American economy has nowhere been better established than by the process of migration, with both human and material resources shifting toward an ever-changing optimum. For many decades the flood of migrants from Europe and Africa made a substantial contribution to American population growth. Much of this migration (being directed toward building our canals, settling the prairies, stocking the plantations) was very selective, tending to bring more males than females, more adults than children. The increments to the labor force were greater, relatively, than those to the population totals. When railroads became a major factor, when canal construction tapered off, and when slavery ended, migration began to include a growing proportion of entire families rather than merely single males.

A second factor at work was the long-term downward trend in birth rates throughout most of the nineteenth century. This decline, of course, accompanied great absolute gains in population and the labor force. (We need not concern ourselves here with Francis Walker's speculations as to how great the growth might otherwise have been, the possible substitution of immigrants for native births, and so on.) The decreases in the United States child labor force began about 1900, after a century of declining birth rates, and are not particularly to be associated with those declines.

A third major factor in population growth is that of mortality.[89] But while short-term peaks in malaria sharply affected the supply of labor in, say, the James River and Kanawha canal, or typhoid that in New Orleans, major changes in mortality had little historical impact on the labor force. The unrepresentative Massachusetts data suggest that little advance was made in the nineteenth century.[90] Mortality reductions have, of course, become a significant force for population growth in the twentieth century.[91] But they exerted little short-term impact on the labor force: the man who enters the labor force today will provide only about 10 per cent more years of work to the economy over his lifetime than did his

[89] Special emphasis on mortality in its direct impact and also in the survival to reproductive ages is given in K. F. Helleiner, "The Vital Revolution Reconsidered," *Canadian Journal of Economics and Political Science*, February, 1957.

[90] The complete expectation of life for white males aged 20 and over in Massachusetts changed hardly at all from 1850 to 1900. *Historical Statistics of the United States*, p. 45.

[91] Cf. the useful review in Mortimer Spiegelman, "Mortality Trends and Prospects and Their Implications," *Annals of the American Academy of Political and Social Science*, March, 1958.

predecessor back in 1900.[92] (The long-run impact on the next generation's supply of labor—and of population—is a further, and deeper, problem for study.)

Beyond these forces affecting both population and labor force change are those that have substantially changed the labor force while bringing only trivial changes in population. First, without question, is the ending of slavery—and with it the sharpest fall in worker rates over the entire record of United States experience. Thus, the over-all participation in the labor force today is well under that prevailing in slave times.[93] Second, is the decline since 1900 in worker rates for children. New value systems—or more accurately, the wider adoption of older ones—set great store by children not working until they had reached 8 years of age, then 10, then 16. Third, is the long-term rise in worker rates for women, with especially pronounced gains after World Wars I and II. The contribution of reductions in fertility to this rise has frequently been overstated—particularly given the increase since 1945 in both the number of women with babies and with jobs. On the supply side, the rise in female worker rates reflects the endless search for a higher standard of material well-being, particularly that euphoric state which is felt to attach to the possession of consumer durables. Given the concurrent shortening of the male work week, and the reduction in income from boarders and lodgers, rising female worker rates were the obvious means toward higher incomes. On the demand side, women's work may be considered as a *pis aller* for the traditional sources of cheap labor—slaves, immigrants, children—as these became increasingly exiguous.

Throughout these long years of population and labor force change, differentials in fertility rates, as in worker rates, among the several groups in the population were reduced. Convergence toward a standard American pattern of fertility and labor force participation tended to follow. That pattern was not a fixed, irretrievable one, but in the process of change and formation as the economy and the social order continuously developed. The process of convergence helps explain the contradiction between what static cross-section data on worker rates and fertility differentials tell us and what the time series on American economic development report. Static data indicate that upper income families

[92] Stuart Garfinkle, "Changes in Working Life of Men, 1900 to 2000," *Monthly Labor Review*, March, 1955, estimates a work-life expectation rising from 39.4 to 43.2.

[93] This is contradictory to the estimate in the major pioneering report by P. K. Whelpton, "Occupational Groups in the United States, 1820–1920," *Journal of the American Statistical Association*, September, 1926, p. 342. The basic source of the difference probably lies in Whelpton's use of 1870 and 1880 ratios of domestic servants to population. The present procedure would allow for a higher proportion under slavery.

have fewer children than lower, also fewer working women. The time series report, however, that the proportion of white women who work has gained since 1830, the proportion of nonwhite women since the end of slavery, and that the largest gains in fertility have occurred during the period of marked income rise since 1940. The only uniformity that more or less reconciles these contradictory statements is the long-term tendency toward a reduction of fertility and worker rate differentials among the various social and economic groups.

Appendix A

WHITE FEMALE LABOR FORCE: 1830–1950

For 1830, at nearly the beginning of the factory system on any significant scale, we can develop a total as the sum of four component estimates.

1. *Factory workers: 60,000.* Contemporary sources give a reasonably complete enumeration of all females employed in cotton and woolen mills, in the manufacture of palm leaf hats, and in the manufacture of shoes, as well as those in industries with few female employees.[94]

2. *Free servants: 80,000.* The largest single group of white female workers—servants—was estimated from a regression against the number of white families, the relationship between the two series for 1850–1930 being a very close one. A description of procedures for estimating the number of white families prior to 1850, and of the various sources used, appears in Appendix B.

3. *Farm workers: 0.* As noted above, examination of the 1820 schedules now in the National Archives showed very few women reported as gainfully occupied, and virtually none in the rural areas where, if anywhere, the farm workers would have been found. The 1870 Census (*Population,* Table xxvii), the first showing data separately for females, showed no female farm laborers except in the Southern states, that group clearly being the nonwhite category. For example Indiana, with 181,491 male farm operators in 1870 reported only 22 female farm laborers. And in none of the Northern and Western states were any but a handful of farmers' wives and female family members included. Even the excellent

---

[94] U.S. Congress, Serial Set 222,223, *Statistics of Manufactures,* 1033. These data were adjusted in some instances to broader totals from the immediately preceding survey by the New York Convention of Friends of the Manufacturing Interest, *Niles Register,* XLII, March–August, 1832, Addendum, p. 7. With 39,000 in cotton and hand weaving, 2,900 in wool, 3,300 in palm leaf hat manufactures, and 4,800 in shoe manufacture, it was assumed that there were no more than 10,000 in other manufacturing, other branches being infrequent employers of women.

1900 Census (*Population*, 1, Table XXXIII) shows the same pattern. Therefore for comparability with later Censuses we include no female family farm workers in 1830. Those who desire to include this group will have to make estimates both for 1830 and for years in which the published Census figures in principle include, but in practice exclude, this group.

4. *Other employees: 25,000.* Analysis of the occupational distribution of females beginning with 1880—when we first have separate Census data for females—suggests that a half-century earlier the significant occupations not covered in (1) and (2) above would have been primarily milliners and seamstresses. An arbitrary 25,000 was added for these latter occupations on the basis of the trend for all mantua makers, seamstresses, milliners, and tailors from 1850 to 1880.

The ratio of these figures to the number of white females 10 and over[95] is 8 per cent.[96]

For 1890 we have the Census reports, while for 1950 we must adjust the Census figures to cover the 10-and-over group.[97]

Year	Per cent of white females in the labor force (Aged 10 and over)
1830	8
1890	13.3
1950	26.0

NONWHITE FEMALE LABOR FORCE: 1830–1950

Our basic source of data is the Census. The major problem in using its reports, however, is that no Census counted among the gainfully occupied Negro slaves the substantial number that worked as domestic

---

[95] 1850 Census, *Compendium*, p. 5. A small number of nonwhite employees are included in the above estimate. The error will be small since the only group where their numbers would be substantial—servants—was estimated so as to exclude nonwhites.

[96] These and other data refer to labor force participation as currently measured. We know that housewives' work was important in the nineteenth-century economy, and it is today—though omitted in our measures. The limitation is analogous to the limitation of national income measures—and just as the income falls, in Pigou's example, when a gentleman marries his housekeeper, so does the labor force. Those who wish to eschew this paradox, and market measures, can simply take the able-bodied population, say 10 and over, as a measure of labor input. But they must do so consistently, rejecting our current measures by the same criteria that they would adjust historical estimates.

[97] 1890: 1900 Census, *Occupations*, p. lxxxiii.

1950: A rate of 28.1 per cent for those 14 and over appears in 1950 Census, *Population*, Vol. II, Part I, Table 120. This was reduced on the basis of labor force survey data. Current Population Reports, Series P-50, nos. 31 and 83, enable us to compute a ratio of 33.9 for females 14 and over in August, 1950, and 31.8 for females 10 and over. The ratio of one rate to the other was applied to the reported Census total for 14 and over.

servants. Of the two Censuses—1820 and 1840—that purported to enumerate the number of gainfully occupied slaves, that for 1840 has various internal indications of inadequacy. (For example, examination of the unpublished schedules shows sizable counties with no occupational entries.)

However, an indicative estimate for 1820 can be outlined. Taking the Census for that year, let us look to a dozen counties in which the failure to count those occupied as domestics must be a minimal problem for our purposes. In these counties, a very large number of slaves were recorded in proportion to the number of adult white males. Consequently, it can be assumed that virtually all gainfully occupied slaves in these counties were in agriculture and few in domestic service.[98]

Thus, if we deduct from the total number of persons reported with an occupation in Jones County, Georgia in 1820 the estimated number of whites and free colored, the residual is 4,218. But the total number of slaves aged 14 and over (males plus females) in the county was only 3,600. It is clear, therefore, that nearly all female slaves plus many (if not all) slave children aged 8–14 were also counted among the gainfully occupied.[99] Similar net balances were computed for the other selected counties, all indicating this type of margin.

Was an unusually high proportion of slaves gainfully occupied in these counties? Possibly so. Yet there is no reason to believe that eleemosynary traditions were stronger in other counties where slaves were present. We will, therefore, take it that the proportion of female Negroes in the labor force in these counties did not exceed that prevailing in other counties. We can reduce this 100 per cent ratio for females 10+ to allow for illness and absence for other reasons, using as an empirical guide the ratios for white males in 1850. We then arrive at something like a 95 per cent

[98] The following counties were used: Jones and Jasper, Georgia; Monroe, Alabama; Feliciana, Point Coupee, St. Charles, Louisiana; Davidson, Tennessee; St. James-Colleton, St. Thomas, Georgetown, Beaufort, South Carolina; Wilkinson, Mississippi. The number of white males aged 10 and over gainfully occupied in each county was estimated from the proportion reported for the state in the 1850 Census—that ratio changing little even in later years. This number was then deducted from the total (male and female, free and slave) reported by the 1820 Census as having any occupation. Since examination of the individual schedules now in the U.S. Archives indicated no white women with occupations reported—and the merest handful of free colored—the balance must have been Negro slaves.

[99] Specific examples may make the point clearer, Micajah Pickett, Sr., of Franklin County Mississippi, reported 27 in agriculture in 1820—a figure larger than that obtained by counting all whites in his family aged 10 and over plus all slaves 14 and over. James Jackson, of Green County Georgia, reported, in 1840, 144 in agriculture, but had only 2 whites in his family and 131 slaves aged 10 and over. Elizabeth McLendon, of Harris County Georgia, reported 14 in agriculture in 1840, but had only 1 white person in the family, 10 slaves aged 10 and over and 4 under 10 years of age.

worker rate for Negro female slaves in the prime age group. A compatible rate for all aged 10 and over would be 90 per cent.[100] The over-all rate, furthermore, has been assumed to apply equally well both to married and unmarried female slaves. The only reasons for married slaves to have been absent from domestic or field work more than unmarried ones are associated with childbirth. But since Negro children were both marketable and marketed under slavery, parturition did not remove Negro females from the labor force engaged in the production of what contemporary markets treated as capital or consumer goods.

Appendix B

SERVANTS

1870–1930: Edwards, *op. cit.*, Tables 8, 10.

1860: 1860 Census, *Population of the United States in 1860* (1864) pp. 663, 667, 675. The totals reported for domestics, laundresses, and servants were added to give an all-servants figure.

TABLE B-1

Families and Servants, 1790–1950

Year	Number of White Families (000)	Number of Servants (000)
1790	558	—
1800	(755)	—
1810	(1,025)	—
1820	(1,380)	(40)
1830	(1,865)	(80)
1840	(2,520)	(200)
1850	3,598	(350)
1860	5,211	(600)
1870	(6,650)	1,033
1880	(8,680)	1,153
1890	11,255	1,544
1900	14,064	1,710
1910	18,002	2,039
1920	21,826	1,801
1930	26,983	2,776
1940	31,680	3,111
1950	38,429	2,848

[100] Contemporary definitions count in the labor force all persons, apart from unpaid family workers, if they work 1 hour or more during the week. Under slavery even elderly and infirm Negroes made sufficient small contributions of labor to reach this standard.

1850: The Seventh Census of the United States, 1850 (1854) p. lxxvi. The 1850 figures relates to free males aged 15 and over. An estimate for all servants was made as follows. The number of female servants in 1860 was computed as 90.6 per cent of the total, and in 1850, at 93.9 per cent. (These percentages were estimated on the assumption of a 3.3 per cent change from one decade to the next—the same as that occurring between 1870 and 1880.) These figures may be contrasted with percentage of 87 per cent for 1870 and roughly 84 per cent for 1880, 1890, and 1900.

1830: Estimated from the relationship for 1850–1930 between number of white families and servants with the regression line assumed to have a zero origin. Particular weight was given to the 1850–1860 trend in estimating 1830, assuming that the level following 1870 was generally higher than in prior years as nonwhite females, freed from slavery, entered the free labor market.

WHITE FAMILIES

1890–1950: 1950 Census, *General Characteristics of Families*, p. 2A-8.

1790, 1850, 1860: The number of free families appears in *Historical Statistics of the United States*, p. 29, and minor adjustment was made for free Negroes.

1870–1880: The change in the average size of family appears in 1900 Census, *Supplemental Analysis*, p. 382, and was used to extrapolate the 1890 average size of white families.

1800–1840: The white population was divided by the estimated size of family. The population figures were from *Historical Statistics*, p. 25. The average size of family was estimated from the regression of the 1790, 1850–1900 figures for (*a*) average size of family, on (*b*) number of children under 5 per 1,000 females in white families. Data on children from Taeuber and Taeuber, *op. cit.*, p. 251.

COMMENT

JAMES N. MORGAN, Survey Research Center, University of Michigan

I shall not presume to criticize Lebergott's methods of measuring labor force participation, nor his measures of fertility, but merely express my awe that he was able to make estimates for early periods.

I have mostly a few small queries, and one or two general interpretative comments:

Is the statement that the factories in Waltham, Lowell, etc. in 1820 offered incomes larger than the imputed value of work on the family farm true for both wives and daughters, and what is the evidence as to the relative rewards from factory and home work?

A table is given on the proportion of white females aged 10 and over who were in the labor force in 1830, 1890, and 1950. What about the proportion of white males who were in the labor force at these dates? With growing use of factory production, presumably a growing proportion of men, too, became employed rather than self-employed.

As to the comparison between Census and *Surveys of Consumer Finances* on labor force participation of married women, I have to report that the situation is worse than Lebergott implies. The table below, which I was able to prepare and send to Lebergott only after his paper was written, indicates that the differences are probably not due to understating of incidental employment only in the *Survey of Consumer Finances*. For women

TABLE 1

Amount of Labor Force Participation of Married Women[1] Who Work,
Census vs. SCF[2]

Circumstances of Employment	Children Under 18		Children, Some or All Under 6		Children, All 6–17 Years[3]	
	Census 1956	SCFS 1957	Census 1956	SCF 1957	Census 1956	SCF 1957
Full Time						
50–52 weeks	43.5	40.0	16.3	16.6	30.5	28.3
40–49 weeks	10.3	13.9	6.1	6.7	7.8	7.8
27–39 weeks	7.9	12.3	9.7	12.0	8.0	13.1
1–26 weeks	12.5	14.0	32.6	37.6	17.0	16.5
Part Time						
27 weeks or more	17.3	11.5	16.5	3.8	22.0	17.0
1–26 weeks	8.5	8.2	18.9	23.4	14.8	17.3
	100.0	99.8	100.1	100.1	100.1	100.0
Number of cases where wife works	—	313	—	215	—	203
Per cent of families where wife works	45.4	—	30.7	—	47.5	—
Per cent of S.U.'s where wife works	—	39.3	—	30.3	—	34.5
Number of cases where there is a wife present	—	807	—	704	—	655

[1] SCF: Head married, two adults present (at least) ⎫ In practice, identical in almost
    Census: Married, both husband and wife present ⎭ all cases
but: SCF is spending units, Census is *families*, i.e., only wives of family heads, not of related secondary units.

[2] Survey Research Center Economic Behavior Program.

[3] SCF includes a few units here with children under 6 where Head is 45 or older.

who report they worked during the last year, the two sources give quite similar distributions on the proportion of the year worked, and full or part time.

My table compared data from two different years, but Lebergott also compared 1955 data from both sources and found a similar discrepancy. There are minor differences, including the fact that the SCF is on a spending unit basis and the Current Population Reports on a family basis, but these differences would not explain the apparent discrepancy in results.

It is useful, however, to know the actual questions used, since labor force participation has proven notoriously sensitive to the questions used, and even to the training of the interviewers.[1] The *Survey of Consumer Finances* has elaborated the question sequences in recent years, and the reason for using the 1958 Survey in the table was that it used more questions.

The sequence, coming after a whole set of questions on sources of income, and income of the head, runs:

Did your wife have any income during the year?
If yes: Was it from wages, salary, a business or what?
How much did she receive? (taken down for each source).

If wife had wages or salary: How many weeks did she work either full time or part time?
When she was working did she usually work full time or part time or what?

The Current Population Survey questions, asked for all persons 14 years old or over, are:

In 1957, how many weeks did . . . work either full time or part time (not counting work around the house)? (Include paid vacations and paid sick leave.)
If none: Even though . . . did not work in 1957 did he spend any time trying to find a job?
What was the main reason . . . did not work in 1957?
(Here boxes to be checked include "ill or disabled", "keeping house", "could not find work", etc. Presumably only "could not find work" would result in the individual being counted in the labor force.)

It appears likely that the Kinsey-like approach of the CPS questions, which do not ask whether the individual had any income, or even whether

---

[1] Gertrude Bancroft, "Current Unemployment Statistics of the Census Bureau," in *The Measurement and Behavior of Unemployment*, published by Princeton University Press for the National Bureau of Economic Research, 1957.

she worked, but rather start by assuming the work and ask first how many weeks she worked, might avoid underreporting more than the SCF sequence. They might also lead to some overreporting in CPS, but in either case the CPS should then have more reports of part time or incidental employment—and this is not the case.

We are left then with some unexplained differences. Perhaps they arise from unemployed or self-employed women. The former are omitted from the SCF definition of working wives. The latter may be omitted if they do not receive an income separate from that of their husband.

After the conference, Conrad Taeuber forwarded the following information from Robert J. Pearl of the Census Bureau: "One immediate source of difference is that the Survey of Consumer Finances apparently excluded unpaid family work (since the introductory question related to income of the wife) whereas our survey as usual included this group. We do not have a breakdown of unpaid family workers by marital status and presence or absence of children, but the over-all annual worker rate for women (per cent of female population with any work experience during the year) would have been reduced by as much as 4 percentage points if the unpaid group had been excluded from our figures."[2]

Table 4 in Lebergott's paper has some interesting aspects which were not discussed. For instance, young and old single nonwhite women reduced their labor force participation between 1890 and 1940. This requires that they have some other source of economic support, presumably their relatives. Does it also imply less available housework? And why should the *increase* in participation of nonwhite women be restricted to married women between 25 and 44 years old? Does this represent factory work, or home work that was previously done by slaves, or what?

Is it possible that there was a slow tendency for the market place to eliminate some nonwhite workers—the very old and the young—who had been utilized when their marginal cost was nearly zero because of slavery, and perhaps for a time thereafter? Were factory jobs that opened to nonwhite women mostly those requiring the strength and stamina of middle-aged people, such as work in commercial laundries?

Noting the large increase in the proportion of married women with children who are in the labor force, it is possible that a desire for more children, or higher quality children, to use Gary Becker's phrase, leads to increased income—from the wife's work, rather than the reverse causation where income determines the number of children? Or perhaps

[2] Letter from Conrad Taeuber to Stanley Lebergott and James N. Morgan, December 23, 1958.

children turn out to cost more than the parents anticipated, given the standards of the culture.

Tables 7 and 8 appear to permit some spurious correlation because durables and the debts associated with durables are mostly bought and incurred earlier in the life cycle than a house, in many cases before the first child is born. The house is generally purchased later, often when the wife has left the labor force to have children. In other words, there are relationships of debt to home ownership and stage in the family life cycle which may cast some doubt on the motivational interpretation given by Lebergott that the wife will go to work to help get a car or durable, but not for a home. Since mortgage payments are mostly made during the period when there are small children, and this is also the period when the wife is least able or able to work, the tables can have a different interpretation.

I agree with the conclusion that the rise in the proportion of women in the labor force can be attributed to "a variety of supply and demand factors, few of which are closely associated with population changes."

A general problem of interpretation has to do with the economic meaning of data on participation in the labor force, particularly in the case of women, and over periods when more and more economic activity was being transferred from the home or farm to the factory or store. This is not to denigrate the importance of the data, or their intrinsic interest, but to suggest that interpretations as to motivation, or as to the economic or welfare implications of the data, must be made in the light of these considerations.

There is a growing body of research on the present-day motivations of women workers, and the impact of their outside work on the home. Certainly, when a wife works it mostly means that she and her husband do more total work. They may also, however, use some of the earned money to pay someone else to do housework. Or they may make use of relatives or friends in various ways difficult to catch in the statistics. Since leisure is also an economic good, but one with no market price nor record of its purchase or sale, welfare implications are difficult to make. Even the total labor force can be affected in different ways. Insofar as women work in food-processing factories, doing for dollars what they formerly did at home without pay, their total work efforts may not increase much, but the records will show more income and more employment.

I do not know just how one should analyze trends in labor force, gross national product, and the like, in the light of these considerations, but some attention might be given to adding to GNP estimates of the value of (*a*) housewives' services at home, and (*b*) leisure, the value of the residual of sixteen hours a day not spent working. Trends in such a measure *in toto* and relative to the total person-hours of work should be most revealing.

JOHN DURAND, United Nations

I want to begin by talking about population and labor force relationships in a more general and elementary way than Lebergott has done. This may help to show how his contributions fit into the general picture.

In the first place, the labor force is not merely *related* to the population, it is a *part* of the population. It is not merely *influenced* by demographic variables, it *is* a demographic variable. Likewise the percentages of labor force members in different sex-age groups of the population, which we call "participation rates," are also demographic variables—not like sex and age, which are inherent characteristics of individuals, but like marital status or farm-residence. The participation rates have a seasonal variation and on occasions they may change considerably from year to year, as we saw during the war, but large short-term variations are extraordinary. Normally these rates change slowly, and in an orderly progression; they have a certain stability and predictability which befits a demographic variable. Consequently, both over long and short periods, the growth of the population is normally the main determinant of the growth of the labor force—or rather, the growth of the adult population. If the annual average labor force in 1956 was about 2 per cent larger than in 1955, it was mainly because the adult population increased roughly in that ratio; and this is the usual state of affairs. And if we can predict the size of the adult population in the year 2,000, we shall not be very far wrong in predicting the size of the labor force.

The growth of the labor force is therefore determined primarily by the fundamental demographic factors of fertility, mortality, and migration. The influences of these factors can be measured in an approximate way by the methods illustrated in Notestein's paper. In his charts, even if they are limited to the female population, we can see in a general way how the changes of fertility, mortality, net immigration, and also the peculiarities of the original age structure, affected the size of the labor force and its numerical relation to the total population during a 25-year period.

For a more accurate measure of the effects of these demographic variables, it is necessary to introduce labor force participation rates into the calculations, and take account of the changes in these rates and their

419

interaction with the changing numbers in the different sex-age groups of the adult population. This analysis can be extended back to earlier periods, and in this way we can get a more exact measure, for instance, of the effect of changing fertility on the number of children in the labor force than Lebergott has given.

For still more accurate measures, we should have to take account of interactions between labor force participation rates on the one hand and the fertility, mortality, and migration rates on the other hand. These interactions, however, are of a secondary order of importance. The level of fertility affects the participation rates of women, and vice versa. Lebergott refers to the studies of the changes during 1890–1930 and 1920–1940 which showed that the decline of fertility could have accounted for only a small share of the large increase in the number of working women. Gertrude Bancroft's new book contains an analysis of the growth of the female labor force between 1940 and 1950 which indicates that the marriage and baby boom had a fairly important restraining influence, but not enough to prevent a very large increase in the female labor force during this decade.[1]

Changing mortality rates can also affect labor force participation rates through the medium of widowhood and orphanhood, but here we are considering influences of really small relative importance. Large-scale immigration or emigration is more important, as it is likely that the migrants will not only be largely in the sex-age groups to which the highest participation rates apply, but also that their participation rates will be higher than those of nonmigrants of the same sex and age. However, in the United States, international migration during the last 30 years has not been large enough to rank as a major factor. Off-farm migration of the native population is now much more important as a factor influencing the trend of the labor force participation rates.

It is also necessary to consider the possibility that the participation rates may be influenced by changes in the rate of population growth. If the increase of the adult population lags behind the demand for labor, participation rates may rise, and if population growth overtakes demand, participation rates may fall. I say *may*; I do not know if it is true, and if it is true, we have no means of estimating the amount of the effect. Lebergott thinks that the increasing female participation rates in the last few decades could be explained partly by the cutting off of immigration. It may be so, but I think it is equally possible that this effect was unimportant.

[1] *The American Labor Force*, Wiley, 1958.

It is also possible, as Lebergott says, that changes in the participation rates for some sex-age groups tend to produce compensating changes in other groups. He refers to increasing female rates being stimulated partly by the loss of other customary sources of family income—income, that is, from employed children and from lodgers. I will not take issue, but I do not think we have any evidence of this.

On the other hand it cannot be denied that the sudden removal of an important segment of the labor force is likely to provoke an increase in participation rates of other segments of the population. We saw this very clearly, of course, during the war.

I am getting over now from the demographic interrelations into "exogenous" factors, if I may be permitted to use the economists' term. As Lebergott says, we have plenty of evidence to show that "exogenous" factors have been responsible for the greater part of the changes of the participation rates in this country during the last 80 years. Sometimes these nondemographic factors are lumped under the heading of "propensity"; I have done this myself, but the term does not do justice to the importance of demand factors; it implies that membership in the labor force is open to all who wish to join, which is obviously not true—except in the sense that anyone can get under the statistical definition by seeking work, even if there is no demand whatsoever for his services.

There are three groups in the population whose participation rates have been greatly affected by changing demographic and exogenous factors: women, children, and elderly men. Lebergott has discussed the first two; to fill out the picture I will only say that the changes in the participation rates of males over 65 have been no less spectacular and persistent. The decrease in average age of retirement—or relinquishment of economic activity—has continued in the 1950's after the interruption during the war. Bancroft's tables show only 35 per cent of white males over 65 in the labor force in 1955, by comparison with 41 per cent in 1940 and 1950, and 67 per cent in 1890.[2]

In Lebergott's very interesting analysis of the trends in labor force participation of women and children, I want only to raise questions about a few details. For one thing, I am somewhat doubtful about the reliability of the evidence from the censuses that child labor was increasing during the late nineteenth century. As for the fascinating estimates of the female labor force in 1830, I wonder what happened to the agricultural component, and I would be glad if he would clarify this question. One more point: I am dubious of comparisons of female participation rates for

[2] *The American Labor Force*, Wiley, 1958.

different groups where age is not controlled. I think this applies to the data on indebtedness and purchases of durable goods on the part of families with and without working wives.

In his conclusions as to the main explanations of the most recent increase in female participation rates, Lebergott says: "On the supply side, the incentive is to be found in the dazzling array of material goods now incorporated into the American standard of living."

Bancroft's emphasis is a little different. She analyzed the female labor force with regard to educational level, occupation, family-income classes, and the like, and found that in general it is not the lower but the upper social-economic groups who are spearheading the present female invasion of the labor market—the Joneses themselves—those same elite pace-makers who have been bearing the standard of the new four-child, three-seated station wagon ideal. Bancroft says cautiously, "the data give some support for the belief that, in addition to the need or desire for income, other motives for labor force activity have assumed importance in recent years."

For the economic consequences, it is pertinent to consider that increasing employment of married women means an increasing frequency of two-worker families, which has an obvious bearing on the shape of the family-income distribution. This is relevant, of course, to the building of models for exploration of economic and demographic relationships, and for prediction of future trends of consumers' expenditures, and so forth.

I have not touched on internal migration or urban-rural and other geographical differences in natural increase and labor force participation rates, and there is hardly any time to talk about these matters now, but they are obviously of capital importance for investigation of labor force and population relationships below the national level. We now have a rich store of material for research on these aspects of the subject in the monumental compilation of historical data and estimates of internal migration and labor force by states since 1870 which recently issued from the University of Pennsylvania.[3]

[3] *Population Redistribution and Economic Growth, United States, 1870–1950*, American Philosophical Society, 1957.

Population Change and Resources: Malthusianism and Conservation

HAROLD J. BARNETT

RESOURCES FOR THE FUTURE, INC.

AND WAYNE STATE UNIVERSITY

1. Social Importance

CONTEMPORARY society holds the belief that there is an imbalance of some kind between the economic availability of natural resources and population growth. More specifically, it is thought that natural resources (hereafter usually "resources") are scarce in an economic sense, and that this makes economic growth more difficult.

Two of America's leading physicians have recently made forceful statements of their beliefs that resources are economically scarce relative to the number of human beings and their consumption of goods. The late Allen Gregg, Director of the Rockefeller Foundation medical division, asked, "Is Man a Biological Cancer?"

> There is an alarming parallel between the growth of a cancer in the body of an organism and the growth of human population in the earth's ecological economy. (*Population Bulletin*, "Hidden Hunger at the Summit," August 1955, Volume XI, no. 5, p. 74.)

A. J. Carlson posed the same dilemma with a different simile:

> The number one problem facing man today and tomorrow is overpopulation and starvation. . . . If we breed like rabbits, in the long run we have to live and die like rabbits. ("Science Versus Life," *Journal of the American Medical Association*, April 16, 1955, Vol. 157, pp. 1437–1441)

Other leading life scientists have also spoken out about resource scarcity and its adverse consequences for social welfare and economic growth. Sir Charles Galton Darwin (grandson of the originator of the modern theory of evolution) is quite pessimistic.[1] He believes that society

[1] *The Next Million Years*, Hart-Davis, London, 1952.

Note: This paper is drawn from a much larger Resources for the Future research project, on the economic theory of resources and growth, in which Chandler Morse and I are collaborating. It is intended that most of the results will be published as a book by Resources for the Future, Inc. I wish to acknowledge helpful comment on this article from Professor Morse, Henry Jarrett, and other colleagues. In addition, the final draft has benefited from criticisms by Professors L. E. Craine, E. M. Hoover, E. S. Mason, T. W. Schultz, and from the editor of this volume, Mr. C. J. Dwyer. But I have not fully accepted all criticisms, and am alone responsible for remaining errors.

as a whole will tend to breed without limit. And, further, it is precisely the poorest intellectual stock, he believes, which will breed at the highest rates. Given a shortage of resources, the result is a tendency of civilization relatively to proliferate its lesser quality specimens and to shrink the numbers of its abler ones. The "weak" shall inherit the earth.

Outstanding men from the other physical sciences have also supported the doctrine of resources conflict. For example, Harrison Brown has recently written:

A substantial fraction of humanity today is behaving . . . as if it would not rest content until the earth is covered completely and to a considerable depth with a writhing mass of human beings, much as a dead cow is covered with a pulsating mass of maggots. (*Challenge of Man's Future*, Viking Press, New York, 1954, p. 221)

Similar views are also widespread among social scientists, although perhaps less so than among the physical ones. We find (ignoring, for the moment, economists and demographers) statements from political scientists, sociologists, the legal profession, and representatives of the other social disciplines. Occasionally, the expressions are of alarm or urgency; occasionally they are as simple and straightforward as some of the physical scientist expressions in flatly asserting a contradiction between a limited earth and a burgeoning population and standard of living. For example, lawyer Samuel Ordway, in a recent book is no less forceful than the physical scientists quoted.[2] More usually, however, the social scientists hedge their statements on the conflict between resource scarcity and economic growth. Examples are recent writings of Craine, Gulick, Griffith, and Hertzler, among others.[3]

The social importance of the doctrine of resource scarcity is thus demonstrated by the simple fact that there is widespread belief in one form or another of the proposition.

But the social importance of the doctrine of resource scarcity goes beyond the fact of wide public belief. In many countries, this belief has, rather naturally, found expression in laws and modes of governmental (and private) behavior. In this country, the platforms of both political parties contain policies for "scarce" natural resources. Public policies based upon the doctrine of resource scarcity are, in part, responsible for

---

[2] *Resources and the American Dream*, Ronald, 1953.

[3] Lyle Craine, "Natural Resources and Government," *Public Administration Review*; Luther Gulick, "The Cities' Challenge in Resource Use," and Ernest Griffith, "Main Lines of Conversation Thought and Action," both in *Perspectives on Conservation, Resources for the Future*, Johns Hopkins University Press, 1958; J. O. Hertzler, *The Crisis in World Population*, University of Nebraska Press, 1956.

federal or state land reclamation programs, resource reservation practices, and controls on rates of use of some natural resources. Prominent examples are: forest reservations, limitations on the use of oil and gas, and preferential tax treatment in certain natural resource industries. Many foreign countries also have public policies based upon the doctrine of resource scarcity. The situation of the oil-rich, underdeveloped countries is particularly interesting. Their problem is sometimes visualized as that of reinvesting the income from their petroleum sales so as to assure the development of their economies before the reserves run out.[4]

Thus the doctrine of natural resource scarcity is an important social question for two reasons: because thoughtful public opinion views it as such; and because public policies based upon these views are being adopted.

2. Contemporary Economist and Demographer Writings

In general, economists and demographers are not in the vanguard of alarmed writers on the resources-growth dilemma. In this sense, their views are similar to those already characterized for other social scientists. Here also there are exceptions, such as demographer Robert Cook, editor of the *Population Bulletin*. Among economists, it is possible to interpret some recent pieces by Spengler and Villard as exceptions; I regard them, however, more as forceful presentations of the natural resources-population dilemma.[5]

Although probably not really alarmed concerning resource scarcity, economists (and, so far as I know, demographers) also generally believe that this scarcity in the economic sense truly exists, and that it is a drag on economic advance. Advances in output per capita from technological improvement and other causes are subject to a degree of offset from this scarcity. Exceptions to the idea of limited natural resources as an obstacle to growth in economic writings are very few. So far as I know, the strongest appear in Erich Zimmerman's monumental volume.[6] Other exceptions take the form primarily of denying major importance to this

---

[4] C. Kindleberger, "Exhaustible Resources, Foreign Trade and Foreign Investment" (M.I.T. manuscript, 1958); S.V. Ciriacy-Wantrup, *Resource Conservation—Economics and Policies*, University of California Press, Berkeley, 1952; A. Scott, *Natural Resources: The Economics of Conservation*, University of Toronto Press, 1955.

[5] Joseph Spengler, "Population Threatens Prosperity," *Harvard Business Review*, January–February, 1956; Henry Villard, "Some Notes on Population and Living Levels," *Review of Business and Economic Statistics*, May, 1955.

[6] *World Resources and Industries*, Harper, 1950. See particularly ch. 50.

negative influence, rather than quarreling with its presence. For example, George Stigler in a recent paper states:

A larger economy should be more efficient than a small economy: this has been the standard view of economists since the one important disadvantage of the large economy, diminishing returns to natural resources, has proved to be unimportant. (Conference on Income and Wealth, National Bureau of Economic Research, Oct. 17–18, 1958)

Similar derogations of the significance of an adverse resource influence in modern industrial societies, although less flatly stated, appear in writings of E. S. Mason and Harold Moulton.[7] In general, however, the major body of literature takes seriously the retarding force of resource scarcity as an important obstacle in economic growth—for example, the recent thoughtful book on Asia by Harold Belshaw.[8]

In view of the wide belief that economic scarcity of resources in fact impairs economic growth in modern societies, it might be thought that it has been theoretically and empirically proved. But this is not the case. Rather, the proposition is assumed to be a factual statement. Either it is considered sufficiently obvious to need no proof, or else there is simple reference to "Conservation" or the "Malthusian dilemma." Elsewhere, Chandler Morse and I have examined the economic theory of resource scarcity as an impediment to growth.[9] And, elsewhere, I have argued it is an hypothesis, not a fact, and made a preliminary and exploratory empirical analysis of whether it is possible to observe any development of resource scarcity in the U.S. economy between 1870 and 1956.[10] The results of these efforts, so far, have not removed my uncertainty as to whether there is necessarily, in a growing modern economy, a development of resource scarcity which operates to retard growth and threaten future welfare.

Stimulated by this finding for modern industrial societies, I have set myself the task of trying to chase down and examine the origins of the doctrine. Perhaps by examination of resource scarcity doctrines *in situ*, I can find elaboration which will show, as modern writing does not, under what circumstances the widespread belief is justified, or which will at least explain why the belief is widespread.

---

[7] E. S. Mason, "An American View of Raw Materials Problems," *Journal of Industrial Economics*, Vol. 1, no. 1, 1952; Harold G. Moulton, *Controlling Factors in Economic Development*, The Brookings Institution, 1949.

[8] *Population Growth and Levels of Consumption*, G. Allen, London, 1956.

[9] Forthcoming *Resources for the Future* book.

[10] "Measurement of Natural Resource Scarcity and Its Economic Effects," paper presented to Conference on Research in Income and Wealth, October 17–18, 1958.

In economic literature, the principal lead for such historical investigation is what has been termed the "first American conservation movement." So closely has resource scarcity doctrine been identified with this movement that the terms "conservation problem" and "natural resource scarcity" are frequently used as synonyms, the former being the more common. For example, two of the major professional books on the economics of natural resources are titled *Resource Conservation—Economics and Policies* (S. V. Ciriacy-Wantrup) and *Natural Resources: The Economics of Conservation* (A. Scott). A. C. Pigou, in his statement that the resource scarcity problem generates a danger which justifies public policy concern, also points to the conservation movement for authority:

> But there is wide agreement that the State should protect the interests of the future *in some degree* against the effects of our irrational discounting and of our preference for ourselves over our descendants. The whole movement for 'conservation' in the United States is based on this conviction. It is the clear duty of Government, which is the trustee for unborn generations, as well as for its present citizens, to watch over, and, if need be, by legislative enactment, to defend, the exhaustible natural resources of the country from rash and reckless spoliation. (*Economics of Welfare*, Macmillan, London, 1946, pp. 29–30; italics in the original)

In general, I think most American economists believe that "conservation" is concerned with the problem of resource scarcity relative to welfare and growth.

Among non-economists, the signs pointing to the conservation movement as a means of understanding the problem of resource scarcity and growth are even clearer. Leading expositors of the resource scarcity view today, in fact, frequently see themselves as descendants of the first conservation movement and inheritors of its reform mission.

Contemporary demographic and economic literature also suggests going back a hundred years earlier and examining Malthus for this inquiry into the origins of the resource scarcity-growth doctrine.[11]

3. Malthus

An elementary statement of the Malthusian view of the economic scarcity of resources and the retardation of growth therefrom is about as follows: The doctrine of resource scarcity and its economic effect reflect natural law. By the laws of nature, resources are limited and population multiplies. In the absence of social preventive checks, population increases to

---

[11] I have also examined other historical writings as possible keys to the resource scarcity gospel. Some of these, particularly works of Ricardo, Mill, G. P. Marsh, and W. S. Jevons, I have found to be of equal or greater importance as origins of the doctrine.

the limits of subsistence. The dynamics of economic growth are thus dominated by the scarcity of resources and the law of population growth. With respect to resource scarcity, Malthus believed,

. . . Man is necessarily confined in room. When acre has been added to acre till all the fertile land is occupied, the yearly increase of food must depend upon the melioration of the land already in possession. This is a fund, which, from the nature of all soils, instead of increasing, must be gardually diminishing. (*An Essay on the Principles of Population*, Ward, Lock, London, 1890, p. 4)

With respect to the law of population growth, Malthus believed that there is

. . . the constant tendency in all animated life to increase beyond the nourishment prepared for it (*ibid.*, p. 2) . . . population invariably increases where the means of subsistence increase (*ibid.*, p. 14)

The theory was, thus, that man's propensity for breeding was in conflict with the world's limited availability of natural resource and his ability to extract economic goods therefrom.

Is Malthus the originator of the doctrine? It appears clear from the *Essay* that his generalization of the problem of population pressure on scarce resources derived more from the contemporary policy problem of the Poor Laws, and from social observation and empirical analysis, than from purely abstract thought. In part, the social conditions of the time generated his ideas, and the ideas were therefore unlikely to be wholly new. Keynes in his sympathetic biography of Malthus states that, "his leading idea had been largely anticipated in a clumsier way by other eighteenth-century writers."[12] Malthus, therefore, did not originate the doctrine that resource scarcity restrains economic growth, but rather provided a clear and forceful statement on an attractive generalized level.

It is also possible to quarrel with the characterization of Malthusianism as the origin of subsequent doctrine on natural resource scarcity and effect on three other grounds. First, the *Essay* is far more an analysis of population than of natural resources, and resource scarcity and its effect are more asserted than demonstrated. Second, while the Malthusian doctrine describes a resource scarcity effect upon economic growth, it does not entail an economic scarcity effect in a stationary society. And, third, Malthus apparently did not raise the problem of depletion at all. All of these points are valid. Their implications, however, do not deny to the Malthus *Essay* the role of intellectual parent of the family of subsequent views on resource scarcity and its economic effect. But they do suggest that resource scarcity doctrine has developed since Malthus.

---

[12] *Essays in Biography*, New York Press, 1951, p. 100.

Although for its subject matter the Malthusian theory far surpassed its contemporaries in logic, precision, and clarity, it is not a complete statement, in the modern economic model sense, of the relation between resources and economic growth. It is useful to attempt the construction of such a model, by using his text as a basis for filling in gaps and providing a modern formulation.

Static model. First, there is posited a social production function consistent with Malthus' view:

$$O = F(R, L, C)$$

where O is physical national output, R is physical quantity of resources employed, L is physical quantity of labor employed, and C is physical quantity of capital employed. The functional relationship is a description of all possible efficient combinations of the inputs to produce output with given techniques and social parameters. Each of the variables—the three inputs and the output—is either homogeneous in quality, or is characterized by an invariant frequency distribution of quality. This difficult assumption is necessary if the function is to be a meaningful, precise mathematical statement.

In order to yield a specific output figure under these conditions, the availability of natural resources, labor, and capital, and the extent of their employments, must first be specified. Under Malthusian assumptions, as they are simplified and imputed to him for exposition here, the following may be specified as the availability and employment of the three inputs. The quantity of available natural resources is fixed; natural resources are indestructible. The available quantities of both labor and capital are variable. If fully employed, labor's marginal productivity equals subsistence, and capital's marginal productivity will be positive. If natural resources are free and not yet fully employed, their marginal productivity will be zero. Once they are fully employed, marginal productivity will become positive. Reservation policies in regard to the supply of any factor from existing stock may be adopted for institutional, psychological, or other reasons. Since these would affect marginal productivities, let it be assumed that each individual reservation policy, if adopted, is persistent and independent of the other reservation policies.

The form of the Malthusian static social production function is required to be such that the marginal productivities of labor and capital individually and together are monotonically declining. And, therefore, the second partial derivatives of output with respect to labor, capital, or both, are negative.

429

Growth model. The final conditions are those needed to convert the above Malthusian static model into a Malthusian growth one. That is, rules are needed for changes in factor quantities and in technological and institutional parameters. For simplicity, the labor force is assumed to be a fixed proportion of population. The population level, in turn, increases exponentially as a function of time, subject to two biological constraints. Its rate of increase may not exceed that permitted by the maximum biological rate of reproduction characteristic of human females (increase from improved longevity is thus ignored); and the level of population may not exceed that set by the biological minimum of food and other subsistence goods required to sustain life. Capital availability increases no faster than population. Natural resource availability is invariant. And technology and institutional conditions are invariant. Finally, we need a time horizon, and for this we assume a very long term. This completes the Malthusian long-term growth model.

In summary, the Malthusian growth model constructed here has five conditions:

A. A very long term
B. An exponential population-increase function and appropriate limits on capital increase
C. Given natural resources
D. Unchanging technology and institutional conditions
E. Homogeneous or constant-composition input and output variables; a law of variable proportions (eventually diminishing marginal productivity) for labor and capital applicable to this static social production function, as stated above under "Static model"

This model is illustrated in Charts 1 and 2. If resource stock is fixed at r_1 and the whole stock is employed, then output increases less than in proportion to increases in labor plus capital. The output expansion path is *EHM*. As labor and capital increase from a_1, their marginal productivity $[\Delta O/\Delta(L + C)]$ declines steadily, reaching zero when labor + capital are equal to a_2. The decline in output per capita from o_1/a_1 to o_2/a_2 may never be reached, since the latter figure may be below the level of subsistence. Or, if o_2/a_2 is above subsistence, population will continue to grow even though output declines, so that eventual stable output might be o_3; then output per capita will be at subsistence, at o_3/a_3, a level below o_2/a_2. Thus while we are sure that output growth will cease someplace on the path *EHM*, we don't know at which point unless

CHART 1

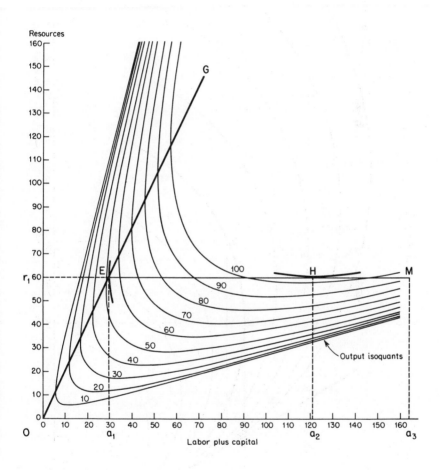

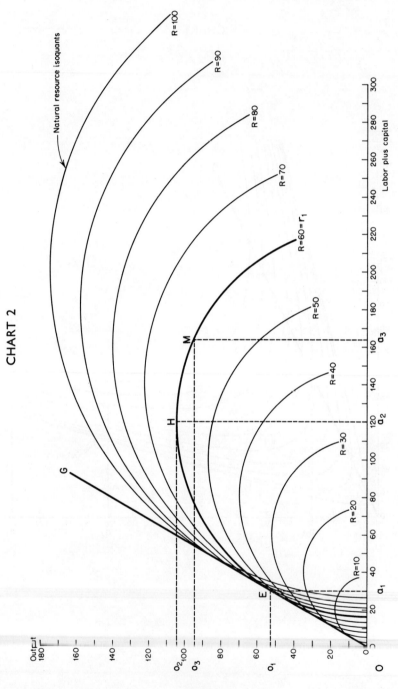

CHART 2

we can define subsistence. Note that alternative social definitions of subsistence are possible.

The charts show that the assumed conditions inevitably produce resource scarcity eventually. But they also show that the mere definition of a fixed physical world does not, in itself, amount to economic scarcity of resources. To be economically scarce, the fixed natural resources must be of small amount relative to $L + C$ and the socio-technical parameters. In our charts "small" is defined as an amount less than r_1/a_1. From this it follows that while a fixed world (or universe) always contains a threat of resource economic scarcity, nevertheless onset of scarcity depends on the other conditions as well. So long as resources are large enough to permit output expansion along the path OEG, resource economic scarcity is not yet experienced.[13]

If economic growth is defined as increasing output, then Malthusianism is a simple, extreme case of a general hypothesis of inhibition of economic growth from limited natural resources. The beginning state of the model is irrelevant to the eventual outcome of population being limited by food subsistence. Timing of the outcome, however, is influenced by the beginning state. Any outside disturbance in effect creates a new beginning state. If the closed model is disturbed by, for example, improved technology, the Malthusian limitation will at that point be avoided. But provided the impulse is a "one-shot" affair, the economy will absorb the impact of the disturbance and immediately thereafter again tend toward a new Malthusian equilibrium combination of total output, population, and subsistence levels of living.

The conditions described are sufficient for an eventual Malthusian outcome of subsistence living and cessation of economic growth, namely, stable population and no increase in output per capita. The following five classes of conditions are also necessary:

A. It is only in the very long term that the model necessarily operates to its equilibrium solution. In a short term, there can be economic growth, since resources do not become scarce until the ratio of population to resources rises beyond a critical level (a_1/r_1 in our charts).

B. Except for persistent population increase and appropriate limits on rate of capital increase, there is not necessarily sufficient labor to drive average returns to the limit of subsistence. The critical population/ resources level has to be reached via population growth. And of course

[13] The charts are drawn to follow R. G. D. Allen's "more general normal type" of production function in *Mathematical Analysis for Economists*, Macmillan, London, 1947, p. 288. In my charts, $O = [2H(L + C)R - A(L + C)^2 - B(R)^2]^{1/2}$, where $H = 2$ and $A = B = 1$.

Malthus' "exponential rate" of population increase and my assumption of capital increase at the same rate yield one case of such growth.

C. Except for limited natural resources, output could rise as fast as, or faster than, population. And, of course, Malthus' "fixed land" is one case which satisfies the requirement of "limited natural resources."

D. Only when the rate of technological and organizational advance is too slow to offset the declining marginal returns to population increase would output per capita be forced down to the subsistence level. And, of course, "fixed technology and institutions" satisfies this condition.

E. Except for the assumption of diminishing marginal returns to labor and capital in the social production function, social output could increase as fast as, or faster than, labor and capital additions.

It is also apparent, however, that while each of these classes of conditions is necessary, the particular conditions are not. The specifications of particular conditions we have given (exponential population growth, fixed land, and the like) are more stringent than absolutely necessary for Malthus' conclusions.

Strategic variables and sensitivity. That the five types of conditions are necessary for the Malthusian scarcity model is an important truth, frequently overlooked. The dynamic forces which tend to drive economic evolution toward Malthus' conclusion are sometimes viewed as a population problem, or a natural resource problem, or a race between technology and population, or in still other simplified ways. Such simplifications do not, of course, deny the existence of the other relations characterized here as necessary, but frequently these relations are admitted only implicitly or not recognized at all. Further, incomplete specification of the entire model permits implicit introduction of other assumptions and views. These latter are sometimes dangerous to sensible analysis, and are partly responsible for a fraction of nonsense in resources literature.

The conditions required for the Malthusian scarcity effect—known as the "Malthusian dilemma"—constitute a multi-variable, dynamic model, containing the variables and kinds of relations described. Every one of them is potentially important. Yet it is true that if one makes certain assumptions, certain of the variables and conditions become unimportant, while others become dominant or strategic.

Time horizon. The assumption concerning time horizon is extremely prejudicial to the question of which variables are strategic. Let an extremely "long term" be assumed as the setting for the analysis. Then the entire outcome of the Malthus model hangs on whether or not the annual rate of population increase exceeds zero—depends, that is, on whether or not population more than reproduces itself, however minutely. Population is the strategic variable, and, given a finite world, the population equation is virtually the only important relation. Assume, for example, a net reproduction rate of 0.016, very roughly the present world rate, a considerable part of which is due to improved longevity. This involves a birth rate less than half that which Malthus' empirical work led him to use. Then the world population would increase *one hundred-fold* in 290 years, and *one thousand-fold* in 435 years. Let the annual net reproduction rate be still lower—set it at 0.001, about 1/30 of Malthus' finding. Then the long term doom from scarcity is only deferred. The 2½ billion living bodies of 1950 generate: 25 billion in A.D. 4300, a ten-fold increase; 250 billion in A.D. 6600, a hundred-fold increase; 2,500 billion in A.D. 8900, a thousand-fold increase. And this numbers game may be played without end, with an unspecified long-term horizon. Consequently, if the time horizon is a very long or an endless one, the crucial question is whether net rate of reproduction is positive, for this makes ultimate population boundless. No other question is very relevant: technological change, capital formation, utilization of the depths of the earth or its atmosphere and solar energy, and so on, are submerged in people and endless time. If time is infinite, so is population; if time is extremely long, then population is extremely large.

Now let the time horizon be a closer one—25, 50, even 100 years. The following world populations result at decade intervals from continuation of the present annual net reproduction rate of about 0.016:

Year	World Population (in billions)
A.D. 1950	2.5
1960	2.9
1970	3.4
1980	4.0
1990	4.7
2000	5.5
2010	6.5
2020	7.6
2030	8.9
2040	10.4
2050	12.2

For these shorter periods, the population variable no longer nullifies the other terms in the model. For the earlier part of the 100 years, population level may be less significant than availability of advanced technology and capital for the lower income areas of the world; employment of new lands, intensity of land use, and availability of chemical fertilizers; institutional arrangements for domestic and international trade and exchange; and other conditions. Even for the final 50 years, population level would not appear to be obviously dominant. It is no longer enough to define scarcity as a finite world, as Malthus did. It becomes necessary to ask how great or how little a volume of resources constitutes economic scarcity.

Rate of population increase. As to the second necessary condition of the Malthus model—annual rate of population increase (r)—this is important for economic growth over moderately distant time periods. This is demonstrated in the following table:

World population (in billions)

Year	$r = .03$ (Malthus)	$r = .016$ (present)	$r = .001$
1950	2.5	2.5	2.50
1975	5.2	3.7	2.57
2000	11.0	5.5	2.63
2025	22.9	8.2	2.69
2050	48.0	12.2	2.77

If explicitly or implicitly one uses the Malthus rate, then Malthus was surely right. Population *is* the strategic variable for periods longer than 50 years or so. On the other hand, one might be inclined to project the present rate of world population increase, a far lower rate than Malthus', and partly reflecting increased life-span. Then population must be considered, but other elements may not be neglected, as they were by Malthus. If one posits $r = 0.001$, then population is not a significant variable, and may be neglected.

For Malthus, the population function is independent of level of consumption (or output), except that consumption per capita may not be less than subsistence levels. This was central and explicit to Malthus' analysis and conclusions, and is necessary to them. For if in consequence of an increase in income per capita the birth rate should fall, scarcity and its effect could conceivably be avoided. The Malthus model absolutely requires that population *not* vary inversely with income.

It may now be seen why Malthus emphasized the population level. For unchecked $r = 0.03$ is a monstrous force. Population multiplies by almost 20 in the first century, by about $2\frac{1}{2}$ million in the fifth, and by the year A.D. 3000 the population mass would exceed the earth's and if closely packed would be five times as bulky.[14] If Malthus did believe $r = 0.03$, then the relative neglect of other variables is understandable. For in this case and given a finite world, none of the other variables is important.

Natural resource availability. The third condition for the Malthus formulation is limited economic availability of natural resources. So far as I can tell, this assumption derived directly from the fact that the world's agricultural lands were of limited physical extent.

Several questions may be asked. Was Malthus unaware that agricultural land varied in economic quality? Malthus *was* aware that agricultural land was not homogeneous. But this was not important to his theory. His thesis was the basic and ultimate inconsistency between a natural birth rate tending to double population each twenty-five years and the food availability from a limited agricultural territory, the earth. For him, there was no question but that the unhomogeneity of land could be ignored. The fixed agricultural land of the globe meant natural resource scarcity. In his own words, ". . . what is true . . . in reference to a single farm, must necessarily be true of the whole earth, from which the necessaries of life for the actual population are derived."[15]

Was Malthus unaware that there were natural resources other than land? His *Essay* hardly mentions them, but we may be sure he was aware of them. But, again, they could be ignored. One reason is that just given for ignoring variations in economic qualities of agricultural land. The other is that his society was primarily an agricultural one, whose major problem was food for subsistence (fish, game, and forests did not figure importantly in his scheme).

These oversimplifications do not disturb me. The mark of good theory is not that it describes reality completely, in all respects faithfully, but that it captures the essence of that part of reality which is under consideration. Good theory, like art, simplifies, abstracts, and highlights. It is therefore, in a sense, inappropriate to ask whether Malthus believed his conditions to be complete and detailed descriptions of reality. Of course he did not. A really good theorist is a hair-splitter only when necessary, or when engaged as a critic. The proper question is whether Malthus believed his theory and conditions to be essentially accurate. And to this, the answer is that certainly he did.

[14] *Any* positive rate of population increase will do these things if one's time horizon is distant enough. Henry Villard, *Review of Economics and Statistics*, May, 1955, observed that the *present* world net reproduction rate would yield a population size equal to the weight of the earth in only a couple thousand years or so.

[15] *Introduction to Malthus*, D. V. Glass, ed., Wiley, p. 145.

Technology and institutions. Malthus assumed that technology and economic organization were, if not fixed, at least not subject to radical change. But the beginnings of the industrial revolution were observable about Malthus even when he wrote the first *Essay,* and there was significant industrial advance as he went through successive editions. In the *Essay* he comments, for example, on the remarkable advances in productivity in textiles. Was it solely beçause of his estimate of r that technological change was given so little attention? There is no way of knowing for certain, of course. An $r = 0.03$ is sufficient reason for ignoring technological change. But, in addition, it would have required prophetic genius, rather than analytical brilliance, for Malthus to appreciate the significance of such phenomena as technological change. The phenomena which entirely transform the equations of the Malthus model are advances which did not take place until after the study was completed and his conclusions had congealed. The important ones are the increase in biological and chemical knowledge, development of the earth sciences, the industrial applications of such knowledge, and the recent atomic energy advances. Such events as Wohler's synthesis of urea, the discovery of cell composition of living things, Liebig's advances in organic chemistry, Mendeleev's periodic table, Mendel's laws, Pasteur's bacteriological discoveries, and the great biological, chemical, and nuclear advances which followed did not take place until much later. Without these advances, there was no reason for Malthus to doubt man's dependence upon naturally fertile soil; to doubt the applicability of a principle of diminishing returns to increments of population; or to place much confidence in man's ability to limit procreation, since in Malthus' view this required sexual continence. It is only with access to the above and other technological changes that, concurrent with striking increases in output per capita and food availability, r begins to decline, land perhaps ceases to be economically fixed, dependence on natural agricultural fertility diminishes sharply, and the single industry principle of diminishing returns, while a truism in a static model, may become anachronistic with respect to changing social output and economic growth.

Law of diminishing returns. The five individual conditions necessary for the Malthusian dynamic model and its unhappy results are being systematically discussed. In each case the interest is briefly to characterize the strategic importance of the condition, the sensitivity of the model results to the individual variables, and the validity of the conditions in contemporary society. The last of the conditions that so concerns us is "the law of diminishing returns." What is necessary at this point is that some of the confusion as to what the "law" is be cleared away. Certainly the diminishing returns principle which is required by the Malthusian formulation is not the one which modern economists view as a natural (although abstract) law; that is, the Malthusian condition is not our familiar, well accepted, necessarily-true "law" at all. There are a considerable number of quite different propositions of diminishing returns extant.[16] I discuss here four which are seemingly or actually embodied in the Malthusian dynamic model.

One of the diminishing returns propositions is the *end result* of the Malthusian economic growth model. Any simple statement of output behavior in the Malthusian theory seems to be itself a statement of the diminishing returns principle. For example, thus: during economic growth, output increases less than in proportion to the increase of population. But it is really inappropriate to use the diminishing returns term so, despite historical sanction. As already described, the Malthusian economic growth model, in the simplest form it could be stated, is a complex of five quite separate types of conditions, all necessary, so that it is misleading to imply that it is a singular principle, and to cloak it with the validity today credited to the "law of diminishing returns." If our entire discussion is viewed as a footnote to the allegation that the Malthusian dilemma is a "law of diminishing returns," then no harm would result. But neither would much good—it is really too lengthy a footnote. In short, it propagates misunderstanding to call the Malthusian results a "law of diminishing returns"—this is not what modern convention and accepted terminology mean by the term. And in any case, it is clear that the proposition so used is not "law." I labor the point not for professional economists, who are no longer much given to the practice, but for non-economists.

A second "diminishing returns" proposition, which is *not* required in my Malthusian formulation, is *static model diminishing returns to social scale*. This proposition, according to modern usage, is that if all factor input quantities are increased proportionately, output will increase by lesser degree. Thus, the social production function is such that if factor inputs are doubled, output will less than double. This is unnecessary to the Malthus model I have constructed. He did not need this condition because in his *dynamic* model he built in the severe limitation of no increase in the factor *land*. With this model, one cannot ask whether outputs will double if all inputs are doubled, since his land input is fixed.

A third principle of diminishing returns, the true "law" of economics,

---

[16] See, for example, T. Schultz, *Journal of Farm Economics*, October, 1932.

is the static law of variable proportions applied to a homogeneous (or invariant composition) output and individually homogeneous (or invariant composition) inputs. This states, for the production of individual commodities, under invariant socio-technical conditions, that after some point additions of a single factor will yield diminishing marginal returns. Formulated rigorously, this is a provable proposition; it is law.

However, the Malthusian model doesn't use this universally acceptable assumption, but rather a fourth proposition which is a dubious modification of it. Malthus requires that the principle be applicable to a whole economy, that is, to a social production function. The condition for the Malthus model is that in a static social production function the marginal productivity of each factor is monotonically declining, and the second partial derivates are negative. The point, briefly, is that the social production function, as distinct from a commodity one, involves unhomogeneous outputs, technologies, and inputs. Recourse to the homely case of limits of ability to raise wheat with men and horses on an acre must be viewed as an analogy, not proof, unless the social production function produces only wheat with acres, men, and horses. This is not the place to elaborate on the difference between a commodity production function and a social one. But its importance is illustrated by the fact that the difference is major in accounting for so-called "external economies."

This discussion of diminishing returns was intended to establish these four points: there are a good many views of diminishing returns; only one of them (the third, above) is the accepted law of diminishing returns; this one is not the Malthusian condition; the Malthusian condition is of uncertain validity.

4. The First Conservation Movement[17]

"Conservation," a coined term, was a part of the "Progressive" political reform platform of the Theodore Roosevelt presidential period. It was also a social movement underlying that reform effort. In terms of ideas, conservation was a wide-ranging melange of views, concerning all the individual natural sciences, economics, political science, public administration, sociology, engineering, art, and public health.

To see it as a political program makes clear features of conservation which are otherwise difficult to understand. How does it happen that the conservation movement moved from natural resources to policies on

---

[17] S. Hays, *The First American Conservation Movement, 1890–1920*, pp. 84f. This recent unpublished Harvard doctoral dissertation is an outstanding *political history* of the movement.

immigration, anti-industrialization, trust-busting, pure food laws, child-labor, Anglo-Saxon supremacy, and so on? One clue here is that it was a successful political movement; these and their architects are rarely consistent in thought or action. Was the conservation movement dominated by its leaders and flavored by their personalities, rather than intellectually led and constructed with scholarly rigor? To ask is to answer: was there ever a successful political movement which was not? Were there manipulation, power alliances, scare propaganda, and other behavior different from the high personal-life ethics of conservation leaders? Again, of course there were—this was American politics. As a successful political movement, conservation was opportunistic, expedient, and compromising in high degree.

As it was a successful political and social movement in American national life, so conservation could not be truly revolutionary in its immediate impact. However, conservation could be, and was, revolutionary in part of its doctrine, and in its *eventual* influence upon American society. The doctrine of "conservation of nature" was an American part of a major revolution in thought in the Western world against the then dominant social philosophy of the self-regulating market economy. Marxism was one European part of that revolution in ideas. In the same period began the now successful revolution against the idea that labor is merely a factor input to the production function in a purely competitive market, and that wages are, according to natural law, merely a factor return from a laissez faire distribution system. And as with labor, so with the "land" factor of classical economics. Conservation views rejected the idea of nature as purely the classical market-place phenomenon "land."

With the vantage of hindsight, Karl Polanyi writing 50 years later, describing the larger revolution of Western society against the self regulating economy, never even mentioning conservation or any of its adherents, has phrased the essence of the conservationists' revolutionary rejection of land laissez-faire with wonderful succinctness and accuracy:

> What we call Land is an element of nature inextricably interwoven with man's institutions. To isolate it and form a market out of it was perhaps the weirdest of all undertakings of our ancestors.
>
> Traditionally, land and labor are not separated; labor forms part of life, land remains part of nature, life and nature form an articulate whole. Land is thus tied up with organizations of kinship, neighborhood, craft, and creed—with tribe and temple, village, guild, and church. . . .
>
> . . . The economic function is but one of the many vital functions of land. It invests man's life with stability; it is the site of his habitation; it is a condition of

his physical safety; it is the landscape and the seasons. We might as well imagine his being born without hands and feet as carrying on his life without land. And yet to separate land from man and organize society in such a way as to satisfy the requirements of a real-estate market was a vital part of the utopian concept of a market economy. (Karl Polanyi, *The Great Transformation: The Political and Economic Origins of Our Time*, Boston: Beacon Press, 1957, p. 178. First published in 1944.)

As might be expected from the features of the conservation movement described above, there is not, in the vast conservation literature of the period 1890–1920, a definitive and rigorous economic analysis of what natural resource economic scarcity is. Rather, scarcity doctrine arises in a variety of ways out of more practical, less academic writings.

Limits. The conservation literature of the period 1890–1920 abounds with quantitative estimates and descriptions of the nation's endowment of natural resources, and exhortations to improve these estimates. One of the important practical contributions of the conservation movement, according to its leaders, was the inception of a program to inventory the nation's natural resource wealth. The historic Governor's Conference and Inland Waterways Conference were responsible for literally thousands of estimates of the physical quantities and characteristics of natural resources within the nation's boundaries. And the non-quantitative discussions continually emphasized that these estimates, and the ones proposed to be made, represented the nation's natural resource wealth. It is quite clear from the record that economic natural resource scarcity was equated with these estimates of finite physical resources within the nation. As with Malthus, finite natural resource physical limits constitute economic scarcity. But the definition of resources differs:

We have a limited supply of coal, and only a limited supply. Whether it is to last for a hundred or a hundred and fifty or a thousand years, the coal is limited in amount. . . . (Pinchot, *The Fight for Conservation*, New York, Doubleday Page, 1910, p. 43)

We have timber for less than thirty years at the present rate of cutting. The figures indicate that our demands upon the forest have increased twice as fast as our population.

Our supplies of iron ore, mineral oil, and natural gas are being rapidly depleted, and many of the great fields are already exhausted." (*ibid.*, pp. 123f.)

The conservationist concepts of limits and thereby economic scarcity are, unlike Malthus', multi-dimensional. Natural resources are specific in type, location, qualities, and relationships, one to another; and economic scarcity (limit) characterizes all the dimensions. Thus one type of natural resource may be more scarce than another, one quality more scarce than another, and so forth.

Ecological balance. As we have learned in the past few generations (in considerable degree from the stimulus of the conservation movement and its educational efforts), there are small and large systems of interdependency among nature's biological organisms and its geological and atmospheric features. Forest watersheds, for example, play an important role in moderating and equalizing water flow from uneven rainfall by initial retention and slow release. In the absence of forest (or other plant) cover, soil is washed into the rivers, rivers flood and cave their banks, and so on. The conception of ecological balance has been widely presented in scholarly and popular literature.[18]

Additional meaning is thereby given to the doctrine of economic scarcity by the conservation view of nature as a system in ecological balance. The analogy of a chain as strong as its weakest link is relevant. Quantities and qualities of individual natural resources are dependent one upon another. In a dynamic world, constraints additional to the over-all limits described above are imposed by the requirement of "balance." This "scarcity" in no way depends upon man. It derives from interdependencies. It would be true in a dynamic world even if man did not in a substantial way modify nature.

Ecological damage and destructive utilization by man. In the conservationist view, stated in an extreme way, nature sans man was a world optimally balanced ecologically. Thus it follows that modern man's activities, however prudent, are necessarily damaging to natural ecological balance, and the ecological system is a weakened one. This, then, constitutes an additional component of the economic scarcity doctrine. The scarcity of limits (above) is initially tighter because of the constraint of balance (above), and is further aggravated by upset of ecological balance from civilized man's presence.

A few examples will be helpful. Civilized man eliminates forests and puts the Great Plains under the plow, and thereby changes nature's balance. Buffalo and other wild-life disappear, soil is lost, and rivers silt. The point here is *not* poor management. It is that nature's ecological system once supported only several million nomadic inhabitants in the United States area, and today it has almost 200 million industrial ones.

The economic scarcities arising from the limits of nature and the constraint of ecological balance are further inevitably subject to aggravation by modern man's destructive utilization of mineral resources. Fossil fuels once burned are forever lost. Metallic minerals can furnish repeated

[18] E. P. Odum, *Fundamentals of Ecology*, Saunders, 1954; J. H. Storer, *The Web of Life*, Signet Books, 1956.

use by secondary recovery; nevertheless they are eventually dissipated by corrosion, wear, and other loss. This generation of additional economic scarcity is thus a necessary consequence in a society which utilizes non-renewable mineral resources. The rate of such deterioration in resource availability can be moderated only as society chooses to consume less of these natural resources.

Waste and wise use. All of the foregoing economic scarcities occur even under conditions of wise use of resources. In conservation doctrine, the above scarcities are in practice inescapable. The limits of the world are physical bounds. The facts of ecological interdependencies are physical. Man's weakening of the natural ecological system occurs because of the physical drains occasioned by his large numbers and industrialized society.

But these scarcity forces are greatly aggravated by waste. In conservation literature, waste is given much attention as a source of economic scarcity of natural resources. This is not to say that there is attributed to waste more importance than "limits" or "ecological balance" or "upset of balance" as the origins of scarcity. Rather, waste is emphasized because the other origins of scarcity tend to be a non-active, constraining type, whereas waste is an active input to the generation of scarcity. In this sense, waste is similar to the pressure of large modern societies in weakening ecological balance and exploiting irreplaceable mineral resources. Like these scarcity forces, waste depends upon man's activities. But unlike them waste is easily avoidable by "wise use." Waste is man's foolishness in aggravating an already existing and ineluctable situation of natural resource scarcity.

What constitutes waste? The conservationist slogan answer of "unwise" or "inefficient" use does not carry us very far. I have therefore distilled four types of "waste" from the enormous conservation literature of the period to illustrate the meaning of the term in conservation doctrine.

Destructive use of natural resource. One type of waste is destructive utilization of a natural resource where it would be possible to procure *approximately the same kind* of product or service by non-destructive use of that resource, of a renewable resource, or of another, more plentiful resource. If arid grazing land is turned to crop production, with subsequent erosion, this is waste. If hydropower dams are permitted to silt with eventual reduction or total loss of their output, this is waste. If coal, oil, or gas, irreplaceable in nature, are used to generate electric power while undeveloped water power sites remain unexploited, this is waste.

The list of examples can be greatly multiplied, by means of the following simple rules I have concocted of what conservationists meant by "waste avoidance" and "wise use":

A. renewable resources, such as forests, grazing land, crop land, water, should not be physically damaged or destroyed;

B. renewable resources should be used in place of nonrenewable ones, insofar as *physically* possible;

C. plentiful mineral resources should be used before less plentiful ones, insofar as *physically* possible.

These rules are not the ones of a laissez-faire economy. Such an economy is guided by revenue maximization and cost minimization in the producing sphere, and utility maximization and freedom of choice in the consumer one. In conservation doctrines, such a society is wasteful and generates natural resource scarcity.

Physical mismanagement of renewable resources. The second type of waste is failure to procure the maximum sustained *physical* yield of useful extractive products from nature's renewable resources. Whereas the first type of waste includes over-exploitation of renewable resources to the point where their capacities are reduced, this type of waste is under-exploitation. Production of crops, fish, livestock, timber, and hydropower should be maximized to the limits of sustained physical yield from the respective resources. In two ways, it is wasteful not to partake fully from nature's ecological bounty. If nature's perennial yield is not used, then this is viewed as waste in an elemental sense, as leaving fruit to rot on the tree or vine is waste. And if the renewable resources are not used to the maximum of their sustained physical yield potential, then non-renewable resources will tend to be drawn upon.

Physical mismanagement of non-renewable resources. As the second type of waste characterized mismanagement of renewable resources, so the third type of waste which generates resource scarcity relates to mismanagement of non-renewable ones. Waste occurs with respect to mineral resources from failure to maximize the physical yield of extractive product from the physical resources which are destroyed. As noted earlier, there is serious doubt whether the pools of oil in the earth should be tapped so rapidly. But to the extent that a pool is tapped and drawn upon, then it is wasteful, and productive of scarcity, not to maximize the volume of petroleum eventually withdrawn from the pool. Again, this is quite a simple and straightforward notion. If a resource is to be used, then let it be used, not spoiled. To conduct oil production in such way as to make only 20 per cent of the pool recoverable, or coal mining so as to leave 50 per cent of the deposit underground and unrecoverable—these are waste and generate scarcity.

Unwise use of the products of resources. The first type of waste, above, resulted from not using resources in proper order of priority, and the second and third from exploiting resources unwisely. The fourth type of waste in conservation doctrine results from unwise use *not* of the natural resource itself, but of the extractive products yielded by it. Gas should be withdrawn for use only, and not flared. Mineral fuels were withdrawn from nature to furnish useful heat; to burn them in furnaces of low thermal efficiency is wasteful. Metals were mined and timber cut to provide useful services; since they are physically recoverable as secondary materials and scrap, they must be so recovered or there is waste. This is further extension to the utilization sphere of the principle of maximizing *physical* yield and minimizing *physical* destruction of natural resources.

445

Unlike the other scarcity forces enumerated earlier, waste is remediable. Waste results from ignorance or apathy of man in his individual behavior; from physical inefficiency in use of natural resources because of improper criteria built into the laissez-faire system; from inefficient government activity and inadequate government intervention in the economic sphere; and other causes.

Social effects of scarcity. What, according to conservation doctrine are the consequences of natural resource scarcity, from the facts: that nature is limited; that nature is an ecological balance; that modern society is damaging to that ecology and necessarily destructive of mineral resources; and that wasteful behavior aggravates scarcity?

As the result of scarcity, major portions of the population are unnecessarily separated from livelihood on the land and association with the land, with resultant evil social consequences. There is a reduction in the relative numbers of the most valuable group of citizenry, the independent farmer, and a weakening of agrarianism—the core of national life. Ethical values are perverted by crass materialism and urban pleasures. There is increased industrialism and urbanism, an undesirable development, and a poor trade for the former agricultural society. The beauty and wonder of Nature are increasingly lost, to ourselves and our descendants. There is psychic damage, to the individual, the family, the community, and the nation.

Effects of scarcity on economic structure. The economic effects of scarcity, in conservation literature, are of two kinds: those involving economic structure and organization of the nation, and those involving productivity, cost, and price.

The conservationists found that, unless remedial steps were taken by government and the citizenry, the forces of resource scarcity, coupled with the high efficiency of the trust form of industrial organization, would produce monopoly, and maldistributions of income among the populace so severe as to be inconsistent with a democratic society. From scarcity and monopoly control there would increasingly develop larger and larger profits—unearned increment. The eventual outcome would be severe maldistribution of land and property ownership, and of income.

Cost and productivity effects of scarcity. In conservation literature, resource scarcity was a powerful force working to reduce labor productivity and to increase the real cost of all products. The growing economy would increasingly press upon already scarce resources. Destructive utilization of minerals would make them more scarce. Encroachment of cities and highways would further reduce available resources. And waste would be the final turn of the screw to grind the American society to poverty and misery. Output per worker would decline steadily. The real cost of commodities would rise steadily. Real income per capita would steadily fall, to subsistence levels.

Interpreting conservation economic doctrine. My purpose in probing into the First Conservation Movement was to improve understanding of this important source of the doctrine of natural resource scarcity, both because the movement was an important development in the nation's history and because much contemporary view derives from that movement. I wanted to unearth the assumptions of this doctrine and observe the logic of the analysis. I was interested in the elements and details from which the crucial scarcity generalizations were compounded And I was interested in the conservation movement's own antecedents and major sources of ideas. The quest, I think, has been at least partly successful. I have dug out premises, ascertained the structure of the analysis, and detailed the conservation theses in various ways. I have learned the important fact that quantitative economic analysis of antecedent nineteenth century economic evidence did not in any rigorous way enter the analysis of economic scarcity and economic effect.

But a word of warning is appropriate. For a variety of reasons, it is extremely difficult to ascertain and interpret the economic doctrine of scarcity of the First Conservation Movement. The leading figures of the movement were not economists, and there is no evidence in their writings that they had any substantial training in economic analysis. This means that there is little or no recourse to rigorous economic formulation and statement, and therefore that the meanings of terms are sometimes uncertain to an economist-reviewer of the literature.

Despite the difficulties and uncertainties, I believe that I have accurately characterized the essential elements in the conservation doctrine of natural resource scarcity. The movement was enormously successful in its own time. And its influence reaches to the present. As in President Taft's time, so today "A great many people are in favor of conservation, no matter what it means."[19] To the extent to which I have been successful, then, the discussion should be not only a useful contribution in its own terms, but also speak, in some degree, to conservation beliefs which most of us hold as revealed doctrine.

The views of most other economists on the conservation movement differ from the interpretive summary I have presented above. So far as

---

[19] *Outlook*, May 14, 1910, p. 57, quoted in J. Ise, *The U.S. Forest Policy*, Yale University Press, 1920, p. 373.

I know, most professional economists who have made important contributions in the economics of natural resources tend to consider conservation as concerned with the economic problem of *time rate of use* of natural resources. I find this interpretation of the conservation movement to be incomplete, and possibly misleading.

Part of conservation doctrine was indeed this familiar proposition: it can be constructed from the Malthusian case by simply assuming that some resources can be, and others necessarily are, destroyed by use. In Chart 1, for example, let it merely be assumed that the resource axis gradually is "eaten away"; or in Chart 2, that resources are used up, and the economy is forced onto lower level resource isoquants. In both cases the expansion paths fall to lower levels. This, essentially, is the time rate of use problem—that there is a fixed stock whose exhaustion and changing availability depend on the time distribution of use.

But part of conservation doctrine, and the *gestalt* in which time rate of use appeared, go quite far beyond the time rate problem. To characterize conservation in this way has two defects. It credits conservation with contributions made earlier and more systematically by Malthus, Ricardo, and Jevons, among others. And it fails to credit conservation with an important and partly successful revolution in social ideas and applied political economy.

The concept of "ecological balance" is importantly different from time rate of use of a stock, and moreover is not even a very familiar idea in academic work on economics of natural resources. The additional idea of ecological damage was also a novel, or at least an undeveloped one, for economic thought. The conservationists even modified the classical notion of "limits": the resource "limits" conceived by the conservation movement as relevant were those within national boundaries, and the economic objective was national self-sufficiency—hardly consistent with the trade assumptions of classical economics. Of the hundreds of papers in the *Proceedings* of the 1908 Conference of Governors in the White House and the three-volume 1909 *Report of the National Conservation Commission to the President*, only four (by count of titles) looked outside the United States, and these did so primarily from the point of view of United States interest.

With respect to "waste" and "wise use," the characteristic economist view is that this conservation doctrine has little meaning and is of no value for economic analysis. With respect to meaning, I continue to differ. The codification I have given to waste has meaning—government administrators could follow these rules (and some do, with results that in my view are frequently unfortunate). Of course, the rules are at variance with economic common sense and understanding if these are based on laissez-faire premises. But this is the essence of the matter—conservation doctrine did, in significant degree, reject laissez-faire, consumer sovereignty principles; it questions the quality, even more than the mechanics, of modern civilization. This is why the intelligent men among them could plead for their view of "wise use" and avoidance of waste, to the mystification of later economists.[20]

5. Two Concluding Observations

In Malthus' time, and to a lesser extent during the period of the conservation furor, a considerable part of "final" or virtually final output was natural, mainly agricultural, goods—foodstuffs, natural fibers, timber, game, and so on. To this extent, increase in these outputs could be, and was, viewed as identical with economic growth. Now as to how these goods would be further processed, again there was a simple answer. They would be *mechanically* shaped from the gifts of nature—the wheat grain would be taken out; the hide separated from the meat; the timber sawed to size; the fibers combed, twisted, and woven; and so forth. Turning to the derivation of the basic substances from nature, man's role here also was a *mechanical* one. Thus, if a man stood on a square mile of land, or a nation on 3,000,000, the natural resources relevant for economic activity could be easily identified and measured. They were acres of crop land or pasture, board feet of standing timber, and the like.

A great deal has happened in advanced Western nations since these times to the meaning of final goods, the methods by which they are produced, and the definition of natural resources. With respect to the meaning of goods, more than 90 per cent of the increase in real GNP in the United States since 1870 has been of nonagricultural origin. With respect to the method of transforming materials into final goods, this has

[20] Where the economist defines the term "conservation" narrowly, with explicit warning of its delimitation, there can be no confusion. I agree, for example, with E. S. Mason, who has recently written, "If . . . conservation is defined as 'a shift in the time distribution of use of a resource in the direction of the future,' we have a set of issues that can be analyzed, but one which represents only a small part of the traditional concern of conservationists." But note that the subject thus defined omits the principal concerns which have rallied the major groups in the historical and contemporary conservation movements, and which have made conservation a major public policy issue. I am arguing that the larger questions can also be defined and merit analysis by economists. I thus think Professor Mason is too strong in his comment that, "If conservation is defined as a 'wise use of resources' nothing escapes its ken, but the invitation to subjective value judgements is so sweeping as to leave little room for rational analysis." Both quotations from "The Political Economy of Resource Use," in *Perspectives on Conservation*, The Johns Hopkins Press, 1958, pp. 157f.

become far less a purely mechanical one, and to a considerable degree a controlled heat or electro-chemical process. Finally, the natural resource building blocks have changed radically—they are atoms and molecules. That is, the natural resource input is to a far less degree acres, and to far greater degree particular chemical compounds.

This has changed the meaning of "natural resources" for societies which have modern technologies and access to capital. We now look more at contained molecules of iron, magnesium, aluminum, coal, nitrogen, and so on, and at their naturally existing chemical combinations, than at acres or board feet. While in a sense, the same ultimate world limits still exist, in a more significant sense they do not. How many taconite iron atoms or sea water magnesium atoms and bromine molecules constitute plenitude, and how many scarcity? In significant degree, further, even the ultimate limits are different from Malthus'. His natural resources were conceived for a two-dimensional world. Ours is a three-dimensional one, sustained by subsurface resources. His society could reach natural resources to only insignificant distances above and below his acres. We have multiplied our "reach" by many thousands.

I am greatly impressed by a "new" form of resource scarcity—the problem of space, privacy, and nature preservation. Actually it is not new, as the following quotation from Mill indicates.

There is room in the world, no doubt, and even in old countries, for a great increase of population, supposing the arts of life to go on improving, and capital to increase. But even if innocuous, I confess I see very little reason for desiring it. . . . A population may be too crowded, though all be amply supplied with food and raiment. It is not good for man to be kept perforce at all times in the presence of his species. A world from which solitude is extirpated, is a very poor ideal. Solitude, in the sense of being often alone, is essential to any depth of meditation or of character; and solitude in the presence of natural beauty and grandeur, is the cradle of thoughts and aspirations which are not only good for the individual, but which society could ill do without. Nor is there much satisfaction in contemplating the world with nothing left to the spontaneous activity of nature; with every rood of land brought into cultivation, which is capable of growing food for human beings; every flowery waste or natural pasture ploughed up, all quadrupeds or birds which are not domesticated for man's use exterminated as his rivals for food, every hedgerow or superfluous tree rooted out, and scarcely a place left where a wild shrub or flower could grow without being eradicated as a weed in the name of improved agriculture. (J. S. Mill, *Principles*, London, 1871, Bk. IV, ch. 6)

It may surprise this audience to learn that by far the largest fraction of contemporary conservationists are concerned with this form of resource scarcity, and not with minerals or agricultural land shortages.

This category of doctrine already includes a "quality scarcity" concern over fouling streams, disfiguring land, and air pollution. And I guess it should also include concern over atmospheric and land contamination by radioactivity.

As to whether this is a proper area for economic analysis, this is obviously a decision for the individual economist. It has been sanctioned as a problem in political economy from Mill to Pigou at least. It is part of the problem of social investment and communal resource use which is increasingly concerning economists. Finally, it is a problem of sizable economic dimensions.

COMMENT

EDGAR M. HOOVER, Harvard University

Barnett's paper has a rare combination of qualities—it is both careful and provocative. I had hoped I might find in it some occasion to pick a quarrel with him, but shall have to leave that to others. I propose to accept his findings about the origin of the scarcity doctrine, and to go on to ask, "What can we now conclude about whether there is, or is not, a 'population problem' or a 'resources problem' to worry about?"

In a commendably rigorous way, Barnett has deflated the Malthusian bogey of population growth eventually reducing the world to a state in which the bulk of the population everywhere is on the edge of starvation. He has shown that no less than five conditions would have to prevail in order to make the bogey operate according to specifications, and that each of the five may be questioned. In essence, there is one loophole on the demographic side, and at least two on the economic side.

Does this dispose of the "population problem" and the "resources problem"? I thought it might be fruitful to try to set up a model, as Barnett has done—but in this case a model defined by the absence of any population or resources problem. More specifically, what are the basic conditions that would give us an economy in which no case could be made for any kind of policy designed to restrict either population growth or resources exploitation? How realistic are these conditions? In just a few minutes I cannot do the sort of model-building job he did, but can merely heave out a few pieces of rough building material.

First of all, we shall not find the necessary basic conditions for complacency in the densely populated backward economies, where population pressure and the resource limitations are all too evident and Malthus would feel right at home. So we have to restrict our inquiry to the range of conditions that might apply in advanced countries.

451

Now, a conceivably sufficient condition for absence of a resources problem would be that resources were not scarce—that is, that they were free goods and exercised no constraint upon output. This can be ruled out as both trivial and incompatible with the conditions of an advanced industrialized economy. (I interpret Barnett's contention about resources scarcity to mean not that no scarcity exists, but that resources are not getting *more* scarce as time goes on.)

On the demographic side, a possibly sufficient condition would be that population growth would automatically slow down to a halt while income was still high. Until about 15 years ago many people might have thought this a realistic assumption or "law" of population growth in advanced countries. In view of subsequent demographic experience, however, it seems exceedingly improbable.

What about the technological escape from Malthus? (Technological progress includes here, of course, the creation of new resources.) Is it enough if we can count on technology advancing indefinitely? No. In order to make population growth a matter of no concern, we should have to assume much more—namely, that the rate of technological advance is positively geared to the rate of population growth. Is this a realistic assumption? I know of no basis for concluding that technical progress responds in this way.

What, then, about the scale economies (internal and external) of larger population? If we could assume that these scale effects operated (apart from technological advance) so as to produce at least constant returns to labor in the social production function, then we should not have to worry about any economic burden from overpopulation. This seems in fact to be a necessary condition for our "no-problem" model, in view of the fact that none of the alternative conditions we have so far considered seems at all likely to apply in the real world.

This question of the form of the social production function is a complex one. We might ask first, what about the growth of capital? If the rate of capital accumulation could be assumed to vary in close response to the rate of population growth, then we could (as Barnett does) simply consider labor and capital together as one input. But this does not seem to be the case, judging from experience. The observed association is slight, if any. Faster population growth can not be counted on to produce correspondingly faster capital accumulation.

So perhaps everything hinges on the scale economies of a larger population per se. What are those based on? Adam Smith had a pretty good answer: the more complex division of labor, which in turn depends on widening the range of contacts among individual units of production and consumption.

But does the "extent of the market," to use Smith's term, depend really on the ratio of population to natural resources? If it did, then we might have here a population-growth effect that would transform diminishing returns into constant or even increasing returns to population.

Actually the range of contacts and division of labor depend on a somewhat different sort of ratio: population relative to area and to the costs of transport and communication. Natural resources, as Barnett points out, have less and less direct association with area. The really crucial factor is the cost of contact. Is it affected by population density?

It is very significantly affected, because most means of transport are themselves subject to economies of scale (that is, traffic density). For example, in the nineteenth century the actual and anticipated growth of population in the United States warranted the building of railroads, which greatly widened the spatial range of division of labor and contributed to an over-all rise in productivity. With a very sparse and static population, this would not have occurred.

I suggest, however, that this experience may not be a very good basis for generalization. Subsequently developed means of contact like motor transport, air transport, and radio do not seem to be anywhere near so dependent on high traffic density to achieve economy. Moreover, it is possible to run into *increasing* costs from traffic density when the amount of space required for transport itself becomes a large factor. Road and also air traffic in our larger urban areas would seem already to be in this stage, and population densities in such areas are in process of thinning out rather than increasing. It would seem, then, that we cannot assume that population growth in technologically advanced countries will continue to produce scale economies to offset against diminishing returns.

Here it is useful to remind ourselves that that peculiarly natural resource, space, plays a unique and dual economic role. On the one hand, space is a "negative resource" or natural handicap—it embodies distance to be bridged in order to effect economically useful contacts. When space in viewed in that aspect, its intensive occupancy by people appears as a source of increasing returns (to population). But at the same time, space has value as elbow room (entirely apart from any useful materials it may contain), and in this aspect increased density of occupancy leads to diminishing returns. In closing, I should like to second and underline Barnett's reference to the steadily increasing importance of this second aspect, especially from the consumer welfare standpoint.

Space-scarcity is in the last analysis inexorable, and is being accentuated in every advanced society by rising standards of income, leisure, and personal mobility.

To sum up: Barnett has shown that, despite the warnings of extreme Malthusians and conservationists, we are not necessarily damned—(at least, not if we can confine our concern to the more advanced countries). I have shown, less adequately, that we are not necessarily saved either. I expect we would both agree that complacency with regard either to population growth or resources use is unwarranted.

THEODORE W. SCHULTZ, University of Chicago

This paper reminds one how indebted we are to talent from the exact sciences for revealing to us the ominous scarcity of natural resources. Barnett's paper opens with a selection of statements of the relationships between population and food (natural resources) drawn from distinguished physical and biological scientists. We expect these to be models of the best in scientific analysis; axioms explicit and exact, concepts clear and identifiable, and the connections rigorous and precise. The thinking of this elite should, therefore, be sobering for such as us. In model one, the growth of the human population in the earth's ecological economy is represented as a cancer. Model two informs us that if we breed like rabbits, in the long run we have to live and die like rabbits. Model three reveals to us that humanity behaves as if it would not rest content until the earth is covered completely and to a considerable depth with a writhing mass of human beings, much as a dead cow is covered with a pulsating mass of maggots. No doubt, the exact mode of thought of scientists gives them bold and compelling imagery. This remarkable talent should not be lost for poetry. Population and food, however, might better be spared.

A major part of Barnett's paper is devoted to an examination of the first American conservation movement. Three things emerge: he finds that this movement made many useful contributions; it did much to shape and advance the doctrine of economic scarcity of natural resources; and economists generally have failed to see the real contributions that this movement made. I shall contend that in reaching these conclusions Barnett may have sold economics short in those areas of analysis where it has some relevant things to say about the ideas attributed to this movement. I am asking for economic criticism.

Economic criticism is important. It is based on a fairly well-defined and established set of standards. There are, of course, other important standards of criticism. However, in the case of the doctrine under review and in examining and evaluating the role that the conservation movement played in it, economic standards are among the appropriate ones and as economists we should have some special competence in this form of criticism. The approach that Barnett uses in this paper does not examine critically the ideas that he attributes to the conservation movement and that presumably support the doctrine under review.

The conservation movement was, as Barnett points out, an assemblage of many ideas. These ideas presumably had some connections with the doctrine of economic scarcity of natural resources. I have no doubt that they did, but I am puzzled because it is not at all clear to me from this paper how these ideas are connected with this particular doctrine.

Any growth in population increases the ratio of the number of people to the area (surface) of the earth, and, of course, also, to the cubic content of the earth. Surely, the doctrine under review was not based on any notion as crude as that, although the poetic images of those scientists to whom I referred at the outset would appear to qualify on this score. What, then, was the substance of this doctrine of economic scarcity of natural resources? Did it pertain to free versus scarce (not free) natural resources, or to natural resources becoming scarcer relative to other resources, or did it encompass both of these relationships? These questions, however, go unanswered, and it is, therefore, not clear what is meant by this doctrine.

For my purposes I shall define this doctrine as representing views based on the belief that natural resources become scarcer relative to other resources as population increases and economic growth proceeds. Resources, whatever their form, natural or otherwise, are here viewed not as free but as scarce components that render valuable services in production.

Barnett observes that the first conservation movement was in opposition to the "then dominant social philosophy of the self-regulating market economy." But they looked upon this malfunctioning of the market economy as affecting adversely all resources and not exclusively or especially that of natural resources. The view that there are absolute limits to the quantity of coal, iron, water, and presumably also to that of agricultural products and wood implies a set of loose connections that may or may not support the doctrine. It is, therefore, the task of economic criticism to make clear that these particular connections in themselves do not necessarily result in, say, coal becoming scarcer relative to labor as population increases and economic growth proceeds. The idea of ecological balance would appear to represent a form of external economies but it does not necessarily support the doctrine. Then, too, the idea of waste and wise use, when it is given economic content, is applicable to each and every resource; it is in no way specific to natural resources. The list of bad social effects of scarcity and of monopoly are not restricted to scarcity or monopoly in the area of natural resources. What this says is: (1) The doctrine means that natural resources become scarcer relative to other resources, and (2) The particular ideas attributed to this movement pertain almost entirely to other issues.

The principal difficulty in classifying and evaluating the ideas of this movement is conceptual in nature. What is needed at the outset is a clear and identifiable concept of economic scarcity applicable to particular natural resources. This concept must specify scarcity in terms of values, that is, in relative prices, and the type of scarcity that is relevant pertains to the changes in values that are associated with increases in real national income (a measure of economic growth) and increases in population. Can one use a classification of products, that is, of raw materials, semi-processed, and finished products? As a very rough approximation, changes in the relative prices of these classes of products may be of some help. But these prices can mislead one seriously. We must specify the prices of the services rendered by a particular natural resource relative to the prices of the services rendered by other resources (of labor and of reproducible durable capital, for example).

Once we see clearly that it is the change in the relative price of the service of a natural resource that is the key to the concept, it follows that it is possible for the evidence (economic growth data) to reveal rising, or constant, or falling relative prices for the services of a natural resource. Presumably, ideas in support of the doctrine of economic scarcity of natural resources would attempt to show that the relative price of the services of natural resources had been rising and would continue to rise. But this is not the burden of the ideas that Barnett attributes to the conservation movement; on the contrary, these particular ideas are not inconsistent either with constant or falling relative prices of the services of the resources under discussion. Accordingly, these ideas do not argue either for or against the doctrine.

Population Change and the Demand for Food

JEAN A. CROCKETT

UNIVERSITY OF PENNSYLVANIA

WHILE a large number of factors affect family food consumption, the present paper is concerned with only five of these: income—clearly the most important single influence, family size, age of head, race, and location of family (whether in a metropolitan area or not, whether in the northern, southern, or western part of the United States), all of which may be considered demographic variables.

Intercorrelations among these variables make it difficult to isolate their separate influences. For example, any measure of the income effect is distorted by the other four variables, unless some way is found of holding these constant in the statistical analysis. Large families spend more for food than small at the same income, but they also tend to have higher incomes. Thus, only part of the higher consumption of large, high income families is properly attributable to income effects, but all will be so attributed unless family size is in some way introduced into the analysis. Furthermore, white families (particularly at low incomes,) spend more on food than Negroes with the same income and family size, perhaps in part because a very low current income is less likely to be considered "normal" by white families than by Negro families. Families with middle-aged heads spend more on food than either young families or old families with the same income and family size, and at the same time tend to have higher incomes. These families include a relatively high proportion of adolescents and fairly active adults, who may be expected to eat more heavily than either the small children characteristic of the younger families or the less physically active adults characteristic of the oldest families. Finally, white families in metropolitan areas in the north spend more on food than in other regions for the same income and family size, and also tend to have higher incomes. These families are faced with higher food prices than in other areas and, as compared with families in small cities, are more inclined to eat meals away from home. Thus the

Note: This paper is based on research undertaken in connection with the Wharton School Study of Consumer Expenditures, Incomes and Savings. The study is based largely on the 1950 survey by the Bureau of Labor Statistics of some 12,500 families in 91 representative cities, and is being carried out in cooperation with that agency. It is financed by a grant from the Ford Foundation.

higher income brackets contain a disproportionately large number of large families, white families, families with middle-aged heads, and families living in metropolitan areas in the north, all of which have unusually large food expenditures, not only because of their higher incomes but also because of their demographic characteristics. The result will be an overstatement of the influence of income unless the demographic factors are effectively held constant when this influence is measured.

An intermixture of the effect of income with that of other variables might not be undesirable if the intercorrelations could be counted on to remain unchanged. But this, unfortunately, is not true. In particular, where cross-sectional and time series information are to be combined we run into trouble on this score. A rise in average income over time is not in general accompanied by the same sort of shift in the age, regional, racial, and family size distribution that we find as we move from lower to higher income groups at a point of time. In fact, we expect a rising income over the next few years to be accompanied by a lower incidence (relative frequency) of middle-aged families and a higher incidence of Negroes.

Since the integration of time series and cross-sectional information is highly useful in demand studies, it becomes a major purpose of cross-sectional analysis to approximate a "pure" or "net" income elasticity for consumption items. A second major purpose is to isolate the effects on consumption of other major variables, including the four demographic factors considered here, so that the impact of distributional shifts in these variables over time may be estimated.[1] Because of the previously mentioned intercorrelations with income it is impossible to approach the effects of the demographic variables without first allowing for the primary effect of income. But even after this is done, correlations exist among the four demographic variables—for example, tendencies toward smaller family size among older people and larger family size among Negroes and in nonmetropolitan areas—making it desirable to hold constant, as far as possible, all of these variables except the one whose effect is being studied.

It is the purpose of this paper to develop procedures for estimating the effects on consumption behavior of shifts in the distribution of families among demographic groups, under the assumption that cross-sectional differences among these groups—holding other variables constant—are

---

[1] This involves the assumption of a reasonable degree of stability over time in the effects of these variables. Only by comparison of successive cross sections can we be sure that such stability exists.

reasonably stable over time. These procedures are applied to the case of food expenditures in the period 1950–1970, with particular reference to expected changes in the age and race-area distributions.

Regressions Computed from 1950 Data for Age and Race-Area Groups

In pursuit of the major aims mentioned above, two types of cross-sectional regressions have been computed for food expenditures from the 1950 BLS data on urban families.[2] The first is based on grouped data[3] and in most cases excludes families with incomes under $1,000. The model used is

$$F = aY^b n^c \text{ or } \log F = \log a + b \log Y + c \log n$$

where F is average family food expenditure (excluding alcoholic beverages), Y is average family money income after taxes, and n is average family size. Regressions of this type are available for various race-area groups, for various age groups, and for various occupational groups.[4]

The second type of regression is part of a larger analysis involving all major categories and some subcategories of consumption and saving. It is based on individual family data and excludes Negro families, the self-employed or not gainfully employed, and families with incomes under $1,000 or over $10,000. The model used is

$$F = a + bY + c_j, j = 1, 2, 3, 4$$

where F and Y are family food expenditures and money income after taxes respectively, and j represents family size. For family size four and over, $j = 4$. Regressions of this type are available for various age-tenure-assets-income change-income expectation groups.[5] Separate studies are

[2] The term "family" throughout this paper is understood to include unrelated individuals as one-person families.

[3] Cross-tabulations published in *Study of Consumer Expenditures, Incomes and Savings*, Vols. III and XVIII, University of Pennsylvania, 1956–1957.

[4] For further discussion, see Jean Crockett, "Demand Relationships for Food," forthcoming in *Proceedings of the Conference on Consumption and Saving*, University of Pennsylvania, 1960.

[5] Since the analysis in this paper of the effects of demographic shifts is based on these two sets of regressions and since both relate to food expenditures, the conclusions derived must also refer to food expenditures rather than caloric intake or some other concept of food consumption. It appears from Mr. Fox's comments that this point has not been clear to him.

Mr. Fox also appears to be laboring under the rather common delusion that an expenditure elasticity, as obtained from cross-section data, is not the relevant cross-section parameter for comparison with an income elasticity of quantity derived from the usual time series data. Price effects in a cross-section study largely reflect quality differences and not differences in prices paid for the same quality by different income groups, so that expenditure figures—but not quantity figures—incorporate quality shifts. Similarly a shift from lower to higher quality over time is reflected by an increase in the price weighted quantity index ordinarily used as the dependent variable in time series analysis.

planned which will cover Negroes, the self-employed, and those not gainfully employed.[6]

Regressions of the first type have an advantage in that, (1) the double log regression (exponential regression) provides a somewhat better fit for food than the linear, (2) the family size effect is handled more precisely than in the second set of regressions, (3) a finer age break is available, and (4) a larger portion of the total population is covered. On the other hand, it is not possible to hold race constant in the age regressions or age constant in the race-area regressions. The effects of area are not in fact held constant in the age regressions presented here, though they will be in work now in progress.

Regressions of the second type make use of the additional information provided by individual observations and hold constant many more variables. For example, the tenure of dwelling unit, the income change-income expectation pattern, and the debt-asset position are all likely to be correlated with age of head, and it is not clear that the cross-sectional correlations will be maintained over time. Thus, the net effect of age is measured more accurately from the second set of regressions. On the other hand, area is not held constant and this is a fairly significant factor in food expenditure. Furthermore, fairly large sectors of the population are excluded and a number of regressions must be combined to obtain an average age effect for that portion which is covered.

In the double log regressions the income elasticity is found to be roughly the same for all age groups, for all area groups among the white families, and for all area groups among the Negroes. Some differences were found in family size elasticities, which were relatively low among the youngest families, relatively high among the oldest families, and a little higher for northern than for southern and western families. Since the differences were in most cases well within the range of sampling error, each elasticity was averaged over age groups, over area groups for white families, and over area groups for Negro families, and a single figure used within each of these three groups. There were significant differences in the elasticities between white and Negro families in the same area; and substantial differences in level occur among age groups and among area groups within both the white and the Negro categories.

The regressions obtained, using average values of the elasticities in the double log regressions, are given on pp. 461–462.

---

[6] For further discussion, see Jean Crockett and Irwin Friend, "A Complete Set of Consumer Demand Relationships," forthcoming in *Proceedings of the Conference on Consumption and Saving*, University of Pennsylvania, 1960.

AGE GROUPS

Double log regressions (excluding families with incomes under $1,000)

(1)	Under 25:	$F = 10.2 \ Y^{0.522}n^{0.317}$
(2)	25–34:	$F = 10.6 \ Y^{0.522}n^{0.317}$
(3)	35–44:	$F = 11.2 \ Y^{0.522}n^{0.317}$
(4)	45–54:	$F = 11.6 \ Y^{0.522}n^{0.317}$
(5)	55–64:	$F = 11.6 \ Y^{0.522}n^{0.317}$
(6)	65–74:	$F = 11.1 \ Y^{0.522}n^{0.317}$
(7)	75 and over:	$F = 10.4 \ Y^{0.522}n^{0.317}$

Linear regressions for white employee families with income between $1,000 and $10,000 and cash assets less than $500

(8) Renters under 35

    a. 1 person family: $F = 255 + 0.192Y - 110$

    b. 2 person family: $F = 255 + .192Y$

    c. 3 person family: $F = 255 + .192Y + 142$

    d. 4 or more person family: $F = 255 + .192Y + 313$

(9) Renters 35–54

    a. 1 person family: $F = 357 + .192Y - 110$

    b. 2 person family: $F = 357 + .192Y$

    c. 3 person family: $F = 357 + .192Y + 142$

    d. 4 or more person family: $F = 357 + .192Y + 313$

(10) Renters 55 and over

    a. 1 person family: $F = 369 + .192Y - 110$

    b. 2 person family: $F = 369 + .192Y$

    c. 3 person family: $F = 369 + .192Y + 142$

    d. 4 or more person family: $F = 369 + .192Y + 313$

(11) Homeowners under 35

    a. 1 person family: $F = 264 + .153Y - 175$

    b. 2 person family: $F = 264 + .153Y$

    c. 3 person family: $F = 264 + .153Y + 176$

    d. 4 or more person family: $F = 264 + .153Y + 372$

(12) Homeowners 35–54

    a. 1 person family: $F = 391 + .153 Y - 175$

    b. 2 person family: $F = 391 + .153 Y$

    c. 3 person family: $F = 391 + .153 Y + 176$

    d. 4 or more person family: $F = 391 + .153 Y + 372$

(13) Homeowners 55 and over

    a. 1 person family: $F = 414 + .153 Y - 175$

    b. 2 person family: $F = 414 + .153 Y$

    c. 3 person family: $F = 414 + .153 Y + 176$

    d. 4 or more person family: $F = 414 + .153 Y + 372$

RACE-AREA GROUPS

Double log regressions (excluding white families with incomes under \$1,000)

(14) White northern metropolitan: $F = 14.9 \quad Y^{0.488} n^{0.335}$

(15) Total northern nonmetropolitan: $F = 13.4 \quad Y^{0.488} n^{0.335}$

(16) White southern metropolitan: $F = 13.9 \quad Y^{0.488} n^{0.335}$

(17) White southern nonmetropolitan: $F = 13.0 \quad Y^{0.488} n^{0.335}$

(18) Total western metropolitan: $F = 13.7 \quad Y^{0.488} n^{0.335}$

(19) Total western nonmetropolitan: $F = 13.8 \quad Y^{0.488} n^{0.335}$

(20) Negro northern metropolitan: $F = 6.78 \; Y^{0.591} n^{0.219}$

(21) Negro southern metropolitan: $F = 6.25 \; Y^{0.591} n^{0.219}$

(22) Negro southern nonmetropolitan: $F = 6.23 \; Y^{0.591} n^{0.219}$

Effect of Distributional Changes on Aggregate Food Consumption

The change in aggregate demand for food between, say, 1950 and 1970 may be separated into several elements: (1) the effect of growth in the total number of families and of change in average family size; (2) the effect of growth in average income (or changes in the shape of the income distribution) within demographic groups; (3) the effect of distributional changes in the population, which would, of course, imply some income and family size changes even if the income and family size distributions within groups remained entirely unchanged; and (4) the effect of shifts in consumption behavior within the demographic subgroups, reflecting not only such factors as changes in relative prices or in tastes, which might affect all population groups more or less uniformly, but also factors causing differential shifts, such as the more complete assimilation of Negroes in the metropolitan North.

This paper is confined to considerations of type (3)—the effect of shifts among various demographic groups, assuming that the characteristics of each group as to food consumption remain unchanged. The interesting problems of type (4), involving either time series analysis or a comparison among successive cross-sectional studies, are beyond our present scope.

INTEGRATION OF DISTRIBUTIONAL EFFECTS INTO AN ESTIMATE OF TOTAL CHANGE IN FOOD CONSUMPTION[7]

The changes in food expenditure arising from demographic shifts, as estimated in this paper, may be integrated into an estimate of the total change in food expenditure (in constant dollars) between two points of time in the following way. We consider a number of population groups, differing in their food consumption patterns, and express aggregate food expenditure as the sum of the expenditures of these groups

$$M\sum_i p_i x_i$$

where M is the total number of families, p_i is the proportion of families falling in the ith group, and x_i is the average expenditure per family in the ith group. If the number of families changes by ΔM, the proportion of families in the ith group by Δp_i, and the average expenditure in the ith group by Δx_i then the change in aggregate food expenditure is given by

$$(23) \qquad (M + \Delta M)\sum_i (p_i + \Delta p_i)(x_i + \Delta x_i) - M\sum_i p_i x_i$$

$$(A) \qquad = \Delta M\sum_i p_i x_i$$

$$(B) \qquad + (M + \Delta M)\sum_i p_i\Delta x_i$$

$$(C) \qquad + (M + \Delta M)\sum_i \Delta p_i(x_i + \Delta x_i)$$

If we assume that the family size distributions within demographic groups remain unchanged and that the relationship of expenditure to income and family size within each demographic group is stable over time (no changes in relative prices or in tastes), then changes in average

---

[7] This section incorporates and further develops remarks made at the Conference in response to the comments of Mr. Fox. The expository approach used is suggested by Robert Ferber's paper in this volume.

expenditure within groups result from changes in income only. In this case (A) may be considered a crude first approximation to the change in aggregate expenditure, reflecting only the change in number of families, while (A) + (B) is a second approximation reflecting changes both in the number of families and in (real) income, but neglecting demographic shifts. (A) + (B) + (C) is then a third approximation, incorporating the effects of demographic shifts.

The first approximation (A) requires no expectational information except the change in number of families. The second approximation requires, in addition, only knowledge of the change in average income, say Δy, if this is assumed to be the same for all groups and if the expenditure-income relationship is linear. In this case the term (B) reduces to

$$(M + \Delta M)b\Delta y$$

where b is a weighted average of the marginal propensities to consume food for the various groups, using frequency weights. If income movements are expected to differ significantly among the groups, then the change in average income for each group must be known.

If the expenditure-income relationship is linear in the logarithms and if the income elasticity (though not the level of expenditure) is the same for all groups, then under the restrictive assumption that each family experiences the same per cent change in income, (B) reduces to

$$(M + \Delta M) \left[\left(1 + \frac{\Delta y}{y} \right)^b - 1 \right] \sum_i p_i x_i$$

where b is now the income elasticity (assumed constant for all groups) and $\Delta y/y$ is the relative change in average income. Again the only expectational information required is the change in number of families and in average income. Under less restrictive assumptions, the expected income distributions for each group must be known.

This paper is concerned with the estimation of (C), which must be added to (A) + (B) to obtain the third approximation mentioned above. Estimates of average expenditures within groups are obtained from equations (1)–(22) and the effects of projected changes in the p_i are computed on the basis of these estimates.

In a linear model if marginal propensities (though not levels) are constant among groups and if the change in average income is assumed to be the same for all groups, (C) reduces to

$$(M + \Delta M) \sum_i x_i \Delta p_i$$

requiring only knowledge of the expected change in the number of families and in the proportion of families within each group. In a double log model with constant income elasticity among groups and the same per cent change in income assumed for each family, the only further knowledge required is the expected change in average income. Under less restrictive assumptions, the expected income distribution for each group is required.

The differences among the demographic groups studied are not large in the case of total food expenditures, and thus the value of (C) will ordinarily be small compared to (A) or (B). However (C) is likely to be relatively much larger for certain food subgroups and for certain non-food expenditures, and the estimation procedures developed here are equally applicable to such items. Furthermore the changes in expenditures for individual groups, as estimated below, are sometimes found to be large, both in relation to (C) and in relation to the initial expenditures of these groups (for example, Negroes in large cities in the north), and may therefore be of some interest to the suppliers of these groups.

Still further refinements may be made if some information is available as to expected shifts in the family size distribution, or in relative prices, or in tastes. If the parameters of the expenditure-income-family size relationships for individual groups show persistent time trends, then a comparison of successive cross-sections might lead to improved estimates of future expenditures. Such time trends might occur if, for example, the observed cross-sectional differences among age groups are only partially age specific and in part cohort specific, or if Negroes become more completely assimilated over time.

MEASUREMENT OF DISTRIBUTIONAL EFFECTS

If by 1970 we have a much larger proportion than in 1950 of families with heads under 25 or over 65, this should have three consequences, all of which may be expected to lower food consumption.

(a) An age effect—these families tend to eat less for the same income and family size than families with middle-aged heads.

(b) An income effect—these families tend to have lower incomes than middle-aged families.

(c) A family size effect—these families tend to have smaller families than the middle-aged.

Similarly, if by 1970 Negroes in small cities in the south constitute a smaller proportion of population than in 1950 and Negroes in metropolitan areas in the north a larger proportion, we may expect (a) larger food consumption for given income and family size, (b) higher incomes, and (c) smaller families. Thus the family size effect, though relatively small for Negroes, partially offsets the other two.

The effect on aggregate food expenditures of shifts among demographic groups is somewhat simpler to estimate from the linear than from the double log model. Let us assume that for families in the ith age (or other demographic) group with family size j:

$$F = a_i + bY + c_j.[8]$$

Then the average expenditure of families of this type is

$$\bar{F}_{ij} = a_i + b\bar{Y}_{ij} + c_j;$$

and the average expenditure of families in the ith age group, without regard to family size, is

$$\bar{F}_i = a_i + b\bar{Y}_i + \sum_j w_{ij}c_j,$$

where w_{ij} is the relative frequency of family size j in the ith age group.

If the number of families is N,[9] then the effect on food consumption of a shift of r_i per cent of these families into $(r_i > 0)$ or out of $(r_i < 0)$ the ith age group is given by

$$0.01 r_i N(a_i + b\bar{Y}_i + \sum_j w_{ij}c_j).[10]$$

The aggregate effect of the total of such shifts is

$$(24) \qquad 0.01 N \sum_i r_i(a_i + b\bar{Y}_i + \sum_j w_{ij}c_j),$$

where $\sum_i r_i = 0$. Note that the three terms in the above expression correspond, respectively, to the age effect, the income effect, and the family size effect of the distributional shift.

If we are interested in the effect of such a shift on 1970 food consumption, 1970 values should be used for the number of families, the average income within age groups, and the family size distribution within age groups. If the change in average income from 1950 to 1970 is approximately constant over age groups, however, the 1950 value of average income may be used, since

$$\sum_i r_i b(\bar{Y}_{i(1950)} + K) = \sum_i r_i b\bar{Y}_{i(1950)}.$$

---

[8] This implies not only linearity of the food-income relationship but the absence of any sizable interactions among the income, family size, and age effects. On the basis of pretests, such interactions appear to be fairly small.

[9] Including one-person families.

[10] In terms of the notation of equation (23), N corresponds to $M + \Delta M$ and $0.01 r_i$ to Δp_i.

We may also ignore changes in the family size distribution of the several age groups if these changes cause the average family size effect, $\sum_j w_{ij}c_j$, to vary by the same amount for each age group. If such simplifying assumptions are accepted as to the nature of the changes in average income and family size distribution for the various age groups, only the number of families N and the percentage points of shift among age groups r_i need be estimated for 1970.

Turning now to the double log model, we assume that for families in the ith age (or other demographic) group

$$F_i = a_i Y^b n^c.$$

For simplicity we may approximate this by writing, for families in the ith age group with family size j,

$$F \approx a_i Y^b j^c, \; j = 1, 2, 3, 4, 5, 6,$$

where $j = 6$ for family size 6 or more.

Let us now consider only those families in the ith age group which have exactly the income Y_{ik}. The average food expenditure (averaging over family size) of such families is

$$F_{i(Y_{ik})} \approx a_i Y_{ik}{}^b \sum_j w_{ij(Y_{ik})} j^c$$

where $w_{ij(Y_{ik})}$ is the relative frequency of families of size j among families in the ith age group having income Y_{ik}. If Y_{ik} is the mean income of families in the ith age and kth income group, if the kth income group has sufficiently narrow limits, and if the family size distribution is about the same for all incomes within the ikth age-income cell, then the average food expenditure of this cell may be roughly approximated by

$$F_{ik} \approx a_i Y_{ik}{}^b \sum_j w_{ijk} j^c,$$

where w_{ijk} is the relative frequency of family size j in the ikth age-income cell.

If the number of families (including one person families) is N, the effect on food consumption of a shift of r_{ik} per cent of these families into $(r_{ik} > 0)$ or out of $(r_{ik} < 0)$ the ikth age-income cell may then be approximated by

$$0.01 r_{ik} N (a_i Y_{ik}{}^b \sum_j w_{ijk} j^c).$$

The aggregate effect of the total of such shifts is roughly equal to

$$(25) \qquad 0.01 N \sum_{i,k} r_{ik} a_i Y_{ik}{}^b \sum_j w_{ijk} j^c,$$

where $\sum_{i,k} r_{ik} = 0$. The aggregation of individual age-income cells, rather than complete age groups, minimizes the distortion arising from the approximation procedure used.

Again the 1970 values should be used for total number of families, as well as mean income and family size distribution within age-income cells, in estimating the effect on 1970 food consumption of distributional changes between 1950 and 1970. However, mean income within income classes is not likely to vary greatly over time except in the highest class, which is open-ended. Note that, to determine the r_{ik}, some estimate of the 1970 income distribution within age groups is required.

Numerical Estimates of the Effect of Shifts Among Age and Race-Area Groups, 1950–1970

The following numerical estimates of the effects of distributional changes in the period 1950–1970 are subject to error from a number of sources, listed below, and are intended primarily for purposes of exposition.

1. The values of a_i, b, and c_j used in evaluating (24) in the age analysis are obtained from the linear relationships (8)–(13),[11] which are based on urban white employee families with incomes between \$1,000 and \$10,000 and cash assets under \$500; they are therefore not properly applicable to the population as a whole.

2. These linear relationships utilize rather broad age and family size groups and neglect rather substantial differences in behavior within these groups.

3. The values of $\bar{Y}_i$ and w_{ij} used in evaluating (24) are based on 1950 data. As indicated above this will lead to substantial error only if the changes between 1950 and 1970 in mean income and family size effect ($\sum_j w_{ij}c_j$) differ considerably among age groups.

4. The values of a_i, b, and c used in evaluating (25) in the age analysis and the race-area analysis are obtained, respectively, from relationships (1)–(7) and (14)–(22), which exclude both non-urban families and white urban families with incomes under \$1,000 and are therefore not properly applicable to the population as a whole. However, an alternative estimate of (25) substitutes observed 1950 food expenditures in the lowest income class for expenditures as computed by combining the age (or race-area), income, and family size effects implied by the regressions. The resulting difference in (25) is very small.

---

[11] Regressions for renters and homeowners are combined, using weights based on frequencies and aggregate income of the two groups.

5. The values of c used in (25) are obtained as the exponents of a continuous family size variable but are applied to a discrete variable. In the computations they were applied to the mean family sizes of the various family size groups rather than simply the numbers 1, 2, 3, 4, 5, 6.

6. A straight line approximation to the double log relationship is used in estimating the mean food expenditure within each income class, and the assumption is made of a constant family size distribution within each age-income (or race-area-income) cell. In other words we neglect the quantity

$$a_i \bar{Y}_{ik}{}^b \sum_j w_{ijk} j^c - \frac{a_i}{N_{ik}} \Sigma Y^b j^c,$$

where the second summation runs over all families in the ikth cell and N_{ik} is the number of families in this cell. This difference, which might be very large if complete age groups were used instead of age-income cells, may still be substantial for the open-end income class.

7. The values of $\bar{Y}_{ik}$ and w_{ijk} used in evaluating (25) are based on 1950 data. While it is reasonable to assume little change in $\bar{Y}_{ik}$ for the closed-end income classes, we may expect some increase in the open-end class. Alternative estimates of (25), allowing for a 10 per cent rise in mean income for this class were insignificantly different. The assumption that the family size distribution remains unchanged within age-income (or race-area-income) cells is probably unrealistic and a source of some error.

CHANGES IN THE AGE DISTRIBUTION

Census estimates are available for the age distribution of males in 1970. Table 1 shows the 1950 per cent distribution of males over 20, the estimated distribution for 1970, and the expected shifts into or out of each age group (expressed as a percentage of total population). These shifts may be used as the r_i of equation (24) on the assumption that *changes* in the age distribution of males over 20 are roughly the same as *changes* in the age distribution of family heads. By applying an appropriate income distribution for each age group, these r_i may be converted to the r_{ik} of equation (25). The 1950 income distributions as obtained from the BLS sample were used in this conversion and are, of course, a poor approximation to the expected 1970 distributions for the shifting families. Even if the assumption is made that each family's real income rises by a given per cent, the effects of this rise on the age groups suffering relative losses do not cancel the effects on the age groups with relative gains because of substantial differences in the initial income distributions.

469

TABLE I

Effect on Food Consumption of Expected Shifts in Age Distribution, 1950-1970

| | Per Cent Distribution of Males over 20 | | | Effect on Food Consumption | | | |
| | | | | In terms of N[c] (1950 dollars) | | Assuming N = 65 million[c] (millions of 1950 dollars) | |
Age Group	1950[a]	1970[b] (estimated)	Difference (r_i)	Linear Model	Double log Model	Linear Model	Double log Model
Under 25	11.72	14.50	2.78 } −0.33	− 3.482N	24.097N	− 226	1,566
25-34	23.81	20.70	−3.11		−34.578N		−2,248
35-44	21.58	18.46	−3.12 } −2.24	−29.501N	−40.543N	−1,918	−2,635
45-54	17.58	18.46	0.88		11.179N		727
55-64	13.60	14.51	0.91 } 2.57	25.289N	9.982N	1,644	649
65-74	8.17	8.74	0.57		4.645N		302
75 and over	3.54	4.63	1.09		7.101N		462
Total	100.00	100.00	0.00	− 7.694N	−18.117N	− 500	−1,178

[a] Derived from Bureau of the Census, *Current Population Reports*, Series P-25, no. 170, Table 1.
[b] Derived from Bureau of the Census, *Current Population Reports*, Series P-25, no. 123, Table 2.
[c] N is number of families, including one person families, in 1970.
Source for last four columns: Tables A-1 and A-2.

This is perhaps the most important shortcoming of the estimated effects of age shifts on aggregate consumption as obtained from the double log model.

Table 1 further shows for both the linear and the double log model the estimated increase or decrease in the aggregate food consumption of each age group and of all groups combined, as compared with what might be expected on the basis of growth in population and income in the absence of shifts in the age distribution.

The computations on which the last four columns of Table 1 are based are shown in Appendix Tables A-1 (linear model) and A-2 (double log model). These tables present for each age or age-income group the age effect, the income effect (based on 1950 mean incomes), the family size effect (based on 1950 family size distributions), and—estimated from these three effects—the typical food expenditure of each age-income group. Also shown are the expected shifts into or out of each group and the resulting changes in food consumption as computed from (24) or (25).

It was indicated earlier that some problems arise from applying to the total population relationships based on a subgroup. This is a serious shortcoming for the linear model, but until further computations are completed, covering the omitted groups, little can be done to correct it. For the double log model, where the lowest income class is omitted, an alternative calculation substitutes the observed 1950 food expenditures of this class for expenditures as computed from equations (1)–(7). Actual expenditures tended to be considerably higher than computed expenditures particularly for families with middle-aged heads. (This may reflect a relatively large deviation of current from normal income for these families.)

It should also be noted that relatively poor fits are obtained in the highest income class, even though these families are included in computing the regressions. Here actual expenditures are systematically lower than computed expenditures. Because of low frequencies and large sampling variation in this income class, it was not desirable to replace computed with observed expenditures here. Instead, computed expenditures were lowered by an amount equal to the mean deviation of computed from observed expenditures. The result of these adjustments in the lowest and highest income classes was to decrease the estimated lowering of aggregate food consumption by 1.6 per cent. A further adjustment, allowing for a 10 per cent increase in the mean income of the highest income class between 1950 and 1970, increased the estimated effect by 0.25 per cent.

It will be noted from Table 1 that the linear model gives a much lower estimate than the log model of the negative effect on aggregate food consumption resulting from the expected shift in age distribution. Some difference might be expected because of the much lower coverage of population groups in the linear model. Negroes, self-employed, not gainfully employed, families with incomes under $1,000 or over $10,000, and families with cash assets over $500 or not reporting cash assets, are all omitted in determining typical expenditure patterns. However, the major part of the discrepancy arises from the much broader age groupings used in the linear model, which conceal important intra-group shifts. While good agreement between the two models is obtained for the 35–54 age group, the lowering of expenditure in the under-35 group is much underestimated because the large shift from the 25–34 bracket to the under-25 bracket is entirely missed. The differences between these two brackets are considerable, however, in terms of average income and family size as well as expenditures for given income and family size. The rise in expenditure for the over-55 group is probably overstated in the linear model, since there is no allowance for the fact that about 40 per cent of the shift into this group goes to the over-75 bracket, which represents one-sixth or less of the total group and has much lower food expenditure than the rest of the group.

CHANGES IN THE DISTRIBUTION OF POPULATION BY AREA AND RACE

Projections are not available, so far as I know, for the distribution of population among the race-area groups to which the 1950 regressions apply. However, the actual movements between 1940 and 1950 are available for roughly the appropriate categories, and estimates of the shifts between 1950 and 1970 have been obtained by simply continuing these trends. An easy correction is available if it is believed that the observed trends will continue at an accelerated or decelerated rate. For example, if the 1950–1970 shifts are expected to occur at half the 1940–1950 rates, the r_{ik}, and hence the final figures on change in aggregate consumption, should be multiplied by one-half.

The 1940–1950 shifts among race-area groups were obtained in the following way. First, the 1940 and 1950 populations in metropolitan and non-metropolitan regions were obtained for thirteen economic areas.[12] It was assumed that "metropolitan regions" corresponded approximately to a combination of the Bureau of Labor Statistics categories of "large

[12] Donald J. Bogue, *Components of Population Change, 1940–50*, published jointly by Scripps Foundation for Research in Population Problems and Population Research and Training Center, 1957, p. 18.

cities" and "suburbs." "Nonmetropolitan regions" differ from the BLS category of "small cities" in that they include both cities with population between 50,000 and 100,000 and rural areas. However, the regressions obtained for BLS "small cities" should give a reasonably satisfactory description of the food consumption behavior of these somewhat larger categories. Four of the economic areas distinguished were found to correspond roughly with the BLS category "north," three with the BLS category "south," and the remaining six with the BLS category "west."[13] The per cent distribution of population among the six regions—metropolitan north, nonmetropolitan north, metropolitan south, nonmetropolitan south, metropolitan west, and nonmetropolitan west—was calculated for 1940 and for 1950.

White population as a per cent of total was then calculated for the north and for the south, in 1940 and in 1950, from the Census table, "Population by Race by States."[14] Negro population as a per cent of total in 1950 was then obtained for urbanized and for nonurbanized areas in three regions: northeast, north central, and south.[15] On the basis of this computation it seemed reasonable to assume that in the south, white persons represented the same percentage of total population in metropolitan as in nonmetropolitan regions. The percentage for the south as obtained from the Census table "Population by Race by States" was therefore applied to both metropolitan and nonmetropolitan regions. (This was 73.1 per cent in 1940 and 75.4 per cent in 1950.) For nonmetropolitan areas in the north, the nonwhite population was taken to be 1.5 per cent of the total in such areas and the remainder of northern nonwhites were assumed to reside in metropolitan areas. On this assumption, white population in northern metropolitan areas was taken to be 94.8 per cent of the total in 1940 and 92.6 per cent in 1950.

Table 2 shows the resulting per cent distribution of population among nine race-area groups for 1940 and 1950, the shift into or out of each group (as a per cent of total population), the expected shift between 1950 and 1970, r_i, based on a continuation of the 1940–1950 trends, and the expected change in aggregate food consumption of each group and of all groups combined. The last was estimated from equation (25) by applying to nonmetropolitan regions the regressions obtained for BLS "small cities" and applying to nonwhite groups the regressions obtained for Negroes.

[13] Regions I, II, III, and V as defined by Bogue were assigned to the north; VII, VIII, and IX to the south; and IV, VI, X, XI, XII, and XIII to the west.

[14] Bureau of the Census, *Statistical Abstract of the United States, 1955*, p. 34.

[15] From Duncan, Otis Dudley, and Albert J. Reiss, Jr., *Social Characteristics of Urban and Rural Communities, 1950*, John Wiley and Sons, Inc., 1956, pp. 30, 60.

TABLE 2

Effect on Food Consumption of Expected Shifts Among Race-Area Groups, 1950–1970

					Effect on Food Consumption (double log model)	
	Percent Distribution			Expected Shift 1950–1970 (r_i) (percent)	In terms of N[a] (1950 dollars)	Assuming $N = 65$ million[a] (millions of 1950 dollars)
Race-Area Group	1940	1950	Difference			
North, metropolitan, white	34.54	33.77	−0.77	−1.54	−18.534N	−1,205
North, metropolitan, nonwhite	1.89	2.70	0.81	1.62	14.930N	970
North, nonmetropolitan, total	15.56	14.49	−1.07	−2.14	−21.736N	−1,413
South, metropolitan, white	5.85	6.84	0.99	1.98	21.980N	1,429
South, metropolitan, nonwhite	2.15	2.23	0.08	0.16	1.184N	77
South, nonmetropolitan, white	12.40	11.72	−0.68	−1.36	−13.434N	− 873
South, nonmetropolitan, nonwhite	4.56	3.82	−0.74	−1.48	− 9.672N	− 629
West, metropolitan, total	8.34	10.70	2.36	4.72	48.904N	3.179
West, nonmetropolitan, total	14.71	13.73	−0.98	−1.96	−20.834N	−1,354
Total	100.00	100.00	0.00	0.00	2.786N	181

[a] N is number of families, including one-person families, in 1970.
Source: Table A-3 and see text.

The computations on which the last two columns of Table 2 are based are shown in Appendix Table A-3. The latter presents for each race-area-income group the race-area effect, the income effect (based on 1950 average incomes), the family size effect (based on 1950 family size distributions), and—estimated from these three effects—the typical food expenditure of each race-area-income group. Also shown are the expected shifts into or out of each group, obtained by applying the 1950 income distribution for each race-area group to the r_i of Table 2, and the expected change in aggregate food consumption as computed from equation (25). The use of 1950 income distributions causes less concern in this case than in the analysis of age shifts; for while the real income of each race-area group may be expected to rise by 1970, the income distribution of the shifting families is likely to be lower than the distribution of the group to which they shift. This is true whether we consider white families moving from nonmetropolitan to metropolitan regions in the south and west or Negroes moving from nonmetropolitan regions in the south to metropolitan regions in the north.

Since white families with incomes under $1,000 were not included in computing regressions (14)–(22) and since the observed expenditures of these families were systematically higher than the computed expenditures based on these regressions, an alternative calculation was made, substituting observed 1950 expenditures for the computed expenditures of these families. This resulted in less than a 5 per cent increase in the relatively small effect on aggregate food consumption. There was no systematic tendency for Negroes in the lowest income class to exceed expenditures as computed from the regressions or for the race-area groups to fall short of computed expenditures in the highest income class. A further adjustment, allowing for a 10 per cent increase in the mean income of the highest income class by 1970, leads to an insignificant decrease in the effect on aggregate food consumption.

It should be noted that the increase in food expenditures for Negroes alone is more than twice as large as that for white and Negro families combined. The partially offsetting decrease for white families is largely due to the shift of these families out of the highest expenditure area, metropolitan regions in the north. Much of this apparent shift may simply represent the movement of urban families out beyond the currently recognized metropolitan limits. If these families retain urban habits of food expenditure, then the effect is to overstate the shift from metropolitan areas in the north and understate the shift from nonmetropolitan areas in the north, which are characterized by much lower levels of food expenditure. For this reason, it is entirely possible that in fact no change or even a small increase should be expected in the food consumption of white families as a result of regional shifts.

In summary, it appears that shifts among race-area groups largely cancel in their effects on aggregate food consumption, though the distributional shifts in consumption are of considerable interest for some purposes. On the other hand, shifts in the age distribution may have effects which require a significant adjustment of the change in food expenditure (in 1950 dollars) which might be expected between 1950 and 1970 on the basis of growth in population and real income.

Appendix

TABLE A-1

Computation of the Effect on Food Consumption of Expected Shifts in the Age Distribution 1950–1970 (linear model)

Age Group	Expected Shift 1950–1970 r_i (per cent)	Age Effect a_i	Income Effect[a] $b\bar{r}_i$	Family Size Effect $\sum_j w_{ij}c_j$	Typical Food Expenditure $a_i + b\bar{r}_i + \sum_j w_{ij}c_j$	Expected Effect on Aggregate Expenditure $0.01 r_i(a_i + b\bar{r}_i + \sum_j w_{ij}c_j)N$
					(1950 dollars)	
Under 35	−0.33	259	649	147	1,055	− 3.482N[b]
35–54	−2.24	372	775	171	1,317	−29.501N
55 and over	2.57	389	559	36	984	25.289N
Total	0.00					− 7.694N

[a] Based on 1950 mean incomes.
[b] N is number of families, including one-person families, in 1970.

TABLE A-2

Computation of the Effect on Food Consumption of Expected Shifts in the Age Distribution 1950–1970 (double log model)

Age Group	Income Group	Expected Shift 1950–1970 r_{ik}	Age Effect a_i	Income Effect^a $\hat{r}_k^b$	Family Size Effect^b $\sum_j w_{ijk} j^c$	Typical Food Expenditure $a_i \hat{r}_k^b \sum_j w_{ijk} j^c$	Expected Effect on Aggregate Expenditure $0.01 r_{ik}(a_i \hat{r}_k^b \sum_j w_{ijk} j^c) N$
		(per cent)				(1950 dollars)	
Under 25	All	2.78	10.23	—	—	—	24.097N^c
	Under–$1,000	0.0211		28.5	1.245	363	
	$1,000–$1,999	.5196		45.9	1.245	585	
	$2,000–$2,999	.9196		59.7	1.298	793	
	$3,000–$3,999	.8073		70.5	1.324	955	
	$4,000–$4,999	.3439		80.2	1.300	1,067	
	$5,000–$5,999	.0984		89.0	1.338	1,218	
	$6,000–$7,499	.0281		98.5	1.388	1,399	
	$7,500–$9,999	.0281		111.9	1.388	1,589	
	$10,000–over	.0142		134.3	1.388	1,907	
25–34	All	–3.11	10.64	—	—	—	–34.578N
	Under–$1,000	–0.0286		28.5	1.263	383	
	$1,000–$1,999	–.2239		45.9	1.348	658	
	$2,000–$2,999	–.6186		59.7	1.390	883	
	$3,000–$3,999	–1.0191		70.5	1.440	1,080	
	$4,000–$4,999	–0.6742		80.2	1.458	1,244	
	$5,000–$5,999	–.2979		89.0	1.445	1,368	
	$6,000–$7,499	–.1524		98.5	1.427	1,496	
	$7,500–$9,999	–.0712		111.9	1.468	1,748	
	$10,000–over	–.0243		140.2	1.488	2,220	

TABLE A-2 (concluded)

Age Group	Income Group	Expected Shift 1950–1970 r_{ik}	Age Effect a_i	Income Effect[a] P_k^b	Family Size Effect[b] $\sum_j w_{ikj}j^c$	Typical Food Expenditure $a_i P_k^b \sum_j w_{ikj}j^c$	Expected Effect on Aggregate Expenditure $0.01 r_{ik}(a_i P_k^b \sum_j w_{ikj}j^c)N$
		(per cent)					(1950 dollars)
35–44	All	−3.12	11.21	—	—	—	−40.543N
	Under–$1,000	− 0.0406		28.5	1.153	368	
	$ 1,000–$1,999	− .2022		45.9	1.286	662	
	$ 2,000–$2,999	− .5001		59.7	1.412	945	
	$ 3,000–$3,999	− .8305		70.5	1.491	1,178	
	$ 4,000–$4,999	− .7185		80.2	1.522	1,368	
	$ 5,000–$5,999	− .3803		89.0	1.527	1,523	
	$ 6,000–$7,499	− .2387		98.5	1.533	1,693	
	$ 7,500–$9,999	− .1051		111.9	1.560	1,957	
	$10,000–over	− .1039		157.7	1.539	2,721	
45–54	All	0.88	11.56	—	—	—	11.179N
	Under–$1,000	.0323		28.5	1.164	383	
	$ 1,000–$1,999	.0845		45.9	1.223	649	
	$ 2,000–$2,999	.1547		59.7	1.319	910	
	$ 3,000–$3,999	.1849		70.5	1.407	1,147	
	$ 4,000–$4,999	.1444		80.2	1.440	1,335	
	$ 5,000–$5,999	.1108		89.0	1.477	1,520	
	$ 6,000–$7,499	.0875		98.5	1.515	1,725	
	$ 7,500–$9,999	.0495		111.9	1.541	1,993	
	$10,000–over	.0314		160.9	1.490	2,771	

55–64					
All	0.91	11.63	—	—	9.982N
Under–$1,000	.0688		28.5	1.099	364
$ 1,000–$1,999	.1582		45.9	1.173	626
$ 2,000–$2,999	.1706		59.7	1.273	884
$ 3,000–$3,999	.1824		70.5	1.323	1,085
$ 4,000–$4,999	.1169		80.2	1.368	1,276
$ 5,000–$5,999	.0789		89.0	1.431	1,481
$ 6,000–$7,499	.0654		98.5	1.441	1,651
$ 7,500–$9,999	.0409		111.9	1.531	1,992
$10,000–over	.0279		152.6	1.413	2,503
65–74					
All	0.57	11.07	—	—	4.645N[c]
Under–$1,000	.1249		28.5	1.075	339
$ 1,000–$1,999	.1436		45.9	1.196	608
$ 2,000–$2,999	.1166		59.7	1.258	831
$ 3,000–$3,999	.0809		70.5	1.299	1,014
$ 4,000–$4,999	.0462		80.2	1.373	1,219
$ 5,000–$5,999	.0193		89.0	1.397	1,376
$ 6,000–$7,499	.0143		98.5	1.429	1,558
$ 7,500–$9,999	.0132		111.9	1.473	1,825
$10,000–over	.0110		152.6	1.435	2,424
75–over					
All	1.09	10.44	—	—	7.101N
Under–$1,000	0.4057		28.5	1.100	327
$ 1,000–$1,999	.3111		45.9	1.185	568
$ 2,000–$2,999	.1461		59.7	1.258	784
$ 3,000–$3,999	.0811		70.5	1.310	964
$ 4,000–$4,999	.0650		80.2	1.415	1,185
$ 5,000–$5,999	.0270		89.0	1.463	1,359
$ 6,000–$7,499	.0270		98.5	1.496	1,538
$ 7,500–$9,999	.0135		111.9	1.416	1,654
$10,000–over	.0135		152.6	1.416	2,256

[a] Using 1950 mean incomes. For each of the first eight income classes, incomes were averaged over all age groups. For the highest income class the mean incomes used are appropriate to the particular age group (or where frequencies are very small to a subset of age groups).

[b] Using 1950 family size distributions for each age-income group. Where frequencies are very small, family size effects have been averaged over adjacent income classes in a given age group.

[c] N is number of families, including one-person families, in 1970.

479

TABLE A-3

Computation of the Effect on Food Consumption of Expected Shifts Among Race-Area Groups 1950–1970 (double log model)

Race-Area Group	Income Group	Expected Shift 1950–1970 r_{ik}	Race-Area Effect a_i	Income Effect[a] $\hat{P}_k^b$	Family Size Effect[b] $\sum_j w_{ik}j^c$	Typical Food Expenditure $a_i \hat{P}_k^b \sum_j w_{ik}j^c$	Expected Effect on Aggregate Expenditure $0.01 r_{ik}(a_i\hat{P}_k^b\sum_j w_{ik}j^c)N$
		(per cent)					(1950 dollars)
North, Metropolitan, White	All	− 0.77	14.87	—	—	—	− 9.267N^c
	Under–$1,000	− .0378		22.9	1.122	382	
	$ 1,000–$1,999	− .0711		36.0	1.189	636	
	$ 2,000–$2,999	− .1319		46.0	1.329	909	
	$ 3,000–$3,999	− .1897		53.8	1.425	1,140	
	$ 4,000–$4,999	− .1435		60.7	1.472	1,329	
	$ 5,000–$5,999	− .0821		66.9	1.483	1,475	
	$ 6,000–$7,499	− .0578		73.6	1.510	1,653	
	$ 7,500–$9,999	− .0331		82.8	1.546	1,903	
	$10,000–over	− .0229		116.6	1.524	2,642	
North, Nonmetropolitan, Total	All	− 1.07	13.44	—	—	—	− 10.868N
	Under–$1,000	− .0834		22.9	1.109	341	
	$ 1,000–$1,999	− .1497		36.0	1.213	587	
	$ 2,000–$2,999	− .2024		46.0	1.367	845	
	$ 3,000–$3,999	− .2875		53.8	1.478	1,069	
	$ 4,000–$4,999	− .1684		60.7	1.504	1,227	
	$ 5,000–$5,999	− .0562		66.9	1.541	1,336	
	$ 6,000–$7,499	− .0595		73.6	1.501	1,435	
	$ 7,500–$9,999	− .0374		82.8	1.531	1,704	
	$10,000–over	− .0255		109.4	1.480	2,176	

South, Metropolitan, White — 0.99, 13,88, 10.990N

All	—	—	—	—
Under–$1,000	.0337	22.9	1.156	367
$ 1,000–$1,999	.0965	36.0	1.235	617
$ 2,000–$2,999	.1767	46.0	1.368	873
$ 3,000–$3,999	.2603	53.8	1.426	1,065
$ 4,000–$4,999	.1859	60.7	1.451	1,222
$ 5,000–$5,999	.1079	66.9	1.484	1,378
$ 6,000–$7,499	.0705	73.6	1.476	1,508
$ 7,500–$9,999	.0342	82.8	1.517	1,743
$10,000–over	.0244	105.6	1.505	2,206

South, Nonmetropolitan, White — .68, 13,03, − 6.717N

All	—	—	—	—
Under–$1,000	—.0438	22.9	1.188	354
$ 1,000–$1,999	—.1022	36.0	1.321	620
$ 2,000–$2,999	—.1544	46.0	1.411	846
$ 3,000–$3,999	—.1523	53.8	1.473	1,033
$ 4,000–$4,999	—.1064	60.7	1.480	1,171
$ 5,000–$5,999	—.0563	66.9	1.509	1,315
$ 6,000–$7,499	—.0375	73.6	1.587	1,522
$ 7,500–$9,999	—.0209	82.8	1.571	1,695
$10,000–over	—.0063	105.6	1.590	2,188

West, Metropolitan, Total — 2.36, 13,67, 24.452N

All	—	—	—	—
Under–$1,000	.1744	22.9	1.092	342
$ 1,000–$1,999	.2719	36.0	1.182	582
$ 2,000–$2,999	.3953	46.0	1.301	818
$ 3,000–$3,999	.5570	53.8	1.404	1,033
$ 4,000–$4,999	.4003	60.7	1.439	1,194
$ 5,000–$5,999	.2636	66.9	1.476	1,350
$ 6,000–$7,499	.1692	73.6	1.492	1,501
$ 7,500–$9,999	.0767	82.8	1.508	1,707
$10,000–over	.0517	109.9	1.414	2,124

TABLE A-3 (concluded)

Race-Area Group	Income Group	Expected Shift 1950–1970 r_{ik}	Race-Area Effect a_i	Income Effect[a] $\hat{r}_k$	Family Size Effect[b] $\sum_j w_{iskj}$[c]	Typical Food Expenditure $a_i\hat{r}_k\sum_j w_{iskj}$[c]	Expected Effect on Aggregate Expenditure $0.01 r_{ik}(a_i\hat{r}_k\sum_j w_{iskj}$[c]$)N$
		(per cent)					(1950 dollars)
West, Nonmetropolitan, Total	All	−0.98	13.76	—	—	—	−10.417N[e]
	Under–$1,000	−.0726		22.9	1.107	349	
	$ 1,000–$1,999	−.1140		36.0	1.248	618	
	$ 2,000–$2,999	−.1820		46.0	1.349	854	
	$ 3,000–$3,999	−.2326		53.8	1.436	1,063	
	$ 4,000–$4,999	−.1591		60.7	1.470	1,228	
	$ 5,000–$5,999	−.1020		66.9	1.503	1,384	
	$ 6,000–$7,499	−.0542		73.6	1.472	1,491	
	$ 7,500–$9,999	−.0349		82.8	1.529	1,742	
	$10,000–over	−.0285		109.4	1.517	2,284	
North, Metropolitan, Nonwhite	All	.81	6.78	—	—	—	7.465N
	Under–$1,000	.0458		45.6	1.038	321	
	$ 1,000–$1,999	.1747		75.5	1.145	586	
	$ 2,000–$2,999	.2259		101.7	1.223	843	
	$ 3,000–$3,999	.1888		122.9	1.260	1,050	
	$ 4,000–$4,999	.1094		142.1	1.313	1,265	
	$ 5,000–$5,999	.0406		160.4	1.278	1,390	
	$ 6,000–$7,499	.0141		178.5	1.304	1,578	
	$ 7,500–$9,999	.0053		204.8	1.411	1,959	
	$10,000–over	.0053		256.6	1.438	2,502	

						$0.592 N$
South, Metropolitan, Nonwhite						
All	.08	6.25	—	—	—	
$ Under–$1,000	.0095		45.6	1.077	307	
$ 1,000–$1,999	.0247		75.5	1.203	568	
$ 2,000–$2,999	.0272		101.7	1.269	807	
$ 3,000–$3,999	.0119		122.9	1.282	985	
$ 4,000–$4,999	.0049		142.1	1.331	1,182	
$ 5,000–$5,999	.0012		160.4	1.398	1,401	
$ 6,000–$7,499	.0003		178.5	1.314	1,466	
$ 7,500–$9,999	.0004		204.8	1.341	1,716	
$10,000–over	—		—	—	—	
						$-4.836 N^{[c]}$
South, Nonmetropolitan, Nonwhite						
All	−0.74	6.23	—	—	—	
$ Under–$1,000	−.1644		45.6	1.094	311	
$ 1,000–$1,999	−.3289		75.5	1.302	612	
$ 2,000–$2,999	−.1771		101.7	1.322	838	
$ 3,000–$3,999	−.0316		122.9	1.297	993	
$ 4,000–$4,999	−.0253		142.1	1.418	1,255	
$ 5,000–$5,999	−.0063		160.4	1.480	1,479	
$ 6,000–$7,499	−.0063		178.5	1.480	1,646	
$ 7,500–$9,999	—		—	—	—	
$10,000–over	—		—	—	—	

[a] Using 1950 mean incomes. For each of the first eight income classes, an average income effect was used for all area groups. For the highest income class, income effects apply to a particular race-area group or to a subset of groups.

[b] Using 1950 family size distributions for each race-area group.

[c] N is number of families, including one-person families, in 1970.

COMMENT

KARL A. Fox, Iowa State University

A major research conference is a speculative undertaking. No one member of its planning committee is sure of the relative importance of all the topics that seem logically related to its central theme. The committee as a whole may succeed quite well in listing topics that are germane. But it cannot always find competent scholars who are willing to divert their energies to preparing papers ideally suited to the conference framework. Frequently it gets instead some papers of good intrinsic quality centered at considerable distances from their ideal locations in the conference structure and oriented at odd angles with its major axes.

My preamble is not directed exclusively toward the present conference. However, by concentrating on the interrelations between two fields, this conference did invite greater risks of heterogeneity and doubtful relevance than do conferences confined to a single discipline or subdiscipline. In some cases demographers with research in process properly oriented with respect to demographic axes may have been led to bring economic factors in by the side entrance; conversely, economists may have been induced to add demographic afterthoughts to research studies originally designed to measure relationships only among economic variables.

I believe some such considerations as these are needed to rationalize the inclusion of Mrs. Crockett's paper in its present (November 7 draft) form in the conference. Considered as a family budget analysis in the tradition of Engel, Bowley, and Houthakker, the research project mentioned in her paper seems well designed and may contribute significantly to our knowledge of the net effects of area, race, and home ownership status upon family expenditure patterns. Her preliminary estimates of elasticities of food expenditures with respect to income and family size look reasonable and interesting when viewed as contributions to the main stream of family budget analysis. However, her conference paper turns the basic study to a use for which it is very poorly adapted; in the nature of the case, she has presented us with a by-product rather than a main product, and I am afraid that the by-product is of little value to either demographers or economists.

Instead of discussing Mrs. Crockett's paper point by point, I will make a largely independent attempt to answer the question implied in her title—namely, what effects do demographic factors have upon the demand for food?

As a demand analyst, I have frequently been irritated—and puzzled—at the failure of well-regarded econometricians to specify which of many possible things they mean by the word "demand" in their empirical studies. A few of the leading time series analysts, including Henry Schultz, Stone, and the former Bureau of Agricultural Economics group (Ezekiel, Waugh, Foote, and others), have been careful to define their terms. Thus, a price-elasticity of consumer demand must be measured by using *quantities* purchased by consumers and *retail prices*; an income elasticity of consumer demand involves *quantities* purchased by consumers and a measure of consumer income. From the basic demand surface expressing quantity purchased as a function of retail price and consumer income one can derive a relationship between *consumer expenditures* and consumer income—but to avoid confusion I believe this should be called an *expenditure* relationship rather than a "demand" relationship.

Measuring "the" demand for food also involves aggregation problems —in practice, the construction of appropriately weighted index numbers of the prices and quantities purchased of individual foods. This point will be elaborated below in connection with Table 3. For the moment I will simply point out that Mrs. Crockett has been quite careless about identifying expenditures with quantities purchased, even to the point of remarking that certain categories of families with above-average food expenditures "eat more food." This last phrase raises still further questions of definition—does more food mean more calories, more pounds, or "more" as measured by some sort of price-weighted index? It is just as important for applied economists to discriminate among these concepts as it is for actuaries to distinguish between crude death rates and age-specific death rates or for electricians to distinguish between volts, watts, and amperes. In general, if an economic variable is worth measuring, it is worth defining.

If these comments appear quibbling, consider some of the figures in Table 1. This table presents analyses made by this discussant several years ago, based on family budget data for Spring 1948.[1] In column (2) we note that the elasticity of food expenditures with respect to disposable personal income was 0.51 with both variables on a per family basis and 0.42 with both variables on a per capita basis. On a per capita basis, the income-elasticity of food expenditures away from home was 1.14, while that of food expenditures for use at home was 0.29. The elasticity of *expenditures* per meal eaten at home (with respect to income per family member) was 0.28, while a weighted average of the income elasticities of *quantities* of food consumed per meal at home was 0.14. The income

[1] Originally published in Karl A. Fox, "Factors Affecting Farm Prices, Farm Income, and Food Consumption," *Agricultural Economics Research*, Vol. III, no. 3, pp. 65-82. July, 1951.

TABLE 1

Food Expenditures and Quantities Purchased: Logarithmic Regressions upon Family Income, Urban Families, United States, Spring, 1948

Item	Relative Importance[a] (1)	Effect of One Per Cent Change in Income upon:		
		Expenditure (2)	Quantity Purchased (3)	Col. (2) minus Col. (3) (4)
		Per cent[b]	Per cent[b]	Per cent[b]
A. Per family:				
All food expenditures		0.51		
At home		0.40		
Away from home		1.12		
B. Per family member:[c]				
All food expenditures		0.42		
At home		0.29		
Away from home		1.14		
C. Per 21 meals at home:[c]				
All food (excluding accessories)	100.0	0.28	0.14[d]	0.14
All livestock products	50.8	.33	.23[d]	.10
Meat, poultry, and fish	29.2	.36	.23	.13
Dairy products (excluding butter)	16.9	.32	.23	.09
Eggs	4.7	.22	.20	.02
Fruits and vegetables	19.0	.42	.33[d]	.09
Leafy, green, and yellow vegetables	4.9	.37	.21	.16
Citrus fruit and tomatoes	5.2	.41	.42	− .01
Other vegetables and fruits	8.9	.45	.35	.10
Other foods	30.2	.08	− .12[d]	.20
Grain products	11.4	.02	− .21	.23
Fats and oils	9.8	.13	− .04	.17
Sugars and sweets	5.2	.20	− .07	.27
Dry beans, peas, and nuts	1.5	− .07	− .33	.26
Potatoes and sweet potatoes	2.3	.05	− .05	.10

[a] Per cent of total expenditures for food used at home, excluding condiments, coffee, and alcoholic beverages.

[b] Regression coefficients based upon logarithms of food expenditures or quantities purchased per 21 meals at home and logarithms of estimated Spring 1948, disposable incomes per family member, weighted by proportion of total families falling in each family income group. The object was to obtain coefficients reasonably comparable with those derived from time series.

[c] Per capita regression coefficients are lower than per family coefficients in this study whenever the latter are less than 1.0. This happens because average family size was positively correlated with family income among the survey group.

[d] Weighted averages of quantity-income coefficients for subgroups.

Basic data from United States Bureau of Human Nutrition and Home Economics, 1948 Food Consumption Surveys, Preliminary Report no. 5, May 30, 1949; Tables 1 and 3.

elasticity of *calories purchased* per meal at home would have been substantially less than 0.14, and the income elasticity of *calories ingested* might have been negligibly different from zero. Thus, the income elasticity of "demand for food" could range from zero to 0.42 or 0.51, depending on what we meant by "more food." A vague question gets an ambiguous answer.

For the moment, let us state our analytical problem as that of anticipating changes in expenditures for food as reflected in the coefficient of 0.28 for "expenditures per 21 meals at home." Specifically, let us ask, as Mrs. Crockett does, what will be the effects of each of a number of demographic and economic factors upon changes in food expenditures (measured at Spring 1948 prices) from 1950 to 1970?

We can rough out part of the answer immediately on the basis of logic and experience. Other things being equal, a 40 per cent increase in population will mean a 40 per cent increase in expenditures for food. Also, from the coefficient 0.28 in Table 1, it appears that a 50 per cent increase in per capita income from 1950 to 1970 should mean something like a 14 per cent increase in per capita expenditures for food. Now, after the two obvious factors—population growth and the income elasticity of food expenditures—have been taken into account, there remain a number of demographic or "distributional" factors, the effects of which are not immediately clear and which have received only limited attention in the economic literature. Mrs. Crockett has used a number of these factors in her research design: race-area groups, home ownership categories, and groupings of families according to the age of the head of the family, family income, and the number of persons in the family. All of Mrs. Crockett's factors other than family income may be classed as demographic variables.

In dealing with these factors, it will be convenient to start with *quantities* of individual food products purchased rather than with food expenditures, and to think in terms of projecting quantities purchased per capita of the entire United States population. In what way do changes in demographic (and income) distributions affect average per capita purchases of a given product (q_1)? We may write, following Mrs. Crockett,

$$(1) \qquad q_1 = f\,[y,\, s,\, A,\, k_{(ra)t}]$$

where *y* stands for family income, *s* the number of persons in the family, *A* the age of the head of the family, and $k_{(ra)t}$ is an adjustment factor that applies to a particular combination of race, area, and home tenure status. Mrs. Crockett has analyses in process based on seven age groups, nine race-area groups, nine income groups, six family size groups, and two home ownership categories; altogether, these cross-classifications would provide 6,804 "cells." If we arrayed these 6,804 cells as of 1950, starting with the one which showed the highest per capita purchases of the given product and ending with the cell which showed the lowest per capita purchases $(q_1, 6,804)$ we would have a suitable basing point from which to measure the effects of demographic and income changes. We would also be in a position to make preliminary judgments as to the probable relative orders of magnitude of changes in per capita purchases that might arise from "likely" changes in the distributions of various demographic (and income) variables.

For example, the variance of q_1 could be broken down into a set of components representing the direct effects of each principle of classification, plus interaction terms and unexplained variation. If the coefficient of variation of q_1 arrayed in this fashion were very large, we would be encouraged to look for sizable effects on its average level in consequence of changes in the distributions of one or more explanatory factors. If the coefficient of variation of q_1 were small, the effects of changes in the distributions of explanatory factors would (in most practical situations) also be small.[2]

[2] This point deserves further clarification. Note that the coefficient of variation (V) of a set of values is defined as the ratio (times 100) of its standard deviation (σ) to its mean (M):

$V = 100(\sigma/M)$. Consider the following sets of values:

| | Quantities Purchased | |
Individual	A	B
1	1	1
2	0	1
3	0	1
.	.	.
.	.	.
.	.	.
9	0	1
10	0	0
$N = 10$	$M = 0.1$	$M = 0.9$
	$\sigma = 0.3$	$\sigma = 0.3$
	$V = 300$	$V = 33$

If in Set A the second individual changes his purchases from 0 to 1, M rises from 0.1 to 0.2 and σ from 0.3 to 0.4, while V falls to 200. If in Set B the second individual changes his purchases from 1 to 0, M falls from 0.9 to 0.8, σ rises from 0.3 to 0.4, and V rises from 33 to 50. The assumed change in Set A is extremely important, as it *doubles* per capita purchases; in contrast the assumed change in Set B is relatively unimportant as it reduces per capita purchases by only 11 per cent.

It follows that per capita purchases of goods desired by (for example) a limited age group may be strongly influenced by changes in age distribution, whereas per capita purchases of goods used in similar quantities by all age groups will be relatively impervious to changes in age distribution.

It is common knowledge that the demand for space in high schools and the demand for wedding rings are highly sensitive to changes in age distribution of the sort we are now experiencing; these demands *per capita of the general population* will show sharp percentage increases in the near future. But it seems intuitively obvious that the demand for food is relatively impervious to changes in age distribution—that, in fact, food may be the least promising of all major commodity groups for the sort of analysis Mrs. Crockett undertakes. Everyone eats; except for pre-school children, average calorie requirements for persons in different age groups are within about 25 per cent of the over-all average for the entire population. The range of variation in protein requirements per person by age groups is rather similar.

In 1955, I made a rough analysis of the effects upon calorie and protein requirements of the change in age distribution of the United States population from July 1, 1940 to July 1, 1953. This analysis is summarized in Table 2. It suggested that calorie requirements per capita of the total population may have decreased by 3 to $3\frac{1}{2}$ per cent during that period

TABLE 2

Age Distribution of the Total Population and Its Effects on Recommended Daily Food Allowances, United States, 1940 and 1953

	(1)	(2)	(3)	(4)	(5)	(6)
	Population Distribution				Recommended Daily Dietary Allowances	
	Actual		Per Cent of Total			
Age Group	July 1, 1940	July 1, 1953	July 1, 1940	July 1, 1953	Calories[a]	Protein[a]
	millions	*millions*	*per cent*	*per cent*	*number*	*grams*
All ages	132.8[b]	160.4[b]	100.0	100.0	—	—
0–4	11.4[b]	18.2[b]	8.6	11.3	1,000	40
5–9	10.6	15.6	8.0	9.7	1,800	55
10–14	11.7	12.4	8.8	7.7	2,600	75
15–19	12.3	10.8	9.3	6.7	3,000	85
20–34	33.0	35.4	24.8	22.1	2,800	60
35–54	34.0	40.6	25.6	25.4	2,500	60
55 and over	19.8	27.4	14.9	17.1	2,200	60
Weighted averages:						
(a) Based on 1940 age distribution					2,400	61.52
(b) Based on 1953 age distribution					2,319	60.08

[a] Based on recommended dietary allowances, National Academy of Sciences, Nat. Res. Coun. Pub. 302, 1953, p. 22. Allowances have been roughly adjusted to Census age groupings and rounded to the nearest 100 calories or 5 grams of protein.

[b] Adjusted for underenumeration of young children. Based on U.S. Census Bureau, Current Population Reports, Series P-25, nos. 93 and 98.

and that protein requirements may have decreased by 2 or 3 per cent. These requirements are based upon calories and grams protein *ingested*; if wastes in food preparation increase with increasing real income, the decline in calories *purchased* per capita would be somewhat smaller. Interestingly enough, according to U.S. Department of Agriculture estimates, calories purchased or available per capita of the total population appear to have declined about $2\frac{1}{2}$ per cent from the 1935–1939 average to 1954—time periods which very nearly correspond to those in Table 2.[3]

A connection may readily be made between the 1940–1953 changes in age distribution of the total population and the 1950–1970 changes in age distribution of males 20 years of age and older as shown in Mrs. Crockett's Table 1. If each pair of population distributions is converted into a Lorenz curve or cumulative percentage frequency distribution, the maximum departures of these curves from the diagonal line of identical distribution are 6.6 per cent for the 1940–1953 comparison and 6.2 per cent for Mrs. Crockett's 1950–1970 comparison. Thus, it seems reasonable to expect that the age distribution effects projected by Mrs. Crockett would not change per capita calorie or protein requirements between 1950 and 1970 by more than 2 or 3 per cent; the net effect on "quantity of food purchased" should be no larger than this. In fact, the constant terms in her equations (1) through (7) show an extreme range of less than 14 per cent in expected food expenditures among families whose heads are in different age brackets. This is much less than the range of 83 per cent (from −58 to +25 per cent of the 1940 average) for the calorie requirements in Table 2, and 1970 projections based on equations (1) through (7) might well show age effects of less than 2 per cent.

If age and income distributions are held constant or turned into a standardized joint distribution, it seems unlikely that changes in race-area-home ownership patterns will have any appreciable effect upon average per capita calorie or protein requirements. If changes in age distribution have a potential of 2 or 3 per cent, changes in these other factors must have a potential (in terms of calories or other nutritive requirements) of a small fraction of 1 per cent. Mrs. Crockett's projections of the effects of expected shifts among race-area groups from 1950 to 1970 are indeed of this order of magnitude.

[3] Calorie figures are shown in Table 2, p. 414, of Karl A. Fox, "Effects of Farm Product Prices on Production and Commercial Sales," in *Policy for Commercial Agriculture*, Joint Committee Print, 85th Congress, 1st Session, November 22, 1957.

Thus, we may summarize the probable effects of demographic factors (including population growth) upon changes in quantities of food purchased from 1950 to 1970 as consisting of the following orders of magnitude: (1) effect of total population growth, an increase around 40 per cent; (2) effect of changes in age distribution, a reduction of not more than 2 or 3 per cent; and (3) effect of changes in other demographic factors, not more than $\frac{1}{2}$ of 1 per cent in either direction. These magnitudes are all estimated independently of changes in income level or distribution.

We could conclude our discussion at this point on the grounds that income is not a demographic variable. However, the consideration of income effects will serve to demonstrate the importance of defining terms and specifying the objectives of measurement when discussing "the demand for food." Mrs. Crockett (based on her November 7 draft) is only one of many economists whose empirical practices in this field are far below their recognized competence in theory and econometric technique.

Table 3 may be helpful in conceptualizing the various measures which relate to "the" demand for food. This work table would be a very large one, as it would include 6,804 columns defined by combinations of family income and demographic categories and perhaps 5,000 to 10,000 rows. For example, if we defined about 2,500 different commodities in terms of the forms in which they are sold in retail food stores, we could also conceive of 2,500 "equivalent prices" of these commodities as they show up in restaurant meals and another 2,500 "equivalent prices" for these commodities as they may enter into farm household use by self-suppliers. I do not know the pricing methods used in the 1950 BLS study or even whether farm households are included in the "non-metropolitan" categories cited by Mrs. Crockett; however, the three sectors of Table 3 would be almost co-extensive and consistent with the food expenditure concept of the Office of Business Economics, except that the latter includes food provided to inmates of institutions and to members of the armed forces.

The continuing downtrend in farm population tends to increase the proportion of our total food purchases that is priced at retail-store or restaurant-meal levels. Also, family budget studies indicate that increases in disposable income per capita tend to increase the proportion of food consumed in restaurants; this also tends to increase total money expenditures for food. In addition, changes in food processing technology in the marketing system, in households, and in restaurants may affect the allocation of total food consumption among the three major categories

491

TABLE 3

Work Table for Studying Effects upon "Demand for Food"
of Changes in Family Income and in Demographic Factors
(based on categories used by Jean A. Crockett)

Commodity[a] and Price		*Average Quantity Purchased in Each "Cell"* (defined by race-area group, age of head, family income group, family size, and home-tenure status) [b]			
		Cell 1	*Cell 2*	*Cell 3*	*. . . Cell m*
A. At retail store					
1	P_1	q_{11}	q_{12}	q_{13}	$\cdot\ \cdot\ \cdot$ q_{1m}
2	P_2	q_{21}	q_{22}	q_{23}	$\cdot\ \cdot\ \cdot$ q_{2m}
.	.	.	.	.	.
.	.	.	.	.	.
n	P_n	q_{n1}	q_{n2}	q_{n3}	$\cdot\ \cdot\ \cdot$ q_{nm}
B. Equivalent price in restaurant meals					
1	rP_1	rq_{11}	rq_{12}	rq_{13}	$. . .$ rq_{1m}
2	rP_2	rq_{21}	rq_{22}	rq_{23}	$. . .$ rq_{2m}
.	.	.	.	.	.
.	.	.	.	.	.
n	rP_n	rq_{n1}	rq_{n2}	rq_{n3}	$. . .$ rq_{nm}
C. Equivalent price for farm household use					
1	fP_1	fq_{11}	fq_{12}	fq_{13}	$. . .$ fq_{1m}
2	fP_2	fq_{21}	fq_{22}	fq_{23}	$. . .$ fq_{2m}
.	.	.	.	.	.
n	fP_n	fq_{n1}	fq_{n2}	fq_{n3}	$. . .$ fq_{nm}

[a] Considering grade-and-cut combinations for meats and similar differentiations for other foods, the number of commodities (n) might total in the thousands.

[b] Mrs. Crockett refers to 9 race-area groups, 7 age groups, 9 family income groups, 6 family size groups, and 2 home tenure statuses, or a total number of 6,804 possible cells. The total United States population would provide an *average* of about 10,000 families per "cell"—i.e., per column of the above work table.

shown in Table 3; the allocation of consumption of particular foods among these three categories may be affected to a much greater extent. Changes in the value which urban housewives, and both the housewife and other members of farm families, place upon leisure or upon the use of their labor in other productive activities will also affect patterns of food consumption and expenditure.

Starting with the raw data required for Table 3, one could obtain any of the measures or concepts associated with demand, including total food expenditures, food expenditures per meal consumed at home, food consumption (as a quantity index weighted by fixed retail prices), or derived demand for resources used in production of farm food products (as measured by a quantity index using fixed farm prices as weights).

Chart 1 illustrates the differences that might arise between changes in "demand for food" as measured by a retail price weighted index of food consumption and in "demand for agricultural resources" as measured by a farm price weighted index containing the same or equivalent quantities of various foods. Marketing charges (transportation, processing, and

CHART 1

Percentage Distribution of Total Retail Cost of "Food Market Basket" among Major Food Categories and between Marketing Charges and Equivalent Farm Values, July–September, 1957

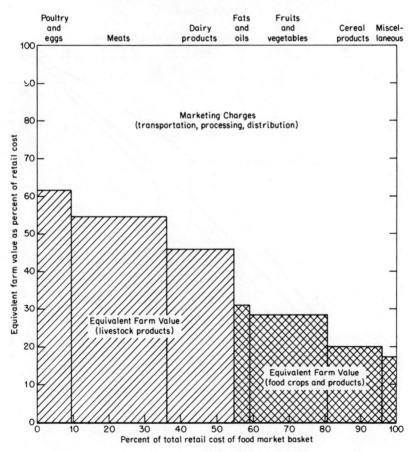

distribution) absorb a very large fraction of the retail cost of foods of crop origin; marketing charges for livestock products take up a smaller percentage of retail cost. Thus, during July–September 1957, livestock products accounted for 54.6 per cent of the retail cost of the food market basket compared with 71.8 per cent of its equivalent farm value; conversely, foods of crop origin accounted for 45.4 per cent of the retail cost and only 28.2 per cent of the equivalent farm value.

Chart 2 compares two Lorenz curves, the solid line relating cumulative frequency distributions of farm values and retail values of seven major

CHART 2

Changes in Age Distribution of U.S. Population from 1950 to 1970 Compared with Differences in the Relative Importance of Food Expenditure Categories at Retail and at Farm Price Levels, July–September 1957
(males over 20)

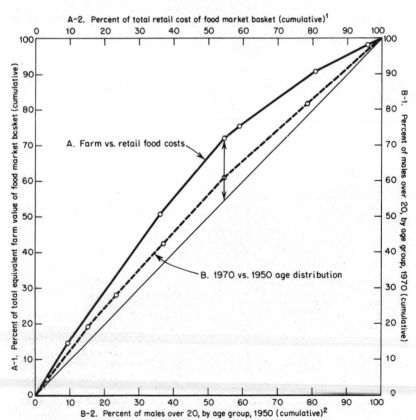

food categories, and the dotted line relating the cumulative frequency distributions of the 1970 and 1950 age distributions for males over 20 years of age as cited by Mrs. Crockett in her Table 1. The maximum departure of the farm-retail food cost curve from the diagonal is 17.2 per cent, almost three times as large as the maximum deviation (6.2 per cent) for the difference between 1950 and 1970 age distributions. It would appear that an error in concept, or pure sloppiness in deciding what one wishes to measure, *could* lead to a distortion in the measurement or interpretation of demand changes almost three times as large as the actual effects of a correctly measured change in age distribution of the total population.[4]

"Total food expenditures" are less well defined than any of the other measures relative to food consumption that have been discussed in the text or represented in the charts and tables. It should be noted that each quantity in Table 3 is subject to influence by its own price, by the prices of closely or distantly competing food products, and by changes in food prices generally relative to prices of nonfood consumer goods and services. Price elasticities of consumer demand for most foods, if measured at such levels of aggregation as "beef," "pork," or "all meat," are less (in absolute value) than -1.0; consequently, we cannot expect food expenditures to remain constant for a specified level of income despite changes in the level and pattern of food prices. The effects of variations in relative prices of different grades and cuts of beef may be negligible in this regard; however, when the retail price of pork drops 20 per cent between two periods or the retail price index for all foods falls 5 per cent in a short time, these price elasticities suggest that food expenditures could fluctuate 3 or 4 per cent above or below the "normal" relationship to disposable income per capita. Price variations of this magnitude are not uncommon, and their potential effects on relationships between food expenditures and income are of the same order of magnitude as potential changes in population age distribution over a 20-year period.

[4] Although this is somewhat to one side of our discussion, it might be noted that the difference between the cumulative frequency distributions of (1) requirements for marketing services and (2) resources used in farm production is even larger than that between the retail and farm value distributions—a maximum departure from the diagonal of 27.8 per cent, or well over four times as large as the maximum discrepancy noted between the 1950 and 1970 age distributions. It appears that the demand for food marketing services could change quite differently from the demand for resources used in farm production—the two types of demand might normally change in the same direction but by quite different percentages.

Population Change and the Demand for Services

ROBERT FERBER

UNIVERSITY OF ILLINOIS

THE objective of this paper is to evaluate the extent to which changes in the size and distribution of the population are able to account for changes in consumer outlays on services between 1936 and 1956. These dates were chosen because cross-section as well as time series data on consumer expenditures are available for those years on a national basis. Two facets of the problem are investigated:

1. The extent to which changes in total outlays for specific services during 1936–1956 are accounted for by the growth in the size of the total population.

2. The extent to which these changes are accounted for by: (a) Shifts in relevant population characteristics, and, (b) Changes in outlay per consumer unit.

Before embarking upon the empirical analysis, it would seem desirable to consider some of the problems involved in an empirical study of this sort.

Measurement Problems

Theoretically the effect of any given change in population numbers or composition can be evaluated in terms of its impact on the amount and distribution of consumer expenditures. Putting this theory into practice, however, reveals numerous obstacles to the attainment of such a goal. For one thing, changes in population are not self-limiting. In most instances, a chain-reaction effect sets in whereby one change leads to a number of other population changes. Thus, an increase in population, which is commonly brought about either by more births or a reduced death rate, implicitly alters the age distribution of the population and varies other distributional characteristics as well. Similarly, a change in, say, the educational distribution serves to bring about changes in the distribution of the population by other characteristics as well.

Second, considerable time may be required both for a particular population change to take place and for its full effect on expenditures to be

Note: The author would like to express his appreciation to Fadil Zuwaylif for assistance with the statistical analysis. He is also indebted to V Lewis Bassie of the University of Illinois and to Philip Golden of *Life* Magazine for reading the manuscript and for helpful suggestions.

apparent. Thus, an increase in birth rates in any one year will alter any number of population distributions for years to come, and many of these will in turn influence expenditure patterns, in part right away and in part with a certain lag.

Third, population changes are not discrete. Before one change has had time to work itself out, others are already under way. Some of these other changes may be brought about in part because of the initial change, while others may be the result of entirely independent phenomena. As a result, the effects of population change tend to become confounded with each other, particularly if two different changes are exerting the same effect on consumer expenditures.

Then there is the perennial chicken-or-the-egg question. Is a particular change in consumer outlays really attributable to a change in population, even if statistical analysis confirms the existence of a relationship, or is it attributable to other, more basic factors which may account for the population change as well? A definitive answer to such a question is not generally possible, in view of the complex interrelationship of demographic and economic events. Population changes are invariably brought about by changes in economic and political conditions which in turn give rise to further shifts in population. The dimensions of the analysis therefore become an important consideration. At the same time, it is clear that only the most intensive type of analysis would permit the tracing of events back to the ultimate causes.

Since resources do not permit such an approach in the present case, we shall content ourselves with an examination of the extent to which changes in consumer service expenditures are associated with population changes. We cannot infer from the results that such net effects as are detected can be attributed solely to a change in the total population, since no attempt is made to evaluate the degree to which the population changes themselves are brought about by nondemographic causes. Similarly, we can measure the extent to which a change in family outlays is associated with a shift in certain relevant population characteristics, but we cannot ascertain the extent to which this shift is brought about by economic or other forces.

For much the same reason, it is much more difficult than appears at first sight to distinguish between effects due to changes in population numbers and effects due to shifts in population characteristics. Not only is there the problem of eliminating the interacting influences of other factors but it is still not clear how much of what remains is truly demographic in nature. In particular, shifts in population characteristics are likely to be brought about by changes in economic and cultural conditions, the influence of some of which is not even measurable. Hence, such demographic effects as are uncovered, though "net" in a statistical sense, are likely to be "gross" in a broader sense.

Both facets of our empirical analysis are subject to these limitations. The population effects which are brought out by the analysis are primarily gross, or apparent, effects. Although the results of both parts of the analysis are based on definitional concepts, this does not remove the inherent limitation noted above. With the results of the cross-section analysis, the difficulty is resolved to the extent that changes in expenditures are attributable to differences in unit outlays of the same population groups. Differences ascribable to shifts in relevant population characteristics, however, only serve to set the stage for more intensive analysis to uncover the factors underlying the observed population shifts.

Effect of Growth in Total Population

The total population of the United States increased by 31 per cent between 1936 and 1956, with almost two-thirds of the increase taking place during the last six years of this period. During the two decades,

TABLE 1

Increase in Service and Total Consumption Expenditures and
Allocation of Increase to Components, 1936–1956

Per Cent Increase in	1936–50	1950–56	1936–56
A. Extent of Increase			
All consumption expenditures, current prices	209.9	38.1	330.2
All service expenditures, current prices	177.0	53.6	324.5
Population	18.3	10.9	31.1
Price of consumer goods and services	83.1	13.7	108.1
Price of consumer services	65.5	21.3	100.8
Deflated consumption expenditures	43.5	9.7	57.4
Deflated service expenditures	41.1	14.5	60.9
B. Allocation of Increase to Components			
Component and category:			
Population, all consumption	15.2	32.0	19.2
Population, services	16.9	24.2	19.4
Prices, all consumption	52.7	39.5	49.3
Prices, services	49.0	44.9	47.4
"Real" change, all consumption	32.1	28.5	31.5
"Real" change, services	34.1	30.9	33.2
Total	100.0	100.0	100.0
	100.0	100.0	100.0

Sources: Population: *Business Statistics, Department of Commerce,* 1957, p. 56. Prices and consumption expenditures: *Survey of Current Business,* July, 1958.

dollar outlays on service expenditures as well as on all consumption goods and services more than quadrupled (Table 1). Much of this increase in outlays on both goods and services is accounted for by the rise in prices, which for goods more than doubled and for services nearly doubled. Nevertheless, the "real" value of outlays per consumer rose by almost 60 per cent.

As a result of these substantial increases in prices and in real consumption per capita, the contribution of the growth in population to increased expenditures on consumer goods or services during this period was relatively small, about 20 per cent.[1] The population effect was much larger during the 1950's, accounting for almost one-fourth of the increase in service outlays and for almost one-third of the rise in expenditures on goods. Increases in price or in "real" consumption were generally not as pronounced during these six years as during the preceding fourteen.

Estimates of the direct contribution of population growth to outlays on the major categories of services indicate a fair degree of variation in the importance of this effect both between categories and between time periods (Table 2). These estimates were derived in the same manner as those for the aggregates in Table 1, with the exception that the number of *households* was used instead of the number of people in obtaining the population effect on increased expenditures for housing, household utilities, and domestic service.[2]

---

[1] To maintain comparability with the analysis of survey data in the next section, the allocation of increased outlays among components may be interpreted within the following framework:

Let: C and C' represent consumer expenditures in period 0 and 1, respectively.
M and M' represent population in periods 0 and 1, respectively.
P and P' represent the consumer goods price level in periods 0 and 1, respectively.
X and X' represent real consumption per capita in periods 0 and 1, respectively.

Define $M' = M + N$, $P' = P + Q$, $X' = X + Y$, N, Q, and Y representing the arithmetic incremental changes in population, price and real consumption, respectively, between periods 0 and 1.
Then:
$$C' = M'P'X' = (M + N)(P + Q)(X + Y)$$
and:
$$C' - C = NPX + MQX + MPY + NQX + NPY + MQY + NQY$$

The first three terms represent the "direct" effects of each factor on increased consumption, and the remaining terms represent indirect (interaction) effects. The allocation to components is, then:

Effect of population $= NPX + 1/2NQX + 1/2NPY + (1/3)NQY$
Effect of price $= MQX + 1/2NQX + 1/2MQY + (1/3)NQY$
Effect of "real" consumption $= MPY + 1/2NPY + 1/2MQY + (1/3)NQY$

[2] Another exception is that the price indexes for the different service categories underlying the calculations for Table 2 were derived by the author based on methods described in another paper. "A Statistical Study of Factors Influencing Temporal Variations in

TABLE 2

Allocation of Increase in Outlays for Main Categories of Services
to Components, 1936–1956
(per cent)

Service Category	Component	1936–50	1950–56	1936–56
Housing	Households	28.4	26.4	28.0
	Price	31.1	46.0	35.4
	"Real" increase	40.5	27.6	36.6
	Total	100.0	100.0	100.0
	Over-all increase	169.5	53.6	314.0
Household utilities	Households	27.5	20.1	25.7
	Price	8.7	14.8	11.4
	"Real" increase	63.8	65.1	62.9
	Total	100.0	100.0	100.0
	Over-all increase	182.6	76.2	398.1
Domestic service	Households	31.5	32.5	34.1
	Price	110.6	63.4	100.5
	"Real" increase	−42.1	4.1	−34.6
	Total	100.0	100.0	100.0
	Over-all increase	163.0	41.7	262.3
User-operated transportation	Population	12.7	22.2	15.6
	Price	27.1	52.2	33.5
	"Real" increase	60.2	25.6	50.9
	Total	100.0	100.0	100.0
	Over-all increase	303.3	59.4	541.9
Purchased transportation	Population	17.9	126.7	26.6
	Price	41.5	295.4	60.8
	"Real" increase	40.5	−322.1	12.5
	Total	99.9	100.0	99.9
	Over-all increase	158.8	108.7	181.1
Foreign travel	Population	19.4	17.4	18.8
	Price	61.5	17.1	43.4
	"Real" increase	19.1	65.5	37.7
	Total	100.0	100.0	99.9
	Over-all increase	142.4	82.2	341.4

Aggregate Service Expenditures" in *Consumer Reactions*, Lincoln Clark, ed., Harper &
Bros., 1958, pp. 394–420. This was necessitated by the refusal once again of the National
Income Division of the U.S. Department of Commerce to make available their price
indexes on the subject. Since the author does not have the resources of the National
Income Division—only a more open-minded attitude—the price indexes must be treated
as rough approximations, particularly for such services as personal business, religious and
welfare activities, and foreign travel.

TABLE 2, concluded

Service Category	Component	1936–50	1950–56	1936–56
Recreation	Population	16.8	30.3	21.9
	Price	54.0	59.9	58.6
	"Real" increase	29.2	9.9	19.5
	Total	100.0	100.0	100.0
	Over-all increase	176.7	40.7	263.6
Personal care	Population	21.5	18.4	20.9
	Price	94.1	42.3	71.9
	"Real" increase	−15.6	39.4	7.2
	Total	100.0	100.1	100.0
	Over-all increase	126.3	76.2	293.8
Clothing and jewelry service	Population	14.2	26.2	19.6
	Price	43.0	51.7	50.1
	"Real" increase	42.7	22.1	30.3
	Total	99.9	100.0	100.0
	Over-all increase	237.9	48.5	317.9
Medical care	Population	15.0	26.5	18.2
	Price	37.7	62.0	43.3
	"Real" increase	47.3	11.5	38.5
	Total	100.0	100.0	100.0
	Over-all increase	215.8	47.9	367.0
Private education	Population	14.7	15.1	15.5
	Price	58.9	39.3	50.8
	"Real increase"	26.4	45.6	33.8
	Total	100.0	100.0	100.1
	Over-all increase	227.8	99.2	552.8
Personal business	Population	19.4	19.4	19.7
	Price	44.2	8.6	31.1
	"Real" increase	36.4	72.0	49.2
	Total	100.0	100.0	100.0
	Over-all increase	140.4	71.1	311.1
Religious and welfare	Population	17.4	23.9	20.4
	Price	76.1	75.8	75.8
	"Real" increase	6.5	0.4	3.8
	Total	100.0	100.1	100.0
	Over-all increase	173.3	54.9	316.9

The increase in total population contributed a relatively small proportion of the expansion in outlays for these services. The population effect seems to have been more important in the postwar period, due in part to the more rapid growth in population during this period and in part to the reduced, and at times, negative, expansion in "real" consumption of services. Even then, however, population growth generally did not account for more than one-third of the total increase in specific service expenditures.

For the two decades combined, the contribution of the total population effect was of the order of 15 to 25 per cent. As a general rule, services for which the population effect was relatively more important were not the ones that exhibited the largest increases in outlays. This is only to be expected when we consider that the relative increase in population was considerably less than the increase in either the price or "real" outlay for such rapidly expanding services as education, medical care, and user-operated transportation. In fact, although population contributed in all instances to the increase in expenditures, in no instance was it the dominant effect.

In interpreting these findings, it must be kept in mind that they measure only that part of the population effect brought about by the over-all (net) change in the *size* of the population. The findings do not necessarily reflect the effect on expenditures of changes in the *composition* of the population, which can be especially important for services or goods used primarily by particular segments of the population, as has been true until recently of private education and foreign travel. To obtain estimates of such effects, however, requires the use of cross-section data, as is attempted in the next section.

These findings possess the further limitation that they do not, and can not, allow for changes in population not associated with any corresponding change in outlays. Thus, the fact that population rose 10 per cent between 1936 and 1946 does not of itself mean that outlays should have risen 10 per cent as a result, distribution effects aside. For these reasons, the figures in Tables 1 and 2 have to be interpreted as rough approximations of the true effect of population, but it is doubtful if the estimates are so rough as to negate the principal inferences drawn from them.

Effect of Population Shifts

METHOD USED

The effect on service outlays of population shifts was determined by a segmental approach roughly similar to that used with the aggregative data, though adapted to the distinctive nature of the cross-section data required for this type of analysis. The approach was based on the premise that the change in aggregate outlays for a particular good or service between any two periods can be compartmentalized, with the aid of cross-section data, into three effects, as follows:

1. The numbers effect—the change attributable to a change in the total number of people, or consuming units.

2. The distribution effect—the change attributable to shifts in the distribution of the population by "relevant" population characteristics.

3. The consumption effect—the change attributable to shifts in the outlay per consumer unit over time.

Because of the absence of price information with the cross-section data, the consumption effect now encompasses both the "real" and price effects of the preceding section.

It can be shown that these effects interact with each other and that, in general, each effect is composed of three sub-effects, or components.[3] These components, which are additive, are:

(*a*) Direct influence of that effect, that is, the zero-order interaction.

(*b*) The interaction of that effect with each of the other (two) effects separately, the first-order interactions.

(*c*) The interaction of that effect with both of the other effects simultaneously, the second-order interaction.

---

[3] The algebraic framework is as follows:

Let: C and C' be aggregate outlays in periods 0 and 1, respectively, not necessarily consecutive.

M and M' be the total number of consumer units in each of those periods.

r_i and r_i' be the proportion of consumer units in each period having the population characteristic, i.

x_i and x_i' be the average outlay per consumer unit of those possessing population characteristic, i, in each period.

Define:

(1) $$M' = M + N, \quad r_i' = r_i + s_i, \quad x_i' = x_i + y_i$$

Then, aggregate outlays in the two periods are:

(2) $$C = M\Sigma r_i x_i \quad \text{and} \quad C' = M'\Sigma r_i' x_i' = (M + N)\Sigma(r_i + s_i)(x_i + y_i)$$

and the change in outlays is, with a little algebra:

(3)

$$C' = C = \frac{\text{Direct influence}}{N\Sigma r_i x_i + M\Sigma s_i x_i + M\Sigma r_i y_i} + \frac{\text{First-order interactions}}{N\Sigma s_i x_i + N\Sigma r_i y_i + M\Sigma s_i y_i} + \frac{\text{Second-order interaction}}{N\Sigma s_i y_i}$$

	Direct influence			First-order interactions			Second-order interaction
Numbers effect	x			x	x		x
Dsn. effect		x		x		x	x
Cons. effect			x		x	x	x

The brackets and x's indicate the segregation of the terms by nature of the effect and of interactions.

Thus, given the necessary data, it is possible to compartmentalize a change in aggregate outlays not only by these three major effects, but also by the manner in which these forces interact with each other to affect outlays. There are, however, two principal problems involved in the application of this method. One problem, a perennial one in empirical work, is securing the necessary data on a comparable basis. In the present instance, this pretty well limited the analysis to the 1935–1936 Bureau of Labor Statistics Consumer Expenditures Study, the 1950 BLS-Wharton Study, and the 1955–1956 LIFE Study of Consumer Expenditures (LSCE). The comparability is not as complete as might be desired between these studies, particularly between the LIFE Study and the other two, but could be made sufficient for the purposes at hand by judicious selection of expenditure classifications.

The second, and somewhat interrelated, problem is the specification of "relevant" population characteristics. By the latter term is meant that population characteristic, or combination of population characteristics, which influences outlays for the particular goods or services under consideration. Ideally, population characteristics are sought which are relevant in a *net* sense—relevant after the influence of other population characteristics have been removed. Ideally, also, that combination of population characteristics is sought which is "most relevant" to the particular set of goods or services in the sense of accounting for the largest degree of variability in expenditures, though for certain purposes it will be at least of equal interest to ascertain the relative degrees of relevance of alternative combinations of population characteristics.

The specification of relevant population characteristics is of basic importance, for it governs the determination of the relative importance of the three effects. The greater the over-all (gross) relevance of a particular characteristic, the greater will be the importance of the distribution effect relative to the two other effects.

One approach to this specification problem is to seek for each category of services the "most relevant" combination of population characteristics. From a practical point of view, however, this approach is unfortunately not feasible, for to ascertain the "most relevant" combination is an undertaking not only far beyond the scope of this study but is also one which would require considerable time and resources.

The second approach is therefore the only practicable alternative. This approach involves selecting certain population characteristics which can be expected on a priori grounds to be relevant to the categories of services under study, and for which the necessary data are available, and determining the importance of the distribution effect of each character-istic, or combination of characteristics in turn. Although esthetically not as satisfying as the "ideal" approach, this approach nevertheless should provide a general idea of the importance of the distribution effect, particularly of its lower limit. It is indeed not unlikely that results obtained in this manner may not be too far from the "true" state of affairs when we consider that, first, the characteristics by which expendi-ture data are presented tend (or are thought) to be the most relevant in general, and second, because of the intercorrelation between most socio-economic characteristics, the estimate of the distribution effect based on only one or two characteristics is likely to be not a net effect, but a larger, gross effect incorporating part of the influence of related characteristics. Though not desirable from a conceptual point of view, this "grossness" of the estimates derived in this manner undoubtedly contributes to securing a more accurate, over-all picture of the importance of the distribution effect.[4]

In practice, it turns out that there is no choice at all, for the only population characteristic for which reasonably comparable data are available at present on at least two surveys is income. The principal reasons for this are the following:

1. Breakdowns of the 1935–1936 data on a national basis are presented only by income. Tabulations are presented also by region, city size, occupation of head, family size, and family composition, in turn, but *only* for families of two or more.

2. The 1950 study contains a wealth of tabulations by population characteristics but deals only with urban areas.

3. Detailed tabulations of the 1955–1956 study are not yet available. Those that are available present data on expenditures by a host of characteristics (but not family size!) all dealing with the total United States, and only income is cross-tabulated with the other characteristics.

As a result, the present analysis deals only with the distribution effect of income. As noted previously, the results in all likelihood pertain to more than the effect of income alone—probably a good deal more, con-sidering the positive intercorrelation between income and such other characteristics as education, occupation, family size, and location—but exactly how much more is difficult to judge.[5]

---

[4] The opposite is also possible, if negative intercorrelation is present, but on balance is not too likely.

[5] The little work that has been done on this subject indicates that the additional distribution effect on other socio-economic variables is likely to be almost negligible once shifts in income distribution have been taken into account. U.S. National Resources

TABLE 3

Data Used in Estimating Effect on Income Redistribution on Expenditures

Expenditure Category		Major Differences in Coverage, if any; General Notes
Early Period	Later Period	

1935–1936 and 1955–1956: Total U.S.

Housing	Housing	Imputed values used for owned homes in 1935–36; mortgage payment in 1955–56.
Household operation	Home operation and improvement (excluding housing and home decoration materials)	Includes furnaces and heating equipment in 1955–56; excludes cleaning and stationery supplies.
Personal and medical care	Personal and medical care	—
Recreation	Recreation	Reading materials included in 1955–56.

1935–1936 and 1950: Urban U.S. Families of 2 or More

Housing	Housing	Imputed values used for owned homes in 1935–36.
Fuel, light, and refrigeration	Fuel, light, and refrigeration	—
Medical care	Medical care	Excludes drugs and supplies.
Personal care services	Personal care services	—
Auto operation	Auto operation	Includes gas and oil.
Admissions	Admissions	—
Gifts and contributions	Gifts and contributions	—
Education, including supplies	Education, including supplies	—
Other transportation	Other transportation	—

1950 and 1955–1956: Urban U.S.

Housing	Housing	—
Fuel, light, and refrigeration	Home heating utilities	1955–56 figure includes cost of furnaces and heating equipment.
Clothing services	Clothing and accessories care	—
Medical and personal care	Medical and personal care	Excludes drugs and medical and personal care supplies.
Auto operation	Auto operation	Includes gas, oil, and auto parts.
Admissions	Admissions	—

Committee, *Consumer Expenditures in the United States*, U.S. Government Printing Office, Washington, D.C., 1941, Appendix C, pp. 185–187. Although this does not imply that these other population characteristics possess negligible distribution effects by themselves, it serves to support that suggestion ventured above that income redistribution incorporates, in whole or in part, the bulk of the effect of shifts in the demographic variables of principal relevance to consumer expenditures.

A list of the tests carried out with these three sets of data is shown in Table 3. This table also highlights the main differences in coverage between the different studies. In addition, two major sources of non-comparability deserve special mention. They are:

1. The sampling unit for the 1955–1956 data was the household (all people residing in one dwelling unit *including* boarders, servants, and the like, though excluding dwelling units with 5 or more boarders), while the sampling unit in 1935–1936 and 1950 was the family or consumer unit (persons in the same dwelling unit dependent on a common or pooled income for major expenditures). Since the average houschold would be larger than the average family, both its income and expenditures would be correspondingly larger. This would manifest itself as an upward bias in the "family" income distribution taken from the 1955–1956 household data and in the consequent estimation of the distribution effect.[6] In a similar fashion, an upward bias would appear in the estimation of the consumption effect, and a relative downward bias in the numbers effect.

2. Expenditure categories differ in various ways between surveys. In particular, the 1955–1956 LIFE data do not cover outlays for education, domestic service, gifts, or purchased transportation, nor do they present separate tabulations on the service component of household operation, auto operation, or clothing services. Foreign travel and personal business expenditures are not covered, or shown separately, in any of the surveys. Hence, several service categories could not be included at all.

Aside from these, there are differences in the methods used to obtain the data, nature, and extent of validity checks made with individual questionnaires, and in a number of other aspects.[7] This discussion is sufficient to indicate that little choice exists in the specification of relevant characteristics and that the results obtained are useful primarily as general indicators of the relative importance of the different effects, given a particular population distribution.

RESULTS

The nature of the results obtained by this approach is illustrated by Table 4, which shows the breakdown of the increase in expenditures for

[6] On the other hand, understatement of incomes in the 1955–1956 study was apparently not infrequent, and seemingly more so than in the 1935–1936 and 1950 studies, which would have some compensatory effect.

[7] For a more complete discussion of these differences between the 1935–1936 and 1950 studies, see the Wharton School monograph by Helen Lamale. The distinctive aspects of the 1955–1956 Life study are reviewed in a general way in the "Objective" section of Volume 1 of the series of reports published by Time Inc., on this study.

TABLE 4

Allocation of Increase in Housing Expenditures from 1935–1936
to 1955–1956 by Different Effects
(dollar amounts in millions)

(1) *Direction of Effect*	(2) *Numbers Effect*	(3) *Distribu- tion Effect*	(4) *Consump- tion Effect*	(5) *Total*	(6) *Per Cent of Total*
Direct	$2,327	$13,997	$−270	$16,054	130.9
First-order					
Numbers and distribution	1,717	1,717		3,434	28.0
Numbers and consumption	−33		−33	−66	−0.5
Distribution and consumption		2,873	−2,873	−5,746	−46.9
Second-order	−470	−470	−470	−1,410	−11.5
Total	$3,541	$12,371	$−3,646	$12,266	
Per cent of total	28.9	100.8	−29.7		100.0

housing between 1935–1936 and 1955–1956 by the type and direction of effect. The data in the body of the table are obtained by applying equation (3) in footnote 3 to the distribution of housing expenditures by income in 1935–1936 and in 1955–1956, as taken from the BLS and LSCE studies, respectively. The figures in the first line of columns 2–4 represent the direct influences of the three effects: $2,327 is $N\Sigma r_i x_i$, $13,997 is $M\Sigma s_i x_i$, and $−270 is $M\Sigma r_i y_i$. The figures in the next three lines represent the first-order interactions, allocated evenly in each case between the two effects involved. Thus, $3,434 represents $N\Sigma s_i x_i$, the first-order interaction between the numbers and distribution effects, and is allocated 50–50 to each effect individually. A similar procedure is followed for $−1,410, the second-order interaction $(N\Sigma s_i y_i)$.

The summation of these effects horizontally shows, in column 5, the total importance of the direct and the various interaction effects, converted into percentages in column 6. The vertical summation of the figures in columns 2–4 indicates, in the "total" line, the net magnitude of the three types of effects, and, in the next line, the relative importance of each.

The over-all sum in the table, $12,266 millions, is the extent of increase in housing expenditures for the populations covered between these two dates according to the survey data. Examination of the components of this sum in Table 4 reveals that income redistribution is seen to account for by far the largest portion of the increase. The growth of population exerts a net positive effect also, whereas the consumption effect is negative. The latter indicates that, on balance, average family outlays for housing, holding income and population constant, declined during these two decades.[8] This may be due in part to the failure of housing prices, particularly rentals, to rise as fast as income, though it is also not unlikely that at least part of these differences is due to lack of comparability between the two sets of data.

Table 4 also indicates that the direct effects are clearly the most important in accounting for the increase in housing outlays. At the same time, the interaction effects are seen to possess some importance, too. The first-order interaction between the numbers and distribution effects contribute $3.4 billion to the increase in outlays. Even more striking is the reduction of $5.7 billion brought about by the first-order interaction between the distribution and consumption effects. This is accounted for by the shift in the income distribution toward higher income levels coupled with the fact that the most pronounced reductions in average family housing outlays were at these levels. It is for this reason that the second-order interaction is also negative.

The results obtained in carrying out the same analysis on the other pairs of categories listed in Table 3 are presented in Table 5. The figures presented in this table correspond to the marginal totals in Table 4— the percentages in column 6 and in the last row of the table. Column 2 of Table 5 also indicates the magnitude of the change involved which, taken with the percentages in columns 4–11, provide a general summary picture of the importance of the different types and direction of effect.

It is important to note that the three main parts of Table 5—Parts A, B, and C—pertain to different segments of the total population, with only Part A referring to the entire population. For this reason, the results in the different parts of the table are not additive, even apart from noncomparabilities in the same category between any two periods, as noted in Table 3, and are not directly comparable with each other.

The results obtained in Table 5 vary substantially with the period under consideration. For both periods together, the distribution effect is by far the most important, accounting for half or all of the increase in each type of outlay. The rise in total population contributes between 20 and 30 per cent while the consumption effect is more erratic, serving to increase recreation and medical and personal care expenditures while reducing outlays for household operation and particularly for housing.

---

[8] Examination of the data indicates that this phenomenon varies substantially with income level and is due primarily to reduced housing expenditures at the higher income levels. Below incomes of $4,000, housing outlays increased between 1935–1936 and 1955–1956. Above this level, housing outlays decreased, with the relative margin increasing rapidly with rising income levels.

TABLE 5

Allocation of Increase in Expenditures for Selected Services by Different Effects

Expenditure Category (1)	Total Net Change in Millions of Dollars (base for percentages) (2)	Total (3)	Type of Effect				Direction of Effect				Second-order Interaction (11)
								First-order Interaction			
			Nos. (4)	Dsn. (5)	Cons. (6)	Direct (7)	Nos. and Dsn. (8)	Nos. and Cons. (9)	Dsn. and Cons. (10)		
A. 1935–1936 vs. 1955–1956: Total U.S.											
Housing*	$12,243	100.0%	28.9	100.8	−29.7	130.9	28.0	−0.5	−46.9		−11.5
Household operation*	10,495	100.0	22.2	83.7	−5.9	112.4	22.1	2.5	−29.7		−7.3
Medical and personal care	7,603	100.0	20.9	63.1	16.0	121.2	18.8	8.4	−38.9		−9.5
Recreation	8,962	100.0	14.0	51.8	34.2	83.5	11.6	7.8	−2.3		−0.6
B. 1935–1936 vs. 1950: Urban families of two or more											
Housing	$11,142	100.0%	43.7	54.1	2.2	84.3	28.9	4.6	−11.0		−7.0
Fuel, light, and refrigeration	2,988	100.0	50.6	28.2	21.2	96.0	19.7	16.5	−20.0		−12.2
Medical care	4,778	100.0	30.9	36.7	32.4	73.9	19.3	17.3	−6.5		−4.0
Personal care	792	100.0	38.5	51.1	10.5	79.6	26.7	7.7	−8.7		−5.3
Auto operation	4,661	100.0	30.7	54.6	14.7	62.2	23.6	5.0	5.8		3.5
Admissions	877	100.0	40.4	69.6	−10.0	86.9	37.5	0.5	−12.5		−9.4
Gifts and contributions	3,532	100.0	33.8	65.7	0.5	84.4	36.0	5.6	−16.2		−9.9
Education*	412	100.0	64.3	142.4	−106.7	185.4	102.0	−15.3	−106.9		−65.2
Other transportation*	1,492	100.0	31.4	41.0	27.6	61.9	17.1	10.8	6.3		3.9
C. 1950 vs. 1955–1956: All urban families											
Housing	$5,368	100.0%	46.5	33.8	19.7	102.0	6.0	3.9	−10.2		−1.7
Fuel, light, and refrigeration*	770	100.0	105.4	65.9	−71.3	112.2	11.1	−9.8	−11.6		−1.9
Clothing services	1,162	100.0	27.6	33.6	38.8	87.8	5.0	5.8	1.2		0.3
Medical and personal care	2,908	100.0	30.7	18.5	50.8	80.8	2.1	7.0	8.7		1.4
Auto operation	4,580	100.0	27.2	31.3	41.5	87.1	4.6	6.1	1.9		0.3
Admissions*	−162	100.0	122.0	128.9	−350.9	−22.0	−27.7	45.3	89.3		15.1

* Results for these categories are probably affected by differences in survey coverages (see pp. 512ff.) and may be of doubtful significance.

Basic sources: 1935–36: U.S. National Resources Committee, *Consumer Expenditures in the U.S.*, 1940. U.S. National Resources Committee, *Family Expenditures in the U.S.*, 1940.

1950: University of Pennsylvania, *Consumer Expenditures, Income and Savings*, 1950, Vol. 18.
1956: Unpublished tabulations from the Life Study of Consumer Expenditures made available through the courtesy of *Life Magazine*.

For the period between 1935–1936 and 1950, the contribution of each effect varies considerably by category, though the growth of population generally increases in importance. Thus, the numbers effect accounts for almost half of the increase in outlays for housing and for fuel, light, and refrigeration, and 30 to 40 per cent of the increase in expenditures on medical care, personal care, and on admissions—categories comparable to those in Part A of the table for which the relative effect of population growth was considerably less.

At the same time, the redistribution of income exerts substantial effect on most of the expenditure categories, and accounts for the bulk of the increase in outlays for such services as housing, auto operation, admissions, gifts and contributions, and education. Changes in consumption patterns, holding income redistribution and population growth constant, serve to increase greatly outlays for medical care and purchased transportation and to reduce sharply expenditures for education (though, as noted later, the latter may well be due to noncomparabilities in the underlying data).

Changes in consumption patterns appear to be considerably more important during the 1950's. These changes account for about 40 per cent or more of the increase in outlays for clothing services, medical and personal care, and auto operation, and apparently kept the increase in expenditures on household utilities substantially below what they otherwise would have been.

The results pertaining to direction of effect are fairly consistent from one period to another. The bulk of the increase in outlays—often more than 100 per cent of the net amount—is accounted for by the summation of the three direct effects, as one would expect. The interaction between population growth and income redistribution generally makes a strong positive contribution to the rise in expenditures, particularly if the 1950's are excluded—reflecting the relatively greater increase of consumer units at the higher-income levels.

The interaction between population growth and consumption tends to be low, reflecting the concomitantly low relationship between these two factors. On the other hand, the consumption-redistribution effect tends to be negative, particularly for both decades combined, as a result of outlays for medical and personal care, utilities, and recreation declining at upper income levels, which at the same time are rising most in importance, while outlays for these services were increasing at the lowest income levels. The second-order interaction exerts relatively little effect in most instances.

To what extent do these results reflect what actually happened and to

511

what extent do they reflect simply sampling errors and noncomparabilities between the three sets of data? Considering the diverse methods used in the three surveys, this is a question which merits serious consideration. Though a complete answer is beyond the scope of this study, useful general inferences nevertheless are possible. For this purpose, Table 6 presents rough comparisons of aggregate expenditures for the services categories and periods covered in Table 5 as derived from the survey data and from the United States Department of Commerce estimates of consumption expenditures. These estimates are rough in that no attempt has been made to correct the survey data for undercoverage of certain items and population groups (such as the highest income levels) nor has any attempt been made to correct for differences in survey and Commerce concepts other than to match corresponding categories of expenditure. The comparisons in this table therefore do *not* provide a basis for evaluating the relative accuracies of these two principal sources of data, particularly columns (4) and (7) which express the survey aggregates (C and C' in each case, respectively) as percentages of the corresponding Commerce aggregates. This table, and these two columns in particular, are useful, however, for highlighting possible shifts in survey coverage between two surveys, taking the Commerce aggregates as the yardstick. Though the accuracy of the latter is at times not clear, the methods used are consistent over time so that the problem of comparability is relatively minor. Hence, to the extent that substantial differences (say, 25 percentage points or more) are apparent in the ratios for a particular expenditure category in columns (4) and (7), some presumption exists for reexamining the comparability of the survey data, though large differences of themselves do not provide conclusive evidence of noncomparability.

Such differences are immediately apparent for housing and household operation (or utilities) where 1955–1956 data are used. In the former case, imputed values were used for owner-occupied homes in 1935–1936 while mortgage payments were the basis in 1950 and in 1955–1956. By 1950, housing prices had probably not increased sufficiently to introduce a substantial error from substituting actual costs for imputed values. However, because of the housing boom in the 1950's, housing prices had risen by 1956 to the point where the imputed value would be substantially above the current cost of an owner-occupied house acquired as little as five years earlier. Hence, the large negative consumption effect for housing between 1935–1936 and 1955–1956, shown in Table 5, may well be spurious. Similarly, the very small consumption housing effect shown between 1935–1936 and 1950 may also be an underestimate; the 1950

TABLE 6

Comparison of Survey and Commerce Aggregative Estimates of Selected Services and Related Expenditures (dollar figures in millions)

A. Total U.S.

Expenditure Category (1)	1935–1936			1955–1956		
	Survey (2)	Commerce[a] (3)	Survey as Percentage of Commerce (4)	Survey (5)	Commerce[a] (6)	Survey as Percentage of Commerce (7)
Housing	$9,506	$7,789	122.0	$21,749	$29,199	74.5
Household operation	5,285	5,160	102.4	15,780	17,816	88.6
Medical and personal care	3,237	3,017	107.3	10,840	11,784	92.0
Recreation	1,643	2,058	79.8	10,605	13,432	79.0

B. Urban families of two or more

Expenditure Category	1935–1936			1950		
	Survey	Commerce[a]	Survey as Percentage of Commerce	Survey	Commerce[a]	Survey as Percentage of Commerce
Housing	$5,337	$4,645	114.9	$16,479	$16,919	97.4
Fuel, light, and refrigeration	1,796	1,529	117.5	4,784	4,584	104.3
Medical care	1,090	1,158	94.1	5,868	4,956	118.4
Personal care	300	238	126.0	1,092	713	153.1
Auto operation	1,168	1,318	88.6	5,829	5,324	109.5
Admissions	353	379	93.1	1,230	1,218	101.0
Education	290	279	103.9	702	1,177	59.6
Other transportation	398	532	74.8	1,890	1,881	100.5

C. All urban families

Expenditure Category	1950			1955–1956		
	Survey	Commerce[a]	Survey as Percentage of Commerce	Survey	Commerce[a]	Survey as Percentage of Commerce
Housing	$13,815	$16,754	82.5	$19,183	$25,054	76.6
Fuel, light, and refrigeration	4,983	5,123	97.3	5,753	7,623	75.5
Clothing services	1,577	1,509	104.5	2,739	3,325	82.3
Medical and personal care	4,562	5,009	91.1	7,470	7,582	98.5
Auto operation	6,077	5,950	102.1	10,657	9,693	109.9
Admissions	1,314	1,362	96.5	1,152	1,435	80.3

[a] Adjustment of Commerce data was based on the following percentages derived (for 1950, estimated) from population statistics and from the consumer expenditure studies:

	1935–36	1950	1955–56
Urban family expenditures as percentage of all families	66	76	81
Urban family expenditure as percentage of all nonfarm families	80	87	—
Expenditures of urban families of two or more as percentage of all urban families	81	90	—
Expenditures of urban families of two or more as percentage of all families	53	68	—

Sources: Commerce data: 1954 *National Income Supplement* and July 1957 *Survey of Current Business*. Table 30. Survey data: Same as Table 5.

513

to 1955–1956 comparison probably yields the most valid results for housing.

For household operation and utilities, the LSCE data seem to provide insufficient coverage, perhaps because these categories include various small items not easily collected in the type of interview used in the 1955–1956 study. Although this is another area in which price increases have lagged considerably behind income increases, the substantially negative consumption effect must be questioned, particularly for a period such as 1950 to 1955–1956, in view of the data in Table 6.

For similar reasons, it seems likely that education expenditures in 1950 are out of line with those in 1935–1936, that admissions in 1955–1956 were probably under-reported (though not recreation in general), and that other transportation expenditures were under-reported in 1935–1936. These various categories, six in all, have been labeled with asterisks in Table 5 to indicate the suspect nature of the results derived for them.

Omitting these suspect categories leaves us with a more consistent set of results—and with a considerably reduced base for drawing generalizations. Nevertheless, certain tendencies are clear:

1. The effect of population growth was most substantial, relatively as well as absolutely, between 1935–1936 and 1950, accounting at times for half or more of the rise in expenditures for selected services. Population growth also contributed strongly to the increases during the 1950's.

2. Population growth was relatively most important in increasing outlays for home-connected items and, to a lesser degree, for medical and personal care.

3. Increased outlays at given levels of income are of substantial importance in accounting for the sharp increases in outlays for medical and personal care and, in the 1950's, for the car owner and for clothing services.

4. The redistribution of population, particularly with regard to income, has been a major influence accounting for the rise in service outlays both from 1935–1936 to 1950 and from 1950 to 1955–1956. It appears to have exerted especially strong effects on the increase in expenditures for housing, medical and personal care, auto operation, and, of course, recreation.

Now, how do these results fit in with those obtained in the preceding section? The answer is, as noted earlier, that they cannot. In part this is because the two approaches explore the problem in different dimensions —the price aspects being covered in the first and population distribution in the second. Perhaps even more important are the differences in coverage between the two sets of data, the Commerce series including institutional purchases as well as family expenditures and being derived in a different manner.

The first source of difference can be reconciled by extending the algebraic framework developed on pages 499–503 to include a price effect, even though data limitations require that one price be used for all income levels.[9] The results do not affect the relative importance of the numbers and distribution effects but do indicate that most of the consumption effect derived earlier is actually due to price increases. Once the effect of price is taken into account, virtually no "real" change in consumption is seen to have occurred during these decades for most services, holding constant population growth and income redistribution. Such modification as may be required in this conclusion because of possible differential price increases in services purchased at different income levels is in all probability relatively slight.

Thus, price is seen to exert major influence in accounting for the increase in survey-based expenditures, the exact proportions coming out to be very similar to, though generally somewhat lower than, the corresponding proportions for the aggregative results in Table 2. This is understandable, for the latter case includes no allowance for distribution effects.

Perhaps the most important reason for observed differences between the aggregative and survey-derived results lies in the inherent lack of comparability between the two types of data, at least as used in this study. The basic difficulty is that the survey data are restricted to certain segments of the consumer population, partly because of the original survey design and partly because of the necessity of reconciling the coverage of pairs of surveys to the type of analysis used here. In addition, the aggregative data include institutional expenditures for consumer goods and services, which are excluded from all the surveys. Then, too, methods generally used to derive the aggregative data are different from those used in consumer surveys.

All things considered, one would expect the aggregative results to ascribe less weight to population change as influencing consumer expenditures than the survey data. This is largely because the survey data

---

[9] Thus, let $x_i = pw_i$, where p is the average price paid by the ith group for the bundle of goods w_i in period O, and $x_i' = p'w_i'$ be the corresponding quantities in period 1. Then, let $p' = p + q$ and $w_i = w_i + v_i$, where q and v_i can be positive or negative. Making the appropriate substitutions in (2) on p. 503 and carrying out the algebra yields an expression analogous to (3) which permits segmentation of the price effect from the "real" consumption effect.

concentrate on the more dynamically changing population group, the urban population. With the urban population growing more rapidly than the total population, the population effect as derived from urban data is bound to be larger than a similar estimate based on total population growth. Then too, the use of the family, or household, rather than the individual as the population unit, tends to increase the effect of population growth by virtue of the faster rate of increase in family formation during the period studied, particularly between 1935–1936 and 1950.

Such an expectation is borne out by a comparison of the "numbers effect" percentages in Tables 2 and 5. The differences that are shown do not necessarily point to discrepancies in the various sets of estimates.[10] Rather they serve to highlight the varying effect of population change and of the other forces among different segments of the population.

Conclusions

The results of this exploratory investigation have to be interpreted with great care. In part, this is because of doubts regarding the reliability and comparability of the basic data used, not to mention that much of the essential data was not available—data on certain types of services and on changes in population distributions. In part, this is also because of the difficulty of interpreting empirical findings on population change.

Notwithstanding these limitations, it is apparent that the growth of population has played an important role in the sharp increase in expenditures for many services during the past two decades. Population growth was of particular importance in affecting the expansion of outlays for housing services and for medical and personal care. In addition there is little doubt that the growth of population and the consequent expansion of markets had a lot to do with the redistribution of incomes during this period, which is the most important single factor in bringing about the tremendous increase in consumer expenditures.

Given the circumstances of these two decades, population growth appears to have supplied a major stimulant to consumer expenditures. At the same time, it is also apparent that population growth does not of itself necessarily insure more expenditures. This is supported by the substantial difference in the relative contribution of population growth to particular outlays, and by the fact that substantial increases in certain

---

[10] Possible discrepancies are clearly not out of the question, however, particularly with regard to the comparability of the expenditure and consumer-unit estimates of the different sources.

expenditures, such as for recreation, can take place with population growth playing a minor role.

From a more general point of view, it should be remembered that the period covered by this study was one of great disturbances. Under such conditions, it is not surprising to find that population growth was of considerable importance on the upside, perhaps even as an independent catalyst. Whether population growth exerts a similar effect during a period of depression is another question.

COMMENT

RICHARD A. EASTERLIN, University of Pennsylvania

The stated aim of Robert Ferber's paper is "to evaluate the extent to which changes in the size and distribution of the population are able to account for changes in consumer outlays on services between 1936 and 1956." In line with this aim he presents several tables of numerical results. The underlying data are chiefly from the Department of Commerce *National Income Supplement*, and three cross-section surveys, the 1935–1936 BLS Consumer Expenditures Study, the 1950 BLS-Wharton Study, and the 1955–1956 *Life* Study of Consumer Expenditures. One can only voice admiration at Ferber's decision to expose himself to the inevitable problems of comparability involved in any attempt to utilize these diverse sources. On his success in overcoming these problems I am not qualified to speak, for lack of detailed familiarity with the basic sources. But the technique of analysis which he applies to these data in order to accomplish his stated objective does seem to raise some questions, for it is not made clear what relation, if any, this technique bears to the conceptual framework of economic analysis.

For expositional purposes, the technique can perhaps best be summarized as follows. The change in money expenditure on a particular category of services is partitioned into two segments, that associated with a change in prices and that attributable to a change in the real volume of consumption. The change in real consumption is, in turn, subdivided into two additional components, the change in the per capita volume of real consumption and the change in size of population. Finally, the population is subdivided into a number of income-size groups, each with its characteristic level of per capita real consumption, and the change in real per capita consumption for the population as a whole allocated between *inter*-group shifts in the relative distribution of population and *intra*-group changes in real per capita consumption levels. Population change is taken to influence total expenditure through two of the foregoing

517

components: the one relating to population size (the "numbers effect"), and that referring to shifts in the relative distribution of population by size of income (the "distribution effect"). The precise procedure followed in the paper differs somewhat, since limitations of the data necessitate the performance of two separate analyses—one in which the change in money expenditure is partitioned into price, population, and per capita real volume components; the other in which the change is allocated among change in population numbers, shifts in the relative distribution of population by income level, and the change in per capita money expenditures at given income levels.

In evaluating the paper, the basic question is: to what extent can the findings derived by this technique be taken as indicative of the influence of population change on service expenditures? Ferber's own answer to this question is not clear. At various points in the discussion he distinguishes between "direct" and "indirect" effects of population change, and also between "gross" and "net" effects. At no place is the meaning of these terms stated explicitly, nor does Ferber make clear to which group or groups of effects his calculations are intended to refer.[1] Suppose, therefore, we examine his procedures with this question in view, that is, to what extent do the findings indicate the influence of population change on service expenditures?

Consider the analysis given in the first part of the paper, where the growth in money expenditure on services is divided into three parts: that due to the change in (*a*) price, (*b*) population, and (*c*) per capita real consumption. Let us take a hypothetical example. Suppose we inject into an assumed initial stationary state a once-over increase in population size with all demographic aspects of population composition—age, sex, family size, and so on—constant. On the demand side, the population increase would make for a proportionate increase in consumption. On the supply side, the growth in labor force arising from the population increase would alter factor proportions. Factor productivity in different lines would be differently affected, as would aggregate productivity, and with relative product prices and the income level consequently changing, the per capita consumption of any given good would alter in an amount depending on the relevant price and income elasticities. For goods requiring relatively large amounts of labor, the over-all effect would presumably be a relative increase in consumption exceeding that in

---

[1] For example, in the discussion of Table 4, the magnitude of the "indirect effect" is identified with the size of the interaction term in contrast with the treatment in the preceding section where the "indirect effect" is said to be omitted in the calculations.

population; for goods requiring relatively little labor, the opposite would be true.

Comparison of the new with the old equilibrium for any given good would reveal a change in money expenditure. Suppose now we were to apply Ferber's technique to determine how much of this was attributable to the change in population. Ferber's analysis would show, I believe, that the change in population gave rise to a roughly proportionate change in expenditure. Whether or not the change would be exactly proportionate would depend on the assumptions used in allocating the interaction terms—and it should be noted they are no more than assumptions. The remainder would be allocated to the price and per capita components —a positive amount if total expenditure rose proportionately more than population, a negative amount if the opposite were true. Now in a very immediate sense one might argue this is quite appropriate—that the change in expenditure does reflect a change not only in population but also in the per capita consumption level and in price. But as one presses back into the underlying causal system, it becomes clear that the price and per capita changes were in turn traceable to the increase in total population, so that at bottom, it is the population change that accounts for the entire change in expenditure.

Stated more generally, one may say that Ferber's method fails to allow for any interdependence among the components distinguished. This is perhaps worth emphasizing since, while he appears to recognize this point in the first part of his paper, in the second part he mistakenly identifies the effect due to interdependence with the size of the interaction terms. In an analysis of the change in *service* expenditure due to population, this interdependence would seem to deserve exploration, since on a priori grounds one might argue that because a number of services tend to employ relatively more labor than the average, the expansion in service expenditures due to population change would be more than proportionate. As a practical matter, the possibility of tracing an effect of this sort seems limited, so that as a working proposition it is perhaps most reasonable to assume that the effect of a change in population numbers, other things, and especially composition, being equal, is a proportionate change in consumption. But if this position is adopted, as seems implicit in the present technique, one might as well recognize as an immediate implication rather than a "finding," that the numerical calculations will show that "services for which the population effect was relatively more important were not the ones that exhibited the largest increases in outlays" (p. 502). This must of course be the case since the population effect on

519

the assumption of proportionality is constant from one good to another, and will thus account for a larger share of the increase in total expenditure if that increase is small rather than large.

More fundamentally, acceptance of the assumption about the proportionate effect of a change in population numbers means that, with regard to the influence of population change on expenditure, the really interesting problems lie in the analysis of the change in the per capita consumption figure. It is here that the influence of the change in population by such demographic characteristics as family size, age, sex, color, residence, and so on, is to be found.

Let us turn then to the second part of Ferber's paper, since it is here that he considers the influence of change in population *composition* on service expenditure. It will be recalled that in this connection he divides the population into a number of income-size groups, each with its characteristic level of per capita service expenditure, and allocates the change in per capita expenditure between inter-group shifts in the relative distribution of population and intra-group changes in per capita expenditure levels. Now when one considers this procedure, it seems a rather strange way of establishing the effects of population change on expenditure, entirely aside from the question of possible interdependence among components. Consider for a moment a situation in which, other things unchanged, the income of all members of the population rises proportionately. To what would the resulting change in per capita expenditure be attributed? Under the present scheme, the answer would be that the population composition by size of income has changed. But the answer offered by economic analysis, and surely more direct, is simply that per capita incomes have risen. If we were to follow Ferber's procedure, I suppose virtually every cause of expenditure change could be encompassed under the heading of "population change." Thus we might talk about the influence of a change in relative prices as the effect of a change in the composition of population by price paid, or the effect of a change in tastes as the influence of a change in distribution of population by taste. This is not mere quibbling over the definitional question of demographic versus nondemographic variables. But it does seem that in any given analysis one must specify what is meant by the effect attributable to "population change," and in particular that this effect should not encompass the classic economic variables of income, or potentially, of relative prices and tastes.

If, then, the change in expenditure attributed by Ferber's analysis to a change in population composition is attributable to income growth (though I do not think the analysis handles even this very well), could one perhaps conclude just the opposite of what Ferber's calculations purport to show, namely, that the influence of changes in population distribution, rather than being reflected under the Table 5 heading of "distribution effect," is included as a residual under that of "consumption effect," so that we do have after all some indication of the effects of change in demographic composition? Unfortunately the answer is no. There is first, of course, the question of the interdependence of components. And even if this is assumed unimportant, which is a big assumption, the category labeled "consumption effect" includes the influence of nondemographic factors such as tastes or price as well as demographic factors.

Our conclusion, then, on the question initially raised—the extent to which the analysis used in the paper succeeds in establishing the influence of population change on service expenditures—is largely negative. To the extent that the analysis does take account of the effect of population change, it is only the roughly proportionate effect on demand of a growth in numbers. The analysis fails to take account of the influence of a growth in numbers on supply, and, through this, on per capita consumption. Nor does it take account of the influence of changes in the typical demographic characteristics of population composition—age, sex, color, and so on. Finally, it mistakenly assigns the effect of income change to population composition.

REPLY by Mr. Ferber

Easterlin's principal criticisms can be classified under two headings: the specific framework used in the analysis, and the general approach taken to the problem.

With regard to the specific framework, I fully agree with Easterlin that the analysis fails to take account of the influence of a number of demographic factors in addition to other possible relevant variables. This point is brought out several times in the paper and the inherent limitations of the results resulting from these omissions are stressed. As is noted in the paper, these variables could not be included because of lack of data, not because of oversight. At the same time, it is worth mentioning once again that such previous work as has been done on this subject indicates that the income factor tends to include the bulk of the effect of shifts in a number of other demographic variables of principal relevance to consumer behavior.

With regard to the general approach, there is also no doubt that it

521

possesses certain major difficulties and that it will yield misleading results under certain conditions. This is only to be expected, for is this not true of any statistical technique if the results obtained from it are interpreted in a vacuum? Similar criticisms can be leveled against such widely used techniques as regression analysis and variance analysis. Yet this does not mean that the techniques themselves are of no value. Rather it seems that the results of these techniques have to be interpreted with regard to the data that are used and the circumstances prevailing during the period covered by the analysis.

These precautions apply as strongly to the present method as to many others, and Easterlin has brought out some examples of such cases. Many other examples could be cited too, but I shall forego doing so for lack of space. Here again, however, I think it only fair to refer the reader to the paper itself where the need for such precaution is stressed in several places. Particular stress is placed therein on the pitfalls and difficulty of ascribing effects due to population or any other factor based on statistical results alone and on the importance of relating results to the dimension of analysis.

I must admit being surprised by Easterlin's allegation that I failed to distinguish between direct and indirect effects and between gross and net effects. The latter distinction is defined on page 504, whereas the distinction between direct influences and interaction effects is spelled out explicitly in footnote 3. Easterlin may have been misled by an occasional slip of mine in substituting the word "indirect" for "interaction"; the two are clearly not the same.

Taking an over-all view, I should like to emphasize, as is stated in the paper, that this is an exploratory investigation using a technique which has received virtually no attention in the past. Because of this, it is all the more surprising that Mrs. Crockett happened to select, independently, virtually the same general technique in her paper, although she applied it in a different manner. Exploratory though her and my results may be, it seems to me that they indicate that this technique has considerable promise and merits more attention in the future.

C O M M E N T on Crockett and Ferber

Elizabeth W. Gilboy, Harvard University

As a non-demographer, I have been impressed by the growing recognition of the fact that demographers and economists cannot work successfully alone, especially when it comes to any sort of prediction. Projections of population change cannot be made without knowledge of economic factors. Similarly, economists are increasingly aware that projections of economic variables require knowledge of demographic changes and their interaction with the elements of the economic system.

Two papers presented at this meeting are concerned with the attempt to evaluate the effects of population change on consumption expenditures. Jean B. Crockett and Robert Ferber are concerned with measuring the influence of demographic variables (total population growth, age of head, race, certain distributional effects, and the like) over time upon specific categories of consumer expenditures—in the first case, food; in the second, services. They both use multiple correlation–variance techniques to estimate the effects of demographic variables upon food and service expenditures from cross-section data; Ferber also experiments with time series.

Mrs. Crockett predicts food expenditures from 1950–1970, making assumptions derived from Census data as to population growth and changes in distributional factors over the period. In using the period 1935–1956, Ferber has the advantage of actual figures for population growth for his experiments with both cross-section and time-series data. He compares the results of the two studies in analyzing the interaction of demographic and economic effects upon services expenditures during this period.

How significant are the results of these investigations? The authors would be the first to admit their inadequacy as predictions, the data difficulties and the heroic assumptions necessary. Mrs. Crockett finds that age and racial factors appear to have quantitatively small effects upon food expenditures over the projected period. Ferber's analysis of time series indicates that population growth seems to have had considerably less effect on service expenditures from 1935–1956 than price changes and consumption effects. The results of his cross-section study show that direct population growth had greater quantitative impact upon service expenditures than the other variables used; this also is true for Mrs. Crockett's study.

As Ferber himself states, the difficulties of comparing the results of his cross-section and time-series studies are truly formidable. With Easterlin, I find difficulty in accepting Ferber's use of three cross-section surveys[1] which are in many serious respects noncomparable, as the basis for estimating consumption and income changes from 1935–1956. I question as well Ferber's use of income distribution changes, derived from these

---

[1] The Consumer Purchases Study, 1935–1936; the BLS Survey of Consumer Expenditures, 1950; the Time-Life Consumer Survey, 1956.

three surveys, to represent population distribution changes, for which there was no available information. This distribution change was found to be an important interaction factor, but can this result be taken with any confidence as an indication of the effects of distributional changes in population? Easterlin questions this, too.

The essence of the critiques of the Crockett and Ferber papers by their discussants, Fox and Easterlin respectively, seems to be that the authors would have done better to engage in a more strictly defined economic analysis per se. Fox points out that aggregate food expenditures are a poor category to select for analysis and that significant results can hardly be expected unless food is broken down into its components. He suggests that relative price differences, the behavior of various subcategories of food expenditures, food eaten at home as compared with food eaten at restaurants, and so on, should all be considered. Easterlin emphasizes that the inclusion of more economic variables would have improved Ferber's analysis.

This is no doubt true, but for the purposes of this conference, explorations into the relations among economic and demographic variables are certainly pertinent. Regarded in this light, the Crockett and Ferber papers provide useful exploratory contributions to a new and difficult field of investigation, the interrelationships of economic and demographic variables. Obviously more work in the area is needed before significant quantitative results can be obtained. The authors concur heartily in this. Both Mrs. Crockett and Ferber note the prevalence of interaction among economic and demographic variables. In the case of food, Mrs. Crockett emphasizes the extent to which income as a variable subsumes the effects of demographic variables such as age and race, with the result that income effects taken alone are greatly distorted. Ferber points out at some length the importance of trying to measure the indirect repercussions of population changes on service expenditures.

The same problem, that of measuring the direct and indirect relationships among economic and demographic variables, is being tackled by Andre Daniere and myself in the consumption research at the Harvard Economic Research Project. Preliminary results, which will be presented at a Wharton School Conference in March, exhibit an extensive amount of interaction and nonlinearity. Using the 1950 BLS Survey data for individual families, we are engaged in a complicated stratification procedure, using some 27 economic and demographic variables, in which these families are grouped and regrouped according to the observed relationships with these variables in succession. So far, the experiments relate only to the effect of five major variables (with subgroups)[2] and a few other economic variables, such as net assets, upon clothing expenditures. Interaction and nonlinearity appear to be widespread and differ within subgroups.

It is hoped that ranges of combinations of variables and subvariables can be found over which additivity and linearity can be reasonably assumed, which, with the use of dummy variables, will reduce substantially the number of variables to be used in an eventual multiple regression analysis. Daniere's preliminary theoretical model for the stratification procedure, while related to variance analysis, is expected to make possible the testing of a wider range of hypotheses than the traditional variance model. The basic hypotheses about the structure of consumption resulting from the detailed stratification procedure should make the interpretation of the final regression results more meaningful.

Our investigation is an extension of the type of analysis presented by Crockett and Ferber on cross-section data. At this stage, it is more disaggregated and includes many more variables. We are faced with the same problems, assuming we get significant measures of reaction among variables: how do we predict on the basis of cross-section results over time? For this we need from demographers estimates of distributional changes in population; from economists, estimates of changes in income distribution. We need also, economists and demographers alike, a more explicit examination of our basic hypotheses and those implied by the statistical and mathematical techniques used.

[2] Disposable income, age of head, family size, family type, tenure.

AUTHOR INDEX

Abramovitz, Moses, 329 *n.*, 332 *n.*
Allen, R. G. D., 433 *n.*
Andrew, Frank, 381 *n.*

Baltzell, E. Digby, 142 *n.*
Bancroft, Gertrude, 416 *n.*, 420, 422
Banks, W. H., 218 *n.*
Barnett, Harold J., 12–13, 423–451
Bash, Wendell H., 90 *n.*
Bassie, V. Lewis, 496 *n.*
Baumol, William J., 324–376
Becker, Gary S., 209–234
Belloc, Nedra, 398 *n.*
Belshaw, Harold, 426
Benedict, Kirby, 385 *n.*
Bensman, Joseph, 139
Beveridge, William H., 258
Birkbeck, Morris, 379 *n.*
Bjerke, Kjeld, 60 *n.*
Blank, David M., 366 *n.*
Bogue, Donald J., 472 *n.*
Borgatta, Edgar, 144 *n.*
Borné, Alfred, 335 *n.*
Bourgeois-Pichat, J., 261 *n.*, 278 *n.*
Bowman, Isaiah, 383 *n.*
Brady, Dorothy, 354, 373 *n.*
Brown, Harrison, 424
Burns, Arthur F., 243 *n.*

Callaghan, M. E., 301 *n.*
Campbell, Arthur A., 86 *n.*, 110
Carlson, A. J., 423
Carus-Wilson, E. M., 384 *n.*
Chow, G. C., 212 *n.*
Ciriacy-Wantrup, S. V., 425 *n.*
Clifford, Jose, 382 *n.*
Coale, Ansley J., 3–14, 133–136, 261 *n.*, 278 *n.*, 352–371
Conrad, A. H., 213 *n.*
Cook, Robert, 425
Coontz, S. H., 215 *n.*, 378 *n.*
Craine, Lyle, 424 *n.*
Crockett, Jean A., 457–483, 523

Dabney, Robert L., 392 *n.*
Darwin, Charles Galton, 423–424
Davis, Joseph S., 258, 357 *n.*
De Wolfe, P., 48 *n.*, 49
Dorn, Harold F., 356 *n.*
Douglas, Paul, 398 *n.*
Duesenberry, James S., 231–234

Duncan, Otis Dudley, 223 *n.*, 473 *n.*
Durand, John, 391 *n.*, 400 *n.*, 419–422

Early, Jubal, 392
Easterlin, Richard A., 517–521
Eaton, J. W., 110 *n.*
Edin, Karl A., 52 *n.*, 54 *n.*, 218 *n.*
Edwards, Alba, 386 *n.*

Farr, William, 257.
Febvay, M., 56 *n.*
Ferber, Robert, 496–515, 521–522
Field, James A., 383 *n.*, 396 *n.*
Franklin, Benjamin, 78
Freedman, Ronald, 72–76, 86 *n.*, 110, 139, 145, 220 *n.*
Friedman, Milton, 345–349, 350–351, 373 *n.*
Friedman, Rose, 373 *n.*
Friend, Irwin, 460 *n.*

Galbraith, Virginia L., 223 *n.*, 241
Garfinkle, Stuart, 409 *n.*
Geary, R. C., 70 *n.*
Gilboy, Elizabeth W., 522–525
Gille, Halvor, 17–34
Gini, C., 77 *n.*
Glass, D. V., 55 *n.*, 56 *n.*, 216 *n.*, 437 *n.*
Glick, Paul C., 296 *n.*
Goldberg, David, 137–151, 220 *n.*
Golden, Philip, 496 *n.*
Goldsmith, Raymond W., 225 *n.*, 354 *n.*, 358 *n.*
Gordon, R. A., 366 *n.*
Gordon, Scott, 377 *n.*
Grabill, W. H., 78, 118
Grauman, John V., 275–282
Grebenik, E., 55 *n.*, 56 *n.*, 216 *n.*
Grebler, Leo, 366 *n.*
Green, Duff, 384 *n.*
Gregg, Allan, 423
Griffith, Ernest, 424 *n.*
Griliches, Zvi, 319 *n.*
Grunfeld, Yehuda, 319 *n.*
Gulick, Luther, 424 *n.*
Gutman, Robert, 113–116
Guttentag, J., 226 *n.*

Hafen, Ann W., 385 *n.*
Hafen, LeRoy R., 385 *n.*
Hajnal, John, 25 *n.*, 356 *n.*
Hauser, Philip, 139 *n.*
Hays, S., 440 *n.*

527

Helleiner, K. F., 408 *n.*
Hertzler, J. O., 424 *n.*
Hexter, M. B., 242
Hill, Joseph A., 87 *n.*
Himes, N. A., 132, 217 *n.*, 218
Hoover, Edgar M., 370, 451–454
Houthakker, H. S., 216 *n.*, 230 *n.*
Hubback, Judith, 50 *n.*, 51, 69 *n.*
Huntington, E., 110 *n.*, 221 *n.*
Hutchinson, Edward P., 52 *n.*, 54 *n.*, 131–133, 218 *n.*, 407 *n.*

Innes, J. W., 90 *n.*
Ise, J., 447 *n.*

Jackson, P. T., 388 *n.*
Jaffe, A. J., 37 *n.*, 89 *n.*, 218 *n.*, 390 *n.*
Jarrett, Henry, 423 *n.*
Johnson, Gwendolyn Z., 36–72, 218 *n.*
Jones, Thomas P., 393 *n.*
Juster, Thomas, 221 *n.*

Kavanagh, K. E., 301 *n.*
Keynes, John Maynard, 326, 355 *n.*, 428
Kindleberger, C., 425 *n.*
Kirk, Dudley, 5, 36 *n.*, 109–110, 223 *n.*, 224 *n.*, 243 *n.*
Kiser, Clyde V., 77–113, 78 *n.*, 89 *n.*, 90 *n.*, 109 *n.*, 137, 138, 139 *n.*, 210 *n.*, 218 *n.*, 239
Korbel, John, 287 *n.*
Kuznets, Simon, 12, 225 *n.*, 324–340, 350–351, 392 *n.*

Lamale, Helen, 507 *n.*
Lamson, H. D., 221 *n.*
Lebergott, Stanley, 366 *n.*, 377–419
Leibenstein, H., 214 *n.*, 233, 237
Long, Clarence D., 398 *n.*
Lorain, John, 383 *n.*
Lorimer, Frank, 6 *n.*, 34–35, 139 *n.*, 261 *n.*

Marshall, T. H., 384 *n.*
Mason, E. S., 426
Mayer, A. J., 110 *n.*
Mayer, Kurt B., 46 *n.*
Meerdink, J., 48 *n.*, 49
Mendershausen, Horst, 354 *n.*
Meyer, J. R., 213 *n.*
Mill, John Stuart, 13, 450
Mills, Robert, 385 *n.*
Mishler, Elliot, 139, 140–142
Mitchell, Wesley C., 243 *n.*
Moberg, Sven, 51 *n.*, 52, 53
Morgan, James N., 390 *n.*, 414, 419
Morse, Chandler, 423 *n.*, 426
Moulton, Harold G., 426
Myers, Robert J., 357 *n.*

Notestein, Frank W., 10 *n.*, 42, 90 *n.*, 91 *n.*, 139 *n.*, 261–275

Odum, E. P., 443 *n.*
Ogburn, William F., 241 *n.*
Okun, Bernard, 215 *n.*, 235–240
Orcutt, Guy H., 287–318, 321–323
Ordway, Samuel, 424
Osborn, Frederick, 139 *n.*

Pearl, Robert, 77 *n.*, 417 *n.*
Philbrick, Edward S., 380 *n.*
Pigou, A. C., 427
Pinchot, Gifford, 442
Polanyi, Karl, 441–442
Potter, R. G., 220 *n.*
Potter, Robert, 139 *n.*
Prais, S. J., 230 *n.*
Pratt, Lois, 140
Price, Paul H., 388 *n.*

Quandt, Richard, 340–345, 351
Quensel, Carl-Erik, 68 *n.*

Raines, Fred, 287 *n.*
Reed, Lowell, 139 *n.*
Reid, Margaret G., 371–374
Reiss, Albert J., Jr., 473 *n.*
Rivlin, Alice M., 287–318, 321–323
Rubin, Ernest, 392 *n.*
Ruggles, Nancy, 155–190
Ruggles, Richard, 155–190
Ryder, Norman, 7 *n.*, 117–131, 123 *n.*, 127 *n.*

Sagi, Philip, 139 *n.*
Sallume, Xarifa, 90 *n.*
Sauvy, A., 261 *n.*
Schachter, Joseph, 252 *n.*
Schultz, Theodore W., 454–456
Scott, A., 425 *n.*
Seligman, Ben B., 109 *n.*
Sharp, H., 220 *n.*
Simms, William Gilmore, 392 *n.*
Simpson, Sophia, 385 *n.*
Singer, Hans, 338 *n.*
Smith, Adam, 452–453
Solow, Robert, 318–323
Spengler, J. J., 223 *n.*, 425 *n.*
Spiegelman, Mortimer, 408 *n.*
Steinberg, J. R., 301 *n.*
Stevenson, T. H. C., 37
Stigler, George J., 228 *n.*, 426
Stolnitz, G., 261 *n.*
Stys, W., 45 *n.*
Suits, Daniel B., 303 *n.*
Swanson, Guy, 76

Taeuber, Conrad, 283–284, 386 *n.*, 417 *n.*
Taeuber, Irene, 386 *n.*
Tarver, J. D., 213 *n.*
Theil, H., 215 *n.*
Thomas, Dorothy S., 223 *n.*, 241, 242, 257–260, 381 *n.*
Thomas, John L., 109 *n.*
Tietze, C., 110 *n.*

Valaoras, V. G., 261 *n.*
Vance, Rupert, 235
Van Den Brink, T., 43 *n.*, 48 *n.*
Van Doren, Carl,, 78 *n.*
Villard, Henry, 425 *n.*, 437 *n.*

Wernick, Murray, 402 *n.*

Westoff, C. F., 82 *n.*, 92 *n.*, 138, 139, 140–142, 144 *n.*, 151–154, 406 *n.*
Whelpton, Pascal K., 78 *n.*, 86 *n.*, 109 *n.*, 110, 118, 132, 138, 139 *n.*, 140, 190–208, 210 *n.*, 218 *n.*, 239, 252 *n.*, 294, 409 *n.*
Whitney, L. F., 110 *n.*, 221 *n.*
Willcox, Walter, 393
Winnick, Louis, 358 *n.*, 366 *n.*
Wolfbein, S. L., 390 *n.*
Woofter, T. J. 82 *n.*

Young, Allyn, 377 *n.*
Yule, G. U., 242

Zantus, Janos, 380 *n.*
Zimmerman, Erich, 425
Zuwaylif, Fadil, 496 *n.*

SUBJECT INDEX

Age distribution of population: consumption function and, 353–354; economic significance of, 9–10; effect on food consumption of expected shifts in (1950–1970), 469–472, heads of households and, 360–361; quantitative significance of demand and, 364–368.

Age structure of population, 262, 275–277; determination of population's births and deaths by, 9–10; economic and demographic relationships and, 281–282; effect of fertility history on, 9–10; mortality and, 278–281; United States (1930–1955), 265–268, 271

Aggregate output, population change and, 324–351

Australia: birth rate trends in, 19, 20; fertility of selected marriage cohorts in, 30, 32; gross reproduction rates in, 21, 22; population structure in, 276; total marital fertility rates and crude birth rates in, 24

Austria: age structure in, 276; birth rate trends in, 18, 19, 20

Average deviation, fertility differentials and, 91

Belgium: birth rate trends in, 17, 19, 20; family size trends in, 27; gross reproduction rates in, 21, 22; total marital fertility rates and crude birth rates in, 24

Birth, estimation of operating characteristics for, 294

Birth cohorts, patterns of family building in, 33–34

Birth control, see Contraception

Birth rates: business cycles and, 223–227, 239, 241–260; changes in, within homogeneous groups, 158–159; child labor force and decline in, 386–387, 408; cyclical changes in consumer durable purchases and, 223–227, 231; reasons for higher levels in, 229–230, 231; time series of, 119–120; trends in, 17–20

Births, population change and, 261–262, 265, 267–274, 275, 283–284; see also Fertility

Boarders, decline in family income from, 403, 409

Business cycles, influence on marriage and birth rates of, 223–227, 239, 241–260

Canada: birth rate trends in, 17, 19, 20;

fertility rates in birth cohorts of, 33–34; gross reproduction rates in, 21, 22

Capital: marginal productivity of, 429; population growth and accumulation of, 452; population growth and formation of, 331, 348

Capital investment, labor force increase and, 325–326

Capital-output ratios, population increase and variations in, 333–334, 342–343, 344

Catholics: fertility of in Netherlands, 49–50; fertility of in United States, 108–110, 111, 208; use of contraception by, 149

Census Bureau, labor force participation of married women and, 390, 415–417

Census data, trends in family size and, 26–28

Chicago, fertility rates in, 86

Child labor; decline in worker rates and, 409; fertility change and, 383–387

Children: economist's view of, 210–211, 231; net cost of, 213–215; trends in labor force participation of, 421–422; utility of, 216

Clothing service, increase in outlays for (1936–1956), 501, 510

Cohort measures, fertility indexes and, 117–131, 133–136

Color, fertility by in United States, 84, 86, 88–89; see also Race

Community size, family size and, 183, 184–185

Conservation movement, 440–449, 454–455

Consumer durables; cyclical changes in births and purchases of, 223–227, 231; spending units and expenditures on, 312–316; working wives and, 400–403, 409

Consumer expenditures, population change and, 496–525

Consumption, population increase and, 13, 331–333, 334–336, 344–345, 347–348

Consumption behavior, demographic variables and, 457–459

Consumption effect, 503, 510–511; housing and, 508–509, 512–513; prices and, 515

Consumption function: age distribution of population and, 353–354; population growth and, 355, 364–366

530

Consumption theory, children and, 210–211, 213–215, 230, 232–234, 235–240

Contraception, 212, 216–217, 230, 231; alternatives to, 210; differential knowledge of, 218–223, 232, 238–239; effect on differential fertility of, 77–78; family planning and, 148–149; income and, 218–221; reduction of fertility by, 7; status and, 75

Convergence, labor force-population relationships in United States and, 404–407, 409–410

Copenhagen, fertility and status in, 61, 62

Cost, scarcity and, 446–447

Crude birth rate, 134

Current Population Report, labor force participation of married women and, 416

Death: population change and, 262, 265, 267–274, 275, 283–284; projection of probabilities of, 292

Debts, families with, 400–403, 418; *see also* Personal debt

Demand: high fertility and, 11: meanings of term, 485; population change and, 352–376

Demography: economic variables, household sector and, 287–323; interrelations with economic and social forces, 282

Denmark: birth rate trends in, 18, 19, 20; gross reproduction rates in, 21, 22; occupational status and fertility in, 61, 62; urban-rural fertility differentials in, 46, 47, 60–61

Dependent variables, *see* Outputs

Dependents: future prospects for in United States, 371; income levels and, 354, 370

Depression: effect of on birth rate, 18, 274–275; effect of on marriage rate, 23; trends in family size and, 29, 32

Detroit, fertility rates in, 86

Detroit Study, 137, 145–147, 152

Differential fertility, 77–116; definition of, 77; European, 36–76; methodological considerations on, 113–116; United States census data and, 155–208

Diminishing returns law, Malthusianism and 434, 438–440

Distribution effect, 503; expenditures of income and, 505–507, 511; housing expenditures increase and, 508–509

Divorce, estimation of operating characteristic associated with, 293–294

Domestic markets, population growth and, 334–336

Ecological balance, concept of, 443, 455

Economic growth: internal migration and, 327; Malthusianism and, 427–429

Economic indexes, birth and marriage rates and, 243–260

Economic structure, effects of scarcity on, 446

Economics, demographic variables, household sector and, 287–323

Economies of scale, 12, 452–453; domestic markets and, 335

Education: effect on child labor of, 385–386; expenditures for, 514; family limitation patterns and, 149, 150; family size and, 143, 147, 154, 156, 165–177; fertility and, 207–208; government expenditures for and population growth, 362–363, 367; increase in outlays for (1936–1956), 501, 510

Educational status: level of fertility and, 50–55, 72; United States fertility levels and, 93, 96–98, 99, 101, 103–108, 111–112

Employment indexes, birth rate and, 243–260

England: birth rate trends in, 19, 20; differential fertility in, 37, 44; family size trends in, 28; fertility and income in 61, 68–69; gross reproduction rates in, 21, 22; occupational status and fertility in, 55, 59, 61; total marital fertility rates and crude birth rates in, 24; urban-rural fertility differentials in, 46, 47

Environment, family size and, 141, 142

Europe: birth rate trends in, 17–20; differential fertility in, 36–76; gross reproduction rates in, 21, 22

Expenditures, *see* Consumer expenditures; Government expenditures

External economies, 346, 349–350, 452–453, 456; production functions and, 440

Factory system: child labor and, 384; women and, 388–390, 410–413

Family, unique function of the, 74–76; *see also* Head of family

Family limitation, 148–149; depression of fertility by, 7

Family planning, 137–138; population increase and, 336

Family size: analysis and testing of differences in, 155, 160–165, 168–169; decline in age at marriage and, 26; future American population growth and, 150–151, trends in, 26–34; use of as independent variable, 230; variables influencing, 140–149, 153–154

Family structure: demography and, 282; fertility and, 139, 140

Family units, use of in models of consumer sector, 295–297

Farmers, *see* Rural inhabitants

Farm workers, 410–411

Fertility: changes in marriage rate and, 23–26; cyclical movements in, 223–228 economic analysis of, 209–240; economic influences on, 5–8; effects on rate of population growth of, 261–262, 265, 267–274, 275, 283–284, 327; family-oriented activities and, 139; growth of labor force and, 419–420; industrialization and, 4, 35; international survey of recent trends in, 17–35; life plan and, 139–140; measurement of, 117 136; planning of, 137–138; population age structure and, 9–10, 276–277; social statuses and, 139; trends in gross reproduction rate and, 22–23; trends in worker rates and, 392, 394–404; variableness of, 132–133; *see also* Differential fertility; High fertility; Low fertility

Fertility rates: reduction in differentials in, 406–407; slavery and, 392–394

Fertility reduction, rise in worker rates and, 409

Finland: birth rate trends in, 17, 18, 19, 20; fertility rates in birth cohorts of, 33–34; gross reproduction rates in, 21, 22; total marital fertility rates and crude birth rates in, 24

Food demand, population change and, 457–495

Food expenditures, demographic shifts and, 463–465

Foreign born, family size variance among, 161

Forest watersheds, 443

France: age structure in, 276; birth rate trends in, 17, 19, 20; fertility in, 23, 29, 31, 32; gross reproduction rates in, 21, 22; occupational status and fertility in, 55, 56, 57, 59; urban-rural fertility differentials in, 60

General fertility rate, 134

Geniuses, proportion in population of, 12

Germany, birth rate trends in, 18, 19

Government expenditures, demographic variables and, 361–364, 367

Governor's Conference, 442

Great Britain: birth rate trends in, 19; educational status and fertility in, 50–51; gross reproduction rates in, 21; occupational status and fertility in, 55, 56, 58, 59; urban-rural fertility differentials in, 60

Gross reproduction rate, trends in, 20–23, 36

Growth of American Families Study, 74, 86, 110–112, 137, 147–151, 208

Head of family: consumer durable expenditures and, 313–316; probability of liquid assets and, 309–312; probability of mortgage debt and, 304–306; probability of personal debt and, 307–309

High fertility, 10 *n.*, 11, 12, 13

Household sector, economic and demographic model of, 287–323

Housing: dependency of expenditures for on demographic variables, 357–361, 366; expenditures for, 500, 507–509, 510, 512–513; fertility by types of, 87

Husband-dominant families, family size in, 145–146, 147, 153

Immigration: female workers and, 392; labor supply and, 378–383, 408; national output and, 326; population increase, 336; *see also* Migration

Income: consumption and, 353–354; demand for space and, 371–373; distribution effect of, 505–507, 511; family size and, 143, 147, 154, 156–157, 160, 177–179, 182; fertility and, 5, 8, 68–70, 104–108, 112, 217–228, 237–240; fertility and growth in, 211–213, 231, 232; population growth and, 452; working wives and, 403–404; *see also* Personal income

Income effect, family food consumption and, 457–458

Independent variables, *see* Inputs

Indianapolis Study, 113–114, 137–138, 144, 208, 218–220, 226 *n.*

Industrial production indexes, birth and marriage rates and, 243–260

Industrialization, 327; fertility and, 4, 5–6, 35; increases in life expectancy and, 8–9, population growth and, 158, 276

Inland Waterways Conference, 442

Inputs: demographic and economic variables of, 299, 303–316, 319–320; stochastic relation of to outputs, 289–291

Institutions, Malthus and, 434, 438

Internal economies, 452–453

International trade, population growth and, 338, 349

Investment, population growth and, 13, 355–357

Investment theory, children and, 210–211, 213–215, 232, 235–240

Ireland: birth rate trends in, 17, 19, 20; fertility and wealth in, 69–70; fertility in, 23

Italy: age structure in, 276; birth rate trends in, 19, 20; fertility decline in, 6; gross reproduction rates in, 21, 22

Japan, fertility in, 6, 276
Jewelry service, increase in outlays for (1936–1956), 501
Jews, fertility among in United States, 108–110

Kinship, family size and, 141, 145, 146–147, 152, 154
Knowledge, growth of output per capita and, 328–330, 343–344, 347, 349 350

Labor: division of, 452–453; marginal productivity of, 429
Labor force: changing supply of, 281–282; employment level and growing, 356; fertility and, 11, 13; immigration and, 378–383, 408; married women in, 397, 399–404, 415–417; population change and, 325–328, 347, 377–422; rate of growth in, 280–281; women in, 388–391, 410–413, 415–417, 418, 421–422
Labor force-population relationships, 394–400
Leisure: family size and, 145, 146–147, 152, 154; women workers and, 418–419
Life expectancy, mortality and, 4
Limits, conservationist concepts of, 442.
Liquid assets, spending units and, 309–312, 313, 314, 316
Living space, 12–13
Lodgers, decline in family income from, 403, 409
Los Angeles, fertility rates in, 86
Low fertility, 10 n., 11

Malthusianism: assumptions about fertility, 209, 212; dilemma of, 433–439; doctrine of resources scarcity and, 427–440; population checks and, 258
Marital status: consumer durable expenditures and, 312–316; probability of liquid assets and, 309–312; probability of mortgage debt and, 304–306; probability of personal debt and, 306–309
Marriage: business cycles and rates of, 241–260; family size and age at, 183, 186–187; fertility and changes in rate of, 23–26; projection of probabilities of, 292–293
Marriage cohorts, cumulative fertility rates in, 29–32
Medical care, increase in outlays for (1936–1956), 501, 510

Micro-economic studies, 316–317, 321–323
Migration: effects on rate of population growth of, 262, 265, 267–274, 283; growth of labor force and, 419–420; influence on fertility differentials of, 206, 207; United States, 379–383, 408
Milbank Round Table, 137
Mineral resources, 445
Mobility: fertility and, 139–140, 141, 142–143, 152–153; population growth and, 326–328, 347
Mortality: age structure and, 278–281; decline in among children, 212, 227, 230, 231; economic forces and, 4, 8–9; effects on productivity of, 13–14; effects on rate of population growth of, 262, 265, 267–274, 275, 283–284; labor force growth and, 419–420; population change and, 9–10, 408–409; reproduction level and, 34
Mortgage debt, families with, 401–402, 418; spending units and, 304–306, 307, 308, 309–310, 311, 312, 313, 314, 315

National Income Division, Commerce Department, 500 n.
Nativity, United States fertility by, 87–88
Natural resources: destructive use of, 444–445; labor force increase and utilization of, 326, 346–347; population increase and pressure upon, 338; *see also* Resources
Nature preservation, scarcity of, 450–451
Negroes: consumer durable expenditures and, 314, 315; food expenditures by, 457, 460, 465–466, 472, 473–475, 482, 483; liquid assets and, 309, 310, 312; mortgage debt and, 304, 305, 306; personal debt and, 307, 308, 309
Netherlands: birth rate trends in, 17, 19, 20; differential fertility in, 37, 42–43, 45; educational status and fertility in, 52, 53; fertility and wealth in, 69–70; fertility by religious groups in, 48–50, 76; fertility in, 23; gross reproduction rates in, 21, 22; occupational status and fertility in, 55, 59
New York-Northeastern New Jersey, fertility rates in, 86
New Zealand: birth rate trends in, 19, 20; fertility increase in, 6; fertility of selected marriage cohorts in, 30, 32; fertility rate of birth cohorts in, 33–34; gross reproduction rates in, 21, 22; total marital fertility rates and crude birth rates in, 24
Non-renewable resources, physical mismanagement of, 445

North America: birth rate trends in, 17, 19, 20; gross reproduction rates in, 21, 22

Norway: birth rate trends in, 19, 20; differential fertility in, 37, 42; family size trends in, 27; fertility in, 6, 29, 30; gross reproduction rates in, 21, 22; occupational status and fertility in, 55, 57, 59, 61, 63–68; total marital fertility rates and crude birth rates in, 24

Numbers effect, 503, 510–511; housing expenditures increase and, 508–509

Occupation, family size and, 143, 156, 180–183

Occupational status: differences in fertility and, 55–60, 61–68, 71–72; United States fertility and, 92–95, 99, 100–102, 104–108, 112

Oceania: birth rate trends in, 17, 19, 20; gross reproduction rates in, 21, 22

Operating characteristics, probability distributions and, 289–290

Oslo, Norway, family size in, 37, 63, 68

Outputs, 288; stochastic relation of to inputs, 289–291; variables of in model of household sector, 298–299, 303–316, 319–320

Participation rates, 419–422

Period measures, fertility indexes and, 117–131, 133–136

Personal debt, spending units and, 306–309, 310, 311, 312, 313, 314, 316

Personal income, relationship to births and marriages, 243–260

Personality, family size decisions and, 140–141, 143

Philadelphia, fertility rates in, 86

Poland: differential fertility in, 43, 45; fertility and wealth in, 61, 69–70, 71

Population, labor force and, 394–400

Population change: basic patterns in, 261–263; fertility patterns and, 131, 150–151

Population characteristics, outlays for goods and services and relevant, 504–507

Population effect, service, and consumption expenditures and, 498–502

Population growth: consumption function and, 355; creation of new knowledge and, 328–330; definition of, 9; economic effects of, 157–158; effect of social change upon, 158–159; Malthus and, 428, 433–437; weighing positive and negative aspects of, 398–399

Portugal: birth rate trends in, 17, 19, 20; fertility decline in, 6; gross reproduction rates in, 21, 22

Price effect, consumption effect and, 515

Prices, increase in service and consumption expenditures and rise in, 498–502

Princeton Study, 137, 138–145

Privacy, scarcity of, 450–451

Probabilities of occurrence, economic behavior of households and, 289–290

Production, population growth and, 325–330, 341–343, 345–349

Productivity: scarcity and, 446–447; variations in fertility and mortality and, 11–14

Prosperity, fertility and, 5–8, 274–275

Protestants: fertility among in United States, 108–110, 111, 208; use of contraception by, 149

Race: consumer durable expenditures and 313–316; probability of liquid assets and, 309–312; probability of mortgage debt and, 304–306; probability of personal debt and, 307–309; *see also* Color

Race-area groups, effect on food consumption of expected shifts in (1950–1970), 472–483

Recreation, increase in outlays for (1936–1956), 501, 510

Regressions, food expenditures and, 459–462

Relative variations, fertility differentials and, 91

Religion: family size and, 144, 149; fertility differences and, 46, 48–50, 76; increase in outlays for (1936–1956), 501; influence on fertility of, 208; United States fertility and, 108–110, 111

Renewable resources, physical mismanagement of, 445

Residence, fertility differentials by, 78–87; *see also* Rural inhabitants; Urban inhabitants

Resources: Malthusianism and limited economic availability of, 434, 437; population change and, 11–12, 423–456; unwise use of products of, 445; *see also* Natural resources

Resources for the Future Project, 423 *n.*

Retirement, decrease in average age of, 421

Royal Population Commision, 55 *n.*, 56 *n.*

Rural inhabitants: child quality among, 229 *n.*; fertility levels of, 46, 60–61, 71; United States fertility of, 78–87, 92–93, 95, 97, 98, 99, 105, 107

Russia, fertility decline in, 6

Savings, population growth and, 330–334, 344–345, 347–348

Scarcity: doctrine of, 442–447; economic advance and, 425–426; economic effects of, 446; productivity and cost effects of, 446–447; social effects of, 446: social importance of doctrine of, 423–425, 455–456

Scotland: birth rate trends in, 19, 20; gross reproduction rates in, 21, 22

Scripps Foundation for Research on Population Problems, 252 *n.*

Second World War, effect on marriage rate of, 23

Servants, 410, 413–414

Services, population change and demand for, 496–525

Slave raising, profitability of, 213

Slavery: domestic servants and, 411–412; female laborers under, 391; fertility rates and, 392–394; labor force replacements and abolition of, 382, 409; value of children under, 385

Social production function, Malthus and, 440, 452

Space, 12–13, 453–454; scarcity of, 450–451

Spain: birth rate trends in, 17, 19, 20; fertility decline in, 6

Spending units, 295–297; consumer durable expenditures and, 312–316; liquid assets and, 309–312, 313, 314, 316; mortgage debt and, 304–306, 307, 308, 309–310, 311, 312, 313, 314, 315; personal debt and, 306–309, 310, 311, 312, 313, 314, 316

Status, fertility and, 59–60, 70–72, 89–99, 145–146, 156–157; *see also* Educational status; Income; Occupational status

Sterility, 148

Stockholm, Sweden, fertility in 1930's in, 5; fertility in from 1917 to 1930, 220

Study of the Future Fertility of Two-Child Families, 110

Subfecundity, 148

Suburbs, fertility, 86–87

Survey of Consumer Finances, 295; labor force participation of married women and, 390, 415–417

Sweden: birth rate trends in, 19, 20; educational status and fertility in, 51–52, 53–55; fertility in, 6, 276; fertility of selected marriage cohorts in, 31; fertility rates in birth cohorts of, 33–34; gross reproduction rates in, 21, 22; income and fertility in, 61, 68; urban-rural fertility differentials in, 46, 47, 60–61

Switzerland: birth rate trends in, 19, 20; family size trends in, 27; gross reproduction rates in, 21, 22; urban-rural fertility differentials in 46, 48

Technology: Malthus and, 434, 438; natural resources and, 449–450; population growth and, 452

Time horizon: reproduction rate and, 434–436; strategic variables and, 433, 434–436

Total fertility rate, 134

Total marital fertility rate, 23–24

Traditionalism, fertility and, 144

Traffic density, increasing costs of, 453

Transportation: economies of scale and, 455; increase in outlays for (1936–1956), 500, 510

Underdeveloped countries: age structures in 278; population growth in, 262–263, 324, 337–338

Unemployment, government expenditures and, 367–368, 369

United Nations, 17

United States: birth rate trends in, 17, 19, 20; differential fertility in, 77–116, 155–208; family size trends in, 27; female population changes from 1930 to 1955 in, 263–274; fertility by geographic area in, 84–87; gross reproduction rates in, 21, 22; population model for, 278

Urban inhabitants: child quality among, 229; fertility levels of, 46, 60–61, 71; fertility in United States of, 78–87, 92–94, 96, 99–104, 105, 107

Utilities, increase in outlays for (1936–1956), 500, 510, 512

Variance, analysis of and differential fertility, 114–116

Vital statistics, trends in family size and, 28–29

Wales: birth rate trends in, 19, 20; differential fertility in, 37, 44; family size trends in, 28; fertility and income in, 61, 68–69; gross reproduction rates in, 21, 22; occupational status and fertility in, 55, 59, 61; total marital fertility rates and crude birth rates in, 24; urban-rural fertility differentials in, 46, 57

Waste: economic scarcity of natural resources and, 444; types of, 444–446

Welfare, increase in outlays for (1936–1956), 501

Western Europe, discussion of family size in, 72–74

Wife-dominant couples, fertility norms and behavior among, 145–146, 147, 153

Women: employment of, 388–391, 410–413, 415–417, 418, 421–422; family size and age of, 183, 188–190

Worker rates: convergence of, 404–407; fertility trends and, 392, 394–404; women and, 389–391, 396–398, 409

World Population Conference, 73

Yugoslavia, age structure in, 276